Interpreting the Middle East

INTERPRETING THE MIDDLE EAST

Essential Themes

edited by

DAVID S. SORENSON

Air War College

WESTVIEW PRESS

A Member of the Perseus Books Group

Find us on the World Wide Web at www.westviewpress.com.

Westview Press books are available at special discounts for bulk purchases in the United States by corporations, institutions, and other organizations. For more information, please contact the Special Markets Department at the Perseus Books Group, 2300 Chestnut Street, Suite 200, Philadelphia, PA 19103, or call (800) 810-4145, ext. 5000, or e-mail special.markets@perseusbooks.com.

Set in 10.5 point Adobe Garamond

Library of Congress Cataloging-in-Publication Data

Sorenson, David S., 1943–
    Interpreting the Middle East : essential themes / David S. Sorenson.
        p.   cm.
    Includes bibliographical references and index.
    ISBN 978-0-8133-4440-9 (alk. paper)
    1. Middle East—Politics and government—21st century. 2. Middle East—Economic conditions—21st century. 3. Middle East—Social conditions—21st century. I. Title.
    DS63.1.S674 2010
    956.05'4—dc22   2009042607

10 9 8 7 6 5 4 3 2 1

CONTENTS

List of Illustrations *vii*

Preface *ix*

1 Interpreting the Middle East, *David S. Sorenson* 1

PART 1
Demography and Historical Memory 31

2 Demographic Development, *Onn Winckler* 35

3 Historical Memory and Contemporary Affairs, *Glenn E. Perry* 61

PART 2
Politics 93

4 Drivers of Political Change in the Middle East
and North Africa, *Dafna H. Rand* 97

5 Civil-Military Relations, *David S. Sorenson* 125

PART 3
Political Economy 157

6 Political Economy, *Chantel Pheiffer and Gregory White* 163

7 Political Economies of the Maghreb, *Clement M. Henry* 185

PART 4
Social Contexts   213

8   Gender, *Amy Elizabeth Young*   219
9   The Islamic Awakening, *Raymond William Baker*   249

PART 5
International Dimensions   275

10 The Israeli-Palestinian Conflict, *Christopher Hemmer*   281
11 Conflict in Western Sahara, *Yahia H. Zoubir*   303
12 The Political Economy of Modern Iraq, *Eric Davis*   337
13 Iran's Regional Foreign Policy, *Manochehr Dorraj*   363
14 Global Energy and the Middle East, *Steve Yetiv*   383

Glossary   *407*
Biographies of Key People   *413*
Chronology of Significant Middle East Events   *421*
Contributors   *423*
Index   *427*

LIST OF ILLUSTRATIONS

MAP

The Middle East and North Africa   x–xi

FIGURES

2.1   Population Growth in Some Middle Eastern Countries, 1950–2025   36

2.2   Total Fertility Rates in Some Middle Eastern Countries, 1960–2008   38

2.3   Percentage of Urban Population Within Total Population in   42
Some Middle Eastern Countries, 1950–2007

2.4   Nationals and Expatriates in the GCC Populations, 1975–2007   48

6.1   Percentage of Total Renewable Water Resources   172
Withdrawn by Region

6.2   Desalination in the Middle East and North Africa   174

7.1   Government Effectiveness   189

7.2   Per Capita GDP, 1961–2006   190

7.3   External Debt as a Percentage of Gross National Income,   192
1970–2006

7.4   Debt Service as a Percentage of Export Revenues   193

7.5   Control of Corruption   195

7.6   Exports as a Percentage of GDP, 1962–2006   197

7.7   Nonperforming Loans as a Percentage of Total Loans, 2000–2006   199

14.1   Oil Prices vs. Spare Capacity, 1990–2006   389

14.2   Consumption, Production, and Import Trends, 1950–2007   398

TABLES

1.1 Freedom House Rankings, 2009   9
1.2 Comparative GDP/Capita for Middle East Countries   15

2.1 Population Growth in Some Middle Eastern Countries, 1950–2025   37
2.2 Major Demographic Indicators for Some Middle Eastern   39
Countries, 1960–2008
2.3 Percentage of Urban Population Within the Total Population in   42
Some Middle Eastern Countries, 1950–2007
2.4 Nationals and Expatriates in the GCC Populations, 1975–2007   46

4.1 Four Drivers   98
4.2 MENA 2008 Gross Domestic Product (per capita) Compared to   101
Political Rights and Civil Liberties

6.1 MENA Commodity Trade, Annual Average 2003–2005   170
6.2 Agricultural Production in MENA, 2002–2004 Average   175

PREFACE

To the potential instructor who is considering adopting this book for class, this is an invitation to read the preface and introduction and judge whether it meets your needs. For the student or the bookstore customer who is opening this book for the first time, this is your invitation to explore the most significant issues that impact both the Middle East and much of the rest of the world.

I chose the contributors for this volume for their ability to generate a chapter that would be informative, incisive, current, and relevant to the debates and discussions revolving around the Middle East. Some are old friends, but most do not know me personally. What they all have in common is that they are internationally recognized experts in their fields. Outside of that criterion, they range considerably. Some have been in the field of Middle East studies for many decades, while others are just starting what will be distinguished careers. Some are Americans, others hold different-color passports. Their ethnicity, native tongue, or nationality did not matter to me; all that mattered was that they delivered a quality product within a relatively short span of time. I am convinced that they did, though it will be up to the readers and critics to judge for themselves.

I can promise that the chapters in this collection are timely, significant, and often controversial. Most involve not only additions to previous scholarship, but laborious efforts in the countries where the authors carried out their fieldwork. Their work is the most up-to-date research into political change, Middle East demographics, economic reform, civil-military relations, post-2003 change in Iraq, the latest thinking on Iran, and other pertinent matters that will benefit both students and professionals, along with the informed citizen.

I thank my editor, Karl Yambert of Westview Press, and my colleagues Chris Hemmer and Evelyn Early, for lengthy discussions and careful readings of my material. I alone am responsible for remaining shortcomings and errors.

MAP 0.1: THE MIDDLE EAST AND NORTH AFRICA

1

INTERPRETING THE MIDDLE EAST

David S. Sorenson

THIS EDITED BOOK provides an introduction to the modern Middle East using five principal themes intended to capture the essence of the contemporary Middle East. Each section of the book represents an issue area that students of the region need to become familiar with: *features of the modern Middle East*, including demographic issues and the impact of historical memory; *interpreting politics in the Middle East*, which has chapters on political change and civil-military relations; *economic development*, where the pertinent chapters discuss the changing political economy of the Middle East; *interpreting the social context of the Middle East*, with contributions on gender and religion in the region; and *interpreting international issues in the Middle East*, the longest section. It covers the Israeli-Palestinian dispute, the Western Sahara conflict, the aftermath in Iraq after 2003, Iranian regional interests, and the international implications of Middle East oil. The book's purpose is broad but simple: to familiarize students of the region with its essential features and to help them understand the debates that frame those features.

PRESENTING THE MIDDLE EAST:
THINGS TO THINK ABOUT

Each chapter in this collection assumes some familiarity with the issues and background.

The Middle East itself is a complex map of different countries, languages, religions, and traditions. It is easy to stereotype, but difficult to capture. There are few constants: Most of the occupants of the region speak Arabic, but there are other major languages as well—Persian (or Farsi), Hebrew, and Turkish, along with dozens of minor languages. Millions of Middle East inhabitants speak Armenian, Berber, Kurdish, Aramaic, and other ancient languages. A majority of the region's citizens are Muslim, but there are numerous sects of Islam, plus other populations of sects sometimes but not universally recognized as Islamic: the Druze, the Alawi (the Alevi in Turkey), and the Imbadi in Oman, to name but a few. A majority of Muslims are Sunni, but around 15 percent are Shia, and those two major branches have offshoots, along with adherence to different schools of Islamic jurisprudence. Most Shia follow the "Twelver" or *Imamiyya* understanding of Shia Islam, but there are also "Fivers" (the *Zaid*) and the "Seveners" (or *Ismailia*) branches, all named after the place of a particular imam in the Shia descendents following Ali, the Prophet's son-in-law. There are also mixed Jewish populations, and while Judaism is not split as clearly into schisms as is Islam, divisions exist. The "secular" Jews, often Western European in ancestry, mix uneasily with the "ultra-orthodox" Jews, many of whom trace their ancestry to Eastern Europe, or the Arab world. Their debates include passionate arguments over observance of the Jewish Sabbath, and the degree to which Israel should be a religious state. There are few Christians in the land where Christianity began, but those who live there are usually members of the smaller sects of the religion, such as the Maronites, Nestorians, or Chaldeans. While the Maronites have influential positions of power in Lebanon, Christians in most of the rest of the Middle East live in tiny communities on the edge of the larger Muslim populace.

The Middle East: Progress and Persistent Problems

For many outsiders, the Middle East appears as a distant and unfamiliar place, filled with conflict and featuring authoritarian regimes run by theocrats or military dictators. Television brings almost nightly scenes of flames and death, and one cannot be blamed for the impression that most of the citizens of the Middle East spend a lot of time attending funerals. For those whose study takes them to the area, worrisome or negative comments—coming from anyone from colleagues to strangers—become an almost daily event.

However, the region is rich in history, tradition, language, culture, and religion. While the region as a whole lags behind some other parts of the world in political freedom and economic development, there are strong signs that it is catching up and, in some cases, rapidly surpassing other areas in progress. In parts of the Arabian side of the Persian Gulf, modern skyscrapers, expansive highways, and luxury automobiles denote clusters of wealth and influence that compete with such high-profile places as Hong Kong and Singapore. New modern buildings and wide streets impress visitors to Amman, Jordan, and Casablanca, Morocco, and in Cairo, though dilapidated neighborhoods such as

Imbaba remain, steel and glass edifices are gradually replacing them. Tourists flock to beaches in Tunisia and Morocco, and are now eying Libya as the next possible vacation spot. Investment from outside the region is finally beginning to move in, spurring jobs and growth opportunities. Every year the region moves up slightly on the Freedom House regional rankings of free nations, though it still remains largely not free.[1] Although Middle Eastern history is littered with the detritus of war, particularly between Israel and its Arab neighbors, Arab and Israeli warriors did not fight a state-on-state major war between the mid-1980s (when Israel invaded Lebanon) and 2006 (when Hizbullah and Israeli forces clashed violently but briefly). There are worrisome signs that violence is still a distinct possibility in parts of the Middle East, and indeed it has been a regular visitor to such places as Iraq and Lebanon, but the bloody and expensive state-on-state wars like that between Iran and Iraq (killing perhaps half a million people between 1981 and 1988) seem less likely.

The Middle East in the twenty-first century presents a decidedly mixed picture of progress and persistent problems rooted in the region's historical mosaics, along with its religious and cultural foundations. The historical record includes long periods of foreign occupation and invasion. Many citizens still recount stories of the depredations of the Mongols, the warriors of Tamerlane, Selim the Grim, Richard the Lionhearted, Alexander the Great, Napoleon Bonaparte, and hundreds of other conquerors, large and small. Most of the Arab world came under Ottoman rule between the early sixteenth century and the end of World War I, when the victorious British and French divided the spoils of the Ottoman Empire between them. Their incorporation of the Middle East ranged from attempted absorption (France regarded Algeria as just another part of metropolitan France) to "protectorate" status, a favorite technique of the British that allowed them to tolerate semi-autonomous rule while "protecting" the country from Britain's rivals.

Under the influence of foreign rule, and too often misruled by its own leaders, much of the Middle East gradually declined in power and influence from the high points of the Umayyad and Abbasid periods, which stretched from around 691 to 1258. Modern Iraq, once the seat of the Abbasid Caliphate, was an example. Faded pictures of early Baghdad, once one of the greatest cities on earth, recall its glory, with towering gilded mosques lining the Tigris River and elegantly dressed men smoking water pipes along its banks. But over the centuries, Baghdad declined from a city of grandeur to one of dust and grime, the faded capital of a regime that only pretended to reflect the grandness of its past. Its most notorious recent ruler, Saddam Hussein, concocted gaudy portraits of himself receiving King Hammurabi's blessings for his depraved rule. The shah of Iran celebrated the 2,500th anniversary of the Persian culture with a lavish party at Persepolis in 1971 costing millions of dollars. One of the invited guests, British Foreign Secretary Michael Stewart, gushed to the shah, "Your Empire was founded by Cyrus. Xerxes extended it and Darius preserved it. Your present ruler seems to me to possess something of the qualities of all three of these mighty kings."[2] Not all Middle Eastern rulers displayed such brazen imitation, but many realized that they stood in the long shadows of their powerful ancestors.

Regions of the Middle East

Geographers normally divide the Middle East into regions, though sometimes such divisions provide more confusion than clarity. Commonly the divisions are the *Persian Gulf*, the *Eastern Mediterranean*, and *North Africa*. The eastern Mediterranean is called the *Mashriq*, from the Arab word for "where the sun rises," but it is also called the *Levant*, a word whose origin is cloudy but seems to come from Greek or French, while North Africa is known as the *Maghreb*, which refers to the setting sun or just "the west." The Persian Gulf is also referred to as the "Arabian Gulf" by the Arab countries on its western shore and by the US Central Command, which has military responsibility in the region for the United States. Their argument is that the "Persians" (Iran since 1936) are on only one side of the Gulf, while Arab countries dominate the opposite shoreline.

These regions are not distinct, and decisions about how to classify the locations of countries within regions can seem capricious at best. Part of the categorization is simply geographical place, but another component is "culture." This much-bandied term signifies such features as language, architecture, diet, religious practices, clothing styles, personal adornment, and a multitude of other things, down to the preferred side of the road to drive on. Cultures are often self-determined, and thus it is vital to understand not just how a cultural anthropologist might consider cultural categorization, but how those who bear such cultures might use them to define themselves. Consider, for example, that Tunisia's founding president, Habib Bourguiba, stated that, in his view, the Maghreb was not just a place on maps, but where the people ate couscous, which placed the Maghreb east of Egypt, also located in North Africa, but Egypt's people do not, as a rule, eat couscous, but rather bread and rice. In the Maghreb, the mosque minarets tend to be square, whereas in many other Muslim countries, they are generally round. Fishing boats in the Gulf are the traditional dhow with a large lateen sail, whereas fishing boats in North Africa tend to resemble the boats on the European side of the Mediterranean. In some eastern Mediterranean countries, an anise-flavored alcoholic beverage known as *araq* or, in Turkish, *raki*, is preferred, but in North Africa wine is favored, and in the Arabian Gulf there is no alcohol tradition.

The Maghreb is not always considered a part of the Middle East, but it shares a postcolonial identity, along with religious and language affinity, with much of the Middle East. Thus in scholarship that does include the Maghreb with the larger Middle East, the term "Middle East and North Africa," abbreviated "MENA" is used. The Maghreb consists of Tunisia, Morocco, Libya, and Mauritania (rarely covered in North African discourse, though). The Maghreb is largely Arabic speaking, though there are areas where the language is Berber, an ancient tongue that predates Arabic. And while there are small pockets of Jews and Christians living in the Maghreb, it is predominantly Muslim. Because of the long epoch of French colonialism, except for Libya, French is commonly spoken in the Maghreb.

The Persian Gulf includes a number of countries with differing cultures, including Saudi Arabia, Bahrain, Kuwait, Qatar, the United Arab Emirates, Oman, Iran, Iraq, and Yemen, although the last country does not have a sea-coast on the Gulf. The Eastern Mediterranean countries include Egypt, Turkey, Syria, Lebanon, Israel, Jordan, and Palestine.

Persian Gulf countries vary considerably. All but Iran are Arab-speaking, but their populations range in size from over 60 million to less than 1 million people. Some have large reserves of petroleum, while others have virtually no oil or natural gas. Some rank as the richest countries in the world on a per capita basis, while others have significant poverty. The gross domestic product per capita for Qatar is $103,500, second in the world only to tiny Liechtenstein, while Yemen's per capita GDP is $2,400, 177th in the world. The currency of the Gulf remains petroleum, with roughly two-thirds of the world's proven reserves of oil and the second largest supply of natural gas, trailing only Russia. While petroleum remains the largest source of income for Gulf countries, many are diversifying their economies, aware that wide price swings characterize the global petroleum market and that at some point reserves will diminish to the point where it is no longer feasible to extract them. Thus countries such as Qatar and the United Arab Emirates are pushing investment in real estate, tourism, banking, and other service industries to cushion themselves for the day that oil and gas run out. Unfortunately, the global recession starting in 2008 undercut those investments, and with recession-induced drops in petroleum consumption, the Gulf countries found themselves in economic freefall.

The Eastern Mediterranean is no more cohesive than the Gulf or the Maghreb. While a majority of the Levant countries are Arabic speaking, two are not: Turkey and Israel (though around 20 percent of Israel's population is Arabic speaking). Egypt is included in the Levant and not the Maghreb, even though Egypt is located in North Africa (though the dividing line between Africa and Asia runs up the Red Sea, placing Egypt in two continents). The distinction may be more cultural than geographical. Egyptians have commonly tied their culture more to the Eastern Mediterranean, where they had empires in the times of the Pharaohs.

Levant countries include Turkey, Lebanon, Israel, Syria, Jordan, and, tangentially, Cyprus, although that island country is a mix of Turkish and Greek inheritance. The dominant economic form is service, though such activities range from a growing private sector in Israel to state-run bureaucracies in Syria. Political latitude varies from "free" in Israel to "partly free" in Jordan and "not free" for Syria, according to Freedom House.

The Middle Eastern Language Mosaic

Language is an important key to understanding the Middle East, because identity is often tied to idiom. Language is sometimes a more powerful identifier than is country, partly because the idea of a modern nation-state is a relatively new one, while Middle East languages trace back for millennia.

Numerous language families exist in the Middle East. The Semitic family is the largest language group, including Arabic, Hebrew, and Aramaic (the language of Palestine at the time of Christ, spoken today in a few mountain villages in Syria). Arabic is the most common language in the Middle East, the official language of twenty-four countries, though some of them lie on the periphery of the Middle East itself (Djibouti, the Comoros Islands, and Eritrea, for example). The official language of Mauritania is Arabic, but the CIA World FactBook for 2010 lists its ethnicity as "mixed Moor/black 40%, Moor 30%, black 30%," while it lists some other Arab countries as "Arab 90%, Afro-Asian 10%" (for Saudi Arabia), or "Egyptian 99.6%, other 0.4%" for Egypt. It is hardly clear whether "Moors" (from the Greek *Mauris* or "Mauritanian") means Arabs or something else.

Written Arabic varies between "classical" Arabic and Modern Standard Arabic, which differ by structure and grammar. Spoken or colloquial Arabic varies considerably from region to region and sometimes even from country to country. The North African versions of Arabic (which themselves vary across countries) differ from "Egyptian" Arabic and "Arabian Gulf" Arabic to the point where visitors from, say, Saudi Arabia can barely understand Arabic as spoken in Morocco. There is some standardization, though. Many Arabs can better understand Egyptian Arabic because Cairo is the center of film production in the Arab world, and so many people throughout the region watch Egyptian movies that they become familiar with Arabic as it is spoken in Cairo.

Hebrew is also a Semitic language, widely used by Israel's Jewish citizens (though not by Israeli Arabs, who constitute 20 percent of the country's population) and in Jewish religious services worldwide. The origin of Hebrew lies in the ancient Canaanite family of languages, and thus is close to Aramaic. Hebrew survived mainly as a literary language, similar to the role that Latin once played among literary Europeans. In the nineteenth century, Jewish communities in Europe revamped and revived Hebrew, and today it is the national language of Israel. Hebrew today is spoken in Israel with differing dialects, one influenced by the Ashkenazi Jews (those of European origin) and the other voiced by the Sephardic Jews, those of original Spanish origin who fled the Spanish Inquisition initially to Arab countries (most went to Morocco), and later migrated to Israel.

Persian is another language in the Middle East, though it is the national language of just one country, Iran. It is one of the oldest surviving languages (albeit in changed form), dating at least to the Achaemenid dynasty, from 559 to 331 BCE. The modern version of Persian is known as Farsi, after the Persian province of Fars ("Pars" in early Greek, but in Arabic script there is no "P" and thus "Farsi"). In Iran, the proper name for its variety of Persian is Modern Iranian Persian, to distinguish the dialect from other versions of Persian spoken in Afghanistan, Pakistan, and Uzbekistan. Though different in structure from Arabic, Modern Iranian Persian is written in modified Arab script, which offers additional letters not found in Arabic.

Turkish, one of the Ural-Altaic families of language, is the official language of Turkey, a tongue carried by the Turks as they migrated east from the Altaic Mountain region of northeast Asia. Turkish began to change as early as the sixth century, borrowing words from other languages (particularly Persian and Arabic), and evolved into a written form using Arabic script. However, Kemal Atatürk, the founding president of the Turkish Republic, tried to steer Turkey from its Muslim and Ottoman roots by revising the Turkish language after World War I. He banned the use of "imported" words in the press and ordered a new Turkish alphabet in Latin script. Today, Istanbul Turkish is the country's official language.

There are dozens of smaller but significant language groupings in the Middle East. They include Berber, an ancient language spoken by over 8 million inhabitants of North Africa, though other estimates put the number as high as 25 million (most North African countries do not count their Berber population separately). At least six dialects of Berber exist, but the three main categories are *Tachelhit*, spoken in southwest Morocco, *Tamazight*, spoken in the Middle Atlas Mountains, and *Tarifit* (or *Rifia*), the language of the Rif area of northern Morocco.

Kurdish is another important language from the same Indo-European language group as Persian. Around 25 million people speak Kurdish in Iran, Syria, Turkey, Iraq, and Central Asia. Kurdish is written in several scripts, depending on the region. In Arab countries, and in Iran, Kurdish is written in Arabic script, whereas in Turkey it is written in Latin script, and in Russia it is written in Cyrillic. Armenian also appears in pockets in the Middle East, spoken by small numbers of Armenians living in Turkey and in parts of the Arab world. Other languages found in the Middle East include Azeri (spoken by almost a quarter of Iran's population), Mazandarani, Circassian, Aramaic, and many others. The languages of the old imperial powers, English, French, and Italian, are also commonly understood in the modern Middle East.

THE THEMES COVERED IN THIS BOOK

The Middle East can be understood in several ways. A country-by-country approach provides the most complex portrait of the Middle East, because despite similarities, each country is quite different even from its neighbors in the area. Jordan and Syria border each other, for example, but other than Arab identity, they have little in common. Syria is a single-party state with no monarchial tradition, and the ruling family is of the minority Alawi faith. By contrast, Jordan is a constitutional monarchy with elections as a regular feature of the political climate, although there are also limits to political participation. Jordan has been supportive of most American policies in the Middle East (though King Hussein opposed the war against Saddam Hussein's Iraq in 1990–1991) and operates its military mainly with American weapons. Jordan is a largely homogenous country with a dominant Sunni majority and a royal family with ties to the family of the Prophet Muhammad. By way of comparison, Syria is a one-party state ruled by the Baath, with a state-managed economy. The Asad family has held the presidency of Syria since 1969, with the office passing to Hafiz al-Asad's son Bashar in 2000. Syria has a Sunni majority, but also a population of Druze and Alawi along with small Christian and Shia populations. Syria is the only Arab country that supported Iran in its war with Iraq in the 1980s, so to compare the two neighboring countries of Syria and Iraq would focus more on differences than on similarities. Thus this book builds its arguments from central themes that allow for both broad commonalities as well as country-by-country comparisons, thus building a richer body of knowledge than would a simple exploration of each Middle East country.

Political Themes in the Middle East

A fundamental activity of those in authority is to distribute resources within the societies they govern. Societies may allocate resources to their members by central authority, or through the collective decisions of the population. Governments vary across the political spectrum, ranging from totalitarian governance to complete participatory democracy, with few pure examples on either end. Societies construct compacts between citizen and governor, though such constitutions vary considerably between those "guaranteeing" rights that actually do not exist to those taking seriously a commitment to govern through popular consent. Some polities separate faith from state; others weld the two together. Some regimes rule from the palace without popular assent, while others serve only with it. Most political systems combine some degree of popular sovereignty with regime imperatives to preserve stability, retain power, and protect the state from threats. Of course governments can and do justify restrictions on popular involvement for all sorts of reasons that may cloud the genuine rationales, which may involve more self-interest than they do the interests of the population.

In the Middle East, democracy was slow to arrive, and it sometimes faltered when it did. In too many cases, Middle Eastern countries failed to make the transition to democracy: Tunisia, Libya, Saddam Hussein's Iraq, and the lower Gulf Arab states rarely entertained any democratic enlargement, while such others as Jordan and Morocco created constitutional monarchies where democracy developed, but under a ceiling set by the royal family. The 2009 Freedom House rankings reflected this lack of democracy in the Middle East.

According to Freedom House, there is but one "free" country in the Middle East, Israel; five countries ranked as "partly free"; and ten considered "not free."[3] Some critics have argued that Freedom House scores for the Middle East do not

TABLE 1.1: FREEDOM HOUSE RANKINGS, 2009

Country	Free	Partly Free	Not Free
Algeria			X
Bahrain		X	
Egypt			X
Iran			X
Iraq			X
Israel	X		
Jordan		X	
Kuwait		X	
Libya			X
Morocco		X	
Oman			X
Qatar			X
Turkey		X	
Saudi Arabia			X
Syria			X
Tunisia			X
United Arab Emirates			X
Yemen			X

reflect democratic progress (Algeria has had several relatively open elections since 2004, and Iraq has also had some) and that relatively democratic Turkey and relatively undemocratic Kuwait have the same scores ("partly free"). Harik argues that "the argument here is not that Arab countries have a stellar record of democratization, as indeed they do not. It is a matter of whether FH's quantitative measurement of democratization across the board is reliable at all."[4]

It may be argued, though, that the emphasis on accountable governance is greater in the West than it is in the Middle East, and that many citizens in the region may prefer the stability central rule can provide to the unsettling nature of democracy. However, there is evidence to suggest that even in countries ruled as absolute monarchies, the public holds values that are not only compatible with democracy, but also encourage it. Says Englehart about the World Values Survey on Saudi Arabia:

> Although Saudi Arabia is the original center of Islam and is governed by an absolute monarchy, its public does *not* have the most traditional value system of any Islamic country—quite the contrary, the Saudi public emphasizes self-expression values more strongly than any other Islamic public. Since these values are closely linked with mass support for democracy, it would be a serious mistake to assume that the Saudi public is uninterested in democratization.[5]

A survey conducted by the Pew Charitable Trust in 2002–2003 found similar support for democracy in some, though not all, Middle Eastern Muslim countries. For example, in response to the statement "It is very important to live in a country where there are honest two-party elections," 75 percent of Turkish respondents and 71 percent of Lebanese said "yes," though only 28 percent of Jordanian respondents answered in the affirmative.[6]

The Politics of Separation in the Middle East. The organizations of human collective life stem from a vast array of sources and have a reciprocal impact on their origins. People organize into communes, cities, villages, or refugee camps because of exigent circumstances, human needs, orders from on high, or accident, and their organizations then create their own needs. Organizations must have some kind of mechanisms to regulate conflict and enhance collective productivity, and to move beyond mere survival. Sometimes, to regulate conflict alone, organizations push wedges between groups of people. They may segregate their societies for religious purposes ("my religion might be compromised or weakened if it comes into contact with yours") or language purposes ("my language must never be adulterated by words from your language") or for other "pragmatic" reasons. But the most common reason for societies to fence away elements of their own group is the quest to gain and keep power. By making certain targeted groups live in special neighborhoods or camps or requiring them to wear special garb or implying that they are "unclean" or "infidels," one is stating that "they are not like us" and must be controlled, segregated, watched, or arrested and sometimes targeted for killing. There is hardly a society in history that has not practiced some form of social ghettoization.

So it is in many Middle East countries. Separate communities existed for those in minority status, as was the case in Europe, North America, China, and elsewhere.[7] In traditional Moroccan cities, for example, the Jewish population usually was consigned to live in the walled-off *mellah* ("salt" in Arabic).[8] Other cities had their quarters for Christians, Jews, Zoroastrians, and others, just as Sunni Muslims lived in the "Muslim Quarter" in traditionally Christian Beirut. Tripoli became a Sunni city with few if any Shia Muslims. Jerusalem is divided into Christian, Armenian, Jewish, and Muslim quarters, with a gate leading to each area.

The most visible and controversial separation in the Middle East is the walling-off of the Palestinian population both within Israel proper and in the Occupied Territories. The "Palestinian population" refers to both Israeli Palestinians (the descendents of those Palestinians who did not leave in 1948) and Palestinians under occupation in the West Bank and East Jerusalem. The partition between Israelis and occupied Palestinians is very physical: A combination of walls and fences separate the state of Israel from the Palestinian territories. The segregation is less formal and often less obvious within Israel, though walks through Tel Aviv or Haifa or Jerusalem reveal distinct neighborhoods, Jewish Israelis in one neighborhood and Palestinians in another, and small villages that are exclusively Palestinian. For some Israelis, such segregation should be state policy. In June 2009, Israel's housing minister, Ariel Atias, argued that it was imperative to stop the alleged spread of Arab Israelis into Jewish neighborhoods: "I see [it] as a national duty to prevent the spread of a population that, to say the least, does not love the state of Israel." He then added that as an ultra-orthodox Jew himself,

> There is a severe housing crisis among the young ultra-Orthodox couples, and in the general population. I, as an ultra-Orthodox Jew, don't think that religious Jews should have to live in the same neighborhood as secular couples, so as to avoid unnecessary friction. There is a severe housing crisis among the young ultra-Orthodox couples, and in the general population.[9]

In Jerusalem, a poll some years ago revealed that a majority of Jewish Israelis claimed that they would not object to giving back Arab east Jerusalem to the Palestinians because "we never go there." Israel is hardly the only state to separate its people, though. To visit a Shia area in Saudi Arabia, one has to drive to such remote places as Al-Qatif, which lies to the north of the eastern city of

Dammam. In Egypt, the small Shia population largely lives in south Cairo, and there are usually distinct Coptic Christian neighborhoods there as well, one consequence of anti-Christian riots in that city dating back to 1321.[10]

Segregation by gender is still common in most of the Middle East, though it certainly is common in other parts of the globe as well. While segregation varies from almost complete in Saudi Arabia to less common in Turkey, Tunisia, Lebanon, and Israel, it is probably more usual in the Middle East than elsewhere. The United Nations calculated "gender empowerment" scores across member nations, and the Middle East and the Arab world in particular rank lower on these scores than any other part of the globe.[11] There are, for example, fewer female parliamentarians in the Arab world than in any other region.[12]

Some argue that the lack of access to jobs, political positions, full legal protection, or societal respect for women may stem from Islamic provisions, as Islam is the dominant religion of the Middle East. However, strictures stemming from interpretations from Islam are only part of the story. "Culture" is the other. Women have served as heads of state or prime ministers in several countries with Muslim majorities (Pakistan, Turkey, Bangladesh, and Indonesia), but these countries are outside of the Arab realm, where gender empowerment is lacking. It is likely that cultural characteristics also limit women's full access to equal protection under the law, or a stairway up the national economic ladder, or a real chance at a seat in parliament. There are changes, to be sure. In 2009 several female candidates successfully contested for parliamentary seats in Kuwait, after being shut out of the game for years. Several Arab women serve in cabinet-level posts, in Yemen, for example. But according to the most recent UN Arab Human Development report, while women have made progress in the Arab world through reform efforts, "reforms often seemed empty gestures to cover up the continuation of an oppressive status quo."[13]

State-Building. Most Middle East countries were colonies of the major European powers. Other countries held the status of protectorate, which was but a short putt away from colonial status. The exceptions include Turkey and Iran, though Iran was under influence from both Russia and Britain from the nineteenth century on, and British intelligence assisted in reinstalling Shah Muhammad Pahlavi in 1953. The colonial experience left a legacy of political institutions built and serviced to meet the needs of the imperial power, and thus independence required a new set of national organizations. However, as postindependence leaders discovered, it was one thing to construct a state structure to collect taxes, to provide for the common defense, and to plan the vast number of activities needed for governance, and yet another to built legitimacy for such activities. This was partly because in many Middle East countries, most politics was local, with respected tribal and clan leaders responsible for the day-to-day application of politics: deciding who got what and how to pay for it. The creation of the strong state moved political power from villages and districts to the national capital, thus weakening the power of the local gentry. It also challenged both urban and rural elites, who often amassed considerable power in the absence of a centralized state. However, the voices of these once-powerful elites faded in the noise of nationalist movements, which were often led by military officers.

The officer corps in many Middle East countries often consisted of working-class men who saw the military as one of the few ladders to success and power, since family ties that they lacked often paved the primary road to wealth and influence. So officers such as Hafiz al-Asad joined the Syrian army, as did Gamal Abdul Nasser in Egypt. In other cases the nationalist story was written by such scholars as Michel Aflaq and Salal al-Din Bitar, whose studies of nationalism in Europe crystallized the ideas that led to the Baath (or "Renaissance") Party in Syria and, later, in Iraq. The soldiers, though, were the original backbone of state-building, which for them was similar to building a military. They created large ministries that governed by power instead of finesse as the state became organized in a top-down fashion resembling a military force where orders flow downward to the obedient followers. The old elites who had sometimes collaborated with the previous monarchy or foreign rulers were cast aside to make way for the modernizers who replaced the privileged networks with their own associations, often drawn from the military. Unsurprisingly the process of state-building often resulted in the strong national security state, with priorities placed on armaments and the preparation for war. Imported armaments flowed in from the industrial countries that paid less attention to the domestic side of state-building than they did to maintaining clients in the Cold War climate. Armaments sometimes provided the means for state-builders to go to war in the name of defending their state, or adding contrived legitimacy to their creations. One consequence was the vast growth of military cemeteries and memorials to fallen heroes, while a less tangible result was the loss of opportunity for education, housing, infrastructure, and other parts of the modern state that were neglected as leaders prepared for the next conflict.

Economic Themes in the Middle East

There is a connection between political stability and prevailing economic conditions in all parts of the world, though that association may be keener in the Middle East than the industrial world because of the fragile nature of both political legitimacy and economic development in many MENA countries. Leaders of strong centrally managed states often justify their power grip through economic requirements, and, reciprocally, weak economic systems seem to require strong state oversight. Too frequently autocratic leadership manages the state economy to retain political power, and thus the economy becomes a reward-and-punishment system for friends and foes. Supporters of the regime get plum positions while opponents find themselves in an economic wilderness. Subsidies and tax incentives go to loyalists, along with lucrative monopoly contracts to collect garbage, construct military bases, and a thousand other state-managed functions. Those not seen as faithful to the regime can find themselves under investigation for corruption, or tax fraud, or a host of other offenses, to be scrutinized and tried in courts run by the government.

The other correlation between politics and economic conditions is that economic failures, perceived or real, pose a clear threat to regime survival. While this is true universally, it is particularly poignant in areas with weak political institutions and brittle economies. In cases where either the state is seen to be responsible for bad economic conditions or where the state actually creates bad economic policy, key groups will withdraw regime support. More significantly, where there is no alternative party, or where the alternative parties do not show a viable difference with the ruling regime, the alternative may become religious. Karasipahi notes that Iranian economic policies under the shah harmed merchant interests and "they were powerless *vis à vis* the state and thus consolidated their ties with the mullahs and clergy."[14] In Turkey in the 1980s, President Turgut Ozal promoted a free market economy that helped to impoverish many lower- and middle-class Turks, who turned to the Islamist parties for support.[15] The curtailing of economic subsidies withdrew one of the few social safety nets in the MENA, empowering religious groups that used their own resources to provide bread and education for those who once bought subsidized bread, sugar, and petrol.

The Range of Economic National Wealth. The Middle East is a mosaic of wealth differences, ranging from Yemen, one of the poorest countries in the world, to Qatar and the United Arab Emirates, which are some of the wealthiest. In between is a wide range of countries, though they tend toward the lower range of economic development.

Economic status is measured in a variety of ways, with none giving a complete picture. The most common is the division of a country's total wealth by its population, gross domestic product per capita. The resultant ratio may be expressed in either the exchange rate figures (national currencies converted to dollars by an index method) or by "purchasing power parity," which standardizes dollar price weights. For 2009, the Middle East economic situation is shown in Table 1.2.

It is evident from this table that wealth measured in GDP per capita varied widely in the Middle East in 2009, from Mauritania, at $2,100, to Qatar, at $103,500, one of the wealthiest countries in the world. At the margins, clear explanations pop up: Petroleum exporting countries are, in general, wealthier than countries with no oil or gas. Population also obviously matters; tiny Qatar, whose population of Qatari passport holders may be less than 10,000, has a

TABLE 1.2: COMPARATIVE GDP/CAPITA FOR MIDDLE EAST COUNTRIES

Country	GDP/Capita (PPP)
Algeria	$7,000
Bahrain	37,200
Egypt	5,400
Gaza	2,900
Iran	12,800
Iraq	4,000
Israel	28,200
Jordan	5,000
Kuwait	57,400
Libya	14,400
Mauritania	2,100
Morocco	4,000
Oman	20,200
Qatar	103,500
Saudi Arabia	20,700
Syria	4,800
Tunisia	7,900
Turkey	12,000
United Arab Emirates	40,000
West Bank	2,900

huge supply of natural gas, and thus a high GDP/capita. Other differences are a consequence of more subtle explanations. Oman has almost no exploitable oil and gas reserves, yet its GDP per capita is higher than that of Libya, which has the largest petroleum reserves in North Africa, with 41 billion barrels of oil. Part of the reason for the differential is that Libya under its leader, Muammar Qadhafi, ran a "stateless" system that could not use oil revenues efficiently, its petroleum sector struggled under decades of international sanctions for Libyan support of terrorism, and even after Libya's efforts to retreat from its fanatical economic and political experimentation, the country remains behind.[16] Oman, on the other hand, avoided the worst features of Arab socialism and has instead used a careful blend of privatization and state investment to stimulate its national economy.

The economic foundations of the Middle East were varied, but a common feature in many was the dominance of a merchant class, a rural elite, and the interests of colonial powers. These actors formed economic systems and institutions that suited their narrow interests, which included amassing wealth and power for themselves while reducing the cost of doing so.[17] One consequence was a sharp class distinction in most countries, with a powerful upper class and an often impoverished working class, with the ranks of a middle class generally filled out only after independence, and largely by members of the growing state bureaucracy. In some ways, the Middle East resembled Europe in the nineteenth century, and thus, like Europe in the twentieth century, the Middle East turned to socialism partly to break the power of the economic elites.

In many ways, Arab socialism and Arab nationalism were sewn from similar cloth, because they stood on a single premise: The Arab world had fallen behind the industrial world, and only a concerted state-centric effort might have a chance to thrust it forward in the postcolonial era. Arab socialism meant that the state opened enterprises vital to growth: cement, steel, shipbuilding, road construction, and such, along with state provision of services to support growth, including health care and education. State planning was the centerpiece of Arab socialism, and much of the construction boom that marked Cairo, Damascus, Rabat, and other cities created vast ministry buildings. The ministry of cement planned and operated national cement enterprises, often presided over by political loyalists rather than experts in cement, or finance, or import rules. Sometimes the loyalists were former or active military officers who ran their ventures like army divisions rather than businesses. Moreover, the goal of Arab socialism was not only to produce things, but also to employ workers whose unemployment might have led them to join political opposition groups. One consequence was the almost inevitable inefficiency that results when state planners rather than market forces determine economic production. Arab socialism mandated steel mills in countries with no iron ore or coking coal (coal), or transportation systems to deliver both raw materials and finished goods. Planning often meant supporting projects that created more jobs over projects that responded to societal demand, thus giving power to planners over entrepreneurs. And since the planners worked for the state, their plans generally worked to advance state interests over other elements of society. As a result the state amassed power under the Arab socialism banner, while the business and agricultural elites, along with religious leaders, saw the state train pass them by. Many migrated, went underground, or simply surrendered to the obvious and got jobs with the government.

Socialism was not limited to the Arab world, though. The state of Israel, founded in part by members of the Jewish socialist community from Europe, also adopted state planning and state-run enterprises. The roots of Israel's state-dominated economy were less ideological than practical: Zionism did not attract private capital, and thus the state had to provide it, along with land to practice the Zionist ideal of kibbutz farming.[18] The founding Israeli Labor Party created powerful state ministries to run the most significant parts of the Israeli economy, along with the state-run airline (El Al), the railroad system, and the powerful Israeli Aircraft Industries, one of Israel's largest single employers.

For a number of reasons, Middle Eastern economic growth spurted during the 1960s, reaching 6 percent per worker per year, at that time the highest in the world, and oil price growth allowed such rates to continue into the 1970s.[19] But ultimately a combination of lower oil prices and economic reform in other parts of the developing world helped the Middle East to fall behind, and exposed the flaws of its economic systems.

While state socialism might have produced high employment levels, it also brought considerable inefficiencies. Because there was little if any need to calculate market forces in investment and management decisions, socialist managers and their political bosses usually made decisions on resource expenditures more on political calculations. They sought to enhance national prestige, reward faithful followers, or build jobs in areas of political unrest. The consequences were often wasteful and corrupted. Jordan provides examples, such as the Jordan Phosphates Mines Company, which was consistently over-manned to soak up unemployment, and the national airline: "Arguably the worst of all excesses was the national carrier (Royal Air Jordan), with a large debt of some $850 million (or the equivalent of 11 percent of GDP) being built up on the reckless acquisition of aircraft, and due scrutiny being warned off by an active royal patronage that reflected the king's personal weakness for flying. Such prestige projects undoubtedly enhance the status of a small country."[20]

State socialism could not last, though. A variety of forces drew power in their combined opposition to state control, albeit for differing reasons. As Rutherford notes, the legal and commercial elites in Egypt shared a consensus with the Muslim Brotherhood that central state power in Egypt should be curbed, and while the business elites wanted fewer regulations and less competition from state-owned enterprises, the Muslim Brothers wanted to rein in the state's coercive power over religious groupings.[21] Whatever the source of opposition, it may be paying dividends for less state control and more opportunities for private investors.[22]

Other challenges to state-managed economies came from outside the region. With globalization came pressures from foreign advisers both from particular countries (the United States supplied advisers from the Agency for International Development) and from multilateral organizations, such as the International Monetary Fund (IMF) and the World Bank. In the 1990s these institutions settled on a general set of guidelines for developing countries, including the Middle East, called the Washington Consensus. At its core were ten recommendations (sometimes called "the Ten Commandments") aimed at reducing state subsidies, privatizing state enterprises, basing currency exchange rates on competition rather than state manipulation, liberalizing trade, and creating other conditions designed to enhance a meaningful private sector. In other words, the Washington

Consensus was really a recipe to either restore capitalism to developing countries that once had it or to implement it in countries where it had never really existed.

The response to the Washington Consensus in the Middle East was decidedly mixed. As Henry and Springborg observe, "The responses of the MENA countries to the Ten Commandments ranged from eager acceptance, to vociferous rejection, to covert compliance with some of them."[23] Privatizing state ventures could lead to unemployment, thus threatening political stability. Ending subsidies had similar problems: In Tunisia IMF-mandated suspension of bread and flour subsidies led to a doubling of the prices for these goods, and thus to riots and thousands of casualties in 1983,[24] and similar riots broke out in Egypt in 1977 and Algeria in 1988 for the same reason. The suspension of subsidies withdrew the state-provided social safety net from the poor, often leaving them no recourse but to turn to the mosques for help, and thus empowering political Islam at the state's expense. One commentary noted that "not only did unemployment and poverty increase, inequality of income also worsened in all of them except Tunisia,"[25] and thus, "There is already a growing body of evidence that economic liberalization and other forms of globalization have opened up a space which is rapidly being occupied by religious groups in the Arab region, some of which are politically motivated."[26]

However, a number of Middle East countries did follow some of the guidelines or developed their own systems for economic reform. Privatization happened in many countries, with states placing national airlines, banks, insurance companies, and other national enterprises on the selling block.

Is There Economic Progress in the Middle East? A current picture of the Middle East shows a mixed economic picture. On the one hand, there has been economic progress in the Middle East. According to a 2009 study by the Brookings Institution, science and technology are gaining ground in the Arab world, with more patents registered and investments, such as that of the Mohammed bin Rashid Al Maktoum Foundation, putting billions of dollars into research and education. Moreover, between 2000 and 2005, high-tech exports rose in Jordan, Morocco, and Saudi Arabia. Egypt now employs more than 40,000 people in information technology companies. Still, economic progress in the Arab world was overshadowed by other regions, the report notes. Ireland outspent Jordan by around 300 percent on research and development, and while 18 percent of Moroccan university students study science or engineering, 40 percent of Malaysians are studying in those fields.[27]

The other side of the story is that Arab economies still rely too much on natural resources, imported technology, and low-skill microenterprises. Foreign direct investment, as a percentage of GDP, is only half that of East Asia. Executives cite the lack of qualified personnel as the largest obstacle to innovation, despite high levels of unemployment in the region. Demographic challenges loom: With 35 percent of the population under the age of fifteen, Arab economies must create 100 million new jobs by 2020 to accommodate the number of Arab youth reaching age eighteen by that year.[28] The lack of globally competitive education in many Middle Eastern countries is also a potential barrier to economic development. The 2003 Arab Human Development Project worried that "education policies in many Arab countries lack an integrated vision of the education process and its objectives. Furthermore, these policies are characterized by inconsistency and a lack of direction. Problems, such as those relating to the content of the curricula, forms of examination, evaluation of students, and foreign languages cannot be settled without formulating a well-defined vision of educational goals and necessities."[29]

The Religious Theme

The Middle East cannot be comprehensively discussed without including religion as a component in the area's life. As in many other world cultures, religious values inform law, guide personal behavior, both individual and social, and provide answers to the most complex questions of life in the Middle East. Religion provides foundations for statehood, and often the constitution (where there is one) states that "Islam is the official religion" in the case of a Muslim country. It also provides the substance of quarrels over how much statecraft should incorporate religion as an instrument for direction and compliance. Disputes over the degree to which Torah or Islamic law should bind members of society break out frequently in most Middle Eastern countries (Christians are tiny minorities in all Middle East countries except Lebanon). Religious law and teachings upon which it is based come from a fundamental understanding in Muslim countries that stems from early Muslim thinking on humanity: that "it is the nature of humans that they need one another and must cooperate to survive," and such cooperation must be regulated by government partly because of the very nature of humans, who, left to their own passions, "would ruthlessly pursue their own interests and diverse passions, engage in constant rivalry and strife without affection or altruism . . . and thus bring about their own ruin."[30] Moreover, since humans are fundamentally incapable of creating their own laws, laws thus must come from God.[31] Since the earliest days of Islam, scholars and government leaders have debated the degree to which divinely inspired law should govern society, and, since 1948, similar disputes have raged in Israel. They include the degree to which the direct revealed word of God is law, as opposed to "secular" law that at least does not contradict direct divine words.

The Mosque and the State

Religion is not a cause in itself of international conflict, but it can be an accelerant of such conflict. Says Ayoob of Saudi Arabia and Iran, two states with strong religious identity,

Contiguous and proximate states at early stages of state making often develop conflictual relations with each other for a number of reasons related to state and regime legitimacy and/or divergent conceptions of the regional balance of power. Saudi Arabia and Iran are no exception to this rule. Their self-proclaimed "Islamic" character does not mitigate but, in fact, adds to their regional rivalry by overlaying it with ideological rhetoric.[32]

The Middle East is the fountainhead of the three most populous religions, and even those adherents who live far from it still look to the Middle East for religious inspiration and guidance. For Jews, Jerusalem and its environs are a spiritual abode, Muslims pray daily toward Mecca and aspire to perform the *hajj*, the religious pilgrimage to Mecca to reaffirm their faith, at least once in their lives, and many of the world's Christians seek pilgrimage at some point to the holy places they read about in scripture. However, religious interpretations have also been and remain a vulnerability for the Middle East. In many countries, weak national identification means that religious identities are worth more than national citizenship, and thus religious adherents are more likely to quarrel over religious identity. So within a country, cohesion is fragile simply because fewer citizens bond through national citizenship while more cluster into religious groupings. In countries with more than one religious club, quarrels between Sunni and Shia or Maronite and Druze or secular and orthodox Jew are more likely to occur, and more likely to range beyond the bounds of state intervention. At the same time, most of these disputes are actually about power more than they are about theology. In Iraq, the Sunni and the Shia fight more about power than they do about the ancient question of who should have succeeded the Prophet Muhammad at his death in 632. But it is easier to fight with someone whose religious understanding is clearly incorrect, according to rival understandings, and thus when Sunni extremists declare the Shia to be apostates, for example, it is easier to blow up their mosques and kill them, even if the real motive is to prevent them from taking power in Iraq.

Religion, for its believers, is a set of milestones, to use the title of Sayyid Qutb's most famous work.[33] Religious interpretations stand ready to remind humankind of its professed values, its pinnacles and valleys, its hopes, and its fears. Religious principles get wide respect because they are old, enduring, and based upon either direct divine message or indirect divine inspiration. The world is full of adherents, and those who profess to truly have no religious beliefs generally range from only 16 percent to 20 percent in global polls. Of course, religious adherence is just a profession of some religious beliefs and does not measure intensity. Intensity of religious belief, as measured by a positive response to a Pew Charitable Trust survey asking the question "Does religion play a very important role in your life?" varies considerably across peoples. According to the survey, the percentages of those answering in the affirmative range from Senegal at 97 percent to the Czech Republic at 11 percent.[34] The survey also found that religion is of far more importance in low-income countries than for wealthy countries. (The United States is an exception, at 59 percent.)[35] This may be one reason why religion is so important both at the personal and at the collective level in the Middle East, and though the Pew survey included Turkey as the only Middle Eastern country, another survey, done for several years by Gallup, found that Middle Eastern countries rank strongly in religious adherence. In response to a question similar to the Pew survey, "Is religion an important part of your daily life?" 100 percent of Egyptians and 98 percent of Moroccans and Emiratis said "yes," as did 86 percent of Lebanese, 83 percent of Iranians, and 50 percent of Israelis.[36] Gallup also found that of the top ten countries in religious adherence, all but the United Arab Emirates were low- to middle-income countries, whereas the citizens of high-income countries displayed less importance of religion (Sweden at 17 percent, Norway at 20 percent, and Hong Kong with 22 percent).[37]

It is impossible to separate religion from politics in almost all countries in the world, though those nations with a Marxist political tradition, such as China, attempt to do so. While Europe is relatively secular, many European political parties have the word "Christian" in them. However, that identity is now associated much more with skepticism about the rival socialist parties than it is with Christian theology. The European political tradition is much more strongly rooted in the logical secular social order of Mill, Saint-Simon, and other European thinkers whose ideas about governance were passed on to Europe's colonies, including the Middle East. The European imperialists may have hoped that the consequence would be a "rationalist" pact between governor and governed, in place of the often-Islamic-inspired rulers the imperialists either replaced or used to rule in their stead. But in colonial countries with Islamic traditions, Islam itself often became a vehicle for an empowered Islamist political opposition to challenge the Islamic credentials of rulers who were not sufficiently grounded in principles of Islamic governance. There was also a Jewish challenge to the idea of Israel as a secular state with a Jewish identity, and though David Ben Gurion, Israel's first prime minister, turned it back, the question has kept Israel from having a genuine constitution. Still, those in Israel who wish for Torah law argue their case with as much passion as do those Islamists who advocate that law based on sharia (law based on Islamic principles) replace the civil law from European secular grounding.

In significant ways, the contest for authority in both Muslim and Jewish countries is a joust between secular rule based on nationalist principles, and religious rule. The dominant tale in early Arab independence movements was Arab nationalism, which in some ways was a doctrine based on foreign roots. Some of the early Arab nationalists were students in Europe in the 1930s, such as Salal al-Din Bitar and Michel Aflaq, who were the ideological godfathers of the Baath movement, and Habib Bourguiba, the founding president of Tunisia, who received his law degree in France. Other Arab nationalists grounded their beliefs in military service, such as Gamal Abdel Nasser of Egypt, Hafiz al-Asad of Syria, and Ali Abdullah Saleh of Yemen. But the influence of the mosque was never far away, and the dramatic loss for the Arab side in the 1967 war opened its doors to more influence as Arab nationalism began to wane.

For the state of Israel, similar challenges were brewing as the nature of Jewish identity, the main stream running through a country founded on collective memory of Jewish tragedy, as the initial secular character came under scrutiny from a growing religious chorus. As Etzioni-Halevy puts it, the Jews who came in the early beginnings of Israel "were proud of their nationality (rather than of their religion). They accepted the main religious symbols (such as the Jewish holidays, or Zion and Jerusalem), but converted them to national symbols. . . . As for the religious Zionists, they rejected the secular interpretation of the Jewish heritage. They also saw the return to Zion, and the establishment of the Jewish state, as the beginning of the redemption, in the religious sense."[38] So was Zionism primarily religious, primarily political, or both? Says Zertal, "Zionism's determination to solve the problem of anti-Semitism through the establishment of a Jewish state, and by the deployment of organizational, diplomatic, economic, and eventually military means, was utterly political."[39] The original compromises between the profane and the religious came through considerable angst between the secular Zionists and the religious adherents over the structure of the legal system, the nature of state education, and a host of other matters that Ben Gurion had to shepherd through a contentious and fragile process.[40]

The International Theme

No region is an isolated island on the globe, and the Middle East is no exception. Events, memories, raw material deposits, and security concerns spill out from the region into the rest of the world, to the point where there are few spots on earth that the Middle East does not touch in some way. That is a part of the international theme, but relations within countries in the area are also obviously international.

The term "flashpoints" was once used to describe issues that divided countries: for example, disputed borders, historical national rivalry, the poaching into a region by an outside power, or the rise of a regime that based its claim to legitimacy by stirring up revanchist arguments against another country. Such flashpoints existed globally, and some got famous names—the "Iron Curtain," or the "demilitarized zone," for example—while others just festered. The Cold War helped to create some of these flashpoints, such as the border between North and South Korea, while others were a consequence of long historical memory that regimes often reinforced for their own purposes. India and Pakistan, Argentina and Chile, China and Vietnam, and the Soviet Union and the People's Republic of China are only a few examples.

Partly because of the end of the Cold War, flashpoints are fewer today, but they still exist. Despite efforts at peace-making, India and Pakistan, North and South Korea, and the states of the former Yugoslavia remain tense. There are also fewer flashpoints in the Middle East, but those that remain are some of the most dangerous on the planet. They include Iran's relationship with its Middle East neighbors, and the evolution of stateless insurgents who use the vast spaces of the Middle East to recruit, organize, and plan.

Some of the conflicts in the Middle East are about land and memory of land, hardly surprising in a region where land valuable to humans is scarce. Roughly 90 percent of Arab lands are desert or semi-desert, useful for limited cultivation and herding, but with temperatures hovering around 120 degrees Fahrenheit or hotter in the summer, even semi-fertile land has limits. Thus claims to arable land are rarely given or sold, except within family, and so when others take land by force, memories of it by its previous owners may last for centuries. When such land has religious attributes, the conflict may become particularly intractable. Thus it is in the present conflict between the state of Israel and the Palestinians who claim the land where Israel stands today was their ancestral home.

For the Palestinians, and the vast majority of the world's Muslims, the creation of the state of Israel by force was a theft of Muslim lands, a violation of the very idea of the *Dar al-Islam*, or abode of Islam, since most Palestinians are Muslims. For the vast majority of the world's Jewish population, though, the birth of the modern state of Israel was a rebirth of the ancient Hebrew kingdom that had wrought Jerusalem as its ancient capital and site of its most sacred space on earth, the Second Temple. Here the physical conflicted space gets even smaller and more intense. For Muslims, the land not only was a part of the abode of Islam, but Jerusalem also was the spot where tradition holds that the Prophet Muhammad ascended to heaven from the mountain to assemble with God's previous messengers and receive God's final revelations. To commemorate these events and to preserve their positions, Jews built the Second Temple (the Babylonians destroyed the First Temple), and Muslims built the Dome of the Rock. These buildings sit next to each other but are leagues apart in the sacred world, whose passions may never allow them to cast shadows over the peaceful world that both religions profess.

Conflicts may arise over land possession, but they quickly become much more complex. The Israeli-Palestinian differences that have flamed since 1948 have generated their own set of stories that help to fuel the embers. Both parties have genuine historical accounts that allow the ghosts of the past to live on. For the Israelis, the story is the Holocaust and the other depredations the Jews of Europe suffered, a series of images captured now at Yad Vashem, the Holocaust memorial in Jerusalem. For the Palestinians, the story is of foreign occupation of Palestine by the British, the French, and the Ottoman Turks, and sometimes stretched even to the Crusaders, whose conquest of Jerusalem in 1099 resulted in rivers of both Muslim and Jewish blood and the conversion of the Dome of the Rock into a church. Thus it is possible to recast Palestinians as jackbooted National Socialists and Jews as Crusaders or as the fictional British Colonel Bogey or symbolic Turkish pasha treating Arabs like children and hanging them if they refuse to obey. While such memories are not a direct cause of conflict, they clearly enhance its violence and give support for those who direct it.

It is still the case, though, that most conflict in the MENA involves arguments over property, often exacerbated by memory. The dispute in the Western Sahara, or the Moroccan Sahara, is about land, even though it may be desolate and sparsely populated. For Morocco, and particularly for the Moroccan monarchy, it is about a claim that the Western Sahara was traditionally a part of Morocco and that the monarchy has an obligation to protect that claim in the name of its right to rule. The Crown justifies that right to rule partly through a claimed heritage to the Prophet Muhammad. It was not by accident that King Hassan II launched his claim to the Western Sahara in 1975 through "the Great Green March," where hundreds of thousands of Moroccans marched into the region carrying the color of Islam with them. It is also not surprising that Algeria and Mauritania, whose postcolonial identities were forged in the language of nationalism and, by extension, republicanism, opposed Morocco's claim. For them, this exacerbated existing border differences with Morocco, in Algeria's case, and gave both an opportunity to support the indigenous claimants to Western Sahara, the Sahrawis. The conflict, sometimes called a "frozen conflict," continues without resolution.

Other conflicts range beyond land, which becomes a part, but just a part, in the overall matrix. The situation between Iran and most of the adjacent countries in the Gulf and Levant is one such case. Iran is an anomaly, a country whose national language, Farsi, is unique to the region. Its religious heritage, "Twelver," or Imamiyya Shia, provides its ruling clerics with a faith-based justification for their right to reign. Iran has no friends in its neighborhood, partly because it has chosen isolation from them, and partly because the "Islamic Revolution" that started in 1979 caused tremors in the region's Muslim countries along with concern in Israel that Iran would try to polish its Islamic credentials by attacking it. Iran compounded all these fears by embarking on a nuclear research program that most analysts believe will result in a nuclear weapons capacity, despite official denials from Iranian leadership.

The "Weapons of Mass Destruction" Genie. During the reign of Shah Muhammad Pahlavi, Iran initiated a nuclear research program. Whether such a program might have led to the development of nuclear weapons was unclear, but it continued at low levels after 1979. Its purpose generated intense sparks of debate, with some arguing that it would produce offensive weapons, while others suggested that a potential Iranian nuclear weapons program mirrored Iran's traditional insecurity because of its neighborhood. The national prestige factor could not be discounted either, an Iranian declaration against its potential tormentors. As Abid-Moghaddam notes, "The national consensus in defence of Iran's nuclear energy programme can be linked to the 'Tobacco revolts' of 1891, . . . the nationalization of the Anglo-Iranian Oil Company in early 1951, . . . and the Islamic revolution of 1979."[41]

The Iranian nuclear program only complicated the already complex environment of the so-called weapons of mass destruction in the Middle East. These weapons, characterized as involving chemical, nuclear, or biological capacity to hurt and kill, have already been used in the Middle East, probably more so than in any other region after World War I. Egypt used them in Yemen in the 1960s, and Iran and Iraq hurled them at each other during the long and deadly Iran-Iraq war of 1981–1988. Despite official denials, Israel began work on a nuclear weapons program in the late 1950s and is believed to have a nuclear arsenal of several hundred weapons and the means to launch them.

Countries develop weapons of mass destruction, and nuclear weapons in particular, for varying reasons. Some of these reasons lead to highly dangerous conditions in security situations, when countries believe that nuclear weapons provide a sense of security particularly against similarly armed rivals, to the danger of either a regional nuclear arms race, to the transfer of nuclear weapons to a third party, or, in the worst case, to a nuclear strike. In other situations, national prestige is also involved: Both India and Pakistan touted their successful nuclear tests around a panorama of national pride, with citizens carrying posters with pictures of mushroom clouds in government-organized rallies.

Arguably the world has moved on from its collective thinking that nuclear weapons bought prestige and a voice at the community table. Nuclear weapons are like the so-called American muscle cars of the 1960s; they were once thought of as cool, but cool has now moved to hybrids instead of powerful V-8 engines. Much of the world has now moved on to competition in the global marketplace of goods, services, and ideas, and countries that still think nuclear weapons matter are lampooned, such as North Korea and Iran. The leaders of these countries preside over broken economies (massive starvation has marked North Korean recent history) and, when queried about his country's economic woes, Ayatollah Ruhollah Khomeini blustered that "economics is for donkeys."[42] Irresponsible rhetoric and brutal rule mark both North Korea and Iran, and they would still be potentially dangerous to their neighborhood without nuclear weapons, but the game changes when "rogue states" get deliverable nuclear weapons. The obvious problem is that nuclear weapons in the hands of quixotic leaders is like a muscle car in the hands of a drunk driver, with potentially catastrophic consequences, and thus the Iranian nuclear program has drawn great focus both inside and beyond the Middle East.[43]

So has the Israeli nuclear program, though for different reasons. Although the behavior of Israeli leaders cannot be compared to that of Mahmoud Ahmadinejad, Israel has launched preemptive wars against its neighbors, attacking

Egypt, Syria, and Jordan in 1967 and Lebanon on several occasions. Iran has not preemptively attacked its neighbors since 1971, when Iranian forces took Abu Musa and the Tunb Islands in the Gulf. While Israel often claimed that its war initiations were defensive (or the prime minister lied about them, as in the 1953 Qibya massacre in Jordan), Israel's adjacent countries did not view them as self-protective, nor did some of Israel's supporting countries. The 1967 war was particularly troublesome because Israel retained territory it took from the surrounding Arab countries, and it still holds some of that territory today. Some argue that that war was defensive for Israel: "The Six-Day War . . . was launched by Israel to safeguard its security, not to expand its territory."[44] Others argue that the Arab states provoked Israel's actions in 1967 by shelling Israeli territory or by appearing to mobilize for war.[45] Yet other interpretations suggest mixed motives for the Arabs. Says Maoz, "Nasser's initial aim in the crisis (of 1967) was clearly to deter Israel from attacking Syria. There is almost no dispute on this point."[46] The reality remains that Israel used military force to attack other countries in the recent past and has nuclear weapons, while Iran has a nuclear program that could produce weapons but has not attacked its neighbors since 1971. The simple reality is that while neither Israel nor Iran's Arab neighbors want Iran to develop nuclear weapons, the levers that they and other countries can use to stop Iran's program are somewhat harder to use because of the Israeli nuclear capacity. And while Egyptian leaders have proposed a nuclear-free Middle East, and US President Barack Obama has called for a world with zero nuclear weapons, both options are highly unlikely to achieve their goals unless there is both a considerable reduction in the tensions that lead to weapons and a global belief that nuclear weapons have no more desirability than do muscle cars.

WELCOME TO THE MIDDLE EAST

The purpose of this introduction is to pave the road for the following sections. The necessary baggage for the trip are a basic understanding of the area's complex history and a willingness to explore ideas. The following sections contain interpretations of the available information about the meaning of history, about demographics, about politics and economics, and about regional security. Let the journey begin.

NOTES

1. Freedom House is a nongovernmental organization founded in 1941 and head-quartered in New York City. It promotes democracy and issues an annual evaluation of democratic progress in the world, ranking countries in three categories, "free," "partly free," or "not free," based on a series of measures indicating levels of political rights and civil liberties.

2. Cyrus Kadivar, "We Are Awake: 2,500 Celebration Revisited," *The Iranian*, January 25, 2002.

3. See "Methodology" on the Freedom House Web site for information on how the survey was conducted: www.freedomhouse.org/template.cfm?page=351&ana_page=341&year=2008.

4. Iliya Harik, "Democracy, 'Arab Exceptionalism,' and Social Science," *Middle East Journal* 60 (Autumn 2006): 664–684.

5. Ronald Englehart, "The Worldviews of Islamic Publics in Global Perspective," www.worldvaluessurvey.org/.

6. "Iraqi Vote Mirrors Desire for Democracy in Muslim World," a Pew Global Attitudes Project Commentary, February 3, 2005, http://people-press.org/commentary/?analysisid=107.

7. Of course, such divisions are common throughout the world, including the United States, as former President Jimmy Carter reminded his audience when he infamously praised "ethnic purity" while visiting a Polish-American neighborhood on his 1976 presidential campaign. The run-down areas north of the airport road in Paris are largely immigrant housing, marred by rioting several years ago by jobless youth. But these divisions impede national unity and, often, when the minority lives and works in substandard quarters and conditions, in the view of the majority, those views give rise to tensions and sometimes violent confrontation.

8. Named because, according to one traditional tale, one of the tasks assigned to members of Morocco's Jewish community was to preserve in salt the decapitated heads of insurgents so they could be mounted on the city walls as a warning to other rebels.

9. "Housing Minister: Spread of Arab Population Must Be Stopped," *Ha'aretz*, July 2, 2009.

10. André Raymond, *Cairo* (Cambridge, MA: Harvard University Press, 2000), pp. 161–162.

11. In a survey of 108 countries by the United Nations Development Programme, while Sweden was ranked number 1, five Arab countries (Morocco, Algeria, Saudi Arabia, Egypt, and Yemen) ranked at the bottom. *Human Development Indices: A Statistical Update 2008*. United Nations Human Development Programme, 2008, p. 44, http://hdr.undp.org/en/media/HDI_2008_EN_Complete.pdf.

12. Ibid., p. 19.

13. "U.N. Cites Arab World's 'Empty Gestures' on Women," *Washington Post*, December 8, 2006.

14. Sena Karasipahi, "Comparing Islamic Resurgence Movements in Turkey and Iran," *Middle East Journal* 63 (Winter 2009): 102.

15. Ibid.

16. Dirk Vandewalle, *A History of Modern Libya* (Cambridge: Cambridge University Press, 2006).

17. For summaries of some of the foundations of Middle East economic systems, see David S. Landes, *Bankers and Pashas: International Finance and Economic Imperialism in Egypt* (Cambridge, MA: Harvard University Press, 1979); Jill Crystal, *Oil and Politics in the Gulf: Rulers and Merchants in Kuwait and Qatar* (Cambridge: Cambridge University Press, 1990); Charles Issawi, *An Economic History of the Middle East and North Africa* (New York: Columbia University Press, 1982); Charles Issawi, ed., *The*

Economic History of the Middle East, 1800–1914 (Chicago: University of Chicago Press, 1966).

18. Ephraim Kleiman, "The Waning of Israeli *Etatisme*," *Israel Studies* 2 (Fall 1997): 146–171. The kibbutzim are collective communities based largely on agriculture, from the Hebrew word for "gathering."

19. Tarik M. Yousef, "Development, Growth and Policy Reform in the Middle East and North Africa since 1950," *Journal of Economic Perspectives* 18 (Summer 2004): 96.

20. Philip Robins, *A History of Jordan* (Cambridge: Cambridge University Press, 2004), p. 145. Jordan's King Hussein was an accomplished pilot who enjoyed flying visitors to Jordan. Once he flew US Secretary of State Henry Kissinger and his wife in a helicopter, and Kissinger's wife, terrified that the king was flying so low, queried, "Do helicopters always fly this low?" The king responded, "Oh, no, they can go much lower," and down went the helicopter. Kissinger's wife's reaction was not recorded.

21. The Egyptian Muslim Brotherhood, founded in 1928 by Hassan al Banna, has agitated through participation in the political process for a government more aligned with moderate Islamist principles.

22. Bruce K. Rutherford, *Egypt after Mubarak: Liberalism, Islam, and Democracy* (Princeton, NJ: Princeton University Press, 2008), esp. ch. 6.

23. Clement M. Henry and Robert Springborg, *Globalization and the Politics of Development in the Middle East* (Cambridge: Cambridge University Press, 2001), p. 26.

24. Kenneth J. Perkins, *A History of Modern Tunisia* (Cambridge: Cambridge University Press, 2004), pp. 169–170.

25. Hamed El-Said and Jane Harrigan, "Globalization, International Finance, and Political Islam in the Arab World," *Middle East Journal* 60 (Summer 2006): 227–228.

26. Ibid., p. 230.

27. Kristin M. Lord, *A New Millennium of Knowledge? The Arab Human Development Report on Building a Knowledge Society, Five Years On* (Washington, DC: Brookings Institution, 2008).

28. Kristen M. Lord, "The Arab World's (Uneven) Progress," *Christian Science Monitor*, February 20, 2009. This figure assumes the current retirement rate remains relatively constant, though if it increases that will reduce the number of new jobs required by 2020.

29. *Arab Human Development Report 2003: Building a Knowledge Society*. Arab Fund for Economic and Social Development, United Nations Development Programme, 2003, p. 54, www.arab-hdr.org/publications/other/ahdr/ahdr2003e.pdf.

30. Patricia Crone, *God's Rule: Government and Islam* (New York: Columbia University Press, 2004), pp. 260–262.

31. Ibid., pp. 263–266.

32. Mohammed Ayoob, *The Many Faces of Political Islam* (Ann Arbor: University of Michigan Press, 2008), p. 48.

33. Sayyid Qutb was an Egyptian Muslim ideologue who criticized President Gamal Abdel Nasser's regime for being insufficiently Islamic and demanded to implement sharia law. Some argue that his political thought inspired Islamist groups such as al-Qaeda.

34. "Among Wealthy Nations, U.S. Stands Alone in Its Embrace of Religion," Pew Charitable Trust, December 19, 2002, http://people-press.org/report/167/among-wealthy-nations-%E2%80%A6.

35. Ibid.

36. "What Alabamians and Iranians Have In Common"; the survey broke the United States into states, and the title reflects the finding that Iranians at 83 percent and Alabamians at 82 percent share a high religious importance, though that number varies within the United States from Mississippi at 85 percent to Vermont at 42 percent. Gallup International, February 9, 2009, www.gallup.com/poll/114211/Alabamians -Iranians-Common.aspx.

37. Ibid.

38. Eva Etzioni-Halevy, *The Divided People: Can Israel's Breakup Be Stopped?* (Lanham, MD: Lexington Books, 2002), p. 108.

39. Idith Zertal, *Israel's Holocaust and the Politics of Nationhood* (Cambridge: Cambridge University Press, 2005), p. 166.

40. Peter Y. Medding, *The Founding of Israeli Democracy, 1948–1967* (New York: Oxford University Press, 1990).

41. Arshin Adib-Moghaddam, *Iran in World Politics* (New York: Columbia University Press, 2008), p. 77.

42. Robert Tait, "Economics Is for Donkeys," *New Statesman*, September 11, 2008.

43. There are debates about whether "crazy states" are forced to become more responsible when they possess nuclear weapons. China, while in the throes of the "Great Cultural Proletariat Revolution," behaved with considerable responsibility when its troops clashed with Soviet troops on a disputed island on the Chinese-Soviet border. A single case does not prove the argument, of course, but it is fodder for further analysis.

44. Avi Shlaim, *The Iron Wall: Israel and the Arab World* (New York: W. W. Norton, 2000), p. 242.

45. Martin Gilbert, *Israel: A History* (New York: Morrow, 1998), chapter 21; Richard B. Parker, *The Politics of Miscalculation in the Middle East* (Bloomington: Indiana University Press, 1993), chapters 1–4.

46. Zeev Maoz, *Defending the Holy Land: A Critical Analysis of Israel's Security & Foreign Policy* (Ann Arbor: University of Michigan Press, 2006), p. 94.

Part 1

DEMOGRAPHY AND HISTORICAL MEMORY

THE MIDDLE EAST is easy to describe, yet difficult to understand. For outsiders, it is tricky to penetrate, its languages difficult to comprehend, its cultures remote from others in the world. Even the very term "Middle East" is hard to comprehend because it is a foreign term, coined by the British to describe the region that lay between Europe and the "Far East," in eastern Asia. At one point it was both the "Near East" and the "Middle East," until the Royal Air Force merged its "Middle East" branch in Iraq with its "Near East" branch in Egypt, and the term "Middle East" won out. The term was also reportedly popularized by American naval strategist Alfred Thayer Mahan, whose theories about maritime "chokepoints" included such places in the Middle East as the Suez Canal. Some who live in the Middle East complain that the term is Western in origin, because for them the Middle East is not "middle," it is home. The problem is that while the term is difficult to interpret, the region itself is even more intricate. Where to begin?

There are several starting points, actually. First, the region generally described as the Middle East is bounded to its west by Egypt, then extends northward along the eastern Mediterranean through Israel, Lebanon, and Syria, and eastward to Iraq, Iran, and Jordan. It extends southward into the Arabian Peninsula, which contains a majority of the world's natural gas and oil. The periphery of the Middle East is more difficult to define, though. For many scholars and policy makers, it should include the countries of North

Africa, though even that list is often in dispute. The majority Arab-speaking countries of Libya, Tunisia, Algeria, and Morocco are most often included in the "greater Middle East," but should North Africa also include Somalia and Mauritania, which combine features of the Arab world as well as sub-Saharan Africa? For the purposes of this book, Libya, Morocco, Algeria, and Tunisia are included in the discussion, and Mauritania is covered where appropriate. The term "MENA" appears frequently in this book as shorthand for "Middle East and North Africa." Some chapters just use "Middle East," but the reader should know that the overarching themes in this book cover the entire region, including North Africa.

This first section outlines some fundamental underpinnings of the Middle East. Chapter 2 in this section, written by Onn Winckler of the University of Haifa in Israel, concentrates on the changing demographics of the Middle East and the policies of Middle Eastern countries that impact population dynamics. As Winckler demonstrates, population growth for most Middle East countries has been high, continuing into the twenty-first century, while other parts of the world have seen population growth slow, dipping below replacement rates. The consequences are significant; a high population growth rate provides young people who are often willing to work for low wages, giving the Middle East a potential advantage over other parts of the globe with aging populations. However, this young population must ultimately retire, leaving the remaining working population to help support it, and thus providing a potential barrier to future economic growth in the decades to come. At present, though, many Middle Eastern countries have not been able to educate or employ enough of their younger population, leading to unemployment and unrest. The problem was compounded by policies in countries such as Egypt that encouraged population growth, which complicated later efforts to put on the population brakes. Whether an army of under- and unemployed youth will fuel extremist movements is open to question, as Winckler indicates. The 2003 bombings in Casablanca were the work of poor youth from the city's slums, and the al-Qaeda message has resonated with poor young males in Jordan's cities. However, radical movements also need a message that is sometimes predicated on actions real or imagined by the state or by the United States. The debate on what draws people to extremist movements is extensive, and while most argue that poverty and economic deprivation contribute, it is but a part of a larger set of phenomena.

One cannot understand the contemporary Middle East without comprehending the role of historical memory. Americans in particular, who have a relatively short history, still get caught into webs of passion over reparations for slavery, the Civil War (sometimes called the "war of Northern aggression" by die-hard Southerners), Pearl Harbor, and other memory points. If anything, Middle Easterners are even more zealous about the images from recollection, because there are so many of them over thousands of years, and because they are embedded with their faith. Islam in particular is full of recollections about past glories and reversals of fortune. Great Islamic empires once stretched from Spain to India and beyond. Within the bounds of those empires Arab culture brought forth some of the most fruitful learning periods in world history. Muslim scientists blazed paths in physics, chemistry, mathematics, and medicine, while Muslim artists developed music, poetry, geometric design, and stunning calligraphy. Muslim theologians debated the meaning of the Quran and the messages left to them by Muhammad, weaving them into traditional society. Muslim strategists debated the art of war, while early Muslim intellectuals set out political doctrines for both rulers and followers to obey. Islamic architecture became a standard for the world. The Arabic language evolved as a language of literature and poetry, and Arabic words such as "algebra" (*al jebr*), "alcohol" (*al-kuhul*), "alfalfa" (*al-fisfisa*), and many others entered other languages, including English. And there is almost universal appreciation among educated people of the classic Persian and Arabic tales contained in *Kitab 'alf layla wa-layla* (One Thousand One Nights) and Omar Khayyam's monumental *Rubaiyat*.

Those splendid days ended ingloriously in a whirl of foreign invasions, internal corruption, and malaise that left many in the Middle East with reminders of what was. As with the defeated American Southerners after 1865, they had but recollections and ruins left behind. Now the future seems to be leaving them behind. In a culture once rich with innovation, the combined efforts of Saudi Arabia, Egypt, Syria, Jordan, Kuwait, and the United Arab Emirates registered 367 patents with the United States between 1980 and 2000, while South Korea registered 16,328 and Israel 7,652 in the same period, according to the Arab Human Development Report. Today the Middle East has almost no universities ranked in the top 500, with only Israeli universities appearing on the list, or the more elite top 100 universities, where only Hebrew University is in the rankings.

As Glenn Perry observes in his chapter, memory also enshrines Islamic events, from the time of the initial revelations to the Prophet Muhammad through the tumultuous period following the Prophet's death in 632. The language of many modern Islamist movements is distilled from these early times and is communicable to almost all Muslims who understand the message of the Battle of Badr or "Ashura" or the thousands of other words that convey down through the years inspirations, hopes, or fears for Muslims and non-Muslims alike. These memories may be ancient in a historical timeline, but they are often as fresh as yesterday in the minds of those in the Middle East. Reinforcements come from the stones left from the Crusader fortifications that dot so many parts of the eastern Mediterranean, from the skeletons of shipwrecks off the Turkish coast at Gallipoli, in the ruins of the Saudi Arabian town of Diriyah, and from the British cemetery at al-Kut, in modern Iraq.

More recent memories come from Europe, and the singling out of a people for extinction. Today the memorial known as Yad Vashem sits on a hill overlooking Jerusalem, a stark monument to Jews who died in the Holocaust and elsewhere. At the end of the tour the architecture transforms into a cornucopia pointing toward the city, with a message: "The horrors remembered in this building justify Jerusalem as a Jewish city." Here memory creates both literal and visual political space.

The Middle East is a complex and fascinating place, and to understand it requires an appreciation for the population dynamics and how those populations understand who they are, and how they compare to the rest of the globe. This section sets out that welcome mat.

2

DEMOGRAPHIC DEVELOPMENT*

Onn Winckler

SINCE THE 1970S, but particularly with the end of the "bonanza oil decade" in the mid-1980s, the "demographic challenge" has become the most acute socioeconomic problem for an increasing number of Middle Eastern countries.

The aims of this chapter are to describe and analyze three major areas. The first is to examine the causes and the process of the intensified rapid population growth in the Middle East region since the early twentieth century, but particularly since the 1950s, when the population growth rates sharply intensified. The second is to examine the fundamental socioeconomic consequences of the extremely high natural increase rates that are characteristic of all the Middle Eastern countries without exception.[1] The final aim is to look at the natalist policies of the Middle Eastern countries since the mid-twentieth century.

CAUSES AND PROCESS OF
RAPID POPULATION GROWTH

According to the most common estimates, the Middle Eastern population numbered approximately 40 million to 45 million in the second century CE— a fifth of the total global population at that time. Subsequently, the region's population fluctuated without a clear trend until the mid-nineteenth century, when a steady rise in number became evident. During the 1840–1914 period, the Middle Eastern population doubled at an average annual growth rate of just under 1 percent.[2]

By 1914, on the eve of World War I, the Middle Eastern population (including Iran and Turkey) was estimated at 68 million.[3] By mid-2008, it had reached 458 million (including Iran, Turkey, Israel, the West Bank, and the Gaza Strip).[4]

Thus, despite the vast emigration from the region, the Middle Eastern population increased almost sevenfold in less than a century.

As shown in Figure 2.1 and Table 2.1, the population growth rates during the second half of the twentieth century and the early 2000s were extremely high in each of the Middle Eastern countries. Egypt's population, for example, increased from 21.8 million in 1950 to 74.9 million in mid-2008, representing an almost fourfold increase in less than six decades. Turkey's population increased from 21.5 million to 74.9 million during the corresponding period, while Iran's population increased from 16.9 million in 1950 to 71.2 million in mid-2007.

Like those of other developing regions worldwide, Middle Eastern populations grew by rates that were particularly accelerated during the 1960s and 1970s. As shown in Table 2.2, during these two decades the natural increase rate in each of the Middle Eastern countries (except Turkey) substantially increased. In Jordan, for example, the natural increase rate climbed from 2.8 percent in 1960 to 3.6 percent in 1980. In Syria the increase was from 3.0 percent to 3.8 percent, while in Iran the increase was from 2.9 percent in 1960 to 3.2 percent in 1981.

This rapid rise was a result of the sharp decline in death rates that occurred in each of the Middle Eastern countries, without a single exception, similar to the vast majority of the developing regions worldwide. Three major components

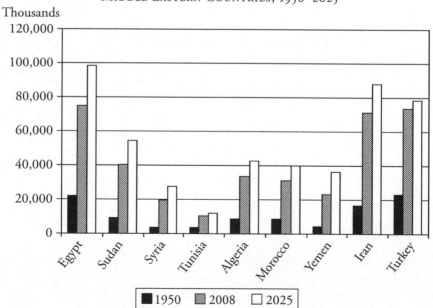

FIGURE 2.1: POPULATION GROWTH IN SOME
MIDDLE EASTERN COUNTRIES, 1950–2025

Thousands

■ 1950   ▨ 2008   ☐ 2025

TABLE 2.1: POPULATION GROWTH IN SOME MIDDLE EASTERN COUNTRIES, 1950–2025

Country	Population 1950 (millions)	Population mid-2008 (millions)	Population 2015* (millions)	Population 2025* (millions)	% Growth 1950–2008	% Growth 2008–2025
Egypt	21.834	74.900	86.219	98.513	243.0	31.5
Syria	3.536	19.748	23.510	27.519	458.5	39.4
Jordan	0.472	6.199	6.923	8.029	1213.3	29.5
Lebanon	1.443	3.973	4.431	4.784	175.3	20.4
Tunisia	3.530	10.384	11.204	12.170	194.2	17.2
Morocco	8.953	31.224(a)	34.330	37.865	248.8	21.3
Algeria	8.753	33.770	38.088	42.882	285.8	27.0
Sudan	9.190	40.218	45.613	54.267	337.6	34.9
Yemen	4.316	23.013	28.288	36.567	433.2	58.9
Turkey	21.484	74.900	82.111	89.557	248.6	19.6
Iran	16.913	71.208(a)	79.379	88.027	321.0	23.6

* Medium variant projection
(a) Data relate to mid-2007.

Source: UN Department of Economic and Social Affairs, *World Population Prospects: The 2006 Revision* (New York, 2007); US Department of Commerce, US Census Bureau, *International Data Base*, www.census.gov/ipc/www/idb/informationGateway.php.

have contributed to the "death revolution" in the Middle East since the mid-twentieth century. First, there was a marked drop in infant and child mortality rates;[5] second was a considerable increase in life expectancy;[6] and third was a very young age pyramid[7]—a direct consequence of the prolonged high natural increase rates.

At the same time, not only did the fertility rate in Middle Eastern societies not decline, but in some of them it even increased. Overall, by the late 1970s, the demographic characteristics of the various Middle Eastern societies were quite similar, with only minor differences among them. This prolonged demographic similarity, however, ended in the mid-1980s (see Table 2.2 and Figure 2.2.). At the beginning of the twenty-first century, four "demographic regimes" prevail in the Middle East:

(a) The first group includes Tunisia, Lebanon, Iran, Turkey, and recently Algeria, all of which have achieved the targeted replacement level, with a total fertility rate (TFR) of around 2.1 children per woman.[8]

(b) The second group includes Egypt, Jordan, Syria, Morocco, and Bahrain—countries that have succeeded in substantially lowering their TFR from around 6 to 7 children per woman during the 1950s and 1960s to between 3 and 3.5 in the early 2000s. Although the fertility rates of these countries have sharply declined during the past generation,

FIGURE 2.2: TOTAL FERTILITY RATES IN
SOME MIDDLE EASTERN COUNTRIES, 1960–2008

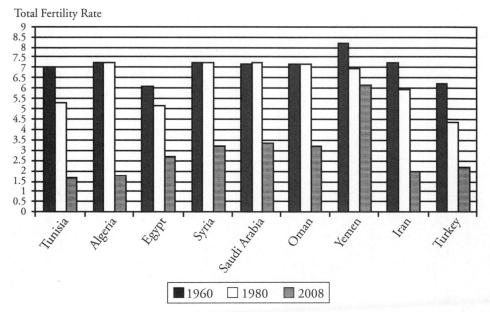

Total Fertility Rate

■ 1960   □ 1980   ▩ 2008

TABLE 2.2: MAJOR DEMOGRAPHIC INDICATORS FOR SOME MIDDLE EASTERN COUNTRIES, 1960–2008

Country	1960				1980				2008			
	CBR	CDR	NI	TFR	CBR	CDR	NI	TFR	CBR	CDR	NI	TFR
Egypt	43	17	2.6	6.1	38	10	2.8	5.2	22	5	1.7	2.7
Jordan	48	20	2.8	6.8	47	11	3.6	7.3	20	3	1.7	2.5
Syria	48	18	3.0	7.3	46	8	3.8	7.3	27	5	2.2	3.2
Lebanon	43	14	2.9	6.3	30	8	2.2	4.1	18	6	1.2	1.9
Tunisia	49	21	2.8	7.1	35	10	2.5	5.3	16	5	1.1	1.7
Morocco	52	23	2.9	7.2	44	12	3.2	6.9	21	5	1.6	2.6
Algeria	50	23	2.7	7.3	48	14	3.4	7.3	17	5	1.2	1.8
Sudan	47	25	2.2	6.7	47	19	2.8	6.7	34	14	2.0	4.6
Yemen	50	28	2.2	8.2	48	18	3.0	7.0	40	9	3.1	6.2
Saudi Arabia*	49	23	2.6	7.2	46	14	3.2	7.3	29	2	2.7	3.7
Oman*	51	28	2.3	7.2	50	13	3.7	7.2	35	4	3.1	5.6
Turkey	45	18	2.7	6.3	32	10	2.2	4.4	19	6	1.3	2.2
Iran	46	17	2.9	7.3	43	11	3.2	6.0	17	6	1.1	1.7

* Nationals only
CBR = crude birth rate per 1,000 people   CDR = crude death rate per 1,000 people
NI = natural increase (%)   TFR = total fertility rate

Sources: Arab Republic of Egypt, CAPMAS, *Statistical Yearbook*, various issues (Cairo); The Hashemite Kingdom of Jordan, Department of Statistics, *Statistical Yearbook*, various issues (Amman); Syrian Arab Republic, Central Bureau of Statistics (CBS), *Statistical Abstract*, various issues (Damascus); al-Jumhuriyya al-Tunisiyya, Wizarat al-Tanmiyya, *al-Nashriyya al-Ihsa al-Sanawiyya Li-Tunis*, various years (Tunis); World Bank, *World Tables*, various issues (published for the WB by Johns Hopkins University Press); UN, *Demographic Yearbook*, various issues (New York); ECWA/ESCWA, *Demographic and Related Socio-Economic Data Sheets for Countries of the Economic (and Social) Commission for Western Asia*, various issues (Beirut, Baghdad, and Amman); ESCAP, *Population and Development Indicators for Asia and the Pacific—2007* (Bangkok, 2008); UNICEF, *The State of the World's Children*, various issues (New York); US Census Bureau, *International Data Base*, www.census.gov/ipc/www/idb/informationGateway.php.

in the early 2000s their TFR still is almost twice the targeted replacement level.

(c)   The third group includes Sudan and Yemen, which are still character-
      ized by the traditional demographic regime with very high fertility rates
      and death rates, similar to those seen in sub-Saharan Africa—the poor-
      est area worldwide.

(d)   The fourth group includes the GCC (Gulf Cooperation Council) oil
      states (except Bahrain),[9] which have created an unparalleled demo-
      graphic pattern of extremely low death rates and extremely high fertility
      rates as a consequence of their unique socioeconomic and political *ren-
      tier* nature.[10]

SOCIOECONOMIC CONSEQUENCES OF HIGH NATURAL INCREASE RATES

The negative socioeconomic consequences of the prolonged high fertility rates
in the Middle Eastern countries are many and varied. The most prominent
was the creation of a wide-based age pyramid, in which half the population,
and in some countries even more, is under twenty years old. The meaning of
this is that even if the fertility rates were to decline to replacement level, the
population would continue to grow, as the number of women of reproductive
age would continue to increase for a number of decades before finally stabilizing. Only at that point would the population decline below replacement
level, or stabilize at replacement level. Hence, the younger the age pyramid,
the longer the time between achieving replacement level and the termination
of population growth. This period is called "the demographic momentum."
Therefore, the population in each Middle Eastern country is projected to
substantially increase in the foreseeable future, even in countries that have
achieved the replacement-level fertility rate in recent years. Thus, for example,
according to the UN medium-variant projection, Tunisia's population will
number 11.2 million in 2015 and will further increase to 12.2 million in 2025,
compared to 10.4 million in mid-2008. Iran's population is projected to number 88.0 million in 2025, compared to 71.2 in mid-2007, while Turkey's population will number 89.6 million in 2025 compared with 74.9 in mid-2008
(see Table 2.1).

The high natural increase rates also dictate a low labor force participation
rate. In addition to the wide-based age pyramid, another factor that prevents
high labor force participation in Middle Eastern countries, oil-based and non-
oil alike, is the very low female labor force participation rate—a consequence
of high fertility rates combined with traditional limitations on female employment.[11] While a prominent development engine of the "Asian Tigers"[12] during

the past generation was their high labor force participation rate—a result of the "demographic gift"[13]—this was not evident in the Middle East, as a result of continued high natural increase rates. In turn, the low labor force participation rate led to a "low income trap" in all non-oil Middle Eastern economies.

Beyond the severe consequences of prolonged high natural increase rates, the rapid population growth in the non-oil Middle Eastern countries led to an ongoing increase in pressure on the natural resources, the most prominent being a steady decline in the ratio of population on the one hand and water and cultivable lands on the other. In Syria, for example, the per capita crops area for the total population declined from 0.76 hectare in 1960 to 0.27 in 2003.[14] For the rural population, the decline was from 1.21 hectare to 0.37.[15] In Egypt, the decline in the per capita crops area was even sharper than in Syria.[16]

Due to the rapid population growth, not only is the available per capita agricultural land constantly decreasing, but the available water for agricultural production is constantly declining as well because of the rapid increase of domestic use. In Jordan, the demand for water already far exceeds supply and the gap is steadily widening. The end result of this process is a steady increase of food imports, which imposes a heavy burden on the balance of trade and on the budget. As early as 1989, food subsidies made up 7 percent of Jordan's governmental expenditure and 3.3 percent of the total GDP.[17] In the other non-oil Middle Eastern countries, with the exception of Turkey, a similar situation existed.

The steady decline in per capita crops area and water available for agriculture led to a rapid urbanization process in each Middle Eastern country. Although the Middle Eastern urbanization process started during the Mandatory period, it has rapidly increased since the mid-twentieth century. In 1950, Kuwait was the only Middle Eastern country where the urban population composed more than 50 percent of the total population. At the dawn of the twenty-first century, with the exception of Sudan, and Egypt to a lesser extent, in every Middle Eastern country the urban population constitutes more than half the total population (see Table 2.3 and Figure 2.3).

The vast majority of the Middle Eastern rural-to-urban migration was directed toward the capitals and a few other major cities. Currently, approximately 25 percent of the total Middle Eastern urban population lives in the three megacities of Cairo, Tehran, and Baghdad, another 25 percent are concentrated in cities of between 1 million and 5 million, and 50 percent reside in cities of less than 1 million. According to the UN projection, the rapid urbanization process in the Middle East will continue during the foreseeable future and by the year 2020 the percentage of the urban population among the total Middle Eastern population will climb to 65 percent, compared to 57 percent in mid-2008.

The rapid urbanization process in the non-oil Middle Eastern countries caused many and varied socioeconomic problems, the most acute being a housing shortage, particularly in the capitals, which has led to a constant expansion

TABLE 2.3: PERCENTAGE OF URBAN POPULATION WITHIN THE TOTAL
POPULATION IN SOME MIDDLE EASTERN COUNTRIES, 1950–2007

Country	1950	1970	1990	2007
Egypt	31.9	42.2	43.5	42.7
Syria	30.6	43.3	48.9	53.8
Jordan	37.0	56.0	72.2	78.4
Lebanon	32.0	59.5	83.1	86.8
Sudan	6.8	16.5	22.6	42.6
Tunisia	32.3	43.5	57.9	66.1
Morocco	26.2	34.5	48.4	55.7
Algeria	22.2	39.5	52.1	64.6
Saudi Arabia	21.3	48.7	76.6	81.4
Kuwait	61.5	85.7	98.0	98.3
Oman	8.6	29.7	66.1	71.5
Turkey	24.8	38.2	59.2	68.3
Iran	27.5	41.2	56.3	68.0

Source: UN Department of Economic and Social Affairs, Population Division, *World Urbanization Prospects: The 2007 Revision* (New York: UN, 2008).

FIGURE 2.3: PERCENTAGE OF URBAN POPULATION WITHIN THE TOTAL
POPULATION IN SOME MIDDLE EASTERN COUNTRIES, 1950–2007

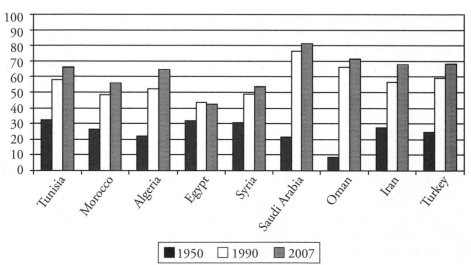

of informal housing; a water shortage caused by a rapid increase in domestic use; sewerage problems; air pollution; and a "transportation explosion."[18] The concentration of huge numbers of poor people in major cities also has distinct political implications as they hold the regime hostage, thus preventing any substantial economic reforms in the form of subsidy reduction. This was the case, for example, in Egypt in January 1977, in Morocco during the early 1980s, in Jordan in April 1989 and again in August 1996, and in Yemen in 1998.

EMERGENCE OF THE "MIDDLE EASTERN ARMY OF THE YOUNG AND FRUSTRATED UNEMPLOYED"

Among the various devastating consequences of rapid population growth in the non-oil Middle Eastern countries, the most severe is unemployment, particularly among the younger generation, which dramatically rose following the end of the "oil decade." The relatively low unemployment rates in most Middle Eastern countries during the 1950s and 1960s can mainly be attributed to the small workforce at that time; the étatist economic approach, which created vast numbers of job opportunities in the public sector; and the implementation of large-scale industrial and infrastructure projects.

The 1973 oil boom changed the socioeconomic situation in all Middle Eastern countries, particularly in the oil economies, turning them into some of the richest worldwide from the early 1980s. In retrospect, the oil decade was the "bonanza" period of the Middle East economies, not only for the oil economies, but for the non-oil economies as well, as reflected by the largest economic expansion in their entire modern history. This rapid economic expansion was due to the sharp rise in aid given by the Arab oil countries to those Arab countries that did not enter into peace negotiations with Israel, an amount that dramatically increased after the Second Baghdad Arab Summit (March 1979). An additional factor was the massive labor migration wave to the Arab oil countries and, to a lesser extent, to Jordan (see below). The end result of the combined rapid economic expansion and the massive labor emigration was a sharp decline in unemployment in the poorer Middle Eastern countries. By 1982, Egypt's unemployment rate was estimated at only 5.7 percent,[19] declining from 8.4 percent in 1976.[20] Jordan's unemployment rate declined from 14 percent in 1972[21] to only 3.9 percent in 1981.[22]

Following the end of the oil decade, and even more so with the drop in oil prices in 1986, the Middle Eastern economies, both oil-based and non-oil, began to rapidly deteriorate. The scale of the deterioration of the non-oil economies was a function of their dependence on the oil economies. Hence, Jordan's economy experienced the worst deterioration as a result of the reduced aid given by the Arab oil states combined with the decline in workers' remittances and later, the effects of the end of the Iran-Iraq War (August 1988).[23] The severe recession was accompanied by a sharp increase in the unemployment rates, which climbed to more than 10 percent in early 1990.[24] The Syrian economy also greatly suffered from the sharp oil price decline and the cut in Arab aid. By the late 1980s, Syria's unemployment rate was approximately 10 percent.[25]

Egypt's economy also suffered from an economic recession starting in the mid-1980s, which was accompanied by an increase in unemployment. According to the 1986 census, the unemployment rate was 14 percent,[26] while according to unofficial estimates the real unemployment rate in 1988 was as high as 20 percent, not including underemployment and hidden (disguised) unemployment.[27] The economic recession of the 1980s hit the North African countries as well. The end result was a sharp rise in unemployment to 16 percent in Morocco in 1989, compared to 8 percent in 1980,[28] and to almost 20 percent in Algeria in 1990.[29] In the late 1980s, the unemployment rate in each of the non-oil Middle Eastern countries climbed to more than 13 percent—twice the rate at the peak of the oil decade in the late 1970s and early 1980s.

The sharp drop in oil revenues during the second half of the 1980s had only a minor effect on the employment pattern of the GCC indigenous workforces. The GCC governments exploited their huge financial reserves from the oil decade to maintain the living standard of their indigenous populations, including their employment in lucrative public sector positions (see below).

In the early 1990s, however, a new unemployment form emerged in all the non-oil Middle Eastern countries—structural unemployment. While unemployment rates had dropped in response to economic growth in previous periods (mainly during the 1950s and again during the oil decade), since the early 1990s open unemployment, not to mention hidden unemployment and underemployment, has continued to climb even in periods of relatively rapid economic expansion. This new unemployment pattern was primarily the result of the mismatch between the number of new job opportunities and the number of new entrants to the workforce.

In Egypt, for example, during the second half of the 1990s, although the economy produced approximately 400,000 new jobs on annual average, the labor force increased by 500,000,[30] reflecting a 20 percent gap between the number of job opportunities and the expansion of the workforce. By the year 2000, Egypt's unemployment amounted to 15 percent to 25 percent—higher than a decade before despite the rapid economic expansion during the 1990s.[31]

This trend of relatively high economic growth rates along with climbing unemployment intensified during the first half of the 2000s. During the fiscal years 2004–2005 and 2005–2006, Egypt's real GDP growth rate amounted to 4.5 percent and 6.6 percent, respectively, namely, more than twice the population growth rate. The unemployment rate, however, continued to increase as the number of new entrants into the workforce skyrocketed to 650,000 annually.[32] Syria achieved an annual average GDP growth rate of 3.3 percent during the

2001–2005 period, more than 1 percent higher than the population growth rate. However, even this growth rate was not enough to maintain the unemployment level, which climbed to 20 percent in 2005—higher than ever before.[33]

A similar process has prevailed in both Turkey and Iran in recent years. In Turkey, despite a healthy economic growth rate, which amounted to three times the population growth rate,[34] unemployment remained above 10 percent.[35] In Iran, the situation was even more severe: Despite the rapid economic expansion since 2004 due to high oil revenues, unemployment remained constant at 12 percent.[36] Thus, even under conditions of extremely high oil revenues, the Iranian economy failed to reduce unemployment, particularly among first-time job seekers.

A similar trend occurred in the North African countries as well. In Morocco, although economic expansion in 2003 and 2004 amounted to 6.1 percent and 5.4 percent, respectively,[37] three times the population growth rate, unemployment did not decline. In Algeria, despite continued rapid economic expansion due to high oil revenues in recent years,[38] unemployment continued to be very high, estimated at 21 percent in 2005.[39] In Tunisia, despite the strong GDP growth rate of 5.4 percent in 2006, unemployment remained unchanged at 14.2 percent.[40]

Unlike Eastern European countries, whose recent adoption of the capitalist economic approach has led to the privatization of many governmental factories and establishments, including mass dismissal of employees, the major source of unemployment in non-oil Middle Eastern economies is the inability of new entrants into the labor force to find employment in the first place. Hence, the unemployment rate among the younger generation, particularly among first-time job seekers, is far above their share in the total workforce. In Algeria, for example, by 2003 about 80 percent of the unemployed were under the age of thirty.[41]

Since the mid-1990s, the vast majority of the non-oil Middle Eastern economies have been forced to deal with a harsh situation: On the one hand, they have successfully implemented macroeconomic reforms along with substantial fertility decline, which combined have brought about an impressive economic expansion of more than twice the population growth rates; on the other hand, even these high growth rates are lagging far behind the rates needed to reduce the current high unemployment level. Thus, it is quite understandable why the 2006–2007 UN Economic and Social Commission for Western Asia (ESCWA) socioeconomic report opened the section on the labor market by stating: "Youth unemployment remained a foremost challenge for policymakers in the region."[42]

INTER-ARAB LABOR MIGRATION: CAUSES AND CONSEQUENCES

One major result of the rapid population growth in non-oil Middle Eastern countries on the one hand, and rapid economic expansion in the oil countries, particularly following the oil boom on the other, was massive intra-Arab labor migration. In 1975, barely two years after the oil boom, the total number of foreigners (including both workers and their accompanying family members) in the GCC countries amounted to 2.76 million. A decade later, in 1986, their number climbed to 5.54 million. During the second half of the 1980s and the first half of the 1990s, despite the slowing down of economic expansion due to low oil prices, the number of foreigners in the GCC countries continued to increase, amounting to 8.74 million in 1994.

During the second half of the 1990s and more so during the early 2000s, not only did the number of foreigners in the GCC countries not decline in response to the labor force nationalization policy,[43] but it continued to increase even more rapidly than during the previous two decades. By 2007, the number of foreigners in the GCC countries amounted to 14.1 million (including both workers and their accompanying family members), representing almost 40 percent of the GCC total population (see Table 2.4).

Why has the number of foreigners in the GCC countries continued to increase in recent years, despite the implementation of the labor force nationalization policy? The answer lies with the GCC *rentier* nature. By guaranteeing the national workforce public sector employment with high salaries and luxurious work conditions, the GCC royal families, in practice, "bought" the loyalty

TABLE 2.4: NATIONALS AND EXPATRIATES IN THE
GCC POPULATIONS, 1975–2007 (THOUSANDS)

Country	Nationals	Foreigners	Total	% Foreigners
		1975		
Saudi Arabia	6,218 (a)	1,565	7,783	20.1
Kuwait	472	523	995	52.6
Bahrain	214	56	270	20.7
Oman	550	132	682	19.4
Qatar	60	97	157	61.8
UAE	170	388	558	69.5
Total	7,684	2,761	10,445	26.4
		1986		
Saudi Arabia	7,849	2,314	10,163	22.8
Kuwait	750	1,072	1,822	58.8
Bahrain	295	140	435	32.2
Oman	816	494	1,310	37.7
Qatar	105	284	389	73.0
UAE	434	1,239	1,673	74.1
Total	10,249	5,543	15,792	35.1

(continues)

Country	Nationals	Foreigners	Total	% Foreigners
1994				
Saudi Arabia	13,053	5,127	18,180	28.2
Kuwait	671	949	1,620	58.6
Bahrain	346	205	551	37.2
Oman	1,511	538	2,049	26.3
Qatar	129	403	532	75.8
UAE	629	1,522	2,151	70.8
Total	16,339	8,744	25,083	34.9
2000				
Saudi Arabia	15,589	5,258	20,847	25.2
Kuwait	832	1,358	2,190	62.0
Bahrain	391	261	652	40.0
Oman	1,778	624	2,402	26.0
Qatar	152	428	580	73.8
UAE	703	2,187	2,890	75.7
Total	19,445	10,116	29,561	34.2
2007				
Saudi Arabia	17,691	6,551	24,242	27.0
Kuwait	1,055	2,345	3,400	69.0
Bahrain	474	235	709	33.1
Oman	1,884 (b)	693 (b)	2,577 (b)	26.9
Qatar	227	680	907	75.0
UAE	864	3,620	4,484	80.7
Total	22,195	14,124	36,319	38.9

(a) Figure relates to 1974   (b) Figure relates to 2006

Sources: State of Kuwait, Central Statistical Office, *Annual Statistical Abstract*, various issues (Kuwait); State (Kingdom) of Bahrain, Directorate of Statistics, *Statistical Abstract*, various issues (Manama); Dawlat al-Bahrayn, al-Jihaz al-Markazi lil-Ihsa, *al-Ta'adad al-'Amm lil-Sukan wal-Masakin wal-Mabani wal-Munsha'at-1991* (Manama, 1992); Bahrain Monetary Agency (BMA), *Annual Report*, various issues (Manama); Sultanate of Oman, Ministry of National Economy, *Statistical Yearbook*, various issues (Muscat); Kingdom of Saudi Arabia, Central Department of Statistics, *Statistical Yearbook*, various issues (Riyadh); Saudi Arabian Monetary Agency (SAMA), *Annual Report*, various issues (Riyadh); State of Qatar, Central Statistical Organization, *Annual Statistical Abstract*, various issues (Doha); State of Qatar, Planning Council, *Qatar in Figures—2006* (Doha, October 2006); ILO, *International Migration and Development in the Arab Region*, by J. S. Birks and C. A. Sinclair (Geneva, 1980); ESCWA, *Demographic and Related Socio-Economic Data Sheets for Countries of the Economic and Social Commission for Western Asia*, various issues (Beirut, Baghdad, and Amman); "al-Simat al-Asasiyya li-Sukan al-Kuwayt wa-Kuwwat al-'Amal fi Nihayat 1994," *al-Iqtisadi al-Kuwayti*, No. 324 (May 1995); Andrzej Kapiszewski, *Nationals and Expatriates: Population and Labour Dilemmas of the Gulf Cooperation Council States* (Reading, PA: Ithaca Press, 2001); Andrzej Kapiszewski, "Business Versus Politics: Local Versus Foreign Workforce in the GCC States," paper presented at the conference *Transnational Migration: Foreign Labor and Its Impact in the Gulf*, Bellagio, Italy, June 20–24, 2005.

FIGURE 2.4: NATIONALS AND EXPATRIATES IN THE
GCC POPULATIONS, 1975–2007

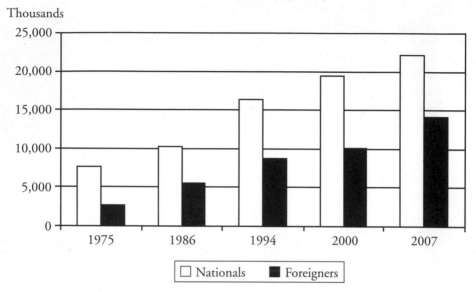

and compliance of their national populations with a policy of "no taxation and no representation."

Consequently, a unique employment pattern emerged in these economies: the dual labor market with a clear dichotomy between nationals and foreign labor. As long as the economic expansion was rapid and the indigenous labor force was relatively small, the dual labor market worked to the benefit of both the indigenous and the foreign workers. The private sector employers, on the one hand, were allowed to recruit cheap foreign labor almost without limitation, thereby maximizing their profits. The national workforces, for their part, were guaranteed the luxury of public sector employment, regardless of their professional background and skill level.

Moreover, the *kafala* (sponsorship) system produced a unique situation in which nationals could earn money strictly by virtue of their nationality.[44] An estimated 600,000 foreign workers in the United Arab Emirates (UAE) obtained work permits in that manner, representing approximately 27 percent of the total UAE foreign workforce. A similar phenomenon prevailed in each of the other five GCC countries as well.[45] However, the dual labor market mechanism prevented the implementation of the labor force nationalization policy.

Hence, in recent years, despite the sharp increase in unemployment among nationals, reaching more than 15 percent in each of the GCC countries, the number of foreign workers has steadily increased.[46] Consequently, the GCC authorities were forced to implement a new employment strategy. They used huge numbers of cheap foreign workers in order to create suitable and sufficient work opportunities for nationals in the private sector, as the number of new employment opportunities in the public sector sharply declined. The new employment policy is most evident in the tourism industry, where foreign workers fill the low-skilled, low-paying jobs as well as the professional jobs, while nationals fill the medium-rank managerial jobs. The new employment policy also was intended to finance the vocational training of national workforces through various taxes imposed on the foreign workers themselves and their local employers.[47] Hence, as noted in the ESCWA's 2006–2007 report:

> [The GCC] workforce nationalization strategies were rendered more flexible with greater emphasis on human resource development and vocational training of nationals than on the quota enforcement of those strategies.[48]

In retrospect, it appears that whatever economic diversification had actually been achieved, it was done at the price of increasing dependence on foreign labor and not through developing advanced industries in which nationals constituted the majority of the employees. The example of Dubai illustrates this phenomenon. In the early 2000s, three decades after the oil boom, Dubai is indeed the most diverse among the Gulf oil economies. However, Dubai's economic diversification was achieved through the rapid increase in the number of foreign workers. By the end of 2006, Dubai's population amounted to 1.422 million, less than 10 percent of whom were nationals.[49]

In general, with regard to the Arab labor-exporting countries, their tragedy is that while during the oil decade the employment relationship between them and the GCC countries was characterized by mutual dependence—as the GCC countries needed the Arab labor force in the public sector due to the need for Arabic speakers—in the mid-1980s this mutual dependence ended. The petering out of this mutual dependence was achieved through sharp improvement in the educational level of GCC nationals, which enabled them to gradually occupy the positions previously held by Arab foreign labor; the gradual replacement of Arab workers by Asians in the private sector; and GCC authorities' use of the job opportunities in their labor markets as an intra-Arab political tool. Hence, following the Iraqi invasion of Kuwait (August 1990), the GCC authorities replaced Jordanian, Yemenite, Sudanese, and Palestinian workers—whose countries did not support the anti-Iraq coalition—with Egyptian and Syrian ones, whose countries supported the US-led anti-Iraq coalition.

In retrospect, it appears that instead of using the amnesty period of the "bonanza oil decade" for preparing their socioeconomic structure for the post–labor emigration era, the Middle Eastern labor-exporting countries chose the easy way out and did almost nothing. The end result was that their economies could not absorb the bulging young workforce and, consequently, unemployment has steadily increased since the mid-1980s.

Yet, it should be taken into account that the massive intra-Arab labor migration benefited the labor-exporting countries as they got rid of a substantial portion of their unemployment while Islamic fundamentalist opposition became stronger than ever before across the Middle East. The combination of growing Islamic fundamentalist opposition and increasing unemployment, mainly among the educated young, could lead to the end of the secular regimes, as was the case in Iran in 1979. Thus, one could say that the massive inter-Arab labor migration constituted a major tool for preserving the current regimes.[50]

MIDDLE EASTERN NATALIST POLICIES

Since the mid-twentieth century, when most of the Middle Eastern countries achieved full independence, and until the present, their natalist approach has changed in line with three variables: The first and the most important has been their economic situation; the second has been the change in both internal and international politics; and the third has been the shift in the worldwide natalist perception. In the following sections, the natalist approach of the Middle Eastern countries will be examined according to developments in the above-mentioned variables.

At the beginning of the process of rapidly accelerated natural increase rates in the 1950s and early 1960s, the leaders of many developing countries worldwide, including those of the Middle East, perceived that population growth was not the core of poverty, in line with the worldwide traditional attitude toward population growth. Therefore, they made no attempts to limit it. As a result, the attempts made by Western leaders to convince those countries of the need to curb population growth because of its long-term devastating consequences were unsuccessful. The vast majority of the developing countries' regimes considered these Western attempts another variant of neocolonialism. In addition, dependency theory was widely accepted during that period in the developing countries.[51] Accordingly, it was widely believed that the end of Western colonialism, combined with the adoption of socialist-étatist socioeconomic policies, would bring about rapid economic development. Above all, at the very time that Western postcolonial countries were trying to advocate fertility decline in their former colonies, they were implementing pro-natalist policies in their own countries.[52]

Although the common approach in the Middle East was pro-natalist, in practice only Turkey and Syria carried out specific pro-natalist measures, which included a ban on family planning propaganda and on distributing and using contraceptives, as well as financial benefits to large families.[53] In Egypt, although some warned that rapid population growth would lead to a neo-Malthusian population trap,[54] the monarchy regime not only did not promote fertility decline, but actually adopted a pro-natalist approach.[55] In contrast to Syria and Turkey, however, the Egyptian regime did not carry out any practical pro-natalist measures. Within the framework of the pro-natalist approach, in the former French North African colonies, the 1920 French law forbidding abortions and the promotion and use of contraceptives was still in force.[56]

The results of the population censuses conducted in many developing countries in the late 1950s and the first half of the 1960s, including in most Middle Eastern countries, showed that the fertility rates were actually higher than previously assumed. In Iran, for example, according to the 1966 census, the total fertility rate in the urban centers amounted to 7.0 children per woman and was as high as 8.2 in rural areas—one of the highest levels not only in the Middle East, but worldwide as well.[57]

At the same time, many developing countries' leaders became aware of the negative correlation between economic development and population growth. In addition, the adoption of socialist policy, including a wide variety of subsidies on health care, education, transportation, energy, and basic foodstuffs, led to a steady increase in governmental expenditures in line with the population growth rates. The change in the demographic perception began in Asia, with South Korea being the first to adopt a national family planning program as early as 1961.[58]

Among the Middle Eastern countries, the first to adopt an official family planning policy was Turkey. Within the framework of the Five-Year Development Plan, covering the 1963–1967 period, Turkey officially adopted an anti-natalist policy. In April 1965, the Population Planning Law was passed. The new law explicitly permitted the use of contraceptives and entrusted the Ministry of Health and Social Affairs with educating the population as to the need of reducing fertility rates and the importance of family planning.[59]

Iran also officially adopted a national family planning policy in 1967,[60] aiming to reduce the annual natural increase rate to 1 percent within two decades, compared to more than 3 percent recorded in the 1966 census.[61] The shah's family planning policy should be examined within the broader context of his "White Revolution," which strove to rapidly transform Iran from a developing into a developed country.[62] His fear was that continued rapid population growth would jeopardize the Revolution's achievements.[63]

Among the Arab leaders, Tunisia's president, Habib Bourguiba, was the first to change the traditional pro-natalist approach. As early as 1961, Tunisia abolished the 1920 French law forbidding abortions and the use of contraceptives.[64] In June 1964, Tunisia officially adopted a declared national family planning policy that included the provision of family planning services within the existing network of mother-and-child health-care clinics, as well as sterilization procedures in public hospitals.[65]

The Egyptian natalist concept changed in the early 1960s as well. On May 21, 1962, Gamal Abdel Nasser presented the National Charter (*al-mithaq al-watani*), in which he stated that the population growth "constitutes the most dangerous obstacle that faces the Egyptian people in their drive toward raising the standard of production."[66] In 1965, Egypt officially adopted a declared family planning policy,[67] aiming to reduce the crude birth rate (CBR) from 41 per 1,000 in 1966 to 30 in 1978.[68] In 1966, Morocco also adopted a declared family planning program.

It's quite obvious that during the 1960s the governments of the most populated Middle Eastern countries became worried not only about the nominal number of their citizens, but about the long-term implications of the demographic momentum as well, primarily in the area of supplying employment opportunities for the rapidly growing workforce and the increasing financial burden of the various governmental subsidies.

However, at that stage, among the Middle Eastern leaders who officially adopted anti-natalist policies, the shah of Iran, Turkish President Cevdet Sunay, and Tunisian President Bourguiba were the only ones to take the political risk of strongly supporting the anti-natalist policy. The leaders of other Middle Eastern countries that adopted family planning policies remained on the sidelines and left the family planning issue to the "professional staff" in the ministries of health and social affairs. Morocco's King Hassan II remained totally silent on the question of family planning.[69] The main reason for the negligible action in family planning and the absence of public support of the policy by the leaders themselves was purely political: While the benefits of fertility decline can be seen only in the long run, the political risk is evident in the short run, particularly from the wide opposition by Islamic fundamentalists to any kind of family planning.

Hence, it was only in Tunisia, Turkey, and Iran that the family planning programs of the 1960s and 1970s were effected, and the fertility rates in these countries indeed declined (see Table 2.2). Although in Egypt fertility rates also sharply declined during the late 1960s and early 1970s, this decline was not a result of the family planning program but rather a consequence of the economic hardship endured following the June 1967 war and the War of Attrition, combined with the fact that more than 1 million Egyptians were in military service at that time.[70] In Algeria, in the early 1970s the opposite pro-natalist policy was adopted by Houari Boumediene, which presented family planning as a "false solution" and a kind of "neo-colonialism."[71]

The oil boom added to the perception of "awareness without action" in the family planning area among the vast majority of Middle Eastern countries due to rapid economic expansion. This new perception was most evident in the case of Egyptian President Anwar al-Sadat, who in practice almost totally neglected the family planning issue, although officially Egypt did not abandon its previous anti-natalist policy.

Following the oil boom, the Middle Eastern oil countries adopted a pro-natalist policy. According to the demographic transition theory, fertility rates would naturally decline following a reduction in infant and child mortality rates, combined with a surge in economic development and women's educational level. Thus, the pro-natalist policy of the Middle Eastern oil countries was aimed at changing this natural evolution and maintaining the high fertility rates despite their tremendous socioeconomic development. Overall, the pro-natalist policies of the Middle Eastern oil countries included: (a) initiating public housing projects whereby the government sold housing at cost or provided land for building while offering highly subsidized loans; (b) encouraging early marriage through large marriage grants; (c) providing full subsidies for education, from first grade through university; and (d) funding allowances for each child of nationals.[72] It should be noted, however, that with the exception of Saudi Arabia, the GCC pro-natalist policies were carried out only on a voluntary basis, without implementing any coercive measures.

Following the 1979 Islamic Revolution, Khomeini immediately halted the Iranian family planning program for three main reasons: First was the belief that rapid population growth by itself is not a socioeconomic problem, but rather an advantage. Second was his basic concept that family planning contradicts the Islamic faith. The third and the most important factor was the onset of the war against Iraq in September 1980.[73] Within the framework of the new pro-natalist policy, the Higher Population Council was abolished; the law of minimum age for first marriage for both females and males was abolished as well; and many women's rights that were introduced during the shah period were abolished. However, despite the radical change in the natalist policy, in contrast to Saudi Arabia, the use of contraceptives was not forbidden by the new Islamist regime.[74]

In the mid-1980s, the natalist approach of the overpopulated Middle Eastern countries radically changed toward fertility decline, heralding a new period that can be called "Demographic Sobriety." The first Middle Eastern country that changed its natalist perception following the end of the oil decade was Algeria. In 1983, under the rule of Chadli Bendjedid, Algeria adopted its first family planning program.[75] Egypt also revised its natalist policy. In 1985, the National Population Council was established, headed by President Hosni Mubarak himself. A year later, in 1986, a new family planning program was announced with the aim of reducing the natural increase rate from 2.8 percent in 1986 to 2.1 percent in 2001.[76] In 1987, Tunisian authorities limited child allowances to families with a maximum of four children and, one year later, in 1988, to those with only three children. A maternity leave of two months at full pay, followed by four months at half pay, was also limited to the first three children.[77] The year 1987 also marked a turning point in the Syrian natalist policy, with the cancellation of the financial benefits given to large families.[78]

The most dramatic change in the natalist area since the mid-1980s has occurred in Iran. In 1988, Iranian authorities decided to revise their natalist perception.[79] A year later, in 1989, Iran officially adopted a family planning program. As in other Middle Eastern countries, the Iranian authorities also recruited religious clerics to support the new policy. The Iranian clerics even presented the aim of fertility decline as a religious obligation in cases where a large number of children harms the family's welfare.[80] The slogan of the Iranian family planning program was: "One is good, two is enough."[81]

Overall, five major factors led to the marked change in the natalist perception of the non-oil Middle Eastern countries after the mid-1980s:

(a) **The collapse of the "economic solution" thesis**. In the mid-1980s, many Middle Eastern leaders realized that "the best contraceptive is a contraceptive"; namely, only a well-organized and declared national family planning program could rapidly reduce high fertility rates.

(b) **The collapse of the intra-Arab labor migration option** mainly as a consequence of the preference given to Asian workers at the expense of Arabs.

(c) **The cut in grants from Arab oil countries** due to the decline in oil revenues.

(d) **The success of family planning programs** in many non–Middle Eastern developing countries, such as "the Asian Tigers," Argentina, and Indonesia.

(e) **The change in the global political economy** toward the Washington Consensus,[82] which naturally promotes fertility decline.

The most dramatic natalist perception change during the 1990s, however, occurred in Oman and, to a lesser extent, in Saudi Arabia. These two countries gradually abandoned their traditional pro-natalist approach and started to promote fertility decline.

Hence, in the mid-1970s only Egypt, Tunisia, Morocco, Turkey, and Iran considered their population growth rate too high and intervened to lower it, while four countries considered their population growth too low and aimed at raising it (Oman, Qatar, Saudi Arabia, and UAE).[83] At the turn of the twenty-first century, however, all of the Middle Eastern countries advocated fertility decline, with the exception of Qatar and the UAE, which implemented a non-interference natalist policy.

SUMMARY AND CONCLUSIONS

Reducing fertility is important not only because of its consequences for economic prosperity, but also because of the impact of high fertility in diminishing the freedom of people—particularly of young women—to live the kind of lives they have reason to value.[84]

Are fertility rates and the overall socioeconomic situation a function of a woman's status and the political regime? Is the core of the demographic problem a political one? The Middle Eastern case supports this assumption, as the fertility rates sharply declined during the past generation in countries that implemented economic liberalization combined with national family planning policies. Tunisia, Egypt, and Turkey are good examples of these kinds of states. In contrast, fertility rates in countries that adopted family planning policy without economic liberalization remained high, with Syria and Yemen being good examples.

Paradoxically, precisely at the stage when the Arab countries could benefit from the "demographic gift," the global economy is entering into the most severe recession since the Great Depression, one major expression of which is a reduction in the demand for goods and services. The implication for Middle Eastern countries is that they will not be able to take advantage of the "demographic gift" for their rapid economic expansion as the Asian Tigers did in the 1970 and 1980s. Since this is a one-time gift, it will be wasted in the coming years and with it, the opportunity for being rescued from their current harsh socioeconomic situation.

What will be the sociopolitical consequences of the mismatch between massive numbers of young educated unemployed and the inability of the regimes to provide enough good job opportunities? Will widespread frustration among the younger generation lead to a reaction that ushers in a new era in which extreme fundamentalist ideologies flourish throughout the Middle East?

NOTES

* This chapter is based on my book *Arab Political Demography*, 2nd ed. (Brighton, England and Portland, OR: Sussex Academic Press, 2009).

1. The natural increase rate refers to the difference between the number of live births and the number of deaths occurring in one year, divided by the midyear population. Population growth rate = natural increase rate ± migration balance.

2. Charles Issawi, *An Economic History of the Middle East and North Africa* (New York: Columbia University Press, 1982), p. 93. See also: Abdel R. Omran and Farzaneh Roudi, "The Middle East Population Puzzle," *Population Bulletin* 48, no. 1 (1993): 5.

3. Issawi, *An Economic History of the Middle East and North Africa*, p. 93, table 6.1.

4. The data for the Arabian Gulf labor-importing countries only refer to the indigenous populations.

5. By 2006, the infant mortality rate in the MENA (Middle East and North Africa) region was 36 per 1,000 live births, compared to 181 per 1,000 live births during 1950–1955. See UNICEF, *The State of the World's Children—2008* (New York: UN Publications, 2008), p. 117, table 1; United Nations, Population Division, "Mortality of Children under Age 5: World Estimates and Projections, 1950–2025," *Population Studies* 105 (New York, 1988), p. 38, table A.2.

6. The life expectancy in the Middle East increased from less than fifty years in the mid-twentieth century to more than seventy-one years in the early 2000s. See UN Development Programme (UNDP), *The Arab Human Development Report*, various issues, 2002–2007 (New York: UNDP).

7. The age pyramid, frequently called age structure, is the way in which the population is distributed across different age and sex groups.

8. The replacement-level fertility rate is defined as the level at which a cohort of people has only enough children to replace themselves. The minimum replacement-level fertility rate under the optimal conditions of low mortality rates is 2.1 children per woman, which is equivalent to a net reproductive rate (NRR) of 1.0 (one daughter for every woman).

9. The GCC organization was established in May 1981 and includes Saudi Arabia, Kuwait, Oman, Qatar, Bahrain, and the United Arab Emirates (UAE).

10. The term "rent" relates to "income derived from the gift of nature." The term "*rentier* state" refers to a situation in which the rental income, which predominates governmental revenues, is external to the domestic economy, and although only a few are involved in its generation, such as in oil and gas industries, the vast majority of the population reap the rental wealth.

11. By the late 1990s, the female labor force participation rate in the Middle East averaged 20 percent—half the rate that prevailed in the developed economies. See Edward Gardner, "Creating Employment in the Middle East and North Africa," *IMF Working Papers* (Washington, D.C.: January 2003); Valentine M. Moghadam, *Modernizing Women: Gender and Social Change in the Middle East*, 2nd ed. (Boulder, CO: Lynne Rienner, 2003), pp. 33–78.

12. The term "Asian Tigers" refers to Taiwan, South Korea, Hong Kong, and Singapore, which have managed to achieve and maintained very high economic growth rates since the 1960s, thus transforming themselves from developing into developed economies within only one generation.

13. The "demographic gift" is a period of an extremely high percentage of the population being of working age (twenty to sixty-five years). This gift period is not only temporary, stretching for no more than three decades, but also a one-time gift. After that, the share of the elderly population steadily increases due to the low fertility rates of the previous years. On the demographic factor of "the East Asian economic miracle," see Geoffrey McNicoll, *Policy Lessons of the East Asian Demographic Transition*, Population Council Working Paper No. 210 (New York: Population Council, 2006).

14. One hectare is equivalent to 1000 m².

15. Syrian Arab Republic, Central Bureau of Statistics, *Statistical Abstract*, various issues (Damascus).

16. Egypt, Central Agency for Public Mobilisation and Statistics, *Statistical Yearbook*, various issues (Cairo).

17. International Monetary Fund (IMF), *Jordan: Selected Issues and Statistical Appendix*, Country Report No. 04/121 (May 2004), p. 102.

18. On the pace and the various consequences of the Middle East urbanization process, see Michael E. Bonine, ed., *Population, Poverty, and Politics in Middle East Cities* (Gainesville: University Press of Florida, 1997).

19. M. Riad El-Ghonemy, *Affluence and Poverty in the Middle East* (London and New York: Routledge, 1998), p. 183.

20. A. S. M. Kashef, "Egypt," in *Social Welfare in the Middle East*, ed. John Dixon (London: Croom Helm, 1987), p. 26.

21. Tayseer Abdel Jaber, "Jordanian Labor Migration: Social, Political and Economic Effects," in *Labor Migration: Palestine, Jordan, Egypt and Israel*, ed. Mohammad Shtayyeh (Jerusalem: Palestine Center for Regional Studies, 1998), p. 85.

22. Muhammad Sa'ad 'Amirah, "Waqi' al-Bitala fil-Urdun wa-Nazara Nahwa al-Mustaqbal," in *al-Iqtisad al-Urduni: al-Mushkilat wal-Afaq*, ed. Mustafa al-Hamarneh (Amman: Markaz al-Dirasat al-Istratigiyya, 1994), p. 224, table 2.

23. During the war, a considerable percentage of the activities in the Aqaba port were related to Iraq, while the Basra port was almost totally paralyzed.

24. 'Amirah, "Waqi' al-Bitala fil-Urdun," p. 224, table 2.

25. *Al-Hayat* (London), January 26, 1992.

26. *Al-Ahram al-Iqtisadi* (Cairo), February 13, 1989.

27. Economist Intelligence Unit (EIU), *Country Report—Egypt*, No. 4 (1988), p. 10.

28. El-Ghonemy, *Affluence and Poverty in the Middle East*, p. 188.

29. EIU, *Country Profile—Algeria, 2004*, p. 36.

30. EIU, *Country Profile—Egypt, 1999–2000*, p. 28.

31. EIU, *Country Profile—Egypt, 2001*, p. 33.

32. *MEED (Middle East Economic Digest)*, April 13–19, 2007, pp. 29–30.

33. EIU, *Country Profile—Syria, 2006*, p. 32.

34. During the 2002–2006 period, Turkey's real GDP growth rate averaged more than 6 percent annually.

35. IMF, *Turkey: 2007 Article IV Consultation—Staff Report*, Country Report No. 07/362 (November 2007), p. 42, table 2.

36. IMF, *Iran—Country Report*, No.08/284 (August 2008), p. 27, table 1.

37. IMF, *Morocco: 2007 Article IV Consultation*, Country Report No. 07/323 (September 2007), p. 16, table 1.

38. By 2005, Algeria's real GDP growth rate was 5.5 percent. EIU, *Country Profile—Algeria, 2006*, p. 33.

39. IMF, *Algeria: 2006 Article IV Consultation*, Country Report No. 07/72 (February 2007), p. 5.

40. IMF, *Tunisia: 2007 Article IV Consultation*, Country Report No. 07/302 (August 2007), p. 5; EIU, *Country Profile—Tunisia, 2006*, p. 33.

41. EIU, *Country Profile—Algeria, 2004*, pp. 36–37.

42. ESCWA, *Survey of Economic and Social Developments in the ESCWA Region, 2006–2007* (New York: UN Publications, 2007), pp. 16–17.

43. The GCC labor force nationalization policy, implemented in the mid-1980s, aimed at gradually replacing foreign labor with nationals, thus reducing both the dependence on foreign labor and the scale of the workers' remittances. On the GCC labor force nationalization policy, see Onn Winckler, "Labor and Liberalization: The Decline of the GCC *Rentier* System," in *Political Liberalization in the Persian Gulf*, ed. Joshua Teitelbaum (London: Hurst, 2009), pp. 66–80; Harry Wes, "Employment Creation and Localization: The Crucial Human Resource Issues for the GCC," *International Journal of Human Resource Management* 18, no. 1 (January 2007): 132–146.

44. According to the *kafala* system, a foreigner was not allowed to work in the GCC countries without local sponsorship (*kafil*).

45. ESCWA, *International Migration and Development in the Arab Region: Challenges and Opportunities* (Beirut: ESCWA, July 2007), p. 8.

46. See ESCWA, *Survey, 2001–2002*, p. 19; Nasra M. Shah, "Restrictive Labour Immigration Policies in the Oil-Rich Gulf: Effectiveness and Implications for Sending Asian Countries," United Nations Expert Group Meeting on Social and Economic Implications of Changing Population Age Structure (UN/POP/EGM/2006/05), May 5, 2006, p. 3; *MEED*, May 6–12, 2005, p. 30; IMF, *United Arab Emirates: Selected Issues and Statistical Appendix*, Country Report No. 05/268 (August 2005), p. 27.

47. On the taxes imposed on foreign labor and their employers since the early 1990s, see ESCWA, *International Migration and Development in the Arab Region*, pp. 7–8.

48. ESCWA, *Survey, 2006–2007*, p. 18.

49. The official Web site of the UAE, www.uaeinteract.com, posted March 1, 2007.

50. On the overall cost/benefit economic balance of the intra-Arab labor migration for the Middle Eastern labor-exporting countries, see Alan Richards and John Waterbury, *A Political Economy of the Middle East*, 3rd ed. (Boulder, CO, and London: Westview Press, 2008), p. 396.

51. Dependency theory maintains that the core of poverty in many developing countries is long-term colonialism, which hampered their socioeconomic development.

52. Joseph Chamie, "Trends, Variations, and Contradictions in National Policies to Influence Fertility," in *The New Politics of Population: Conflict and Consensus in Family Planning*, ed. Jason L. Finkle and C. Alison McIntosh (New York: Population Council, 1994), p. 37; Kelley Lee and Gill Walt, "Linking National and Global Population Agendas: Case Studies From Eight Developing Countries," *Third World Quarterly* 16, no. 2 (1995): 259.

53. Adnan Habbab, "Family Planning in the Syrian Arab Republic," paper presented at the First Regional Population Conference of ECWA, Beirut, February 18–March 1, 1974, pp. 5–6; Ayşe Akin, "Emergence of the Family Planning Program in Turkey," in *The Global Family Planning Revolution: Three Decades of Population Policies and Programs*, ed. Warren C. Robinson and John A. Ross (Washington, D.C.: World Bank, 2008), pp. 86–87; Erhard Franz, *Population Policy in Turkey: Family Planning and Migration between 1960 and 1992* (Hamburg: Deutsches Orient-Institut, 1994), pp. 48–50.

54. The core of the Malthusian theory (published in 1798) is that while population increases at a geometric ratio, the means of subsistence increases at an arithmetic ratio. Thus, any given country that would not be able to lower its population growth rates at some point in the future would not be able to live above subsistence level.

55. Azriel Karni, "Temurot be-Yahas la-Piquah 'al ha-Yeluda ba-Mizrah ha-Tikhon," *Hamizrah Hehadash* 17 (1967): 230 [in Hebrew].

56. United Nations Department of Economic and Social Affairs, *Fertility, Contraception and Population Policies* (New York: UN Publications, 2003), p. 20.

57. Richard Moore, "Family Planning in Iran, 1970–1979," in *The Global Family Planning Revolution*, p. 34. On Iran's demographic developments since 1900 and until 1966, see Julian Bharier, "A Note on the Population of Iran, 1900–1966," *Population Studies* 22, no. 2 (July 1968): 273–279.

58. Peter J. Donaldson, *Nature Against Us: The United States and the World Population Crisis, 1965–1980* (Chapel Hill and London: University of North Carolina Press, 1990), p. 117.

59. Franz, *Population Policy in Turkey*, pp. 55–56; Akin, "Emergence of the Family Planning Program in Turkey," p. 91.

60. Prior to adopting the anti-natalist policy, Iran, in contrast to Turkey, never implemented a pro-natalist policy. Hence, since the early 1950s, the International Planned Parenthood Federation (IPPF) initiated voluntary family planning services in Iran.

61. Moore, "Family Planning in Iran," p. 37; Rodolfo A. Bulatao and Gail Richardson, *Fertility and Family Planning in Iran*, Discussion Paper Series No. 13 (Washington, D.C.: The World Bank, 1994), p. 21; Imperial Government of Iran, *Fourth National Development Plan, 1968–1972* (Tehran, 1968), pp. 66–68, 324.

62. On the "White Revolution," see Rouhollah K. Ramazani, "Iran's 'White Revolution': A Study in Political Development," *International Journal of Middle East Studies* 5, no. 2. (April 1974): 124–139.

63. Richard Moore, Khalil Asayesh, and Joel Montague, "Population and Family Planning in Iran," *Middle East Journal* 28, no. 4 (Autumn 1974), p. 397.

64. United Nations, *Fertility, Contraception and Population Policies*, p. 20.

65. On the earlier stages of the Tunisian family planning program, see Robert J. Lapham, "Population Policies in the Middle East and North Africa," *Middle East Studies Association Bulletin* 11, no. 2 (May 1, 1977): 7–8.

66. *Al-Ahram*, May 22, 1962. The English translation appears in Nissim Rejwan, *Nasserist Ideology: Its Exponents and Critics* (New York: John Wiley & Sons, 1974), pp. 195–265.

67. On Egypt's family planning program during the second half of the 1960s, see Gad G. Gilbar, "Family Planning Under Mubarak," in his *Population Dilemmas in the Middle East* (London and Portland, OR: Frank Cass, 1997), pp. 117–119; Saad M. Gadalla, *Is There Hope? Fertility and Family Planning in a Rural Egyptian Community* (Cairo: American University in Cairo Press, 1978), pp. 213–219.

68. Steven K. Wisensale and Amany A. Khodair, "The Two-Child Family: The Egyptian Model of Family Planning," *Journal of Comparative Family Studies* 29, no. 3 (1998): 505.

69. Lapham, "Population Policies in the Middle East and North Africa," p. 6.

70. Gad G. Gilbar, "Nasser's Soft Revolution," in his *Population Dilemmas*, pp. 84–85.

71. Youssef Courbage, "Economic and Political Issues of Fertility Transition in the Arab World: Answers and Open Questions," *Population & Environment* 20, no. 4 (1999): 370; Philippe Fargues, "Demographic Explosion or Social Upheaval?" in *Democracy Without Democrats? The Renewal of Politics in the Muslim World*, ed. Ghassan Salamé (London: I. B. Tauris, 1994), p. 165.

72. Baquer Salman al-Najjar, "Population Policies in the Countries of the Gulf Cooperation Council: Politics and Society," *Immigrants & Minorities* 12, no. 2 (1993): 212; Gregory III Gause, *Oil Monarchies: Domestic and Security Challenges in the Arab Gulf States* (New York: Council on Foreign Relations, 1994), p. 54; United Nations, "Qatar," *World Population Policies* III (1990), pp. 39–40.

73. Yasmin L. Mossavar-Rahmani, "Family Planning in Post-Revolutionary Iran," in *Women and Revolution in Iran*, ed. Guity Nashat (Boulder, CO: Westview Press, 1983), p. 253.

74. Homa Hoodfar and Samad Assadpour, "The Politics of Population Policy in the Islamic Republic of Iran," *Studies in Family Planning* 31, no. 1 (2000): 20.

75. Lee and Walt, "Linking National and Global Population Agendas," p. 264; Louisiana Lush et al., "Politics and Fertility: A New Approach to Population Policy Analysis," *Population Research and Policy Review* 19, no. 1 (2000): 9.

76. Kamran Asdar Ali, *Planning the Family in Egypt: New Bodies, New Selves* (Austin: University of Texas Press, 2002), pp. 30–31.

77. United Nations, "Tunisia," *World Population Policies* III (1990): 159–160; Muhammad Faour, "Fertility Policy and Family Planning in the Arab Countries," *Studies in Family Planning* 20, no. 5 (1989): 260.

78. ESCWA, *Population Situation in the ESCWA Region—1990* (Amman: ESCWA, May 1992), p. 192.

79. Hoodfar and Assadpour, "The Politics of Population Policy in the Islamic Republic of Iran," p. 22.

80. See Islamic Republic of Iran, *National Report on Population*, submitted to the International Conference on Population and Development, Cairo, 1994, pp. 13–14.

81. On the implementation of the Iranian family planning program since 1989, see Yassaman Saadatmand, "Socioeconomic Factors and Population Policies of the Islamic Republic of Iran," *Journal of South Asian and Middle Eastern Studies* 33, no. 4 (Summer 2000): 17–20.

82. The Washington Consensus, which emerged during Ronald Reagan's presidency, maintained that only private sector–led export-oriented economies can promote economic performance in developing economies.

83. ESCWA, *Population and Development: The Demographic Profile of the Arab Countries* (Beirut: ESCWA, October 2003), p. 3.

84. Amartya Sen, *Development as Freedom* (Oxford: Oxford University Press, 1999), p. 226.

3

HISTORICAL MEMORY AND CONTEMPORARY AFFAIRS

Glenn E. Perry

NOWHERE ELSE IS William Faulkner's much-quoted statement that "the past is never dead" and is "not even past" more applicable than in the Middle East. History affects the present in at least two obvious ways. In the first place, past events have created objective realities that shape the world today. But more important for our purposes is the memory of the past, whether accurate or imagined. History is entangled with myth, a term that in its broadest sense includes real historical events that are deeply embedded in popular culture and memory. McNeill calls this "mythistory," as "the same words that constitute truth for some are . . . myths for others."[1] Such memories provide a prism through which contemporary events are interpreted and analogies for presenting one's actions to others. Conflicting narratives of the past account in large part for conflicts among peoples as well as for the existence of different peoples. And, as Willner demonstrated in her study of charismatic leaders (but also, I suggest, equally applicable to many other situations), such a person "evokes, invokes, and assimilates to himself the values and actions embodied in the myths by which that society has organized and recalls its past."[2]

The relationship of historical memories to what actually happened in history varies from situation to situation. The memory may reflect the real past (itself not always scientifically established and, even if it is, seen from diverse vantage points that give it totally different meanings), but it often is a distorted memory, sometimes consciously inculcated by propagandists and, notably, by school textbooks and teachers in the process that political scientists call "political socialization." False memories crop up among collectivities as they do among individuals. When Murat Belge, a Turkish professor of literature, spoke

61

of his country's "very unhealthy relation with our history," which he called "basically a collection of lies,"[3] he could with nearly equal accuracy have said the same about many other countries' versions of their histories. In the famous words of Ernest Renan, "Getting its history wrong is part of being a nation."

What happened in the past sometimes has been lost to memory. While some may suggest that this can remain part of a collective subconscious, such an idea is highly problematic. Psychologists recognize the importance of a forgotten past for an individual, but collectivities that transcend many generations are a different matter. However true an account of the past may be, one must doubt any claim that it has an impact on a people lacking awareness of it. Thus while archaeologists have produced much evidence that the early Sumerian city-states practiced a greater degree of democracy than did the much later Athens, any claim that such a democratic past is relevant to attempts to democratize Iraq today[4] seems highly fanciful. Southern Iraqis likely are descended to a considerable extent from Sumerians, who however belonged to a radically different culture that largely was replaced by that of Semitic peoples from the third millennium BCE on. Admittedly, to adopt Lewis's terminology, a past that is not "remembered" can sometimes be "recovered" (or even "invented").[5] A recovered history can become absorbed into the history of a people. Lewis emphasizes such cases as the story of Masada, where Zealot Jewish rebels against Roman rule in 66 CE allegedly chose to commit mass suicide rather than surrender—which, if true, did not remain part of Jewish memory over the centuries—and Cyrus, the sixth-century BCE founder of the Persian Empire, whom Iranians only in modern times learned of via the Bible and Western sources. While truth may be largely irrelevant to a myth's utility in bolstering national identity, this is quite different from equating a practice in the fourth millennium BCE with a "historical tradition" of democracy relevant to democratization today.

Philosophers and theologians espousing a pessimistic view of human nature have identified several specific components that sometimes provide a rationale for accepting a less than desirable world. Thus St. Augustine finds humankind to be characterized by such flaws as self-love, greed, domination, and lust. What such writers may have overlooked in human nature is a tendency for conflict among large groups to be underpinned by selective historical memories—sometimes cultivated for that purpose—that give those on all sides a sense of collective identity and justify their own actions while delegitimizing and often demonizing their opponents. Divergent historical *memory* enables each side in a conflict to see itself as upholding a righteous cause.

SPECIAL RELEVANCE TO THE MIDDLE EAST

Awareness of historical events varies everywhere. But in the absence of survey research on this matter it seems that references to many events in both the seventh century CE and the twentieth century CE evoke even more powerful memories among people of varying levels of education in the Islamic world than does the past in other societies. Lewis recently noted that

> we in the Western world, and particularly in the United States, don't seem to attach much importance to history. And even what happened three years ago has become ancient history. . . . In the Muslim world, on the contrary, they have a very lively sense of history . . . and a surprisingly detailed knowledge of history. If you look at, for example, the war propaganda of Iran and Iraq during the eight-year war between those two countries . . . this is propaganda addressed to the largely illiterate general public [and] it is full of historical allusions . . . not telling them historical anecdotes, but a rapid, passing allusion to a name or an event in the sure knowledge that it would be picked up and understood.[6]

For Arabs and Muslims in the Middle East and beyond, a series of events starting in the seventh century CE have a special kind of resonance in the popular mind.

THE UNFORGETTABLE TRANSFORMATION

It seems plausible to suggest that no other cluster of events in world history remains so alive in the minds of so many people today as those related to the rise of Islam in the seventh century CE. Western civilization has no common historical memories of its own rise that evoke anything even remotely as powerful as do these Islamic memories, although for many Western Christians there are comparable memories of a religious nature related to events that preceded the emergence of the West by several centuries. And the religious memories of Christians, whether Western or otherwise, lack the same sort of political dimension that is equally important in Muslim memories. Perhaps the nearest parallels in modern Western nations to the intense historical memories of the Muslims are the specifically national ones—such as those connected with, say, Valley Forge or Plymouth Rock in the case of Americans—which in fact may be interpreted as part of a thinly veiled national religion. Indeed, the Islamic calendar begins at this point in history, specifically in 622 CE, the year of the *hijrah*—the migration (literally, "the breaking of ties" with idolatrous blood relatives) of the first Muslims from persecution in their native city of Mecca to establish the Islamic *ummah*, or community, in Yathrib, which henceforth would be named Medina ("the City")—constituting Year One. Only a few dozen people participated in the hijrah, but it became a formative event for an ummah that today incorporates nearly a fourth of the world's population. And the life of Muhammad—said to be the only prophet who "was born in the full light of history"—is documented in great detail in massive collections of *hadith*s (news reports) whose reliability is deemed to vary from the "strong" to the "weak," with each report supported by a chain of oral sources, or *isnad*s, about his sayings and actions that provide the basis for much of the Islamic legal system, known as the *sunna*, or custom. This provides a model for the behavior of all faithful Muslims. For that matter, a whole genre of literature, the *sira* (biography), is devoted to Muhammad's life.

According to the judgment of some non-Muslim writers, Muhammad ibn Abdillah (born around 570 CE)—who, for Muslims, is the final messenger of God to humanity and whose name is not mentioned without adding "God bless him and grant him salvation" (sometimes shortened in English works to "pbuh," from the translation "peace be upon him")—is the most influential person who ever lived.[7] Not only was he the founder of a religion, but he also was the creator of a state that expanded after his death to dominate much of the world. As a result of this new religion, a vast zone extending from the Atlantic Ocean to the Persian Gulf speaks a common language (unimaginable had not the existence of untranslatable scriptures in this language prevented it from breaking up into mutually unintelligible tongues, as happened with Latin), while the Islamic world in general uses this language for religious purposes. In addition, the languages other Muslims speak and write have come to be infused with Arabic vocabulary (often pronounced differently, as in the Arabic "w" ["waw"] becoming a "v" in Turkish and Persian) and, in many cases, use the Arabic alphabet. The speech of Muslims who are unable to converse in the language of their scriptures is nevertheless peppered with Arabic phrases such as "*salam alaykum*" ("peace on you") and "*in sha' Allah*" ("if God willed"). And the cultures of these diverse peoples have all been influenced by Arabs in many other ways. Muslims everywhere mostly have Arabic names. The memory of Muhammad is so great that, according to numerous calculations, his name has become the most widely used among living people today (and far back in the past), for the name of the final messenger of God is given by Muslims to so many baby boys. If Muhammad ("the praised one") is not what a Muslim man is known by, it (or such a variant as Ahmad, "the more praised one") likely is part of his whole name. It came as a surprise to many people a few years ago to discover that even in England Muhammad was second only to Jack as a boy's name and that, as Muslim immigration continued, it was soon expected to be first.

MEMORIES OF EARLY ISLAMIC EXPANSION

The conquests (literally, "opening" [*fath*; plural, *futuh*]) of countries that ensued with such rapidity immediately after Muhammad's death in 632 CE permanently transformed a vast part of Eurasia and Africa. (The "opening" and "closing" of the American frontier provides an analogy in English usage as well as being another subject of mythistorical memory.) The expansion occurred quickly. By 711 CE, Islamic armies were in Spain, and they reached Tours, in today's France, in 732 CE. An Arab army "opened" Sind in 711 CE too, thus Islamicizing what today includes much of Pakistan. Contact was made with a Chinese army in 751 in the Battle of Talas in today's Kazakhstan. One might think accounts such as this could be only fairy tales.

More remarkably, these territories would be fundamentally changed in that the vast majority of the descendants of the people who were conquered would eventually possess a historical memory of being an integral part of the "openers" themselves. Naipaul thinks it strange that Pakistanis, whose biological forebears underwent conquest by the Arabs in the seventh century, now see history through the eyes of the conquerors and have, in effect, become their adopted descendants.[8] Except for the vast scale of Islamization, this is no different from the way people have changed their identities through assimilation, as in conversion of individuals of various backgrounds to Judaism over the centuries, or—for that matter—the way descendants of recent immigrants to the United States think of their country's founding fathers.

Fuller is quite on the mark in pointing out that even "if Islam had never existed," the struggle to control the Middle East would have been fundamentally the same as it is today.[9] He points out that the same sort of resistance to Western domination, of which Islamist movements provide the vanguard today, could instead have been led by an Orthodox Christian religiopolitical movement. In this case, Monophysite Christianity would be more likely, as Middle Eastern peoples under Roman rule who had embraced Monophysitism were bridling at the bit of the orthodoxy (in today's terms, including both the Orthodox and Roman Catholic churches and the latter's Protestant offshoots) adopted at the Council of Chalcedon in 451 CE that was being imposed when Islam arose. Another heterodox movement, Nestorianism, which previously had gained adherents in the Roman Empire's Eastern provinces, now was the dominant form of Christianity in the Sasanian Empire; had it not been uprooted in the Roman territories, it too conceivably could have provided the same sort of challenge to the Chalcedonian-dominated Roman Empire that the historical memory of peoples subordinated to Hellenism since the time of Alexander the Great seemed to evoke. And in Iran other new religions that grew out of Zoroastrianism—Manichaeism and, in the sixth century CE, the allegedly communistic Mazdakism, both of which represented the dissatisfaction of the times and, in turn, faced brutal suppression—might have served a similar purpose. But, as Fuller recognizes, Islam provides a common identity for otherwise diverse peoples—eventually as far afield as Indonesia—that no other faith or ideology likely ever would have been able to match. It is true that the prospects of the ummah uniting as one state, as originally envisaged, appear to be nil, but while there are many conflicts within it, Muslims everywhere become disturbed and in many cases volunteer to fight when their brethren in Bosnia, Palestine, or Afghanistan are seen as victims of non-Muslims.

The territorial expansion of the Islamic faith and identity and of Islamic rule continued long afterward. But these early futuh—starting with the immediate conquest of the Sasanian Empire and of the Roman Middle East except for the more hellenized Anatolia, which came to be known as "the Land of Rome"—created a vast area that would forever form the core of Islamic lands. Of the territories incorporated into Islamic rule during this early period, the Iberian Peninsula and some small footholds in Europe, notably Sicily, never became predominantly Muslim (although they were illustrious centers of Islamic civilization) and would be lost by the end of the fifteenth century CE. Almost simultaneously, the territories that today form the Republic of Turkey (and for centuries, the Balkan Peninsula) were added to those already under Muslim rule; both Turkey and some parts of the Balkans (and northern Cyprus) became predominantly Muslim. Islam also spread to vast areas of Southeast Asia and sub-Saharan Africa. In addition to the early conquest of Sind, most of the Indian subcontinent came under Muslim rule, with Islam eventually predominating in much of it. Otherwise—with the exception of part of Palestine, in which the state of Israel was created in 1948 but where a struggle continues on various levels, notably the demographic (and perhaps some parts of Central Asia that now have large Slavic, non-Muslim populations)—what the early caliphs (those who came after the Prophet and succeeded him as the political leader of the ummah but not as a prophet or messenger) conquered is solidly part of the Muslim world today, and in some cases, increasingly Muslim in a demographic sense.

In a major part of this region there ensued an ethnic/linguistic transformation that resulted in what today is called the "Arab world." This extends as far as Arabic replaced the tongues spoken at the time of the Conquest, such as the closely related Aramaic, which had become the lingua franca of much of the region centuries earlier and the everyday tongue of the bulk of people in the Fertile Crescent, where arabicization (south of the mountainous Kurdish region) would prove more thorough than almost anywhere else outside the Arabian Peninsula. In Egypt, where a language only distantly related to the Semitic tongues was spoken (but which had been affected by Semitic intrusions from early times), arabicization would be almost total, although the Arab identity probably never became as intense as in the Fertile Crescent. Although the Berber languages survive among a part of the population of North Africa, the Arab/Arabic zone today extends across the northern tier of African countries (where Islamization would become more complete than in Egypt and the Fertile Crescent) and southward to include major parts of the populations of Mauritania and the Sudan. Although the genetic makeup of the population of the Arab countries today undoubtedly is derived mainly from the populations that underwent the conquest of the seventh century, with the subsequent immigration of Arabs from the Arabian Peninsula being relatively small (although it continued long after the futuh, as exemplified by the migration of Bedouin tribes to North Africa in the eleventh century CE), the basic identity of the people (at least the identity that distinguishes them from other Muslims, say, Iranians or Senegalese) is Arab. Although I will qualify this below, insofar as they have adopted an Arab identity, the main historical memory of the people whose lands the Arabs conquered in the seventh century is not of being overrun by outsiders but of being part of the conquest itself. There is much truth in renowned Orientalist Sir Hamilton Gibb's definition of Arabs as "a people clustered around an historical memory" and his statement that "all those are Arabs for whom the central fact of history is the Mission of Mohammad and the memory of the Arab Empire, and who in addition cherish the Arabic tongue and its cultural heritage as their common possession."[10] He might have specified "as their mother tongue," as hundreds of millions of non-Arab Muslims also cherish it as the language of their scriptures and of prayer.

EVOKING MEMORIES: RECENT EXAMPLES

So powerful is the memory of early Islam that the events related to it are invoked again and again. The names given to military campaigns, to revolutionary movements, and the like would seem like mere sounds to most outsiders but evoke powerful memories for Muslims. Sometimes such evocative names provide an important weapon in their own right. The Battle of Badr, in which the Muslim community in Medina attacked the Quraysh of Mecca in 624 CE and provided the ummah's first military victory despite the Muslims' being drastically outnumbered (it is said, with the help of angels who appeared on the battlefield at a crucial time), continues to provide an analogy again and again. Thus when Egyptian President Anwar al-Sadat launched his surprising military offensive across the Suez Canal in 1973 in an attempt to jump start the liberation of Israeli-occupied Sinai, he provided his forces and his image makers in the Arab/Islamic world a significant asset by naming the move "Operation Badr." And when Egyptian forces surprised the world by actually seeming to be defeating the formidable Quraysh, as it were, of the new age, the Israelis, it was predictable that stories would emerge that angels had come to the aid of the Egyptian army in a repetition of the original Battle of Badr.

So entrenched is this battle fought by the Prophet Muhammad in Islamic historical memory that since 1973 the term "Operation Badr" has been used in at least two additional wars. One was the offensive launched by Iran in 1985 in an attempt to defeat Saddam Hussein's Iraq. The Pakistani army carried out another "Operation Badr" in Kashmir in 1999, while more recently "Badr" has been the name used by a militant Kashmiri group. During the 1980s, the Iraqi government invoked the title of Sura (Chapter) 8 of the Quran—al-Anfal, "The Spoils of War," which relates to the Battle of Badr—by calling the campaign against the Kurdish insurgency "Operation Anfal."

The hijra also is evoked. Thus the Muslims who fled to Pakistan when the Indian subcontinent was partitioned in 1947 called themselves *muhajirun* or *muhajirin* (emigrants, actually a variant of "hijra"), the word used for those who broke ties with Mecca and fled to Medina in 622 CE. Similarly, the word *ansar* (helpers), applied to the local Muslims of Medina, is recurrently used in modern situations. The derogatory value of the word *munafiqin* (hypocrites)— evoking memories of those in Medina who were accused of merely pretending to convert to Islam—served the Islamic Republic of Iran well as a way of mocking the violent opposition group that called itself the Mujahidin ("pursuers of jihad") in a way that those who do not understand the structure of Arabic words may fail to notice.

Also, it is notable that the Shiite Iraqi opposition organization established in Iran during the 1980s, the Supreme Council for the Islamic Revolution in Iraq (SCIRI), now called the Islamic Supreme Council of Iraq (ISCI), set up a military force called the Badr Brigade (later called the Badr Organization). With ISCI one of the main components—along with the Dawa ("Call") Party—of the coalition, which has dominated the parliament and cabinet since the 2005 elections, the Badr Organization is an important militia that controls many parts of southern Iraq. The powerful historical memories evoked by the term "Badr" also are shown by its use as the name for a Palestinian military force attached to the Jordanian army. And the name of the other main component of the Iraqi Islamic Front, the Dawa Party of Prime Minister Nouri al-Maliki—the party was famous for its attacks on French and American embassies in Kuwait in 1985—also evokes powerful historical memories, as the word "Dawa" has been used for organizations devoted to spreading Islam, and particularly Shiism, during the past millennium at least.

The Battle of Hudaybiyyah (628 CE), in which the Prophet entered into a ten-year truce with the Meccans, serves as another notable example of an event that is deeply embedded in the memory of the Islamic world. This agreement became a model for treaties with enemies, shaping the writings of medieval jurists in the field of international law, or Siyar.[11] When Egyptian President Sadat made peace with Israel in 1979, Muhammad's truce provided a ready-made way to legitimate his action.

Evoking the Arab/Islamic "opening" of countries in the seventh century CE, the word "fath" (for those who know no Arabic: note that the "t" and "h" here are separate consonants, not "th" as in the word "thin") appears again and again in contemporary politics. The appearance of the word *fath* in Sura 61 of the Quran, "The Battle Array," revealed during the Muslims' military struggle with the Meccans and promising an approaching victory for the faithful, reinforces its resonance. The guerrilla organization founded by Yasir Arafat and his associates during the 1950s, which eventually transformed itself into the ruling political party in the Palestinian National Authority that emerged during the 1990s, is usually transcribed into English as "Fatah" or "al-Fatah." It is an acronym—in reverse—for the Movement for the Liberation of Palestine. As vowels normally are not written in Arabic, the acronym can be read with an "a" following the second consonant, depriving it of any meaning, but it can also be read without the vowel (*fath*) to imply the goal of repeating the amazingly quick and decisive defeats of the awesome armies of the Roman (Byzantine) Emperor Heraclius in the 630s that transformed Palestine into an Arab/Islamic land. The word *fatah* has continued to provide the name for new organizations such as Fatah-al Intifadah and Fatah-Islam that try to rival their namesake.

Muammar Qadhafi called the overthrow of the Libyan monarchy he carried out on September 1, 1969, the Great al-Fateh Revolution (at least as it usually is written in English), while the country's leading institution of higher learning became, as widely transliterated from the Arabic, al-Fatah University. In fact, he used the closely related word *fatih* (literally, "opener"), a reference to its occurrence on the opening day of the month. But the word also evokes something more powerful, the name of the opening Surah (Sura al-Fatiha) of the Quran.

Perhaps even more remarkable than the expansion of the Muslim Arabs in the early seventh century at the expense of the Roman Empire were the simultaneous victories over the other great empire of the time, the Sasanian, which succeeded a series of empires centered in Iran going back to Cyrus the Great and the Achaemenids. Within a few years, the Persian Empire would totally succumb to the Muslim Arab invaders. The Battle of Qadisiyyah (636 CE), in which the Arab Muslims defeated the Persian Zoroastrians, was another great step in the fath. It remains a vivid force in the historical memory of Arabs and Muslims, and it has been widely invoked in recent times. To Saddam Hussein, when his forces invaded Iran in 1980, the adoption of Qadisiyyah as a name for this campaign was supposed to refer to his own replay of the conquest of the Iranians and to evoke solidarity of Arabs against Persians. It would have been more appropriate if he had been attacking secular Persian nationalists who did not see themselves also as descendants of the original Muslim liberators of their land from Zoroastrian rule.

But others, including the Islamic Revolutionary leadership in Tehran, had a different memory of Qadisiyyah. They saw themselves as part—indeed as a new vanguard of—the Muslim ummah that overthrew the Sasanian *kafir*s (non-Muslims, literally "disbelievers") at Qadisiyyah and elsewhere in the seventh century. In their view, they had recently replaced a kafir regime in Iran and now faced another kafir enemy coming from Baghdad, and indeed saw this as providing a unique opportunity—though coming from the opposite direction—to proceed in the footsteps of their seventh-century ancestors in again taking Iraq for Islam. Secular Arab nationalists saw the defeat of the Sasanians by the Muslim

Arabs in the seventh century as a continuation of a process that had already started by the time Muhammad began to receive his revelations, in which Arab tribesmen defeated Persian forces in the Battle of Dhu Qar at the beginning of the century. In any case, the historical memory of Qadisiyyah was vivid for each side, although seen through different prisms: pan-Arab in one case and pan-Islamic in the other.

FURTHER MEMORIES OF GREATNESS

The historical memory of a time when the Arabs and Muslims were at the center of world power and of cultural creativity haunts their descendants during an era of weakness. Smith once pointed out that history (concern with this world) is more important for Islam than for Christianity and Hinduism and that while the reality of success during the Middle Ages matched Muslim expectations, a basic "tension" has emerged between the expectation of greatness on the one hand and the reality of weakness on the other in modern times.[12]

For secular Arabs whose historical memory of greatness is one of the Arabs as such having been at the center of history during the centuries immediately following the rise of Islam, the emergence of a unified, free, socialistic Arab world was the goal, summarized in the slogan "unity, freedom, socialism" of one movement representing this idea, the Baath ("Rebirth," "Renaissance") Party. Smith pointed out that "Arab Islam" has little historical memory of this later Islamic greatness as represented by the empires of the Ottomans and Safavids.[13] But for others, the historical memory is that of a Muslim primacy that endured for several centuries after its center was shifted from the Arabs to other Islamic peoples, notably Turks. The broader Islamic world has a memory of political and military power that peaked as late as the sixteenth century, when the Ottoman, Safavid, and other Islamic states were far more powerful than any Western countries (whose world power extended mainly to the seas), while some Muslim sultanates in southern India, as Hodgson tells us, were the equals of European powers, and the closest thing to "an 'international' language . . . [was] not the relatively parochial French or Latin but Persian."[14] Although he characterizes "world history since 1500 . . . as a race between the West's growing power to molest the rest of the world and the increasingly desperate efforts of other peoples to stave Westerners off," McNeill concludes that there was no "decisive collapse" of the "millennial balance" between the Middle East (and India and China) and the West until the mid-1800s.[15] Indeed, there is much historical memory of that in the Islamic world.

MEMORIES OF DIVISION

Vivid memories remain of a violent split that occurred during the formative period, known to Muslims as the *Fitnah* ("Chaos"). The First and Second Fitnahs are particularly important in Muslim memory. Relating to the succession to leadership following the death of the Prophet Muhammad, these struggles for power represent the beginning of a permanent sectarian division within the Muslim community and have shaped doctrines relating to such matters as revolution versus acceptance of the status quo, as one group of Muslims, from which Sunnism would emerge, accepted the legitimacy of a series of caliphs, and those known as the *Shiat Ali* ("Party of Ali," Shiites) believed that the Prophet's son-in-law and cousin, Ali ibn Abi Talib, had been designated as the beginning of a series of imams (leaders) of the community. The First Fitnah (or Islamic Civil War) involved a military struggle for power between Ali and Muawiyyah, nephew of Uthman, the third caliph, from the same Umayyad clan that had led the opposition to and persecution of the Prophet in Mecca and who mostly had conveniently converted to Islam only after the Prophet returned triumphantly to his native city. Muawiyyah, who had established his capital in Damascus, met the forces of Ali at Siffin, on the Euphrates River, in 657 CE and finally agreed to a proposal to arbitrate the conflict on the basis of the Quran. Ali was duped in the process, and a majority of the arbitrators decided in favor of his Umayyad rival.

Following his death, Ali's son Hasan, revered by Shiites as the second imam, was content to stay out of public life. But then Hasan's brother Husayn asserted his claim to leadership, clashing with the forces of the irreligious Umayyad caliph Yazid (Muawiyyah's son) in what came to be known as the Second Fitnah. In 680, Yazid's army attacked and massacred Husayn and a small group of his followers at Karbala, in southern Iraq, as they were proceeding to Ali's former capital at Kufa to claim Husayn's birthright. Husayn's head was taken to Damascus as a trophy. This was the grandson of the Prophet Muhammad, much beloved by him, and the story was told that one of the men who saw the severed head pointed to the lips, exclaiming that he had seen the Prophet himself kiss them.

The memory of Fitnah always continued to haunt the Muslim community and to provide a rationalization for political thought. According to one interpretation, one reason for the predominance in Islamic political thought over the centuries, as represented in the writings of such men as al-Mawardi and al-Ghazali, of the idea that Muslims should submit to any ruler, however bad, and that even a bad ruler is preferable to no ruler is the memory of the Fitnah experienced during Islam's first century. The Khawarij or Kharijites, Islam's third sect, originally were allied with Ali in opposition to the Umayyads at the Battle of Siffin but broke with him, because of the moderation he exhibited in being willing to accept arbitration as a solution, and then went on to proclaim that they were the only real Muslims and made war on the others. Memory of Kharijite extremism is said to have provided another reason for later Muslim thinkers to shy away from delegitimizing bad rulers as long as they professed to be Muslims (and more generally not to declare any sinners to be non-Muslims but to leave that decision to God). With their extreme beliefs, the Khawarij did not survive. The Ibadi sect, which is dominant in Oman and has a few members among the Berbers of Libya and Algeria, represents an outgrowth of the Khawarij, but if it is to be deemed a branch of the Khawarij at all, it is so moderate as to represent a rejection of the very essence of the movement. However, as Eickelman has shown, the memory of the Khawarij, together with the confused idea that they survive in Oman, has provided an issue of potential significance for some Sunni Muslims.[16]

The memory of the Kharijite specter has evoked accusations against some Islamic movements in recent decades. One minuscule group that emerged in Egypt during the 1970s, calling itself the Society of Muslims, promulgated the idea that its members were the only true Muslims, declaring others *takfir* (loosely translated, "excommunicated"; declared to be kafirs), and adopted the idea of withdrawal (hijrah) from mainstream society to separate communities in the desert. Indeed, a more important figure in the evolution of Islamist movements, Sayyid Qutb (hanged for his dangerous ideas during the era of President Gamal Abdel Nasser, another topic of great historical memory for some radical groups in the Islamic world today), went beyond the moderate Islamism of the Muslim Brothers to proclaim that Egypt had returned to the pre-Islamic Arabian condition of *jahiliyyah* (literally, "ignorance"), that is, was no longer Muslim—in effect, a kind of excommunication. As such a doctrine paralleled that of the Khawarij of old, President Sadat and others labeled the new Muslim extremists *Khawarij*, a very derogatory word in the lexicon of the many Muslims who retained some historical memory of the early Islamic Fitnah. The slur came to be thrown more loosely at Islamists in general, including the moderate Muslim Brothers, rather like the way some militant proponents of private enterprise in the United States sometimes accuse anyone who favors, say, national health insurance, of being a Bolshevik.[17]

MEMORY OF THE FITNAH: IMAM HUSAYN AND KARBALA

Shiism's historical memories are centered on the martyrdom of Husayn, which often has been called the equivalent of the Crucifixion for Christians. The annual celebration of Ashura (literally, "the tenth" [day of the Islamic month of Muharram]) and another celebration forty days later each year evoke strong feelings for Shiites in general. The martyrdom is portrayed in passion plays (*taziyyah*s). Some people beat their chests or strike their heads until blood runs in order to experience the pain inflicted on Husayn. It has become a powerful occasion for mobilization of Shiite populations, with governments that are afraid of their people, as in Saudi Arabia and in Iran under the shah, attempting to prevent such celebrations. Yazid, the Umayyad caliph responsible for the

Karbala massacre, is reviled as the ultimate evil ruler, and for a contemporary monarch, such as Muhammad Reza Shah, to be labeled "the Yazid of our age" is to evoke one of the most powerful historical memories. Considering the small extent of doctrinal differences that seem relevant today (the dispute over the succession from which the break between the sects arose is largely academic now, as few Sunnis are much concerned about reestablishing the caliphate, while Twelver Shiites believe they must wait for the coming of the Mahdi), it might be appropriate to say that in cases where sectarian differences become salient in struggles for power, this is largely a matter of divergent historical memories.

The way Husayn's martyrdom is remembered, together with the political significance of the event, has undergone a dramatic change in recent decades. Historically, Shiites have concentrated on mourning for Husayn, remembering Karbala as demonstrating to the weak that they must learn not to revolt against injustice. Thus the celebration of Ashura has served to bolster the status quo. Other Shiite doctrines were given the same conservative twist. The belief in the *ghaybah* ("absence") of the Twelfth Imam, Muhammad al-Mahdi, in 874 CE (whether one considers this historical or mythical memory) and that he will return as the Mahdi ("Rightly Guided One") to restore justice in the world was understood to mean that Shiites should be content with an unjust world in which their opponents would remain in charge for the time being, because only the Mahdi could make things right. According to one interpretation, the doctrine of the Twelfth Imam was invented to rationalize living under Sunni rule.[18]

Illustrating a transition from the traditional teachings that bolstered the status quo to radical movements calling for change in the name of Islam, some religious leaders in recent times have turned the meaning of Karbala upside down by stressing Husayn as a model revolutionary who resisted injustice. Revolutionary Shiite scholars such as Ayatollah Ruhollah Khomeini understood revolution as a way of hastening the return. And something like this was already true in the case of other revolutionary Shiites, an early example being the preaching of Sayyid Musa al-Sadr, an Iranian scholar of Lebanese ancestry who helped shake the generally underprivileged and politically marginal Shiites of Lebanon out of complacency during the 1960s and whose mysterious disappearance during a visit to Libya evoked the historical memory of the ghaybah.[19] In Iran, one Western anthropologist saw a dramatic shift in the way Husayn was remembered during the months preceding the fall of the shah in 1979.[20] In large part, the success of the Islamic Revolution in Iran may be understood in terms of the ability of Khomeini and his followers to use historical memories concerning Husayn and the doctrine of the Twelfth Imam. More recently, Ayatollah Ali Sistani invoked Karbala (and particularly the participation of Husayn's sister Zaynab in the battle) in calling on women to vote in the 2005 Iraqi election.[21] As for the imamate in particular, Khomeini came to be known as Imam Khomeini, and while the word "imam" in Arabic simply means "leader," particularly a prayer leader, and although the ayatollah of course never made any claim to being the Twelfth (or other) Imam, the use of such a title undoubtedly evoked messianic associations in the minds of many people.[22]

To some extent, the historical memory of Husayn's martyrdom at Karbala transcends the Sunni-Shiite divide. Indeed, Shiism (the Party of Ali) emerged during the period of the First and Second Fitnahs over the question of succession, with Shiites rejecting the legitimacy of the first three caliphs (Abu Bakr, Omar, and Uthman). Sunnism would eventually develop among those who rejected the Shiite position on this matter. But it is anachronistic to refer to the Shiites' opponents at this early date as Sunnis (as Western journalists often do in their background analyses), for the term "Sunni" (and much of the theology of Sunnism) did not emerge until much later as a label (the full term being "People of Sunna [custom] and Jamaa [community]") for those who accepted the legitimacy of the actual leaders of the community (only the first four of whom were granted the status of having been truly "rightly guided"), including the "sinners" among them, it being left to God at the last judgment to determine whether they were truly Muslims. Keep in mind that Ali, whom Shiites consider the first legitimate ruler following the Prophet's death, also was the legitimate fourth caliph from the Sunni point of view. And although Sunnis do not accept Husayn's claim as the legitimate head of Islam, he has at times been a hero for some Sunni as well as Shiite Muslims, as illustrated by his (and his brother Hasan's) many famous namesakes among rival Islamic sects. By contrast, one has to look long and hard to find any Muslim—Sunni or otherwise—named for the Umayyad Caliph Yazid. Admittedly, some Sunnis have praised Yazid or have blamed Husayn for sacrificing himself and others for a hopeless cause. But the idea of Husayn as a model revolutionary has been adopted by numerous secular-minded and even some religious Sunni writers in modern times, at first with greater ease than for Shiites.[23]

PERSISTING AND INVENTED MEMORIES OF ANCIENT TIMES

As Middle Eastern history did not start with the rise of Islam, memories of pre-Islamic times persist too. It might not be too much of an oversimplification to suggest that much of the ideological debate in modern times (the nineteenth century CE on) has involved attempts by "modernists" to invoke memories—sometimes, to repeat Lewis's terms, "remembered" history but more often "recovered" or "invented"—of the ancient world against those committed to maintaining the continuity of the world that came into being with Islamization and arabicization during the medieval period. The process of arabicization gradually brought not only the Arabic language but also an incorporation of most of the peoples in territories west of Iran into the Arab self. In other words, Egyptians, Syrians, and the like became Arabs, not because the pre-Arab population disappeared and not mainly because so many immigrants from Arabia settled there but rather because the existing populations in such countries slowly adopted the Arabic language and an Arab identity. In North Africa, arabicization eventually produced mainly Arab countries, and the Berbers quickly embraced not only the religion of Islam but also became a driving force in expanding the Islamic state, particularly into Spain. And yet many Berbers (including perhaps 40 percent of the population of Morocco today) kept a memory of their own past and thus of their separate Berber identity.

Some historical memories persisted even among the original Arabs as well as the arabicized peoples. For Muslims, the period before Islam, particularly in Arabia, which was characterized by idolatry, is called the *jahiliyyah*, or "Age of Ignorance." We have already seen how this word is used as a term of reproach. But it also is the Arabs' "heroic age." It was a time of great poetry, with which Arabs continue to be entranced. And there is much mythistorical memory of early prophets and such in ancient Arabia in the Quran. The Quran preserved the memory of the ancient city of Iram or Ubar and of its destruction that otherwise was known only in legend—comparisons with Atlantis have been made—until remote sensing made possible by satellites and the space shuttle helped explorers uncover it in the early 1990s in southern Oman, along what in ancient times had been the route over which frankincense was shipped to the Mediterranean world.[24]

As for countries such as Iraq and Egypt, which arabicized in the centuries after the rise of Islam, their pre-Arab pasts did not go away. Pharaonic Egypt left too much evidence of its existence for the country's later inhabitants to be unaware even if their scriptures had not told them about it. But contrary to some who recently have argued the opposite, there does not seem to have been much interest in it until the work of modern Western Egyptologists. Islam preserved Egyptians' memory of the Pharaohs, but of a negative sort. Joseph is the topic of a whole *surah* (chapter) in the Quran. Moses is one of Islam's messengers/prophets. The Pharaohs, for Islam, are villains. "Pharaoh" is mentioned in the Quran as "wielding kingpins who were (all) so arrogant in the land and increased the scourge of torment on them" (Sura 89, T. V. Irving translation). Identifying with them poses a dilemma for Muslim Egyptians who might otherwise feel a sense of continuity with their ancient ancestors. Only in modern times did a kind of local nationalism—sometimes labeled Pharaonism—develop in which some Egyptians identified with the country's whole history, arguing that the essence of a distinctly Pharaonic culture had survived. This reached its height during the "liberal" period of the 1920s and early 1930s, when a secular Egyptian nationalism disassociating Egypt from the Arabs seemed to be ascendant. As

the Christian West often sees its own civilization as a lineal descendant of the ancient Near East (which is true, though not more for the West than for Islam),
Pharaonism and similar movements connecting with the ancient world became a
rationale for adopting Western culture and denying the Arab identity,[25] leading
some Egyptian writers in the pre-1952 "liberal age" to fancy that, unlike the Semitic Arabs, they were "European" in culture and even in race. But for both pan-
Arabism and pan-Islamism this represents a deplorable failure to identify with
the larger community that has come into being since the seventh century CE.
Thus after assassinating Anwar al-Sadat (seen by some as having deserted Arab/
Islamic causes in favor of a Pharaonic Egyptian identity), Khalid al-Islambuli
proclaimed that he had "killed Pharaoh."

A memory of pre-Islamic identities was invented in Fertile Crescent countries too as a way of disassociating with Arabism. Some Lebanese, mainly Maronite Christians, pushed the idea that they form a distinct Phoenician nation
that has existed continuously since ancient times, bolstering their rejection of
being considered part of Syria. For many of them, the idea of being Phoenicians is accepted uncritically, having been drilled into them in school.[26] (Ironically, the pan-Syrian ideologue Anton Saadah, founder of the Syrian National
Party in the 1930s, considered Syria as a whole, including Lebanon, to share
the Phoenician heritage.) There are many problems with this notion. The
people of such cities as Tyre and Sidon were Canaanites like their neighbors farther south, and the appellation "Phoenician" may have been a mere Greek innovation. While there has been some movement of populations over the
millennia, it seems likely that the Lebanese today have much Phoenician blood
in their veins. Recent DNA studies point to a major "Phoenician" genetic influence on the populations of places all around the Mediterranean that were colonized by Tyre and Sidon in ancient times.[27] But the idea that modern Lebanese
are simply Phoenicians is purely a modern invention. As Salibi points out, any
similarity between the Phoenicians and today's Lebanese—a judgment that
could be applied equally well to Pharaonist arguments about cultural similarities between modern Egyptian peasants and those who preceded them three
millennia ago—results from geography, which, "in some respects, can be as important as history."[28]

Particularly in the Fertile Crescent, there has been an opposite modern tendency on the part of those who stress their Arab identity. Invoking the dominant linguistic theory explaining the rise of Semitic languages in terms of the
recurrent movement of tribes out of the Arabian Peninsula, these modern
Arab nationalists sometimes stretch the term "Arab" to include all such early
Semitic peoples. After all, linguists consider Arabic, the last Semitic tongue
committed to writing, to be older than the others, such as Akkadian, Amorite,
Hebrew, and Aramaic. It is not difficult to jump from this to the obviously
simplified idea that Arabic is the parent Semitic language. According to this
way of thinking, the Akkadians, Phoenicians, and others become Arabs too.

Thus the Baathist regime in Iraq after 1968, though committed in principle to the idea that Iraq is an integral part of a larger Arab nation, stressed the notion of all the pre-Islamic Semites having been Arabs and consequently of the continuity of Mesopotamian/Iraqi civilization. Although the fact that the earliest known Mesopotamian people, the Sumerians, were not Semites makes it difficult to fit them into such a scheme, aside from the likelihood that later Mesopotamians/Iraqis are in part their biological descendants, the Sumerians too were presented as ancient Arabs. And identification with the Babylonians in particular went against the grain of Islamic traditions, presumably influenced by the Old Testament, which presented them in a bad light. The reconstruction of ancient Babylon during the period of Saddam Hussein's presidency is probably the best-known example of the phenomenon, but the Baathist regime promoted an extensive cultural program stressing Iraqi Arabs' ties to their country extending back to the Sumerians.[29]

The peoples of Egypt and the Fertile Crescent were subordinate to Hellenism during the centuries from Alexander the Great to the rise of Islam. Iran, by contrast, reestablished its independence under the Parthian and Sasanian empires, and the latter in particular may be seen as a restoration of the Persians' national greatness under the Achaemenids. (The Sasanians actually occupied the eastern parts of the Roman Empire, including Egypt and much of Anatolia, at the beginning of the seventh century CE but were pushed back at about the same time Muhammad was receiving his first revelations.) But Roman rule in the Middle East continued to represent the domination of the Hellenic culture over the indigenous peoples even after the Romans, with their capital now in Constantinople, adopted a Middle Eastern religion, Christianity. The form of Christianity that gained the status of orthodoxy and official Roman support, with the Council of Chalcedon in 451 CE, accepting the idea that Christ has two interrelated natures, human and divine, put it at odds with the non-Hellenic population of the Middle East. The revolt of the Middle East against the Romans came in the form of adopting non-Chalcedonian forms of Christianity—first, Nestorianism (the idea that Christ has two completely separate natures), which emerged as the dominant form of the faith in Sasanian lands, including Mesopotamia, after it was extirpated in Roman-ruled territories, and then Monophysitism (the idea of Christ as having only a divine nature) continued the indigenous resistance to Roman-backed orthodoxy. Thus the advance of the more tolerant Arab Muslim invaders—it is hard to say whether the concept of their being Semitic kinsmen would have been understood by people living in those days—was hardly opposed by most Syrian and Egyptian Christians and may have seemed more like liberation from oppressive Orthodox Christian rule. These Christians remembered who they were under Islamic rule, and they were tolerated and given autonomy. In modern times some of them adopted a secular identity as Arabs. The Jewish minority too was generally happy to have the Arabs liberate them from Roman oppression (they allied themselves with the Sasanians at the beginning of the seventh century, and Emperor Heraclius ordered them to convert to Christianity), and they preserved their own historical memory and identity while enjoying a generally decent if not utopian condition under Islamic rule.

The Arab/Islamic Conquest of the Fertile Crescent and Egypt and the failure of the Jewish and Monophysite Christian population to oppose it has been interpreted as a final stage in the recurrent resistance to the subordination to Hellenic domination since the fourth century BCE. Arnold Toynbee includes such developments as the Jewish revolt under Macabee leadership in the second century CE and even the attempt of the Arab Queen Zenobia to take over the Roman Empire, as well as the schism within Christianity, as chapters in the story of anti-Hellenic resistance over the millennium preceding the Arab/Islamic defeat of the Romans.[30]

IRAN: HEIRS OF THE ACHAEMENIDS OR OF THE PROPHET?

An even more important case in point is the Iranian historical memory that competes with Islam for the soul of the country. Two rival versions of historical memory have been at the heart of recent Iranian history. It may be ironic that Iran became more completely Islamic than did much of the Arab world, where large minorities became arabicized while remaining Christian. Only tiny Zoroastrian, Christian, and Jewish minorities remain in Iran. Not only did the decrepit nature of the Sasanian state at the time provide a major explanation for its quick capitulation to the Arab/Islamic armies in the seventh century CE, but a rigid caste system apparently weakened the will of its population to resist, and indeed there is reason to think that Iranians were looking for a new faith to replace Zoroastrianism, as Nestorian Christianity was showing signs of replacing this ancient Iranian faith.[31] But Persian (and related Iranian tongues) persisted in Iran (in contrast to the Fertile Crescent, where Semitic tongues related to Arabic went back three millennia, making the transition relatively easy), along with a strong historical memory among Iranians of being distinct from their fellow Muslims in the Arab world. The perpetuation of the ancient name of the country—meaning "land of the Aryans"—preserves a distant prehistorical memory of a migration from the north that explains the similarity in some basic vocabulary and grammatical structure between Persian and most of the languages of Europe and northern India and distinguishes the Iranians from the Arabs. Thus while the Arab and Islamic identities of Arabs are closely woven together (with even Christian Arabs sometimes sharing in the same historical memory and treating Islam as part of their national identity), Iran since its conversion to Islam has demonstrated a Janus-like quality, an Islamic face alternating with an Achaemenid/Sasanian one.

Representing the notion that Islam is a hindrance to modernization and in an attempt to distinguish Iranians from the Islamic world generally, the Pahlavi dynasty, which ruled from 1925 to 1979, was committed to a worldview that made Iran distinct from the rest of the Islamic world and emphasized its history going back to ancient times. The dynasty's taking the name Pahlavi—another word for "Middle [immediately pre-Islamic] Persian"—provided one indication of this, as did the fashion during that period of giving children names such as Cyrus and Darius. Taking the title "Shah of Shahs and Light of the Aryans," Muhammad Reza Shah—whose two names oddly represented the Islamic and the specifically Shiite historical memory, respectively, as Reza is the name of one of the twelve Shiite imams—tried to evoke the perception that he not only was in the same line as Cyrus the Great but also the great movement of Indo-European peoples from central Eurasia four millennia ago. Willner deals with the way the events leading up to 1970 pitted the shah's myths of Persian kingship against the Shiite worldview of Khomeini.[32]

The grand, extravagant celebration at Persepolis in 1971 of the supposed 2,500th anniversary of the founding of the Iranian monarchy obscured the fact that Muhammad Reza Shah represented an upstart dynasty founded by his father rather than a continuous line of kings going back to Cyrus the Great. In fact, following the Islamic conquest there was a nearly thousand-year hiatus in statehood for any geographical unit resembling Iran. When the Safavid state emerged in 1502 it was ruled by a Turkish dynasty that purported to be a universal empire based on Shiite Islam rather than on Iranian nationhood. And even when Muhammad Reza Shah formed a close relationship with Israel in violation of the sensibilities of the Muslim world, generally he played it down, a case in point being the classification of what in fact differed little from an embassy as a mere "mission."[33]

There were precedents for Persian particularism from the beginning of the Islamic period. While the bulk of the population of the conquered Sasanian Empire converted to the religion of their Arab conquerors fairly quickly, they did not become Arabs (the Aramaic-speaking, in other words, Semitic, people of Mesopotamia providing the exception). Within the Islamic community during the religion's formative centuries, the idea of the equality of all without regard to such differences failed to prevent the ethnic division between Arabs and Persians from becoming a major factor in Islamic society and politics, as the Arab conquerors during the Umayyad period acted like an aristocracy and required Persians and others to take on a subordinate status as *mawali* (clients) of Arab tribes when they converted to Islam. This led many Persians to join the Alid (Shiite) opposition to the Arab-dominated Umayyad state (although the conversion of Iran to Shiism did not occur until the sixteenth century). The Persian mawali were one factor in the overthrow of the Umayyads in 750 CE and the establishment of a new dynasty, the Abbasids, who, although they were Arabs too, created a new order in which Persians were able to attain important positions. And at least one writer speaks of the Persians as the conquerors of Islam rather than the reverse.[34] Non-Arabs, particularly Persians, sometimes demonstrated a sense of superiority, as in the medieval literary movement known as the Shuubiyyah ("pertaining to the peoples").

The Persians' memory of a great past of their own going back to the days of the Achaemenids (even if they had forgotten about Cyrus the Great) underwent renewal as a new variation of their Indo-European tongue, which came to be known as New Persian (as opposed to Middle Persian or Pahlavi, which withered as a literary language following the Islamic conquest, and the Old Persian of Achaemenid times), emerged by the ninth century CE, using the Arabic alphabet and incorporating much Arabic vocabulary. During subsequent centuries Persian would rival Arabic as the primary language of Islam. Arabic always would be the language of religion throughout the Islamic world, but in other fields Persian would become the lingua franca of the Islamic peoples living to the north and east of the Arab countries—that is, not just in Iran but in the Ottoman Empire and the Moghul Empire, where it was the official language, and in central Asia. Persian poetry—whose masters were an ethnically diverse lot, not just Persians or Iranians—for many centuries achieved perhaps unsurpassed literary accomplishments. Iranians' pre-Islamic historical memory was perpetuated in the writings of Ferdowsi's *Shahnama* (Book of Kings), written around 1000 CE. Relating legends of rulers from mythical times to the Islamic conquest, this national epic has had a tremendous impact on the consciousness of the Persian-speaking world. With its emphasis on an Islamic historical memory, the 1979 Revolution did not look favorably on this purely Iranian national story but found it impolitic to ban it. The same is true of the ruins of Persepolis, the Achaemenid capital, which remains a place of national pilgrimage, although originally some of the revolutionary leaders planned to destroy the pagan—and monarchical—site that was not part of the pan-Islamic historical memory they preferred.

Pre-Islamic traditions such as national festivals also survived Islamization. A case in point is the Iranian New Year, or *Nowruz* ("New Day"). Despite the emergence of a regime that emphasizes Iran's Islamic identity rather than a past that extends back to when the country's religion was Zoroastrianism (if not before), the festival of Nowruz was too deeply imbedded in national consciousness even for an Islamist regime to have dared to ban it even if it originally wished to do so. A day of rejoicing, it is still a bigger holiday than any of the Islamic ones, and it is said that when it coincides with Ashura, which involves mourning for Husayn, "the Zoroastrian soul of Iran wins in spite of the wishes of Iran's clerical rulers."[35] Perhaps, however, such a testimony to peculiar Iranian national memories is put in better perspective by the fact that Nowruz is celebrated in a wide geographical zone that includes not only non-Persian Iranian peoples, such as the Kurds, but also among Turks. For that matter, Egypt and the Sudan have a popular holiday, celebrated without regard to religion, that goes back to Pharaonic times, Shamm al-Nasim ("smelling the

breeze"), to commemorate the beginning of spring. The survival of such a tradition is easily understandable considering that Islamic holidays are determined by the Islamic lunar calendar, which causes them to shift from season
to season.

But neither the wide use of Persian as a world literary language nor the sense
of the distinctiveness of the Persian people should be interpreted to imply any
necessary hostility between them and other Islamic peoples, such as Turks and
Arabs. The idea that each people, identified by a national language, should form
its own independent political unit hardly existed anywhere in premodern times.
Indeed, the political entity called Iran is the early sixteenth-century creation of a
Turkish dynasty, the Safavids. While the distinction between Turks, Persians,
and other ethnic groups was always significant, it does not seem that Persians
objected to rule by Turkish shahs either in the Safavid period (which lasted until
the early eighteenth century) or during the rule of the Qajars, another Turkish
dynasty, which took power at the end of the same century. This was not a state
based on the principle of nationality and nationalism but rather on the ideology
of Twelver Shiism. While there have been breakaway movements in the Kurdish
region—unlike the Azeris, most Kurds are Sunni Muslims—and while there
have been revolts among the Azeris, the goal each time was change in, not seces-
sion from, Iran.[36] Even today, the Leader (or Jurist), Ayatollah Ali Khamenei,
the country's top leader under the Islamic Republic, is of Azeri extraction, as are
other major figures in Iranian politics.

As for Iranians and Arabs, two opposite misconceptions sporadically alternate.
I used to be regularly horrified by American journalists who kept calling Iran an
Arab country. That misconception is now often replaced by an opposite one—
the mistaken idea that there is and always has been a deep Arab-Persian antagonism. Indeed, the sense of Iranian distinctiveness emerged early in Islamic
history. Contrary to the Islamic doctrine of one ummah in which ethnic distinctions make no difference, early Iranian converts to Islam, after all, had been dis-
criminated against during the Umayyad period. And it was natural for the
Persian heirs of a great imperial tradition to feel superior to the tribes of the desert
who, to their amazement, conquered the Sasanian Empire. But one should remember that the word "Arab" has had different meanings over time. The word
today applies to diverse arabicized peoples who have come to speak Arabic, such
as Egyptians and Syrians, many of whom sometimes share the Persian condescen-
sion toward Bedouins (that is, Arabs in the narrow sense of the word).

Both sectarian and ideological differences (as well as the natural tendency of
some of its smaller neighbors to be wary of the Iranian giant) have sometimes
been mistaken as Arab-Iranian antagonism. In fact, Arab Shiites have historically tended to be closer to Iranians than to their fellow Arabs. The Arab Shiites
of Lebanon have always had important ties to their Iranian co-religionists. Shiite
ulama (religious scholars) were imported from Lebanon when Iran converted to

Shiism. And many of the Iranian ulama families claim to be descendants of the Prophet Muhammad, which, insofar as this is true, makes them partly of Arab descent.

Ideology puts people on both sides of the ethnic divide in the same camp. The Baathist regime in Iraq bitterly disliked revolutionary Iran but gave refuge to Iranian dissidents such as the Mujahidin-i Khalq, while hundreds of thousands of Iraqi Shiite opponents of the Baathist regime took refuge in Iran. And there is no reason to think that the conservative Arab regimes and their supporters would have liked a radical Islamic regime any better if it had arisen in Egypt rather than in Iran. President Nasser of Egypt (actually, the wife of this preeminent Arab nationalist hero was of Persian origin, while Muhammad Reza Shah's first wife was the sister of Egyptian King Farouk) clashed with the shah, but his successor, President Sadat, developed a close relationship with him. Unlike many Arabs in Syria and Jordan, Iranians would not have wanted their country to unite with Nasser's Egypt, but a lot of anti-shah Iranians admired Nasser as a spokesperson for Third World causes. And many Arabs—including Sunnis—admired Khomeini and saw him as a model for leading revolutions in their own countries, although—unlike in the earlier case of the Arab charismatic hero Nasser—this did not extend to wanting to abolish state boundaries. Some polls in the aftermath of the remarkable fight the Iranian-backed Lebanese Shiite resistance group, Hizbullah, carried out against the Israelis in 2006 showed its leader, Hasan Nasrullah, to be the most popular figure in the Arab world, and there were varying levels of support for Iranian President Mahmoud Ahmadinejad.[37] The most powerful person in post-2003 Iraq likely is Ayatollah Ali Sistani, an Iranian Shiite scholar residing in Najaf. A 2008 University of Maryland poll of Arab opinion showed a mere 8 percent saying that Iran's growing power was their major concern in relation to the consequences of the war in Iraq, while only 29 percent (as opposed to 44 percent who expressed a positive view and 12 percent who said it would not matter) thought the consequences of Iran's acquisition of nuclear weapons would be negative for the Middle East.[38] A BBC World Service Poll showed a higher level of "mainly positive" evaluations of Iran's role in the world in Egypt than in any of the other twenty-seven countries surveyed.[39] Thus, while Arabs and Persians are conscious of being two different peoples, this is not the same as saying there is a deep conflict between them.

TURKISH MEMORIES

Turks are relative newcomers to the Middle East, particularly to what now is the Republic of Turkey. Descended, as one myth has it, from a man who mated with a female gray wolf (a mythistorical memory invoked by the name of one small ultra-rightist movement, the Gray Wolves, in recent decades), the

Turks lived in Mongolia in ancient times. Linguistically they are related not only to the Mongols but also to diverse peoples (termed "Uralic-Altaic" by modern students of language) whose trajectories of migration took them to such countries as Hungary and Finland. The Huns who attacked the Roman Empire in the third century CE may have been the first Turks to appear in western Eurasia. Turks entered the Middle East in early Islamic times as slaves imported for use as soldiers (known as *mamluk*s, literally, "owned"), and such mamluks, who continued to import Turkish slave boys for military use, soon became the real rulers, initiating a process that resulted in Turks forming the ruling class throughout most of the Islamic world for about a millennium. Then free Turkish tribes, already converted to Islam, began to move in, as in the case of the Seljuk Turks, who defeated the Romans at the Battle of Manzikert in 1071, beginning the process of Turkifying and Islamizing Anatolia and parts of the Balkans. Turkish tribes settled in Anatolia, but the much more numerous Anatolian peoples, many of them hellenized as a result of more than a millennium of Macedonian-Greco-Roman rule, were not exterminated or expelled (at least until the uprooting of Greeks and Armenians in the early twentieth century, the subjects of special historical memories that persist today). So the Turkification process must have been mainly a matter of assimilation, that is, people's languages, religions, and identities changed. One Turkish dynasty, the House of Osman (Ottoman), emerged in the thirteenth century CE on the frontier of a disintegrated Seljuk realm to become one of the largest and longest lasting states in history, the Ottoman Empire. It survived until the end of World War I, when its breakup resulted in the establishment of the Turkish Republic in the region that, ethnically, was mainly Turkish.

New mythistorical memories artificially were imposed by the ideology of the new republic that contrasted with anything in the past. Among most Muslims, ethnic identity survived incorporation into the Islamic ummah, but the Turks of the Ottoman Empire, at least those who were educated or were part of the ruling class, gave such primacy to being Muslims that they lost interest in Turkishness. The word "Turk" was relegated to use as a derogatory term for the lower classes. Members of the Ottoman elite were insulted when Christian Europeans called them (and Muslims in general) Turks and probably were totally confused when their country was referred to as "Turkey." According to Lewis,

> Save for a few fragments, all [of the specifically Turkish heritage] was forgotten and obliterated in Islam until its partial recovery in European scholarship in the eighteenth and nineteenth centuries. There is no Turkish equivalent to Arab memories of the pagan heroes of old Arabia, to Persian pride in the bygone glories of the ancient Emperors of Iran, even to the vague Egyptian legends woven around the broken but massive monuments of the Pharaohs. . . .

Even the very name Turk, and the entity it connotes, are in a sense Islamic. . . . Its generalized use to cover the whole group, and perhaps the very notion of such a group, dates from Islam and became identified with Islam; and the historic Turkish nation and culture, even in a certain sense the language . . . were all born in Islam. To this day the term Turk is never applied to non-Muslims though they be of Turkish origin and language . . . or citizens of a Turkish state like the Christians and Jews of Istanbul.[40]

The nineteenth century CE saw the emergence of Turkish identity, partly as a result of Western—notably Hungarian—research on the origin of the Uralic-Altaic peoples and their languages that renewed the Ottoman Turks' previously forgotten historical memories. This took the form of pan-Turkism or pan-Turanism (from the romantic term "Turan" for Central Asia), calling for Ottoman leadership of and even unification of a vast region extending to the Pacific Ocean. Pan-Turanism contended with pan-Islamism, as some Ottomans aspired to lead the whole Islamic world and many Muslims looked to them as the last remaining significant independent Islamic state and increasingly took the Ottoman sultans' claims to the caliphate seriously. Some also espoused the dream of pan-Ottomanism (or simply Ottomanism), in which all peoples and religions would live in equality and identify with the Ottoman state. But with defeat by the Allied powers in World War I and the breakup of the Ottoman Empire, all these dreams were dead.

Mustafa Kemal, later known as Kemal Atatürk, led a fierce resistance movement during the early 1920s that succeeded in thwarting Allied plans to divide up what would become today's Republic of Turkey. Along with this, a new national identity, with accompanying mythistorical memories, was born. The new national concept emphasized Turkishness but dropped its pan-Turkish aspect in favor of a Turkish nation limited to the borders of the new republic. Non-Turkish ethnic groups such as the Kurds, an Indo-European people belonging to the Iranian subfamily who predominate in the eastern part of Anatolia, were told that they too were Turks (just "Mountain Turks") and experienced attempts to extinguish their separate historical memories and identities.

Along with this territorial Turkish nationalism came an artificial set of new historical memories to bolster it, although some of the most extreme pseudoscientific ideas eventually were dropped or played down. While in fact the Hittites, who long dominated much of Anatolia, starting in the early third millennium BCE, were an Indo-European people rather than a part of the Uralic-Altaic migration that started nearly two thousand years later, in the new ideology of Turkism they were declared to have represented an early Turkish presence in Turkey. Many of the people who underwent Turkification in Anatolia in the second millennium CE indeed must have been descendants in part of Hittites, but the Kemalists included the Sumerians—inhabitants of southern

Mesopotamia in the earliest recorded times, as Turks too, apparently because of the agglutinative nature of both Turkish and Sumerian (which, however, linguists do not consider to be related to Turkish or any other known language). And so the Turks' Sumerian heritage was fancifully invoked in the name of such an important institution as the Sumerbank, established in Turkey during the 1930s. In attempting to rid the Turks of certain Islamic influences, the Kemalists adopted the idea of the Turkish sociologist Ziya Gokalp, who made a distinction between civilization and culture, arguing that it was necessary to become part of the only viable living civilization, the Western, but to preserve Turkey's own national culture, which was said to have been radically different from the foreign Islamic culture adopted in previous centuries and more like the cultures of modern Western countries. Thus to westernize the Turks' culture was to bring them back to their original one. Much effort was devoted not only to ridding Turkish of the Arabic alphabet in favor of a basically Latin one but also of the many Turkish and Persian words that had entered Turkish. If the substitutes were borrowed from French or even if it proved impossible to replace an Arabic word, that too was fine, for in Atatürk's "sun language" theory Turkish was the original language from which all others had emanated as peoples moved outward from Central Eurasia over the millennia, and so such words really were Turkish.[41]

JEWISH HISTORICAL MEMORIES AND ZIONISM

A unique case of invoking ancient memories to undo the world that emerged in the seventh century CE is that of Zionism and the establishment of a Jewish state of Israel in Palestine in 1948. For Jews, the historical memory of Palestine has focused on its Jewish period, which ended in 135 CE with the defeat of the Jewish Rebellion against Roman rule and the exile of much of the Jewish population. There is hardly any consciousness of Palestine as an Arab land for many centuries. In fact, some of the leaders of the Zionist movement, which emerged among European Jews in the late nineteenth century with the goal of establishing a Jewish state in Palestine, imagined that it was an empty country, partly representing a more general European attitude at the time toward "natives" of non-European lands. Only for a short time during the early twentieth century did some of the Zionist leaders, particularly David Ben Gurion, focus on the likelihood that the Arab Palestinians were descendants in part of ancient Israelites who had converted to Christianity and Islam and become arabicized (undoubtedly true, though missing from anyone's historical memory). The historical memory of the West regarding Palestine is also limited to the ancient period, a fact that has contributed to a lack of comprehension of the Arab/Islamic rejection of the Zionist project. Thus at the beginning of the Palestinian Uprising in 1987, one member of the US Congress allegedly demanded to know who these Palestinians were. Some say it was fundamentalist Protestants, with their historical memory of the country derived only from the Bible and a belief that the "return" of the Jews is a prerequisite to the Second Coming, who really invented Zionism long before the nineteenth century, as the Jews traditionally believed that such a project was forbidden until the coming of the Messiah.

The Jewish community established in Palestine that eventually formed the state of Israel devoted much attention to archaeology, looking for proof of the biblical narrative as a way of reinforcing historical memories. Only in recent years has a more objective approach known as biblical revisionism—disputing much of the Old Testament account—emerged among Israeli archaeologists, such as Israel Finkelstein and Neil Asher Silberman.

Much of the Jewish memory of the past two millennia is well known. Those in the Christian world often suffered, culminating in the Holocaust during World War II. It was from among these Jews that the modern Zionist movement arose. The Jews of the Islamic world—*Mizrahi* (Oriental) Jews—were only later recruited as immigrants to the Jewish state. They were culturally and racially different from their European co-religionists. The Jews of the Arab countries in particular underwent the same process of arabicization as other inhabitants of these countries after the seventh century CE and, had Zionism not emerged in Europe, might have developed the historical memory of being Arabs of the Jewish faith. Those who immigrated to Israel mostly have supported hawkish political parties, although they have intense historical memories of contemptuous treatment by European Israelis. Even now, some supporters of Israel have expressed worry over small beginnings of a Mizrahi movement that has adopted an "Arab" identity.[42]

MEMORIES OF YESTERDAY

Many other intense historical memories have continued to accumulate during the past century, notably those connected with weakness and victimization. For anyone who is aware of the bitterness with which many Arabs remember the duplicity of European powers during the First World War, it should not have come as a surprise in 2001 to hear Osama bin Laden's statement that "our nation has been tasting this humiliation and contempt for more than eighty years," that is, since about the time of the First World War. He might have referred to events going back much further, including the colonization of Islamic lands from North Africa to Southeast Asia that started in the nineteenth century and earlier. But for many Muslims and Arabs the end of any semblance of a Muslim great power, which the Ottomans had been in the past, at the end of the First World War was a horrible tragedy for the ummah. Even Ayatollah Khomeini, despite being a Shiite, lamented the plot of the enemies of Islam that brought about the demise of "the great Ottoman Empire."

With the rise of India and China and the apparent reemergence of Russia, most of the major civilizations today have an emerging "great power," but not Muslims. Lustick has provided a superb analysis of how Western powers have strived to deprive the Muslim world of this sort of enfranchisement in the world power structure,[43] while Huntington has argued for the need for a Muslim great power to establish a world order based on civilizations at a time when he sees the "blip on the radar screen"—as he describes recent Western ascendancy—coming to an end. [44] Huntington further reminds us that the West gained superiority only through its "organized violence" and not because of any broader superiority, noting that it tends to forget this but that "non-Westerners never do."[45]

Whether from the perspective of Arab nationalists or Islamists, events slightly "more than eighty years" before 2001 are remembered with lamentation and anger. Arab nationalists have a memory of the way their predecessors struggled for liberation from Turkish rule in the First World War in an alliance with the British, who however betrayed them by entering into the secret Sykes-Picot Agreement to divide up their lands (as well as by issuing the Balfour Declaration, announcing support for a Jewish national home in Palestine).[46] For other Arabs, however, the Hashemite princes who betrayed the Islamic Ottoman state by collaborating with British imperialism to become their clients were not innocent victims, although the Arab and Islamic peoples were. For Palestinians, but also for other Arabs and Muslims, memory of the Arab/Islamic loss of Palestine in 1948—the *Nakbah* ("disaster") of the Palestinian people, itself a further stage of developments going back to the betrayals of 1916–1917—is more intense than that of any other set of events in recent historical memory. The apparently permanent incorporation of the rest of Palestine into the Israeli state since 1967, with the subordination of its people explained in terms of being an occupation, provides icing for the cake of bitterness.

Iranians continue to suffer nightmares about the encroachments of Russia, Britain, and the United States during the past century. Russia proved to be a dangerous expanding neighbor during the nineteenth century, while Britain long was looked on as a more benevolent power that would protect Iran from its northern neighbor, but the 1907 Anglo-Russian agreement to divide the country into spheres of influence made it hard to say which was worse from the Iranian point of view. When Iranians resisted British attempts to make their country essentially a protectorate in 1919, London helped bring a new local despot to power in the form of Reza Shah Pahlavi, and when the latter showed a preference for Germany, the country came under British and Russian occupation in 1942. Americans still were regarded as an anti-colonial power and as friends of Iran, but they increasingly supported the new shah against the parliament. In 1953—in cooperation with the British—they overthrew the constitutional government and turned the shah into an ally against the Iranian people and helped turn him into an autocrat during the following quarter century.[47]

The Islamic Revolution of 1979 and the subsequent clash between Washington and Tehran cannot be understood except in light of the popular Iranian historical memory of all this.

CONTROLLING AND KILLING MEMORIES

Much of what people remember is what they are told is true. Thus controlling memories of the past serves an important purpose in keeping the masses devoted to nationalistic and ideological causes. Those who accept the official version of the past likely will be devoted to pursuing a cause with great moral fervor, while their enemies, with their own narrative, believe with equal sincerity that they are combating evil.

Palestinians and Israelis provide extraordinary examples of such divergent memories. Suggesting that this exemplifies the way states generally play "a major role in developing such a collective memory," Nets-Zehngut recently documented the way such Israeli institutions as the Information Center, "established in the early 1950s as part of the Prime Minister's Office," propagated versions of the past, particularly a standard narrative portraying the Arabs as always having stood in the way of peace and as having full responsibility for the Palestinian refugee problem, while Palestinian infiltrators were presented as simply being sent by Arab countries to harm Israel, with "the state's dissemination of the Zionist narrative in general" being fed to the public "through the education system, the media . . . and through the center . . . substantially supported . . . by most of the intellectual community, including academics, artists, writers, and war veterans, who disseminated the Zionist narrative among the public."[48] Thus "the past became an instrument for the needs of the present, to establish (or sustain) a collective memory of conflicts that would enable the memory consumers (the public) to cope with the conflict and contribute their part to the struggle."[49]

The purpose of erasing historical memories and creating false ones sometimes dictates the destruction of physical evidence and the creation of evidence designed to evoke false memories. Destruction of monuments and other cultural artifacts—as well as cemeteries—in war and during military occupations sometimes is motivated by the desire to destroy memories of the enemy.[50] Benvenisti has presented a remarkable, far-ranging account of how the state of Israel has changed the landscape of its territory to create the illusion of an uninterrupted Jewish presence while wiping out evidence of a Palestinian presence.[51] Palestinians, including those in Israel, are making renewed efforts to promote the memory of the Nakbah, and the day Jewish Israelis celebrate their "independence" Palestinians have started to celebrate as the Nakbah, but legislation was pending in the Knesset in summer 2009 making this a crime punishable by up to three years in prison.

CONCLUSION

Much of what happens in the contemporary Middle East—and particularly the discussion of such matters—would be incomprehensible to anyone lacking knowledge of history. The events of the early Islamic period are of particular importance, as they provide a lens through which the world today is seen and are regularly invoked to elicit powerful responses. The Arab/Islamic conquests also eventually brought into being two changes that determine the identity of most people in the Middle East and much of the rest of the world. The first was the emergence of an Arab world, united in language and other facets of culture but more fundamentally in terms of identity. The second change was the Islamization of not only the Arab world but of a vast region that extends much farther. Islam also shapes identity, making it impossible for Muslims everywhere not to be concerned with issues beyond their own state borders, as in Palestine or Bosnia. However, the formative period of Islam also involved some intra-ummah struggles that are perpetuated in the form of sectarian divisions.

Those who want to play down their Arab and Islamic heritages often have attempted to evoke ancient times, making the modern Middle East partially understandable as a field in which the ancient is invoked against the medieval in struggles to determine the shape of the modern world. In Iran in particular, a kind of identity going back to the pre-Islamic era never disappeared as it did in the Fertile Crescent and even in Egypt and North Africa. In the past century, the myth of continuity with the Achaemenids has contested the image of Iran as an Islamic country. Even in the Arab countries, those pushing for local nationalism and for Westernization sometimes have invoked identity with ancient Egypt, Phoenicia, and the like. Arab nationalists, as exemplified by the Baathist regime in Iraq, have sometimes stressed the Arab nature of their countries before the Arab conquest, arguing that all the waves of Semitic peoples coming from Arabia in ancient times were essentially Arab. Similarly, the Kemalists in Turkey developed the myth that the pre-Islamic peoples in what is now Turkey were Turks too. The conflict over Palestine during the past century has revolved around different historical memories of the country, one focusing on the ancient period and excluding its continuing history and its long-established population at the beginning of the Zionist project.

NOTES

1. William H. McNeill, *Myth History and Other Essays* (Chicago: University of Chicago Press, 1986), p. 19.

2. Ann Ruth Willner, *The Spellbinders: Charismatic Political Leadership* (New Haven, CT: Yale University Press, 1984), pp. 62ff.

3. Sabrina Tavernise, "On the Bosporus, a Scholar Tells of Sultans, Washerwomen and Snakes," *New York Times*, October 25, 2008, p. A5.

4. See Benjamin Isakhan, "'Primitive Democracy': Mideast Roots of Collective Governance," *Middle East Policy* 14, no. 3 (Fall 2007); Glenn E. Perry, "The Middle East's 'Primitive Democratic' Tradition," *Digest of Middle East Studies* 9, no. 2 (Winter 2000): 18–53.

5. Bernard Lewis, *History—Remembered, Recovered, Invented* (Princeton, NJ: Princeton University Press, 1975).

6. Bernard Lewis, "Islam and the West: A Conversation with Bernard Lewis," Pew Forum on Religion & Public Life, June 6, 2006, Pew Research Center Publications, http://pewresearch.org/pubs/30/islam-and-the-west.

7. See, for example, Charles Issawi, "The Historical Role of Muhammad," in *The Contemporary Middle East: Tradition and Innovation*, ed. Benjamin Rivlin and Joseph S. Szyliowicz (New York: Random House, 1965), pp. 87–95; Michael H. Hart, *The 100: A Ranking of the Most Influential Persons in History*, rev. and updated (New York: Citadel, 2000).

8. V. S. Naipaul, *Among the Believers: An Islamic Journey* (New York: Alfred A. Knopf. 1981), pp.142–143.

9. Graham E. Fuller, "A World Without Islam," *Foreign Policy*, January–February 2008, pp. 46–53.

10. Quoted by Issawi, "The Historical Role of Muhammad," p. 94.

11. Majid Khadduri, *War and Peace in the Law of Islam* (Baltimore and London: Johns Hopkins University Press, 1955), pp. 202–203.

12. Wilfred Cantwell Smith, *Islam in Modern History* (Princeton, NJ: Princeton University Press, 1957), pp. 17, 21–26.

13. Ibid., p. 99.

14. Marshall G. Hodgson, *The Venture of Islam: Conscience and History in World Civilization, Volume 3: The Gunpowder Empires and Modern Times* (Chicago and London: University of Chicago Press, 1974), p. 47.

15. William H. McNeill, *The Rise of the West: A History of the Human Community* (Chicago: University of Chicago Press, 1963), pp. 707–709.

16. Dale Eickelman, "National Identity and Religious Discourse in Contemporary Oman," *International Journal of Islamic and Arabic Studies* 6, no. 1 (1989): 1–20.

17. Jeffrey T. Kenney, *Muslim Rebels: Kharijites and the Politics of Extremism in Egypt* (Oxford: Oxford University Press, 2006).

18. W. Montgomery Watt, "The Significance of the Early Stages of Imami Shi`ism," in *Religion and State in Iran 1785–1906*, ed. Nikki R. Keddie (New Haven, CT, and London: Yale University Press, 1983), pp. 27, 31.

19. See Fouad Ajami, *The Vanished Imam: Musa al-Sadr and the Shia of Lebanon* (New York and London: Cornell University Press, 1986), pp. 123ff.

20. Mary Hegland, "Two Images of Husain: Accommodation and Revolution in an Iranian Village," in *Religion and Politics in Iran: Shi`ism from Quietism to Revolution*, ed. Nikki R. Keddie (Cambridge, MA, and London: Harvard University Press, 1980).

21. Ahmed H. Al-Rahim, "The Sistani Factor," *Journal of Democracy* 16, no. 3 (July 2005): 50.

22. See Willner, *The Spellbinders*, pp. 78ff.

23. See Hamid Enayat, *Modern Islamic Political Thought* (Austin: University of Texas Press, 1982), pp. 184ff.

24. John Noble Wilford, "Phoenicians Left Mark of Genes, Study Finds," *New York Times*, October 31, 2008, p. A11.

25. See Abdeslam M. Maghraoui, *Nationhood and Citizenship in Egypt, 1922–1936* (Durham, NC: Duke University Press, 2006), pp. 59–60, 70ff; also see Nadav Safran, *Egypt in Search of Political Community: An Analysis of the Intellectual and Political Revolution of Egypt, 1804–1952* (Cambridge, MA: Harvard University Press, 1961), pp. 143–147.

26. Kamal Salibi, *A House of Many Mansions: The History of Lebanon Reconsidered* (Berkeley, Los Angeles, and London: University of California Press, 1988), pp. 167–181.

27. Wilford, "Phoenicians Left Mark of Genes, Study Finds."

28. Salibi, *A House of Many Mansions*, p.178.

29. On this phenomenon, see Amatzia Baram, *Culture, History and Ideology in the Formation of Ba`athist Iraq, 1968–89* (New York: St. Martin's, 1991).

30. Arnold J. Toynbee, *A Study of History*, Volume IX (London, New York: Oxford University Press, 1954), pp. 301–302.

31. Richard N. Frye, *The Heritage of Persia*, Mentor Books edition (New York: New American Library, 1963), pp. 264ff.

32. Willner, *The Spellbinders*, pp. 78ff.

33. Trita Parsi, *Treacherous Alliance: The Secret Dealings of Israel, Iran, and the U.S.*, with a new preface by the author (New Haven, CT: Yale University Press, 2007), pp. 27ff.

34. Frye, *The Heritage of Persia*, pp. 263ff.

35. Parsi, *Treacherous Alliance*, p. 6.

36. See Richard W. Cottam, *Nationalism in Iran: Updated Through 1978* (Pittsburgh: University of Pittsburgh Press, 1979), pp. 118ff.

37. See Gareth Porter, "Politics: Iran's Anti-Israel Rhetoric Aimed at Arab Opinion," Inter Press News Agency, March 9, 2009, www.ipsnews.net/news.asp?idnews =46037; Dan Morrison, "Persian Populist Wins Arab Embrace: Iran's Ahmadinejad Is Attracting Fans Across the Middle East for His Fiery Rhetoric," *Christian Science Monitor*, June 21, 2006.

38. Shibley Telhami, principal investigator, 2008 Annual Arab Public Opinion Poll: Survey of the Anwar Sadat Chair for Peace and Development at the University of Maryland (with Zogby International), conducted March 2008 in Egypt, Jordan, Lebanon, Morocco, Saudi Arabia (KSA), and the UAE, 2008 http://sadat.umd.edu/surveys/ 2008%20Arab%20Public%20Opinion%20Survey.ppt, accessed July 11, 2009.

39. BBC World Service Poll, "Israel and Iran Share Most Negative Ratings in Global Poll," www.globescan.com/news_archives/bbccntryview, accessed July 18, 2009.

40. Bernard Lewis, *The Emergence of Modern Turkey*, 2nd ed. (London, Oxford, and New York: Oxford University Press, 1968), pp. 8, 323ff.

41. Ibid., pp. 357ff.

42. See Meyrav Wurmser, "Post-Zionism and the Sephardi Question," *Middle East Forum* 12 (Spring 2005), www.meforum.org/article/707, accessed August 6, 2009.

43. Ian S. Lustick, "The Absence of Middle Eastern Great Powers: Political 'Backwardness' in Historical Perspective," *International Organization* 51, no. 4 (Autumn 1997): 653–683.

44. Samuel P. Huntington, *The Clash of Civilizations and the Remaking of the Modern World* (New York: Simon & Schuster, 1996), p. 51.

45. Samuel P. Huntington, "The Age of Muslim Wars," *Newsweek*, December 17, 2001, pp. 46–51.

46. For the classic statement of this position, see George Antonius, *The Arab Awakening: The Story of the Arab National Movement* (New York: G. P. Putnam's Sons, 1946). For a more succinct, recent summary, see Arthur Goldschmidt Jr. and Lawrence Davidson, "The Roots of Arab Bitterness," in *The Contemporary Middle East: A Westview Reader*, ed. Karl Yambert (Boulder, CO: Westview Press, 2006), pp. 27–40.

47. See James Bill, *The Eagle and the Lion: The Tragedy of American-Iranian Relations* (New Haven, CT, and London: Yale University Press, 1988), p. 425.

48. Rafi Nets-Zehngut, "The Israeli National Information Center and Collective Memory of the Israeli-Arab Conflict," *Middle East Journal* 62, no. 4 (Autumn 2008): 656–657.

49. Ibid., p. 669.

50. See Robert Bevan, *The Destruction of Memory: Architecture at War* (London: Reaktion Books, 2006); Glenn E. Perry, "Cultural Cleansing in Comparative Perspective," in *Cultural Cleansing in Iraq: Why Museums Were Looted, Libraries Burned and Academics Murdered*, ed. Raymond W. Baker, Shereen T. Ismael, and Tareq Y. Ismael (London: Pluto Press, 2010).

51. Meron Benvenisti, *Sacred Landscape: The Buried History of the Holy Land Since 1948*, trans. Maxine Kaufman-Lacusta (Berkeley, Los Angeles, and London: University of California Press, 2000).

Part 2

POLITICS

Politics in the Middle East is highly complex and differentiated, as it is in other regions of the world. It is deeply shaped by tradition, environment, and interpretations of historical memory that reinforce the central power of the state. Thus it is not surprising that the magnifying glass that scholars and pundits generally direct at Middle Eastern politics focuses on the rates of democratization and political inclusion, almost to the exclusion of other issues. Yet while it is true that the Middle East in general lags behind other regions in its adaption of democratic governance, it faces other challenges as well. The area has also made significant progress on many political indicators, despite numerous challenges to such development.

The Middle East's political heritage is a combination of monarchical rule, colonial influence, and imported tradition. Republicanism was one of those imported traditions, though from distinctly mixed roots. The lore of revolution was another root, though it also had deep foundations in the Middle East, and thus some monarchies in the Middle East came to violent ends, as they did in Europe earlier. Often the revolutionaries modeled their ideas of governance on previously successful revolutions, and thus strong central states run by republicans replaced strong central states run by kings, shahs, and imperial stooges. Often in the 1950s revolutions got support from the citizens, as they frequently got rid of the so-called foreign yoke, and the state built on this support with benefits through socialism rather than through the secret police (which, however, the republican state did keep). Democracy as a widely desired good was not nearly as common in the early genesis of independent states in the developing world. The political compass pointed more at the Soviet Union and post-1948 India than at France or the United States, and thus many Middle Eastern countries developed the strong national security-oriented socialist state, usually with a single party representing, or purporting to represent, the "toiling masses."

Because the bulk of this class had lived in poverty, the state attempted to provide free or highly subsidized housing, food, water, and health care. Massive gray apartment blocks sprang up in many Middle Eastern cities as both the urban and rural populations found themselves mobilized into the ranks of the ruling party, and thus eligible to receive government largesse. Because their lives became marginally better than they had been under the previous regime, few citizens demanded accountable governments. Instead, they lined the streets for military parades, or stood out of the way when military coups brought regime change. Whether the leaders took the title of "king" or "president," they served mostly without the benefit of popular consent, not so much because rulers crushed public participation in politics, but because of the lack of a public voice. Their strongest rivals were other generals, or other elite politicians who coveted the presidential or monarchical palace.

The benefits of autocratic rule were stability and the chance for predictability when one clan was able to keep a grasp on power for a protracted period of time. In Egypt the National Democratic Party has retained the presidency for decades, starting with Muhammad Naguib in 1952 through the current regime of Hosni Mubarak. In Syria the Baath Party took power in 1963, and after Hafiz al-Asad assumed power in 1970, Syria underwent a period of stability that differed markedly from the continual coups that preceded him. The al-Saud family in Saudi Arabia, the al-Sabah family in Kuwait, the al-Thani family in Qatar, and many other dynasties provided a straight path from one year to the next, and while citizens might have grumbled privately about regime excesses, the steadiness the palace provided was highly valued, partly because it refereed traditional tribal and regional conflicts.

In other cases, events interrupted democracy in its nascent forms. Iran experimented with democratic rule in the 1950s. It was limited participation, heavily weighted toward the political Left and powerful rural elites, but it was still democracy. That ended in 1953 when military elements in Iran, the US CIA, and British intelligence conspired to end the rule of Prime Minister Mohammad Mosaddeq and to restore Shah Muhammad Pahlavi as Iranian ruler. The shah suspended democratic rule and continued his father's development of a Western-leaning Iran, ultimately alienating most key sectors of

Iranian society in the process. The Shia elite ultimately ousted the shah in 1979 and installed their own limited version of popular suffrage, though it was directed from the top down and participation was constricted, as the elections of 2009 demonstrated. Now Iran joins a majority of Arab countries in the Middle East ranked as "not free" by Freedom House, a nongovernmental organization created in 1938 and based in New York City. While critics have questioned Freedom House's judgment of certain countries, the fact remains that the Middle East has a higher percentage of nondemocratic countries than any place in the world, with more than 60 percent of the population of the Middle East living in "not free" countries. It should be stressed that "not free" does not necessarily mean "despotic," and no country in the Middle East can approach Kim Jong-Il's North Korea or the nation of Myanmar in brutal rule. In some cases the population seems content with the ruling family: For example, there are many praiseworthy stories about Sheik Zayid bin Sultan Al Nahyan of the United Arab Emirates and his benevolent attitude toward his people.

Turkey and Israel, two countries without colonial heritage, took different paths to democracy, and while for Turkey that path was circuitous, both countries achieved levels of answerable authority. Israel inherited a democratic tradition from its European migrants, and Israeli democracy emerged as a vibrant if often chaotic system. Post-Ottoman Turkey developed democratic norms more slowly as the Kemalist tradition emphasized a secular Turkish identity with minimum public participation. Democracy did emerge, though periodically interrupted by military coups. Islamist-leaning parties ran afoul of the Kemalist legacy, which the military inherited and enforced, though the 2002 victory of the Islamist-oriented *Adalet ve Kalkınma Partisi*, or AKP, caused concern within the secular ranks in Turkey. But despite slightly veiled threats, the military largely stayed in the barracks, although individual officers were charged with attempting a coup. The AKP survived legal challenges as well, and continues in power. For Israel, democracy struggled with religious identity, but Israelis clearly preferred a democracy to a theocracy, and Israeli religious parties ultimately compromised with the secular polity.

Israel's struggles with the role of faith in politics are reflected elsewhere. Most Muslim Middle Eastern countries compromise between secular requirements and religious preferences, for example, by sanctioning religious courts for "personal status" matters, including divorce, alimony, and child custody questions, while applying civil law to the remainder of cases. Some in Islamic countries want more Islam in the polity, by which they mean the application of sharia to regulate both state and personal behavior. Such commentary is sometimes viewed outside the region as a call for more discrimination against women or non-Muslims, or a call for violent punishment for the guilty, but often what the advocates of religious law often are demanding is less corruption and favoritism for the privileged members of society. This struggle extends beyond the Middle East to other systems, including that of the United States, where the size and scope of the state brings cries for more accountability and transparency for the large majority who often feel that politics bypasses them.

In this section, Dafna H. Rand considers the reasons for political change in a region where change of any kind has been unhurried. She argues that traditional explanations for both liberalization and democratization do not adequately convey the reasons political transformation is occurring in the area. Her research, based on fieldwork in Morocco and Kuwait, reveals surprising reasons for political change that question some established theories about why developing countries alter their political systems. Change in the Middle East has resulted in political standoffs along the way between those who foster and those who resist change. Moreover, change even in limited democratic openings appears to run along dynastic lines in some Middle East countries, and in Tunisia economic progress has resulted not in political openings but political closings. For Rand, despite considerable work in building theories to explain political change in developing countries, there remains work to be done. It would appear, though, that the Middle East possesses unique political patterns that models developed in other political contexts may not fully appreciate.

The role of the armed forces in politics is critical in all parts of the world, including the Middle East. David Sorenson dissects the relationship between the military and the state in a region where they frequently have been one and the same. The postmodern Middle East state often evolved under the tutelage of a small coterie of military officers who switched attire from uniforms to suits (or robes, in Qadhafi's case) and moved into the presidential mansion. Hafiz al-Asad, Gamal Abdel Nasser, Muammar Qadhafi, Reza Khan, and others assumed political power through coups, while in Israel Yitzhak Rabin and Ehud Barak rode the prestige of the Israeli Defense Forces to the office of prime minister. In most of the Middle East, the armed forces play a vital supportive role in the political life of their country and are often involved deeply in its economy as well. Moreover, in decisions about war and peace, which are fundamentally political, the senior military officers in many Middle East countries have the last say in deciding on war and, once decided, how to wage it.

4

DRIVERS OF POLITICAL CHANGE IN THE MIDDLE EAST AND NORTH AFRICA

Dafna H. Rand

INTRODUCTION

To many, political change often conjures up dramatic events, whether the storming of the Bastille in 1789 or the fall of the Berlin Wall exactly two hundred years later. To political scientists, political change is a linear transformation—from closed systems of governance to systems that allow for greater individual liberty and popular sovereignty. One element of this process involves democratization, characterized by an increase in political participation and greater contestation of executive power. A second element involves liberalization, the expansion of individual and group rights such as freedom of press, expression, and association.[1] These standard definitions of political change have become so pervasive that international organizations such as Freedom House annually grade countries along these two dimensions of political rights and civil liberties.[2]

This chapter questions these conventional conceptions of political change when it comes to the domestic politics of the Arab Middle East and North Africa (MENA) in the twenty-first century. In MENA, authoritarian rule stubbornly persists, particularly in the nineteen core Arab countries, home to approximately 300 million people. Democratization and liberalization have not fully materialized in any of the states in the region. Yet domestic political change is rapidly occurring, transforming the politics of many MENA states.

Moreover, the three most enduring scholarly explanations for the sources of liberalization and democratization do not capture the experiences of the MENA states.[3] These arguments, which focus on the roles of economic growth, elite leadership, and civil society as catalysts of change, are not satisfying explanations for the political trends occurring in MENA in the twenty-first century. Meanwhile, the recent regionalist political science literature—while carefully capturing the particularities of MENA—alludes to but does not focus on the drivers of political change. Some Middle East regional scholars have even made the absence of change their central dependent variable, analyzing the dynamics that sustain authoritarianism in the region.

Rather than simply apply ill-fitted democratization theories on the region, or accept the status quo bias of some academic theories on MENA, this chapter offers a new framework. In particular, four drivers are leading to changed political conditions in many states in the region, albeit slowly. These drivers originate "from below," catalyzed by the collective actions of citizens or political groups, or "from above," initiated by the authoritarian regime itself. These drivers are generating political changes in two main areas: procedural political rights, rules and laws affecting the ability of citizens to choose and change those who govern them; and civil liberties, specifically freedom of press, expression, and association. Sometimes the political changes touch on both areas. Table 4.1 introduces the four drivers:

TABLE 4.1: FOUR DRIVERS

Drivers from Below	free expression
	electoral representation
Drivers from Above	hereditary succession
	bureaucratic de-democratization

First, in some states, individuals and the media are taking advantage of the relatively permissive atmosphere to push the limits of free expression, including freedom of speech and freedom of press. Second, parliamentary candidates, both independents and those affiliated with political movements or parties, are increasingly adept at using elections, however unfree, to mobilize and solidify public support. These parliamentarians legitimately represent wide swaths of the population, even if they have limited power to affect the regime's policies. Third, the succession from fathers to sons (or half-brothers) in states such as Bahrain, Kuwait, Qatar, Morocco, and Jordan over the past fifteen years has created a cohort of younger leaders. Lacking the credibility of their fathers, these sons buttress their rule by instituting reforms, typically by expanding civil liberties and social and economic rights. Fourth, in some states, the autocrats are deliberately using rule-of-law changes—to political parties, constitutions, parliaments, the courts, or the presidency—to de-democratize. These "reforms" tend to restrict rather than expand citizens' procedural democratic rights, challenging Western assumptions about rule-of-law reform.

In some states, more than one of these drivers is occurring concurrently. In other states, none have emerged. The commonality uniting all four drivers involves the unpredictable, fluid situation they pose for MENA autocrats: Try as they might to contain the scope of the political change to ensure their regime's survival, they often must respond with improvisational measures. Unlike authoritarian regimes in earlier eras of modern history, today's MENA autocrats must tread carefully; in what has become a terra incognita for autocratic survival, their strategic responses to these political drivers could trigger unintended consequences.

This chapter deliberately brackets one external source of change influencing the region, most dramatically expressed in Iraq in 2003. Focusing only on the domestic drivers of political change, this chapter does not consider the role of international intervention, from the dramatic toppling of Saddam Hussein to the more frequent and less newsworthy Western military support for MENA regimes. Recent Western democracy promotion policies represent another form of international intervention. This chapter focuses on MENA domestic politics for the sake of parsimony, and should not be misread as an attempt to ignore the continuing international influences on the region. Each of the four drivers and the political changes they trigger are highly contingent on geopolitical factors, which range from the price of oil to unresolved regional conflicts to the US-led campaign to eliminate violent extremism.

This chapter first argues that the most prevalent theories explaining the origins of democratization and liberalization are hard to apply to MENA political systems. Second, it argues that MENA regionalists intent on explaining the logic of authoritarianism leave little room for theorizing or testing hypotheses about change. It then outlines each of the four drivers present in some MENA states and explains how the drivers are creating trends toward political change by focusing on specific cases from the region. These drivers are not novel. They are reminiscent of political changes that have occurred in other authoritarian regimes, whether in nineteenth-century England or in late twentieth-century Eastern and Central Europe. Nonetheless, these political changes are shaping MENA citizens' expectations and redefining the ways in which their rulers govern.

THREE ENDURING THEORIES
OF POLITICAL CHANGE

The Modernization Thesis

Three theories explaining the origins of liberalization and democratization continue to prompt the most prolific debates, both among academics and policymakers. The first theory originated in Lipset's 1959 observation that the "more well-to-do the nation, the greater the chances it will sustain democracy."[4] Since Lipset's time, scholars have debated how economic development might encourage the development of democracy. Empirically, Lipset found a correlation: A state's average wealth, degree of industrialization and urbanization, and level of education were higher in democracies. Subsequent scholars—who became known as modernization theorists—went further, suggesting a causal link between economic growth and development and democratization. Democratic transitions occur, they argued, when gross domestic product (GDP) per capita is relatively high and income inequality is relatively low.[5] Moore amended modernization theory, positing that the presence of an independent middle class, a bourgeoisie, generated democratic development by "balance the crown."[6]

Modernization theory has endured, inculcating many of the assumptions of modern social science, even though its theses have not withstood empirical examination. For example, rather than a simple correlation between economic development and democratization, Diamond found that, while poor countries and high-income countries show a statistical correlation with democracy, in middle-income countries the correlation disappears.[7] Przeworski, Limongi, and their co-authors found that dictatorships almost always survive in very poor countries (whose per capita GDPs are under $1,000). In mid-level countries, with per capita GDPs between $1,001 and $7,000, dictatorships often break down. Yet when incomes reach $7,000, the trend reverses and a dictatorship is much more likely to survive. Przeworski and Limongi concluded that the causal power of development in generating democracies cannot be very strong.[8] Instead, democracies likely appear randomly with regard to levels of development, though dictatorships might be more likely to survive in very poor and very wealthy countries.

Despite the growing evidence that the relationship between development and democracy is complex and contingent on other factors, modernization theory remains a consequential thesis. To policymakers, particularly those working in institutions such as the World Bank and the US Agency for International Development, economic development and economic neoliberal reforms are still regarded as critical foundations for democracy and good governance, whether in sub-Saharan Africa or in MENA states. Moreover, many MENA experts— including the regional intellectuals who wrote the United Nations Development Programme's Arab Human Development Reports—are championing new correlates of modernization theory. Rather than focusing purely on economic development, they are pointing to income inequality, the absence of strong middle classes, and gender inequality to explain the repressive political structures prevalent in the region.[9] Scholars such as Fish are demonstrating statistically how women's rights deficits might contribute to MENA's nondemocratic political systems.[10] Policy practitioners continue to fund women's rights programs and private enterprise projects in MENA, investing in these projects for the sake of eventual political reform.

   Though modernization theory remains pervasive, especially in policy circles, evidence from MENA offers very little support for its initial assumptions and its recent addendums. It is difficult to decipher any correlation between the socioeconomic indicators in individual MENA states and each one's level of authoritarianism. Both the poorest and richest countries in the region remain persistently authoritarian, whether Kuwait, with a GDP per capita (2008 estimates) of $40,943, or Yemen, with a GDP per capita of $2,404.[11] As Table 4.2 suggests, there is no correlation between those states in MENA with the highest per capita GDP and those states with the greatest degree of political rights and civil liberties, as measured by Freedom House's 2008 rankings:

TABLE 4.2: MENA 2008 GROSS DOMESTIC PRODUCT (PER CAPITA) COMPARED TO POLITICAL RIGHTS AND CIVIL LIBERTIES

	GNP		
Country	GDP (PPP)	PR	CL
Qatar	$86,669	6	5
Kuwait	$40,943	4	4
UAE	$39,076	6	5
Bahrain	$33,988	5	5
Oman	$26,094	6	5
Saudi Arabia	$24,119	7	6
Libya	$14,593	7	7
Lebanon	$12,063	5	4
Tunisia	$8,020	7	5
Algeria	$6,927	6	5
Egypt	$5,904	6	5
Jordan	$5,171	5	4
Syria	$4,668	7	6
Morocco	$4,432	5	4
Iraq	$3,427	6	6
Yemen	$2,404	5	5
Sudan	$2,335	7	7
Mauritania	$2,108	4	4
Palestine	$1,700 (approx.)	5	6

PR represents political rights and CL represents civil rights, both measured by Freedom House in 2008. On the 1 to 7 scale, 1 represents the greatest degree of rights and 7 represents the least. GDPs per capita (purchasing power parity) are from the International Monetary Fund's 2008 World Economic Outlook Database.

What about the middle class and women's equality—two factors identified by champions of modernization theory as important preconditions for democratization and liberalization? As the case of Tunisia (and Singapore) demonstrates, the presence of a strong middle class does not necessarily affect the degree of authoritarianism. In Tunisia, the middle class composes 60 percent of the population. Over 60 percent of Tunisian households own their homes and, according to the International Monetary Fund, the country has enjoyed steady economic growth of 5 percent to 6 percent over the past few years. These socioeconomic indicators differentiate Tunisia from its North African neighbors. Tunisia is also at the vanguard in the Arab world in terms of promoting women's legal and social rights. The 1956 Personal Status Code banned polygamy and mandated education for girls. Today, Tunisian women run and own businesses, file for divorce, and serve in the highest level of government.[12]

Yet, despite Tunisia's relatively unique standing in terms of economic development, a pervasive middle class, and women's rights, the Tunisian regime under President Zine al-Abidine Ben Ali has infamously suppressed its citizens' political and civil rights. In 2008, Freedom House rated the degree of political freedom in Tunisia as a 7 on a scale with 7 as the least free and 1 as the most free. Freedom of association and assembly are guaranteed in the constitution, but the government restricts them in practice. The few remaining opposition parties and independent civil society organizations that are genuinely independent of state influence, such as the Progressive Democratic Party and the Tunisian Human Rights League, can barely operate. The state severely curbs their activities and harasses or arrests their activists. Ben Ali's government censors most print and television media and aggressively monitors the Internet.[13]

As the Tunisian case exemplifies, facets of modernization in the MENA region, whether economic growth, a strong middle class, or advanced women's rights, do not necessarily correlate with or engender liberalization or democratization. In fact, there is some evidence that Tunisians' economic satisfaction is actually contributing to the ease with which Ben Ali has been able to strengthen his authoritarian rule since he seized power in 1987. Because they enjoy a high standard of living, Tunisians might have been more likely to passively accept Ben Ali's de-democratization measures, such as the 2002 constitutional revisions that enabled his fourth presidential term in 2004 and, most recently, his fifth term, won in the October 2009 elections.

Tunisia represents only one extreme case where economic development appears to coexist with, if not sustain, repressive one-party authoritarianism. Yet throughout the region, the assumptions underlying the modernization thesis do not hold. Although recent scholarship questions the possibly overly simplistic rentier state theory, there is an undeniable dearth of democracy among the oil-rich states in the region, whether Algeria, Kuwait, Bahrain, Saudi Arabia, or Qatar.[14] During the oil boom year of 2008, for example, the GDP per capita of authoritarian Qatar—over $86,000—was one of the highest in the world. Given the complex relationship between natural-resource wealth and political rule, the MENA states with economic wealth fueled by oil extraction do not easily fit into the expectations of the modernization thesis or its recent addendums.

The Elite Actors Thesis

The second enduring explanation for the source of liberalization and democratization highlights the role of elite actors. In their 1996 foundational texts, O'Donnell, Schmitter, and Whitehead extrapolate from the experiences of South American and Southern European countries to argue that authoritarian breakdown occurs when members of the regime and the opposition divide into camps of hard-liners and soft-liners. According to the initial "transitology thesis," democratic transition occurs when soft-liners within the regime agree to a pact with soft-liners among the opposition, defining rules to govern the exercise of power on the basis of mutual guarantees to enhance the interests of all. To transitologists, the breakdown of authoritarianism is not motivated by a normative preference for democratic rule. Rather, democracy is simply a convenient compromise institution.[15]

While the initial transitology thesis has been challenged, its main contribution—the insight that elite actors negotiate a democratic political solution to serve their mutual interests—has become a dominant assumption in comparative democratization research. Second-generation elite-actor theorists, such as Weingast and Przeworski, use game theoretic models to show how democratic institutions are the result of strategic choices individuals and parties in contention make while trying to maximize their own welfare.[16] Even members of former authoritarian regimes, Przeworski argues, "comply with present defeats because they believe that the institutional framework that organizes the democratic competition will permit them to advance their interests in the future."[17]

Can the elite actor paradigm of political change explain recent events in any of the MENA states? This paradigm assumes, with some exceptions, a gradual progression from authoritarian regime breakdown to democratic transition to an eventual democratic consolidation.[18] In real cases, both within MENA states and beyond, such a teleological process rarely materializes. In the MENA context, few countries have experienced the breakdown or end of autocratic regimes. In those regimes that have collapsed—for instance, due to coups in Tunisia (1987) or Qatar (1995)—new autocrats quickly emerged in their stead.

Moreover, many of the elite actor models use as their template military regimes, where splits between officers lead to negotiated settlements, with one side "going back to the barracks" and submitting to the other side's political rule. Such a scenario did occur in Mauritania in 2005, ushering in a democratic experiment that was quickly reversed by another coup in 2008. On the whole, in MENA states today there are few full-fledged military regimes akin to the Argentinean or Brazilian ruling juntas of the 1970s and 1980s. More often, a MENA dictator or king relies on absolute military loyalty, as well as the loyalty of the internal security services, to buttress his standing vis-à-vis other elites or challengers. Even when the MENA elites surrounding the autocrat break into factions, they all abide by the fundamental rules of the game that keep the autocrat in power.[19]

Thus, there is a reason that no Arab state is mentioned anywhere in the seminal works on authoritarian breakdown by the early transitologists or more recent scholarly work on authoritarian breakdown and decision-making by Weingast, Przeworski, or Geddes.[20] The elite actor theory assumes that authoritarian regimes might easily dissolve into competing factions, but MENA regimes are not that brittle. MENA autocrats are remarkably successful at co-opting members of their clique, or party, or other elites who might pose a threat, and thus stanching factionalism within the regime itself. When challengers do arise, the regime's security apparatus quickly subdues them. Thus, the expectation that elite actors will voluntarily choose democratic institutions as a strategic means of maximizing self-interest—though an influential theory within political science—seems far-fetched when applied to the modern MENA context.

The Civil Society Thesis

A third pervasive explanation for political change emphasizes the role of grassroots participation in civil society organizations (CSOs). From Tocqueville to Putnam, many have argued that the stronger the associational life (whether church groups or bowling leagues), the more likely citizens will develop the social trust necessary to build responsive political institutions.[21] According to this "civil society thesis," democracy is sustained by the social capital developed through civic associations. Civil society is defined as the place where "a mélange of groups, associations, clubs, guilds, syndicates, federations, unions, parties, and groups come together to provide a buffer between state and citizen."[22] Moreover, this thesis posits that voluntary associations foster democratic attitudes and concern for the public good and teach a culture of self-governance.

Civil society currently falls short as a factor that could systematically introduce change to MENA political systems. Civil society organizations—whether unions, professional associations, women's groups, human rights groups, or aid associations—are neither new nor rare in the Middle East.[23] They have burgeoned exponentially since the end of the first Gulf War, but without any commensurate increase in democratic life.[24] By 2008, 40,000 CSOs existed in Morocco and over 20,000 in Egypt.[25] According to the United Nations Development Program, the MENA region boasts over 150,000 organizations.[26] Yet there is little evidence that CSOs are shaping regimes' policies or weakening authoritarianism. Some MENA scholars are even tentatively suggesting that civil society organizations in the region might instead reinforce authoritarian patterns of nepotism and clientelism among the citizens and buttress nondemocratic institutions. Jamal's recent research on Palestinian civil society finds that in the 1990s, many West Bank associations allied with the Palestinian National Authority (PNA) reinforced the PNA's authoritarian practices. Jamal surveyed more than four hundred members of PNA-affiliated associations and non-PNA associations in the West Bank. She found no correlation between individuals' civic engagement and interpersonal trust—elements of social capital—and their support for democratic institutions.[27] Jamal's work contributes to the growing skepticism among MENA scholars regarding the transformational potential of civil society organizations in MENA to foster democratic habits and social trust or to establish a foundation for future political change. In the MENA context, civil society associations, especially those affiliated with ruling parties, can sustain and reinforce authoritarian norms.

It is also difficult to assess the civil society thesis's applicability to MENA because many MENA regimes co-opt independent civil society organizations and try to build (often redundant) layers of organizations loyal to the regime and ruling parties. With the growth of registered civil society organizations in Egypt, Morocco, Jordan, Tunisia, and Yemen since the late 1990s, the regimes in these countries have become increasingly adept at controlling these groups' activities. Autocratic regimes carefully circumscribe the activities of independent CSOs and they create CSOs that are shells for government affiliates or parties, often dubbed "government organized nongovernmental organizations" or GONGOs. According to some analysts, twenty years ago Egyptian President Hosni Mubarak considered it advantageous to have 5,000 small CSOs rather than five big ones. The presence of myriad competing CSOs could weaken the collective organizing capacity of any one group. Therefore, Mubarak fostered the growth of thousands of new CSOs in the 1990s.[28] By 1997, Egypt had 14,000 to 15,000 private nonprofit organizations, in addition to many more youth clubs, professional syndicates, and trade unions—by far the largest number of CSOs in the Arab world.[29] While Mubarak initially encouraged the growth of redundant CSOs, in 1999 he changed course. Without consulting representatives from civil society, he began passing a series of measures to enable the government's broad control over CSO activity. The new laws now limit the amount of foreign funding CSOs can receive and ensure that the government oversees the registration of new CSOs. This oversight authority enables the regime to frequently deny the legality of new CSOs without explanation.[30]

Meanwhile, Tunisian President Ben Ali stretches the limit of what is considered a CSO. He boasts of 8,000 Tunisian civil society organizations while in reality only 7 or 8 are independent of the ruling party, the Democratic Constitutional Rally (RCD). The regime strictly limits the finances, membership, recruiting, and activities of the few remaining independent CSOs, such as the Tunisian Human Rights League and the Tunisian Association of Democratic Women. Tunisian society was once characterized by strong associational life. Today, activists dodge arrest.

Civil society organizations are susceptible to increasing manipulation and co-optation by MENA regimes.[31] The demarcation between independent civil society groups and authoritarian regimes and their allies (such as ruling parties) has blurred. Therefore, the neo-Tocquevillian expectation that civic associations can foster representative institutions and build social trust seems unlikely to materialize in MENA in the near future.[32]

REGIONAL SCHOLARSHIP AND THE AUTOCRATIC RESILIENCE THESIS

Given that the MENA cases were largely left out of the formulation of comparative democratization theories, it is not surprising that the most common explanations for the origins of liberalization and democratization do not capture the politics of most states in the region. Yet while the generalists' theories of political change are ill suited to the experiences of MENA, most of the recent research by MENA regional experts focuses not on change, but rather on explaining its absence. Offering hypotheses for the political statism in the region, many of these "authoritarian resilience" scholars focus on the cleverness of MENA's autocrats particularly how they use economic and electoral means to wield power?

Some MENA experts have concluded that durable autocrats are capable of almost always outwitting and outmaneuvering other actors, including the international community and political opposition.[33] According to Bellin, the autocrats' "robust and politically tenacious coercive apparatus" will overcome "any opposition with strength, coherence, and effectiveness."[34] It is now en vogue to explain autocratic durability in the region by focusing on authoritarian institutional machinations. Earlier MENA scholars located explanations for authoritarianism in external rents, the natural resource curse, Islamic cultural or religious doctrines, or foreign patronage. Today's MENA scholars are particularly interested in how autocrats construct electoral systems to ensure favorable outcomes and how authoritarian elections in MENA are used to promote patronage or to express class, tribal, or religious identity, rather than political representation.[35]

Yet the notion that MENA's autocrats are extraordinarily successful at staying in power—and forestalling political change—is unsatisfying: How can the region's autocrats be so robust if, at the same time, they face a shortage of political legitimacy, as many regionalists also argue?[36] Moreover, the authoritarian resilience proposition tends to paint the region with very broad strokes. This perspective leaves little room for explaining how and when subtle change might occur, and how disparate trends influence different states in the region.[37] For instance, why does authoritarianism in two of the region's monarchies, Jordan and Morocco, look so different from the authoritarian rule in another, Saudi Arabia? While authoritarian resilience theorists are producing important research on autocratic elections, fraudulent voting, electoral rules, elites, clientelism, and the differences between republics and monarchies, there is still a dearth of regional theories focused on change. Even in a region anomalous in its persistent authoritarianism, new trends emerge. The political systems are dynamic. Explanations focused on the status quo are therefore instructive, but ultimately insufficient.

FOUR DRIVERS OF MENA POLITICAL CHANGE

The following section identifies four drivers of current political change in the region as a starting point for understanding the dynamism of MENA politics. Each driver is generating a trend toward change that could yet reverse course. Moreover, each driver has only fully emerged in a few countries in the region, and in some states, none of these drivers have yet emerged. Each driver prompts a series of questions, which create a foundation for further research.

Free Expression

The first driver involves expanding one particular category of civil liberties—freedom of press, speech, and association. This expansion of free expression typically originates when the government relaxes the limitation on citizens' rights to associate and express themselves, whether through peaceful protests or through more daring online, television, or print media. Yet once the floodgates are opened a crack from above, a groundswell emerges from below. Journalists, bloggers, and activists respond by testing the limits of permissible expression. Global communication and pervasive Internet and satellite television access also enable civic groups and press outlets to grow in numbers and to build transnational alliances with nongovernmental colleagues. An autocrat's permissive attitude toward freedom of expression is paramount. Yet the driver itself is the demand of entrepreneurial and courageous individuals at the grassroots level, who organize, report, and communicate in a global information marketplace.

Moreover, a MENA autocrat's initial willingness to open space for free expression has no bearing on his willingness to augment political procedural rights. In some cases, a regime's tolerance for greater free expression coincides with an emphasis on social reforms (affecting women or minorities), neoliberal economic reforms, or development projects. Thus far, however, the regimes that tolerate greater free expression are not augmenting electoral contestation and judicial independence or strengthening political parties.

The expansion of freedom of expression in MENA is no facade, but it still has its limits. It is governed by an inscrutable and invisible red line. Individuals or members of the media who cross this line—often by expressing anti-regime, anti-Islam, or other controversial sentiments—have incurred fines and even jail sentences. The invisible red line is not solidified, however. Activists, journalists, and private citizens repeatedly test this line. In many cases the regimes and their defenders (particularly in the courts and in the ministries of communications) are improvising, unsure themselves of the limits they want to impose on the newly expanded freedoms of expression. Therefore, while the autocrat himself might be originally responsible for the trend by relaxing the limits on free expression, he can often be found scrambling to contain and manage its consequences, whether by instituting new press codes or highly restrictive laws of association. This driver of change requires the autocrat to carefully navigate, maintaining his rule while countering increasingly vocal social forces.

Free Expression in Morocco under King Mohammed VI. Over the past ten years, journalists and individuals in Kuwait, Bahrain, Qatar, Algeria, Egypt, Morocco, and Lebanon have begun to push the boundaries of free press, free association, and free speech, responding en masse as their regimes have relaxed controls over such freedoms.[38] Morocco presents one salient example, where the bottom-up drive for free expression has reached unprecedented heights. After acceding to the throne upon the death of his father, King Hassan II, in 1999, the young King Mohammed VI immediately enacted a series of noteworthy reforms. Revising the family status laws to increase women's rights and establishing the first reparations council in the Arab world, to compensate political victims who had been incarcerated and tortured during his father's reign, both earned him acclaim abroad.

Yet the king's relaxation of media restrictions and censorship on free expression has generated the most resonant changes to Moroccan society over the past ten years. During the thirty-year reign of King Hassan II, many considered Morocco a "prison kingdom." Political opponents were arrested and tortured; dissent was strictly forbidden. King Mohammed VI's accession to the throne in 1999 immediately invigorated the press and even individual citizens to freely broach once-taboo subjects. For the first time in Moroccan history, the press reported on the *makhzen*—the clique surrounding the king that often operates as a shadow government—as well as corruption in the palace, the king's wealth, and the role of Islam in political and social life. The public now sees pictures of royal family members in the media and learns about the private lives of some members of the royal family, including the king's wife.[39]

Outside of the active press, Moroccans themselves have seized upon the greater opportunity for free expression. On the main street of the capital city of

Rabat, across from the parliament, unemployed students gather almost daily to protest the dearth of jobs. Noisy demonstrators regularly fill the streets of Rabat and Casablanca in sympathy for the plight of the Gazans (2008), to protest terrorism after a scourge of attacks struck at home (2003), or to advocate for or against the proposed revisions to the personal status laws (2000).

King Mohammed VI thus tentatively sanctioned an opening ten years ago. Since then, activists, journalists, and private citizens have repeatedly probed the extent of this opening. The regime adheres to inconsistent red lines—sometimes allowing press freedom and sometimes imprisoning journalists and seizing newspapers for seemingly arbitrary offense. Since King Mohammed VI came to power, authorities have censored thirty-four media outlets and imprisoned twenty journalists.[40] As a result, many journalists engage in self-censorship to avoid finding themselves in court. In September 2008, one day after publishing an article critical of the special favors the king sometimes accords his citizens, Moroccan blogger Mohammed Erraji was arrested and sentenced to two years in prison. The first Moroccan blogger to be jailed for his writings, Erraji was released on bail less than a week later by an appellate court.[41] Individuals also test the limits of free speech. A student in southern Morocco was sentenced to eighteen months in prison for replacing "King" with "Barcelona" in the country's national motto "God, Country, King" (in reference to the popular soccer team).[42]

Since 2005, increasingly the Moroccan regime responds harshly when the media or individuals approach sensitive subjects. In 2007, the Ministry of Interior seized and destroyed 92,000 copies of the independent weeklies *Nichane* and *TelQuel* at the printers because they contained an editorial considered disrespectful of the king. According to the Committee to Protect Journalists, Morocco counted among the ten worst global "press backsliders" in 2007.[43] In August 2009, the Moroccan authorities questioned a dozen journalists and seized two privately owned newspapers that had published an opinion poll about the king's reign and articles about his health. The most puzzling aspect of the seizure of the two weeklies, *Nichane* and *TelQuel,* is that the poll they published indicated favorable public attitudes toward the king; 91 percent of Moroccans surveyed judged King Mohammed VI's performance positively, while 49 percent said Morocco had become more democratic under his leadership.[44] Yet, defending the censorship, Communication Minister and Government Spokesman Khalid Naciri argued that using the king as the subject of an opinion poll violated the constitution and showed disrespect to the royal family.[45] Thus, the pendulum might be swinging back toward greater censorship as the Moroccan regime realizes the ramifications of greater tolerance for free expression.

Many Moroccans argue that the king's vacillation between the expansion and the contraction of free expression reflects his own uncertainty. King Mohammed VI might have originally experimented with greater civil liberties to offer Moroccans and opposition organizations a circumscribed avenue for free expression. From king's perspective, allowing society to collectively "vent" might stanch the more dramatic anti-regime sentiment and activism. The king might consider it relatively low-risk to augment free expression, whether in newspapers or on blogs, or to allow greater free association for protesters and activists. By contrast, engaging in political reform would require fragmenting the authority and overwhelming power vested in the monarchy.

Whatever King Mohammed VI's initial intentions, however, now that the media, civil society organizations, and individuals have tasted their newfound freedoms, he is in a bind. King Mohammed VI may find reversing the relaxation of free expression impossible, especially without tarnishing his reputation at home and abroad. Thus far, the international community has largely applauded King Mohammed VI's reforms while keeping mum about the lack of political reform in Morocco. Allowing the expansion of free expression has helped distract global attention from the fact that the king has done nothing to enhance his citizens' procedural political rights. Any further backtracking on free expression will likely damage his reputation in the West as a reformer.

Further Research. The Moroccans' zeal for free expression raises the question of the potential links between civil liberties and political freedoms. Today, though organizations, journalists, and other private individuals are allowed to express themselves freely, the opening has stopped at the palace's gates. Morocco remains a hereditary monarchy with power concentrated around King Mohammed VI and the makhzen, bypassing the prime minister altogether. The king appoints the prime minister and can dissolve the parliament at will, though King Mohammed VI never has done so.

Thus far, the bloggers, journalists, and CSOs are permitted greater freedom of expression, as long as they do not challenge the hegemony of the monarchy. Yet King Mohammed VI might not always be able to monitor the line between free expression and democratic activism. A society increasingly accustomed to free expression will likely develop new patterns of political behavior. During the September 2007 parliamentary elections, for example, almost a fifth of Morocco's voters went to the polls and defiantly defaced the ballots or deliberately left them blank—an act considered a protest against Moroccans' still limited political rights. This type of political self-expression might reflect a society increasingly accustomed to free expression. Further research should investigate the links between free expression in MENA and demands for greater procedural political rights.

Electoral Representation

A second driver of political change involves the growth of electoral representation in regimes where the executive holds disproportionate power over the legislative body and all other institutions. In MENA, many political parties, movements where parties are banned, and individual candidates are increasingly interested in representation: They have demonstrated a savvy ability to contest elections, take advantage of electoral rules, and win the public's trust by serving constituents' demands. Many of these parties or movements have a nonsecular or conservative ideological affinity, whether Jordan's Islamic Action Front, Bahrain's al-Haq and al-Wefaq movements, Morocco's Justice and Development Party, or Kuwait's Islamic Constitutional Movement (known as HADAS, its Arabic acronym). Yet the effectiveness of these movements often has little to do with their ideological positions or their views on the role of Islam in political life. In fact, the West's perception of these political parties or movements as monolithic opposition parties is often inaccurate. These movements are shifting coalitions, inclusive of different factions and ideological viewpoints. Often individual candidates are more credible than the parties, and the former typically contest elections as independents.

A commonality uniting many of these individual candidates and the movements and parties with which they are affiliated is their desire to be credible representatives of their people. They seek to address the needs and beliefs of non-elites outside of the capital cities. In Egypt, Jordan, Morocco, Bahrain, and Kuwait, such candidates and movements have become increasingly popular, earning respect by challenging their regimes on issues such as corruption, unemployment, and nepotism. These candidates compete for every last electoral seat, even though the parliament in which they seek to serve has a very limited role in policy making.

The first driver of change involves the expansion of civil liberties—such as freedom of press, speech and association. This second driver directly affects the procedural political realm—in particular the legislature. Moreover, while the first mechanism is in part enabled by a regime's tacit acceptance of a freer press and strong civil society organizations, the second mechanism is often unwittingly forced upon the regime. In Egypt, Kuwait, Jordan, Bahrain, and Morocco, parties and individuals fiercely compete in parliamentary elections, regardless of the limited scope of parliamentary power. In rare cases such as Kuwait, parliamentary deputies utilize extant (though limited) procedural democratic rights such as a no-confidence vote, or the threat to hold such a vote. With these limited rights, they can sometimes put pressure on the regime. More frequently, however, these representatives try to leverage their populist appeal to deter the autocrat from enacting unpopular policies, whether subsidy cuts, reductions in public sector employment, or suspect social and foreign policies.

Kuwait's Political Stalemate. The increasingly assertive members of the Kuwaiti National Assembly (MPs) and their confrontation with the al-Sabah family offer the most developed example of electoral representation in the region. Although Kuwait has had a representative parliament since 1962, the emir is constitutionally able to dissolve the assembly and call for new elections. The emir has twice exercised this right unconstitutionally, indefinitely suspending the National Assembly for a number of years in 1976 and 1986.

Although political parties are officially banned in Kuwait, over the past ten years, a fluid coalition of Islamists, both HADAS affiliates as well as members of the Salafi Islamist groups, and tribal confederation representatives have increasingly asserted a powerful opposition voice in the National Assembly. In the 1980s and early 1990s, the MPs affiliated with the various tribal confederations offered the government stalwart loyalty in the National Assembly. Yet, over the past ten years, the tribal MPs have become increasingly autonomous, challenging the al-Sabah family's social, economic, and foreign policies. Many tribal MPs have allied with the well-organized HADAS movement, which grew in power over the 1990s. Together, this bloc delayed for six years former emir Jaber al-Sabah's attempts to grant women suffrage. The reform eventually passed in 2005 when a handful of Islamist MPs changed their position to support women's enfranchisement. Over the past decade, a group of HADAS, tribal affiliates, and Salafi MPs successfully blocked neoliberal economic reforms advocated by the technocratic branch of the al-Sabah family. This coalition has also protested the government's attempts to privatize some industries, which would reduce the jobs available in Kuwait's vast public sector, its largest employer. To many MPs, a large public sector allows them to provide jobs to their constituents—a key source of their popularity. As Herb noted, "Kuwait has more political participation, and as a result less foreign investment, more corruption, and less privatization than its less democratic neighbors."[46]

Since 2006, the increasing strength and sense of empowerment among the elected representatives culminated in what many Kuwaitis now call their "political crisis." Between 2006 and 2009, the emir dissolved the National Assembly constitutionally three times, immediately calling for new elections in 2006, 2008, and 2009. The three elections held in three years—and the six governments formed in less than four years—were the result of a standoff between the al-Sabah family and many MPs. The crux of the recent crisis involved the al-Sabah family's unwillingness to allow senior members of the ruling family, in particular the prime minister and nephew of the emir, Sheikh Nasser al-Mohammed al-Ahmed al-Sabah, to face no-confidence votes in the National Assembly or to submit to ministerial interpellations in parliament, public events Kuwaitis call "grillings." This tension goes back to 2006, when a group of powerful opposition MPs, members of HADAS, and their tribal and Salafi allies demanded to interpellate the prime minister and challenged the al-Sabah family's choice of other ministers. In some cases, MP pressure triggered ministerial resignations. In March 2007, fearing that lawmakers would open a corruption investigation against Health Minister Sheikh Ahmed al-Abdullah al-Sabah, the prime minister called for a new government. In June 2007, the oil and transportation ministers resigned over corruption allegations brought on by the MPs.[47] In early 2008, education minister Nouriya al-Sabeeh was threatened with a no-confidence vote by the National Assembly, which subjected her to an interpellation.[48] The MPs again accused the prime minister of mismanagement in December 2008.[49] Since then, National Assembly MPs have persuaded the prime minister not to appoint as ministers certain individuals (including some members of the ruling family) whom they consider incompetent or corrupt.[50]

The standoff in the Kuwaiti National Assembly involved elected representatives leveraging their populist credentials to confront the regime, despite the MPs' limited constitutional rights. Many of these MPs are also savvy about mastering electoral rules. For example, HADAS quickly tailored its campaign strategy to take advantage of the increased number of voters available after women's enfranchisement in 2005. Similarly, many opposition candidates benefitted from the 2006 reduction in electoral districts from twenty-five to five, a reform it had originally helped to engineer.[51]

In May 2009, after a competitive campaign, Kuwaitis again voted for change. Forty percent of those elected are new, including the country's first four female MPs. The Kuwaiti voters punished various organized political parties, Islamists and liberals alike. They did, however, return some of the most outspoken MPs, those responsible for the showdown with the government, thereby setting the stage for yet another confrontation. Sheikh Nasser has yet again been named prime minister.

The political crisis will therefore not abate. To some, the standoff between the MPs and the al-Sabah family seems ineffective and chaotic, with MPs constantly shifting alliances, swamping the floor with uncoordinated motions, and pursuing personal vendettas.[52] Nonetheless, the MPs have thus far succeeded in shaping the agenda and impeding some al-Sabah policies, going further than any other parliamentarians in the Arab world to reshape the political boundaries between the autocratic regime and the elected legislators.

Further Research. It is not surprising that a boisterous parliament filled with representatives who competitively contest elections would emerge in Kuwait, with its long history of parliamentary life and a citizenry generally accepting of the al-Sabah family's rule. Is Kuwait, therefore, an anomaly in the region? Future research should investigate whether the evolution of electoral representation in Kuwait is a harbinger of similar legislative politics that might emerge in other MENA monarchies, especially Jordan, Morocco, and Bahrain. Similarly, further research should analyze whether electoral representation requires the organizing leadership of political movements or parties, whether the Kuwaiti HADAS, the Bahraini al-Wefaq, or the Moroccan Justice and Development Party. It might be that MENA opposition parties are not as salient as Western analysts believe that they are. In the 2009 elections, the Kuwaiti electorate chose an unprecedented number of "clean independents" who eschew any connection to the HADAS, Salafi, or other political movements.

Hereditary Succession

Over the past nine years, a series of sons have succeeded their fathers in Syria, Jordan, Morocco, Bahrain, and Qatar (as well as a half-brother in Kuwait). Analysts argue that similar father-son transitions are imminent in Egypt and Libya. The transfer of power from fathers to sons represents a third driver of change distinct to MENA, enacted in a top-down manner. While none of the familial successions have triggered democratization, the rise of a generation of sons is subtly changing the nature of political rule in MENA. The fathers who came to power in the 1960s and 1970s based their legitimacy on hereditary claims in dynastic monarchies, leadership in national independence movements, or pan-Arab nationalist credentials, but the sons cannot rely on the same sources of authority. In the twenty-first century, the combination of globalization and democratic norms puts on the defensive those who come to power through familial succession. When the sons in Bahrain, Qatar, Syria, Jordan, and Morocco assumed power between 1995 and 2000, they immediately faced domestic challengers, as well as questions about their legitimacy at home and abroad. Most of the sons responded to their credibility deficits by initiating social or economic reforms—augmenting women's rights (Morocco), liberalizing the press (Qatar), or opening up the economy (Jordan). In very rare circumstances, a few sons introduced limited political reforms, such as promulgating a new constitution (Bahrain and Qatar).

The sons share much in common. As a cohort, they are relatively young and enjoy extensive international ties; in fact, most of them were educated abroad. Yet they also share a functional approach to ruling. In Syria, Qatar, Bahrain, and Morocco, the fathers ruled by primarily relying on repressive tactics to confront opposition challengers. Although the sons are willing to use force, many also utilize reforms as carrots, allaying the domestic opposition and burnishing their image as responsive rulers on the international stage. Reforms in the area of social and economic life have enabled the sons to engineer loyal constituencies, among both elites and the populace. Their priority, as a cohort, toward economic reform can be attributed to increasing pressure from international actors such as the International Monetary Fund. In addition, a clique of Western-educated technocrats with neoliberal economic views typically surrounds the sons, encouraging them to repeal the statist economic policies enacted by their fathers.[53]

It is therefore no surprise that MENA regimes ruled by sons compose the majority of the regimes labeled "liberalized autocracies" by Brumberg, who identifies a distinct type of autocratic system unique to MENA, characterized

by "guided pluralism, controlled elections, and selective repression."[54] Moreover, whereas only seven of the nineteen MENA Arab states discussed in this
chapter earned a label of "partly free" in the 2008 Freedom House rankings,
six of these seven states are ruled by one of the sons.[55]

The Rise of the Sons. During their first two years of rule, both Syrian President Bashar al-Asad and Bahraini Emir-turned-King Hamad al-Khalifa demonstrated the reformist tendencies of the sons as a cohort, though the two
leaders' reform experiments produced different outcomes. Immediately after
succeeding his father, Hafez, in June 2000, Syrian President Asad released
hundreds of political prisoners and—for the first time in decades—allowed
the publication of three independent newspapers. He even permitted a group
of pro-democracy intellectuals to hold salon-style public meetings.[56] This experimentation with political openness contrasted starkly with his father's repressive rule and displeased the old-guard regime elites, the bulwark of the
Hafez al-Asad regime. When Bashar recognized that he could go no further in
allowing free political debate, he decided to invest instead in economic liberalization, seeking new legislation to allow the privatization of Syrian banks.[57]
Again the old guard protested, ultimately convincing the new president to
cease his economic reform program. This power struggle between Bashar and
the old guard might have continued indefinitely, had US policy in the region
after September 11, 2001, not intervened.[58] Shortly after the 2003 Iraq war,
the Bush administration escalated its threatening rhetoric toward Syria. In
light of American accusations that the Syrian regime was supporting terrorists
and Iraqi insurgents, the old guard played on nationalist sentiments and
forced Bashar to abandon his reform agenda.

In Bahrain, the new emir, Hamad al-Khalifa, also embarked on a reform program immediately after succeeding his father. Emir Hamad wanted to make
peace with the Bahraini Shia majority who had taken to the streets in the late
1990s, launching popular protests to signal discontent with the repressive rule of
his father (and Sunni) Emir Isa al-Khalifa. In 2001, the new emir invited Shia opposition leaders to participate in writing a national charter document, which pre-
scribed power-sharing and national reconciliation and was submitted to a public
referendum. Emir Hamad abolished the thirty-year-old state security laws that
underpinned the policies of mass incarceration, arrest, torture, and exile that were
widespread during his father's reign. Yet, a year later, to the outrage of many Shia
leaders, Emir Hamad reneged on his promise to allow the opposition to participate in revising the constitution. Instead, in early 2002, he unilaterally promulgated a new constitution, which maintained the imbalance between the legislative
and executive branches and officially transformed Bahrain into a kingdom.

Since 2002, the now-renamed King Hamad has been reluctant to engage in
any additional political reforms. He has instead focused on bolstering Bahrain's

foreign relations, particularly with the West. Discriminatory policies toward the Shia majority persist, fueling the opposition movements' critique of Hamad's regime. Yet many of his father's fiercest critics, particularly leaders of the al-Wefaq society, have been mollified for now by their limited participation in political life and their election to the Council of Representatives.

Future Successions and Further Research. While both Bashar al-Asad and King Hamad immediately turned to reforms upon coming to power, the outcome of each reform initiative diverged. In Syria, the old guard opposed to domestic reform initiatives prevailed. In Bahrain, King Hamad hoped that a series of highly touted reforms would suffice, and he has since resisted calls for additional reforms. In Morocco, Jordan, and Qatar, limited reform programs continue, though they do not touch the realm of political institutions or contestation. In both Morocco and Jordan, the kings focused on market reforms to attract international investors. While King Mohammed VI immediately made administrative, human rights, and women's rights reforms upon coming to power, in recent years he has focused on economic development. In Qatar, Crown Prince Hamad bin Khalifa al-Thani ousted his father in 1995 in a nonviolent palace coup. To justify his power grab, he loosened the strict media censorship laws, promulgated a constitution, and created a partially elected legislature. In recent years, the new Qatari Emir has invested in economic development and educational advances.

In MENA, therefore, succession from father to son typically prompts a flurry of reforms. Aging autocrats foreseeing the end of their rule may also choose to reform proactively, in anticipation of tumultuous successions. Muammar Qadhafi ruled for forty years in a closed system that allowed for no dissent or opposition. He championed a rejectionist and violent foreign policy. Yet in 2003 he decided to moderate his foreign policy positions—dismantling his nonconventional weapons and normalizing ties with the West. Many analysts presumed that Qadhafi's concern for a smooth succession in part contributed to this foreign policy reversal.[59] Though Libya remains a closed and repressive police state, Qadhafi's son Seif Qadhafi, one of the main contenders for succession, has already intimated that he would favor substantial economic reforms should he succeed his father.[60]

If concern about facilitating familial succession prompts reformist behavior, then Egypt's President Mubarak might also initiate reforms to enable the succession of his son Gamal Mubarak. The younger Mubarak has already been selected as one of the ruling National Democratic Party's deputy secretaries general. Will the younger Mubarak, age forty-two, follow the pattern of the other sons and embark upon reforms when he comes to power? He is already surrounded by a group of devoted supporters—"the gang," a group of businessmen and academics interested in reform.[61] Should political rule transfer from father to son in Egypt, the most populous state in the Arab world, the father/son balance in the region will shift decidedly. As the cohort of sons grows, the most important question about their rule is not whether they will continue to enact economic and social reforms, but whether they will experiment with political reforms as well.

Bureaucratic De-Democratization

While most existing theories of political change envision a one-directional movement toward greater liberalization or democratization, in MENA there are no such guarantees. Some states in the region have become more authoritarian in recent years, with autocrats limiting the civil and political rights of opposition actors and citizens. In many states, autocrats introduce rule-of-law measures to ensure that every political institution (such as the courts and political parties) remains loyal to the regime. Rule-of-law reforms often impose draconian controls over civic activity, limiting the rights of groups to organize or to register. Autocrats are increasingly changing electoral laws, revising constitutions, and modifying regulations regarding party activities—often to institutionalize unlimited term limits and/or to reduce the competitiveness of elections. In short, in many MENA states, rule-of-law reform has come to connote the deepening of authoritarianism.

Tunisia's Creeping Authoritarianism. In November 1987, Zine al-Abidine Ben Ali initiated a bloodless coup and swiftly wrested power from the aging President Habib Bourguiba, who had ruled since independence in 1956. Justifying the regime change, Ben Ali called for a new era of political reconciliation, a "*changement*," in which the institutions would "guarantee the conditions for a responsible democracy, fully respecting the sovereignty of the people."[62] To signify the new era, he renamed the ruling party the Democratic Constitutional Rally (RCD). Ben Ali immediately canceled a state security law that Bourguiba had used to repress Islamists and leftists and adopted a press law to ease restrictions on the press.[63] He also eliminated the constitutional provision of "presidency for life" that had enabled Bourguiba to rule for thirty years. As a sign of reconciliation, a range of political parties, including those representing Islamists, issued a National Pact "to define a common denominator and a maximum of principles on which all Tunisians can agree."[64]

Yet the experiment with political pluralism did not last long. In 1989, Ben Ali called Tunisia's first multiparty elections. The government reported that candidates affiliated with the Islamist al-Nahda movement garnered 15 percent of the vote, although they likely won at least 25 percent. This show of force worried Ben Ali, and beginning in 1990, he unleashed a campaign of repression against al-Nahda, arresting its leaders and driving them into exile.

Since then, he has launched a more subtle institutional and legal campaign to weaken any political opposition, including all of the secular, nationalist, and leftist political parties. Since 1992, Ben Ali has introduced a series of laws of association to limit the independence and monitor the activities of all civil society organizations in Tunisia, which was once home to the most vibrant civil society in the Arab world. The Tunisian Human Rights League, once a popular national organization, now consists of a few lone activists issuing communiqués in their downtown Tunis office. The new laws ensure that the ruling RCD party dominates Tunisian political and civic life.[65]

Ben Ali has dramatically retreated from his initial promises of a "changement" engendered by pluralism and liberalization. In 2002, he revised over half of the 1996 constitution, adding eighteen new articles. The changes directly enabled Ben Ali to run for a fourth term by abolishing Article 39—originally written by Ben Ali himself in 1988 to limit the presidency to three terms. The 2002 constitution also raised the upper age limit of presidential candidates to seventy-five, a necessary fix because Ben Ali was sixty-five years old at the time. Together these two revisions allowed him to run in 2004.[66] Preventing any promising competitors from running enabled the president to easily win a fifth term in the October 25, 2009, elections. Ben Ali came to power disavowing the notion of "presidency for life"; he will now serve as president until at least 2014, for twenty-seven years.

Moreover, over the course of the 1990s, Ben Ali perfected the technique of building layers of pro-regime institutions, while packing the courts and the Chamber of Deputies with loyalists in order to sideline any opposition to the RCD. Tactics of intimidation have concomitantly curtailed free speech, press, and association.[67] Civil liberties have eroded to the point where many Tunisians fear expressing their political opinions even to their neighbors.

Further Research. As discussed above, Tunisia is distinct in North Africa, given its relatively advanced socioeconomic development coupled with its stark authoritarian rule. Yet neighboring regimes are watching Ben Ali's tactics carefully. Nearby, the Mubarak regime in Egypt also recently experimented with dedemocratizing constitutional revisions in 2005 and 2007. These revisions, put to a popular referendum, reorganized the rules of electoral contestation in order to protect the hegemony of the presidency and the ruling National Democratic Party. In Algeria, President Abdelaziz Bouteflika also revised Article 74 of the country's constitution in November 2008 to legally enable his third term.

The Tunisian case offers the most extensive example of a MENA regime dedemocratizing by introducing rule-of-law reforms. Yet, in the future, MENA rulers are just as likely to consolidate power and deepen their control over institutions as they are to gravitate toward liberalization or democratization. Further research should consider the conditions enabling deliberalization and de-democratization. In particular, it is likely that the relatively lackluster Western response to illiberal rules-of-law contributes to this trend. The region's autocrats have learned that repressing dissidents and throwing protesters in jail provokes outrage by Western governments. However, the more subtle and superficially "legal" means of de-democratization, such as electoral changes or constitutional revisions, rarely prompt any international response.

CONCLUSION

This chapter has made three claims. First, applying off-the-shelf theories regarding liberalization or democratization, founded in the experiences of other regions, offers limited explanatory power when it comes to current and future political change in twenty-first-century MENA states. Second, much of the current literature on MENA political systems focuses on unearthing the electoral and institutional mechanisms sustaining authoritarianism. This literature, though informative, leaves little room for assessing, measuring, or interpreting subtle shifts that occur within authoritarian systems over time.

Third, this chapter has delineated four drivers of change currently emerging in the region, transforming MENA politics even as authoritarianism endures. Two drivers emanate from the bottom up, while two derive from the top down. First, a populist drive for free expression is enabling individuals, the press, and organizations to test the limits of some regimes' tolerance for dissent. As the Morocco case suggests, sometimes the autocrat must scramble to respond to the free expression, ensuring that the expansion of civil liberties does not spill over into the political realm. Second, elected representatives are increasingly cultivating populist credentials, competing for every last vote to take advantage of even limited electoral rights in nondemocracies. As the current stalemate in the Kuwaiti National Assembly exemplifies, the strengthening of electoral representation in authoritarian regimes might not introduce democratic checks and balances. Nonetheless, parliamentarians no longer rubber-stamp ministerial choices. Moreover, they bring to parliament societal clout, which in the long term might deter some regimes from enacting unpopular policies.

Third, succession of rule from father to son has occurred in approximately a third of the MENA states over the past ten years. As a cohort, the sons are experimenting with a new model of authoritarian rule. They often rely on social and economic reforms to placate opponents and create allies, whether technocrats interested in economic reform or feminists invested in women's rights. Finally, a fourth driver of change involves illiberal reforms often used by the regime to codify and institutionalize executive control. In Tunisia, institutionalized de-democratization through rule-of-law reform has successfully stifled civil liberties and eliminated any opposition actors. Whether Tunisia's deliberalization and de-democratization will occur in other MENA regimes remains among the most critical—and as yet unanswered—questions about the region's politics in the twenty-first century.

While delineating four new ways to conceptualize change in the region, this chapter has also made clear that these four drivers and their outcomes remain fluid. How MENA autocrats respond to the bottom-up drivers will largely shape the extent and type of political change that ensues. The top-down drivers remain subject to autocratic decision-making and the pressures of succession. Finally, while this chapter has deliberately sidelined international influences—whether regional conflicts, Western democracy promotion, or global economic recovery—these factors will also determine the extent of political change over the next ten years.

NOTES

1. Many academics use liberalization to describe a process of economic and market reform. Here the term is used to refer to the expansion of civil liberties.

2. "Freedom in the World, 2008," Freedom House, www.freedomhouse.org/template .cfm?page=15.

3. While definitions of the region vary, this chapter focuses on nineteen Arab states in MENA: Algeria, Bahrain, Egypt, Iraq, Jordan, Kuwait, Lebanon, Libya, Mauritania, Morocco, Oman, Palestinian Territories, Qatar, Saudi Arabia, Sudan, Syria, Tunisia, United Arab Emirates, and Yemen. For the populations of each country, see UN Population Division, *World Population Prospects: The 2006 Revision* (2007), http://esa.un.org.

4. Seymour Martin Lipset, "Some Social Requisites of Democracy: Economic Development and Political Legitimacy," *American Political Science Review* 53, no. 1 (March 1959): 69–105.

5. Yi Feng and Paul Zak, "Determinants of Democratic Transitions," *Journal of Conflict Resolution* 42, no. 2 (2003): 162–177, and Dietrich Rueschemeyer, Evelyn Huber Stephens, and John D. Stephens, *Capitalist Development and Democracy* (Chicago: University of Chicago Press, 1992).

6. Barrington Moore, *Social Origins of Dictatorship and Democracy: Land and Peasant in the Making of the Modern World* (Cambridge, MA: Harvard University Press, 1966).

7. Larry Diamond, "Economic Development and Democracy Reconsidered," in *Reexamining Democracy: Essays in Honor of Seymour Martin Lipset*, ed. Gary Marks and Larry Diamond (Newbury Park, CA: Sage Publications, 1992).

8. Adam Przeworski and Fernando Limongi, "Modernization: Theories and Facts," *World Politics* 49, no. 2 (January 1997): 155–183.

9. See the United Nations Development Programme, "Arab Human Development Report 2004: Towards Freedom in the Arab World," and "Arab Human Development Report 2003: Building a Knowledge Society," http://arabstates.undp.org/subpage .php?spid=14. For the views of Washington policy makers see "Economic and Political Development in the Middle East: Managing Change, Building a New Kind of Partnership," in *Restoring the Balance: A Middle East Strategy for the Next President* (Washington, DC: Brookings Institution/Council on Foreign Relations, 2008).

10. Steven Fish, "Islam and Authoritarianism," *World Politics* 55, no. 1 (2002): 4–37.

11. 2008 GDP per capita purchasing power parity figures come from the International Monetary Fund's World Economic Outlook Database, www.imf.org.

12. "Tunisia: Background Notes," US Department of State, updated February 2008, www.state.gov/r/pa/ei/bgn/5439.htm.

13. "Tunisia," Freedom in the World 2008, Freedom House, www.freedomhouse.org.

14. For the classic articulation of the rentier thesis, see Hazem Beblawi, "The Rentier State in the Arab World," in *The Arab State*, ed. Giacomo Luciani (Berkeley: University of California Press, 1990), pp. 87–88. Recent large-N, cross-regional studies evaluating the rentier thesis have found equivocal statistical corroboration. See Michael L. Ross, "Does Oil Hinder Democracy?" *World Politics* 53 (April 2001): 356–357, and Michael Herb, "No Representation Without Taxation? Rents, Development, and Democracy," *Comparative Politics* 37, no. 3 (April 2005): 297–316.

15. See Guillermo O'Donnell, Philippe C. Schmitter, and Laurence Whitehead, eds. *Transitions from Authoritarian Rule: Prospects for Democracy* (Baltimore: Johns Hopkins University Press, 1986).

16. Adam Przeworski, "Democracy as a Contingent Outcome of Conflicts," in *Constitutionalism and Democracy*, ed. Jon Elster and Rune Slagstad (Cambridge: Cambridge University Press, 1988), and Barry Weingast, "The Political Foundations of Democracy and the Rule of Law," *American Political Science Review* 91 (1997): 245–263.

17. Adam Przeworski, *Democracy and the Market: Political and Economic Reforms in Eastern Europe and Latin America* (Cambridge: Cambridge University Press, 1991), p. 19.

18. In the original theory posited in their 1986 volumes, O'Donnell, Schmitter, and Whitehead did identify some cases of stalled democratization, where authoritarianism would endure.

19. Volker Perthes differentiates among the "core-elite," "intermediate elite," and "sub-elite" in *Arab Elites: Negotiating the Politics of Change*, ed. Volker Perthes (Boulder, CO, and London: Lynne Rienner, 2004).

20. Barbara Geddes, "What Do We Know about Democratization after Twenty Years?" *Annual Review of Political Science* 2 (1999): 115–144.

21. Alexis de Tocqueville, *Democracy in America*, trans. and ed. Harvey C. Mansfield and Delba Winthrop (Chicago: University of Chicago Press, 2000), and Robert D. Putnam, *Making Democracy Work: Civic Traditions in Modern Italy* (Princeton, NJ: Princeton University Press, 1993).

22. Augustus Richard Norton, "The Future of Civil Society in the Middle East," *Middle East Journal* 47, no. 2 (1993): 211.

23. See Norton, "The Future of Civil Society in the Middle East," and Saad Eddin Ibrahim, "Civil Society and the Prospects of Democratization in the Arab World," in *Civil Society in the Middle East, Vol. 1*, ed. Augustus Richard Norton (Leiden, Netherlands: Brill, 1995), pp. 41–42.

24. Sean Yom, "Civil Society and Democratization in the Arab World," *Middle East Review of International Affairs* 9, no. 4 (December 2005).

25. These largely self-reported numbers are questionable, complicated by the varied definitions of what constitutes civil society organizations (CSOs). Drizz Khrouz, "A Dynamic Civil Society," *Journal of Democracy* 19, no. 1 (January 2008): 42–49.

26. Salim Nasr, "Arab Civil Societies and Good Governance Reform: An Analytical Framework and Overview," Working Paper of the UNDP Dead Sea Conference, UNDP Programme on Governance in the Arab Region, Jordan, February, 2005, p. 8.

27. Amaney Jamal, *Barriers to Democracy: The Other Side of Social Capital in Palestine and the Arab World* (Princeton, NJ: Princeton University Press, 2007).

28. Yom, "Civil Society and Democratization in the Arab World."

29. Robert J. LaTowsky, "Egypt's NGO Sector, A Briefing Paper," *Education for Development* Paper 1, no. 4 (1997): 1.

30. James G. McGann, "Pushback against NGOs in Egypt," *International Journal for Not-for-Profit Law*, 10, no. 4 (August 2008), www.icnl.org/KNOWLEDGE/IJNL/vol10iss4/special_3.htm, and Mohamed Agati, "Undermining Standards of Good Governance: Egypt's NGO Law and Its Impact on the Transparency and Accountability of CSOs, " *International Journal for Not-for-Profit Law* (April 2002), www.icnl.org/knowledge/ijnl/vol9iss2/special_4.htm.

31. As the authors of the Arab Human Development Report of 2004 observe: "Civil society faces the same problem as the political community vis-à-vis the authorities who seek to control civil organizations, directly or indirectly, by using a dual strategy of containment and repression. In addition, many CSOs become extensions of political parties, which use them as fronts through which to expand their political influence at the popular level. This in turn limits the CSOs' initiative and independence of action" (p. 17).

32. The civil society thesis does not assume a time frame, however. It might take over a generation for civil society organizations to cultivate greater social capital and foster democratic institutions. Therefore the MENA CSOs established in the early 1990s could yet influence the region's politics.

33. For the best articulation of the resilience of authoritarianism thesis, see Eva Bellin, "The Robustness of Authoritarianism in the Middle East: Exceptionalism in Comparative Perspective," *Comparative Politics* 36, no. 2 (2004): 139–157, and Holger Albrecht and Olivier Schlumberger, "Waiting for Godot: Regime Change without Democratization in the Middle East," *International Political Science Review* 25, no. 4 (2004): 371–392.

34. Bellin, "The Robustness of Authoritarianism in the Middle East," p. 142.

35. See Ellen Lust-Okar, *Structuring Conflict in the Arab World: Incumbents, Opponents, and Institutions* (Cambridge: Cambridge University Press, 2005); Ellen Lust-Okar, "Why the Failure of Democratization? Explaining 'Middle East Exceptionalism,'" Working Paper, 2006; Ellen Lust-Okar and Amaney Jamal, "Rulers and Rules: Reassessing Electoral Laws and Political Liberalization in the Middle East," *Comparative Political Studies* 35 (2005): 337–366; and Lisa Blaydes, "Electoral Budget Cycles under Authoritarianism: Economic Opportunism in Mubarak's Egypt," unpublished manuscript available at http://blaydes.bol.ucla.edu/Budget.pdf.

36. Michael Hudson's observation about Arab politics, made thirty years ago, still applies today: "The central problem of government in the Arab world . . . is political legitimacy. The shortage of this indispensable political resource largely accounts for the volatile nature of Arab politics and the autocratic . . . character of all present governments." See Michael Hudson, *Arab Politics: The Search for Legitimacy* (New Haven, CT: Yale University Press, 1977), p. 2.

37. There are numerous additional critiques of the "robustness of authoritarianism" argument. The most trenchant is offered by Lisa Anderson, who points out that asking

"why authoritarianism persists" is "little more than the inverse of the democracy question. . . . Many of the same factors that had been deployed to explain democracy's fragility—the availability of external rents, the limited popular mobilization for democracy—were adduced to account for the robustness of the coercive machinery and the stability of the regimes. That there was a tautological character to this argument is not surprising; after all, 'authoritarianism' is little more than a residual category in most political science." Lisa Anderson, "Searching Where the Light Shines: Studying Democratization in the Middle East," *Annual Review of Political Science* 9 (2006): 201.

38. In all of these countries, the Freedom House civil rights rating has improved since the mid to late 1990s.

39. See, for example, "Le Salaire du Roi," *TelQuel* 156–157, December 2004, or Sanaa al-Aji, "How Moroccans Laugh at Religion, Sex, and Politics" (Translation mine), *Nichane,* December 2006.

40. "Morocco—Annual Report 2008," Reporters without Borders, www.rsf.org/article.php3?id_article=25439.

41. Naoufel Cherkaoui, "Interview with Moroccan Blogger Mohammed Erraji," *Maghrebia,* September 16, 2008, www.magharebia.com/cocoon/awi/xhtml1/en_GB/features/awi/features/2008/09/16/feature-02.

42. "Morocco—Annual Report 2008."

43. "Backsliders: The Ten Countries Where Press Freedom Has Most Deteriorated," Committee to Protect Journalists, www.cpj.org, May 2, 2007.

44. Muhammed Kurayshan, "Behind the News," Al-Jazeera Television, August 5, 2009, and *Bayane Al -Youm*, Rabat, August 7, 2009.

45. "Moroccan Press Fear Clampdown over Reports on Ruling Monarch," BBC News, September 23, 2009.

46. Michael Herb, "The Ambiguities of Democratization: Parliaments in the Gulf," paper presented at the annual meeting of the ISA's 49th Annual Convention, "Bridging Multiple Divides," San Francisco, March 26, 2008.

47. "Kuwait Country Report," *Freedom in the World 2008*, Freedom House, www.freedomhouse.org/template.cfm?page=22&year=2008&country=7426.

48. The author witnessed the parliamentary grilling of al-Sabeeh in January 2008.

49. Abdullah Al Shayji, "The Pains of Kuwaiti Democracy," *Gulf News*, December 7, 2008.

50. Nathan J. Brown, "Pushing Toward Party Politics? Kuwait's Islamic Constitutional Movement," Carnegie Paper, No. 79, Carnegie Endowment for International Peace, January 2007, p. 5.

51. Nathan J. Brown, "Kuwait's 2008 Parliamentary Elections: A Setback for Democratic Islamism?" Web Commentary, Carnegie Endowment for International Peace, May 27, 2008.

52. Rania El Gamal and Ulf Laessing, "Kuwait Liberal MPs Call for End to Ban on Parties," Reuters, October 31, 2008.

53. Perthes, *Arab Elites*.

54. Daniel Brumberg, "The Trap of Liberalized Autocracy," *Journal of Democracy* 13, no. 4 (October 2002): 56–68.

55. See *Freedom in the World 2008*, Freedom House.

56. "Profile: Syria's Bashar al-Assad," BBC News, March 10, 2005.

57. Eyal Zisser, "Does Bashar al-Assad Rule Syria?" *Middle East Quarterly* 10, no. 1 (Winter 2003).

58. Ellen Lust-Okar, "Reform in Syria: Steering Between the Chinese Model and Regime Change," in *Beyond the Façade: Political Reform in the Arab World*, ed. Marina Ottaway and Julia Choucair-Vizoso (Washington, DC: Carnegie Endowment for International Peace, 2008), p. 74.

59. For an assessment of the possible motives behind Muammar Qadhafi's decision to dismantle his country's WMD program, see Dafna Hochman, "Rehabilitating a Rogue: Libya's WMD Reversal and Lessons for U.S. Policy," *Parameters* 36 (Spring 2006): 63–78.

60. Muammar Qadhafi has apparently cooled to the proposition of domestic economic reforms since 2003–2005. His son, however, has a clear reformist agenda. See "Qaddafi Son Says Libya Wants to Invest in U.S.," Associated Press, November 21, 2008.

61. Daniel Williams, "Clearing the Path for a Scion of Egypt: Hosni Mubarak's Son Climbs Party Ranks as Country's Leaders Undercut His Rivals," *Washington Post*, March 10, 2006.

62. Larbi Sadiki, "Bin Ali's Tunisia: Democracy by Non-Democratic Means," *British Journal of Middle Eastern Studies* 29, no. 1 (2002): 63.

63. Khalil Zamiti, "La societe Tunisienne: absolutisme et democratie après la deposition du president a vie," *Peuples Méditerranéens* 47 (1989): 125–135.

64. Président Ben Ali, "Discours de monsieur le president de la république a la Chambre des Députes a l'occasion de l'anniversaire du 7 novembre," *Le Pacte National* (1988): 6. See also "Lettre d'Ismail Khelil au President de la République," *Le Renouveau*, August 5, 1988.

65. Personal interview, US Embassy, Tunis, Tunisia, May 8, 2007.

66. Personal interview, Tunisian democracy activist, Tunis, June 5, 2007. See also "Les Principaux amendements a la constitution approuves par referendum," Agence France-Presse, May 27, 2002.

67. Mokhtar Trifi, "Nous espérons que la visite de M. Sarkozy en Tunisie n'aura pas un caractère purement économique," *Le Monde*, April 27, 2008.

5

CIVIL-MILITARY RELATIONS*

David S. Sorenson

In December 1948, Syrian President Shukri al-Quwatli was on an inspection tour of Syrian army camps, and in one encampment he sensed a strong odor emanating from a camp stove. He was appalled to learn that the burning cooking fat he smelled was not the traditional Arab *samna* but rather bone waste sold to the army by an unscrupulous contractor. Quwatli immediately arrested the colonel responsible for supply, but the move backfired, and several days later the colonel's superior officers arrested the president, took over the government, and reinstalled the cashiered colonel as head of army supply.[1]

This almost-forgotten episode brings to light the often fragile balance between the army and the state in many Middle Eastern countries. This chapter delves into the relationship between the professional military and the civilian society in the Middle East and North Africa (MENA). It focuses on the varying roles the armed forces play in the political and economic lives of their individual countries, and offers explanations for how those roles evolved and continued. It considers the delicate balance between professional soldiers and civil authority in a region where military power was often the backbone of new nations, and where "civilian" leadership often consisted of retired military officers who had come to power behind the barrel of a gun.

UNDERSTANDING CIVIL-MILITARY RELATIONS

The state of civil-military relations is one of the most critical issues for any political system.[2] Put simply, the military is almost always the most powerful element in a given country, capable of either shooting its way into political power or reaching out from the barracks to influence civilian rulers without actually toppling them; often the mere threat of a coup is sufficient to gain civilian compliance. Civil military relations is also about political control in the military sphere. Feaver puts it well: "The civil-military challenge is to reconcile a military strong enough to do anything the civilians ask them to do with a military subordinate enough to do only what civilians authorize them to do."[3] It thus involves a delicate balancing act between keeping the soldier out of the executive mansion and doing the bidding on the battlefield of those who do live in the executive manor.

Throughout history, soldiers often equated politics and war, believing that military sway over governance was essential to the power to wage war. In retrospect, the modern state with its plethora of power over society was born from the requirements of warfare. The textbook example is Napoleon's France, which became a model for other European powers to follow. However, civilian society was not always willing to trust the state's operation to those who would direct most of its resources into war-making, and thus civil-military relations is rooted in the contest for state authority between warriors and civilians who believed that the modern state should support commercial interests first. The emergence of British liberalism brought additional concerns about state power over individual rights, and thus an offspring of liberalism, the American Constitution, along with long-standing political tradition, has largely kept the American professional military from participating in partisan politics. Democracies and some autocracies throughout the world have usually accepted this military separation from power. However, in other cases, the professional military plays an active and sometimes dominant role in a country's political and economic life.

Locating Patterns of Civil-Military Relations

Traditional models of civil-military relations paint a space between civil governance and the professional military, though the distance of that space varies across cases. Some theorists, inspired partly by the work of Huntington,[4] and others argue that the professionalization of the modern military will create a force to prepare for and engage exclusively in warfare, and that military modernization, professional military education, and procedures for recruiting professional soldiers will keep the military in the barracks and out of politics.

The political lore of the United States initiated and maintained a strong distrust of the professional soldier,[5] and so while Huntington offers a raison d'être for military political neutrality, his theory does not explain civil-military relations in cases where the military already operates or influences the political power levers. Moreover, a number of inquiries have found that few militaries, particularly those in developing countries, achieved the levels of professionalism displayed by the US military.[6] Other studies have asked whether efforts to professionalize the armed forces have actually led to less military involvement in civil rule, usually concluding that the military professionalization concept is either not descriptive of national conditions or is otherwise unhelpful in untangling non-American civil-military relations.[7] Thus new approaches have emerged to frame and understand comparative civil-military relations. Feaver suggests that civilian masters and military "servants" negotiate civil-military relations (principal-agent theory),[8] while Schiff advances "concordance theory," which examines relative tripartite agreement (concordance) between the military, the national political elite, and the citizenry to explain military behavior relative to domestic society.[9] Other research explores the role the military plays relative to civilian leaders in war-making, in both threat assessment[10] and the decisions and execution of war policy.[11]

Civil-military relationships obviously vary across countries, ranging from complete military dictatorship to total control of military affairs by civilian governance, ranging between:

- Almost complete military control.
- The civil-military teeter-totter, where civilians and the military vie for national political control, taking turns at the power apogee.
- Almost complete control of military affairs by civilians.

These are idealized categories, of course, but they are useful starting points.

The first category used to be fairly common in the world, with military dictators ruling most of Latin America, sub-Saharan Africa, parts of Europe, and Asia. The waves of democratization from the 1970s through the 1990s swept away most juntas, and now only Myanmar (once known as Burma), Fiji, and a small number of sub-Saharan African countries remain under total military rule. Some countries do come under temporary control of the military as a consequence of a coup, as in Thailand when a military coup drove Prime Minister Thaksin Shinawatra from power in September 2006 and in Mauritania, where the military ousted Prime Minister Yahia Ould Ahmed El-Ouakef in August 2008. The army took over in Bangladesh in January 2007 after years of political violence and corruption, and banned political activity until December 2008 while clearing out false voter registrations and arresting corrupt businesspeople and politicians. The Honduran military ousted a leftist president in June 2009 and replaced him with the president of the Honduran congress. But in those cases, after the military deposed leaders they disapproved of, the soldiers usually returned to the barracks after brief periods of rule and allowed elections to take place. In recent years military coups leading to long-term military rule have been rare.

The second category is more common in many developing countries today, where the military gained prominence in the process of achieving independence (where the country was a former colony or protectorate) but relinquished control to civil authority while bargaining to remain influential in political and economic life. The military was a central part of the liberation storyline, which allowed it to burnish its credentials as a nationalist symbol. Military leaders use this image to justify their right to leverage both political and economic outcomes. For example, Pakistan's military claimed guardianship of Pakistan's identity, utilizing that claim through four coups since independence, and Pakistan's military and its associated intelligence services remain strong in Pakistan's civil space. As Staniland notes, "Even when civilian control in some sense endures, the military frequently acts as a domestic political cudgel rather than solely as the shield of the state against external foes. This position includes a crucial role as a veto player in civilian decision making."[12] The Philippine military-civilian relationship has similar characteristics, if not as many coups. There are also cases where civilian rulers utilize the armed forces to enhance their own political standing. Weak civilian politicians may embrace a popular military or tacitly craft roles for soldiers that allow them high visibility in a civilian regime. In such cases, even symbolic support by ribbon-bedecked generals and admirals in aviator sunglasses standing next to a civilian head of state on a reviewing stand can convey a not-too-subtle message of military support.

The relative power the military exercises in any given polity is conditional on several dynamics, including internal and external threats, political traditions, and the martial culture that shapes the values of the armed forces. In advanced democracies, the military normally exists to provide national defense and has very little influence in politics. The traditions and requirements of the military and the culture of democracy rarely mix well, which is why most modern democracies place their militaries under civilian political control. For mature democracies, as Kohn notes, the challenge for civilian leadership is exercising authority over military and security decisions, contrasting with weak, immature democracies where the challenge for civilians is to defend themselves against civilian erosion of political power to the military, particularly in the face of a strong military, "sometimes preying on society rather than protecting it."[13]

Security Conditions

Almost all states face some kind of external threat, though such threats range considerably in intensity. For many modern states, the external threat may be smuggling in goods or illegal immigrants, which is the case now in much of post–Cold War Europe. In other cases, however, the threat may be another state's expansionist ambitions, or a terrorist group based in a neighboring state or area. The traditional argument relating to civilian control of the military is that the greater the external threat, the more stable civilian control over the military.[14] Conversely, if the nature of the threat is *internal*, then the military may demand more political influence. External threats force the military to focus on its role as provider of arms to defend the nation, thus potentially limiting its role in domestic governance. Internal threats often require political solutions, putting the military in a situation where it may want to engage in internal policing to mitigate the inside threat, or to respond politically or economically to address the conditions that initially generate the internal peril. There is also the potential for contestation between the professional military about both the nature of the threat and the potential response to it—strategic assessment is often bitterly played out between political and military leadership.[15] In many countries, military leaders as professionals insist on the right to make decisions about deploying military force, as, for example, the Pakistani military insists upon in a quarrel with Pakistan's civilian president.[16] In democracies, however, elected civilian leaders are normally empowered to send their countries to war. The gray areas of war power involve the power of the national military relative to civilian authority in influencing force-commitment decisions. Those decisions first order the initiation of force employment, then determine the length and shape of such employments, an area where the military may and indeed should advise, but civilians ultimately finalize choices. In some situations, strong civilian oversight limits the power of military advice, yet in other situations, military leaders, as specialists in armed violence, have a disproportionate influence.

Political Tradition

National memory of shared political traditions helps to explain civil-military relations. For example, American civil-military relations originated from a traditional trepidation of centralized political authority and the need to check such power by giving the military a subordinate role in political affairs. China has a similar tradition of fearing the military, partly due to its predatory nature in the country's wars, where the difference between soldiers and bandits became blurred,[17] and thus Mao Zedong's dictum that "the (Communist) Party command the gun, and the gun must never be allowed to command the Party."[18] Moreover, scholars composed the elite of Chinese society, and soldiers resided in the lower societal rungs. However, in such countries as Argentina, Japan, and 1930s Germany, the armed forces embodied popular imagination as manifestations of the nation and thus were often able to control or strongly influence the state's political direction. In the former Soviet Union, the Red Army pushed away the previous blight of defeated Russian armies, reorienting tradition from national shame to patriotic pride, and kindled popular imagery with massive parades on national days with tanks, missiles, and other military paraphernalia as bemedaled veterans watched from atop Lenin's tomb. In many developing countries, such as Indonesia, Egypt, and Algeria, the military formed from liberation movements, thus enhancing its credentials as genuinely nationalistic and thus worthy to lead.

The Gradual Disappearance of the Permanent Military Coup

Strong civilian institutions and public support for them often limit the probability of a military coup, a direct power grab by soldiers. Although coups still occur, they usually happen in states with limited democracies or autocracies, and usually the officers who launch them try to right the ship of state as they think it should be, hold elections, and then return to their bases. They usually choose not to govern directly, often because their coups undo carefully constructed institutional relationships and are thus considered undesirable by those members of society who have benefited from institutional relations.[19] Moreover, military officers may find it difficult to manage a country using lessons learned from running an army, and military rulers frequently face a loss of legitimacy abroad, given the general unacceptability of military governance.[20] Thus military leaders may stand in the shadows of civilian rule, but they remain close to the seat of power, exercising gravitational pull over regime decisions while not actually making them.

The Military and the National Economy

In many countries the military plays a significant role in the national economy, both as a consumer and as a producer. The defense budget is a significant part of the national economy, and the military appetite for resources may dampen macroeconomic growth, particularly in developing countries where infrastructure and industrialization lag behind those of the developed world.[21] Military spending may also reduce available funds for social welfare items.[22] Additionally, the military often owns and operates factors of production—farms, factories, or services—sometimes producing its own goods, or in other cases generating income for military-related pursuits. In other cases, the military uses its societal position to skim money from economic enterprises, or controls the licenses necessary to operate a business, or provides security to companies for a price. Corruption has enriched many a military officer in countries where there are few checks on military power. The civil-military implications of military involvement in the economy include martial acquirement of political power to protect its economic interests, and competition with the private sector for goods and services, where the military may have a pronounced advantage because of its political position.

INTERPRETING CIVIL-MILITARY RELATIONS IN THE MIDDLE EAST

The roots of military power are deep in the Middle East. They involve both heroic stories and cautionary parables about force and society. In early Islamic times, Arab conquerors developed a special status in the lands they took. As Bonner notes, "The Arabs remained, ideally and also to a large extent in reality, a privileged, urban-dwelling warrior group."[23] Kennedy observes that because the Arab armies had considerable status within society, the state paid their salaries, perhaps preventing the rise of a European-style landed military aristocracy not dependent on the state for sustenance.[24] The role of the soldier as heroic savior of the land, the faith, and the expansion of horizons is also deeply embedded in Middle East lore. The earliest Islamic expansion from Arabia, led by Khalid ibn al-Walid, one of Islam's most able soldiers, in the first part of the sixth century, remains legend today in much of the Middle East, as do the exploits of Tariq ibn Ziyad, who sent his troops across the Mediterranean into Spain in 711.[25] The struggle against the Crusades also strengthened the status and influence of the warrior class, and, for Chamberlain, such events "transformed collections of pastoralist peoples into standing armies, inspired them with a sense of mission on behalf of Islam, and used them to create an empire in the agrarian world."[26] The tradition of a strong military in politics continued with the rule of the Mamluks, former battle captives who evolved into a warrior caste that founded a dynasty in Cairo that lasted from 1250 to 1517. The danger of a powerful military caste comes in part from the experience of the Ottoman conquerors of the Mamluks, with their military corps, the *Yeni Ceri*, known as Janissaries. The Janissaries, probably founded in the fourteenth century, grew in political stature over the centuries, dominating political decisions in Ottoman Turkey, gaining considerable authority over the sultan, abandoning their military duties, and sometimes murdering sultans who tried to resist them.[27] Finally Sultan Mahmoud II turned on the Janissary corps in 1826 and slaughtered them in one of the first acts of civilian control over the military in the Middle East. The military forces used for this were then subjected to considerable reform that emphasized military professionalism over military politics.[28]

Many modern Middle Eastern nations came into being under military tutelage. The lore of postimperial liberation movements, almost always led by military officers, burnished the standing of the warrior class in Middle East society. Some were built on the ruined foundations of failed regimes, as was the Turkish Republic under Kemal Atatürk on the ashes of the Ottoman Empire, or Egypt under Gamal Abdel Nasser, who as an army colonel led the Free Officers Movement that toppled the government of King Farouk in July 1952. Muammar Qadhafi, a colonel in the Libyan military, overthrew the Sanusi monarchy of King Idris in 1969 and announced that he was freeing Libya of a monarch who was tied to foreign influence. Hafiz al-Asad, a Syrian air force pilot, took the reins of Syria in 1970 during the Corrective Revolution, pushing Arab and Syrian nationalism as a justification for his Baath Party's right to rule the country. Military officer Reza Khan ended the Qajar dynasty in Persia in the 1920s. The Iraqi military toppled Iraq's King Faisal II in 1958 in the name of Iraqi nationalism, arguing that the Baghdad Pact, which tied Iraq to the United States and the United Kingdom, was a surrender of Iraqi sovereignty. The Jordanian Arab Legion, founded in 1921, long before Jordan's official founding in 1946, had a significant role in the founding of Jordan in 1946.[29]

In such countries, military "professionalism" takes on a different cast than it does in the traditional Huntington understanding. In the Middle East, soldiering is not just about preparing for and making war, it is about carrying the national flag well beyond the battlefield and into the capitol building. Often the point of war was nation-building where nations either had not existed or had existed in prostituted form, the illegitimate offspring of imperialists and their national lackeys. Thus professional identity for many senior military officers by necessity includes political involvement. While the military dictator may be rare, the officer corps is generally a powerful force behind the civilian national leader, and consequently officers' roles are circumscribed not by professional identity, but rather by negotiations defined by the interests held by both camps.

In other states, though, civilian founders feared that the military would assume excessive political power to challenge democratic decision making: Israel's first prime minister, David Ben Gurion, cautioned, "It is not up to the military to decide on the state's policy, laws and governmental arrangements,"[30] though later Israeli prime ministers would find out that this could be difficult in practice. Lebanon's civilian architects, Bishara al-Khoury and Riyad al-Sulh, kept the country's armed forces small and politically neutral in the wording of the National Pact, Lebanon's founding document, partly because prior to independence, the French-trained Lebanese military had been a source of French influence. It was also the case that the founders of both Israel and Lebanon likely realized that new democracies with strong militaries run a risk of reverting to military dictatorships resulting from the potential failures of democratic governance to deal decisively with the inevitable problems facing new nations.

The Military as Nation-Builders

As was the case in many postcolonial societies, countries in the Middle East had little national identity outside of revolutionary movements. Identity was often based on tribe, religion, or region, rather than on "nation." Saudi Arabia was an example, with four relatively autonomous regions (Najd, Asir, Hejaz, and Ash Sharqiyih), and Libya with three regions (Tripolitania, Cyrenaica, and Fazzan), and little to integrate them except opposition to the Italian occupier. Jordan has traditionally been divided between the original nomadic population (the Bedouins, or "East Bankers") and the immigrants who came from Palestine (the "West Bankers"). In Syria, elite divisions instead of geography separated the country, with a commercial urban class and a landlord class vying for power, until the military took over, wrapping itself in the cloak of Arab (and Syrian) nationalism.[31] As Vatikiotis notes, "In Egypt, Syria, and many other Middle Eastern countries, the nation-state concept is a relatively alien superstructure, imposed upon an existing society that functioned on the basis of Islamic and local traditions, which were not congenial to the nation-state idea."[32]

By contrast, Middle Eastern militaries were one of the few institutions that could disseminate national unity through education, technology, national symbolism, and an appetite for revolution against local rural, urban, and religious elites. The armed forces often recruited nationally, bringing together personnel from different areas and of different languages. They trained together, fought together, and often died together in battle. As an example, Hashim finds that Iraq in 1921 was a society cleaved by ethnic and tribal divisions, but the creation of the Iraqi army in that year, through the use of conscription, helped to inculcate a sense of Iraqi nationalism in young men drawn from Iraq's disparate regions.[33] Libya's young military leaders were able to accomplish similar integration, in similar ways, after the 1969 coup.[34]

The social impact of the military as an integrative force is mixed, though. While Sunni and Shia fought together in the 1981–1988 Iran-Iraq war, and a disproportionate number of Shia infantry troops died fighting for Saddam Hussein, the rift between the two groups remained wide after 2003. In Israel, the Israeli Defense Force (IDF) was once a nation-building agent, binding the "revisionist" and "labor" Zionists; it is becoming a dividing force. Israel has a minority Arab population whose members cannot serve (with a tiny exception) in the IDF, thus exacerbating the divisions within Israel between Jew and Arab (Israeli Druze may serve, though). Moreover, the split within Israel between the Jewish secular and the ultra-orthodox *(haredi)* also spills into the role of the military. The problem for Israel, according to Etzioni-Halevy, is that the state exempts haredi students from military service, exacerbating the growing rift in Israel between the secular and ultra-orthodox: "To a greater and greater extent, the military is turning from a nation binder, to a nation divider."[35] While the Lebanese military began as an integrated unit, the civil war of 1975–1989 rent the country into sectarian factions, and many Lebanese military officers took off their national uniforms and joined a militia of their religious persuasion. It took considerable effort to reconstitute a national army after the civil war ended.

The Middle East state is a relatively recent phenomenon, and national identity has been slow to adjust beyond local distinctiveness, so the national military often had a vacuum to fill. Said Egyptian President Hosni Mubarak on the fiftieth anniversary of the 1952 revolution: "The graduation of this new batch of military academy cadets coincides with the 50th anniversary of the glorious July Revolution that was carried out by a group of loyal sons of Egypt, Armed Forces officers who were motivated by the strong patriotic feelings and lofty loyalty to the people to make their blessed revolution."[36]

The Lebanese military also generated considerable public image through its role in a very small but significant action during the 1948 war. Before that war, as Khalaf notes, "members of the military claimed little status or social prestige,"[37] but a singular event changed this. While Lebanon officially did not participate in the 1948 war, it allowed its officers and men the opportunity to join the Liberation Army, which engaged with Israeli forces in May of that year near the small village of Malikiyya, on the Lebanese-Palestinian border.[38] When Israeli forces cut off Liberation Army supply lines in the area, regular units of the Lebanese military intervened to break the blockade, one of a few Arab military successes in a war in which Israeli forces ultimately prevailed. The resulting triumph became a rallying call to honor for the Lebanese military, enabling them to use Malikiyya as a platform from which to try to bridge the wide chasms that divided Lebanon. Malikiyya was a multi-ethnic campaign fought by a unified military, and thus, as Barak claims, "these qualities (army unity), which stood in contrast to the actual fragmentation of the army, the paralysis of the central government in Beirut, and the occupation of large parts of the country's territory by foreign forces, enabled this episode to be praised again as a symbol for the army's unity, discipline, *esprit de corps* and professionalism."[39] Thus Lebanese soldiers were able to translate the Malikiyya myth into a significant political and economic role not only as liberators, but as unifiers. That role lasted for years, until the civil war and the questionable neutrality of the Lebanese army began to call Malikiyya into question. Still, in a country without a majority religious group, with weak political institutions, and lacking a national identity forged in war or an independence movement, the military used Malikiyya as one of the more effective symbols of national unity, even though that symbol was forged in a battle of small importance and largely forgotten by military historians. The military also enhanced its image in 1952 when its commander, Fouad Chehab, refused to let it govern when political paralysis threatened to pull the country into partition. Chehab understood the danger of allowing the largely Christian army to become enmeshed in Lebanon's confessional political system, even in the wake of disorder sparked by charges of corruption in Bishara Khoury's government.[40] The closest Lebanon got to military rule was when Chehab surrounded himself with former and current soldiers, using his military background to reform Lebanon's then-chaotic political system, a style that Khazen described as "a mild form of 'military rule.'"[41]

Jordan's military was able to cultivate similar images of its national status from its participation in the Battle of Karameh, in March 1968, when Israeli forces raided the town to eliminate Palestinian militants living there. But combined Jordanian-Palestinian forces drove out the Israeli invaders, inflicting more than one hundred casualties, and thus allowing the Jordanian armed forces to embellish their national credentials.[42] For both Egypt and Syria, the heroic images of their militaries on the opening days of the 1973 war are artistically captured in two similar dioramas in Cairo and Damascus showing triumphant Arab warriors crushing the Israeli foe in true socialist realism (both dioramas are gifts from North Korea).

The military had other advantages beyond possessing national symbols in nation-building. The military officers who often led independence movements in developing countries were "high modernizers" who placed a premium on science and technology, as Cook observes. They also believed that only those who were steeped in science and technology had the right to rule, a criterion often met best by the military.[43] In newly free countries, the officers of the armed forces usually possessed high levels of education (often in the former colonial country), along with the organizational skills and societal integration mechanisms to rule directly or indirectly. Where there were no contending classes of business or rural elites, the officers took a dominant role in the nation, as they did in Iraq, for example, carrying their understanding of Arab ideals forward as a national story line.[44]

The Military as Negative Symbol: the Wrong Stuff

In some cases, the professional military was not a symbol of national unity and identity, but instead was seen as representative of foreign domination or influence. The case of Pahlavi Iran is instructive here. The national Pahlavi dynasty was formed by a soldier, Reza Khan, who adopted as a role model the Western-inspired modernizer Kemal Atatürk, and invited the United States and Britain in to establish oil concessions.[45] Khan, who renamed himself Reza Shah, built his army on a Western model, bringing in Western advisers and purchasing Western military equipment for his troops.[46] Once in power, Khan used his military, sometimes ruthlessly, to cement his hold on the country.[47] His son, Muhammad Reza Shah, continued the path of Western-inspired modernity after Britain and the United States mobilized retired and active military officers to return him to power in 1953. Muhammad Reza Shah lavished funds on his military, consuming one-third of total American arms sales at the end of his reign.[48] Such foreign dependence clashed with the shah's empowering narrative of Persian nationalism, helping his secular, westernized pillar to collapse under the bulldozer of the Shia revolution in 1979.

Thus after the 1979 revolution, many of the westernized secular military leaders went before firing squads, and distrust of the military remains to this day in the Islamic Republic of Iran. While there is a regular Iranian military, Artesh ("army" in Persian), consisting of the traditional three branches (army, navy, air force), there are also the Army of the Guardians of the Islamic Revolution; the Islamic Revolutionary Guard Corps (IRGC), also with three branches; and the Basij, a 300,000-strong paramilitary force affiliated with the IRGC, which counts President Mahmoud Ahmadinejad as a former member. Al-Quds, the IRGC's guerrilla warfare component, is another locus of authority whose funding line is tied directly to the supreme leader. The power of the Basij was obvious during the upheavals following the June 2009 election when they, and not units of the Artesh, took to the streets to beat back the demonstrators protesting Ahmadinejad's allegedly fixed electoral victory.

The military never regained the status it had under the shah, and national identity days feature parades of Basij or Army of the Guardians units more than they do tanks and airplanes. As Crane, Lal, and Martini argue, "While the Artesh remains the critical military force, the IRGC has become an increasingly powerful political participant."[49] The powerful role of the IRGC is evidenced by both the senior government positions its members hold and its custodianship of

Iran's nuclear programs.[50] The political role for the IRGC has also increased under Supreme Leader Ali Khamenei, who, unlike his predecessor, Ayatollah Ruhollah Khomeini, lacked strong clerical and revolutionary credentials. Thus Khamenei "desperately needs the military's support," according to Ganji.[51] Consequently, Iran's military budget has doubled during Khamenei's reign, to over 5 percent of GDP, and numerous high-ranking officers serve in the Iranian Majlis and have run and won in local elections.[52] The IRGC's power, already considerable, increased even more after the disputed elections of 2009. While the outcome divided even the powerful cleric class, the IRGC emerged as the leading power broker in Iran, particularly after taking control of the Basij militia in 2007. According to one analysis, "Its aggressive drive to silence dissenting views has led many political analysts to describe the events surrounding the June 12 presidential election as a military coup."[53]

MILITARY POWER AND POLITICAL POWER

Huntington's argument, noted earlier, argues that professionalism and tradition keep the American military largely confined to pursuing the art of conflict. However, Kamrava finds that introducing military professionalism in the greater Middle East has not led to "the military's depoliticization and increased subordination to civilian control."[54] While there are no military dictatorships in the Middle East, the military generally has more political and economic influence there than in the United States.

When it relinquishes national political rule, the military often remains behind the curtains, watching to ensure that its understanding of national identity remains in place. While most former military officers shed their uniforms and donned business suits or robes upon assuming the presidency of their countries (Gamal Abdel Nasser in Egypt, Hafiz al-Asad in Syria, Muammar Qadhafi in Libya), they usually ruled with the assistance of former military colleagues, and the military often served to protect their rule as much as it did to protect the country. Of course, former military leaders also kept a wary eye on their fellow officers still in uniform, understanding that other officers could blaze the same path to the presidential palace that they had. Still, the close bonds that many of these officers developed in the military served them well in the political realm. Technically, they become civilians after leaving the military to assume their new political positions. However, their base of support often continues to be the military, which can crowd out other potential groups in the contest for authority and influence.

The Military and Middle East Democracy

In the Middle East, as elsewhere in the developing world, the military often protects the status quo, and where the status quo involves centralized governance, such protectors rule. Thus the path to democratization in the Middle East often runs through the military barracks because senior officers often fear that democracy may erode their often privileged positions in politics and society, or that democracy will open doors to old enemies (Islamists, Marxists, or reformers, for example).

There may be ways to encourage the military to accept the coming of democracy, though in some cases the military may choose not to oppose democratic advances, and thus democratic reformers may have to engage the military in some sort of pact to move it out of the path of reform. Cook proposes that such pacts would give the military a portion of the power it had before the advance of democracy, even though such pacts would limit the progress of pluralist participation. However, he argues that as democracy takes root, the military's privileged position may wither away, as it has in Turkey.[55]

Turkey's democracy has progressed forward through cycles that saw a gradual diminishing of military influence over the results of public choices. The Turkish military has historically intervened to preserve its understanding of a secular republic, challenging an Islamist vision of Turkey, but at the same time restoring democratic rule after doing housecleaning in the name of Kemalism. Coups, though, appear to be things of the past. Thus, the military tacitly threatened unspecified action when the parliament, dominated by the Justice and Democracy Party (Adalet ve Kalkınma Partisi, or AKP), moved in an Islamist direction by passing legislation repealing a headscarf ban in Turkey's public universities in 2007, but there was no coup. The next year, Turkey's Constitutional Court heard a challenge to the AKP's legal status to govern because of its religious identity, and senior military officers were widely believed to have encouraged the state prosecutor's charges. The court dismissed the charges by a single vote, and though the outcome may have been a veiled reminder of the military's limits on testing secularism, the military did remain in the barracks after the decision. Does that portend a change in Turkish civil-military relations?

As Satana notes, the Turkish armed forces has undergone evolutionary changes since the 1960s, departing from its predominant role as protector against internal threats (real or imagined) to Turkey and embracing more traditional roles such as external defense and peacekeeping.[56] Although domestic terrorism from both left- and right-wing extremists and violence from the Partiya Karkerên Kurdistan (PKK, or Kurdish Worker's Party) began as internal threats, they now extend to the Iraq-Turkey border, as PKK fighters have taken refuge in neighboring Iraq, from where they launch cross-border attacks against Turkey. Turkey's military is also growing as a professional armed force, with an expensive weapons procurement strategy and strengthened professional military education.[57] Because of this, and because of public support for Turkish democracy, Satana argues that "the continued role of the military in 'guiding,' but not directly controlling, the political system will change as the transformation is complete and as internal factors permit."[58]

It might be argued that a military retreat from politics would pave the road to democracy, but the Algerian case indicates that in addition to removing the military impediment to democracy, countries also require civilian institutional foundations. Algerian military leaders have never been far from the seats of power since independence in 1962. As noted earlier, Algeria's armed forces gained legitimacy through the struggle for independence, enjoying access to privileges and benefits, though their reputation suffered from their inability to curb insurgent violence as well as its own brutality during the country's 1992–2004 civil war.[59] The military's powerful position after 1992 limited presidential initiatives and actions. As Roberts notes, "The army's top echelon . . . was now tending to control the defense ministry. From this position, it was able to box in and hamstring the presidency, sabotage its peace initiatives, and dominate the political arena."[60] After Abdelaziz Bouteflika assumed the presidency in 1999, it took him five years to bring the Algerian General Staff under control, which occurred only after the 2004 general election forcing the retirement of General Staff head General Mohamed Lamari.[61] Thus Bouteflika was able to reduce the military role in Algerian political space; however, for Roberts, the result was an opening of public dialogue once restricted under military influence, without any other democratic implications.[62] This is partly because Algeria retains weak civil political institutions, and so demilitarization alone was insufficient to allow democracy to advance. Moreover, should Bouteflika not run for reelection in 2009 (pending as of this writing), the result could be a return to military rule, particularly if Algerian security forces are not successful in stamping out the vestiges of violent Islamism that remain after the military has returned to the barracks.

Demilitarization may not pave a democratic road, but instead could strengthen its obverse, strong state rule, by removing the soldier as a check to single-party governance. In Egypt, for example, during Nasser's time, the military controlled the important ministries, an officer served as vice president, and military officers sat on newspaper editorial boards.[63] But the aftermath of the disastrous 1967 war began the process of demilitarization, largely due to the harm the loss did to the military establishment. President Anwar al-Sadat accelerated the decline of military influence with his "corrective revolution" beginning in 1971, when Sadat replaced officers loyal to Nasser in his cabinet with civilians, further lessening the military's political role.[64] But this apparent withdrawal to the barracks did not open doors for liberal reforms, largely because Sadat and his successor, Hosni Mubarak, shared worldviews with their former colleagues in uniform, many of whom served in his cabinet.[65] As one analyst noted, Egypt's professional military has eschewed direct interference in Egyptian political space, as it did in Turkey, but its leaders have a role in "avoiding chaos" in society.[66] A similar situation exists in Syria, where many military commanders bore fealty to President Bashar al-Asad's father, Hafiz al-Asad, and that loyalty continued on to the son (those who challenged Bashar's assumption to power were arrested or relieved of their duties).[67] Members of the Syrian senior military retain considerable domestic political power without running the state directly, with close ties to Syria's economy, and considerable leverage in Lebanon, which was largely under the control of the Syrian armed forces between 1992 and 2004.

Military Coups and Shadow Military Power

There are a number of cases where the military has either launched a coup or acted in ways to challenge ruling authority short of a complete takeover when it believes that its understanding of national identity or its power base is threatened. The goals for the military in such cases may be to replace political civilian leadership with political military leadership, or it may be to remove a leader the military considers unfavorable and to replace that person with someone acceptable to the armed forces. Consider the situations in Syria, Mauritania, Turkey, Saudi Arabia, Morocco, and Israel.

Syria's new civilian government came under attack very early in its life, when the Syrian military suffered devastating defeat in the 1948 war with Israel. Syrian troops went into battle with insufficient supplies, and these and other indicators of poor preparation and leadership led to riots and the resignation of Prime Minister Jamil Mardam. From that point on, the Syrian military played significant roles in both removing and replacing leaders they deemed insufficiently nationalist. They also launched coups to protect their own interests, as, for example, after the "cooking fat" crisis of 1949, noted at the beginning of this chapter.[68] The military had to fight for its vision of nationalist identity because the nascent Baathist groups were often dominated by the intelligentsia or the various "Arab clubs" that had genuine mass appeal in post-Ottoman Syria.[69]

Elements in Jordan's armed forces also attempted a coup against King Hussein in April 1957, after the king and his prime minister, Suleiman al-Nabulsi, disagreed publicly over Jordanian membership in the Arab Solidarity Agreement with Egypt and Syria. Chief of Staff Ali Abu Nuwar sided with Nabulsi, and his troops surrounded Amman, but officers loyal to the king preempted the effort.[70] The Iraqi military also launched numerous coup attempts against Saddam Hussein, with at least four between 1988 and 1990 alone, and likely there were others, as evidenced by the periodic execution of senior officers.[71] And the Saudi Arabian military has attempted coups—in 1955, 1962, 1969, and 1977—over various issues, including infiltration by pro-Nasser officers.[72] Because of concerns about the loyalty of the regular Saudi Arabian military, the country's royal family has relied for decades on the Saudi Arabian National Guard, initially formed by King Abdul Aziz al-Saud on the basis of tribal loyalty, and often placed geographically in positions where it can protect the al-Saud family from a military coup.[73]

In August 2008, four Mauritanian generals, fired by the civilian leadership, launched a coup and took power themselves. General Mohamed Ould Abdel Aziz, head of the presidential guards, proclaimed himself president, and the other three generals formed a "state council," after arresting and detaining President Sidi Ould Cheikh Abdallahi, whom Mauritanian voters had elected after General Abdel Aziz ousted the last government in 2005. The ruling generals accused the Abdallahi regime of corruption and compromise with radical Islamists. Mauritania, which has seen ten coups or coup efforts since independence in 1960, had suffered from several terrorist attacks in 2007, causing a drop in tourism and resulting in the cancellation of the Paris-to-Dakar road rally, which drew considerable prestige and revenue for the country.[74]

While Mauritania's military has a long history of coups, it also has been willing to hand back power to civilians through elections. After the August 2005 coup, the plotters, led by General Eali Ouled Mohammed Vall, first demanded a two-year period of military rule through the Military Council for Justice and Democracy. However, during that term, which the ruling junta shortened to nineteen months, the council passed a number of measures that not only allowed for local elections, but also limited military participation in future elections. After the nineteen-month period, the council stepped down to allow elections in March 2007. This was more typical of Mauritanian coups; for example, a 1978 coup resulted in Mauritania's first civilian government (though it was a dictatorship), with the military returning to the barracks. An unsuccessful 1978 coup underscored the tensions between the black and Arab populations of Mauritania, as the coup leaders were black soldiers who apparently resented the Arab domination of the military (though the high cost of Mauritania's conflict with Morocco over the Western Sahara also played a role). Still, the coups seemed to be less about acquiring military power than they were about expressing grievances against particular civilian regimes.

Morocco's professional military attempted at least two coups against King Hassan II in 1971 and 1972. The first coup, allegedly inspired by corruption within the royal family, took place at the king's palace in the summer of 1971, and the monarch escaped. The second involved an effort by the Royal Moroccan Air Force to shoot down Hassan's personal plane as it returned from Paris in 1972. Again, the king barely survived the effort, and numerous military leaders were executed or imprisoned, or "committed suicide."[75] Since that time, King Hassan and his heir, King Mohammed VI, have distrusted the Moroccan military, though Mohammed VI has relaxed his position somewhat, choosing to equip his forces with modern weapons, possibly to keep them loyal.[76]

The coup is the most likely but not the only method for the military to attain power. In Lebanon's case, a military government emerged briefly in 1952, when General Fouad Chehab briefly became prime minister after a government deadlock. Later General Michel Aoun received an appointment as prime minister (traditionally reserved for a Sunni Muslim), even though he was a Maronite Christian, from President Amin Gemayel, who broke Lebanese political protocol after a divided parliament could not choose a successor for him.[77] Aoun did appoint a military cabinet consisting of officers from the major Lebanese religious groups. The experiment did not last long, as factional rivalry erupted between parts of the Lebanese army and militia forces allied with Syria, and ultimately Syrian forces ousted Aoun.[78]

Although coups are the most notorious means for the military to attain power, they can exercise political power in less direct ways, through "shadow power," standing in the shadows behind the national leadership, whispering advice, and being ready to pounce should they not get policies to their liking. Turkey provides an example. Before the founding of modern Turkey, the Ottoman Empire relied on its military to maintain control over a substantial portion of the Middle East and the Balkans. The Ottoman military scored some spectacular successes during World War I—the campaign against the British Commonwealth forces at Gallipoli, for example—though the allies did defeat them in the end. The legend of Gallipoli, though, burnished the legendary status of General Mustafa Kemal, who also led Turkish forces against the Greek invasion and against Russian forces in eastern Turkey just after World War I. Kemal translated his battlefield triumphs into political success by building Young Turk cells in the military to conquer the remnants of the Ottoman Empire and becoming president in 1923. Kemal, whose name the parliament changed to Kemal Atatürk in 1938, pushed many reforms to end the religious power of the Ottoman Empire, believing that secular Europe (where he had studied) was a model for Turkey's future. He abolished the caliphate, a symbol of Turkey's inheritance of the core of the Sunni tradition, along with religious dress, schools, orders (dervishes, for example), courts, and all other trappings of official Islam. The secular state he established became institutionalized in Turkish politics, and the Turkish military became the self-appointed guardian of Turkish secularism.

The Turkish military toppled the government in 1960 after Prime Minister Menderes pushed for a larger private sector. The soldiers again intervened in 1980 after Turkey's economy teetered on the brink of collapse. The military did restore democracy once again, but after years of economic malaise, more voters were turning to Islam, and several Islamic-oriented parties rose to challenge the secular tradition. This trend, coupled with the rise of Islamist splinter groups, fund-raising by Islamic groups outside of Turkey from expatriate Turkish workers, and the growth of illegal Islamist schools, was especially worrisome to the military.[79] Said one Turkish general, "Destroying fundamentalism is of life or death importance," as the military feared that the visible symbols of Islam in government, "could give Turkey a bad name."[80] When Refah (Welfare) Party head Necmittin Erbakan became prime minister in a coalition government in 1995, the military intervened to pull its plug two years later. The Islamist-oriented followers of Refah turned to a new leader, Recep Tayyip Erdoğan, the former mayor of Istanbul, who helped to found the third incarnation of a Turkish Islamist-oriented party, the Justice and Democracy Party (AKP). In the November 2002 elections, the AKP won a sizeable victory with 34 percent of the total vote, giving it a majority of seats in parliament.

After the AKP landslide win in the 2002 national election, military opposition to the ruling party took a different tack. Rather than launching a coup, as it had done previously, the armed forces moved behind the scenes to weaken AKP power. In 2007, the military joined other secularist forces to prevent Abdullah Gül, the foreign minister, from becoming president. In 2008, the military appeared to join forces with the Constitutional Court to declare the AKP unconstitutional. While the association between the military and the court judges was difficult to prove, much attention focused on a secret meeting in March 2008 between the second-highest judge of the court with General Ilker Başbug, commander of Turkish land forces. The meeting, which occurred just after the AKP had changed Turkish law to permit the wearing of headscarves in Turkish public universities, incensed many in the military, and shortly after the meeting between the judge and General Başbug, the court's chief prosecutor announced indictments against the AKP party and seventy-one of its officials, including the prime minister and the president.[81] The play swung the other way several months later when Istanbul's chief prosecutor, Aykut Cengiz Engin, filed indictments against eighty-six people, including two senior retired generals, for plotting a coup against the AKP, while party officials strenuously denied any connection to the indictments.[82] Only six months later Turkish authorities claimed to have discovered yet another coup plot (the tenth that year), as they announced the detention of over forty people, including three retired generals.[83] Whether this was a true military plot or a coup effort planned by military officers working in league with criminal elements in Turkey, as reported by some of the Turkish press, was unclear.[84] Still, the red flags that went up after this spate of arrests of senior military, active and retired, reminded observers that the Turkish military still guards its image as the protector of secular Kemalism.

The Israeli armed forces also have used their influence to remove civilian leaders with whom they have disagreements. Quarrels between the prime minister and the professional military in Israel are common, usually resulting in the resignation of the chief of staff of the IDF. However, senior and retired IDF officers can also work to either change prime ministerial policy or to defeat the prime minister should that fail. The first term of Benyamin Netanyahu was instructive in the latter case: By 1999, three years into his term, Netanyahu had drawn the ire of Chief of Staff Amnon Lipkin-Shahak over a number of policy issues, and the military rallied behind both Lipkin-Shahak and former general Ehud Barak to help defeat Netanyahu in 1999. As Peri notes, Netanyahu lost the election for many reasons, but reserve and retired IDF officers played a critical role.[85]

Limiting the Military in Politics. The military may own the country's guns, but unless it is willing to shoot its way to political power, countervailing forces in most countries limit military influence.

In Egypt, the Muslim Brotherhood have gained power through the ballot box, and while the Brotherhood is banned as a party (Egypt prohibits religious-based political parties), members have run for parliament as independents, and in the June 2007 elections they gained most of the one-third of parliamentary seats up for contestation. The Brotherhood has proposed strict limits on executive power, insisting that the military stay out of politics and that the defense minister be a civilian.[86] In Turkey, the AKP's growing influence has challenged the traditional power of the army, with the AKP-dominated parliament passing a bill that for the first time allowed civilian courts to prosecute military officers. Shortly after passage of the bill, a court charged a Turkish colonel with participating in a coup attempt.[87]

The Power of the Paramilitary. The study of civil-military relations focuses largely on the state-supported military, but many countries have rival military forces, some responsible for domestic security, often under the interior ministry, while others represent religious groups, tribes, or other subnational forces. They exercise considerable political power and often rival, if not exceed, the national military in such power. They are also a political check on the professional military. Iran offers an example, as noted earlier, where one of the most powerful elements in Iranian society is the paramilitary IRGC, with over 150,000 troops and naval and air units. In the 2005 elections, the IRGC favored Mahmoud Ahmadinejad over his rival, Mohammad Khatami, and IRGC units worked to maximize voter turnout. The IRGC also exercises considerable influence through its membership on the Supreme National Security Council and through a large number of informal networks connected to top leadership.[88]

Some Middle East countries adopted the French gendarmerie model, where a civilian armed force is used to maintain domestic order. Algeria has such a force, as does Morocco. The gendarmerie are often attached to the ministry of defense and trained and equipped by the regular military, but they hold a separate functional domain and are often more important to the national government than are the regular military. Some countries have troops attached to the ministry of the interior (unlike the US Department of the Interior, which manages national land, most interior ministries are for internal policing). Sometimes the state has to call upon the gendarmerie in matters affecting domestic security, where the use of the national army might divide it. In 1958 Lebanese President Camille Chamoun called upon the Lebanese gendarmerie to tamp out sectarian violence, but the gendarmerie were poorly equipped for the situation, and Chamoun had to call in private militia forces.[89]

In some Middle East countries, private militia forces like the ones Chamoun called upon are often more powerful than the national military and receive much more political support. This has been true historically in Lebanon, where powerful families have their own private militias. These militias are usually the belligerents in Lebanon's tragic civil war, with the regular military usually standing on the sidelines during these conflicts. Private armies have also been dominant in the occupied Palestinian territories and in Iraq. Militias may be more significant in countries where tribal relations remain strong, since militias are often associated with particular tribes. Since tribal power is often inverse to national power, weak national governments create a power space with a weak national military, and tribal militias often fill that vacuum. Sometimes these militias adopt national defense as a mission, as have Hizbullah in Lebanon and Hamas in Gaza. Such claims blur an already fuzzy line between legitimate national defense forces and militia forces and, moreover, militias often compete with national militaries for resources, including people, with the potential to weaken both forces.

THE MILITARY AND THE NATIONAL ECONOMY

The national military is an important national economic actor. The armed forces are often among the largest consumers in the country, and their cost alone has a significant economic impact. The military is a more attractive employer in difficult economic times, and economic crises sometimes provoke the military to end civilian rule, as noted earlier in the 1960 and 1980 Turkish coups.

The Iranian IRGC provides an example of how the military can penetrate the national economy. Its members have not only competed for political office, but also used their powerful political ties to gain access to the national economy. Their members got permission to import embargoed goods (Western clothing, appliances, and construction materials, for example) and sold them at a profit. They have other commercial interests, including operating the Imam Khomeini International Airport, taking it over by force from the Turkish company that built it.[90] Other officers, along with Revolutionary Guards and law enforcement officers, have financed large projects in Tehran's suburbs and gained access to low-interest loans to finance their many endeavors.[91] According to another report, "The corps has become a vast military-based conglomerate, with control of Iran's missile batteries, oversight of its nuclear program and a multibillion-dollar business empire reaching into nearly every sector of the economy. It runs laser eye-surgery clinics, manufactures cars, builds roads and bridges, develops gas and oil fields and controls black-market smuggling, experts say."[92]

The military also found a role to play in other Middle East countries. As Jordan's economic conditions deteriorated sharply in the 1990s, the Jordanian military was able to take a larger role in supplying economic benefits to the population. As Baylouny notes, though, "The narrow group of the military substituted for previous welfare provided to a broad segment of the population. In the atmosphere of general economic crisis, welfare to one section of the population was welcomed. While new economic policies themselves generated substantial protest, the increasing numbers and economic benefits of the military proceeded without objection. The result contributed to the demise of political liberalization."[93] The recipients, probably fearful of losing their welfare benefits from the armed forces, became reluctant to protest against unpopular regime policies. The Jordanian military provided more than just transfer payments; it was also a major source of employment throughout Jordanian history, employing over 30 percent of all village men in 1960, making it Jordan's largest employer after agriculture. It steadily increased, such that by 1975, 25 percent of Jordan's total labor force was in the armed forces, gaining not just jobs but also the benefits such as health care and retirement pensions that came with service.[94] The Royal Jordanian military also helps to stimulate the economy by offering civilian training in radar technology, supporting the flying element for the national police, and collecting revenues through the customs service.[95] The Tunisian military offers similar training for civilian air traffic controllers. In Egypt the military forces raise much of their own budget through a number of enterprises. They own and operate bottled-water plants, a garbage bag factory, Cairo's largest mall, and medical facilities, and employ soldiers as well as civilians in these enterprises.[96] The military also produces washing machines, clothing, and stationery, and engages in infrastructure construction, with Law 32 of 1979 allowing the military to take the off-book revenue from these activities and place it in special private bank accounts.[97] This makes the defense ministry a profit-making institution, though it is also part of the state, with full access to state benefits, including favorable commercial rulings, subsidies, and the occasional wink from state inspectors in cases of code violations. The military may also receive contracts from former officers for business activities. Moreover, retired Egyptian generals are "well taken care of," often getting lucrative jobs in the private sector after they leave the service.[98]

The impact of such activity is questionable. Militaries are rarely efficient in the marketplace, and military enterprises are no exception. Unlike private entrepreneurs, military operators can get operating funds directly from the state rather than having to raise them in the capital marketplace, and often the state provides a buyer for military-produced goods—often the state itself. Since private operations often cannot compete with such influence, the military enterprise becomes a monopoly.

Middle Eastern militaries often consume a larger portion of national resources than in other parts of the world. Saudi Arabia spends around 10 percent of its GDP on national defense, Oman 11.4 percent, Yemen around 6.6 percent, Qatar 10 percent, Syria 5.9 percent, and Israel 7.3 percent, compared to the United States at around 4 percent.[99]

Egyptian military spending also attempted to fuel the country's economy. Egypt runs a tank plant in Helwan, a suburb of Cairo that employed over 5,000 workers to coproduce American-designed M1A1 tanks between 1993 and 1998.[100] The costs of coproducing this tank were justified by arguing that one of the plant's many benefits was that it would create 21,950 jobs over its operational life.[101] While the jobs created did expose workers to a higher level of technology than they might have found in Cairo, the tanks themselves contributed little to the country's economic growth, and, moreover, pressure to keep the plant operating meant that it continued to manufacture more tanks than the Egyptian army could buy (Turkey refused an offer to buy them for its own military), so the unwanted tanks were parked in a huge warehouse.

WAR, POLITICS, AND CIVIL-MILITARY RELATIONS

War, as Clausewitz reminds, is ultimately about defending or advancing political objectives. A decision about war is thus a political one, to be made by those responsible for governance, and in democratic or semi-democratic systems, it would be expected to be made through the lens of public accountability. However, such a decision also obviously involves the military, which under democratic conditions operates only with the guidance of civilian authority accountable to the polity. What often emerges is a delicate dance between elected officials (or civilian officials in non-free countries) and military leaders about decisions for war. In an ideal situation for democracy, elected officials make the decision and the military salutes smartly and carries out civilian orders. But it does not usually work out that way in the Middle East. In a complex network of factors, including the power of the military over strategic assessment, the armed forces often trump civilian authority in military force decisions.

For Brooks, explanations for Egyptian actions in the 1967 war lie significantly in the reality that Egypt's military, spoiling for war with Israel, not only doctored strategic assessment, but also kept key civilians, including President Gamal Abdel Nasser, isolated from their decision making: "Political officials were so marginalized from the military command that they were often left in the dark about key decisions even when they had profound diplomatic implications."[102] The result was a disaster for Egypt, and it spread to Jordan when Nasser, apparently believing false reports of military victories over the Israelis from his generals, encouraged Jordan's King Hussein to join the fight,[103] and thus disaster for the Arab side in the 1967 war also befell Jordan.

Israel is the only country in the Middle East regarded as "free" by the Freedom House annual survey, but Barak and Sheffer argue that most Western models of civil-military relations are inadequate to understand even Israel: "Western 'ideal types' of civil-military relations are inapplicable to Israel since they presuppose a predominant civilian sector. What is needed, hence, is a more down-to-earth approach that would start from the premise that the civilian sector in Israel is weak compared to its security counterpoint and explains the causes for this situation."[104] Other studies confirm that the Israeli armed forces have exercised considerable latitude on decisions to use force, often at the expense of civilian elected officials. Some of this power stems from the broad grant of authority from Israel's Basic Law, a document that substitutes for a constitution. The Basic Law grants considerable power to cabinet members and to the chief of the general staff of the Israeli Defense Forces in particular.[105] This has had consequences for Israeli civil-military relations, which are reflected in cases where the military not only used force on its own initiative, but also resisted using force even in the face of orders from the prime minister. The so-called Sebastia incident showed the latter tendency. In 1975 Prime Minister Yitzhak Rabin ordered Chief of Staff Mordechai Gur to clear away an illegal Jewish settlement in the West Bank, but Gur refused, citing the potential of high casualties. Gur implied that he would resign if Rabin ordered him to remove the settlement with Israeli military forces, and without support from defense minister Shimon Peres, Rabin backed down.[106] The IDF's power in politics grew as the settlement issue became more divisive, polarizing Israeli political space and sowing chaos: Israel had six prime ministers between the 1991 Madrid conference and 2006, and as a result "the military was sucked into filling the political leadership vacuum; its political power grew and its involvement in national policymaking expanded."[107]

Other cases demonstrate the lack of civilian oversight and its consequences. Schiff claims there is no clear authority for civilian politicians over the Israeli armed forces: "Often, rules are made to define the scope of military authority and then changed depending on the particular government cabinet. All this precludes the possibility for a distinct and well-regulated civilian authority to enable control of the military."[108] Sela considers Israeli deployments and operations in south Lebanon symptomatic of the lack of political oversight for the military, particularly in operation Peace for Galilee, Israel's expansion beyond its "security zone" in 1996, which resulted in heavy civilian casualties in Lebanon and confrontation with Syrian forces. Says Sela of the situation, "That the political system allowed the operation to expand beyond the promised limits of 45–50 km into a full-fledged war, including a confrontation with the Syrian forces in Lebanon and the siege of Beirut, before questioning the military's conduct, attests to the blindness and ignorance of the politicians when confronted by a determined coalition of generals—retired and in uniform—in the IDF and Ministry of Defense."[109] Maoz arrives at a similar conclusion when examining the relationship between Israel's security community and its civilian political leadership: "It (the security community) has also succeeded in concealing numerous blunders and continuous policy failures or in diverting attention from the ineffectiveness of many of the policies it supported. The cabinet, the parliament, the judiciary and the civilian bodies that are authorized to conduct policy planning and policy evaluation . . . lack the ability and the will to properly oversee policy in these areas."[110] Political scandals further weakened civilian governance, with President Moshe Katsav accused of sexual misconduct, Prime Minister Ehud Olmert accused of taking bribes from an American benefactor while mayor of Jerusalem, and Justice Minister Haim Ramon found guilty of sexual harassment of a female Israeli soldier and forced to resign.[111]

It is also true that the Israeli military has almost always complied with operational directives from civilian authorities. Even during times of military crisis, the armed forces have obeyed civil political instructions, as they did during the 1967 war, when Defense Minister Moshe Dayan chastised the IDF chief for calling in air strikes without civilian permission, or the 1973 war, when the IDF chief's call for preemptive air strikes was ignored by both the defense and prime ministers.[112]

Lebanon's military has also engaged in internal operations (its only field of battle in Lebanon's history, with the brief exception of Malikiyya) without much consultation with political authorities. A case in point was the 1976 decision to take the Tall al-Za'atar area southeast of Beirut from the Palestinian militias operating from it. The initial objective came from a coalition of Christian militias, but the Lebanese army, which was starting to disintegrate, worked with the Tanzim, a splinter group from the larger Christian Kata'ib militia, but without consultation or approval of Lebanese party leaders.[113] In response to this uncoordinated action by the army, Lebanese President Bashir Gemayel pushed for a Joint Command Council of the Lebanese Forces in August 1976 to create a military chain of command that would be separate from the militias. There was considerable opposition to the creation of the joint command, but ultimately it succeeded. One consequence was that the government used the Lebanese armed forces to attack a stronghold of Chamoun's "Tiger" militia in July 1980, resulting in the deaths of 150 to 500 mostly Christians, while forcing the integration of the Tigers into the regular army. As Snider concludes, this was the first time the Maronites of central Lebanon were represented by a central organization, the Lebanese armed forces.[114]

CONCLUSIONS

The role of the military varies from country to country in the modern Middle East, but in all cases it is greater in the political, economic, and security spheres than in the North American or European context. Such a relation is not necessarily undesirable, though, as the military can play a positive role in guiding an often fractured polity toward national unity and identity. In many cases soldiers played a critical role in liberation and national integration, binding tribe and region together into a semblance of a modern state. The military, which often had its roots in the underclasses, sometimes rose to challenge elite power and dominance of state and economic power. However, once established, the armed forces did not always return to the parade ground, but rather remained as a shadow behind the executive, ready to remove the head of state should it not abide by the military image of proper rule. The military often maintains a significant role in war-making power, and thus military force is sometimes used without much input from civil authorities, sometimes to unproductive and costly ends.

The modern Middle East is engaging in global patterns of political and economic practice, though at a slower rate than other regions. Democracy and market-driven economies are expanding in the region, and along with those trends are the patterns of a modern military whose increasing professionalism is likely to reduce the shadow governments that have dominated much of the Middle East narrative in the decades since independence.

NOTES

* This chapter reflects only the views of the author, and not those of any US government agency. The author is grateful to Douglas Pfeiffer, Daniel Hughes, and Christopher Hemmer for helpful comments. Any remaining errors or interpretations are the author's responsibility.

1. Patrick Seale, *The Struggle for Syria: A Study of Post-War Arab Politics, 1945–1958* (New Haven, CT: Yale University Press, 1965), pp. 42–44.

2. The term "armed forces" generally refers to the professional active national military, whose primary responsibility is the national defense against outside forces. It normally does not include gendarmerie forces, which often have support from the active military but serve as domestic police agents. It also does not usually include militia forces, whose identity is often at the subnational level, as, for example, Hizbullah's armed wing. Iran does have militia forces at the national level, the Basij, discussed in this chapter, who serve the religious leadership. In this chapter the focus is on the professional military, but it also includes the influence of the militia or paramilitary when those forces have clear support from the armed forces, or when they assume roles normally taken by the state military. In this chapter, though, parastate militaries like the Basij, their parent organization, the Revolutionary Guards, and other such militia often encroach on traditional military roles and missions, and thus they are included in the discussion.

3. Peter D. Feaver, "The Civil-Military Problematique: Huntington, Janowitz, and the Question of Civilian Control," *Armed Forces & Society* 23 (Winter 1996): 149.

4. Samuel P. Huntington, *The Soldier and the State: The Theory and Politics of Civil-Military Relations* (Cambridge, MA: Belknap Press of Harvard University Press, 1957).

5. See Richard H. Kohn, *Eagle and Sword: The Beginnings of the Military Establishment in America* (New York: Free Press, 1975).

6. David E. Albright, "Comparative Conceptualization of Civil-Military Relations," *World Politics* 32 (July 1980): 555–557; Amos Perlmutter and William M. LeoGrande, "The Party in Uniform: Toward a Theory of Civil-Military Relations in Communist Systems," *American Political Science Review* 76 (December 1982): 780; Harold A. Trinkunas, "The Crisis in Venezuelan Civil-Military Relations: From Punto Fijo to the Fifth Republic," *Latin American Research Review* 37, no. 1 (2002): 41–76 (Trinkunas argues that Huntington is also not usefully applied to democracies because it ignores the institutions placed by civilian officials to control military power, p. 44).

7. Monica Serrano, "The Armed Branch of the State: Civil-Military Relations in Mexico," *Journal of Latin America Studies* 27 (May 1995): 423–448; Agola Auma-Asolo, "Objective African Military Control: A New Paradigm for Civil-Military Relations," *Journal of Peace Research* 17, no. 1 (1980): 29–46; Jeremy T. Paltiel, "PLA Allegiance On Parade: Civil-Military Relations in Transition," *China Quarterly* 143 (September 1995): 784–800.

8. Peter D. Feaver, *Armed Servants: Agency, Oversight, and Civil-Military Relations* (Cambridge, MA: Harvard University Press, 2002).

9. Rebecca L. Schiff, *The Military and Domestic Politics: A Concordance Theory of Civil-Military Relations* (New York: Routledge, 2009).

10. Risa A. Brooks, *Shaping Strategy: The Civil-Military Politics of Strategic Assessment* (Princeton, NJ: Princeton University Press, 2008).

11. Eliot A. Cohen, *Supreme Command: Soldiers, Statesmen, and Leadership in Wartime* (New York: Free Press, 2002); Kurt Dassel, "Civilians, Soldiers, and Strife: Domestic Sources of International Aggression," *International Security* 23 (Summer 1998): 107–140; Todd S. Sechser, "Are Soldiers Less War Prone than Statesmen?" *Journal of Conflict Resolution* 48 (October 2004): 746–774.

12. Paul Staniland, "Explaining Civil-Military Relations in Complex Environments: India and Pakistan in Comparative Perspective," *Security Studies* 17 (April-June 2008): 331.

13. Richard H. Kohn, "How Democracies Control the Military," *Journal of Democracy* 8 (October 1997): 140–141.

14. See Michael C. Desch, *Civilian Control of the Military: The Changing Security Environment* (Baltimore: Johns Hopkins University Press, 1999).

15. Risa A. Brooks, *Shaping Strategy*; Christopher W. Hughes, *Japan's Remilitarisation* (London: International Institute for Strategic Studies, 2009), ch. 3; Jing-Dong Yuan, "Deferring to the National Interest: Arms Control and Civil-Military Relations in China," in *Chinese Civil-Military Relations*, ed. Nan Li (London: Routledge, 2006), pp. 40–60.

16. "Zardari in Power Struggle with Army over India Détente," *London Daily Telegraph*, June 26, 2009. According to the story, Zardari wanted the Pakistani military to divert resources away from the Indian border to fight insurgents in Pakistan. "Analysts said last night that they did not expect Mr Zardari to win his fight to redeploy the army."

17. See, for example, Frank A. Kierman Jr. and John K. Fairbank, *Chinese Ways in Warfare* (Cambridge, MA: Harvard University Press, 1974); Jen Yu-wen, *The Taiping Revolutionary Movement* (New Haven, CT: Yale University Press, 1973).

18. *Selected Works of Mao Tse Tung*, vol. 2 (Peking: Foreign Languages Press, 1967), p. 224.

19. Staniland, "Explaining Civil-Military Relations," pp. 334–338.

20. Keith Hopkins, "Civil-Military Relations in Developing Countries," *British Journal of Sociology* 17 (June 1966): 179.

21. Karl DeRouen Jr. and Uk Heo, "Modernization and the Military in Latin America," *British Journal of Political Science* 31 (July 2001): 475–496.

22. These arguments are distilled in Stephen J. Scanlan and J. Craig Jenkins, "Military Power and Food Security: A Cross-National Analysis of Less-Developed Countries, 1970–1990," *International Studies Quarterly* 45 (March 2001): 159–187.

23. Michael Bonner, *Jihad in Islamic History: Doctrines and Practice* (Princeton, NJ: Princeton University Press, 2006), p. 60.

24. Hugh Kennedy, *The Armies of the Caliphs: Military and Society in the Early Islamic State* (London: Routledge, 2001), p. 195.

25. Tariq ibn Ziyad left his name on the mountain he sighted while crossing the sea, the "Mountain of Tar," in Arabic, *Jebel Tar*, which became "Gibraltar."

26. Michael Chamberlain, "Military Patronage States and the Political Economy of the Frontier," in *A Companion to the History of the Middle East*, ed. Youssef M. Choueiri (Malden, MA: Blackwell, 2005), p. 152.

27. Karen Barkey, *Empire of Difference: The Ottomans in Comparative Perspective* (Cambridge: Cambridge University Press, 2008), pp. 219–220; Daniel Goffman, *The Ottoman Empire and Early Modern Europe* (Cambridge: Cambridge University Press, 2002), p. 51; Glenn W. Swanson, "The Ottoman Police," *Journal of Contemporary History* 1 (January-April 1972): 243–260.

28. David B. Ralston, *Importing the European Army* (Chicago: University of Chicago Press, 1990), ch. 3.

29. P. J. Vatikiotis, *Politics and the Military in Jordan: A Study of the Arab Legion, 1921–1957* (New York: Frederick A. Praeger, 1967), p. 5. Not all Middle East states experienced a military role in the creation of statehood; many Arab Gulf states evolved from powerful trading and merchant families, with weak militaries. As Al-Rasheed notes about Saudi Arabia in the early 1960s, "The Sa'udi army was still in a state of infancy, incapable yet of training its own officers, let alone producing 'Free Officers.'" Madawi Al-Rasheed, *A History of Saudi Arabia* (Cambridge: Cambridge University Press, 2002), p. 112.

30. Yoram Peri, *Generals in the Cabinet Room* (Washington, DC: US Institute for Peace, 2006), p. 25.

31. James L. Gelvin, *Divided Loyalties: Nationalism and Mass Politics in Syria at the Close of Empire* (Berkeley: University of California Press, 1998); Patrick Seale, *The Struggle for Syria: A Study of Post-War Arab Politics, 1945–1958* (New Haven, CT: Yale University Press, 1986); Philip S. Khoury, *Syria and the French Mandate: The Politics of Arab Nationalism, 1920–1945* (Princeton, NJ: Princeton University Press, 1987), chapters 22, 23.

32. P. J. Vatikiotis, *The Egyptian Army in Politics: Pattern for New Nations?* (Bloomington: Indiana University Press, 1961), p. 121. Egypt may not be an apt example, though, given its long history as a unified state, albeit under foreign rule for much of its history.

33. Ahmed Hashim, "Saddam Husayn and Civil-Military Relations in Iraq: The Quest for Legitimacy and Power," *Middle East Journal* 57 (Winter 2003): 12–13.

34. Dirk Vandewalle, *A History of Modern Libya* (Cambridge: Cambridge University Press, 2006), p. 94.

35. Eva Etzioni-Halevy, *The Divided People: Can Israel's Breakup Be Stopped?* (Lanham, MD: Lexington Books, 2002), p. 66.

36. Quoted in Steven A. Cook, "The Unspoken Power: Civil Relations and the Prospects for Reform," Analysis Paper 7, Saban Center for Middle East Policy at the Brookings Institution, September 2004, p. 4.

37. Samir Khalaf, *Civil and Uncivil Violence in Lebanon* (New York: Columbia University Press, 2002), p. 216.

38. For a discussion of the debate in Lebanon, see Matthew Hughes, "Lebanon's Armed Forces and the Arab-Israeli War, 1948–49," *Journal of Palestine Studies* 34 (Winter 2005): 24–41.

39. Oren Barak, "Commemorating Malikiyya: Political Myth, Multiethnic Identity, and the Making of the Lebanese Army," *History and Memory* 13 (Spring/Summer 2001): 73. An embarrassing counter to Malikiyya occurred in July 1978 when the Lebanese military tried to counter the influence of the pro-Israel South Lebanese Army, which ambushed them in the small village of Kawkaba, forcing a hasty retreat that Parker called "a serious embarrassment for the Lebanese government" and the Lebanese army. Richard B. Parker, "Kawkaba and the South Lebanon Imbroglio: A Personal Recollection, 1977–1978," *Middle East Journal* 50 (Autumn 1996): 548–558, esp. 557.

40. Michael C. Hudson, "Democracy and Social Mobilization in Lebanese Politics," *Comparative Politics* 1 (January 1969): 258–259.

41. Farid el Khazen, *The Breakdown of the State in Lebanon, 1967–1976* (Cambridge, MA: Harvard University Press, 2000), p. 178.

42. W. Andrew Terrill, "The Political Mythology of the Battle of Karameh," *Middle East Journal* 55 (Winter 2001), 91–111; James L. Gelvin, *The Israel-Palestine Conflict* (Cambridge: Cambridge University Press, 2007), p. 199.

43. Cook, "The Unspoken Power," p. 4.

44. Hashim, "Saddam Husayn and Civil-Military Relations in Iraq," p. 14.

45. See Nikki R. Keddie, *Modern Iran: Roots and Results of Revolution* (New Haven, CT: Yale University Press, 2003), ch. 5.

46. See Amin Banani, *The Modernization of Iran, 1921–1941* (Stanford, CA: Stanford University Press, 1961), ch. 4; Guity Nashat, *The Origins of Modern Reform in Iran, 1870–80* (Urbana: University of Illinois Press, 1982), ch. 4.

47. Stephanie Cronin, *The Shah and the Creation of the Pahlavi State in Iran, 1910–1926* (London: I. B. Tauris Academic Studies, 1997).

48. Barry Rubin, *Paved with Good Intentions: The American Experience in Iran* (New York: Oxford University Press, 1980), p. 196. Military spending was so high under the shah that it slowed other sectors because of shortages in goods like cement and other building materials (Keddie, *Modern Iran*, p. 164). While the shah spent billions for military weapons, he did not trust his military, fearing a coup, and thus keeping his top military officers divided and distrustful of one another. This split probably helped to prevent a coup against the shah in 1979, paving the way for the Islamic revolution that followed. See Mohsen M. Milani, *The Making of Iran's Islamic Revolution* (Boulder, CO: Westview Press, 1988), pp. 218–221.

49. Keith Crane, Rollie Lal, and Jeffrey Martini, *Iran's Political, Demographic, and Economic Vulnerabilities* (Santa Monica, CA: Rand Corporation, 2008), p. 13.

50. Shahram Chubin, *Iran's Nuclear Ambitions* (Washington, DC: Carnegie Endowment for International Peace, 2006), p. 49.

51. Akbar Ganji, "The Latter-Day Sultan," *Foreign Affairs* 87 (November/December 2008): 56.

52. Ibid., pp. 56–58.

53. "Hard-Line Force Extends Grip Over a Splintered Iran," *New York Times*, July 21, 2009.

54. Mehran Kamrava, "Military Professionalization and Civil-Military Relations in the Middle East," *Political Science Quarterly* 115 (Spring 2000): 68.

55. Steven A. Cook, "The Promise of Pacts," *Journal of Democracy* 17 (January 2006): 72–73.

56. Nil S. Satana, "Transformation of the Turkish Military and the Path to Democracy," *Armed Forces & Society* 34 (April 2008): 366.

57. Ibid., pp. 366–371; author interviews, Ankara, Turkey, March 2006, March 2007.

58. Satana, "Transformation of the Turkish Military," pp. 382–383.

59. Daniel L. Byman, "Friends Like These: Counterinsurgency and the War on Terrorism," *International Security* 31 (Fall 2006): 99, 104.

60. Hugh Roberts, *Demilitarizing Algeria* (Washington, DC: Carnegie Endowment for International Peace, May 2007), p. 11.

61. Ibid., p. 11.

62. Ibid., p. 19.

63. Imad Harb, "The Egyptian Military in Politics: Disengagement or Accommodation?" *Middle East Journal* 57 (Spring 2003): 278–279.

64. Steven A. Cook, "The Unspoken Power," p. 8.

65. Ibid., pp. 10–11.

66. Author interview, Egyptian think tank, Cairo, March 2009.

67. Cook, "The Unspoken Power," pp. 24–25.

68. Seale, *The Struggle for Syria*, ch. 5.

69. Gelvin, *Divided Loyalties: Nationalism and Mass Politics in Syria at the Close of Empire.*

70. Vatikiotis, *Politics and the Military in Jordan*, pp. 125–131.

71. Hashim, "Saddam Husayn and Civil-Military Relations in Iraq," pp. 20–21. Some in the Iraqi officer corps began to unify against Saddam after disasters befell the Iraqi military in the Iran-Iraq war, and Saddam had to retreat from some wartime policies after senior officers confronted him. Charles Tripp, *A History of Iraq* (Cambridge: Cambridge University Press, 2002), pp. 240–242, 249.

72. Joshua Teitelbaum, "A Family Affair: Civil-Military Relations in the Kingdom of Saudi Arabia," (draft) Workshop 12, Robert Schuman Centre for Advanced Studies, Florence, Italy, March 19–23, 2003, p. 12. Cited with author's permission.

73. Ibid., pp. 12–13. The regular Saudi Arabian military bases, particularly for the air force, are often located in remote areas (though there is a training base in Riyadh), whereas the Saudi Arabian National Guard bases are in major cities.

74. "Mauritanian Army Stages Coup, Junta Takes Charge," *New York Times*, August 6, 2008. Security concerns also caused organizers to cancel the 2008 rally.

75. Marvine Howe, *Morocco: The Islamist Awakening and Other Challenges* (New York: Oxford University Press, 2005), pp. 110–112. The royal Boeing 727, flying in from a trip to France, was intercepted by four Moroccan fighter planes, which repeatedly strafed the transport. The pilot, himself a Moroccan air force officer, falsely called out over his radio to the fighter pilots that they had killed the king, and thus there was no reason to down the 727. The fighter planes landed at their air base, but their commander immediately ordered them into the sky once again, this time under strict instructions to down the 727. The crippled 727, meanwhile, with only two of the three engines still running, was just about to land when the fighters again attacked it, but the king and the plane made it safely to the ground. The next day the vice chief of the Royal Moroccan Air Force was shot and killed by security forces while playing golf with the American Air Attaché. A number of Moroccan fighter pilots were also either executed or imprisoned for long terms. Personal communication with the author.

76. David S. Sorenson, "Civil-Military Relations in North Africa," *Middle East Policy* 14 (Winter 2007): 108–109. The air force, responsible for the last coup on King Hassan, did particularly well, with a sale of American-built F-16 fighters, ordered in 2008, to be delivered in 2010. Author interview, Rabat, Morocco, March 2008.

77. "Military Cabinet Named in Lebanon," *New York Times*, September 23, 1988.

78. Aoun went into exile in France but would return to Lebanon in 2005, immediately confounding both his enemies and supporters by linking himself politically to Syria and Hizbullah.

79. Metin Heper and Aylin Güney, "The Military and the Consolidation of Democracy: The Recent Turkish Experience," *Armed Forces & Society* 26 (Summer 2000): 640–641.

80. Mehran Kamrava, "Military Professionalism and Civil-Military Relations in the Middle East," *Political Science Quarterly* 115 (Spring 2000): 74.

81. "Paper Soldiers," *The Economist*, June 28, 2008, pp. 57–58.

82. "Turkish Prosecutor Unveils Coup Plan Indictment," *New York Times*, July 14, 2008.

83. "Turkey Detains Dozens in Coup Probe," Al-Jazeera, January 8, 2009; "Arrests of Officers in Turkey Stoke Uneasiness in Military," *New York Times*, January 8, 2009.

84. "Directive From Lieutenant Colonel," *Yeni Safak Online*, OpenSource, January 11, 2009; "Turkish Court Arrests Prominent Journalist in Ergenekon Probe," *Hurriyet*, January 12, 2009.

85. Peri, *Generals in the Cabinet Room*, ch. 5.

86. Bruce K. Rutherford, *Egypt after Mubarak: Liberalism, Islam, and Democracy in the Arab World* (Princeton, NJ: Princeton University Press, 2008), pp. 172–173.

87. "Marching Along," *The Economist*, July 4, 2009. Not all political parties went along with the bill. The Republican People's Party argued that the Constitutional Court should invalidate the law, as did Chief of Staff Başbug.

88. Crane, Lal, and Martini, *Iran's Political, Demographic, and Economic Vulnerabilities*, pp. 14, 18, 19.

89. Samir Khalaf, *Civil and Uncivil Violence in Lebanon* (New York: Columbia University Press, 2002), p. 115.

90. Crane, Lal, and Martini, *Iran's Political, Demographic, and Economic Vulnerabilities*, pp. 13–14.

91. Ganji, "The Latter-Day Sultan," pp. 58–59.

92. "Hard-Line Force Extends Grip Over a Splintered Iran," *New York Times*, July 21, 2009.

93. Anne Marie Baylouny, "Militarizing Welfare: Neo-Liberalism and Jordanian Policy," *Middle East Journal* 62 (Spring 2008): 278.

94. Baylouny, "Militarizing Welfare," pp. 287–288.

95. Author interview, Amman, Jordan, March 2009.

96. Author interview, Cairo, Egypt, March 2009.

97. Harb, "The Egyptian Military in Politics," pp. 285–286.

98. Ibid.

99. Figures from the 2008 CIA World FactBook. Other Middle Eastern countries rank below the United States, such as the United Arab Emirates at 3 percent, Tunisia at 1.4 percent, and Algeria at 3.3 percent.

100. Author interviews, Cairo, March 1996, March 2006.

101. "Military Aid to Egypt: Tank Coproduction Raised Costs and May Not Meet Many Program Goals," US General Accounting Office, National Security and International Affairs Division, B-253412, July 27, 1993, p. 3.

102. Brooks, *Shaping Strategy*, p. 83.

103. Kenneth M. Pollack, *Arabs at War: Military Effectiveness, 1948–1991* (Lincoln: University of Nebraska Press, 2002), p. 298.

104. Oren Barak and Gabriel Sheffer, "The Study of Civil-Military Relations in Israel: A New Perspective," *Israel Studies* 12 (Spring 2007): 11.

105. Yehuda Ben Meir, *Civil-Military Relations in Israel* (New York: Columbia University Press, 1995), pp. 30, 43.

106. Ibid., pp. 114–115.

107. Peri, *Generals in the Cabinet Room*, p. 30.

108. Schiff, *The Military and Domestic Politics*, p. 117.

109. Avraham Sela, "Civil Society, the Military, and National Security: The Case of Israel's Security Zone in South Lebanon," *Israel Studies* 12 (Spring 2007): 60.

110. Zeev Maoz, *Defending the Holy Land: A Critical Analysis of Israel's Security & Foreign Policy* (Ann Arbor: University of Michigan Press, 2006), p. 556.

111. Israel's professional military officers have also had their share of scandal and blame, including the lack of preparation for the 1973 war, the failure of Israeli occupation of southern Lebanon (where the prime minister withdrew forces in 2000), and most recently, the IDF's failures of performance in the 2006 Lebanon war. Moreover, there are allegations that IDF Chief of Staff General Dan Halutz sold his stock portfolio just before Israel launched its counterattack against Lebanon.

112. Ben Meir, *Civil-Military Relations in Israel*, pp. 128–129.

113. Lewis W. Snider, "The Lebanese Forces: Their Origins and Role in Lebanon's Politics," *Middle East Journal* 38 (Winter 1984): 6–7.

114. Ibid., pp. 8–10.

Part 3

POLITICAL ECONOMY

THE MIDDLE EAST presents a decidedly mixed picture of economic progress. Just on the Arabian Peninsula images joust, with pictures of Yemeni children searching for useable trash, an image that clashes vividly with towering buildings, wide freeways, Ferraris, and artificial islands on the other side of the peninsula. The income levels in the region range from Qatar with a 2009 GDP per head of $103,500 to Yemen with a 2009 GDP per capita of $2,400. Most Middle East countries are between these extremes, though the Arab countries outside the Arabian Peninsula are closer to Yemen than to Qatar. The Israeli economy is comparable to advanced European economies, and Turkey's economy has been growing steadily over the past decade.

Most Middle Eastern countries are products of the post–World War II era, and as the new leaders of these countries grappled with how to govern them, the question of economic development was paramount in their minds. Much of the Arab world had been part of the British, French, or Italian empires, and the colonial masters had left a mixed economic legacy. Agriculture was the primary economic activity, but newly empowered nationalist leaders envisioned economic transformation to industrial power, hoping that a strong economy would not only burnish their legacies but also help to preserve independence. Colonial powers had used the weak economies of their developing world outposts to sell imperial products and to extract agriculture and raw materials at pittance prices. This relationship had formed the bonds between colony and colonialist, and to break them new Arab leaders believed they had to develop autonomous economies. So new steel mills, shipyards, cement factories, and other trappings of industrialization sprang up in newly independent countries, along with an economic theory to run them. That theory was "Arab socialism."

"Socialism" generally refers to state ownership of a large chunk of the means of production, and now tends to have a highly negative connotation. It casts images of commissars operating steel mills and planning done by mindless bureaucrats administering factories that grind out locomotives and stoves simply to meet quotas. It is thus useful to recall that socialism was once a favored form to operate a national economy and that its European roots took hold in much of the Middle East. Socialism as practiced by most Arab countries and in Israel was an antidote to earlier economies dominated by powerful urban factory owners and rural landlords whose cozy relationships with the state regime kept them in power and retained their influence at the expense of the average working person. Wealth in much of the Middle East concentrated in the ownership class, who built luxurious villas, imported expensive cars, and played polo with the British on Jazeera Island in Cairo.

Socialism promised relief to the average worker from the patterns of exploitation that they often experienced. Socialism offered an end to cramped and dingy living conditions, long work hours in often hot and dusty shops and factories, or long hours picking cotton or harvesting hemp or pistachios. In the 1950s, socialism promised rapid economic growth in a region where economic expansion had been slow compared to Western Europe, North America, or the Soviet Union. And it fulfilled that promise. Economic growth in countries that adopted Arab socialism spurted forward, with factories sprouting up from rice fields or desert pastures.

Many interpreters thought Arab socialism was an imported concept, extracted from the intellectual salons of Europe or infiltrated into the Middle East by the former Soviet Union in an effort to expand its strategic influence. Such analysis missed much of the point of Arab socialism, though. While some of its core ideas did come from outside the Arab world, its foundations rested on Arab traditions and culture. Although Marxist elements crept into understandings of Arab socialism, there were also elements of Islam that formed some of its pillars. Socialism's Arab defenders did not reveal its Marxist origins because they were trying to avoid the eschatological links between their largely nationalist movements and the religious foundations of their countries. So Arab socialism emphasized Arab identity and Arab national aspirations over the economic leveling aspects European socialists flaunted.

In Israel, socialism was the underpinning of the powerful labor movement Histadrut. However, Histadrut and its associated political parties moved beyond the socialist narrative and emphasized Jewish construction and Jewish society rather than a class-based construction of national economic power. Still, the Israeli economy had to accommodate hundreds of thousands of Jewish immigrants from all over the world, the destruction of Arab infrastructure during the 1948 war, and limited resources. Thus the new state supported the kibbutzim that provided an agricultural basis, while industry grew under state planning and funding.[1] The state of Israel supplied the communications systems, the state-owned airline, El Al, and the Israel Aerospace Industries, which has a shadowy existence as a parastatal company, through strong connections with the state.

Some Middle Eastern countries avoided the socialist road, maintaining a private sector that was often dominated by powerful families with links to the rulers. In most of the Arab Gulf states, the merchant and trading clans dominated the state's economic life. These states drew in such wealth through petroleum sales, though. While the merchant class amassed huge fortunes, the native citizens also did well, partly because there were so few of them (most Arab Gulf countries have fewer than 1 million citizens), though much of the menial labor came from other countries in the form of migrant workers attracted by salaries that were more than what they could have earned in Pakistan, Nepal, or Bangladesh.

Socialism, though, had its limitations. No matter how much skill went into planning, state-run operations rarely had the sophisticated touch of the market. It could not replicate the signals that markets send to society to determine rates of production, quality of goods and services, price charged, and other choices made in the private sector. In the post–Cold War age, market economics took on new life globally as the demise of the Soviet Union finally ushered out most of the interest in socialism and state-run economies. "Privatization" became the new buzzword in many developing regions, including the Middle East. In Israel the grip of the powerful labor organization Histadrut waned as its associated Labor Party lost ground to the conservative Likud Party in the 1970s. While some elements in the Israeli economy remain in state hands, much was privatized. In Egypt, Jordan, Tunisia, and Morocco, privatization became more popular, particularly as the World Bank and the International Monetary Fund demanded a reduction in the state's role in the economic sphere. Although there were costs associated with privatization (unemployment grew as state firms contracted or closed, and newly created private air carriers experienced a rash of accidents, for example), the lure of private ownership was difficult to resist. Foreign investors, once severely limited in Middle Eastern countries, took advantage of the new private sectors in many Arab countries, forming joint ventures with them. Such ventures went against the historical grain of avoiding outside involvement in the Arab world in particular, but they did bring in both capital and expertise. For the first time since its founding, in 2009 the Arab Republic of Egypt employed more people in its private sector than it did in the state segment. In other cases, Gulf oil money became a vehicle for modernity, turning such once-sleepy city-states as Dubai and Doha into world-class cities with amenities not found in more traditional places such as Hong Kong and Singapore.

Economic reform did result in the development of market-oriented economies, but with those changes came a return to some of the classic problems of markets. Inequalities once lessened by socialist economics grew once again, and newly empowered entrepreneurs sometimes misread market signals and started enterprises without adequate capital or through corrupt bargains with the state. There was insufficient regulation to control the new capitalists, and charges of mismanagement and outright corruption grew. In the Middle East, as elsewhere, adaption from state economics to free-range capitalism took an uneven road.

Chantel Pheiffer and Gregory White focus on the transition in the MENA from colonial dependencies to independence-driven economic reform. They note the initial attraction of import substitution industrialization (ISI), used to propel countries into the machine age and reduce the demand for industrial imports. In the 1970s, though, Egypt and Tunisia led the way toward private ownership, which added market dynamics to Middle Eastern economies, but the corruption that marred statist economies marched forward into privatization, often compromising the results. Pheiffer and White also note the continuing importance of the agricultural sector in the MENA, which is a critical source of employment because of the lack of modernization. As a result, MENA countries that depend on agricultural labor are vulnerable to a number of potential disturbances, including drought and competition from more efficient agricultural producers. Water scarcity is a particular problem in the region, with renewal water amounts in the MENA expected to drop to a small fraction of the available water elsewhere in the world. Global climate change, modeled by some scientists to increase both drought and flood conditions, is expected to make the agricultural situation in the MENA worse, potentially throwing millions of people out of work and increasing dependency on agricultural imports. Moreover, such a situation will be particularly worrisome in the MENA due to the continuing high population growth, so it is likely to speed emigration from the MENA (and the Maghreb in particular) to wealthier countries in Europe.

In his chapter, Clement Henry analyzes the particular economic trajectories taken by the North African states of Algeria, Tunisia, and Morocco. He documents the rise of the state sector that the postcolonial movements spawned, and additionally tracks the role of powerful patronage networks that so often benefited from ties to ruling families and parties. Those elites were parts of the old French-educated bourgeoisie in Morocco and Tunisia, while in Algeria the revolutionaries moved into the positions of colonial rulers and resumed their rent-seeking behavior, creating, as Henry notes, a rentier state even before Algeria's petroleum boom began. Here a "rentier state" is an entity that "rents" its resource base to largely foreign buyers; thus, the state becomes an "allocation" state rather than a "production" state, free from the need to derive income from the populace. Petroleum is the most common commodity rented, but other examples include phosphates in Morocco and Suez Canal ship passages in Egypt.

According to Henry, privatization in these countries took a twisted path. Both Algeria and Tunisia initially engaged in state socialism, so reform, when it came, had to disassemble large patronage dependencies. But in Morocco the monarch preserved the French-initiated private sector, carefully transferring it to Moroccans after independence. As a result, Morocco experienced a less difficult privatization trip than either Tunisia or Algeria, though Tunisia's transformation was easier because founding president Habib Bourguiba had curtailed the state sector through a strong central bank, and the promotion of exports ultimately allowed Tunisia to surpass Morocco's economic growth. Algeria had the most difficult transition, hampered by a strong hold of the state sector and the devastating civil war. Privatization in Algeria was further complicated by the rise and fall of Abdelmoumen Rafik Khalifa, whose failed ventures into airlines and banking in Algeria indicated the vulnerabilities of rapid privatization. Dependence on oil rents continues for Algeria. Moreover, as Henry notes, the vibrancy of civil society that enabled construction and enhancement of the European Union is noticeably lacking in the Maghreb.

The value of Henry's chapter ranges beyond the Maghreb, for, as he notes, the three paths to economic reform resemble paths taken in the greater Middle East: Morocco's road to reform resembles that taken by Jordan, Saudi

Arabia, and Iran at the time of the shah, while Tunisia has taken economic measures similar to those of Egypt. Algeria, on the other hand, resembles such weak economic states as Iran, Libya, and Syria.

Economic conditions in the MENA are not only critical to the region itself, but to the rest of the globe as well. Stable economic growth and modernization of domestic economies may slow the flow of economic refugees to other parts of the world, and national economies that provide constant growth rates are probably less likely to experience domestic turmoil. In short, a secure future for the MENA is probably going to be influenced more by economic conditions than by political changes, a lesson that needs to be learned by those who try to shape the area from the outside.

NOTE

1. The kibbutz movement was communalist in origin, with members believing that the establishment of agriculture-based communes fulfilled traditional Jewish interpretations of equality and shared sacrifice. The Israeli population still living on a kibbutz has shrunk to around 120,000 of an Israeli population of over 7 million.

6

POLITICAL ECONOMY

Chantel Pheiffer and Gregory White

THE POLITICAL ECONOMY of the MENA region is an example of "everything's the same, but it's different, too." It is possible to identify broad similarities for the region's political economy, even as there is striking heterogeneity from country to country. Moreover, profound imbalances within a given country's domestic economy often shape that country's situation in the international economy. Obviously, a rural-urban divide challenges any domestic economy, but more subtle differences might stem from different colonial legacies and ongoing state-society relations. For example, Italy's brutal colonial administration profoundly affected Libya's political economy and the diverse experiences of regions such as Tripolitania, Fazzan, and Cyrenaica. In turn, the Qadhafi regime since the 1969 coup has influenced the respective regions differently.[1] It is true that rentier states elsewhere in the region—countries that rely on selling a natural resource, such as oil, for crucial national revenue—may exhibit similarities to Libya. Yet one would be hard pressed to argue that the United Arab Emirates' reliance on oil rents has affected it in a fashion similar to Libya's. The bottom line is that unpacking the profound differences across the region becomes a crucial challenge in efforts to understand its political economy.

In addition to the differences stemming from the unequal distribution of hydrocarbon reserves and the differing impacts of the European colonial legacy, other factors that contribute to the diversity of the region's political economy are the varied experiences with decolonization, Cold War competition, geopolitical conflicts such as the Persian Gulf war, the character of internal economic reform, and, obviously, the political structure of the respective regimes.

At the same time, many of the long-standing issues confronting the region's political economy are uniform. The region's geographical situation makes water security an ever-present challenge. Along with the Sahelian regions of Africa, the MENA continues to confront the greatest hydrological challenges of any region in the world. Furthermore, demographic and population issues exhibit crucial similarities. Although the rapid rate of population growth has slowed in the past decade, the MENA still experiences higher rates than the rest of the developing world—about 2 percent compared to 1.4 percent for the less developed world as a whole. Nevertheless, the population is very young, and the UN projects that the region will have 372 million people by 2020.[2] By contrast, other regions, such as Latin America, are expected to experience a decrease in population.

As Richards and Waterbury quip, the region's political economy can be described as: little rain, much oil, and many young people.[3] As a result, the problem for the region has been (and will continue to be) providing employment for rapidly growing populations, securing adequate levels of industrial activity, sustaining beleaguered agricultural sectors, and using natural resources in a responsible, sustainable fashion.

Instead of examining the region on a country-by-country basis or even on a subregional basis, this chapter offers a thematic approach. It discusses in the next section the predominance of statist responses to economic policy in the postindependence era. This requires an examination of the colonial legacy as well as contemporary trends in state and private sector activities. This is followed by a focus on crucial economic sectors, ranging from energy to industry, agriculture, and the service sector. The subsequent section turns to macrosystemic issues such as water, food, and the environment, with the penultimate section addressing demographic and population issues. The chapter concludes by considering the prospects for regional integration and immigration.

COLONIAL LEGACY AND STATIST INHERITANCE

The range of diversity in the MENA's colonial legacy defies easy generalization. The predominant colonial powers in the nineteenth and twentieth centuries were France and Great Britain, with less extensive colonial efforts by Italy and Spain. In addition, the Ottoman Empire obviously transformed the region, albeit to differing degrees, until its dismantling after World War I. The variability of colonial administration affected not only the kinds of political regimes nurtured and sustained, but also profoundly influenced the character of economic development. This is not to suggest that European colonialism shaped the region's governments and societies in a one-sided fashion. Instead, the development of the region's political economies was the product of a complex array of outside influences intertwining with local and regional political and economic dynamics.[4]

Not surprisingly, colonial administration was fundamentally intent on developing the economy for the colonial project. Efforts were devoted to developing infrastructure; facilitating resource extraction, taxation, and revenue enhancement; and maintaining order. This tradition of external intervention was driven largely by "multilateral great power politics." According to Carl Brown, "For roughly the last two centuries the [MENA] has been more consistently and more thoroughly ensnarled in great power politics than any other part of the non-Western world."[5]

Upon independence political leaders in the region inherited a state that was highly authoritarian and interventionist.[6] In virtually every context, the new national authorities made an ostensible effort to engineer development and move out of the "backwardness" of the colonial era.[7] Be it Turkey's Atatürk, Tunisia's Bourguiba, or Egypt's Nasser, postindependence leaders championed statist solutions rooted in import substitution industrialization (ISI). The ISI strategy is designed to transform national economies previously devoted to exporting primary commodities. In ISI's ideal form, economic policies substitute the domestic industrial production of commodities that once were imported, implement trade barriers to imports, and pursue efforts to add value to primary goods, with the overall goal of creating an industrial economic base, generating economic growth, and spurring employment. In theory, for example, rather than simply export raw cotton, the state could establish factories designed to refine cotton into textiles and perhaps turn to clothing manufacture, too. As a result, employment would stay within the domestic context, and revenues could be derived from the value added to product by domestic labor. Further, the fledgling industries would link into other sectors, such as machinery and perhaps infrastructural sectors.

ISI was the preferred solution throughout the developing world in the '50s and '60s. To a certain extent, the strategy derived its ideological legitimacy from the Soviet Union; more profoundly, it also received sustenance from European social democracy, corporatist frameworks, and Asian developmentalist state theory. In some instances, in fact, forms of ISI strategy in the MENA continued for decades, well into the 1990s and the first decade of the 2000s. Ranging from the Arab socialist regimes (for example, Egypt, Algeria, Syria, and Iraq) to the liberal monarchies (Jordan, Morocco, and pre-1979 Iran) to the rentier oil monarchies of the Gulf (Saudi Arabia, Kuwait, Oman, and the UAE), the state eschewed neoclassical economic rostrums of comparative advantage and export-promotion strategies.

As hydrocarbons took on their central role in the international economy after World War II, oil exporters found that the rents earned from the exports also fueled the growth of the state and its role in the domestic economy. As discussed below, even countries lacking oil rents were affected as they provided migrant labor to the oil-producing economies. The central role of oil rents in the region's economy became abundantly clear when the Organization of Petroleum Exporting Countries implemented controls on oil production after the

1973 Arab-Israeli war. The cut in production by the Saudi Arabia–led cartel, made in retaliation for US support for Israel, caused a spike in oil prices that affected advanced-industrialized economies around the world. In turn, the price spike also created "petrodollars"—cash that was wired from oil-producing countries to European banks and, in turn, lent to developing economies seeking ready infusions of cash. The increase in such lending contributed to the crushing debt burden many highly indebted poor countries (HIPCs) experienced by the '80s and '90s.

By the early '80s, however, a new emphasis on neoliberal policies emerged. Energized by the election of British Prime Minister Margaret Thatcher in 1979 and US President Ronald Reagan in 1980, there was a deepening of the argument for the importance of the privatization of state-led industries, promotion of export-oriented industries, cuts in state subsidies to industry and agriculture, and reduction of spending on education, health care, and infrastructure. Ultimately called the "Washington Consensus" by British economist John Williamson, the policies were ill-suited for the factor endowments of MENA economies. In other words, much like asking a heavyweight boxer to run a marathon, MENA economies were urged to adopt neoliberal policies. By the mid-1980s, implementation of the policies was often conditioned on adopting structural adjustment packages from the World Bank and International Monetary Fund. In exchange for crucial lending and/or refinancing of debt, countries were required to adopt austerity measures—for example, devaluing domestic currency to make exports cheaper, cutting subsidies to state enterprises, and selling state-owned industries. The resulting dislocation caused "bread riots" in many countries, as the cuts in state subsidies to bakeries resulted in sharp rises in bread prices. Some countries were relatively well positioned to move toward at least partial privatization and economic liberalization. Tunisia and Egypt, for example, had engineered gradual economic openings in the '70s. Known as *infitah* in Arabic, market forces were supported in some industries—such as light manufacturing, electronics, and pharmaceuticals. Nonetheless, the legacy of statist politics remained profound for the region's economies.

By the end of the 1990s, MENA countries were unevenly positioned to participate in free trade agreements with the European Union and the United States. Tunisia, Morocco, Egypt, Jordan, and Bahrain inked agreements with Brussels and Washington. Generally speaking, the arrangements allowed for industrial imports into European and North American markets. Far greater restrictions were placed on agricultural exports, as growers in Florida or Spain would hardly abet the full import of Moroccan citrus or Tunisian olive oil into tightly protected developed economies. Exceptions to agricultural quotas took the form of specific, annual quotas—for example, in the 1990s, Morocco was permitted to export 155,000 tons of tomatoes annually to Europe. There were also key geopolitical dimensions to the agreements, as Europe and the United States sought to bolster strategic partners in the region.

One final point concerning the region's statism is the profound corruption evident. MENA economies are no different from other economies around the world in this regard, yet corruption by state officials as well as private sector actors seeking political favors remains rife. And it would not do to leave corruption unmentioned as a powerful force. The absence of the rule of law in many authoritarian contexts—for example, compromised judicial systems, imprecise property rights, and enfeebled parliaments—often holds economic policy hostage. This becomes especially salient in the rentier economies, as a "resource curse" often leads to corruption and poor development performance.[8]

SECTORAL ANALYSES

Agriculture

Agriculture remains an important sector of MENA economies. In contrast to the agricultural sector in many developed countries, where it is has become a capital-intensive business that relies heavily on mechanization (for example, tractors and large machinery), agriculture in many MENA economies remains labor-intensive. This is not to say that the agricultural sectors of North African and Middle Eastern countries do not employ mechanized technology, but relative to the agribusinesses in Europe and the United States, the process of farming and commodity production still relies heavily on manual labor. Therefore, since the agricultural sector in the region utilizes its abundant factor endowment (labor) relatively intensively, it is a critical source of employment for the region. Farming also continues to be a means for sustenance, in addition to its role as an important source of income. Although seasonal unemployment can be high, the agricultural sector still employs a large proportion of the labor force in countries such as Yemen, Syria, Turkey, Sudan, Morocco, Iran, and Egypt.

For reasons discussed below—and in the following section—the agricultural sector faces many difficulties. Between 1950 and 1980, the percentage of the labor force employed in agriculture fell drastically, and since 1980, agriculture has come to employ less than a third of the labor force in most MENA countries.[9] For hydrocarbon-rich countries, the role of the agricultural sector has declined more than in their lower-income counterparts. Yet in the region generally, water scarcity (as discussed below), competition on the international market, the centrality of hydrocarbons and phosphate extraction to revenue generation, and increasing urbanization have been detrimental to the sector's long-run productivity and profitability.

Like many developing areas, the MENA continues to suffer from depressed world prices for agricultural commodities. As a result of heavy subsidization of important agricultural commodities by countries in the EU and the United States, farmers in the MENA often have difficulties selling their crops on the international market. The export of low-priced crops by advanced-industrialized countries—known as "dumping"—drives down the prices farmers in the MENA are able to ask, making traditional small farming a relatively unprofitable way of life. In an attempt to compete with large-scale, mechanized, genetically engineered farming, MENA farmers have had to change not only *what* they produce, but also *how* they produce it. Farmers in the region are increasingly importing fertilizer, pesticides, and insecticides to increase the productivity of their farms. Unfortunately, a drive for such increased production reduces overall fertility of land in the long run and can have negative ecological spillover effects.

Furthermore, access to fertilizer, insecticides, and pesticides is often a difficult endeavor. Because many small farmers make little or no profit from farming, they often need credit to purchase inputs. Credit can be scarce in rural areas and although micro-credit extension programs, such as those offered by the Grameen Bank, have made a large difference to many small farmers in rural regions worldwide, in the MENA, the Grameen Bank has programs only in Morocco, Tunisia, Egypt, Saudi Arabia, Lebanon, and Yemen.[10] Many farmers in the MENA region remain in dire need of credit to afford the ever-increasing costs of farming.

An unattractive agricultural sector has contributed to a marked trend of rural-urban migration in the MENA, which in turn has further contributed to the reduced importance of the agricultural sector in the region's economies. Partially because of rural poverty, wage work has become a more attractive mode of living for many. As other sectors such as manufacturing and hydrocarbon extraction have accelerated, more people are choosing to migrate to urban centers for work. Problematically, however, industries such as hydrocarbon extraction are not labor intensive. As the agricultural sector continues to release labor, capital-intensive industries do not absorb all the workers. The reduction in the size of the agricultural sector therefore contributes to the region's chronic employment problem. Young people especially are increasingly attracted to urban areas in search of work and increased living standards and are often disappointed by the lack of employment opportunities.

Primary Commodities

The Middle East and North Africa's most important and most valuable primary commodity is its supply of hydrocarbons. In fact, MENA economies remain relatively closed to the rest of the world with regard to trade, but the hydrocarbon sector is the exception to this trend. MENA trade figures— leaving out oil exports—show that trade in the region declined from about 53 percent of GDP in the 1980s to about 43 percent in 2000, with intra-region trade making up only about 10 percent of GDP.[11] However, oil exports increased dramatically during this period, leading to large revenue generation for many MENA countries. In 2004, MENA oil and gas export revenues totaled $313 billion, and they are projected to double by 2030.[12] Yet it is also important to note that hydrocarbon production has not been without negative influence on the economies and countries of the region. Problematically, hydrocarbon production is a capital-intensive industry and therefore does not utilize the region's aforementioned labor abundance. Although government revenue has increased because of expanding hydrocarbon sectors in many countries, unemployment has not necessarily improved as a result. Revenue generated from hydrocarbon production has also in large part not trickled down to the majority of the population. Although GDP has risen for many MENA countries, development indicators have not improved proportionately. The apparent abundance of oil in the region has made many MENA economies overly reliant on oil revenue and has discouraged economic diversification in the region, making MENA economies dependent on imports—especially for food—and incredibly vulnerable to world price fluctuations.

Although oil production generates most of the region's revenue, the export of minerals and metals is becoming a more important source of income for the region as well. In fact, Morocco is currently the world's largest exporter of phosphate and is responsible for approximately 40 percent of the world's total phosphate production. Similarly, Jordan also has significant phosphate reserves, and phosphate exports are likely to serve as an increasingly important source of income for other phosphate-rich countries in the region.[13] The MENA also exports a small amount of food and agricultural raw materials, but by and large the MENA region is a net importer of these goods. Fuel is the only primary commodity of which the MENA is a net exporter (see Table 6.1).

Manufacturing

As with primary commodities, the experience of the manufacturing sector in the Middle East and North Africa is diverse. Globally speaking, however, the manufacturing sector has not emerged to an appreciable extent in many countries, owing to the colonial legacy, a reliance on rents from primary commodities, the lack of a vibrant middle class, and a statist legacy. In some instances, depending on the sector and the country, robust efforts have emerged. For example, Jordan, Egypt, Tunisia, and Morocco have developed reasonably significant light-manufacturing sectors in textiles and shoes. Other manufacturing sectors include agribusiness, pharmaceuticals, chemicals, and electronics. Most of the firms that develop in the region, outside of the state-run industries, are small and medium sized—fewer than twenty people in most instances.

The degree to which MENA lags behind other regions or countries in terms of developing its manufacturing sector is astounding. Manufacturing activity on a country-by-country basis is far below what one sees for other countries,

TABLE 6.1: MENA COMMODITY TRADE,
ANNUAL AVERAGE 2003–2005 (IN BILLIONS)

Food	
Exports	6.9
Imports	29.5
Net exports	−22.6
Agricultural raw materials	
Exports	1.6
Imports	4.0
Net exports	−2.4
Metals and minerals	
Exports	5.8
Imports	19.7
Net exports	−13.9
Fuels	
Exports	268.8
Imports	14.3
Net exports	254.5
All commodities	
Exports	283
Imports	67.5
Net exports	−215.6
Exports of all goods	383.6

Marian Radetzki, *A Handbook of Primary Commodities in the Global Economy*, (New York: Cambridge University Press, 2008), p. 32.

based on per capita incomes. As Richards and Waterbury explain, if one examines manufacturing value added (MVA)—a category that shows the economic productivity stemming from manufacturing activity—total MVA for the entire MENA region is only slightly larger than that of Mexico, and three-fourths of South Korea's MVA. Four MENA countries—Egypt, Saudi Arabia, Turkey, and Iran—account for more than 70 percent of the region's MVA, yet Italy's MVA is 7.5 times that of Turkey, 12 times Egypt's, and 17 times Iran's. In short, manufacturing remains an economic sector lagging in terms of employment creation.

In other contexts, such as military hardware, some countries in the region have developed significant armament industries. Egypt, Turkey, Israel, and Iran have developed such sectors for differing historical and geostrategic reasons. Given the region's political instability, the lucrative nature of the industry, and ties to actors with explicit interests in the region—primarily permanent members of the UN Security Council—there is no reason to suggest that military activity will decrease in the future.

Future prospects for the manufacturing sector depend on the ability to attract investment—especially direct foreign investment—and maintain a stable climate of production.

WATER, FOOD, AND ENVIRONMENTAL CONCERNS

The MENA's renewable freshwater reserves have been persistently lower than the global average. This fact was not surprising or alarming until the past few decades. With the advent of technology in the '60s that made extracting underground water inexpensive, however, aquifers quickly became overburdened with the unregulated use of water resources. Renewable water resources in the region fell from 3,500 cubic meters per capita in 1960 to about 1,250 cubic meters in 2009, and it is projected to reach a low of 667 cubic meters by 2025. When compared to the global average of water availability, as Figure 6.1 illustrates, the MENA's dire condition becomes startlingly apparent. Global averages are estimated at 8,462 cubic meters per capita (2006), almost seven times that of MENA; by 2050, when global averages are expected to drop to around 6,000 cubic meters, the Middle East and North Africa region is projected to have 550 cubic meters of water for every person.[14]

Water scarcity is one of the region's most serious development problems and will likely become increasingly problematic as both the quantity and quality of water continue to decrease.

High temperatures and low rainfall naturally render the MENA region exceptionally dry. As a result, water is always in very high demand for domestic, agricultural, and industrial use. Unfortunately, the price of water in the region does not reflect how scarce this resource actually is, and as a result water is used much more rapidly than it will be replaced. The fixed water supply in the MENA region requires careful planning and perpetual consciousness of its use, but current trends in usage and inadequate attempts at harnessing alternative sources have only served to exacerbate the problem.

In addition to overuse, misuse of water in the region has had a significant effect on the depletion of water sources. As noted above, the shift in agricultural production from producing sustainable crops to the production of high-value, water-intensive crops has increased water stress in the region. As the region has

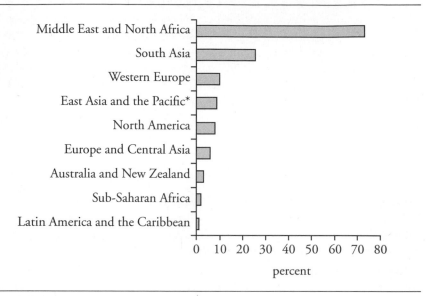

FIGURE 6.1: PERCENTAGE OF TOTAL RENEWABLE
WATER RESOURCES WITHDRAWN BY REGION

*including Japan and Korea
World Bank, *Making the Most of Scarcity: Accountability for Better Water Management Results in the Middle East and North Africa*, 2007, available at www.worldbank.org.

become integrated (albeit unevenly) into the world economy, demand has led many MENA countries to shift production from traditional, sustainable foods to producing much more hydrophilic crops intended for export. Wheat and rice production in the region has decreased while high-value crops such as fruits and vegetables are being produced on a greater scale. Fruits and vegetables typically account for 20 percent to 30 percent of agricultural exports in the region but make up a much higher percentage in some countries. In Morocco, for example, 80 percent of agricultural exports consist of fruits and vegetables and, when quotas are obtained, are transported to European markets.[15] Irrigating fruits and vegetables requires large amounts of water, and given the region's decreasing supply, large-scale production of such crops is clearly unsustainable.

In addition to the problem of water quantity, water quality is also of growing concern. The quality of "fresh" water is deteriorating, as countries seek to solve scarcity issues by reusing water. Recycling water that is not consumed—water that flows out of homes, factories, and irrigation systems as wastewater—significantly reduces the water's quality. In the agricultural sector, for example, the repeated use of irrigation water greatly increases salinity, undermining productivity. Furthermore, as urbanization continues to expand, increased waste and pollution, in combination with inadequate sanitation systems, contribute to the deteriorating quality of water and therefore a reduction in the amount of water available for consumption and irrigation. MENA countries spend, on average, 1 percent to 3.6 percent of their respective GDPs on sanitizing and managing inefficient water and irrigation systems. Government spending on water has made up between 20 percent and 30 percent of total spending in Algeria, Egypt, and Yemen in recent years.[16] Unfortunately, because money spent on the water sector is often used to correct defective systems or to maintain current inefficiency, returns on these "investments" are marginal or nonexistent.

Water is also a serious security issue in the region. All the major rivers in the MENA cross at least one international border—nine countries share water from the Nile—and 60 percent of the total surface water in the region is shared by more than one country. As a result, there is significant potential for water conflict in the region, magnified by the increasing strain of water scarcity. Because many MENA countries share water sources, actions that affect the quantity or quality of rivers have serious implications for downstream neighbors. Interrupting the flow of rivers, polluting, or extracting disproportionate amounts of water has caused disputes in the region for decades. Turkey's Southeastern Anatolia Project in 1990, for example, through which Turkey attempted to dam parts of the Tigris and Euphrates rivers north of the Syrian border, caused Iraq and Syria to ally to secure an ongoing water flow. Conflict between Israeli and Palestinian officials about the use of and access to water also remains a major obstacle to the peace process. As water becomes more scarce, conflict over access most likely will intensify and could have particularly serious political implications for the region.

Despite the fact that many MENA countries have, in the past few years, become more conscious of the need for water management and have attempted to reform the water sector, actual change has been slow. Resistance to reform often comes from powerful urban and farming interests who benefit from the current inefficiency; subsistence farmers and poorer households on the outskirts of cities often lack the organization and information to form effective lobbies. MENA's future with regard to water is becoming increasingly alarming, but a constant relocation of priorities continues to leave the water issue largely unattended.

Many of the countries in the region border some large body of water, but attempts to make water from these sources usable have been challenging. As Figure 6.2 illustrates, Saudi Arabia, Kuwait, and the UAE are among the biggest users of desalination technology—about 50 percent of the world's total capacity. Yet desalination is very expensive and energy-intensive.

As water availability decreases, MENA countries will likely rely more heavily on desalination for usable water. Yet, whether it will be a net benefit for the region is not yet clear. For example, as Algeria continues to develop desalination plants on a large scale, it will be important to weigh the high energy and technological costs against the benefits of making salt water usable. MENA countries will have to investigate the potential long-term consequences of becoming reliant

FIGURE 6.2: DESALINATION IN THE MIDDLE EAST AND NORTH AFRICA

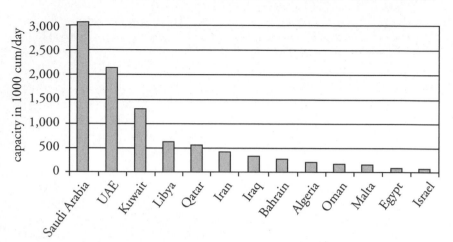

Source: David Hall, Kate Bayliss, and Emanuele Lobina, "Water in Middle East and North Africa (MENA): Trends in Investment and Privatization," 2002, www.waterconserve.org.

on desalination technology, the opportunity costs of such expensive projects—potentially diverting funds from social and development programs—and implications for energy use and emissions. For many countries, such as Algeria, harvesting water from seawater may seem to be the most sensible solution to water scarcity, given extensive seaboards. The World Bank has, however, warned that this technology is not sustainable in the long run because of its high cost and greenhouse gas emissions. Furthermore, employing desalination projects without regulating groundwater extraction may just be substituting one evil for another.

Food security, closely related to that of water, is also precarious. As noted above, many of the countries in the region were predominantly agrarian during the colonial period. Over the past five decades, however, with rapid industrialization and rising oil prices, the region has become increasingly dependent on extracting and exporting hydrocarbons and phosphates for economic growth. As a result of this shift, the agricultural sector has become a much smaller contributor to economic growth. Land available for crop production has decreased, the number of people employed in the agricultural sector has declined, and higher per capita income has shifted consumer tastes away from many traditionally produced crops such as wheat to goods such as livestock products and red meat.[17] These factors, in addition to intensified competition on the world market, have led to a surge in food imports.

The lack of water in the region has also been a major contributor to the increase in food imports in the region. Ironically, however, not only is MENA one of the largest food importers in the world, but it also has become one of the

Table 6.2: Agricultural Production in MENA,
2002–2004 Average (1,000 t)

Country or Region	Meat and Dairy Products	Total Cereals	Wheat	Fruits and Vegetables
Algeria	2273	3404	2356	4678
Djibouti	26	0	–	29
Egypt	6517	17781	6882	22302
Jordan	366	95	45	1355
Lebanon	535	144	118	1676
Morocco	2167	7279	4682	7119
Somalia (2004 only)	2319	369	–	240
Sudan	5851	4626	304	3027
Syria	2403	5801	4742	4240
Tunisia	1286	1672	1376	3260
Turkey	12078	31743	19839	36236
West Bank & Gaza	314	71	48	779
Yemen	497	489	114	1309

Source: United Nations FAO, "Impact of Trade Liberalization on Agriculture in the Near East and North Africa," p. 32.

largest food producers. Most MENA countries produce high-value crops in which they have a comparative advantage for export, while relying on trade for food security by importing lower-value staples and cereals for consumption (Table 6.2).

Because it is easier to import food than it is to import water, MENA countries are essentially importing the "virtual water" that is contained in food to sustain the consumption of a growing population.[18] Net food imports generally make up around 15 percent to 20 percent of total imports, with wheat as the most popularly imported foodstuff.

In 2005, the UN Food and Agricultural Organization (FAO) reported that agriculture used approximately 88 percent of water in the region, with 4 percent left for industrial use and 8 percent for domestic use. Water for domestic and industrial use has much greater economic value than water used for agriculture (families are willing to pay more for water for household use than farmers are willing to pay for farming). Hopes for food self-sufficiency are rapidly vanishing.[19]

For some countries, the dependence on international food sources is extreme: Many Gulf countries, such as Kuwait, import 100 percent of their staple foods. Although these oil producers are able to sustain their food imports with relatively reliable hydrocarbon revenues, others are not as fortunate. Yemen, which does not have significant oil deposits or high-value exports and lacks land and water to grow its own food, is forced to import about 80 percent of grain crops.[20] Farming in MENA requires both land and large amounts of water to irrigate crops, and, while countries like Egypt can extract enough water to "make the desert bloom," others have little choice but to foot a high food bill, often resulting in a deeper debt burden.[21]

Finally, anticipated climate change will likely impact food and water security further. If carbon emissions continue at their current rate of increase, the region will likely suffer from an increase in the number of dry days, a decrease in the number of frost days, and more frequent heat waves. Climate scientists have also projected increasing floods and droughts for the region as a result of more irregular rainfall. These factors could result in shortened growing seasons and could seriously affect the production of crops. The 2008 FAO Cairo report anticipates a 15 percent to 25 percent decrease in maize yields with a 3°C to 4°C (5.4° to 7.2° F) increase in temperature, and as much as a 25 percent to 35 percent fall in the yield of other regional crops. Sea level rise will likely decrease the amount of arable land in areas such as the Nile Delta and the Gulf Coast of the Arabian Peninsula, and the problem of desertification could render even larger parts of this already arid region barren. In addition, some models project that a 3°C (5.4°F) rise in temperature could cause as much as an additional 155 million to 600 million people to suffer from water stress in the MENA region, and as groundwater continues to experience stress from salinization and a rapid extraction rate, the region becomes increasingly endangered.

With the serious increase in water stress in the region, the agricultural sector will likely have to make do with less, which will lead to a further reduction in the size and importance of agriculture to MENA economies. Although some countries have shown signs of smarter water use with regard to irrigating crops—for example, new technologies such as drip irrigation—current trends project a greater dependency on food imports, which makes the region vulnerable to international price changes and price shocks. Therefore, not only will MENA economies be reliant on external forces for their income—for hydrocarbon and mineral exports—but food consumption will also be highly susceptible to international price changes.

DEMOGRAPHY, IMMIGRATION, AND GENDER

The makeup of the MENA population is an important factor in the region's economy. Although there is significant variation and diversity among countries, it can generally be characterized as young and increasingly urban. The population is growing at an average rate of 2 percent per year, compared to the world average of 1.4 percent. Although the population growth rate is lower than it has been in decades, significant growth is a source of both concern and great opportunity for the region.

The high population growth from the '70s and '80s, and current above-average growth, is placing considerable strain on economies in the region. Although a dramatic reduction in fertility rates in the 1990s has led to a tamer population growth, MENA still has a total population of about 310 million people. Not only do more people need basic access to limited—and diminishing—resources, such as water and land, but demand on government subsidies also increases as food imports go up.[22] Moreover, staggering unemployment continues to plague many countries in the region. In Algeria, for example, where 70 percent of the population is between the ages of fifteen and sixty-five, unemployment reached an official rate of 22.5 percent by 2005.[23] The numbers are likely higher. Unemployment has increased in Tunisia (14.1 percent), stayed about the same in Morocco (10.2 percent) and Turkey (9.9 percent), and decreased slightly in Israel (7.3 percent) since 2004.[24]

The MENA's "youth bulge" consists of a population that is disproportionately young. It is estimated that about one in every five people in the region falls into the "youth" category—between fifteen and twenty-four years in age. These statistics are, however, fairly rough and may be significantly higher depending on local, more inclusive definitions of "youth." In 2005, the total number of youth was estimated at nearly 95 million, and this age group continues to grow faster than any other age bracket in the region. The number of youth in the region is expected to continue its growth and peak at 100 million by 2035.[25]

The current size of the population is the product of several interrelated factors. In the late nineteenth and early twentieth centuries, the region's overall mortality rate began to fall, which resulted in a larger total population, while at the same time the fertility rate remained high throughout much of the twentieth century. Following a similar pattern, the current number of young people has come to make up a large proportion of the MENA population as a result of declining child mortality rates in the 1980s. It was not until the 1990s that the birth rate started to decrease from an average of 6 children per woman to the current 2 children per woman. As a result, the population was larger not only because fewer people were dying, but also because more children were being born in a relatively short period of time. Although it has slowed, the population continues to grow at a rate significantly higher than that of many other developing regions. The slowing of population growth can be partly attributed to a rise in per capita income, a conventional demographic pattern around the world, as well as the increased role of women in the labor force (examined below).

Because young people make up such a large part of the region's population today, they especially continue to face tough challenges. Unemployment has been a chronic problem and a particularly hard burden to bear. For a country to have a large young population is not in itself troublesome and can in fact be a significant source of human capital for countries. Where economies have well-developed labor-intensive industries such as manufacturing or agriculture, large populations are quite beneficial. In the MENA region, however, where this is often not the case, thousands of young people are left discontented, resentful, and angry with current governments. As a result, high rates of unemployment and poverty have often resulted in social unrest and have led some to theorize that the "youth bulge" is a cause of riots, terrorism, and even war. Even if one avoids a deterministic and fatalistic conclusion, the radicalization of youth in the face of economic stress is not uncommon. Where youth lack a positive outlook on their futures and experience political unresponsiveness by regimes, political and economic strife oftentimes result in demonstrations and raids in cities.

According to the World Bank, the MENA region had 12.9 million emigrants in 2005, representing 4.2 percent of the population that year. At the same time, 9.6 million people moved into the region, contributing 3.9 percent to the population. Net movement, therefore, was negative. Most of those who left the region entered the Organisation of Economic Co-operation and Development (OECD)—a grouping of the thirty richest countries in the world. A much smaller fraction of those emigrating chose to move intra-regionally or to other countries.

For the Maghrebi countries of Tunisia, Algeria, and Morocco, most migration has historically been oriented toward Europe. This orientation began in the aftermath of WWII, as European countries sought inexpensive labor to power economic reconstruction and growth. By the '70s, however, as European economies reeled from recession and oil shocks, emigration to Europe slowed. Nonetheless, Maghrebi communities remain prominent throughout Europe. A second destination for emigration has been the oil-producing countries of the region, as migrants have traveled to work in oil sectors as well as adjacent service sectors. Algeria, Libya, and countries in the Gulf have experienced significant immigration from neighboring countries. In both contexts, immigrants repatriate significant portions of their earnings back to home economies. Sending countries, therefore, have come to rely on remittances, which can dwarf the flows of capital associated with foreign direct investment and multinational corporation activities. Profound problems occur, again, when receiving countries' economies slow—or when anti-immigration sentiment increases because of concerns about a perceived threat to "societal security." According to the World Bank, Morocco, Egypt, Algeria, Iraq, Iran, West Bank and Gaza, Jordan, and Tunisia were listed as the top 10 emigration sources in 2005.

Finally, women's roles in the region have changed significantly in the past few years. In terms of social indicators such as education, literacy, life expectancy, and maternal mortality, there has been considerable change. In addition, the role of women in the labor force has also increased and women have had greater contributions to the economy. In Algeria, for example, 60 percent of students enrolled in tertiary education in 2007 were female. and 60 percent of lawyers and 70 percent of judges in that year were female.[26] In general, women throughout the region have received more education, have had greater access to contraception, and have experienced deeper access to labor markets; as a result, women are getting married later and, as discussed above, having fewer children. On average, the total fertility rate (TFR) in the region was 6 children per woman in 1960, dropping to 2 children per woman in 2006. For Iran, Lebanon, Tunisia, and Turkey, TFR was below the replacement rate of 2.1 children per woman.[27] In many respects, it appears that MENA women are much more empowered and are achieving greater equality than ever. At the same time, however, progress has not been as complete or widespread as it could be, and economic—and especially political—barriers still exist for women on a large scale.

Even though women are being employed more often and in more important positions, as in the case of Algeria, women, in great majority, still fill the bottom rungs of the labor market in clerical and administrative positions. They are, therefore, the first ones to be affected by layoffs and unemployment surges.[28] Freedom scores for MENA countries also show that there is still a significant gap between the political freedoms for men and for women. Women are often subject to unequal citizenship rights; they are largely disenfranchised and are remarkably underrepresented in government and elected positions. Women hold no seats in parliament in Saudi Arabia and Qatar, and only 4.4 percent in Turkey, 6.4 percent in Morocco, and 7.9 percent in Jordan. Tunisia by far has the most female representation, with 19.3 percent. Furthermore, the ratio of estimated female-to-male earned income for most countries in the region is around 0.30. That women make up the majority of the illiterate population and continue to be both politically and economically marginalized in MENA countries constitutes a profound challenge for future development.

FUTURE PROSPECTS—TOURISM, SECURITY, AND REGIONAL COOPERATION

In recent decades, despite (or perhaps because of) the region's political turmoil, tourism has developed as an economic sector. The reasons for developing a country's tourism are rather obvious and straightforward. Visitors bring in valuable foreign currencies such as dollars and euros. In turn, job creation within the sector can provide important dynamism to struggling economies. Tourism can also provide valuable links to adjacent economic sectors such as transportation and construction. Finally, tourism may also provide an entrée for direct foreign investment, as international firms invest in hotels, utilities, and transportation infrastructure. By many measures, MENA countries certainly possess important and enviable endowments that appeal to a wide array of tourist demands. Warm, sunny climates combine with breathtaking beaches. Mountain, desert, and coastal terrains provide an array of diverse adventure opportunities. An extraordinary patrimony of Greek, Punic, Roman, Berber, and Islamic historical sites offers worlds of exploration for educational tours. Finally, although it is true that in some instances a city's exotic appeal is not borne out by experience—Casablanca's modern grime and traffic are a far cry from Rick and Ilsa's cinematic encounter—the region boasts culturally rich, cosmopolitan, and charming cities with ample opportunities for exploration.

Despite this abundance, MENA tourism has been stymied not only because of political calculations, but also because of internal instability. For some countries—for example, Algeria, Libya, Yemen, and, of course, Iraq—travel remains unsafe and insecure. For other countries, geopolitical forces such as Iraq's 1990 invasion of Kuwait and the subsequent Operation Desert Storm can result in the cancelation of many trips by tour operators. The sector is clearly vulnerable, rather than merely sensitive.[29]

At the same time, security challenges can—paradoxically, perhaps—facilitate and even enhance the tourism sector. For example, Islamist challenges to Tunisia's regime prompted a deepening preoccupation with security and the further encrustation of Zine el-Abidine Ben Ali's police state. As Tunisia's then–interior minister Abdullah Kallal told *Jeune Afrique* in 1992, "We don't have petrol. We have sun, and the sun needs security." On the ground, security has to be provided for visitors so they feel safe, not to mention the importance of creating a perception that the country is safe to visit.[30] More than twenty years ago, Richter and Waugh argued that terrorism and tourism are "logical companions," stemming from tourists' vulnerability to terrorist attacks and the sector's vulnerability to the economic impact of insecurity.[31] Nonetheless, the evidence on the impact of terrorism on tourism is unclear. While studies have shown that terrorism affects tourism negatively and may make tourists choose locales on the perception that they are safe,[32] others such as Hazbun have shown a more nuanced interpretation.[33] In this regard, terrorism and insecurity may affect the flows, but sectors often adjust and provide striking flexibility by turning to new customers or shifting poles to new, enclaved destinations. In 2008, the *New York Times* travel section anointed Tunisia as No. 3 in a list of places to travel, writing:

> Tunisia is undergoing a Morocco-like luxury makeover. A new wave of stylish boutique hotels, often in historic town houses, has cropped up alongside this North African country's white-sand beaches and age-old medinas, drawing increasing numbers of well-heeled travelers.[34]

Complicating the appeal of the tourism sector is the mix between geostrategic calculations and the impact on tourism. In other words, crisis management, tourists' risk perception and travel behavior, and the impact of incidents on destinations are reasonably well studied. What is less well treated is the implication of a country's participation in region-wide efforts to combat terrorism under the frameworks proffered by North Atlantic governments. North African governments, for example, have actively participated in arrangements such as the Trans-Sahara Counter Terrorism Initiative (TSCTI), an effort initiated by Washington in 2005 and which the new African Command began administering in 2008. The participation of governments in the region has been secured through a combination of military assistance, economic aid, and trade agreements. On the part of advanced-industrialized countries—effectively members of the North Atlantic Treaty Organization (NATO)—such assistance is a calculated effort to bolster allies in the global war on terror (GWOT). Although the Obama administration has eschewed the use of "war on terror" rhetoric and is perceived as less bellicose than the Bush administration, the United States does not appear to be changing appreciably its regional security efforts. In addition to the concerns posed by purportedly ungoverned spaces—such as wide swaths of Africa's Sahel—NATO governments also have a keen intent to continue to secure access to oil and other strategic assets.[35]

This prompts several concerns. If, for example, a country's participation in a strategic framework brokered by NATO is perceived as providing support for a government that eschews democratic reforms or is acting in a fashion inimical to social justice—for example, inflaming ethnic tensions or developing a form of crony capitalism—then a kind of "neo-authoritarianism" is deepened. In turn, neo-authoritarianism—sustained through flawed or inexistent elections, harassment of political opposition, and provision of prebends (payoffs) to elites close to ruling circles—becomes part of the basket of grievances voiced by regime critics.[36] It is true that opposition forces need not be violent, but violent efforts to attack a regime are certainly fueled by such grievances.

Assessing the degree to which a government's participation in a geostrategic framework affects the tourism sector is no doubt difficult. The distorted political dynamic that results from participating in a GWOT arrangement may not necessarily inhibit tourism development. In fact, it might even dynamize the sector in important ways. As a country becomes perceived as a loyal ally of North Atlantic countries, it may gain credibility as safe to visit. In this regard, for example, Jordan's and Morocco's carefully cultivated statuses may indeed assuage anxious tourists. Understanding the interplay between tourism and security in the MENA region requires a careful examination of the sector's development.

In sum, for decades, political economy concerns were often separated from security matters. In recent years, however, the overlap of the two sets of concerns has become more and more evident. Tourism, free trade agreements with strategic partners, access to hydrocarbon resources, war economies, and (ideally) recon-struction of war-torn polities reveal the manner in which security matters are now central to the political economy of the Middle East and North Africa.

NOTES

1. Lisa Anderson, *State and Social Transformation in Libya and Tunisia, 1820–1980* (Princeton, NJ: Princeton University Press, 1986); Dirk Vandewalle, *A History of Modern Libya* (New York: Cambridge University Press, 2006), p. 246.

2. "State of World Population," www.unfpa.org/arabstates/overview.cfm.

3. Alan Richards and John Waterbury, *A Political Economy of the Middle East*, 3rd ed. (Boulder, CO: Westview Press, 2008), p. 2.

4. See Lisa Anderson, "Absolutism and the Resilience of Monarchy in the Middle East," *Political Science Quarterly* 106, no. 1 (1991); Roger Owen, *The Middle East in the World Economy 1800–1914* (New York: Methuen, 1981); Crawford Young, *The African Colonial State in Comparative Perspective* (New Haven, CT: Yale University Press, 1994).

5. Quoted in Clement Henry and Robert Springborg, *Globalization and Politics of Development in the Middle East* (New York: Cambridge University Press, 2001), p. 8.

6. John Waterbury, "Twilight of the State Bourgeoisie?" *International Journal of Middle East Studies* 23, no. 1 (1991): pp. 1–18; Giacomo Luciano, *The Arab State* (Berkeley: University of California Press, 1990).

7. Alexander Gerschenkron, *Economic Backwardness in Historical Perspective* (Cambridge, MA: Harvard University Press, 1962).

8. Terry Karl, *The Paradox of Plenty: Oil Booms and Petro-States* (Berkeley: University of California Press, 1997).

9. Richards and Waterbury, *A Political Economy of the Middle East*, p. 63.

10. Available at the Grameen Foundation, www.grameenfoundation.org.

11. Farooq Mitha, "Economic Reform in the Middle East and North Africa (MENA)," 2007, http://works.bepress.com/farooq_mitha/1.

12. Fatih Birol, *World Energy Outlook*, International Energy Agency, 2006, www.worldenergyoutlook.org.

13. Richards and Waterbury, *A Political Economy of the Middle East*, p. 22.

14. World Resource Institute, "Middle East and North Africa Face Increasing Water Scarcity," 2007, http://earthtrends.wri.org.

15. Gregory White, *On the Outside of Europe Looking In: A Comparative Political Economy of Tunisia and Morocco* (Albany: State University of New York Press, 2001); UN Food and Agricultural Organization, "Impact of Trade Liberalization on Agriculture in the Near East and North Africa," IFPRI/IFAD Report 2007 (Rome: UNFAO), p. 32.

16. World Bank, *Making the Most of Scarcity: Accountability for Better Management Results in the Middle East and North Africa* (Washington, DC: IBRD, 2007), http://go.worldbank.org/WDPAMJ5290.

17. Agricultural Outlook (June-July 1999), "Imports Rising in Middle East and North Africa" (Washington, DC: Economic Research Service of US Department of Agriculture), www.ers.usda.gov.

18. World Bank, *Making the Most of Scarcity*, p. 42.

19. Richards and Waterbury, *A Political Economy of the Middle East*, p. 145.

20. World Bank, "Food Crisis in the Middle East and North Africa," June 2008, www.worldbank.org.

21. Andrew Martin, "Mideast Facing Choice Between Crops and Water," *New York Times*, July 21, 2008, p. A1.

22. "Middle East: Population Growth Poses Huge Challenge for Middle East and North Africa," *International Herald Tribune*, January 18, 2007, p. A1.

23. Richards and Waterbury, *A Political Economy of the Middle East*, p. 57.

24. Ibid.

25. Ragui Assaad and Farzaneh Roudi-Fahimi, "Youth in the Middle East and North Africa: Demographic Opportunity or Challenge?" Population Reference Bureau, 2007, www.prb.org.

26. Michael Slackman, "Algeria's Quiet Revolution: Gains by Women," *New York Times*, May 26, 2007, p. A1.

27. Farzaneh Roudi-Fahimi and Mary Mederios Kent, "Fertility Declining in the Middle East and North Africa," Population Reference Bureau, April 2008, www.prb.org.

28. See Karen Pfeifer and Marsha Pripstein-Posusney, "Arab Economies and Globalization: An Overview," in *Women and Globalization in the Arab Middle East: Gender, Economy & Society*, ed. Marsha Pripstein-Posusney and Eleanor Abdella Doumato (Boulder, CO: Lynne Rienner, 2003).

29. See Robert Keohane and Joseph Nye, *Power and Interdependence*, 3rd ed. (New York: Longman, 2001), for a distinction between sensitivity and vulnerability.

30. Sevil Sönmez, "Tourism, Terrorism and Political Instability," *Annals of Tourism Research* 25, no. 2 (April 1998): pp. 416–456.

31. Linda Richter and William Waugh, "Terrorism and Tourism as Logical Companions," *Tourism Management* 7, no. 4 (December 1986): pp. 230–237.

32. Konstantinos Drakos and Ali Kutan, "Regional Effects of Terrorism on Tourism in Three Mediterranean Countries," *Journal of Conflict Resolution* 47, no. 5 (October 2003): pp. 621–641.

33. Waleed Hazbun, "Explaining the Arab Middle East Tourism Paradox," *Arab World Geographer* 9, no. 3 (2006): pp. 2006–2018.

34. Denny Lee, "The 53 Places to Go in 2008," *New York Times*, December 9, 2007, Travel, p. 1.

35. Michael Klare and Daniel Volman, "The African 'Oil Rush' and U.S. National Security," *Third World Quarterly* 27, no. 4 (2006): pp. 609–628.

36. Cédric Jourde, "Constructing Representations of the 'Global War on Terror' in the Islamic Republic of Mauritania," *Journal of Contemporary African Studies* 25, no. 1 (January 2007): pp. 77–100.

7

POLITICAL ECONOMIES
OF THE MAGHREB

Clement M. Henry

MOROCCO, ALGERIA, AND TUNISIA exhibit three distinctive patterns of control over their respective economies that more nearly resemble those of their Middle Eastern neighbors than each other. Indeed, the Maghreb is a veritable laboratory of approaches to the economic challenges of globalization. Morocco is a bit more like the other monarchies than the republics in its immediate neighborhood. Like Jordan, Saudi Arabia, or Iran at the time of the shah, Morocco has preserved and supported a vigorous private sector, whereas Algeria and Tunisia engaged in socialist planned-economy experiments after independence. Algeria, however, is a weak state, resembling Libya, Syria, or Iraq more than Tunisia, whereas Tunisia more closely resembles contemporary Egypt in rebuilding a private sector. The Maghreb, in short, displays a diversity of approaches to economic development. Such diversity has unfortunately hindered the region's economic integration, and each model is deeply dysfunctional, producing growth rates that cannot keep up with new generations in need of constructive employment.

This chapter will first examine the three distinctive trajectories of these core Maghreb units and identify the strengths and weaknesses of each political economy in light of the common challenges they face. Algeria, the weakest of the three states, also has the greatest economic potential. Economic integration would benefit all three countries if its weakest link could effect a simultaneous political and economic transformation. Current trends of social and political alienation in both Algeria and Morocco are also of concern and need to be reversed if the region is to evolve in harmony with its northern Mediterranean neighbors. Political change is much needed in Tunisia and could have a salutary impact on its Maghreb neighbors.

POSTCOLONIAL TRAJECTORIES

The three core Maghreb countries achieved independence from France under circumstances that would define their respective postcolonial trajectories. Each had engaged in a struggle against French colonialism, but just as the length and intrusiveness of the colonial occupation varied, so also did the constellations of emergent social strata and political leadership.

Tunisia

In the 1960s, Tunisia offered a paradigmatic illustration of a little country about to "take off," following the prevailing conventional wisdom about economic development popularized by Rostow.[1] American academics could point to modernization dialectics in Tunisia in that heady era of modernization theory, when political science graduate students waved "Think Hegel" placards in some of the innumerable student demonstrations in Berkeley, California.[2]

The Tunisian colonial dialectic was modeled on that of Hegel's slave, who first emulates the master but then, failing to achieve recognition, revolts and resists, playing the role of a stubborn slave. Through hard work meeting the master's demands, however, the slave can achieve freedom. The master then comes to depend on the slave. By analogy in the colonial situation, an early generation of traditional elites (the Young Tunisians) would try to assimilate to their colonial masters but would not be accepted as equals. In reaction, a subsequent generation of more broadly based notables would resist the colonizer like a stubborn slave, by insisting on constitutional reforms in the name of traditional values (Old Destour Party). More activist elements of the national resistance, however, would hive off to mobilize rural village strata in a modern nationalist party (the Neo-Destour). The victorious forces of Habib Bourguiba would recover the sons of the resistant notables under the hegemony of a rural (Sahel) elite of French-educated leaders and administrators. They enjoyed widespread legitimacy at independence, and their members and sympathizers within the French protectorate bureaucracy would ensure a smooth transition.

After independence the ruling Neo-Destour Party would systematically promote economic "take-off" by means of state planning in the absence of an effective Tunisian private sector. But despite their well-intentioned efforts and relatively efficient administration, the Tunisians achieved slightly less rather than more economic growth than their Maghreb neighbors.[3] The rural property-owning core constituency would, however, modify state socialism after 1969 into a mixed economy developing a private sector dependent on the party-state monolith. The restructuring of the elite during the colonial period determined this postcolonial trajectory, although the eventual outcome of Zine el-Abidine Ben Ali's police state might have been avoided, had the more liberal elements within the Neo-Destour succeeded in their efforts in the early 1970s to subject President Bourguiba to institutional controls.

Morocco

France gradually pacified and colonized Morocco from 1912 to 1934, more than a generation after the rapid conquest of Tunisia in 1881. Consequently, the colonial dialectic did not have as much time to restratify Moroccan society, and traditional elites achieved power at independence, whereas their modernizing counterparts would remain a minority.

Whereas Bourguiba easily eliminated Tunisia's traditional monarch, the Moroccan sultan, exiled by the French for refusing to rubber stamp decrees granting co-sovereignty to the settlers, returned in 1955 as the country's national hero.[4] He then succeeded in dividing and balancing off various nationalist factions while enlisting support from the same core of rural notables that had buttressed French rule under the protectorate. The emerging Moroccan state, being dependent on a variety of constituencies, was less monolithic than its Tunisian counterpart. On the other hand, the king's *makhzen* (royal household, literally a "magazine" or granary)[5] enjoyed relative autonomy and selectively negotiated to acquire settler property and distribute it among its strategic clients. Decolonization occurred more gradually than in Tunisia, and the state as such acquired a much smaller share of the former French properties. The king took over some of the richest lands and became the kingdom's largest landowner. Commercial and industrial properties were nationalized only in 1973, almost two decades after independence, and the proceeds went not to the Moroccan state but to various groups of private entrepreneurs, not least of which was the makhzen, which acquired the Omnium Nord-Africain (ONA), the largest French holding company, and dominant interests in major banks.

The king was able to divide and rule by co-opting political elites promoted by the independence struggle. The property of the departing French settlers and business interests offered further patronage resources the makhzen could distribute to Fassi (from the city of Fez) and other notables deserving of royal favor. By the late 1970s a variety of interlocking conglomerates became visible to discerning Moroccan scholars.[6] They appeared to be useful extensions of makhzen patronage networks.

Algeria

Algeria's more protracted and intrusive colonial situation did not give rise to French-educated elites who could enjoy stable sources of social support like their Tunisian or Moroccan counterparts. Messali Haj's Parti Populaire Algérien/ Mouvement pour le Triomphe des Libertés Démocratiques (PPA-MTLD) developed significant social roots in Algeria after the massacres of Algerians in May 1945,[7] but it never acquired the organizational depth of the Neo-Destour in Tunisia. Algerian intellectuals were hopelessly marginalized in the repressive colonial settler state and subsequently surprised in 1954 by the outbreak of the revolution. Even the few self-educated intellectuals who were its historic leaders did not survive the protracted guerrilla warfare to lead independent Algeria. The hard core of Algerian leadership that emerged from the guerrilla military infrastructure developed principally on the Moroccan and Tunisian frontiers. Civilian political structures, promised originally by the Front of National Liberation's (FLN) congress, assembled in the Soummam Valley in August 1956, never took root either before or after independence, when FLN apparatchiks co-opted by the hard core promised each year a reorganization of the party. The FLN remained a "mirage," in the words of one of Algeria's intellectuals, co-opted by President Ahmed Ben Bella in 1963 and imprisoned by President Houari Boumediene in 1965.[8]

Consequently, the party-state constructed after independence remained considerably weaker than its Tunisian and Moroccan counterparts, which relied on the administrations established under their respective French protectorates. The abrupt departure just before independence of a large majority of Algeria's settler population, including most government officials, further weakened the old colonial administration. Those who moved into their offices, largely vacated during the summer of 1962, tended to view their new assignments as personal property, much like the apartments, villas, yachts, and other possessions that had been left behind to be vandalized. Much has been made of the idea that petroleum wealth undermines state capacity, but the disorderly rent-seeking of Algeria's immediate postcolonial period predated substantial hydrocarbon revenues. Algeria was a rentier state before it became a petro-state.[9]

After Colonel Boumediene's "readjustment" of the revolution in 1965, his "Oujda clan" tried to strengthen the state's administrative capacities, but agrarian reform, initiated in 1971, further undercut any emerging administrative elite. Algeria embarked on a more ambitious policy of state-led industrialization than its Tunisian neighbor, though it had much less administrative capacity. Consequently, large projects were favored over greater multiplicities of small projects that would have required more managers. The dramatic rise of oil revenues in 1973–1974, following the founding of a national oil and gas company that took majority control over French oil interests in 1971, further whetted Algeria's industrial ambitions. Advised by the same French economist who had served Tunisian planners (poorly) until 1969, when Tunisia moved away from state socialism, Algeria engaged its limited state capacities in "industrializing industries." But it could not even control its own oil fields from competing clans within the military establishment. *Mafiosi*, as Belaid Abdesselam, the czar of Algerian industry, described them in one of his political memoirs,[10] infiltrated the entire industrializing enterprise. Unfortunately, Boumediene died in December 1978, before Abdesselam, already criticized for the shortcomings of Algerian industrial policy, had time to build up the light industries that in theory were to emerge from the foundations of heavy industry. Successors would reverse course without fundamentally altering the political core of the regime, based on an evolving military and intelligence establishment.

The administrative capacities of all three regimes were largely set by their respective patterns of transition to independence: an orderly transition in Tunisia backed by a consistent strategy of modernization; a more gradual transition in Morocco accompanied by pluralism verging on paralysis as King Hassan II, who succeeded Mohammed V in 1961, balanced divided elites and survived attempted military coups; a chaotic transition in Algeria resulting in minimal administrative capacities as factions took possession of the vacated administrative infrastructure. The respective profiles are mirrored in Figure 7.1, a World Bank summary measure of government effectiveness recorded since 1996.[11]

It is hardly coincidental that Tunisia registered the strongest economic performance over the entire postcolonial era. Figure 7.2 presents the evolution of per capita gross domestic product in constant (2000) dollars for the three countries

FIGURE 7.1: GOVERNMENT EFFECTIVENESS

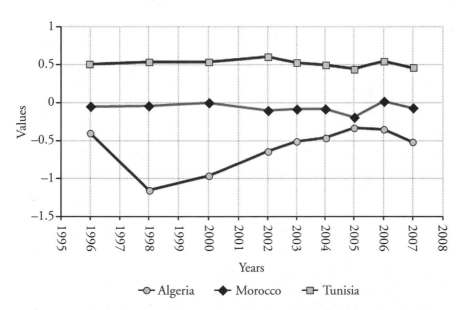

Source: World Bank, World Development Indicators 2008, cited in United Nations Development Programme on Governance in the Arab Region, www.pogar.org.

from 1961 to 2006. The strong single-party system was better able to adapt to the changing international climate, meet the challenges of globalization, and take better advantage of the opportunities than its neighbors. Only in the 1960s, when Tunisia had engaged in ambitious state planning, were its average annual growth rates slightly less than those of its neighbors. During the entire period, Tunisian GDP increased almost tenfold, whereas Algeria's and Morocco's increased only sixfold and sevenfold, respectively. With vastly increased hydrocarbon revenues in the 1970s, Algeria outperformed Tunisia during that decade, and Moroccan growth surpassed Tunisia's in the 1980s, the decade of painful readjustment; but then Tunisian growth was twice that of its neighbors in the 1990s, annually averaging 4.8 percent. But even these growth rates could not meet the region's principal challenge of generating sufficient jobs to reduce high unemployment rates.

FIGURE 7.2: PER CAPITA GDP, 1961–2000

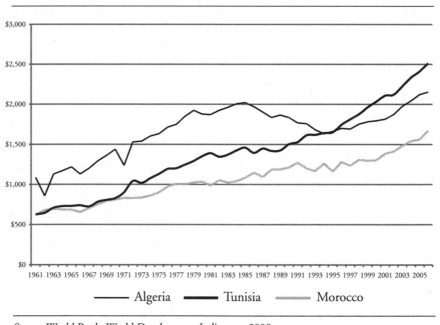

Source: World Bank. World Development Indicators, 2008.

STRENGTHS AND WEAKNESSES
OF THE BUSINESS-STATE MODELS

Algeria and Tunisia were one-party states that originally practiced state socialism once they consolidated their respective regimes, whereas Morocco carefully preserved the private sector enterprise and colonial settler agriculture that had emerged under French protection. While gradual transfers into the hands of Moroccans preserved the continuity of businesses in that country, state socialism destroyed older colonial enterprises in Algeria and Tunisia.

There were also significant differences, however, between Algeria and Tunisia. Some indigenous elites in both countries had prospered during the colonial period, much like their cousins in Morocco. But the wealthy Algerian entrepreneurs were usually viewed as French collaborators rather than welcomed into the revolutionary family, whereas their Tunisian counterparts were permitted to survive in the more flexible regime of Destour socialism. A residual private sector survived the years of intensive state planning in Tunisia (1961–1969), while Algeria's private sector vanished to France. State investment did, however, generate new private sector contractors and other businesses associated with the state enterprises. Young Tunisian entrepreneurs, led by such earlier pioneers as Bechir Belkhiria,[12] emerged in the 1970s in Tunisia, and Algeria's private sector finally began to achieve respectability in the 1980s, as the official socialist ideology lost its luster.

The international debt crisis sparked in 1982 by Mexico's default brought a halt to any economic take-offs the "development decade" of the 1960s promised, as well as high-commodity rents in the 1970s. From the mid 1970s easy credit from international banks recycling petrodollars had mitigated any declines in overseas development assistance, but rents fell sharply and international credit tightened in the 1980s. Morocco was most immediately vulnerable because of its mounting fiscal and current-account deficits but in a sense would have an easier time adjusting to the neoliberal demands of the international financial institutions. Despite a heavier debt burden, its average GDP growth rates in the 1980s surpassed those of both Algeria and Tunisia.[13] Having engaged in less excessive state planning and investment than its eastern neighbors, it had relatively less enterprise to privatize and faced fewer issues of deregulation.

Tunisia effectively managed the transition from a planned economy of state enterprises to a mixed economy in the 1970s. The transition was easier than Algeria's in the 1980s because Destour socialism had engaged less fully with fewer resources in the 1960s in the drive for industrializing industry than Algeria, which had been flush with oil revenues in the 1970s. Even at the height of his enthusiasm for state planning, Bourguiba also supported a strong central bank that checked the excesses of the planners, whereas Algeria effectively subordinated its banking system and state treasury to the needs of industrial development. As a result, it faced much greater problems of economic adjustment in the 1980s and 1990s, once oil and gas revenues plummeted.

Figure 7.3 shows the measure of indebtedness under which the Maghreb countries labored during those difficult decades. External debt as a percentage of gross national income (GNI) peaked earlier for Morocco, but Algeria would experience greater economic hardship in the late 1980s and early 1990s when its debt servicing requirements far exceeded Morocco's, as shown in Figure

7.4. Algeria's debt service ratio reached 76.6 percent of its export earnings in 1988. To pay off the debt, the government simply cut back on consumer imports, leading to the riots in October 1988 that ended the official single-party regime. The debt crisis subjected the economy to much greater pressures than Morocco had experienced in 1983, when its foreign exchange needs led it into negotiations with the International Monetary Fund (IMF). Algeria was in deeper water because it had never accepted the "advice" of international financial institutions, preferring to borrow freely from international private sector banks rather than suffer possible restrictions under subsidized lending.

Another interesting development shown in Figure 7.3 concerns Tunisia. In the first decade of the 2000s its debt crept once again over the 60 percent mark of GNI, though its debt servicing requirements remained well below the 28 percent of its export earnings that had obliged the country in 1986 to seek a standby agreement with the IMF.[14] The growing debt is symptomatic of the shortfall in

FIGURE 7.3: EXTERNAL DEBT AS A PERCENTAGE OF
GROSS NATIONAL INCOME, 1970–2006

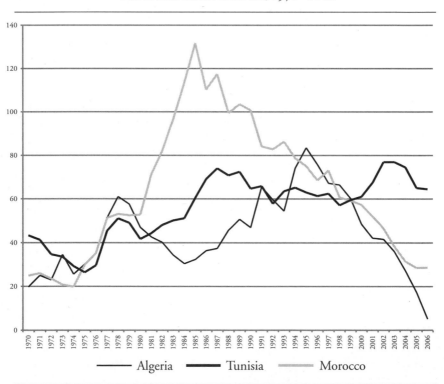

Source: World Bank. World Development Indicators, 2008.

Tunisian private investment, discussed further below. The debt service of Algeria also dramatically increased in 2006, but only because the country was using its windfall oil and gas revenues to pay off the remaining external debt, diminished to barely 5 percent of GNI in Figure 7.3.

Morocco

Confronted with rising fiscal and trade deficits, Morocco resorted to painful cuts in administrative personnel, engaged in an ambitious privatization program, and managed after a number of failures, starting in 1983, to complete its IMF adjustment programs by the mid-1990s to reduce its dependence on the IMF and reduce its debt servicing requirements to below 10 percent of GNI. As noted earlier, however, its overall economic performance compared favorably with those of its neighbors during this period. Morocco could engage in relatively credible programs of neoliberal reform because it had retained a relatively strong

FIGURE 7.4: DEBT SERVICE AS A PERCENTAGE OF EXPORT REVENUES

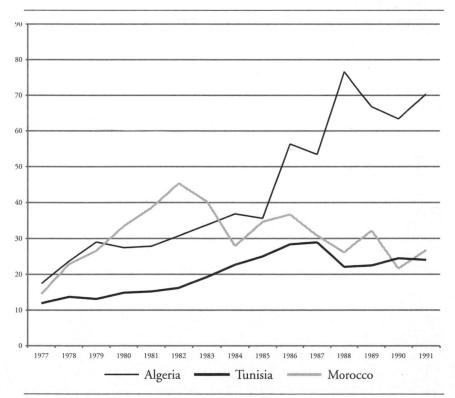

Source: World Bank, World Development Indicators, 2008.

private sector that the makhzen had carefully brought under its control. The regime's patronage requirements, to keep core civilian and security constituencies content, could be met through informal family control and shifting alliances within the top (predominantly Fassi) establishment. Curtailing administrative prerogatives perhaps reduced the authority of an earlier generation of royal clients, thereby enabling the makhzen to retain greater flexibility. To an international financial community more concerned with privatizing and deregulating markets than ensuring their competitiveness, Moroccan oligopolistic controls were an acceptable substitute for discarded administrative ones.

At the core of the private sector lay strategic conglomerates, notably the ONA under the control of the makhzen, and a Moroccanized financial system that had brought Moroccan partners into the French financial establishment. Commercial banks allocate the capital that makes or breaks business enterprises, and this authority was wielded through their owners. In the late 1980s the makhzen's hand became increasingly apparent in changes of ownership, notably of the Banque du Commerce Marocain (BCM). The strongest of Morocco's big private sector banks, BCM subsequently took over the flagship of another leading conglomerate, Wafabank. Although Morocco also actively engaged in promoting a stock market that is far more vibrant than those of its Maghreb neighbors, stock market capitalization remains modest, and markets relatively thin. Despite official efforts, as in Tunisia, to promote young entrepreneurs, businesspeople probably have more difficulty getting financial support in Morocco than in Tunisia.

One sign of the relatively closed character of credit markets in Morocco is the concentration of the banking system. Relatively fewer banks in Morocco (and Algeria) than in Tunisia command larger market shares. The World Bank rates Morocco lower than Tunisia on its Legal Rights Index and Credit Information Index, and only 2.4 percent of Moroccan adults (and 0.2 percent of Algerians) are included in the public credit registry, compared to Tunisia's 14.9 percent. Another World Bank study concluded that only 28 percent of Moroccan adults had some access to financial services, compared to 31 percent of Algerians and 42 percent of Tunisians.[15] Young entrepreneurs and others who do not enjoy prestigious political connections may have better chances in more closely governed Tunisia than in Morocco to start their own businesses. Political favoritism perhaps undermines business ethics in all three countries, however, to judge from the nonperforming loans, discussed below, that their respective banking systems have accumulated. The World Bank does not publish data for Algeria, where the banks are in far worse shape than in Morocco or Tunisia, but the latter have also accumulated substantial shares of nonperforming loans.

The strength of Moroccan state-business relations has been to reinforce the regime's ability to deregulate without losing strategic control of the economy. The makhzen is able to extract sufficient resources to service its patronage needs.

The cost of relying on relatively narrow networks of business conglomerates over the years has been neglect of public infrastructure, especially in the countryside. From a starting point at independence that was weaker than Tunisia's but stronger than Algeria's, Morocco now trails at a considerable distance behind its neighbors on all indicators of functional literacy and educational attainment. Even though the country's degree of urbanization is catching up with the others', female illiteracy remains high even for youth ages eighteen to twenty-four. Only 60 percent of the youth had attained literacy in 2005, compared to 86 percent and 92 percent of their Algerian and Tunisian counterparts.

Another indicator of the monarchy's narrow social bases may be the perceptions of corruption that hurt its business reputation. Figure 7.5 presents the perceptions of outside experts and businesspeople collected by the World Bank, and they pretty much agree with the findings of Transparency International. Morocco was only barely ahead of Algeria, despite the fact that it was one of only three countries in the Arab world to tolerate a fully established chapter of Transparency International.[16] Tunisia's grip on corruption also seemed to be diminishing, although it remained—barely—in positive territory, ranking slightly better than the world average.

FIGURE 7.5: CONTROL OF CORRUPTION[17]

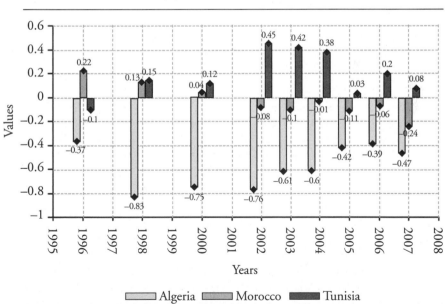

Source: World Bank, World Development Indicators 2008, cited in United Nations Development Programme on Governance in the Arab Region, www.pogar.org.

The World Bank's Country Assistance Strategy progress report gave Morocco high marks for its reform efforts, as did the IMF, but the reforms were not reflected in its World Bank ranking on the ease of doing business—only 128th among 181 countries and not much higher than the Palestinian West Bank and Gaza, Algeria, or Syria.

Tunisia

Tunisian state-business relations also enabled it to weather the adjustments of the 1980s. Whether running a "socialist" model of industrialization, a "liberal" model of import substitution, or, by the 1990s, a neoliberal model of export-oriented growth, the state has always exercised tight control and centralization. In 1987, when foreign currency reserves had dwindled to less than two weeks' worth of essential imports, Tunisia embarked on a radical stabilization plan with the IMF that transformed a state banking system overnight into one still regulated, to be sure, by the Tunisian Central Bank, but by managing market forces rather than directly allocating credit. Such reform was possible because the central state, even during Bourguiba's final year in office, remained an unquestioned "monument without cracks"[18] that was simply continuing economic reforms from above as during the early period of state socialism. His successor by quasi-constitutional coup, President Zine el-Abidine Ben Ali, gave the economic reform his unquestioned support.

From the early 1970s, Tunisia encouraged foreign direct investment, notably in the apparel industry, where European investors hired Tunisian labor in offshore sweat shops. Although it enjoyed some oil revenues in the 1970s, just as Morocco enjoyed a boom in phosphate revenues in that decade, the rents were never sufficient to dwarf the country's traditional agricultural exports, much less discourage new manufacturing. Although Tunisia continued after its break with state socialism in 1969 to encourage import-substituting industries, the state was also sufficiently strong to balance the demands of inefficient textile producers with those of apparel exporters and thereby pursue systematic policies of export-oriented growth in the 1980s and 1990s. The vaunted administrative efficiency of the Tunisians also enabled them to absorb a share of the European Union's Middle East Development Assistance (MEDA) that was quite disproportionate to the country's small population. In the early years of MEDA (1996–2003), disbursements to Tunisia exceeded those to any other Middle East country, with the possible exception of Palestine.[19]

Evidently efficient state management enabled Tunisia to vault ahead of Morocco, constrained by its oligopolistic groups mired in import-substituting industrialization and protected by their brothers and cousins in government. Tunisian and Moroccan exports as a percentage of GDP were neck and neck through the mid-1960s, but Tunisia took off in the 1970s to double Morocco's rate by the end of the decade. Morocco never caught up with Tunisia, whose exports surged past those of hydrocarbon-rich Algeria after 1976. Only in 2008, as oil prices temporarily surged, did Algeria catch up with Tunisia, each exporting goods and services worth 48 percent of its GDP, while Morocco, despite considerable progress, lagged at 33 percent, as Figure 7.6 indicates. Tunisia has displayed consistent progress over the years because it already diversified into apparel exports in the 1970s, while its modest oil and gas revenues offered a cushion for economic diversification. Both Tunisian hydrocarbons and Moroccan phosphates enjoyed peak rents in 1974, reaching almost Algerian heights, as the chart indicates, but these rents did not distract rational Tunisian policy makers from continuing to diversify their export bases in manufacturing and textile processing. Algeria's exports, by contrast, went lock in step with oil prices.

Tunisia suffered, however, from idiosyncratic rule after 1987 that threatened to undermine the state. The president who retired Bourguiba was a former military intelligence officer, hardly up to Bourguiba's political stature, much less inheritor of any historic legitimacy,[20] yet he exercised the same cult of personality.

FIGURE 7.6: EXPORTS AS A PERCENTAGE OF GDP, 1962–2006

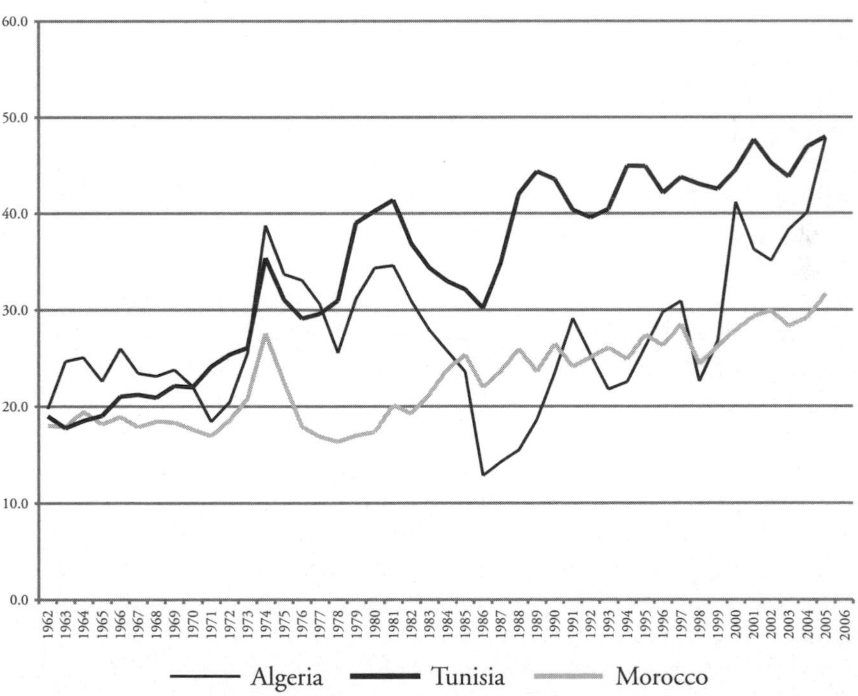

Source: World Bank, World Development Indicators online (October 2009).

Sustaining the act required a vastly increased police force, one that dwarfed both Algeria's and Morocco's even in absolute numbers, for a population one-third the size of each of the others'.[21] It is impossible to estimate the real costs of Tunisia's vast infrastructure as a police state or the extent to which it takes funds that might otherwise be invested in productive expenditures. However, one sign of the political environment, as reported by the World Bank, is the diminishing level of Tunisian investments in their private sector. It may be not so much the foreign investor as the local who is most concerned about good governance or its lack. The World Bank noted that "special treatment of well-connected individuals is a growing concern of the Tunisian business community and may partially explain the low level of domestic private investment"—a finding hotly contested by the Tunisian government.[22]

Tunisian banks were perhaps offering credit to a wider public than their Moroccan counterparts, but the World Bank insisted that "low levels of public accountability" were "strengthening the hand of 'insiders' . . . and discouraging risk taking by less well-connected entrepreneurs." Moreover, the banks were even more heavily saddled with nonperforming loans than their Moroccan counterparts, a sure sign that soft loans had been distributed too generously to friends of the regime. Figure 7.7 presents the available data; Algerian banks were in even worse shape, but there are fewer data. Tunisia's cozy single-party system seemed unable to bring nonperforming loans under control despite almost two decades of financial structural adjustment financed by the World Bank.[23] Efforts to privatize the Tunisian banking system also foundered because the two principal public sector banks were too encumbered with political patronage obligations. And even so, by 2005 private sector bank portfolios were just as riddled with nonperforming loans as public sector banks' because the government informally controlled them and could extract favors for its clients. By contrast, Morocco had been able to privatize the Banque Marocaine du Commerce Extérieur, placing it in reliable hands. Both regimes carefully vetted their bankers, whether the banks were publicly or privately owned, but with greater discretion in Morocco.[24] The CEO of Tunisia's leading privately owned bank, by contrast, was forced to resign in 1993 when he made statements that could be interpreted as opposing President Ben Ali.

Indeed the banking system seemed to be more highly politicized in Tunisia than in Morocco, just as nonperforming loans took a greater toll on the Tunisian system. Tunisia's presidential monarch and entourage, despite much adverse publicity, probably had accumulated fewer resources than the Moroccan makhzen and hence were in greater need of the leverage a banking system could provide. Inefficient financial allocation, however, limited Tunisian growth. Private investment was not forthcoming in sufficient volume, limiting economic growth. The government tried to compensate by borrowing funds but was again, as in the mid-1980s, reaching limits—with external loans again exceeding 60 percent of gross national income.

FIGURE 7.7: NONPERFORMING LOANS AS A PERCENTAGE OF TOTAL LOANS, 2000–2006

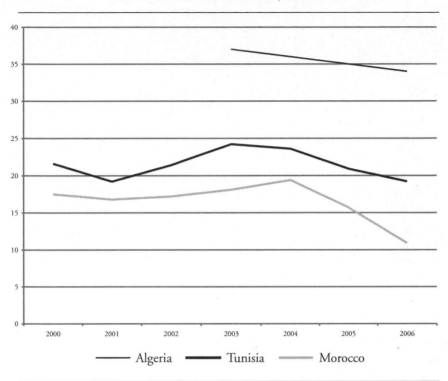

Sources: World Bank, World Development Indicators; IMF, Article 4 Consultations, various years.

In short, Tunisia's superior administrative efficiency could not compensate for the heavy-handedness of a police state. With an estimated 110,000 police personnel—or more than ten for every thousand inhabitants—the Tunisian per capita policing levels far exceeded those of the country's Mediterranean neighbors to the north as well as to the south.[25] But it was probably not so much the actual security expenditures that limited economic growth as it was the atmosphere of surveillance and fear that corroded the business and university climate. Tunisia's economy grew on average at a somewhat higher rate than its neighbors', but its average of 5 percent annual growth was not sufficient to diminish the chronic unemployment, notably of the youth, including those with a university education.

While the regime seemed secure as long as patronage kept the political elite loyal, the prospects for a genuine take-off of the Tunisian economy to the Asian levels needed to stem unemployment seemed remote, and the corruption at the summit of the presidential family projected a more vulnerable image than the

Moroccan monarchy. Meanwhile, private Tunisian investors were deterred from investing in their own country.

Algeria

In the final years of Chadli Bendjedid's presidency Algeria made valiant reform efforts to convert from official state socialism under the auspices of a single-party regime into a market-oriented multiparty political economy. Prime Minister Mouloud Hamrouche, a former protocol officer in the presidential entourage, presided over these ambitious restructuring efforts but was removed from office in June 1991, before they could be fully implemented. The effort to move from an administered to a market economy had stepped on too many powerful toes within the country's core military leadership. And the reform team he had supervised in the presidency before officially taking office in October 1989 did not enjoy significant support either within Algeria's marginalized private sector or within the wide spectrum of some sixty parties constituted under the revised constitution of 1989. A tacit understanding with the Islamic Front of Salvation gave the Hamrouche government temporary relief from active opposition, but efforts to transform public enterprises into market-oriented firms could not succeed in such a short time period. Ambitious financial reform resulted in a powerful and autonomous central bank on paper, but subsequent administrations would undermine its autonomy. Perhaps the biggest impediment to sustained reform was the private sector of the economy, which theoretically had the most to gain from restructuring the public sector.

Under the socialist regime the private sector barely survived, with about half of the little credit offered by the banking system going to registered veterans recognized as guerrilla freedom fighters (*moujahidine*) in the war for independence. In 1992, the first year for which comparable data are available, the Algerian private sector was receiving credit amounting to only 7 percent of GDP, compared to Morocco's 42 percent and Tunisia's 66 percent.[26] Algeria may have had many small privately owned firms, but few of them benefited from the formal banking system.[27] The private sector was virtually invisible in the political economy: It enjoyed neither the oligopolistic influence wielded by Moroccan conglomerates nor the dependent patronage relays operated by the Tunisians.

Algeria's liberal reformers did manage, however, to abolish various state monopolies, notably concerning foreign trade, and subsequent reforms undertaken under the 1994 IMF standby agreement further liberalized trade by reducing duties on imports. The results, however, were not what the liberal reformers had intended. Instead of promoting a more competitive local economy, economic liberalization resulted in new oligopolies of importers commanded by the ruling core of generals and their friends.

The civil war that raged between 1992 and 1998, after the generals halted parliamentary elections being won by the FIS (Front Islamique du Salut, or Islamic Salvation Front), had two major consequences for the political economy. First, under cover of widespread loss of life and destruction the authorities liquidated much of the public sector, with losses of hundreds of thousands of jobs. Second, the violence facilitated control of lucrative import markets by some of the ruling clans. Curiously, too, this violent restructuring of the political economy led to the appearance of a young and dynamic private sector.

Abdelmoumen Rafik Khalifa was a young pharmacist, born after independence, who used his father's connections to enter the lucrative pharmaceutical import market.[28] He then gained permission in 1997 to open a private bank and used his personal connections to attract substantial deposits from various public funds, including workers' pensions. The bank enjoyed spectacular growth, gathering up to 8 percent of the total deposits of the Algerian commercial banking system by the end of 2002. Khalifa Bank in turn financed Khalifa Airways, a private airline that by the turn of the millennium rivaled the state-owned Air Algérie. It rapidly achieved a reputation for much better service than its competitor, having lured away some of the better flight personnel with better salaries. Khalifa, the "golden boy" of Algerian business, cemented his reputation by sponsoring soccer clubs and showbiz extravaganzas with Catherine Deneuve, Gérard Depardieu, and other French stars. A master of public relations, he set up a cable TV network and, perhaps now coming into competition with regime heavyweights, also bought a German construction company to be positioned for lucrative state contracting once the state's oil and gas revenues ballooned in the new decade. A spectacular business conglomerate emerged, burnishing President Abdelaziz Bouteflika's image as a brave reformer, elected in 1999 to rescue Algeria from the dark decade of civil strife.

When the news broke in January 2003 that the Banque d'Algérie had frozen Khalifa Bank's foreign assets, a local press polemic ensued over the political motivations for attacking the golden boy and whether he had double-crossed Bouteflika in preparations for the 2004 presidential campaign, rather than any concern about how such featherweight enterprises, built on feckless public sector deposits and nonperforming loans, could have survived for so long. By the summer of 2003 Khalifa enterprises had vanished, airline and all, and the golden boy took refuge first in Paris, then London. The Algerian authorities have not shown serious intent to have him extradited back to Algiers for a trial that could embarrass too many of their core leaders. Trials of minor figures related to the banking scandal were conducted in 2007, and some of the testimony raised issues of regulation and control that implicated the top officials of the finance ministry, the central bank, and the presidency, while exonerating the former governor of the bank, whom the court had unjustly convicted in absentia.[29]

Nor was Khalifa Bank the only private sector bank to fail in 2003. Union Bank and Banque Commerciale et Industrielle d'Algérie (BCIA) were also shut down, and by 2006 none of the seven privately owned Algerian banks chartered between 1997 and 2002 was still operating. Khalifa alone lost at least

$1.5 billion, and the losses of BCIA cost the state an additional billion. The only surviving private sector financial institutions were subsidiaries or affiliates of foreign banking groups.

Despite liberalization and efforts to build up the private sector, the political economy rested more than ever on state favors and patronage manipulated by the military hard core and their friends. The mafia castigated by Belaid Abdesselam when he served in the 1970s as Boumediene's economic czar had taken new forms but continued to prosper, living off the hydrocarbon and other rents to the state that had accrued. Reelected to a third term by a landslide in 2009 after having his rubber-stamp parliament amend the constitution, President Bouteflika consolidated his power with the help of key military allies, but there was little effective power to wield. The private sector remained fragmented and dependent on political favor. The vestiges of the FLN remained part of the quasi-official ruling coalition but had even less institutional weight or respect after being purged in 2003–2004 and then readmitted to the ruling coalition. The leader who had purged it became prime minister but was subsequently replaced by the leader of the ruling coalition's rival party. Algerians had become so disinterested in their parties that a large majority abstained in the 2007 parliamentary elections.

Algeria's primary challenge in the new decade of relative peace was to avoid major social unrest by spending the hydrocarbon revenues. Riots lasting several days immobilized parts of Oran in July 2008, and unauthorized demonstrations in January 2009 against Israel's three-week war on Gaza enabled political Islamists to raise slogans of the banned FIS. Fortunately for the authorities, widespread popular anger was as disorganized as the ruling political parties. The World Bank monitored Algeria's Programme Complémentaire de Soutien à la Croissance, a massive public investment program, in 2005 and 2006. In agreement with the government, the bank was to advise on accounting and management techniques for efficient use of the funds, especially in the sectors of transport and public works, water, education, and health. Deliberately ruled out, however, was any analysis of the distributional impact of public spending, the role of civil service in the efficiency of public services, and the evaluation of strategic options for the use of hydrocarbon resources.[30] The final report did, however, gingerly suggest that "large front-loaded budget authorizations" carried certain risks, and it urged slowing the process and attending more to the upkeep and maintenance of projects that had often been underestimated or ignored in previous budgets. Of course, "large front-loading" facilitated the commissions and other forms of political patronage associated with big Algerian projects since the 1970s.

One Algerian asks whether the oil rents and the Khalifa affair illustrate corruption of the political system or a political system of corruption, and he suggests that it is the latter.[31] Indeed, Algeria has exhibited a chronically weak set of state institutions that have always been "prey to rapacious political clans and clienteles," ever since the French administration was captured in 1962. Boumediene achieved a measure of control over them in the 1970s but even this incorruptible leader had to tolerate the corrupt activities of colleagues: *"Personne n'est en mesure de résister à la tentation de goûter au miel"*[32] ("No one can resist the temptation to taste the honey") is his famous saying. Bouteflika has attempted to repeat his former master's feat, albeit without any coherent national project like "industrializing industry." As Marx once said, paraphrasing Hegel, history never quite repeats itself, as recall of the revolutionary moment of enthusiasm turns into a farce.

DIVERGENCES AND POSSIBLE CONVERGENCES

The three North African trajectories hardened into distinctive postcolonial political economies. Morocco, least intensively colonized, displayed the greatest continuities in economic development, replacing French with Moroccan business elites close to the palace. The presidential monarchies, by contrast, destroyed the old elites but displayed striking differences in their administrative capacities to replace them. Favored by a strong national party at independence, the Tunisians infiltrated and then took over and managed the colonial state apparatus, whereas the Algerians seized and virtually destroyed theirs.[33] The strong Tunisian state nurtured a politically connected business class of entrepreneurs and contractors that was newer and less concentrated than its Moroccan counterpart. Being more dispersed, the Tunisian entrepreneurs tended to be more dependent on the ruling party and various state agencies than the Moroccan oligarchs, who enjoyed direct connections with the makhzen. Each business community served as a source of regime patronage, but in Tunisia the wiring still ran through the ruling party.

Personality cults, first of Bourguiba, then of Ben Ali, undermined the party as a source of legitimacy, but it remained a useful patronage channel under its various reincarnations.[34] It not only mobilized masses but also vetted key economic actors, such as bank managers. In Algeria, by contrast, the FLN had never been a mass party, although its self-co-opting club of revolutionaries used it to channel patronage before Algeria officially converted to a multiparty system in 1989. In fact, the FLN never enjoyed the Destour's supremacy because the state, enriched by petroleum revenues, offered many other outlets, such as the ministry for revolutionary veterans (moujahidines). Public sector jobs alone constituted almost 60 percent of total employment in 1990[35] but diminished to 28.7 percent in 2000 after the dismantling of much public enterprise during the tragic decade of violence. The government was still substantially larger than those of Tunisia and Morocco, which employed only 12.0 percent and 6.7 percent of their respective workforces.[36] Government jobs were a major source of political patronage needed in Algeria to keep the masses in line. Algeria's government also offered much juicier morsels for its elites, such as tenders for major contracts and project management. A former prime minister estimated in 1990 that Algerian expenditures for development in the 1970s and early 1980s (while oil revenues were plentiful) had netted corrupt Algerian officials some $26 billion, roughly the equivalent of the country's external debt at the time.[37]

In Algeria, patronage derived from command of the state treasury, which depended on hydrocarbon revenues for at least 60 percent of its income, whereas patronage in Tunisia and Morocco depended more on interactions between the state and private sector businesses. Tunisia and Morocco had stronger states and more structured private sectors. Put differently, the two former French protectorates had stronger traditions of private property rights than Algeria, for which private property had literally been theft, equated with colonial exploitation.[38] The resulting patterns of patron-client relations were therefore more durable, grounded in private property, in the two former protectorates. The private sector lacked any real autonomy, but it buffered changes in the corridors of power. In the more egalitarian Algerian society, networks depended on exchanges of favors, effects of family, friendship, and transient power relationships, rather than on the more durable but asymmetrical exchanges of loyalty for goods and services characteristic of classic patron-client relationships.

Despite foreign exchange reserves reaching $140 billion in 2009—sufficient to cover three years of imports—Algeria's political economy remains fragile. Elected to a third term in April 2009, President Bouteflika has concentrated power but remains in need of effective intermediaries to channel popular demands and implement an economic strategy of diversifying the economy. The reserves cushion the economy but growth remains slow, incapable of offering employment to an increasingly frustrated youth.

The Khalifa affair dramatically illustrated the emergence of new economic interests centered on the various private monopolies accumulated in the import sector. The golden boy clearly had influential friends within top military circles. These included Larbi Belkheir, who had served as the director of Chadli Bendjedid's presidential cabinet and éminence grise of the regime until President Bouteflika redeployed him to be Algeria's ambassador to Morocco in 2005. As late as the spring of 2003, after a government sequestrator was put in charge of the Khalifa Bank, General Belkheir was still pressing for refinancing the bank rather than liquidating it.[39] Virtually the entire *nomenklatura* of the Algerian political elite had been involved in the bank's patronage networks. The full story of the Khalifa group's emergence and disappearance illustrates the system of corruption under which Algeria is governed, but it also carries another implication.

The traffickers and their influence peddling implicated the entire regime. The nomenklatura clearly desired to stabilize their influence by acquiring stakes in a dynamic private sector. The fragile networks of influence and power need to be grounded in private property relationships. How else could the revolutionary generation still in power pass on its legacy of power and influence to its sons and daughters?

The liberalization of foreign trade undertaken by the Hamrouche reform government (1989–1991) in theory opened up lucrative import businesses to skilled entrepreneurs, but in practice, once the reformers were dismissed from office, each sector came to be dominated by a few actors enjoying strategic connections with the Algerian military. In short, state monopolies gave way to private sector monopolies protected by those in power, by force when necessary. For instance, in the pharmaceutical sector that Khalifa penetrated, at least four of the other five major actors had important military or police connections.[40] By 2008 the six firms had roughly 60 percent of the sector, but new legislation was finally promoting rather than discouraging the domestic production of generic drugs.

Political elites needed stability to ensure that the conversion of their transient political influence into economic goods and services could be kept in their families. Some conglomerates, such as Issad Rebrab's Cevital, already offer some foundation for a competitive private sector. Rebrab is involved across a number of sectors, including the press, where he owns one of Algeria's principal French-language newspapers.[41] Rebrab, too, like others who benefited from privatized state monopolies, had his start in imports (iron bars for reinforced concrete) with help from political allies, but he moved to import-substituting industries and currently intends to export some of the household appliances that are to be manufactured in Setif in a joint venture with Samsung. New would-be conglomerates, such as Mohamed Abdelouahab Rahim's Groupe Dahli, competing for a megaproject to develop Algiers, also need legality, a comfortable and transparent business environment, and property rights above all. As Rahim argues, speaking of financial markets and reflecting the perspective of a new entrepreneurial class, "The informal market creates chaos. We have become the world's garbage heap. We need a bit of organization."[42]

TOWARD A MAGHREB OF OLIGOPOLIES?

Maghreb unity has long been a popular aspiration, but the loose-knit Union du Maghreb Arabe has stagnated since 1989, and trade between its three core countries actually diminished from 2 percent to 1.2 percent of their total trade in 2004. The World Bank still argues the virtues, however, of deeper, broader economic integration of the core Maghreb countries with the European Union. Economies of scale and competition within the market of 75 million people would lead to greater growth as well as a better bargaining position with the northern countries. The Bank estimated in 2006 that a free trade area accompanied by concerted reforms of services and investment climates could raise per capita growth rates between 2005 and 2015 by an additional 57 percent,

38 percent, and 51 percent for Algeria, Morocco, and Tunisia, respectively, compared to the growth rates projected under the status quo. Such reforms, in fact, could impel average annual per capita income growth rates in the range of 6 percent in all three countries—sufficient to make a significant dent in the region's serious unemployment problem.

Technocrats of the three countries participated in the writing of the report and would no doubt find large areas of agreement with colleagues in their home countries. But the border between Algeria and Morocco remains closed, despite Morocco's entreaties, except for infrequent and expensive cross-border flights by the two national airlines between Casablanca, Oran, and Algiers. Although Morocco would agree to open the border without Algerian acquiescence in Morocco's occupation and annexation of the former Spanish Sahara, the Algerians have refused to forgive Morocco for having falsely accused the country of promoting Islamist terrorism in the kingdom. Technically Algeria would be the principal beneficiary of the World Bank's proposed reforms, but a legacy of distrust persists from the 1963 border war between the two countries, which was fueled in part by vigorous ideological opposition between the monarchy and the Democratic and Popular Republic.

One way out of the ideological cul-de-sac would be to depoliticize integration and work on functional cooperation. Such efforts were attempted and failed in the late 1960s, however, and again seem doomed to fail in the absence of vigorous parastatal actors. The Union du Maghreb Arabe (UMA) has been paralyzed over the past two decades, despite obvious economic interests in functional integration, which has failed to materialize. Where such processes bore fruit, as with the European Union that originated from an iron and steel community, rich varieties of interest groups made the critical contribution of discovering convergent interests and, even when they disagreed, acquired a stake in transnational institutions that reduced their transaction costs.[43] Civil society in the Maghreb, however, does not feature the rich variety of relatively autonomous interest groups that supplemented governmental efforts to build the European Union. The numbers of NGOs (nongovernmental organizations) were increasing in all three countries, but they enjoyed little autonomy in the former single-party states, where the authorities systematically instrumentalized associational life.

Algeria led the way in absolute numbers, totaling 58,000 associations in 2001, or roughly 187 per 100,000 inhabitants, compared to much lower associational densities of 103 and 54 in Morocco and Tunisia, respectively.[44] As a seasoned Algerian journalist recently observed, however, "This civil society has been artificially manufactured and it constitutes, in its overwhelming majority, a simple clientele of local administration and security services."[45] Tunisia, too, despite a much richer associational past, now resembles Algeria. Fewer than a half dozen of Tunisia's 7,500 associations counted in 2001 are really autonomous, and they are subject to continual harassment by police thugs and infiltration by ruling party loyalists. Only in Morocco is some space allowed for NGOs to breathe, for their very divisions help to legitimate the monarchy. Business associations have occasionally demonstrated real initiative in conjuring up collective action against incumbent cartels, in the textile and apparel industry, for instance, as ably demonstrated by Melanie Cammett.[46] Shortly after she wrote, however, the old guard regained control of the Confédération Générale des Entreprises du Maroc (CGEM), the umbrella organization of Moroccan private sector business. And the controls over associational life in neighboring countries were not about to be lifted. In Algeria the shadowy presence of al-Qaeda served to justify a state of emergency that has been in force since 1992, just as the specter of political Islam also served incumbent leaderships with excuses to violate human rights in Morocco and Tunisia.

How then might the reforms suggested by the World Bank come about, assuming Algeria and Morocco could reach agreement on opening their borders, without the sorts of active interest groups that propelled Europe's economic integration? The story of the Khalifa group suggests one possible sort of convergence of interests that might lead toward a Maghreb of enterprises. As the nomenklatura that benefited from market reforms in the 1990s tries to consolidate its conversion of political influence into economic enterprises, it may push for a more credible legal framework to guarantee the hard-won property rights it wishes to pass on to its children. In coming years new and more firmly based Khalifa groups may come to dominate a growing private sector. The Khalifa experience itself anticipated the vision, and its negative outcome has not destroyed the underlying interests that supported its enterprises. Private sector development was viewed as a miracle to the ex-socialist elite expecting miracles. "We were all just fooled," claimed the hardnosed incoming prime minister, Ahmed Ouyahia, on June 3, 2003.[47] Were the Algerian private sector to develop along Moroccan lines, the traditional antitheses between a medieval monarchy and a progressive popular socialist regime would vanish under the power of their collective media representations.

Another catalyst that might stir reforms along the lines of the World Bank technocrats could be a change of regime in Tunisia that liberated its highly developed civil society. Tunisia is economically and administratively the most advanced of the three countries, and its police state serves as a model for Algeria's search for law and order. The president's family, however, seems far more economically dysfunctional than the Moroccan monarchy, and tight police surveillance is needed to repress the resentments of a business community. Tunisian businesspeople can exit in the sense of not investing but they cannot exercise voice: They are silent but refuse to become visible in major projects when it is generally known that the president's family members will extort a good 25 percent of commissions to implement any major investment. The leader's family even tried to steal funds from Yasir Arafat's widow.

Were the dysfunctional ruling family of Tunisia to be somehow removed, its patron perhaps retired like Bourguiba for medical reasons if not by fair and free elections, the Algerians would observe a new model in place of Tunisia's unnatural police state. The press would be liberated along Algerian lines but with greater underlying transparency, as the preponderant one-party regime adapted to new collective leadership. Tunisia's evolution would become more visible. In a more gradual way the Tunisian single-party nomenklatura has quietly converted its political prestige and influence into solid property holdings that are better guaranteed than in Algeria. With the return of a liberated judiciary and a strong state temporarily corrupted by excesses of personal power, Tunisia could show its Algerian counterparts the way to better security for their newly gained holdings. Such business-friendly reforms are part of the concerted efforts proposed by the World Bank, leading to a Maghreb of enterprises in which oligopolies would become more competitive in the expanded markets.

Algeria is obviously the center of any prospective Maghreb, but all three countries face dire threats of revolt by a younger generation of unemployed. It was not Algeria or Morocco but rather the slightly more affluent Tunisia that supplied the four suicide bombers who blew themselves up in Iraq in April 2009.[48] The national visions of the 1960s have worn thin everywhere, and all three regimes as currently constituted face dismal futures unless they can harness the demographic "bulges" of youth reaching their respective labor markets. Perhaps—at least one might hope—the colonial trajectories discussed in this chapter have outlived their usefulness.

NOTES

1. Walt Whitman Rostow, *The Stages of Economic Growth, a Non-Communist Manifesto (Cambridge and New York: Cambridge University Press, 1960).*

2. Charles Micaud with Leon Carl Brown and Clement Henry Moore, *Tunisia: The Politics of Modernization* (New York: F. A. Praeger, 1964); Clement Henry Moore, *Tunisia Since Independence: The Dynamics of One-Party Rule* (Berkeley: University of California Press, 1965); Moore, *Politics in North Africa* (Boston: Little, Brown, 1970); Elbaki Hermassi, *Leadership and National Development in North Africa: A Comparative Study* (Berkeley: University of California Press, 1972). Moore taught at Berkeley, where Hermassi was a graduate student given access to an earlier draft of his 1970 publication. Readers may judge how carefully the graduate student used the text.

3. From 1961 to 1970 Tunisia's gross domestic product (in constant 2000 dollars) increased by 36.9 percent, whereas Algeria's and Morocco's increased, respectively, by 39.5 percent and 39.2 percent. Source: World Bank Development Indicators 2008, author's calculations.

4. Had Tunisia achieved independence a generation earlier, in 1943, its traditional ruler, Moncef Bey, might have achieved a status comparable to that of Mohammed V of Morocco and then succeeded in balancing off various factions of the Destour Party.

5. The "granary" consisted of reserves of wheat that precolonial sultans stored for favored tribes during hard times.

6. The outstanding reference is Mohammed Said Saadi, *Les groupes financiers au Maroc* (Rabat, Morocco: Okad, 1989).

7. Mohammed Harbi, *Aux origines du Front de libération nationale: la scission du P.P.A.-M.T.L.D.: contribution à l'histoire du populisme révolutionnaire en Algérie* (Paris: C. Bourgois, 1975), pp. 88–99. Messali Haj created the MTLD in 1946, to succeed the PPA, which France had banned in 1939.

8. Mohammed Harbi, *Le FLN, mirage et réalité* (Paris: Éditions J.A., 1980).

9. For more on this theme, see C. M. Henry, "Algeria's Agonies: Oil Rent Effects in a Bunker State," *Journal of North African Studies* 9, no. 2 (Summer 2004): 68–81.

10. Belaid Abdesselam, *Le hasard et l'histoire: entretiens avec Belaid Abdesselam* (interviewed by Mahfoud Bennoune and Ali El-Kenz), vol. 2 (Algiers: 1990).

11. Government effectiveness is a subjective governance indicator aggregated from a variety of sources and measuring perceptions of the following concepts: bureaucratic quality, transaction costs, quality of public health care, and government stability. Estimates range between -2.5 and 2.5; higher is better.

12. From the same Sahel village as chief planner Ahmed Ben Salah, Belkhiria decided upon a private business career in the early 1960s, unlike his classmates, who almost universally gravitated into government service of one form or another. Tunisian business groups celebrate his exemplary career.

13. From 1981 to 1990 Morocco's GDP grew by 33.3 percent in constant 2000 dollars, whereas Tunisia's and Algeria's increased by only 25.7 percent and 21.6 percent, respectively. Source: World Bank, WDI 2008.

14. Figure 7.4 stops at 1991, the last year of available statistics from Algeria. In 2006 Tunisia's debt servicing amounted to only 14.4 percent of its export earnings.

15. World Bank, "Getting Credit," Finance For All research project 2007, http://econ.worldbank.org/WBSITE/EXTERNAL/EXTDEC/EXTRESEARCH/0,,contentMDK:21546633~pagePK:64214825~piPK:64214943~theSitePK:469382,00.html, Table A.1, Composite Measure of Access to Financial Services.

16. The other two full national chapters—no longer simply "national chapters in formation"—were those of Lebanon and Palestine.

17. Control of corruption is defined as "a subjective governance indicator aggregated from a variety of sources and measuring perceptions of the following concepts: corruption among public officials, corruption as an obstacle to business, frequency of 'irregular payments' to officials and judiciary and perceptions of corruption in civil service." Estimates range between -2.5 and 2.5; higher is better. Source: World Bank.

18. An expression once used by Bourguiba to play up the importance of having a strong state. Several Tunisians stressed the significance of the expression to the author during his fieldwork in those vintage Bourguiba times,1960–1962.

19. Aid per capita to Tunisia amounted to 77 euros 1995–2003, almost double Morocco's receipts and far more than Egypt's or Syria's. Patrick Holden, "Strategic Intervention or Showcase: EU Aid (MEDA) as a Force for Change in Morocco?" pp. 541–567, www.fscpo.unict.it/EuroMed/EDRC5/ecofincom03.pdf, cites official MEDA data on p. 555.

20. Hedi Baccouche, who also came from Ben Ali's home village of Hammam-Sousse, had protected Ben Ali immediately after independence from being sanctioned

for a relative's alleged collaboration with the French colonial power and enabled him to get a scholarship for Saint-Cyr, the French military academy. In need of some historical legitimacy, Ben Ali made another former Tunisian student leader, Tahar Belkhodja, write about his mythical exploits as a young officer defending against the French bombardment of Sakiet Sidi Youssef in 1958 as a condition for publishing his book in Arabic. Belkhodja had served as minister of the interior in 1980–1983, and Baccouche was Ben Ali's first prime minister, the reputed brains behind Ben Ali's coup, before being dismissed in favor of a more pliable successor.

21. See Michel Camau and Vincent Geisser, *Le syndrome autoritaire: Politique en Tunisie de Bourguiba a Ben Ali* (Paris: FNEP, 2003), pp. 204–205, for various estimates of the police force in 2000. Tunisian police density exceeded that of Montserrat, the country with the highest density at 7.8 per 1,000 inhabitants in an online data set that included the major European countries, Japan, India, and Hong Kong, but not China. See www.nationmaster.com/red/graph/cri_pol_percap-crime-police-per-capita.

22. World Bank, Country Assistance Strategy Progress Report, Report No. 38572-TN, August 13, 2007, p. 4.

23. The World Bank supported reforming Tunisia's financial system in 1991, if not earlier. See Economic and Financial Reforms Support Loan, Loan No. 3424, December 13, 1991. A Tunisian Financial Stability Assessment paper published by the IMF in June 2002 (Country Report 02/119: www.imf.org/external/pubs/ft/scr/2002/cr02119.pdf) indicated that nonperforming loans declined from 34 percent in 1993 to 25 percent in 1996 and 19 percent in 1999, but it seems the progress could not be sustained. A. Bedoui, p. 28, reports that the nonperforming loans had increased under Ben Ali from 15.9 percent in 1989 to 39.4 percent of outstanding loans in 1994.

24. There was more overlap between politicians and bankers in Morocco than in Tunisia, however, as discovered by Matias Braun and Claudi Raddatz, "Banking on Politics," Policy Research Working Paper No. WPS 4902, April 15, 2009, www-wds.worldbank.org/external/default/WDSContentServer/IW3P/IB/2009/04/15/0001583 49_20090415165247/Rendered/PDF/WPS4902.pdf.

25. Camau and Geissner, *Le syndrome autoritaire*, pp. 203–205, give a range of 80,000 to 133,000 police in 2000. Earlier, between 1972 and 1976, the combined police and constabulary had doubled from 6,600 to 13,000 officers.

26. In the early 1980s total credit to the economy amounted to 65 percent to 70 percent of Algeria's GDP, but balance sheets of the public sector banks suggested that no more than 5 percent of their loans were going to the private sector, half of which was constituted by the moujahidines.

27. In 2000–2005 the World Bank counted 580,000 small or medium-sized enterprises in Algeria, or 18.7 for 1,000 inhabitants, whereas Morocco had only 450,000, or 15.4 per 1,000 inhabitants. World Bank, *World Development Indicators 2008*.

28. His father, Laroussi Khalifa, had served as cabinet director of Abdelhafidh Boussouf, the Provisional Government's minister of armaments and general communications, the famous MALG, from 1958 to 1962.

29. Mohammed Hachemaoui has written an excellent summary of the available evidence—all of it published in the Algerian and French presses—in an unpublished manuscript, *Généalogie du système de corruption en Algérie*. The present narrative draws

heavily on his analysis as well as the author's observations from fieldwork in Algiers in January and February 2003, when the scandal first broke.

30. World Bank, *People's Democratic Republic of Algeria: A Public Expenditure Review: Assuring High Quality Public Investment*, Report No. 36270-DZ, August 15, 2007, 2 vols., 1: 9.

31. Hachemaoui, *Généalogie du système de corruption en Algérie*.

32. Cited by Hachemaoui, *Généalogie du système de corruption*, p. 61. Further, President Boumediene is quoted on p. 301 as saying at an important public debate in 1976, "Il est difficile de mélanger le miel sans le goûter!" ("It is difficult to mix honey without tasting it!") And his foreign minister at the time, Bouteflika, admitted three decades later that "Il n'y en a pas un seul qui n'a pas mis le doigt au miel" ("Everyone has put his fingers in the honey pot"). *El Watan*, July 28, 2008, www.elwatan.com/Bouteflika-et -les-voleurs, accessed April 27, 2009.

33. In one telling remark in 1977, Boumediene is quoted as saying, "Ruser pour voler l'Etat semble être devenu la règle, comme si l'Etat était un Etat étranger" ("Plotting to steal from the state seems to have become the rule, as if the State is a foreign state"). Hachemaoui, *Généalogie du système de corruption*, p. 301, added the italics and cites *Révolution Africaine*, September 28–October 4, 1977, cited by Luis Martinez, *La guerre civile en Algérie*, p. 21.

34. In celebrating the fifty-third anniversary of Tunisian independence in 2009, two youths presented President Ben Ali with a CD containing the party-state's latest mobilization effort, a Youth Pact signed by 1,322,929 youth. A coalition of official parties organized the campaign to collect the signatures, and the official ruling party apparently mobilized the masses more effectively by staying in the background. See *La Presse*, March 21, 2009.

35. World Bank, *Unlocking the Employment Potential in the Middle East and North Africa: Toward a New Social Contract* (Washington, DC: World Bank, 2004), p. 98.

36. Elizabeth Ruppert Bulmer, "Rationalizing Public Sector Employment in the MENA Region," World Bank, Working Paper Series No. 19, 2000, p. 5.

37. In his *L'Économie algérienne: défis et enjeux*, 2nd ed. (Algiers: Editions Dahlab, 1991), Adelhamid Brahimi attempts to document his accusation, which had been widely reported in the Algerian press.

38. Pierre-Joseph Proudhon, *What Is Property?* (1840).

39. *Algeria interface*, June 13, 2003, cited by Mohammed Hachemaoui, *Généalogie du système de corruption*, p. 231

40. Djillali Hadjaj, *Corruption et démocratie en Algérie* (Paris: La Dispute, 1998), p. 170, cited by Hachemaoui, *Généalogie du système de corruption*, p. 173.

41. *Liberté* is traditionally understood to be owner Rebrab's mouthpiece, although he recently reinstalled his chief editor and promised him greater editorial freedom. The French-language press collectively claims roughly as many readers as its Arabic-language counterparts—each in the neighborhood of 750,000, many of whom are the same bilingual readers.

42. "Groupe Dahli: Le montant levé en deçà des espérances," *El-Watan*, February 22, 2009. The CEO said, "Le marché informel engendre le chaos. On est devenu la poubelle du monde. Il faut un peu d'organisation."

43. The seminal sources are Ernst B. Haas, *Beyond the Nation-State: Functionalism and International Organization* (Stanford, CA: Stanford University Press, 1964), and Robert O. Keohane, *After Hegemony: Cooperation and Discord in the World Political Economy* (Princeton, NJ: Princeton University Press, 1984).

44. Selim Nasr, *Arab Civil Societies and Governance Reform: An Analytic Conference*, United Nations Development Programme, Conference on Good Governance in the Arab Countries, Dead Sea, Jordan, February 6–7, 2005, pp. 8–9.

45. Abed Charef, "Zerhouni fait une 'découvre,'" *Le Quotidien d'Oran*, July 10, 2008.

46. Melanie Claire Cammett, *Globalization and Business Politics in North Africa: A Comparative Perspective* (Cambridge: Cambridge University Press, 2007).

47. Hachemaoui, *Généalogie du systéme de corruption,* p. 231.

48. "Petraeus: Tunisian Militants Behind Recent Attacks in Iraq," *Boston Herald*, April 24, 2009.

Part 4

SOCIAL CONTEXTS

IN THE TITLE of this section, "social" refers to the formal and informal norms that govern social groups. All societies require social thermostats to regulate interactions between members; sometimes they take the shape of formal regulations generated from the political process, while others are informal norms generally recognized as valid by the social order ("don't wear a Speedo to a formal dinner party"). While such norms and rules vary considerably from almost anarchy to Stalinist control, all societies need them to function. They extract social standards from many sources: from religion, interpreted history, environment, or perhaps the mind-sets of powerful or persuasive individuals. Over time such things become regulators for societal interactions, roughly lumped together as the "social context."

The social context of the Middle East is no different from other milieus, with its norms, rules, and consequences. They must be understood at two levels: the objective and the source, where "objective" is a category impacted by formal and unofficial norms of behavior, while "source" probes the origin and shaping influences for the objective. In this section, the objective is the status and condition of gender relations in the Middle East, and the source is the corpus of Islam. This is not to assume that these two wellsprings are tied for the purposes of this book, because although religion clearly shapes gender relations, it shapes much more in the Middle East, and, likewise, gender relations are conditioned as much by social memory, fears, and biology as they are by interpretations of faith.

The Middle East is the wellspring for three major religions, but while Christianity thrived in Europe, it remains a small part of the religious fabric of the Middle East. Judaism found a home in the state of Israel, though Islam is the dominant religion of the Middle East. For the Arab countries, Islam is not just the majority religion in all of them, but it is predominant in all but Lebanon (around 60 percent Muslim) and Israel, though around 23 percent of Israel's population is officially listed as "non-Jewish," almost all of whom are Muslim Arabs. In Saudi Arabia, 100 percent of the population are Muslim, in Tunisia it is 98 percent, and in Egypt 90 percent of the population adhere to Islam. In Turkey 99.8 percent of the population are Muslim.

As in all societies, creed plays a significant role in Middle Eastern life. As in Europe or Thailand, or North America, religious temples dot the landscape. While Cairo has a few old synagogues left from its Jewish population (around forty families remain there now) and distinctive Coptic Christian churches, its mosques are a dominant feature, ranging from grand structures with towering minarets to tiny neighborhood mosques that are barely noticeable to passersby. These buildings are the most obvious part of religion in the Middle East, but it is the ideas that spring from text and teachings that hold the most significant influence. And since Islam is the dominant religion of the Middle East, that is the focus of this section.

It is difficult to overstate the role that Islam has had and continues to have in shaping the modern Middle East. Its postmodern role has only accelerated, passing by the older ideas of Arab nationalism and socialism, left in the dust of failed military campaigns and economic laggardness. "Islam is the solution" rings more frequently in the minds of engineering students at Cairo University who cannot finds jobs in their own country, or soldiers poorly equipped to deal with invisible foes, or merchants who cannot find customers in the wake of a global economic recession. To understand the power of this message, one needs to watch a crowd gather for a Shia ceremony at the Husseini Mosque in Cairo or at the President Saleh Mosque in Sanaa, Yemen, or the Umayyad Mosque in Damascus. Even the massive congregational mosques in Istanbul, once largely visited mostly by foreign tourists, now have more of the religious faithful who seem intent on rediscovering their religious grounds.

It would be a mistake, of course, to associate Islam's appeal with only the dispossessed, though they may embrace it more firmly. Islam penetrates the lives of almost all Muslims, in ways that are deeper than usually are found in Christian parts of the world. A February 2009 Gallup survey showed that the peoples of the Middle East placed almost uniform high importance on religion, while the citizens of Europe generally placed religion in the "least important" category. Islam pervades public speech, with references to God in common greetings and wishes. In many cases Islam is the official state religion: Article 2 of Part 1 of the Egyptian Constitution states, "Islam is the religion of the state," and Article 6 of the Moroccan Constitution similarly notes that "Islam shall be the state religion. The state shall guarantee freedom of worship for all." The last sentence indicates the effort at tolerance of other religions connected to Islam, though interfaith relations in the Middle East have been tested.

Islam may be the newest of the three religions of Abraham (Ibrahim), but it has been the subject of over 1,400 years of thought. Scholars throughout the Muslim world have decoded the complex language of the Quran, and the meanings of the sayings and deeds of the Prophet Muhammad. They work through text and recorded memory to decipher the meaning of "obligation," "vengeful," "martyr," and other passages as they shape laws based on their comprehension of centuries-old words. Islam has particularly empowered the jurist, who interprets Islamic legal responsibilities for Muslim communities. The jurists query about the proper role for Islam in the political sphere as well as in the household. They consider the proper role of banking within an Islamic context, and whether a just economic system requires economic security for the poor and dispossessed. They explore the proper relationship between the sexes, raising one of the most controversial aspects of Islam.

Amy Elizabeth Young brings frameworks from cultural anthropology to reflect on gender relations in the modern Middle East. She notes that while it is common, even among scholars, to attribute the shaping of gender relations to religion, their roots are also located in tribal society. Traditions run deep in the Middle East, as they do in China, where it could be argued that similar patrilineal structures formed from the clay of antiquity. The value of women as home-tenders conflicts with their upward aspirations, not just because religious strictures mandate such roles, but also because that is the way things have been. Indeed, as Young notes, Islam sends a mixed message for Islamic society on gender, with some passages emphasizing the equality of men and women as believers, and a number of Muslim countries have made strides in advancing women's interests. Arab socialism also pushed for gender equality, and in some cases state education also served to help level gender differentials, though male and female literacy rates differ considerably, as Young observes. Some private efforts, along with state attempts, have improved women's education in the Middle East, but sometimes those endeavors create a backlash, so that, for example, women may have higher levels of education than do men in some Middle East countries, but barriers to their employment erase that advantage. Finally, as Young notes, gender issues and gender relations differ widely across countries, and thus there is no general fix available to those who wish to push gender equality forward. For those outside the region who wish to effect change, Young correctly warns that there are numerous agents of change within the region and that outside assistance only complicates some already complicated situations.

The emphasis of Raymond William Baker's chapter is the Islamic Awakening, which is unfolding in the Middle East and beyond. Islamic voices span a broad range of understanding and interpretation, but many in the middle are gaining influence at the expense of both semisecular Arab regimes and extreme visions of Islam. While the term "political Islam" may generate fear in the minds of those outside the region, its language is largely about political accountability and a return to a moral vision of faith that many Muslims find lacking in their current political leadership. Egypt's Muslim Brotherhood and Turkey's Justice and Development Party (Adalet ve Kalkınma Partisi or AKP) reflect a moderate current within Islamic thinking. While moderate Islamist interpreters share a vision with extremists of the need to push back the historic veil of *jahiliyyah* (or pre-Islamic paganism), they deny that Islamic text and memory justify the spasm of destructive actions taken, often against other Muslims, but also against the "far enemy." Baker questions the American response to the currents of political Islam, noting that for the George W. Bush administration, Islamist movements became coagulated into one lump, largely to be resisted under the rubric of a "global war on terrorism." Such a broad-brush reaction to September 11 and other actions of Islamist violence only helped to mobilize Muslims who may have been on the fringes of political Islam, propelling many of them to move from reformers to advocates of violence empowered by the tradition of Islamic resistance to outside occupiers. Baker acknowledges the shift in the language of the Obama administration but also notes a traditional caution in the Muslim Middle East about poisoned honey. Moreover, as Baker warns, the new administration should avoid the intellectual trap of believing that Islam is fighting the outside world because it refuses to alter its historical worldview. While all Muslims look to the seventh century for inspiration, as Christians look to the time of Christ for similar encouragement, Islam, like Christianity, has undergone considerable transformation during its 1,400-year history and continues to evolve both socially and theologically. Although some of those transformative paths may lead back to the *Salifiyyist* narratives of Taqi Al Din Ahmad ibn Taymiyya or Sayyid Qutb, they have also led to the thought of Islamist modernists whom Baker interprets in his groundbreaking earlier work *Islam Without Fear* (Cambridge, MA: Harvard University Press, 2003), who have countered theologically the violence that the Salifiyyists too often justify.

The social context of the Middle East is actually adjunct to the political, economic, and international spheres located there. The dynamics of those fields are contingent on currents in society, which also move in connection with the political and economic lives of the countries in the area. None of these issue areas can be understood in isolation from the other wheels in the Middle East clock of life.

8

GENDER

Amy Elizabeth Young

Whoever says whatever our parents do, or decisions they make are the best? or that we have to accept every word of our elders as if it is a verse from the Qur'an? I don't deny the benefits of experience, but that does not mean what they say are the ultimate words of wisdom. They are humans and make mistakes too! Such idealistic view of parents or elders, absolute obedience and unquestioning respect only leads to dictatorial rule in the family.[1]

This statement by a nineteen-year-old Iranian may seem familiar to us as the kind of statement against parental authority common among young people in any or all societies in the world. It may be surprising to some readers, however, that this decisive statement is made by a female blogger, part of a new cohort of young women who are using the Internet to surpass the limits to their mobility and ability to express themselves that have been imposed on them by state and society and, perhaps, family. And the statement may take on extra weight when one remembers that the Middle East has the youngest population in the world; in Iran, comparable to other countries in the region, two-thirds of the population is under the age of thirty.[2] If these young people are choosing not to accept the words, traditions, and rule of their elders, this presages a great deal of change for the Middle East in upcoming years.

This chapter is about gender in the Middle East, a realm that is certainly undergoing great change and transformation today and will continue to do so into tomorrow. Women's issues may well be the most stereotyped and least understood aspect of the Middle East in the contemporary era. Since the 1970s and 1980s, numerous scholars, almost all of them female,[3] have published works showing the astonishing variety of forms of agency among women in the Middle East: in their families, communities, labor force, politics, and civil society. This work continues today and has provided a wealth of information about the forms of power and authority to which women have access (and from which they are barred) and how and when they can mobilize them in service of personal, familial, political, and legal transformation. Another transformation is taking place as well: the explicit recognition that "gender" is not a synonym for "women." Recent works have also begun to explore masculinity in the Middle East and to account for how family and society produce gendered roles and expectations that are simultaneously interrelated, complementary, reinforcing, and contested.

This chapter addresses some of the most salient gender issues in the region as they affect both men and women, drawing primarily on anthropological and historical works. In particular, I would like to address gender as part of past and current discourses of modernization and modernity in the Middle East. Abu-Lughod makes an excellent case for why I will not provide a general definition of either modernization or modernity here: These terms can only be defined within the specific contexts of what they purport to be or, more significantly, what they purport *not* to be.[4] In other words, these terms are always opposed to something else: the primitive, the premodern, the traditional, even the non-West. Gendered roles and expectations as they exist today do not come directly from "culture" or "religion" and have not arisen sui generis within groups in the Middle East. Rather, gender is part of the story of modernity discourses associated with colonialism, postcolonial nation-building, competing political factions, development programs, conflict, and other overarching factors in the region. These have emphasized particular notions of gender and family over others and institutionalized them through so-called modern laws and state practices; moreover, political factions and states have used certain notions of gender to promote their ideologies. This chapter will examine the predominant ideal structure of gender and family in the region before moving on to discuss how this has been acted upon by larger forces within the societies of the Middle East making claims about modernization and modernity. Then we will return to the topic of youth and social change and ask to what extent these notions of gender are being contested, dismantled, renegotiated, or reinforced.

GENDER AND THE FAMILY

Gendered roles and identities begin in the family. Much of the Middle East operates generally on a patrilineal, patrikin, and patriarchal family system ideal: religious and national identities are passed from father to children, children tend to be more closely located and related to their father's side of the family, and older males tend to have authority over younger males and all females.

Even Judaism, which is famously matrilineal in the sense that religious identity is passed from mother to child, is otherwise guided in the region by patrilineal understandings of kin relation and patriarchal social norms. Anthropologists have analyzed this as deriving from the tribal origins of some Middle Eastern societies and claim that this structure continues to have salience today, among Christian and Jewish as well as Muslim groups. This normative structure continues to have cultural, legal, and political (as well as analytical) traction despite vast change. Although it is important to remember that there are individual and cultural exceptions to this ideal, it nevertheless remains the foundation for laws and practices around gender and family despite the fact that most Middle Easterners do not characterize themselves as members of tribes, come from families that have lived in cities for generations, or are otherwise living in family and community structures that bear little resemblance to this ideal.

This notion of a tribe-based Middle Eastern society is accompanied by a corollary emphasis on the corporate nature of life and identity: Scholars assume that individuals in the Middle East think of themselves as a part of their family and group as much as, or more than, they think of themselves as individuals. In her theory of "patriarchal connectivity," Joseph nuances this understanding by describing the Arab individual as living in a tight-knit world of connections to others in the family, in which "maturity is signaled in part by the successful enactment of a myriad of connective relationships . . . [which are] not only functional but necessary for successful social existence."[5] In other words, individuals do see themselves as connected to others, but they hold multiple connections at multiple levels, and the individual self is both a part and a product of them. Joseph's concern is on "selving" within these connective family environments and the ways in which gendered selves develop within notions of family that are both connective and patriarchal and based on relationships of control between family members. She names this "patriarchal connectivity" with emphasis on elder male control of the family. However, she points out that the selving process is influenced by both males and females:

> Connectivity and patriarchy intertwine in variable ways. I caution, however, against seeing men or fathers as prime movers or causes of these complex relationships. Each person, including women and juniors, is an active participant, both caused and causative of the relations of inequality in patriarchal systems. The actions of persons are always embedded in relational matrices.[6]

Rather than characterizing the family as oppressive to women and men through a strict gender system, Joseph reminds us that it is more productive to examine the nature of roles and relationships between and across all individuals within the family. For one, we can distinguish between individuals' access to *power* versus access to *authority*. The female life cycle is in many ways one of increasing power within the family over the life span. Although daughters and sons are often pampered and indulged in early years, girls quickly become directed toward playing the female role in the household, performing chores, cooking, and serving the needs of males.[7] Though both daughters and sons may attend school, girls are still expected to do housework outside of school times, whereas sons may run free in the neighborhood and play. As they near adolescence, the freedom of girls to move around outside the house may be circumscribed or at least monitored.

It is as a young wife that a woman's power is generally at its lowest. She joins a family outside the natal family with which she is familiar, and her major source of security is the kindliness of her husband as she competes for space within the existing web of family connections in the household, ruled over by her new mother-in-law. If her mother-in-law perceives her as a threat to her own relationship with her son, this new wife will especially suffer; young married men often have to perform a balancing act between the needs of mother and wife, and those of the mother often triumph. However, this new wife knows that eventually, as she becomes the mother of sons to continue the patriline, her status in the family will rise. Toward the end of her life, when she has power over and through her grown male sons, she will experience the fullest sense of power in her lifetime.

Women's selving thus occurs in a context within which they must negotiate power within relationships of control that change over their lifetime. According to Kandiyoti,

> Women's life cycle in the patriarchally extended family is such that the deprivation and hardship she experiences as a young bride is eventually superseded by the control and authority she will have over her own subservient daughters-in-law. The cyclical nature of women's power in the household and their anticipation of inheriting the authority of senior women encourages a thorough internalization of this form of patriarchy by the women themselves.[8]

Women who face change and disruption that may affect their connective relationships and forms of selving are likely to "bargain with patriarchy" in ways that reinforce what they believe to be their traditional roles.[9] Women have great power in the domestic sphere, especially as their sons grow and establish families over which older women have great power, but they have little real authority in structural or institutional terms. They tend, thus, to cling to their roles in these relationships and the structures that support them, even if these are oppressive or harmful to them as individuals. This extends to policing the activities and decisions of younger women in the family.

Male selving proceeds within this same structure of patriarchal connectivity but according to a different pattern. The early childhood years of boys involve close identification with their mothers and other female family members. Gregg reports from a psychology study by Bouhdiba and a study on sexuality by Ouzi that "a mother and her children of this age [late childhood] may share their status as juniors and victims of patriarchal control and conspire to circumvent the father's authority."[10] But in preadolescence, at the same age when girls are identifying closely with their mothers through increasingly helping with household chores, boys are identifying increasingly with male relatives, accompanying them to their shops or to prayers or other activities outside the home. Boys begin to identify more with their patriline and may even, as former co-conspirators, become increasingly suspicious of their mothers, whom they perceive as outside the patriline and perhaps disloyal to it. This feeling is complicated, however, by a strong sentiment of loyalty to the mother in Islam, coming from the tradition of the Prophet Muhammad's stating that "Paradise is at the feet of the mother." There is also a close emotional connection; as Bouhdiba writes, "In an Arabo-Muslim setting the mother appears even more as a font of affection, all the more precious in that it is a restful oasis in the arid social desert" of negotiating new and sometimes anxiety-inducing norms of masculinity.[11]

Adolescence can also be a time of sexual experimentation for boys, including encounters and sexually symbolic games with friends and close male and female kin, or prostitutes, as they grow to see themselves as men with a sexual role to play in continuing the patriline. Marriage, however, marks the commencement of true manhood. Like women, men experience selving within relationships of power; unlike women, they slowly begin to assume authority over others through relationships of control. As Joseph writes, "Males and elders are privileged to enter the boundary of the self of others, shape its contours, and direct its relationships. The connective patriarch may view his wife (wives), sisters, junior siblings, and children as extensions of himself."[12] In fact, one reason for the unrest among young men in many Middle Eastern societies today is that they are increasingly unlikely to marry, and assume authority over their own family, until a much later age than in the past—perhaps as late as their thirties and forties. They are therefore in a long period of limbo between boyhood dependence and manly independence as married men with their own families. Several Gulf countries, Saudi Arabia, UAE, Bahrain, and Qatar, even have marriage funds available to help young men defray the costs of weddings.[13] Another gender difference is that the power of men within the family wanes with age as they are supplanted economically—and, increasingly today, in education level—by their grown sons, and is reduced by the growing power of their wives as mothers of those sons. Thus, during Abu-Lughod's ethnographic fieldwork among the Awlad Ali Bedouin group in Egypt, she recorded the following about Haj Sagr, the patriarch of one family with which Abu-Lughod was particularly close:

> Yet, Sagr pointed out, women want sons as much as men do. Hadn't I noticed, he asked me, giving his wife a glance, that as women get older, they use

their children to dominate their husband? They pay less and less attention to their husband. They tell him to go to hell. A woman raises her sons to displace him. Once she has grown sons, she doesn't need a husband at all.[14]

Again, this is an ideal-type family structure and set of relationships between males and females within the family. This family has undergone great change in recent decades, the most marked of these being the increase in nuclear families at the expense of extended families. Change has also come about through particular modernization schemes put forth by various political factions, which will be discussed later in this chapter. Family structure also varies according to rural versus urban location, ethnicity and its relation to the state, and other factors discussed elsewhere in this volume. For now, it is important to know how this family operates and informs the sense of self and actions of gendered individuals in families and communities, as well as how it remains in practices across the Middle East. Two examples concerning the importance of honor clarify this point.

Demographic trends throughout the region resulting in late marriage ages for both men and women make it difficult to maintain virginity before marriage. In numerous studies from Morocco, for example, males make it clear that they desire premarital sexual relationships and free interaction with women as girlfriends outside of marriage. Yet these same males expect to marry a virgin, as virginity suggests that a woman respects family and community ideals, is religious, and will be able to serve as an appropriate role model for her own daughters someday. Thus hymen reconstruction is the leading surgical procedure in Morocco, despite its high cost, so that women who are no longer virgins can appear to meet the expectations of bridegrooms and their families. Some, alternatively, engage in sexual activities that do not destroy the hymen, such as oral and anal sex, to circumvent the need for hymen reconstruction.[15] The seeming hypocrisy of these double standards, and the emphasis on the *appearance* of virginity no matter the reality, underline two themes of this section of the chapter. First, the gendered roles and expectations of individuals in the family continue despite social change. Although both men and women seek out sexual intercourse before marriage, both carry within themselves the expectations of the larger society and hold themselves and their peers to these expectations.[16] Second, appearance is important because undertaking the responsibility for maintaining appearance upholds these gendered expectations. When marriage takes place, and those involved are assured that the all-important hymen is still intact, social norms about marriage, family, and gender are underlined and reproduced.

A second example involves honor crimes, a term applied to an array of practices, from the killing of family members because of so-called honor violations to forced marriage. Honor killings appear to be more prevalent in Muslim societies than elsewhere and are stereotypically associated with Islam. Many Muslim groups do not practice honor killings, however, and most interpreters of religious texts argue that Islam does not permit the practice. Furthermore, those societies with the highest incidences of honor killings are outside the Middle East.[17] The use of the term "honor crimes" is tricky, moreover, in that it legitimizes the stated justification of the perpetrator rather than representing the perspective of the victim. It appears that so-called honor crimes often have a much different justification:

> Besides the general and familiar association of women with property in the "honour" paradigm, there are many instances in which the primary motivation for an "honour crime" is more directly something other than "honour"— a brother's arguments with his sister over inheritance, for example, or a husband's desire to be rid of a wife, with a murder not so much covered up as proclaimed as a matter of "honour" in the expectation of a minimal punishment and less disapprobation from at least some sections of society than otherwise would have been the case.[18]

In spite of the problematic nature of the term, the latter part of the above quote gets to the heart of why the issue must nevertheless be addressed. The category "crimes of honor" does exist legally across the region (as elsewhere) and mitigates the sentence of a perpetrator of an honor crime; likewise, it is a socially recognized and, to some extent, accepted category that some individuals and groups in the Middle East use to explain and justify male violence against women. Honor crimes relate to the patriarchal belief that sexual activity within the family can and should be regulated by elder males. It is worth noting that "within the family" allows for honor crimes against males as well, which do indeed occur, though not with the frequency of those against females.

But the patriarchy explanation does not treat the complexity of the issue. The example of honor killings among Kurds in Iraqi Kurdistan shows the intersection of law, politics, and ethnicity on the problem of honor killings and how they also pose obstacles to activists attempting to reform the law. According to Begikhani, the political configuration of Iraqi Kurdistan is an obstacle to addressing the issue: Kurdistan is an area of Iraq governed by two Kurdish political parties in a "fratricidal confrontation" that has led to the division of the region into two separately administered areas.[19] Before 1991, Iraqi law governing the region recognized and mitigated for the category of honor killings. With the establishment of the Kurdish regional government in 1992, women's rights advocates began to pursue reform of the law, a difficult task given the split administrations and competition for power between enemy governments. In 2003, the parliaments began to take reform seriously and reduce the occurrence of mitigation in some cases. But this only applies to limited numbers of crimes and has not been widely accepted by the society.

Although, and perhaps because, Kurdish society is undergoing migration and resulting social change, tribal affiliation is still an important, and indeed unifying, source of identity for most Kurds. One tradition growing out of this tribal structure is that of the *komelayeti*, a council of representatives who rule on disputes within the community, pass judgment, and enforce sanctions. They often rule harshly on honor-related issues, such as calling for the death of individuals involved in illicit sexual unions. These councils cling to their role and traditional sanctions as a bulwark against social and political change and as an affirmation of their special Kurdish identity in light of the fact that Kurds do not have their own homeland. The unofficial civil war between political parties also means that these parties court the support of such tribal governing structures, so they have been reluctant to interfere with the power of the komelayeti and meet the full request for reform made by women's groups. Additionally, these phenomena intersect with an Islamist discourse that sees new human rights–informed criticisms of komelayeti rulings as a sign of Western cultural imperialism against the Kurds and Muslims in general. The complexity of this issue, even in one particular location in the Middle East, illustrates that the ideal-type, patriarchal family structure can be manipulated, reinforced, and even expanded by larger political, legal, and historical circumstances.

NATIONALISM, STATE-BUILDING, AND THE "MODERN" FAMILY

Anthropologists, feminists, and other scholars of women have long interrogated inequality between males and females as an issue of the private versus public sphere. Women are believed to be associated with the private, domestic sphere of the home, whereas men are associated with the public, external sphere of larger society. In reality, the lines between these spheres—and gendered roles within them—are blurred, in the Middle East as elsewhere. One of the purposes of veiling, for example, is to allow women to maintain the modesty and protection of the private sphere as they move into the public sphere for education or work.[20] The jobs that men and women perform in the public sphere serve the primary purpose of allowing them to support their family and reproduce the family in the private sphere. Further, the private sphere of the family and women's roles within it have been co-opted by states through legal and other institutions that allow states to govern the family in its home. All of this has been accomplished through discourses of modernization and the state-building process.

Most of the Middle East was under colonial rule until the early to midtwentieth century. In fact, the Middle East was by and large created through colonialism, during which European powers laid down new borders over the remains of the Ottoman Empire and brought new combinations of people under increasingly centralized bureaucracies. These new borders and administrative units lasted for the most part beyond the official end of colonialism and formed the nucleus of state-building efforts into the postcolonial period. Since this period, the legacies of several "isms"—including nationalism, secularism/leftism, and Islamism—have continued to shape the lives of individuals in both the private and public spheres. Women's issues, and the perceived low status of women in family, society, and religion, were an important part of the colonial discourse of otherness and inferiority (while, ironically, those colonizers who held such perceptions about the Middle East were staunch opponents of burgeoning feminism in Europe). Women's issues were, therefore, an inevitable part of the nationalist response as well.[21]

Women played an active role in nationalist movements to end colonialism, and this participation both depended on and expanded gendered norms of women's roles in the family and community. In the case of Morocco, for example, Allison Baker writes that, during the active resistance to French colonial rule, women were able to operate under the radar of the French by taking advantage of traditional beliefs about their feminine identity—namely, that as women they were incapable of participating in political or military action.[22] They used the custom of wearing veils and long robes in public, and their right of refusal to search by male soldiers, as a means of secreting weapons, communications, food, and other supplies to men involved in the resistance. At the same time, however, they were able to move beyond traditional gender roles, occupying new roles within the resistance movement and new physical spaces outside the home and even noting "a dramatic improvement in their relations with men."[23] There were two broad classes of women taking part in the resistance movement: bourgeois women helping with the ideological work of the nationalist movement, and lower-class women taking part in the armed resistance. Generally, independence brought a shock to women who had participated in the armed resistance. Many were divorced or repudiated; Widows who had lost their husbands in the movement were often relegated to marginal social status, and others were forced to return to their traditional roles and expectations of remaining quietly at home, tending the house and children. Elite nationalist women, on the other hand, experienced a kind of emancipation, encouraged by their families to further their education, and continuing to be active, albeit in limited capacity, in the nationalist movement.

In Egypt, as in many other places, determining the direction of women's role in the public sphere was up to elite and middle-class, rather than working-class or rural, women.[24] This class split has continued in politics today (although it can be overstated by critics):[25] The few women who do have some role in politics or as heads of associations tend by and large to be middle- to upper-class women, and there is a lesser role for lower-class women except in more localized, grassroots political efforts. Elite women continued to live the dream of earlier nationalist efforts and discourses founded on the notion that it was necessary to modernize the family in order to modernize the nation. A modern nation was in turn necessary for competing with and eventually driving out the colonial powers. Writers during and after the colonial period advocated the nuclear family and education for both males and females so that both could play an important role in the family and nation, arguing in particular that more educated women made for better wives and mothers. For Najmabadi, this transition from premodern to modern Iran in the nineteenth century took the form of images and texts by reformists hoping to transform women from "house" (in other words, part of the household) to "manager of the house." Educated women could help their husbands build and manage modern households and educate children, and be true helpmates in the home, leaving their husbands to focus on working outside the home and building a modern Iran.[26] Women were also encouraged to leave behind patterns of female homosociality within the space of the home and neighborhood. Rather than interact with multi-generational and multi-class groups of extended family members, neighbors, and servants, the modern woman should concentrate on her new duties of management and keeping order within her small, bourgeois, nuclear family. Reformists may have felt threatened by homosocial worlds of female solidarity and the "sexually explicit language of that world that is often hostile to men."[27]

Why the focus on women? As Fleischmann explains,

> Reformist, Western-oriented men were seeking to modernize *themselves*, albeit through focusing their attention on women . . . and reflexively turned their attention to women, targeting them as the backward, atavistic embodiments of all that was wrong with "tradition" and traditional culture and religion.[28]

The focus of their concern, however, was not dismantling patriarchal control of the family but rather improving women's status so they could better serve the family and, by extension, the nation. In the postcolonial years, in many cases, elite nationalists became state-builders, as they moved into positions of power or leadership in government and established political parties that institutionalized such ideologies of modernity. Algeria, as described by Lazreg, provides a good example of how nationalist anticolonial rhetoric was transformed into state-building rhetoric based on gender difference. The socialist Ben Bella government, morphing out of the FLN (National Liberation Front, the revolutionary body that led the fight for Algeria's independence from France), wrote the following in the 1964 Charter of Algiers:

> For centuries the Algerian woman was maintained in an inferior condition justified by retrograde conceptions and erroneous interpretations of Islam.

Colonialism aggravated such a situation by triggering among us a natural re-action of self-defense that isolated women from the rest of society. The war of liberation enabled the Algerian woman to assert herself by carrying out responsibilities side by side with man, and taking part in the struggle.[29]

The charter further states, "Algerian woman should be able to participate effectively in politics and the building of socialism. . . . She should be able to put her energy in the service of the country by taking part in its economic life, thereby genuinely promoting herself through work."[30] Women's new ability, by virtue of their being side by side with men rather than their intrinsic worth as citizens of a new nation, now allowed them the opportunity to work hard outside the home (in addition to domestic duties) for the economic good of the state. In other words, Lazreg points out, women's role in state-building, as in resistance, became one of service and sacrifice. In 1963, Ben Bella even asked that women donate their gold and silver jewelry, their most significant personal source of wealth and status, to the National Bank. Lazreg writes, "Women, as a group, were seen as necessary to the building of the state, but as contributors, not participants. . . . Sacrifice, not duty complemented by right, was the cornerstone of the new state's view of women."[31] In later decades, as the socialist government lost legitimacy against powerful Islamist discourses and violence, women were expected to sacrifice again—this time giving up their hopes for a family code that would guarantee and support their rights within the family and community.

WOMEN AND POLITICAL MOVEMENTS

So to recap, we have an ideal-type family based on relationships between indi-viduals that reinforce and are reinforced by a patriarchal system of control. And we have nationalisms that compete with, co-opt, and attempt to control this patriarchal family, and the gendered individuals within it, for their own pur-poses. Now we turn our attention to two political trends or movements that mediate this relationship between family and state: secularism and Islamism. These terms are vast oversimplifications of complex ideologies and historical re-alities, both useful and limiting as a set of binary oppositions that only make sense in contrast with each other. So-called secularists come in many forms and can even advocate for religion within certain spheres. So-called Islamists come in many forms and have a variety of agendas as well, some relying on secular in-stitutions to achieve their goals. In other words, these terms are problematic as oversimplifications but discursively useful as oppositions that shape the dis-courses on gender, family, and state. In this section, I will discuss certain aspects of secularism and Islamism in the Middle East and look more closely at two important areas of debate within and between them as relates to gender. The first is reform of family law, also referred to as personal status law, as it delineates status, rights, and responsibilities to individuals based on their position within the family. The second involves the participation of women in study and (re)interpretation of religious texts.

In the postcolonial period, from the 1950s to the 1970s and beyond, nationalism was joined by another political movement and ideology: secularism in the form of left-leaning politics, which most saliently took the form of Arab socialism and Baathism, mainly in Egypt, Iraq, and Syria, but also building opposition leftist parties or movements among nationalist political regimes in Morocco and pre-revolution Iran, as well as among the Palestinians. Individuals across the region, both men and women and particularly young adults and students, were swept up in the fervor of left-leaning politics. Class issues were certainly part of the enthusiasm: Non-elites generally found more room to participate in left-leaning parties and political movements than they had in earlier nationalist efforts, and working-class women were valorized for their contributions to economic production outside the home. As in much of the postcolonial world, leftist political discourse opened up for women the possibility that they could have a greater role in the public sphere and equality with their male comrades. These dreams faded, however, as activists realized that, in the leadership of political movements as well as in their personal lives, male colleagues were unwilling to live up to the equality espoused by their slogans and platforms.[32] Thus female activists began forming women's associations that would specifically address women's inequality in all societies in the region. During this broad phase of women's political history in the region, women's activism expanded from a primary focus on education for girls and charitable giving to include a variety of issues, such as political participation, violence against women, access to educational and job opportunities, and legal reform.

It would be impossible to summarize briefly the political context of women's rights efforts to organize around particular goals, including family law, in the entire region; some broad patterns can be noted, however. One pattern is state feminism, in which state leaders make the top-down decision to "emancipate" women through laws and education—for reasons similar to the modernization processes discussed above. State feminism has been the rule in Tunisia and Turkey, as well as Iran before the 1979 revolution. Family codes in Tunisia and Turkey are among the most egalitarian in terms of family relations, but state efforts to enforce secular laws are currently being challenged as undemocratically formed and actually anti-woman in many senses. The prohibition on veiling in public spaces in Turkey, for example, is named as a major hardship for Muslim women who choose to veil. A similar kind of state feminism appeared in the Arab socialist/Baathist regimes of Syria, Iraq, and Egypt but has been reversed in Iraq since the American invasion and has had a checkered history in Egypt's successive regimes. This Arab socialist narrative sought more egalitarian laws for women not only for the sake of modernization but also as part of a socialist emphasis on harnessing women's productive and reproductive labor, a view that women were a wasted national resource to be cultivated. In the rentier states of the Arab Gulf, family law issues have taken a backseat to concerns with political participation as well as other basic civil/political rights and economic rights (for example, to employment, to own businesses, etc.). Iran and Saudi Arabia currently have the most restrictive laws on "morality," including surveillance of women's dress and interactions between males and females, but Iran is also in the forefront of the region in terms of women's education and employment, political participation, and access to contraception. The societies with the longest histories of powerful women's rights movements, with the primary goal of personal status/family code reform, are Egypt, Morocco, Algeria, and Jordan. The Palestinians could be included in this group as well, although the immediate and dire political and economic concerns of the Palestinians, under Israeli military and economic occupation, always threaten to override the focus of female activists on legal and social change for women alone.[33]

Despite this complexity, one clear trend is that secularism has gone hand in hand with a certain set of demands for legal reform that emphasize the need for *equality* between men and women in the family. Whatever rights women had achieved in the public sphere were all but meaningless to secularist activists as long as a patriarchal vision of the family—upheld by certain interpretations of religious texts—remained in place.

Islamism has also facilitated women's political activity in ways that scholars are only beginning to analyze and understand. There have not been enough studies of these religio-political movements in the Middle East from a gender perspective to indicate their agendas by and for women, both within their political parties and movements and in society in general. Ethnographic research by White among female Islamists in Turkey, however, lends support to the view that women and men within Islamist associations are not always of the same mind on women's and family issues.[34] For male Welfare Party members in Turkey, there was an emphasis on the importance of a woman's remaining at home to take care of the family rather than working, and veiling became the outward symbol of this role. In private, women strained against these limits and complained that they wanted more access to education, jobs outside the home, and permission to come and go as they pleased. Indeed, many young women became active in the party as a means of doing something that would allow them to escape their restricted role within the family. White writes of the dangers of blindly assuming, as we so often do, that Islamist women share cultural expectations of their roles:

> One manifestation of the implicit contradiction between conscious activist intentions and the varied cultural expectations hidden under the canopy of

populism is the difference in construction of women's rights, privileges and motivations by activist women and their male colleagues within the Welfare Party. While many activist women I interviewed in Umraniye [a lower-class neighborhood of Istanbul] were engaged in the Islamist project in order to carve out new areas of autonomy within the traditional expectations of their community, male activists in the next office were motivated in part by a desire to reinforce traditional female roles and to enhance their own autonomy vis-à-vis women—for instance, by supporting polygyny, which is illegal in secular Turkey. The women were very much interested in using party activism to advance the position of women, particularly through education and work outside of the home.[35]

The strong political presence of women within such politico-religious movements represents a real threat to more secularist movements and their vision of women's political participation and legal reform. In Morocco, women's rights associations that are linked to leftist and secularist political factions increasingly refuse to allow women from the Islamist political party to come to their political participation training, for fear that they will use the tools they have gained to promote an Islamist agenda once they have obtained some political power. According to Ertürk, Turkey is characterized by this same enmity between Islamist women's groups and secularist women's groups.[36] She points, for example, to the controversy over the turban (head covering) of the first woman elected to the Turkish parliament, Merve Kavakçı, in 1999. As a secular state, Turkey has a policy that prohibits religious clothing and symbols in public spaces such as government buildings and universities. Kavakçı wears a headscarf and appeared at her swearing-in ceremony to be told that she could not enter the parliament building and take her seat without removing her headscarf. Although the important goal of electing women to parliament was met (albeit a woman representing the Islamist Virtue Party), secular feminist groups nevertheless supported the state's treatment of her,[37] which included preventing her taking the oath as a member of parliament and eventually withdrawing her Turkish citizenship after discovering she had not disclosed her dual US citizenship when she registered as a candidate in the election. For Ertürk, this and other examples show the isolation of Islamist women even when they gain power through their parties and organizations, despite the fact that secularist women's groups opposed to them share this isolation as well: "Consequently, Islamist women, at least those in the mainstream, find themselves a part of the establishment—although in a rather awkward fashion. This situation brings to light the patriarchal contradictions in their lives, thus bringing them closer to their secularist sisters in their stance vis-à-vis patriarchy."[38]

Two brief examples will illuminate the very different emphases of women within these two broad camps in terms of the relationship between family and religion. First, reform of family law, or personal status law—the body of laws that regulate marriage, divorce, child custody, and inheritance and that concern what we call "women's rights"—is a hotly debated topic between secularists and Islamists, as it gets to the heart of perceptions of Islam's place in the family and therefore in the state. The Middle East is under great external pressure—from North American and European governments, aid agencies, the UN and its millennial goals for ending poverty, and even occupying military forces—to reform laws regarding women and their status in the family and in society. There is also pressure from within—from human rights and women's rights organizations and, in some cases, political parties—to improve women's status. There is also pressure from certain religious groups to keep laws the same or make them even more conservative, reflecting how closely family law is identified with sharia, or Islamic law. The legal codes of most countries in the region—for example, tax, labor, and penal codes—are secular and externally derived, many of them holdovers from the colonial era. The only vestiges of sharia are in the family/personal status codes. It is important to keep in mind that family codes are not commensurate with sharia—they are, rather, based on interpretations of jurisprudence, combined with colonial and customary law, and subject to various reinterpretations and modernizations by states since the end of the colonial era. Thus, the family code in each country is different from all others in the region, although each claims that its family code is based on sharia.[39] In most Muslim majority countries, other religious groups are subject to their own family code as well. In Morocco, for example, the Jewish community is exempt from the laws of the Moroccan family code and is governed instead by the Hebraic Code developed by the Jewish community's political and religious leaders; and in Egypt, family matters concerning the Coptic Christian minority are handled in separate family courts. Nevertheless, the symbolic importance of family law as having some relation to sharia is great, and it is the driving force behind the desire of many religious movements to preserve the family code as is or fight against its secularization. Family law also holds the symbolic importance of protecting the Muslim family (and patriarchal oversight of it) against influence or change by external (read: Westernizing) forces.

Morocco's 2004 reform of the family code is the most radical recent revision of women's rights in the region. It exemplifies the concurrence of decisions, political and social structures, and even unpredictable events that allow for a change to family law. The 2004 reform included several significant provisions: It expanded women's rights to file for divorce, including for what we might call "irreconcilable differences"; removed the requirement that a female contract her marriage through a male representative or *wali*, usually a father or other male relative; raised the minimum age of marriage to eighteen for both males and females; required court oversight of polygamy in a way that makes it more difficult to practice; further protected women's rights to retain custody of their children after divorce and remarriage; and set wives and husbands as equal heads of household, removing the legal requirement that wives obey their husbands. Although there are many loopholes in these provisions and their implementation depends greatly on the discretion of individual judges, these reforms on paper represent a major shift in the understanding of how law oversees the family realm in Morocco.

These reforms did not arise in a vacuum, however. They were strongly supported by King Mohammed VI as well as the bulk of civil society, including strong human rights and women's rights organizations. They were also generally supported by Islamist groups because of a particular confluence of political and other factors that encouraged Islamist support.[40] But by and large the reforms were the fruition of decades of work by women's rights and human rights activists and associations. Their emphasis was on equality between men and women in the family as an extension of the equality guaranteed for all citizens by the Moroccan constitution and called for in the UN Convention for the Elimination of All Forms of Discrimination Against Women (CEDAW). In other words, the state should govern the family through imposing equality in place of Islamic notions of complementary roles and responsibilities for women and men.

A second example is the participation of women in studying and (re)interpreting religious texts. All of the major religious groups in the region practice some form of gender segregation or discrimination, especially in more "orthodox" versions of the religion. In Islam, women and men pray in separate spaces in the mosque and enter separate doors to get to them; women are most often seated behind or above men so that men will not be distracted by the sight of women when they should be focused on prayer. Among certain Jewish groups, this same pattern guides the ritual separation and immersion of women during their menstrual cycles.[41] Christian sects in the region also practice certain forms of segregation, most notably in barring women from the highest positions of leadership. Thus, the emerging discourse that the advancement of women's status is best accomplished through religion rather than secularism requires explanation.

Segregation is also present in women's relations to religious texts; they have not been (or at least less often than men) readers or interpreters of religious texts but are now demanding this role. El-Or has written extensively about the lack of religious "literacy" among Orthodox Jewish women in Israel and recent efforts to correct this imbalance: "The field of study and knowledge is the weak link in the chain separating the world of women from the world of men."[42] Muslim women are likewise engaging in study and reinterpretation of texts, either through formal or informal study groups in homes and mosques or as scholarly authors of works calling for new interpretations to complement or replace centuries of male jurisprudence that inform family law today. In study groups, women are using the segregation characteristic of Islamic worship and practice as a means of empowerment, bringing women together for support, education, and agency through submission to and understanding of their religious belief. Mahmood has written of piety movements in Egypt and how women are finding what may be—especially to Western feminist scholars—surprising kinds of agency through submission to the "patriarchal assumptions" at the heart of their religious belief.[43] She gives the example of two women in a study group discussing the cultivation of the Islamic virtue of shyness or modesty.[44] This is a virtue for both men and women but is especially valued in women, and the women in the study group are discussing a story from the Quran of a woman who exhibited this special form of modesty. In the discussion, one woman explains how shyness was difficult for her to cultivate because it went against her personality, but through teaching herself to *act* and *speak* with modesty, she was able to develop it as a personality trait that came to feel natural. Her friend compared this with learning to wear *hijab*, or the veil: First one feels awkward, but over time the bodily act of wearing the veil comes to feel so natural and such a part of oneself that one does not feel comfortable without it. Mahmood notes that classical understandings of feminism would argue these women are forcing themselves to comply with patriarchal norms in a kind of betrayal of self. But Mahmood argues that these forms of submission, through bodily acts, are a form of agency, that women are acting in ways that allow them to *be* educated, pious, and respectable.[45] From this perspective, gendered segregation in religious practice in the Middle East may be seen as a catalyst for development of the self that then enables new forms of engagement in the public sphere.

Despite the complexities of these practices, one clear trend is that Islamism has gone hand in hand with a certain set of actions and interpretations of texts that emphasize the need for *complementarity* between men and women in the family. Whatever rights women had achieved in the public sphere, and whatever transformations in the family were wrought through family law reform, these were all but meaningless without mutual respect between males and females for the unique roles that they have been formed to play in the family and in society.

States in the Middle East have been quick to intercept the tools of piety movements for their own agendas, including the study-group setting in which women seek to interpret religious texts for personal transformation. The overlap between this religious issue and larger structures can be seen in the example of the *morshidat* in Morocco. These are women who have been trained by the Ministry of Islamic Affairs and Endowments to go into neighborhoods and lead prayer meetings and study groups, with the intent of ensuring that a certain kind of Islam is being discussed and disseminated—a kind of Islam espoused by the state. This program grew directly out of the May 2003 bombings, when an extremist group killed thirty-three people and injured one hundred others by attacking tourist sites and a Jewish community center in the heart of Casablanca. Political leaders and the press expressed very public concern about how the preaching and teaching of extreme beliefs in Islam may have led to or encouraged this kind of terrorism, not seen in Morocco before. The state immediately reacted by rounding up so-called extremists and building up the very powerful Ministry of Islamic Affairs and Endowments to oversee all religious teaching in Morocco. Mosques received approved topics to cover in Friday prayers, the state aired television programs with a particular kind of interpretation of Islamic texts, and cassette tapes with unapproved teachings were banned. In 2006, the morshidat program began, with the dual purpose of extending the state's oversight of religious teaching into homes where women were studying Islam and of supporting the state's plan for legal reform and an improvement in the status of women. The morshidat are an important symbol of how women can fill leadership roles within the religion if only with the support of the state.

Abu-Lughod uses an examination of contemporary television serials and a critical reading of Egyptian nationalist and reformer Qasim Amin to argue that, in fact, today's secularists and Islamists are both children of modernity discourses. Islamists seek a return to a "purer" form of the Islamic family and castigate the inculcation of Western values in Egyptian society today. Yet,

> What is characteristic of the Islamists is that they stigmatize sexual independence and public freedoms as Western but much more gingerly challenge women's rights to work, barely question women's education, and unthinkingly embrace the ideals of bourgeois marriage. Yet the latter three are elements of the turn-of-the-century modernist projects that might well carry the label "feminist" and whose origins are just as entangled with the West as are the sexual mores singled out in horror.[46]

One aspect of modernity from which both secularists and Islamists have benefited, according to Ertürk, is that modernization processes have created a space of competing discourses, which has had the effect of "broadening the space for autonomous individual action beyond what is intended by the various political discourses."[47] In other words, one of the major effects of modernization has been to create a variety of discourses and perspectives from which one can choose and on which one can act. Yet, at the same time, modernization has developed or strengthened powerful institutions (such as laws and courts) that limit the actions one can take. Thus the limits imposed on families by law have increased, as has the ability of individuals and families to act on and contest the law. That these limits may constrict rather than expand gender roles is a critique of modernization that has not been taken seriously enough by scholars.[48]

EDUCATION, AND DEVELOPMENT

How have states managed to pursue their own agendas despite these competing secularist and Islamist trends? One way is by linking international discourses of education and development to, once again, modernity and modernization. Education begins in the family through enculturation; as seen in the first section, boys and girls learn their different roles within the family early on, primarily at the hands of mothers and other female family members who provide care for them. As compulsory early childhood education is now the norm across the region, however, the state early on intervenes in the education process and does its part in forming gendered citizens. Education has played into nationalist projects across the region in the modern era, especially in the postcolonial period as newly delineated states attempt to form citizens as members of a new state with new borders and a new mix of populations.

A fascinating compilation of articles on contemporary textbooks in Muslim-majority countries shows the variety of ways in which the state attempts to shape family identity and roles into citizen identity and roles through textbooks. In Jordan, Saudi Arabia, and Oman, for example, textbooks seek to instill certain civic values that reflect Islamic and family norms such that individuals will care for society in ways similar to those in which they care for family members. This can lead to contradictions when it comes to the gendering of family members and citizens, however. In Jordan, for example, textbooks include statements about the importance of equity and harmony between family members (especially husband and wife) that fit the kinds of civic values the state would like to instill. Yet these are confused, in both "Islamic texts" for religion classes and "civic texts" for classes outside the religion curriculum, with statements questioning women's role in the public sphere, suggesting that they should instead be taking care of the home; encouraging women to veil; stating the importance of the mother's role in teaching children about Islam; and overall hinting at the "threat of social fragmentation hang[ing] over the heads of women" if they do not live according to these ideals.[49] These restrictions on women do not mesh with more general statements about equality between men and women, or with socioeconomic realities that require women to work outside the home or act as head of household when husbands are unemployed or working abroad. The confusion may mesh well, however, with Jordanian political realities, as the state pushes for family law reform yet must placate the Islamist and tribal groups that oppose it.[50]

The late twentieth century was remarkable for an increased presence of women in schools throughout the region. Compulsory education efforts attempted to keep children in school until some level of literacy was achieved; these were most successful in the Gulf states of United Arab Emirates, Bahrain, Kuwait, and Qatar, as well as Turkey and Jordan, all of which have literacy rates above 85 percent, and Israel, with a literacy rate of 97 percent.[51] These efforts were less successful in North Africa (Tunisia 74 percent, Egypt 71 percent, Algeria 70 percent, and Morocco 52 percent) and Yemen (54 percent). The uneven and difficult implementation of compulsory education can be seen, however, in the starkly different literacy rate for males and females in those states that do not have high literacy. In Morocco, for example, 66 percent of males are literate compared to 44 percent of females; likewise, in Yemen, 70 percent of males are literate versus only 30 percent of females. In states with high literacy rates, there is still some gender difference; in Bahrain, for example, male literacy is at 89 percent and female at 80 percent. Despite compulsory schooling throughout much of the region, girls tend to drop out of school earlier than boys, often in grade school around the age of adolescence and especially in rural areas. Sometimes this is because families need girls at home to perform chores or to prepare for marriage and the management of a household. More often, it is because families fear what may happen to girls during long commutes to and from school each day.

During the late twentieth century, the numbers of women present in higher education surpassed those of men in several Middle Eastern countries, especially those in the Gulf region,[52] and some states are considering instituting quotas to help ensure that 50 percent of university slots are reserved for males. But these statistics for women in higher education do not necessarily match the social world that awaits them after graduation, one of high unemployment and discrimination against women in hiring, as well as the expectation that women's ultimate goal is to marry and manage the household. Critics have claimed that the presence of women in the workforce takes away employment from men, which, again, stands in the way of men's being able to set up a household and marry. Some husbands make it clear that they do not wish to have an educated wife, and families fight raising the legal age of marriage to eighteen in several societies by claiming that waiting for girls to finish their education before marrying leaves them open to loss of virginity and other problems that may interfere with their ability to marry well. Since, depending on context, a woman's economic future may lie with her husband and family, these are serious issues to be considered. Other critics have claimed that Middle Eastern societies are not working hard enough to take advantage of skilled and educated women, that biases remain against employing them, and that laws (supporting maternity leave, claims of sexual harassment, etc.) are not sufficiently in place to promote and protect women's employment. Thus men are represented in paid employment at two to three times the rate of women; women continue to fill the ranks of the unwaged or informally employed; and these trends show little sign of changing in the near future.

In general, as the populace in the Middle East grows more educated, its expectations for employment and material success are unmet. This segues well into the second topic of this section: education's ties to numerous development issues that are also gendered. Social indicators are increasingly tied to females, especially the education level of mothers; in its 2004 "State of the World's Children" report, for example, UNICEF listed girls' education as the most urgent goal in accomplishing the UN's Millennium Development goals, encompassing a wide variety of antipoverty, health, human rights, and development issues.[53] Illiteracy is a major development issue as it affects so many other aspects of life, such as employment. Men are unable to start or financially maintain families. Divorced or repudiated women are present among the homeless and impoverished population, as many of them are illiterate and have no employment skills that would allow them to support themselves and their children. The political, economic, and social complexity surrounding illiteracy in the Middle East can be seen in the wide variance in literacy rates across the region, noted above.

Whether in an oil-rich kingdom in the Gulf region or a resource-poor state in North Africa, there are development issues shared widely that have an enormous effect on gender and family, including urbanization, migration, unemployment, overpopulation, and lack of infrastructure. Their effects vary, however, across the region. A brief look at one of these problems, overpopulation, shows how development, education, and earlier themes from this chapter are tied together and represent yet another gender issue in the Middle East. Population growth rates have been among the highest in the world since the 1980s.[54] This became a problem as economic opportunities began to decline, wars and conflicts increased debt and diminished states' abilities to care for their populations, and refugee populations from neighboring regions swelled. Yet larger families were prized widely in the region, especially in rural areas and among families who feel that muslims are required to reproduce and expand the Muslim population. Birth rates also tend to rise during and after times of conflict, as people attempt to replenish their dead and wounded population, sometimes at the behest of state propaganda.

Since 1988, Iran has taken the lead in the region in establishing a model family-planning program. After the 1979 revolution, family planning programs were not abandoned but were also not promoted, and Ayatollah Khomeini "called on women to reproduce and find satisfaction in motherhood."[55] After his death, the Khamenei regime decided to promote family planning, anxious about growing debt after the Iran-Iraq war, growing poverty, and a growing refugee population from Afghanistan and elsewhere. They did so through conducting public education campaigns and distributing free contraception to married women and men, as well as promoting literacy, education, male participation in family planning, and issuing *fatwas*, or religious rulings, claiming that Islam required healthy families over plentiful families. Religious leaders pointed to the Prophet Muhammad's own use of early withdrawal as a family planning technique, and this remains the favored method in Iran, followed by condom use and then surgical techniques. Couples are encouraged not to have children before the age of eighteen or after the age of thirty-five: "Not too late, not too soon, not too many" is a ubiquitous slogan. Tober et al. credit the partnership between health officials and religious leaders in producing a plan that is culturally and religiously acceptable, and the program has been greatly successful in diminishing the birth rate.[56]

This must be understood within a larger context of women's increasing presence in employment, education, and government in Iran, many of them working through the Islamic regime to demand rights and access to the public sphere.[57] Ali calls into question this link between the public presence of women and improved family planning numbers as yet another twist in discourses of modernity, using the Egyptian family planning program as an example.[58] Contraception has been associated with femaleness, and women have been more likely to seek out contraception as they must carry, feed, and provide primary care for children. To bring men into family planning schemes, Ali argues, the Egyptian state had to convince them that family planning is a good strategy for modernizing the nation, that modern families should be characterized by communication and choice between husbands and wives in the nuclear family unit. Egyptian state ad campaigns, technically directed and funded by USAID and Johns Hopkins University, ridicule "backward" men who mistreat their wives and force them to have more children than the men can provide for, contrasted with "modern" men who help with chores around the home and eagerly consult their wives about contraception. Such discourses efface structural problems leading to high birth rates, linked to poverty, underdevelopment, and discrimination against certain groups in Egypt, and instead place the blame for high birth rates on individual families and, in particular, men. Other discourses invoke men's protective nature by reminding them of their responsibility to ensure the health and well-being of their wives and children, again underlining men's patriarchal authority within the family.

Despite a government interest in family planning since 1984, Yemen has had negligible success in decreasing the birth rate or promoting contraception use. Chase and Alaug argue that the conservative Yemeni state refused until recently to address rights issues that prevented women from accessing contraception.[59] These included private sphere issues, such as male control of women's movement and violence against women that disrupt their ability to make choices about contraception; but also public sphere issues, including disparate access to state health facilities between urban and rural areas and the expense of increasingly privatized health services. Now the government is attempting a rights-based approach that deals with both the public and private sphere simultaneously: "Conceptualized in this manner, rectifying a rights violation—even one in the 'private' sphere—is seen as fundamental rather than ancillary to accomplishing the goal of advancing women's health status and, in that way, also impact on an issue such as population growth to the benefit of Yemen's overall economic goals."[60]

These different approaches nevertheless share a common theme: State needs necessitate intervention in the private sphere of the family and relationships between husband and wife. As with other topics discussed in this chapter, one way states accomplish family planning is through education and discourses of modernity that equate family with nation. And again we see women being positioned as subjects rather than agents of these discourses whereas men's participation in family planning is necessary to realize the state's vision of modernity in the form of development.

GENDER AND CONFLICT

The Middle East is one of the most heavily conflicted regions in the world, and it is impossible to treat the topic of gender without a consideration of how it is impacted by conflict. Inter- and intranational conflicts in Iraq, the Palestinian territories, Morocco/the Western Sahara, Algeria, and Turkey have accounted for hundreds of thousands of deaths in recent years; even more wounded; displacement of hundreds of thousands of people; and long-term physical damage resulting from rape, torture, imprisonment, and other brutalities. The trickledown effects of conflict in the region include high unemployment rates, disruption of education opportunities for a generation of Palestinian and Iraqi youth, environmental hazards, poverty, and increased violence within families.

Feminist scholars have shown that state conflict and violence are highly gendered.[61] For one, military conflict can reflect two idealized notions of masculinity: first, the strong, patriotic male who is loyal to his nation; second, the protective male who fights to preserve his family and way of life. In fact, some feminist scholars have questioned whether war is itself an outgrowth of this masculine ideal of defending the land and home against aggression.[62] Feminine images and metaphors are often used within resistance movements and in the media to provoke this masculine notion of protectivity: mothers who have lost children, the "motherland" that must be defended, family honor that must be protected. The homeland can even be sexualized through notions of romantic love: Rohde shows that, at the beginning of the Iran-Iraq war (1980–1988), the newspaper of the ruling Baath Party of Saddam Hussein, *al-Thawra*, published poems in which "the war becomes an act of love, carrying overt sexual connotations, between a male soldier and his beloved, the homeland."[63] That such imagery serves its purpose in recruiting male soldiers is suggested by a letter written by a soldier to his girlfriend in 1982:

> During these days I and my comrades give concrete form to a love, which equals my love for you, and that is the love for the homeland. Oh my dear, this love which is nothing but love . . . I will always be [committed] like you are committed to me. I will turn my memory of touching your tender fingertips into a firm embrace of my rifle, and the heat of my love for you into a fire in which I burn my enemy.[64]

Moreover, males and females interact with conflict, and experience its consequences, differently. As conflict increasingly involves civilian communities, a phenomenon that grew exponentially in the latter part of the twentieth century, more women and children are brought into the front lines of conflict.

Women's bodies are sites of victimization, through sexual assault by soldiers or local men who take advantage of chaos. But they are also sites of protest through such varied means as giving birth to a new generation of fighters or men to replace those lost in war; physical intervention as military fighters attempt to pull individuals out of households for arrest or questioning and women stand in their way; and, increasingly, as fighters and even suicide bombers themselves. That this latter role represents a real shift in expected gender roles—both on the part of communities involved and the scholars who analyze conflict—is seen in the shocked reactions worldwide to female suicide bombers among the Palestinians. Men, on the other hand, are actively involved in combat, or can face remonstration if they are not. The masculinity provoked by the symbolic systems of war transfers to the home, as men increasingly attempt to control their families as a response to their lack of control on the conflict front. Males also make up the vast majority of people arrested, tortured, and imprisoned, leaving lasting physical, psychological, and emotional scars.

Much of the region has experienced some form of conflict—much of it organized military conflict—since the end of the colonial period. The gendered experiences of conflict among Palestinians in a variety of contexts are particularly telling for how long-term conflict can affect gender status and roles within the family and community.[65] Peteet writes of Israeli violence as a kind of rite of passage that facilitates a boy's transition to manhood. Because of the masculine ideal of defending and protecting family and community, men who have been actively involved in resistance activities during the time of the first intifada (1987–1991) make this transition and experience increased status within the family and community. Peteet writes of older fathers, emasculated by their lack of active participation in the resistance, who defer to their young adult sons in family decisions, or of how young men fresh out of prison or bearing the marks of Israeli torture are asked to play the highly respected role of mediator in community disputes.[66] The older generation of men, on the other hand, feel like failures because of their inability to protect their families and the larger community—whether Palestinians in the occupied territories or in refugee camps in Lebanon—from violence.

Women, on the other hand, are generally less directly involved in the resistance as objects of violence and therefore do not benefit from this transition to greater status and power. In fact, as Peteet points out, their position is rather ambiguous if they are taken away from the home to prison, where they must interact with strange men (soldiers) and face the threat of sexual as well as physical violence.[67] Rather, women's gender roles as mothers are reinforced during times of conflict in Palestinian communities as they take on any of the following identities: the mother of a martyred son who has been killed in combat or resistance against the Israelis, the reproducer of the nation who will bear and raise the next generation of resisters and fighters, the mother who shames Israeli soldiers as they interrogate a young boy for throwing stones at them, the mother who publicly mourns all the lost children of Palestine, and so on. While there is a certain status for women in playing the role of mother of the nation, this can be a double-edged sword. Women are further identified with the wife/mother role, constraining them from a wide range of involvement in the resistance movement or the freedom to make life choices that may not involve reproduction at all. And when, through movements to enact legal reform or improve women's status in the public sphere, female activists insist on benefits for women such as maternity leave, paid compensation for "caring labor" within the family, and benefits as wives and mothers of "martyrs," these attempts often are blocked or denied by the Palestinian leadership.

Thus conflict carries with it the possibility of reinforcing idealized gender roles at the same time that it carries the possibility of disrupting these roles. Women are increasingly active in the resistance in the occupied Palestinian territories and even play a role in violent activities such as suicide bombings. Yet, at the end of the day, men can experience a clear boost in status for their active involvement in conflict while women receive ambiguous praise at best. And in the home, the effects of conflict are to reinforce gender roles and place stress on the family system as families attempt to live under violence, lack of employment and educational opportunities, alcoholism, trauma, and so forth.

CONCLUSION

Maroon writes of how cell phone usage is changing the ways in which especially young people experience space and time in Morocco.[68] Before cell phones, appointments with friends were difficult to set up, often necessitating hanging around a café for several hours hoping a friend would show up, but with no way to immediately contact him or her to ensure a meeting would take place. And whereas previously it might have been difficult to keep in close touch with someone who lived in a different part of a city, now technology allows that relationship to continue and the odd meeting to take place. For Maroon, this has a special effect on gender relations within the family, as women are able to access a wider social sphere (including relationships with men) that formerly their fathers, brothers, and other family members might have circumscribed.[69] Young people can have conversations and plan meetings with friends and lovers without parents even knowing. This anecdote shows the potential for new communication and other kinds of technologies to disrupt many of the gendered patterns of sociability described in this chapter.

Likewise, such technologies are allowing individuals and groups to communicate with the world. Back to the example that opened this chapter, Nouraie-Simone describes how young Iranian women are using the option of anonymous blogging to complain about the restrictions placed on women today:

> For educated young Iranian women, cyberspace is a liberating territory of one's own—a place to resist a traditionally imposed subordinate identity

while providing a break from pervasive Islamic restrictions in public physical space. The virtual nature of the Internet—the structure of interconnection in cyberspace that draws participants into ongoing discourses on issues of feminism, patriarchy, and gender politics, and the textual process of self-expression without the prohibition or limitation of physical space—offers new possibilities for women's agency and empowerment.[70]

The Iranian government has had some difficulty preventing those complaints from reaching the outside world, as seen in the aftermath of presidential elections in the summer of 2009. This possibility provides a release for frustrations but also allows individuals with common concerns about rights and the roles of men and women in society to be in contact with one another and possibly work together—at least virtually—for change. This, too, has great potential to disrupt gendered patterns of interacting with others in society and with the state.

Examining these technologies, and the role of young people, is a good reminder that patterns of gender identities and relations are always complex and changing and reflect social norms of the time. In summary, I hope that readers will draw two major conclusions from this chapter. The first is that many factors come together to impact gender in the Middle East. One cannot simply point to "religion" or "culture" or "tradition" or "patriarchy" to explain certain laws or family traditions or political structures that guide the lives of gendered individuals. Second, individuals in the Middle East themselves are best situated to understand the history of "gender" within certain contexts and how this category has been invoked and manipulated through discourses of modernity for a variety of political objectives. There are social movements and associations across the region addressing social and political problems, despite political oppression or other obstacles. There are activists working hard to change laws and policies that affect women and men. There are volunteers working diligently to improve illiteracy rates and ensure that women and men have better access to economic and social support. There are religious scholars debating the place of gendered roles within families in a time of rapid change and upheaval. Our job is to learn about them and from them and to understand "gender" against the contexts in which it is invoked in the Middle East.

So often discussions of gender in the Middle East morph into discussions of the need to save women in the Middle East, at least the Muslims among them. I therefore close with a statement made by Abu-Lughod in her reflection on the question "Do Muslim women really need saving?" asked in response to the American invasion of Afghanistan:

When you save someone, you imply that you are saving her from something. You are also saving her *to* something. What violences are entailed in this transformation, and what presumptions are being made about the superiority of that to which you are saving her? Projects of saving other women depend on and reinforce a sense of superiority by Westerners, a form of arrogance that deserves to be challenged.[71]

NOTES

1. Fereshteh Nouraie-Simone, "Wings of Freedom: Iranian Women, Identity, and Cyberspace," in *On Shifting Ground: Muslim Women in the Global Era*, ed. Fereshteh Nouraie-Simone, pp. 61–79 (New York: Feminist Press at the City University of New York, 2005), p. 75.

2. UN Development Programme, *Arab Human Development Report 2002: Creating Opportunities for Future Generations* (http://hdr.undp.org/en/), pp. 35–37; Nouraie-Simone, "Wings of Freedom," p. 65.

3. Many male scholars of the Middle East, including anthropologists conducting on-the-ground ethnographic research, have claimed that their oversight of women in scholarly analyses is due to their inability to access female informants in highly sex-segregated societies like those of the Middle East, a notion that Lila Abu-Lughod challenges in her review article on anthropology of the Middle East. Lila Abu-Lughod, "Zones of Theory in the Anthropology of the Arab World," *Annual Review of Anthropology* 18 (1989): 267–306.

4. Lila Abu-Lughod, "Introduction: Feminist Longings and Postcolonial Conditions," in *Remaking Women: Feminism and Modernity in the Middle East*, ed. Lila Abu-Lughod, pp. 3–31 (Princeton, NJ: Princeton University Press, 1998).

5. Suad Joseph, "Introduction: Theories and Dynamics of Gender, Self, and Identity in Arab Families," in *Intimate Selving in Arab Families: Gender, Self and Identity*, ed. Suad Joseph, pp. 1–17 (Syracuse, NY: Syracuse University Press, 1999), p. 12.

6. Ibid., p. 14.

7. For a comprehensive compilation of psychological and other studies of gendered life cycles in the region, including those by scholars from the region, see Gary S. Gregg, *The Middle East: A Cultural Psychology* (Oxford and New York: Oxford University Press, 2005).

8. Deniz Kandiyoti, "Bargaining with Patriarchy," *Gender and Society* 2, no. 3 (September 1988): 279.

9. Ibid.

10. A. Bouhdiba, *Sexuality in Islam* (London: Routledge and Kegan Paul, 1985), and Ahmad Ouzi, *Saykulujiyyat al-murahiq* (Psychology of Adolescence) (Rabat: *Majallat dirasat nafsiyya wa tarbawiyya*, 1986). Cited in Gregg, *The Middle East*, p. 225.

11. A. Bouhdiba, p. 221, cited in Gregg, *The Middle East*, p. 228.

12. Joseph, "Introduction," p. 13.

13. For an overview of demographics regarding age of marriage, see Hoda Rashad, Magued Osman, and Farzaneh Roudi-Fahimi, "Marriage in the Arab World," Population Reference Bureau: www.prb.org/pdf05/MarriageInArabWorld_Eng.pdf, accessed October 2009.

14. Lila Abu-Lughod, *Writing Women's Worlds: Bedouin Stories* (Berkeley and Los Angeles: University of California Press, 1993), p. 162.

15. Abdessamad Dialmy, *Sexualité et Santé Sexuelle au Maroc* (unpublished).

16. Douglas A. Davis and Susan Schaefer Davis, "Dilemmas of Adolescence: Courtship, Sex and Marriage in a Moroccan Town," in *Everyday Life in the Muslim Middle East*, ed. Donna Lee Bowen and Evelyn A. Early, pp. 84–90 (Bloomington and Indianapolis: Indiana University Press, 1993); Soumaya Naamane Guessous, *Au-delà de Toute Pudeur: La Sexualité Féminine au Maroc* (Casablanca: Eddif, 1997); Carla Makhlouf Obermeyer, "Sexuality in Morocco: Changing Context and Contested Domain," *Culture, Health, and Sexuality* 2, no. 3 (2000): 239–254.

17. Lynn Welchman and Sara Hossain, "Introduction: 'Honour,' Rights and Wrongs," in *"Honour": Crimes, Paradigms, and Violence against Women*, ed. Lynn Welchman and Sara Hossain, pp. 1–21 (London and New York: Zed, 2005).

18. Ibid., p. 8.

19. Nazand Begikhani, "Honour-Based Violence among the Kurds: The Case of Iraqi Kurdistan," in *"Honour": Crimes, Paradigms, and Violence against Women*, ed. Welchman and Hossain, p. 209.

20. Women who veil for this reason claim that the veil protects them from sexual harassment, gossip, and the suspicion of their family members as they move outside the home. It is important to note that individual and scholarly explanations of veiling are complex and can be a combination of factors including: personal choice, cultural trends/fashions, religious belief, and/or political statement. There is disagreement as to whether veiling is mandated or suggested by Islam. For an exceptionally comprehensive and nuanced treatment of the role of veiling for Muslims, see Fadwa El Guindi, *Veil: Modesty, Privacy, and Resistance* (Oxford and New York: Berg, 1999).

21. Leila Ahmed, *Women and Gender in Islam* (New Haven, CT, and London: Yale University Press, 1992). See in particular her chapter "The Discourse of the Veil," pp. 144–168.

22. Alison Baker, *Voices of Resistance: Oral Histories of Moroccan Women* (Albany: State University of New York Press, 1998).

23. Ibid., p. 9.

24. Nadje Al-Ali, *Secularism, Gender and the State in the Middle East: The Egyptian Women's Movement* (Cambridge: Cambridge University Press, 2000).

25. Margot Badran, "Independent Women: More than a Century of Feminism in Egypt," in *Feminism in Islam: Secular and Religious Convergences*, pp. 116–140 (Oxford: Oneworld, 2009).

26. Afsaneh Najmabadi, "Crafting an Educated Housewife in Iran," in *Remaking Women: Feminism and Modernity in the Middle East*, ed. Lila Abu-Lughod, pp. 91–125 (Princeton, NJ: Princeton University Press, 1998), p. 102.

27. Lila Abu-Lughod, "The Marriage of Feminism and Islamism in Egypt: Selective Repudiation as a Dynamic of Postcolonial Cultural Politics," in *Remaking Women: Feminism and Modernity in the Middle East*, ed. Lila Abu-Lughod, pp. 243-269 (Princeton: Princeton University Press, 1998), p. 259.

28. Ellen L. Fleischmann, "The Other 'Awakening': The Emergence of Women's Movements in the Modern Middle East, 1900–1940," in *A Social History of Women and Gender in the Modern Middle East*, ed. Margaret L. Meriwether and Judith E. Tucker, pp. 89–139 (Boulder, CO: Westview Press, 1999), p. 100.

29. Marnia Lazreg, *The Eloquence of Silence: Algerian Women in Question* (New York and London: Routledge, 1994), p. 143.

30. Ibid., p. 144.

31. Ibid., p. 146.

32. Saskia Wieringa, "Introduction," *Women's Struggles and Strategies*, ed. Saskia Wieringa, pp. 1–12 (Brookfield, VT: Gower Books, 1988).

33. Julie Peteet, *Gender in Crisis: Women and the Palestinian Resistance Movement* (New York: Columbia University Press, 1991).

34. Jenny White, *Islamist Mobilization in Turkey: A Study in Vernacular Politics* (Seattle and London: University of Washington Press, 2002).

35. Ibid., p. 234.

36. Takın Ertürk, "Turkey's Modern Paradoxes: Identity Politics, Women's Agency, and Universal Rights," in *Global Feminism: Transnational Women's Activism, Organizing, and Human Rights*, ed. Myra Marx Ferree and Aili Mari Tripp, pp. 79–109 (New York and London: New York University Press, 2006).

37. Ibid., p. 98.

38. Ibid., p. 111.

39. Juliet Combe, *La Condition de la Femme Marocaine* (Paris: L'Harmattan, 2001).

40. Janine A. Clark and Amy E. Young, "Islamism and Family Law Reform in Morocco and Jordan," *Mediterranean Politics* 13, no. 3 (2008): 333–352.

41. Tova Hartman and Naomi Marmon, "Lived Regulations, Systemic Attributions: Menstrual Separation and Ritual Immersion in the Experience of Orthodox and Jewish Women," *Gender and Society* 18, no. 3 (June 2004): 389–408.

42. Tamar El-Or, *Next Year I Will Know More: Literacy and Identity among Young Orthodox Women in Israel*, trans. Haim Watzman (Detroit: Wayne State University Press, 2002), p. 29.

43. Saba Mahmood, *Politics of Piety: The Islamic Revival and the Feminist Subject* (Princeton, NJ: Princeton University Press, 2005).

44. Ibid, pp. 155–161.

45. Ibid.

46. Abu-Lughod, "The Marriage of Feminism and Islamism in Egypt," pp. 243–244.

47. Ertürk, "Turkey's Modern Paradoxes," p. 83.

48. Mervat Hatem, "Modernization, the State, and the Family in Middle East Women's Studies," in *A Social History of Women and Gender in the Modern Middle East*, ed. Meriwether and Tucker, pp. 63–87.

49. Betty Anderson, "Jordan: Prescription for Obedience and Conformity," in *Teaching Islam: Textbooks and Religion in the Middle East*, ed. Eleanor Abdella Doumato and Gregory Starrett, pp. 71–88 (Boulder, CO: Lynne Rienner, 2007), p. 80.

50. Clark and Young, "Islamism and Family Law Reform in Morocco and Jordan."

51. http://unstats.un.org/unsd/demographic/products/socind/literacy.htm.

52. http://unstats.un.org/unsd/demographic/products/indwm/tab4d.htm.

53. http://www.uniccf.org/sowc04/index.html.

54. United Nations Development Programme, Arab Human Development Report 2002, pp. 35–38.

55. Diane M. Tober, Mohammed-Hossein Taghdisi, and Mohammed Jalali, "'Fewer Children, Better Life' or 'As Many as God Wants'?: Family Planning among Low-Income Iranian and Afghan Refugee Families in Isfahan, Iran," *Medical Anthropology Quarterly* 20, no. 1 (2006): 50–71.

56. Ibid.

57. Valentine M. Moghadam, "Islamic Feminism and Its Discontents: Toward a Resolution of the Debate," *Signs* 27, no. 4 (Summer 2002): 1135–1171.

58. Kamran Asdar Ali, "Modernization and Family Planning Programs in Egypt," *Middle East Report* 205 (October–December 1997), www.merip.org/mer/mer205/mer205.html.

59. Anthony Tirado Chase and Abdul Karim Alaug, "Health, Human Rights, and Islam: A Focus on Yemen," *Health and Human Rights* 8, no. 1 (2004): 114–137.

60. Ibid., p. 132.

61. Wenona Giles and Jennifer Hyndman, "Introduction: Gender and Conflict in a Global Context," in *Sites of Violence: Gender and Conflict Zones*, ed. Wenona Giles and Jennifer Hyndman, pp. 3–23 (Berkeley and Los Angeles: University of California Press, 2004).

62. Cynthia Enloe, *The Morning After: Sexual Politics at the End of the Cold War* (Berkeley: University of California Press, 1993).

63. Achim Rohde, "Opportunities for Masculinity and Love: Cultural Production in Ba'thist Iraq during the 1980s," in *Islamic Masculinities*, ed. Lahoucine Ouzgane, pp. 184–201 (London and New York: Zed Books, 2006), p. 192.

64. *al-Thawra*, July 21, 1982; cited in Rohde, "Opportunities for Masculinity and Love," p. 192.

65. Peteet, *Gender in Crisis*.

66. Julie Peteet, "Male Gender and Rituals of Resistance in the Palestinian 'Intifada': A Cultural Politics of Violence," *American Ethnologist* 21, no. 1 (February 1994): 31–49.

67. Julie Peteet, "Icons and Militants: Mothering in the Danger Zone," *Signs* 23, no. 1 (Autumn 1997): 103–129.

68. Bahíyyih Maroon, "Mobile Sociality in Urban Morocco," in *The Cell Phone Reader: Essays in Social Transformation*, ed. Anandam Kavoori and Noah Arceneaux, pp. 189–204 (New York: Peter Lang, 2006).

69. Ibid.

70. Fereshteh Nouraie-Simone, "Wings of Freedom: Iranian Women, Identity, and Cyberspace," p. 61.

71. Lila Abu-Lughod, "Do Muslim Women Really Need Saving? Anthropological Reflections on Cultural Relativism and Its Others," *American Anthropologist* 104, no. 3 (September 2002): 783–790, pp. 788–789.

9

THE ISLAMIC AWAKENING

Raymond William Baker

ISLAM IS TODAY narrating an epoch-defining story. It has moved millions across the Islamic world. For all those who have responded, no matter their diversity in almost every other respect, this story of Islam is a Quranic story. It is at the same time a worldly story. The Quran, all Muslims know, was given to humanity by God. Jesus, the savior of Christianity, returned to his father in heaven. The holy Quran, however, remained on earth to provide guidance in human affairs. This difference is crucial for all that has come from the message of Islam.

The first verse of the Quran commands Muslims to "read, recite."[1] Muslims are *not* called to worship the Quran. Rather, they are summoned to use their minds to understand the guidance the Quran provides for the ordering of their worldly as well as spiritual affairs. In this effort, they also find assistance in the hadith (prophetic traditions) that record the exemplary sayings and actions of the Prophet Muhammad, who was both religious and political leader of the first community of Muslims.

Community-building is at the heart of Islam's message. It is quite impossible to be a Muslim alone. All five basic obligations of Muslims have a collective dimension: the *shahada,* bearing public witness to the oneness of God and to the Prophet Muhammad as his messenger; the *salat,* five prayers each day and the community prayer on Friday; the *saum,* fast during the month of Ramadan; the *zakat,* obligatory financial support for the community's less fortunate; and the hajj, pilgrimage to the holy city of Mecca for those who have the means to make it at least once in their lifetime.[2] These fundamental requirements of the faith reinforce the bonds of the ummah, community of believers, and enhance the capacities of individuals to live well together as Muslims and to make their lives part of something larger. Muslims around the globe all pray in the same direction to Mecca, no matter where they find themselves. Every year, some 2 million Muslims give this symbolic union physical reality when they come together in Mecca from the ends of the earth to share the experience of walking the ground where the Prophet Muhammad received the revelation. When they set aside money for zakat, Muslims know that they are fulfilling an obligation along with their fellow Muslims worldwide. Fasting, too, during the month of Ramadan enhances this sense of a faith shared with the world's 1.3 billion Muslims.

All of these practices strengthen community and remind Muslims of the larger purposes of their collective lives. Muslims are called not only to worship God but also to act through their communities as God's vice regents on earth to complete the "building of the world."[3] The divine mandate to humankind, *Istikhlaf* in the language of the Quran, charges humanity with developing the earth to its fullest. This distinctive responsibility distinguishes humans from all other creatures. It means that, as they make their history, Muslims are explicitly called to have one eye on the sacred text and the other on the mundane human and natural world around them. The message of Islam calls them to pay attention to the real-world imperatives of their particular times and places as they act in the world to build just societies that develop and preserve the earth. In this sense, the scholarly traditions that Islam fostered have been at once spiritual and worldly.

Worldly Islam today calls ordinary Muslims to reform and resistance as the path to fulfilling their responsibilities of Istikhlaf. The millions who have responded include Sunnis, who represent about 85 percent of the world's Muslims; Shia, who comprise 15 percent; as well as those from both main branches who have turned to Sufism, Islamic mysticism. The major division in the ummah between Sunni and Shia arose early and it is instructive that the divisive issue was one of political succession rather than theology, at least initially. The great Sufi orders (*turuq*) are spread throughout Islamic lands, with important orders in such diverse places as India, Central Asia, and Africa as well as the Arab, Turkish, and Iranian heartland areas. They played an important role in earlier waves of Islamic renewal in the eighteenth and nineteenth centuries, as they do today.[4] A diffuse and pervasive Sufi influence makes itself felt throughout much of the Islamic world. All these, whatever tensions occasionally arise among them and however distinctive their traditions become, are communities of Muslims, part of the ummah. They all recognize that there is but one God and that he is one (*tawhid*),[5] they all revere his Prophet Muhammad, and they all pray toward Mecca. All have been touched by the Awakening and contributed to it. The Awakening is neither Sunni, nor Shia, nor Sufi. It is neither Arab, nor Iranian, nor Turkish. It is all of these things. It is an *Islamic* Awakening, *Sahwa Islamiyya*, of worldwide scope.

Yet, this story of Islam for our time has yet to be heard in the West. The West is not listening. This is not the first time for such massive inattention. In the late '60s and early '70s Western scholars and policy makers, convinced of their own vision of the Islamic world's secular future, failed to hear the announcements of Islamic intellectuals and activists of the early emergence of the contemporary Sahwa Islamiyya. That powerful force reshaped life throughout the region in subsequent decades and in ways quite contrary to Western expectations.

Today the most important story from Islamic lands tells how this Islamic Awakening, with its call for reform and resistance, has taken hold in the lives of millions of common people, making itself felt on the mass as well as elite level.[6] The centrist intellectuals and movements at the heart of the Awakening, the *Wassatteyya*, or transnational Islamic mainstream, have succeeded as no other force in giving voice to the everyday dreams of ordinary people for a better life as Muslims. In doing so, the Wassatteyya has made itself the guiding force of the mass Islamic Awakening, ensuring its worldly as well as spiritual role.[7] The Wassatteyya is inclusive, though not without definition. It is not owned by particular individuals or movements but rather speaks for the oldest, mainstream trend in Islamic thought. The Wassatteyya finds its most fundamental sources in the Quran[8] and the Sunna, enriched further by both the insights of Sufism and of that great "ocean" of interpretive scholarship that constitutes *fiqh* (understandings of Quran and Sunna, the work of specialists).[9] In each age this Islamic mainstream has taken new forms and drawn diverse individuals to its banner, depending on the needs of time and place. The lifeless typologies and "bucket thinking" typical of Western social science are of limited use in characterizing so fluid and adaptive a phenomenon as the Wassatteyya.[10] It is best thought of, to borrow Muhammad Abduh's evocative image, as a river out of Islam, representing the moderate mainstream of Islam, from which all sorts of tributaries flow.[11]

In our age of Islamic Awakening, the Wassatteyya raises the banner of reform of Islamic thought and legitimate resistance to imperialism and colonialism. In doing so, it opens a space between mainstream scholars and movements that represent its contemporary incarnations and traditionalists who cling to rigid and inflexible versions of the heritage. The Wassatteyya stands apart even more clearly from extremists, who have little regard for the heritage as they innovate with radical distortions of Islamic thought and tarnish legitimate struggles of resistance with what centrists have denounced as their indiscriminate "war on the world."[12] However, it would be a mistake to rigidify and universalize these categories. They are simply useful starting points to *begin* thinking about the Wassatteyya in our own time and to determine how it differs from other trends. It is important to keep the designations flexible. The center itself is moving and what is mainstream in one context may well not be in another. Moreover, particular movements and individuals may well float between these markers and display the characteristics of more than one. The categories that differentiate themselves apart from the mainstream have more the character of eddies in a flowing river than fixed islands, permanently set apart.

The Islamic mainstream has found leadership in the work of such diverse figures as the Egyptian Yusuf al Qaradawy, who heads the Union of Islamic Scholars; Turkish Prime Minister Recep Tayyib Erdoğan, whose Justice and Development Party has Islamist roots; and the former Iranian President Mohammad Khatami, who speaks for reforming the Islamic revolution from within. No one scholar or public figure can speak for the Wassatteyya in all its variety, nor can any single movement. At the same time, a catalog of all centrist Islamic scholars and movements across the Islamic world would overwhelm this brief chapter. But it might be helpful to just mention the centrist Islamist movements in the Arab world since they are almost always overlooked with the standard focus on Arab extremists. In addition to the venerable Muslim Brotherhood in Egypt, there are important centrist Islamist movements in a variety of sites in the Arab Islamic world, notably the Renaissance Party in Tunisia, the Justice and Development Party in Morocco, the Reform Party in Algeria, the Jordanian Islamic Action Front, the Ummah Party in Kuwait, and the Yemeni Reformist Union.

Mainstream Islamists have taken the lead in an innovative transnational Islamic project of reform and renewal to bring Islamic discourse and practice fully into the twenty-first century. At the same time they insist on thoughtfully preserving the best of the heritage. Not surprisingly, Egypt, Turkey, and Iran, three great demographic and cultural reservoirs at the heart of the Islamic world, have each played important, complementary roles in the Awakening. Outside this triangle, developments to the west in North Africa, to the north in Central Asia, and to the east in Southwest Asia have made the Awakening a presence in the lives of Muslim-majority communities in these areas. In each of these cases, and others like them, including growing Muslim minority communities in both East and West, the Islamic Awakening takes varied forms. They are all Islam. They all give force and vitality to the reform and resistance the Awakening heralds.

Yet once again the West, led by the United States, hears only its own very different drumbeat. For the eight years of George W. Bush's leadership, the United States was obsessed with a quixotic and ill-conceived Global War on Terror. This war justified violent intrusion of American power into the very heart of the Arab Islamic world with the overtly imperial aim of transforming the entire region by force. The Bush administration fixed world attention on the "noisy," criminal Islam that provides the indispensable enemy required to make such imperial wars on Islamic lands seem defensible. In 2009, during the early months of his presidency, Barack Hussein Obama gave the war a cumbersome new name, replacing Global War on Terror with Global Counterinsurgency Against Extremism. He also strengthened its diplomatic and economic dimensions, while speaking a new, more nuanced language that took more realistic account of the limits of American power. However, even on the rhetorical level, as yet there has been more continuity than change in his vision of America's role in Islamic lands.

For all its symbolic importance, Obama's historic address to the Islamic world in June 2009 did not resolve this fundamental question of continuity or change in US *policies* toward the Islamic world.[13] It is most important for what it reveals of the limitations of the new administration's thinking. In Cairo, Obama delivered two messages: the first on Islam as religion and civilization, the second on the policy issues that bedevil American relations with the Islamic world. Undoubtedly, this dualism came naturally to Obama, for it mirrors one familiar to and taken for granted by Westerners of the separation between religion and politics, a legacy of the West's Christian heritage. It is, however, strange and unnatural for Muslims, given the insistent worldly character of Islam that is anchored in the Quran's continuous presence on earth. For Obama's Muslim audience, this difference inevitably threw into relief the sharp contrast between the president's two messages. The first could not have been more welcome for its new language of rightful respect and appreciation for Islam, despite some troubling echoes in the ring of the words. The second message on policies, however, brought almost no change at all. The contrast between the two messages defined the almost universal reaction to Obama's address among ordinary Muslims. Would the words that lifted their spirits, they asked, be expressed concretely in more balanced and more just policies?

From his Cairo platform Obama addressed the Muslim world as a man of color with a personal history that connects him to the Islamic world. To great effect, the new American president translated the symbolism of his person and his biography into a historic call for a new relationship between the West and Islam. The speech was remarkable in many ways. No American president had ever before spoken with such respect and understanding of Islam and the meaning of the Islamic heritage for humankind. The Quranic passages the president recited summed up the most uplifting dimensions of Islam's universal message and meaning for the moral and material progress of humanity. They were quoted with an aptness that was breathtaking in its impact. No shoes came flying through the air, like those hurled in anger by an Iraqi journalist during a speech delivered in Iraq by President George W. Bush in 2008. Instead, the world heard a youthful voice from the balcony of the university hall call out, "We love you, Obama." Here was a widely felt, emotional response to the president's stunning new rhetoric of respect and depth of appreciation for what Islam has brought to human history and what Muslims, at their best, have contributed to build the world.

However, for many thoughtful public intellectuals and scholars, notably from the Arab world, even these sweet words about Islam left a lingering aftertaste. Was the aftertaste simply the effect of well-justified suspicions of American intentions? After all, George W. Bush had described Islam as a religion of peace[14] and invoked good Muslims to offset the bad Muslims that Osama bin Laden represented. Was there poison in the honey yet again, they asked? Had Obama, described by Henry Kissinger as a master chess player in the realpolitik tradition,[15] adeptly changed the subject from politics and policies to faith and culture and thereby obscured the real sources of Muslim grievances with America? And just how deep was the commitment to these changed views of Islam? After all, many of the same intellectuals invited to hear Obama had heard Condoleezza Rice's striking admission in an address at the American University in Cairo on June 20, 2005, that America's record of supporting regional tyrants for six decades was wrong and would be reversed.[16] They had heard her unequivocal pledge of American support for democracy, only to see it abandoned with little show of anguish just months later when the local tyrants pushed back and internationally supervised elections brought Hamas to power in occupied Palestine in 2006. The United States refused to recognize that peaceful electoral outcome and actively sought to undermine and reverse it. America favored democracy for the Arabs, it turned out, provided such support did not impede the dirty work of useful tyrants or produce electoral outcomes not to American or Israeli liking. Thoughtful listeners in Cairo University's great hall and outside wondered whether Obama's respect for Islam and empathy for Muslims would suffer a similar fate.

Obama's second message on specific policies was far less ambiguous and far more negative. A coldness crept into Obama's voice and even his physical demeanor changed markedly as he laid out his policy vision. Here the message was continuity, all the more chilling for what had come before. Though obscured by his words on the faith that moved his worldwide Muslim audience in such a powerful way, Obama had laid the foundations for policy continuity from the outset in the way he framed the sources of tension between Islam and the West. The president opened his address by pointing to those "tensions rooted in historical forces that go beyond any current policy debate." There would be attention to more distant history and a promised better future. However, with these carefully chosen words, he quite deliberately set aside the most recent past of the clear and aggressive imperial policies of George W. Bush. Obama did acknowledge the earlier record of Western colonialism and Cold War exploitation of Islamic peoples, only to suggest, however, that America had moved beyond those historical failings. He cautioned his listeners against adopting the stereotype of America as "an interested empire." His very presence in Cairo promised a new beginning.

Yet, almost immediately Obama made it clear that the basic framework he proposed for going forward represented little change in the recent American policies that were most painful to Muslims worldwide. The core policies of a militarily driven "interested empire" would continue, with only tactical adjustments. There were, as has been widely noted, some striking new phrases and even small departures on some specifics, most notably on the language the president used to address the question of Palestine. However, the essential narrative that undergirded the American imperial policies after 9/11 remained completely intact; so too did the justificatory story of America's one-sided support for the state of Israel.

It has been easy enough for those so inclined to exaggerate the policy changes Obama's speech signaled. All one has to do is pull out some of the more striking passages that contrast with the aggressive discourse of the first four years of George W. Bush. Among such departures, the president acknowledged, in 1953 "in the middle of the Cold War, the United States played a role in the overthrow of a democratically-elected Iranian government."[17] Most notable were changes in the way Obama spoke about the Israeli-Palestinian question. Obama did catch up in important ways on some clear realities long acknowledged by rational people around the world, though rarely in America and never by American presidents in the early months of their terms: The West Bank is occupied, Hamas should not be labeled a terrorist organization, Palestinians are suffering without a state of their own, all three of the great monotheistic faiths should be welcome in Jerusalem, further Israeli settlement activity must cease. It is a measure of the backwardness of American political discourse on the Arab-Israeli conflict that any of these ideas represent breakthroughs. Yet they do and Arab analysts and policy makers, in particular, may well be advised to seize on these improved American formulations to consolidate whatever gains they represent, as some of the more astute commentators have argued.[18] Yet, it is also important to see clearly the limitations of the Obama formulations. The United States still has a very long walk to line up with the international consensus that has for decades considered *all* Israeli settlements illegal under international law and has stood firmly for the full national rights of both Israelis and Palestinians. In Obama's remarks there was nothing at all on the core issues of the character or borders of the Palestinian state envisioned in his two-state solution, the status of the existing Israeli settlements, the critical question of sovereignty over Jerusalem, and the right of return of Palestinian refugees.

Moreover, to take the incremental and marginally positive elements in Obama's speech as the heart of his message on policy toward the Islamic world requires inattention to the underlying narrative within which these phrases were embedded. The problem with Obama's address was not one of words versus implementation. It was the words themselves and the story they told. To put the matter starkly, neither George W. Bush nor even Dick Cheney has cause for any serious problems with the fundamental narrative framework for policy that President Obama laid out. On these most essential issues of America's direct imperial role in Islamic lands there is almost seamless continuity between the vision Obama projected in Cairo and the policies of Bush's second term when the current era of counterinsurgency and more restrained language began. Rather than change the policies, Obama has embraced the change of military tactics to carry them out that Bush charted in his second term, notably the shift from high-tech "shock and awe," associated with General Colin Powell, to "counterinsurgency," associated with General David Petraeus. Obama has retained Petraeus as head of CENTCOM (US Central Command) and a key player on a military and security team dominated by holdovers from the later Bush years.

When President Obama turned in his Cairo speech from generalities about Islam to actual policies at the heart of tensions with the Islamic world, the thread of the old grand narrative that justified the militarism of the War on Terror ran through all his remarks. Yet again, the world heard the familiar story of America as a gentle giant, sleepwalking in all innocence and good intentions across the globe, uninterested in bases or resources, though notably lingering in the Islamic world. The giant moves protectively, hand in hand, with a very small, vulnerable junior partner with a tragic past and threatened future, a tiny ward that does only what it must do to defend itself. In this familiar fable, the inhabitants of distant lands are unable to understand such a powerful yet selfless and well-intentioned force for good and all the gifts the giant and his diminutive companion seek to bring to the world and one of its most troubled regions. Out of jealousy and envy some among these misguided peoples respond to his misunderstood presence in the region with murderous strikes on the very symbols of the giant's benign power back home, killing thousands. They do so from their sanctuary in a far-off mountainous land. The giant has no alternative but to respond. The self-defense of a betrayed innocent fully justifies the death and destruction the giant is forced to rain on that distant refuge for the evil-doers, just as it rationalizes, despite some equivocations, extending the assault, with all the calculated fury of the giant's unrivaled power, to neighboring lands also must be secured and rescued from evil.

Nearly all of the misguided rigidities of the Bush years reemerged in this unchanged narrative from the mist of the warm rhetoric about Islam. With his underlying narrative Obama affirmed all of the basic arguments that rationalized the military-driven imperialism of the Bush years, centered on Afghanistan and Iraq, and that today justifies its extension to the border regions between Afghanistan and Pakistan (the so-called Af-Pak theater), now rightly called Obama's War. In Cairo, Obama said it clearly: The Afghani people are better off without the Taliban, the Iraqi people are better off without Saddam, and so the wars must continue, not just for self-defense but also so the troops can come home from these pacified, secured lands. In this familiar narrative violence begins with 9/11 and the irrational and unforeseeable attack that brought the twin towers down. The core problem of the area is the violent extremism of Islamist movements rather than the provocative work of imperialism, colonialism, or brutally repressive client regimes. America seeks neither oil nor bases but rather the transformation of the region into an island of peace, democracy, and prosperity, open to global investment and trade. Israel acts only to defend itself and to survive the essential threats it faces. The age-old conflicts and irrational hatreds that define the Islamic world have made the realization of this disinterested and benign vision unattainable without the cleansing, transforming assertions of American and Israeli power to end terrorist states, to annihilate terrorist movements, and to eliminate the capacity of extremists to threaten Israeli security and to export terrorism to America's shores.

There was no room at all in the narrative for even a hint that US foreign policy is the main motivation for the various forces, and not just the extremists, that resist American policies in the Islamic world. Any reasonable accounting of the sources of tension would include US and Western exploitation of the region's energy resources, unqualified support for Israel and its expansionist aims, US active support for the brutal police states that rule in much of the Arab and Islamic world, US support or compliant acquiescence in the oppression of Muslims by other great powers, like Russia, China, and India, and the US military presence in Afghanistan, Iraq, and other Muslim countries.[19] The unchanged narrative gives no space to even acknowledge the horrific price paid for the false gifts of "freedom and progress" by the Muslim peoples of Afghanistan and Iraq, not to mention Palestine. There was no repudiation of the disastrous and explicitly imperial policies of the Bush years that took the lives of hundreds of thousands of Muslim civilians, as well as over 4,000 young men and women from the American military. The president did not mention the terrible and totally disproportionate violence unleashed on the essentially defenseless people of Gaza just six months before his address or the separation wall or the rampant Israeli settler violence against Palestinians on the West Bank.[20] The only violence that must be ended, he said clearly, was Palestinian resistance. In politics and foreign policy, narrative is everything. But there was no new narrative here. The president displayed no new thinking to make sense of the moral and political failures of US foreign policy in the region and to guide a more rational and modest foreign policy course, an alternative to the violent pathways of colonization and empire. There was instead a more elegant retelling of the old story that had brought Muslims such pain by a confident and charismatic president with a warm smile and a gift for words.

Nothing in this characterization of the ill-conceived Global War on Terror and Obama's ownership of the concept under a different label is meant to suggest that criminal Islamic minorities are not real and dangerous. They are. However, they are not Islam and they are not a majority of Muslims. Nor do they constitute an existential threat to the United Sates. Nor can they be countered by a "war" in any reasonable meaning of that phrase. The record is now clear that the initial assault on Afghanistan on October 7, 2001, the subsequent invasion of Iraq on March 20, 2003, and now Obama's ongoing war in the Af-Pak theater have all deepened the enmity toward the United States of ordinary people throughout the Islamic world. They have also proved a recruitment boom for extremists. Bloody military interventions and the civilian deaths and maimings in large numbers that they inevitably inflict are a stimulus rather than a cure for extremism.

It is no contradiction to recognize at the same time that it would require stunning inattention to the obvious to deny the Islamic rationalization of the murderous logic that brought the twin towers down. Criminal political acts were first thought out in an Islamic vocabulary of jihad (struggle for the faith) and *jahiliyyah* (condemnation as un-Islamic, atheist, or pagan), traceable to important Islamist thinkers such as the Pakistani Maulana Abul Ala Maudidi and, even more emphatically, the Egyptian Sayyid Qutb. However, for all the power of such Islamic rationalizations, it is important to acknowledge the quite distinctive and highly distorted character of these readings of the sacred texts by the extremists who draw on their work. The Wassatteyya condemns in clear and unequivocal terms the terrifying and indiscriminate violence of the extremists' "war against the world." They explain the ways this terrible instrument violates Islamic mainstream values and the restraints that Islam, properly understood, places on the conduct of war. In sharp contrast but with equal clarity, the mainstream endorses the legitimate violence of Islamic resistance movements that confront foreign occupation with bravery and impressive inventiveness against overwhelming odds. In Islamic terms, they argue forcefully that there is an obligation to actively resist occupation and colonization that falls on both the collective shoulders of Muslim communities anywhere Muslims are attacked (*fard kifaya*) and on the individual shoulders of all Muslims directly suffering such injustices in their own homeland (*fard al ain*).[21] It should be noted that resorting to the violence of resistance, as understood by leading centrist Islamic intellectuals, must always be purposive and pragmatic and never an end in itself. They argue that campaigns of resistance must be conducted with an eye to their likely effectiveness in achieving liberation as measured against their costs to the ummah in lives and treasure. Such violence is also constrained by commitments to both proportionality and the morality of means. There are, for example, quite explicit exclusions of such targets as children, women, the aged, farmers, and other innocent civilians who have nothing to do with the fighting.[22] A right of resistance, subject to parallel strictures, is also recognized by international law as legitimate for peoples under occupation, whatever unilateral and arbitrary laws and motions the US Congress or the Israeli Knesset may pass.

Centrist Islamists have no illusions as to the deadly character of the extremist challenge to their own project of Islamic reform and legitimate resistance to foreign intrusions.[23] The *amir*s (leaders of militant groups) promise their followers to take hold of a world spinning out of control and to use any and all means to do so. The circle is vicious. Western policies, driven by an imperial agenda, act as a major incitement for the most violent Islamist militants. Their crimes then focus media and expert attention in the West all the more strongly on extremism, which inevitably becomes the face of Islam for alarmed Westerners and justifies further military interventions. It also means that almost all of our efforts in the West to understand the Islamic world go into assessments of this Islamic threat. In this way, even the best Western work on Islam risks reinforcing a narrow security perspective that threatens to leave the mainstream in the shadows while casting the spotlight on extremists. Efforts to lean against this unfortunate outcome have been far too modest in number and impact.[24]

Unlike extremists, ordinary Muslims center their aspirations on the prospect of living decent, self-directed lives with adequate means, a measure of freedom, and a cultural environment of their own making. National battles for basic rights and freedoms across the region now draw inspiration from Islam. Islam is an active participant in struggles against domestic tyrannies. Islam also enables millions to say to the West: We will be free, we will be modern, but we will not be you. Islam inspires ordinary people to courageous and unpredictable actions in accord with these words. Today very little understanding of these developments is reaching the West, and not for the first time.

Convinced of history's direction, my generation of graduate students who began their careers in the early '70s believed that our Western, secular experience provided a mapping of the future of the Arab Islamic world. From that experience, ahistorical models were extracted and labeled development theory. With eyes riveted on an imported, inevitable, and secular future for Muslim societies, we missed the importance of the Islamic wave that now defines politics in much of the Islamic world. Today, with our gaze firmly fixed on the criminal, marginal Islamist minorities represented by al-Qaeda and on the mayhem they periodically cause, we ignore the normalcy of ordinary lives and the everyday dreams of common people in the Islamic world.

In the '60s area studies were motivated by a sense of the United States as an emerging superpower with global responsibilities. The challenge from the Soviet Union impelled an unprecedented national effort to secure our rightful role in the world. We needed people to understand the lands beyond our borders to help facilitate their transformation along the modern lines that we and not the Soviets had pioneered. We considered ourselves the vanguard of a great global ascent. To be sure, the rhetoric of global responsibility provided a screen for a rising imperial assertiveness. Talk of underdeveloped countries slid easily into condescending assumptions of underdeveloped peoples.

Yet, however unhappy these pretensions and their racist implications in the '60s, things are much worse today. Now the call is for counterterrorism specialists, fluent in Arabic and trained in counterinsurgency. The terrorism specialists, with their special focus on the Arab world, are preparing themselves to face a vast and nameless army of Islamic extremists that must be confronted abroad, they tell us, with as much violence as is needed, in order to avoid another 9/11 at home. America's aim now is not to develop backward societies. Now we must demolish imagined enemies and protect the "homeland," whatever the cost to societies and people in the Islamic world. The old centers for development and modernization now take a backseat to a new generation of centers for terrorism and security studies at some of the West's most prestigious universities.

During all these many years of my life in Cairo hardly a day has gone by without two or three Middle East stories in the major global news outlets. Over four decades my American family, friends, and students repeatedly and always with a sense of the novelty of the moment have commented on "what a fascinating time to be living and working in the Middle East"—responding to the latest disaster, upheaval, or war. Yet, from the vantage point of my direct experience, the most important story in the Arab Islamic world today makes no impression at all. From my vantage point in Cairo, where I first settled into a personal and professional home some forty years ago, I would tell that epoch-defining story something like this: Ordinary people throughout the region are struggling resolutely every day using whatever means available to them to create better lives for themselves and their children. They actively yearn for more just economic and political systems. They seek to create societies rooted in inherited Islamic values but open to the world, pluralistic and tolerant, and with greater freedoms and more widely shared prosperity.[25]

What makes these everyday struggles so remarkable is that they take place in circumstances of domestic tyranny and foreign invasions. The Arab Islamic world groans under authoritarian rule while facing periodic assaults from the West. These realities of everyday life inevitably mean that the struggles for ordinary lives are waged under quite extraordinary conditions. It is these exceptional circumstances and not the dreams themselves that make the lives of Arab Muslims, in particular, seem so different and so incomprehensible. In the conditions in which Muslim peoples find themselves it is precisely these perfectly understandable battles for normalcy that foster resistance, including the forceful resistance that so many in the West find baffling. These are national and not civil rights struggles. The occupiers leave no room for nonviolent resistance. There is no constitution or even shared values to appeal to, as the occupiers no less than the local dictators routinely ignore international human rights law. How can one live a normal life in the face of such tyranny and degrading oppression? Does it make any sense at all to fault Arab citizens and the movements they support for the duality of their commitments, at once to the fulfillment of quite common everyday dreams of adequate food, shelter, health care, and education for their children while at the same time fostering resistance to local tyrants and foreign invaders, using force as circumstances require? Their situation demands no less.

None of this is meant in any way as a whitewash of Islamist resistance movements. The record of the human rights violations of both Hizbullah and Hamas have been fulsomely documented by the most respected regional and international human rights organizations.[26] These acts of criminality have been extensively covered in the international press. Those on the short end of a power imbalance are often brutalized by their circumstance and often engage themselves in brutalities. Clearly, there have been excesses, at times criminal excesses, by both Hamas and Hizbullah, and they do tarnish the cause of resistance. They also sow confusion about the Islamic justifications for legitimate defense and rightful conduct in warfare, for, as we have seen, Islam is brought directly into these battlefields. Yet, for all of these shortcomings both movements are legitimate movements of national resistance, however their adversaries seek to label them.

These unlikely and unforeseen resistance movements have made Muslims important players in world history once again. Unequal contests against local tyrants and foreign invaders have become part of the meaning of the Islamic Awakening, though they are not the whole of it. At the same time, centrist movements also work to renew Islam and reform Islamic thinking and practices in ways that will determine how the expanded role of Islam will be played. Resistance movements of Islamic inspiration against occupation are a source of well-deserved pride throughout Islamic lands. In parallel fashion, centrist Islamist movements have asserted themselves in local struggles for greater freedom and more social and economic justice, while at the same time working to renew and reform Islamic thought. Achieving balance between these conflict imperatives of the moment is neither easy nor always achieved. Yet, on both reform and resistance, the Islamic Awakening has registered considerable advances, and those tangible gains, no matter how costly, have raised the status and enhanced the appeal of centrist Islamist forces.

The strategic vision, developed by neoconservative intellectuals, that drove the Bush vision of imperial America is now in ruins. There is no longer unabashed talk of remaking Islam and Muslims themselves with benign and incontestable imperial power. However, the hapless Global War on Terrorism, conceptually incoherent and defining an impossible mission for the US military, limps along as an excuse for strategic direction. Regrettably, as his Cairo address indicated, President Obama has made the war on terrorism his own. Attention has been shifted now to the ruined Afghanistan, given the necessary importance with the artificial Af-Pak construction that brings into the equation Pakistan's nuclear weapons and the oil of Central Asia. Suddenly, with these enhancements even poor and tortured Afghanistan can once more be conjured up as a threat to civilization and provide the rationale for the wars of counterinsurgency now envisioned.[27] In short, despite the change in administration, the very same arguments that justified invading Iraq have been recycled with only minor modifications. The same disaster, foreseeable then and clearly visible now, awaits us in the mountains of the Af-Pak territory.[28]

Disaster in Iraq has taught us little. It is simply untrue that there were no signs that invading Iraq would have horrific consequences, and not just for Iraqis. Nor is the argument that we should have known better an instance of Monday-morning quarterbacking, though I must add that I have never quite understood this phrase as a way of blocking analysis of misguided policies. It has been my good fortune to have college coaches as friends. Even when they win, they spend hours poring over tapes of the last game to understand any mistakes made, though they did not cost the game or throw overall strategy into question. When they lose and basic strategy is in question, the tapes just keep rolling and not just on Monday morning. We should have zero tolerance for those, including Obama, who urge us to "look forward" and not waste time cataloging the costs of a failed strategy and holding criminals and fools accountable. How can you move forward in any reasonable way if you don't know where you have been and exactly what you have done and who you have become in the process? It might also be a good and generous idea to mention every so often that those hundreds of thousands of everyday citizens who poured into the streets of their capitals had it right. It is self-serving nonsense when elite policy makers and pundits whine that in the buildup to war "we were all fooled." Clearly, those demonstrators who took to the streets to protest the criminal invasion *before* it took place were not fooled.

The facts on the ground were there for the viewing. They still are. So are the lessons to be learned from them, if the right questions are asked. Why didn't the overwhelming military strength and technological advantage of the United States and Israel translate into the unchallenged dominance of Islamic lands? By what alchemy does Islam translate the visible weaknesses of Muslims into the surprising and formidable strengths of Islamist movements of resistance?

The simple and straightforward answer is the power of Islamic identity. It is a power that cannot be defeated by military means. At just this point Western scholarship averts its eyes. Islam is always a proximate and never an ultimate explanation for both neoconservative and liberal analysts. Neoconservative theorists of Islam, for example, argue that the forces that drive Islamic movements are rage and envy. Islamic movements in their view are purely reactive and the reactions come in instinctual, nonthinking ways. It is the glittering spectacle of Western prosperity and democracy that generates these impulses and, while they may find reinforcement in certain retrograde elements of faith and tradition, Islamic movements are essentially caused by factors outside Islam. The liberal mainstream agrees, though this school attributes the rise of Islamism to uneven development, oil wealth, or simply poverty. Islamic movements are always understood in terms of some other substratum of influences, never Islam itself.

We need a new approach that places Islam at the center of any assessment of Islamic movements. Islamic theorists of global Islam take precisely this approach. The power of Islamic identity always remains the clear focus of their analyses. No movement of Islamic inspiration can possibly be understood without careful attention to the distinctive features of Islamic thought and action. In assessing the surprising strength of such movements, almost always facing very formidable odds, we need to pay close attention to the ways efforts at resistance take shape and evolve. Islamic movements are always movements of resistance and they are always part of the larger pattern whereby the ummah as a whole defends itself. Such movements invariably join their resistance struggles against others to more fundamental internal efforts at renewal. Thus, Islamist movements in all their forms are always movements of Islamic reform, and in this capacity they contribute to the larger pattern of adaptation and absorption that has always been an important factor in the survival of the Islamic ummah through the centuries.

These distinctive features of Islamic movements differentiate them from other political and social movements. They are most clearly imprinted in the remarkable pattern whereby defeat is transformed into more expansive and more effective resistance. We are more surprised by these outcomes than we should be. There are profound lessons in adoption and adaptation to be learned from the 1,400-year history of Islam. These cultural and historical lessons have direct relevance in very practical ways. Islam has thrived in the new conditions of globalization. This remarkable adaptation belies the persistent myth of Islam as "stubbornly resistant to change, except on its own terms."[29] It is striking that even one of the most perceptive of American critics of US imperial policies in the Islamic world, Andrew Bacevich, cannot shake this all-pervasive stereotype. Neither the assertion nor even the qualification is accurate. In fact, since the late eighteenth century Islam has undergone four successive waves of sweeping reform and renewal.[30] It has been in a constant state of change, often adopting ideas and concepts from others, always adapting with great flexibility to its environment. In the fourth such wave underway since the late '60s the environmental changes brought on by the forces of globalization have sharply accelerated the pace of resistance, as cascading changes envelop us all. Islam can in no way dictate or determine the terms or character of these changes, as Islamist intellectuals calmly acknowledge. Yet, Islam has responded with successful adaptations, often in the most adverse circumstances of apparent weakness and vulnerability while remaining Islam. These persistent adaptations help one understand just how the message of the Quran has survived these fourteen centuries and, more important, how its relevance has sharply and unexpectedly increased in our own time.

Islam in the global age is a force to be reckoned with, as both Israelis and Americans have discovered. But the power of Islamic identity cannot be measured in the usual ways. Nor is that power tied to any particular individual, movement, organization, or state, though its deepest reservoir throughout the ages has been the Islamic mainstream. Islam is unpredictable in both the timing and locus of its actions and reactions. Islamist theorists explain Islam in the world as a living rather than mechanical entity. It has a capacity for self-organization, without the need for overt leadership or stable hierarchy. Islam takes on extraordinarily variable forms, while still remaining recognizable as Islam. Those forms emerge from creative adaptations to radically different circumstance, whether of domestic tyranny or foreign occupation or minority status in Western societies. Yet, the imprint of the circumstances never eclipses the Islamic character of what emerges, whether in the Arab countries, Turkey, Iran, or any other places Muslims have built Islamic communities.

The 1,400-year history of Islam as interpreted by mainstream Islamist thinkers reveals recurrent patterns of adaptation, absorption, and authenticity. Like a living organism, Islam attends to its own survival, making sure that essential needs are fulfilled in whatever conditions it finds itself. As a spiritual presence, Islam requires only the Quran and a community of Muslims who respond to its divine message. Islamic communities are self-generated and self-organized. Therefore, they inevitably have distinctive features. Yet, all such communities recognize themselves and are recognized by others as part of the larger Islamic ummah. Wounded in one setting, Islam may well respond in another, physically quite distant, though still a part of the ummah. This unpredictable spatial displacement makes the response all the more effective. Timing, too, is flexible. The riposte to assault may not be immediate but it will come. For these reasons, it is quite impossible to read the character of an Islamic community simply as an imprint of the environment in which it exists. Nor can such movements be analyzed primarily by the character of the struggles in which they engage or by the means they employ in asserting the power of Islamic identity. There is always and everywhere an elusive excess of meaning and that meaning always points to a distinctive Islamic dimension that goes beyond the character of the environment and the struggles it generates. If we are to understand the Islamic world, there is no escape from the study of Islam itself, particularly its startling capacity to create communities that adapt to their environment and absorb elements from it while remaining recognizable as part of the larger Islamic ummah. The place to start in developing such understanding is the Islamic mainstream.

It is the Islam of the Wassatteyya that gives distinction to the most important of Islamic schools of centrist thought, notably the New Islamic trend in Egypt. The nineteenth-century reformist spirit of Muhammad Abduh, shaded with just the right amount of more active resistance of Gamal Eddine al Afghany, pervades the critical intellectual work of the New Islamists of Egypt. To be sure, the school has been hampered from the first by the climate of repression in Egypt. The Free Officers coup that ended the monarchy in 1952 and made Egypt a republic soon targeted and repressed the Muslim Brotherhood, the organization of Islamic activists founded by Hassan al Banna in 1928. The Brothers initially threw their support to the young officers, rallying the street to the new regime. However, when the Free Officers, led by Gamal Abdel Nasser came to see the Brothers as a rival for power, the regime brutally repressed them. At the same time, the new rulers eviscerated the power of the traditional religious establishment and made it a docile instrument of authoritarian rule. While for the most part the West reacted with hostility to the nationalist character of the Nasserist order, this anti-Islamic dimension was welcomed.

With the passing of Nasser and succession of Anwar al-Sadat in 1970, an opening was created for serious Islamic work. Sadat turned to Islamists to counter the influence of the more left-leaning Nasserists and Islamists were released from prisons and returned to public life, under highly circumscribed terms and with only very limited freedom. Rather than a political party, a group of centrist Islamist intellectuals constituted themselves as an inventive "intellectual school," representing a new Islamist trend. With time these Egyptian New Islamists acquired a deep influence in Egypt and beyond its borders, primarily because of their intellectual work. One of the major Islamist intellectuals of our time, Yusuf al Qaradawy, has played a key role in the work of the school. That contribution is matched only by another of the major Egyptian New Islamists, Shaikh Muhammad al Ghazzaly, who was arguably the single most influential and creative centrist Islamic thinker of the twentieth century. However, the New Islamists are quite genuinely, as they describe themselves, an intellectual school with a galaxy of impressive thinkers that includes Muhammad Selim al Awa, Kamal Abul Magd, Fahmy Huwaidy, Muhammad Selim al Awa, and Tareq al Bishry. Few other trends in Islamic political thought, or for that matter political thought in general, can match the combined intellectual weight of these thinkers.

This "intellectual school" has addressed the most pressing issues of our age with an inventive, creative, and highly literate spirit in the best traditions of classic Islamic scholarship. All those who ask whether Islamic moderation, suited to the global age, is possible are advised to study their work on such pressing, large issues as Islam and cultural integrity in the information age, Islam and democracy, Islam and the rights of minorities and women, Islam and imperialism. Here we have a tolerant and inclusive Islam of the long and deep breath that rises from Sunni Islam but speaks to all Muslims. There is a calm tenacity at the heart of this intellectual school that gives it remarkable staying power and very broad appeal.

In sharp contrast the colors of Iranian Shia Islam are bolder and more assertive. Yet, for all the difference, it is instructive that Egypt's New Islamists have paid close and appreciative attention to the contributions to the Islamic Awakening by the Iranian Islamic revolutionaries. The overthrow of the shah's regime, corrupt, brutal, and American-imposed, represented a signal and quite unexpected political victory. The revolutionaries themselves, we know, were caught unprepared for their startling success. The 1979 Iranian revolution redefined the meaning of Islamic resistance for our contemporary era.[31]

Inevitably, the Iranian revolution enhanced the status of Shia Muslims everywhere and compensated for their minority status and the hardships that has entailed. Yet, the major intellectuals who prepared and guided the revolution sought to avoid a narrow sectarian discourse. Ali Shariati, a figure almost as important to the revolution as the Ayatollah Khomeini, played a central role in readying Iranians, especially young people, to play a revolutionary role with a broad Islamic rather than narrow Shia appeal. Shariati brought with him a highly complex and innovative rereading of the history of Shia Islam in Iran. He laid a firm ground for rejection of quietism and corrupt compliance of traditional Shiism with his call for a struggle of "religion against religion" as the defining character of the coming battle.[32] For Shariati it was a distorted Shia Islam as much as a Western-imposed dictatorship that was the enemy to topple. To that end Shariati drew heavily not only on critical strands in Shiism but also on the Western revolutionary tradition, particularly the Third World version appropriated by Frantz Fanon for the Algerian revolution.

Khomeini himself was almost as far from a traditional cleric as the very modern, cosmopolitan Shariati.[33] In Islamic terms he was an iconoclast and an innovator and used both dimensions of his charismatic persona to appeal to the suffering Iranians. Khomeini's most controversial and problematic innovation was the pivotal notion of the *vilayet al faqih* that justified the rule of the ayatollahs in Iran. It is less well known in the West that many of Iran's leading Shia scholars rejected the notion at the time of the revolution because of its authoritarian implications. They continue to do so now, just as Sunni mainstream scholars do, citing its authoritarian and elitist implications. Shariati and Khomeini, each in their own way, were innovators in shaping Islam's role as a major means of resistance in the late modern world.

No comment of the French philosopher Michel Foucault evoked more derision and scorn than his observation that there was afoot in revolutionary Iran a "spiritual power."[34] In fact, Foucault had a point, though his innocence of a deep knowledge of either Iran or Islam skewered its expression. In Islam the worldly and the spiritual are inseparable, so the power afoot in Iran was more properly thought of as a new, revolutionary Islamic identity. To be sure, it was in important ways a problematic expression of that identity. For the Islamic mainstream a critical downside of the Iranian experience is the authoritarian, top-down character Khomeini gave it, hijacking the genuine social revolution symbolized by Shariati that was under way.[35] By these lights, the resistance to these dictatorial tendencies on Islamic ground within Iran represents the most promising dimension of the Iranian experience, represented by such reformist figures as former President Khatami. For all the unsettling contradictions of the Iranian revolution and its continued travails at present, it did provide a riveting display of the power of Islamic identity in opposing a brutal, Western-imposed regime. Even today, after all the tarnishing of the revolution, that power continues to exert its appeal and not just in Shia communities.

The power of Islamic identity took a quite different form in Turkey, though one just as unexpected and almost as influential. The Kemalist regime that ended the Ottoman era was militantly secular. Kemal Atatürk, the founder of modern Turkey, sought quite explicitly to create a Western political order and society in modern Turkey. That militant secularism continues to attract many in the West as the appropriate model for the region's political transformation. However, the Turkish secular model was always something of an airbrushed mirage. The real driving force behind the Atatürk revolution was Turkish hypernationalism. It demonstrated many of the ugly features of all such nationalism. Atatürk actively encouraged the ethnic cleansing of Anatolia. Greeks, Armenians, and Kurds were all unwelcome in an ethnically homogeneous Turkey. The results were predictable and quite deplorable. Leaving these terrible nationalist excesses aside, the West has chosen instead to focus on and herald the parallel moves to weaken Islam's hold on the Turkish people.[36] These actions were widely celebrated as an essential part of Turkish modernization and a preferred path for others in the region. Islam was to be contained in the private sphere and its social and political influence all but eliminated. The new Turkey would be an ethnically homogeneous *and* secular nation rather than the organizing center of a multi-ethnic political empire. Turkey would look to the West rather than the Islamic world to build its national future. The Turkish experience seemed to confirm Western development theory that the nation-state defined modernity and religion was a thing of the past. From this perspective, the Islamic legacy was a burden to be set aside, by force if necessary. A violent, cataclysmic clash with Islam seemed to be in the making.

It never came. Islam in Turkey responded instead with the pacific, yielding Sufi Islam. The major figure of Turkish Islamism, Said Nursi, provided an intense and perceptive spirituality that speaks of the divine in Sufist terms that are at once universalist and intimate. Only very rarely do signs of Nursi's political intelligence and strategic sense emerge. Nursi proved to be the fountainhead of a liquid, supple Islam of Sufist inspiration that held its ground in Turkey by giving way. The Islamic wave in Turkey never had the character of an intellectual reorientation in the ways of Egypt's New Islamists nor of a torrent or a flood in the Iranian style to overwhelm the ramparts of a hostile, repressive regime. For all the violence of the secular revolutionaries, they were Turks and their revolution carried the banner of Turkish nationalism. To confront that menace and the danger of the eradication of Islam in Turkey, Islam instead soaked deeply, like water, into the soil of Anatolia, the very soil from which Turkish nationalism itself arose. Secularization went forward on the surface while Islam penetrated even more deeply the roots that nourished the hearts and souls of the Turkish people. Islam not only survived, it flourished. With time, Islam could assert itself in a more overtly political way. Nursi's mantle passed to others and Turkish Islamists experimented with a variety of flexible political forms. Sufism thrived in the shadow of militant secularism and paved the way for Turkey's democratically elected government with Islamist roots to assume power in 2003. Prime Minister Erdoğan and his Justice and Development Party are the beneficiaries of Nursi's Sufi-inspired triumph for Islam in modern-day Turkey.

In the end, the West must come to terms with these vital and living forms of Islam that have already reshaped the region. Not even the power of the world's sole superpower recklessly and brutally deployed under the Bush administration could succeed in remaking the Islamic world by force along Western lines. Illusions about an Islam made in the West and re-exported to the region that periodically seduce the denizens of the Rand Corporation and other such think tanks will have to be abandoned. Muslims can and will rally in the end to isolate the extremists. But they will do so to preserve Islam itself and with an agenda that they themselves forge and not according to Western dictates.

By not paying attention to the Islamic Awakening and to Islam's epic story for our own time, we deny ourselves the opportunity to make better sense of the Islamic world. We also lose potential partners in the Islamic world. Yet, to the limited degree that we have faced our own most recent failings, the focus has been on the shortfalls of the military and the intelligence effort in the context of inept, ideologically driven political leadership.[37] These are important beginnings. Yet, it seems deeply regrettable that so little attention has been paid to the colossal intellectual failure to develop a reasonable understanding of Islam and the Islamic world that actually informs our broad policy toward the world's Muslims.

The simple truth is that the United States is very much an interested empire and our interests implicate us deeply in developments in the Islamic world. Our adeptness in devising ways of looking at the Islamic world that allow us to escape from responsibility for our own actions, either through demonizing Muslims or morphing them into incomplete copies of ourselves, have had disastrous consequences for the Islamic world and for ourselves. The view of Islam as "Islamo-fascism" channels our fears and passions into the drive for cruel and unfeeling wars. After our bombing Baghdad, killing civilians by the uncounted hundreds of thousands, and allowing the looting of incomparable cultural treasures, is any place on earth safe from our self-righteous, misguided, and self-interested anger? On the other hand, the inevitably failed quest for those mythic moderates channels our reason and empathy into dead-end searches for pale, ghostly imitations of ourselves. Dialogues become invidious indictments of putative moderates to live up to our images of who they should be. Calls for understanding mask efforts to remake others in our own image and to refashion their history to duplicate our own. Inevitably, such clones of ourselves will be at best marginal in their societies and at worst simply counterfeits suitable only for the role of agents for a foreign power. What is most disconcerting about both of these approaches to the question of Islam and the West is the way they steer us away from a critical look at what has gone wrong with our own policies. Even more damaging is the way that both approaches blind us to the existence of genuine, autonomous Islamist centrists with whom we do share some important commitments, though not all, and who do represent potential partners for joint projects of mutual interest.

Surely one would think that the calamities of the Bush years would have provoked massive inquiries, robust congressional hearings, painful Truth and Reconciliation commissions as to just how we got so much wrong in Palestine, Afghanistan, and Iraq. People are ready to face these realities. Many already have. Millions of Americans, and others around the world, recognized that the unprovoked war on Iraq was a crime. They saw through Colin Powell's charade at the UN in presenting the "evidence" for Saddam's link to al-Qaeda terrorism and possession of weapons of mass destruction. They knew that war is *never* a cakewalk and that there would be no flowers for the troops. The world had never seen anything like it. Massive protests took place in Western capitals before the war was launched. Ordinary citizens could not restrain an imperial president and the American military machine, though they did remind the world that not all Westerners, not all Americans, are "war fighters."

Despite the prejudicial embedding of journalists with our military and the deadening hand of the news conglomerates, enough investigative journalism and real scholarship has been produced that we now know that we were indeed systematically lied to in the buildup to the war of choice against Iraq. We all know that the planners of that catastrophe had no grasp of the realities of the world into which they recklessly plunged. This is no small matter. Clearly we failed in the most flagrant ways to understand the Islamic world into which we have blundered with such terrible arrogance and such deadly violence. Yet, there has been no radical rethinking of the underlying causes for our massive failings. We have, however, increased our military budget and launched planning and weapons development programs for the new wars of counterinsurgency, which are really the old colonial wars with a new label. Most of these unending wars to come will target Islamic lands.

Our situation as a nation is that we now find ourselves a massive presence in an Islamic world we do not understand, where we cannot distinguish our friends from our enemies unless they are shooting at us. Incoherence in intellectual understanding leads to incoherent policies on the ground. The contradictions of current policies that refuse fundamental rethinking are quite astonishing: We use unarmed drones to bomb areas as part of a counterinsurgency strategy in the Af-Pak theater that has winning the people's hearts and minds as a central aim. Our mindless drones bomb funeral processions and wedding celebrations with soul-numbing regularity. We can do better in both understanding and policies, though national political institutions appear to be incapable of generating such new understanding and new ways of relating to the Islamic world. It is time for the social movements that animate civil society and have been responsible for the most important democratic advances America has achieved to make the intellectual, moral, and political effort themselves to rethink America's global role, with particular attention to the Islamic world, and to enforce a reorientation away from these continued foreign policy disasters.

The resources for such a reorientation are at hand. Empires inevitably generate some version of the white man's burden, just as they always conjure up some horrific threat, emanating from the "natives," by which to cow their own population and justify the terrible violence, for the most part against civilians, with which they achieve their ends. Yet, at the same time, empires also inevitably create domestic critics, especially when losses in treasure and lives mount. Opposition to empire takes root first in these narrow nationalist terms as imperial overreach comes to be seen as a threat to the national interest. Invariably, however, there are also those who see farther and recognize a common human interest in resistance to imperial and colonial projects and the violence they entail, whatever their national origins. Such individuals and groups have made themselves a presence in the West and they are open, in theory at least, to cooperation in resistance to empire and in the building of a somewhat better, somewhat more equitable, and somewhat more democratic world. Despite the failures to restrain imperial and colonial policies, recent years have seen precisely such developments, including important beginnings in the United States and Israel. Even more remarkable is the appearance in those Islamic lands under assault of individuals and groups who recognize that, while empire and colonization must be resisted, there are potential allies for those struggles on the other side of the battle lines. These possibilities of joint effort came into view in the clearest way during the massive protest in Western capitals against the US-led attack on Iraq. Leading Islamist intellectuals of the center regularly remind their peoples that there are intellectuals, activists, and ordinary citizens in the United States and Israel who stand against the war-making policies of their governments.

It is the role of humanistic scholarship that is by definition anti-imperial and anticolonial to document these unlikely developments and to provide the knowledge base to help turn them into cooperative, activist efforts in the human interest. There have been some important beginnings to generate scholarship of this kind, but the record thus far remains unimpressive. The work of positive, humanistic learning that can underwrite willful acts of cooperation across the battle lines has hardly begun. A critical dimension of the work ahead is seeing more clearly how existing transnational movements that seek to transcend narrow nationalisms can find common ground and cooperative projects on behalf of a more just world system, yet to be created. The massive antiwar movements in the West that sought to prevent the Iraq war are one such resource. The Wassatteyya in the Islamic world is another. Both share anti-imperial and anticolonial commitments, often at variance with the diverse national settings out of which they grow. At the same time, they confront critical differences, notably on social and cultural issues. Progressives in the West find Islamic notions of the unity of politics and faith as well as the role of women difficult to fathom. Islamists find not only particular issues, such as gay rights, at variance with their convictions, but also a general Western cultural arrogance even more damaging to genuine cooperation. Part of the difficulties on both sides is quite simply the lack of a nuanced understanding of the respective positions of the possible partners. Yet, in the end, even when these misperceptions are set aside, serious differences remain.

There are ways around these barriers. Western peace and justice activists have years of experience in cooperating with diverse groups on specific campaigns for social progress and against war, while understanding that differences would preclude joint action in other arenas. The Islamic Wassatteyya has a parallel tradition of overcoming conflicts on "branch" issues while cooperating on "root" issues. Centrist Islamists have also developed a sophisticated Fiqh of Priorities, which allows them to set aside less critical matters in the interest of such large questions as war and social justice. There are moments when these possibilities of mutual understanding and cooperation flash before us like lightning in the sky, despite all the blinders we normally wear. Yusuf al Qaradawy saw one such moment when he addressed his audience of sheikhs, callers to Islam, and the massive Muslim publics that respond to the words he was quite prepared to say—"No to the unjust and illegitimate war of aggression against Iraq"—*in tandem with* the millions of protesters on the streets of European and American capitals.[38]

America is neither a sleepwalking nor gentle giant. It is no longer possible, if it ever was, to see Israel as a beleaguered David, crouched defensively against overwhelming odds. It in no way justifies the vileness of the crime committed against innocent American civilians on 9/11 to recognize that the United States is a global power, deeply involved in the Arab and Islamic worlds, in pursuit of its own interests. The United States' closest regional ally is a nuclear power with a world-class military that is more than a match for all Arab armies combined, a dominant regional power that has occupied the lands of all its neighbors in the course of its brief history and is today relentlessly colonizing the remnants of historic Palestine under its occupation. Americans are not demeaned as a people when they acknowledge that the involvements of their government in the Islamic world have very often been enacted with more of the violence and greed of an empire than the wisdom and restraint of a democratic republic. It is time to recognize that there is precious little in the record of American involvements in the Islamic world that reflects the largeness of purpose and humane generosity that Americans like to think they represent in the world. Israelis need to face their own hard choices between exclusionary and expansionist ultranationalism and democracy, between a greater Israel and an Israel at peace with a respected place in the region and the world. The truth is that many in America and in Israel have begun to face these harsh truths.

For their part, the vast majority of Muslims do reject the extremists and their "war on the world." They recognize that millions in the West side with them against dictatorships, imperial wars, and colonial occupations. But they also believe, with good reason, that today the real danger extremism represents in their lands is overshadowed by the greater violence and deeper wounds of imperial and colonial projects for which the United States and its closest regional ally bear primary responsibility. Despite such ugly realities, glimpses of the kind of understanding and genuine cooperation needed to transcend them have appeared in existing transnational movements, both Islamic and Western, that have the potential to create new spaces for global cooperation in the human interest. To underwrite these efforts, there is serious work ahead for that broad tradition of worldly, humanistic scholarship to which both Islamic and Western civilizations have contributed.

NOTES

1. Quran 96:1.

2. Shia Muslims consider jihad a sixth pillar.

3. Quran 2:30; Quran 57:7

4. See, in particular, John O. Voll, Foreword in J. Spencer Trimingham, *Sufi Orders in Islam* (Oxford: Clarendon Press, 1971).

5. "Say; He is Allah, The One and Only; All, the Eternal, Absolute. He getteth not. Nor is He begotten." Quran 112:1–3.

6. See Tareq al Bishry, "The Islamic Revival Added Much to our Lives." July 26, 2006, ISLAMMEMO; See also Yusuf al Qaradawy, *The Islamic Awakening* (Cairo: 1999).

7. For a discussion of the importance of the popular expressions of the Awakening, as well as of the guiding role of the Wassatteyya, see Bishry, "The Islamic Revival."

8. Quran 2:143

9. See the striking, mainstream characterization of the role for contemporary thinkers of the "ocean" of Fiqh from all schools in Yusuf al Qaradawy, *Fiqh of Jihad: A*

Comparative Study of Its Rulings and Philosophy (in Arabic) (Cairo: Dar al Wahba, 2009), pp. 20–29.

10. The phrase, with the meaning intended here, was coined by Robert M. Sapolsky in his teaching company lecture series "Biology and Human Behavior: The Neurological Origins of Individuality, 2nd Edition," www.teach12.com/ttcx/CourseDescLong2 .aspx?cid=1597.

11. The underlying image runs through the major work of Muhammad Abduh, *The Theology of Unity,* trans. Ishaq Musaad and Kenneth Cragg (London: Allen & Unwin, 1966).

12. See the statement of Yusuf al Qaradawy in response to the 9/11 attacks, "Islam on Line," September 27, 2001.

13. For the full text of the Obama speech, see *New York Times,* June 4, 2009.

14. See, for example, 2002-SEP-17, at www.whitehouse.gov, accessed September 2009.

15. In an interview with *Der Spiegel* Kissinger made the comment in explicit reference to Obama's Cairo speech to the Islamic world. Cited http://presstv.ir/detail .aspx?id=99988&sectionid=3510203, accessed July 18, 2009.

16. For a transcript of the secretary's remarks, see http://merln.ndu.edu/archivepdf/ NEA/State/48328.pdf, accessed July 18, 2009. The secretary said: "For 60 years, my country, the United States, pursued stability at the expense of democracy in this region here in the Middle East—and we achieved neither. Now, we are taking a different course. We are supporting the democratic aspirations of all people."

17. See *New York Times,* June 4, 2009.

18. For an astute analysis along these lines, see Manar al Shorbaby, *Three Voices of Obama: Arabs in the Post Black and White Era* (in Arabic) (Cairo: Safir, 2009).

19. Statement Before the House Armed Services Subcommittee on Terrorism, Unconventional Threats and Capabilities, presented September 18, 2008, http://armed services.house.gov/pdfs/TUTC091808/Scheuer_Testimony091808.pdf, p. 1, accessed October 15, 2008.

20. See Ira Chernus, "Palestinian Violence Overstated, Jewish Violence Understated. Time to Change the Story," June 25, 2009, www.tomdispatch.com/post/175088, accessed July 30, 2009.

21. Qaradawy, *Fiqh of Jihad,* especially pp. 110–114.

22. For a pointed representative discussion of such purposive violence and the rules that circumscribe its use, see Yusuf al Qaradawy, *Islam and Violence* (in Arabic) (Cairo: Dar al Sharouq, 2004), especially p. 26.

23. The major Egyptian centrist thinker Selim al Awa pronounced unequivocally that "if Islam were to come to power by force, it would be far worse than the current situation. Those who are in power today are in dialogue with us, which is far better than being slaughtered in the name of Islam." *Al Ahrar,* March 23, 1992.

24. An important contribution along the lines needed is John L. Esposito and Dalia Mogahed, *Who Speaks for Islam: What a Billion Muslims Really Think* (New York: Gallup Press, 2007).

25. Rami al Khouri, "The Arab Story: The Big One Waiting to Be Told," *Daily Star,* July 21, 2007.

26. On Hizbullah human rights violations, see, for example, "Israel/Lebanon Under Fire: Hizbullah's attacks on Northern Israel," Amnesty International, September 14, 2006, http://web.amnesty.org/library/index/engmde020252006; "Lebanon: Hezbollah Rocket Attacks on Haifa Designed to Kill Civilians," Human Rights Watch, July 18, 2006, http://hrw.org/english/docs/2006/07/18/lebano13760.htm; "UN Envoys: Israel and Hezbollah Broke Human Rights Law in War," *Haaretz*, October 3, 2006, www.haaretz.com/hasen/spages/769953.html; "Israel/Lebanon: Hezbollah Must End Attacks on Civilians," Human Rights Watch, August 5, 2006, http://hrw.org/english/docs/2006/08/05/lebano13921.htm. On recent Hamas human rights violations, see, for example, www.hrw.org/en/news/2009/08/05/gazaisrael-hamas-rocket-attacks-civilians-unlawful; Human Rights Watch, "Gaza: Hamas Should End Killings, Torture," Euro-Mediterranean Human Rights Network, April 22, 2009, www.euromedrights.net/pages/571/news/focus/69818; Aug 6, 2009mhttp://www.earthtimes.org/articles/show/280431,rocket-attacks-on-israel-war-crime-human-rights-watch-says.html ; http://www.lightstalkers.org/human_rights_watch_on_gaza, 13 Jun 2007.

27. Juan Cole, "Armageddon at the Top of the World: Not!: A Century of Frenzy over the North-West Frontier," July 27, 2009, www.tomdispatch.com/post/175100/juan_cole_empire_s_paranoia_about_the_pashtuns, accessed August 12, 2009.

28. See the assessment of the former CIA station chief in Kabul, Graham E. Fuller, for an incisive analysis of the failed US approach to Afghanistan, "Obama's Policies Making Situation Worse in Afghanistan and Pakistan," May 10, 2009, www.huffingtonpost.com/graham-e-fuller/global-viewpoint-obamas-p_b_201355.html.

29. See Andrew J. Bacevich, "9/11 Plus Seven," September 9, 2008, www.tomdispatch.com/post/174974, accessed August 16, 2009.

30. See Tareq al Bishry, *The Characteristics of Islamic Political Thought in Contemporary History* (in Arabic) (Cairo: Dar al Sharouq, 1996), especially pp. 58–59.

31. See Alastair Crooke, *Resistance: The Essence of the Islamist Revolution* (New York and London: Pluto Press, 2009).

32. Ali Shariati, *Religion Versus Religion*, trans. Cyrus Bakhtiar (Chicago: Kazi Publications, 2000).

33. See Fahmy Huwaidy, *Iran from Within* (Cairo: Al Ahram Center for Publishing and Translation, 1987).

34. Michel Foucault, "What Are the Iranians Dreaming About" (in French), *Le Nouvel Observateur*, October 16–22, 1978.

35. See Huwaidy, *Iran from Within*.

36. Stephen Zunes, *Tinderbox: US Foreign Policy and the Roots of Terrorism* (Monroe, ME: Common Courage Press, 2003), especially pp. 19–21.

37. See Anonymous (Michael Scheuer), *Imperial Hubris: Why the West Is Losing the War on Terror* (Washington, DC: 2004).

38. Qaradawy, *Fiqh of Jihad*, p. 717.

Part 5

INTERNATIONAL DIMENSIONS

It MAY BE a stretch to argue that international relations were invented in the Middle East, but certainly relations between the earliest forms of states happened in the region many millennia ago, as evidenced by cuneiform tablets found in dusty ruins of libraries in ancient city-states. Such records tell of the fate of city-states under attack, as evidenced by the desperate plea from the king of Ugarit for help to repel an invasion by the "Sea People" around 1800 BCE (it never came, and the Sea People demolished Ugarit). These tablets and companion papyrus documents tell of treaties and trade agreements, and even proposals of marriage to bond ancient kingdoms together—the young widow of King Tutankhamen requested that the Hittite king send her an eligible husband. The Middle East has set a pattern of international relations that many other nation-states have followed.

The participants in Middle Eastern international relations may be formal states, or they may be "semi-states," such as the Palestinian Authority, which has some of the functions of a state but lacks the formal recognition necessary to claim status as a genuine state. In other situations the parties are substate actors who wish to change power at the top of their state, or at least to influence national leadership, sometimes by recruiting the assistance of another state. Lebanon's Hizbullah party is a case here, a Shia group that channels resources from Iran (sometimes through Syria) to maintain its influence in its home country.

International relations are about how nations interact to achieve power, influence, and status. They are about understanding how countries and substate actors gain and keep the instruments that allow them to get others to do their bidding, or to prevent them from doing the bidding of others. The chapters in this section indicate the levels of analysis necessary to gain such an understanding of the complex patterns of international affairs in the Middle East. These chapters consider particular issues such as the Arab-Israeli differences, resource issues such as those posed by Middle Eastern petroleum, and the situations evolving from two particular countries that have dominated the Middle Eastern news cycle: Iraq and Iran.

If a single issue has pocked the landscape of the Middle East and beyond, it is the relationship between the state of Israel and the Palestinian population that was largely displaced as a consequence of the 1948 and 1967 Arab-Israeli wars. Approximately 700,000 Palestinians fled or were driven from the land that became Israel in May 1948, and hundreds of thousands more fled as Israeli forces took the West Bank of the Jordan River and East Jerusalem from the state of Jordan and Gaza from Egyptian administration in 1967. The large majority of those who left ended up in squalid refugee camps in Lebanon, Jordan, Syria, and other Arab countries, while those who remained in the West Bank and Gaza came under Israeli occupation. As Christopher Hemmer demonstrates in his contribution to this volume, both the Israelis and Palestinians have defined the subsequent situation as a contest between two "rights" to the land and the identity that goes with it. This is much more, of course, than just a contest between identities. The Israeli-Palestinian conflict is a magnet for attention well beyond the direct players. In the larger Arab world, the Palestinian situation is one of the most important issues that citizens pay attention to, and a lens through which they judge their leaders and others, including the United States. However, as Hemmer notes, a resolution that would be even minimally satisfactory to the parties has proven to be intractable despite often heroic efforts.

There are many "frozen" conflicts in the world, disputes that get little attention until they explode into global consciousness. The dispute over the region known as the Western Sahara is one such conflict, a former colony abandoned by an imperial power, only to be claimed by several contesting parties. The Western Sahara is a desolate part of North Africa, which has a small population but is rich in phosphates and has one of the world's largest fishing grounds off its coast. When Spain withdrew its colonial claim in the early 1970s it left a vacuum that was quickly filled by three countries—Morocco, Mauritania, and Algeria—and by an indigenous group, the Sahrawis, whom the Popular Front for the Liberation of Saguia el-Hamra and Río de Oro (in

Spanish, Frente Popular para la Liberación de Saguia el-Hamra y Río de Oro, or the POLISARIO Front) claims to represent. The conflict is now largely between Morocco and the POLISARIO, although Algeria and Morocco remain divided over Morocco's claim to the territory as the "Moroccan Sahara." Yahia Zoubir has dissected this conflict, noting its importance not just to North Africa, but also to outside powers, including the United States. The United States has tried, as Zoubir notes, to maintain good relations with both Morocco and Algeria, and thus tried to broker an end to the conflict through the mediation of former secretary of state James Baker. However, thus far there has been no solution to the dispute, which impedes cooperation between two key North African states and is costing Morocco considerable treasure.

Iran stands in the greater Middle East as a lonely outpost of Shia governance and a majority language, Farsi, which is the national tongue of only Iran. Ancient Persia before 1936, Iran is a mélange of ancient temples, poetry, *chelo* (the unique Persian steamed rice), lush mountain forests, uninhabited deserts, and a storied set of political traditions. Its public image of the fierce visage of Ayatollah Ruhollah Khomeini betrays a rich civilization that sent its martyrs to the gallows in 1904 for demanding constitutional democracy. For the United States, Iran was a constantly misunderstood country where Americans believed what they wanted to believe in the face of clear contrary evidence. Like the British before them, American Cold War–era policy makers supported the Pahlavi dynasty because they believed that its modernist tendencies correlated to support for American Cold War aspirations. Their chosen leader, Muhammad Reza Pahlavi, catered to this support, pushing Iran into his vision of European-style modernity, banning Islamic attire, marginalizing the Shia clergy, and pushing reform through his "White Revolution." American leaders and their myopic vision of Iran never saw the end coming even as President Jimmy Carter praised Iran as an "island of stability" in the Rose Garden right before the Islamic Revolution put an end to American hopes. That political movement fueled itself on generations of Iranian hatred for those held responsible for its long history under or near foreign thumbs. Khomeini and his successor wasted few words on "The Great Satan" while quietly reaching out to the United States and other regional countries when doing so suited Iran's interests. Khomeini turned over much of the Iranian economy to fellow Shia clerics, who mismanaged much of it, thus alienating many former regime supporters. Iranian leadership then began a journey down the nuclear path, either because they genuinely felt insecure or because they wanted to draw attention away from the failure of Iran's economy. The United States took the lead in opposing the Iranian nuclear specter, and the state of Israel hinted at preemptive action to prevent Iranian nuclear weaponization. Iran's 2009 presidential elections gave outside players some hope that the long-sought Iranian "moderates" might at last prevail, though those hopes wound up on familiar rocks of despair when Mahmoud Ahmadinejad won a disputed contest. What followed was a continuation of the waiting game where the United States, Israel, and the Arab Gulf countries eyed Iran nervously, unsure what the next step should be.

Manochehr Dorraj analyzes the foreign relations of the Islamic Republic of Iran, noting both continuities and change from the pre-1979 Iran of the Pahlavi dynasty. He dissects the debates within the Islamic Republic's ruling circles about engagement with both Iran's neighbors and with the West, and the United States in particular. The Khatami presidency saw a thawing of tensions between Iran and the enemies it made after 1979. However, the election of President Mahmoud Ahmadinejad in 2005 quenched Khatami's efforts at rapprochement and instead embarked on an anti-American and anti-Israel campaign accompanied by a refusal to open Iran's nuclear research facilities to international inspection. The consequences have been a crippling set of economic punishments that Iran seems determined to endure, though, as Dorraj indicates, Iran may stop short of a workable nuclear weapon in exchange for both the lifting of sanctions and a restoration of international prestige that Iranians have sought since 1979.

A headline word count in any major American or European newspaper would probably rank the word "Iraq" ahead of the name of any other country for the past two decades. Iraq has riveted American attention in particular, and although US military forces are drawing back from the country, Iraq will not go away quickly in American minds. It will continue to draw attention, for its oil, for the potential of its violence, and for the impact that the Iraq situation will have in the Middle East. It may become the graveyard of failed American expectations of being able to build stability where the forms of governance reflect the need to maintain some level of tranquility in a country welded together by foreign influences. It may yet reach those expectations and, more important, reach the expectations of its own people, for security, for a better life, for all the things citizens of troubled states desire. But it must overcome the curse of so many other states that were constructed for the pleasure of a faraway imperial power that ignored the separateness of Iraq's three principal regions while expediting the recovery of oil for the Royal Navy and ultimately Great Britain. Britain installed an imported monarchy, borrowed from the Hashemi family, which once ruled Mecca. That rule came to a bloody end in 1958 as Iraq joined the legion of Arab countries embracing Arab nationalism. Its last ruler, Saddam Hussein, also came to a violent end in December 2006, hanged in the same prison where he had executed many of his victims.

Initially Iraq was an American problem after the 2003 invasion that toppled Saddam, but, as has so frequently been the case in modern American combat, the public tired of the cost in lives and dollars, so President George W. Bush set a timetable for American withdrawal. That announcement was accompanied by a "surge" in American forces, which appeared temporarily to stem the endemic violence that tore the country from region to region. But the American withdrawal, which continued at a more rapid pace under President Barack Obama, did not address the chronic problems of the Iraqi state.

Iraq has large deposits of petroleum and is the only Middle Eastern country to have two of the world's great rivers running through it. Those rivers nourished some of the greatest civilizations in ancient history, and the life-giving water continued to irrigate the land for most of Iraq's thousands of years. But a combination of Saddam's agricultural follies and dams on the rivers in Turkey combined to reduce the flow of the Tigris and Euphrates rivers to the point that Iraq was importing food in 2009. Iraq's capacity to lift and process raw petroleum was also crippled by mismanagement during the Baath era and by the economic sanctions that gradually strangled much of Iraq's economic capacity.

But while the headlines have underscored Iraq's tragic internal violence and the political challenges, the connected issue of the country's political economy has been almost ignored. However, as Eric Davis emphasizes in his chapter, an understanding of Iraq's political economy is crucial to comprehending much of Iraq's modern history and political climate. The power of the central regime in Baghdad, the bloody war between Iran and Iraq, and the cleavages between linguistic and religious groups in Iraq all have ties to economic factors. Thus, for Davis, the road to Iraq's future must also be paved partly through a better understanding of Iraq's future economic prospects.

One of the currencies of the Middle East is petroleum; indeed, for many of the world's people that is what the region is best known for. Images of tankers streaming out of the Straits of Hormuz or flames of natural gas flaring from wells are common from the Middle East, where over two-thirds of the global oil reserves and some of the largest natural gas deposits lie. It was oil, according to then–US defense secretary Richard Cheney, that propelled the United States to rescue Kuwait from Saddam Hussein's clutches in 1990. The reason for this interest is obvious: The global economy is fueled with oil and gas, for transportation, electricity generation, chemicals, and a host of other uses. And one of the petroleum paradoxes is that the countries that use the most petroleum do not have adequate supplies, while the countries that have petroleum do not use much of it; the Middle East is one of the lowest producers of carbon dioxide because of its low levels of industrialization. Most Middle Eastern oil and gas instead moves by ship or pipeline to Europe, North America, and Asia to fuel the appetites of industrialization and service. The consuming countries lack their own petroleum and because their economies run on Middle Eastern fuel, they find that they must adjust their foreign and economic policies to this reality. Many oil-consuming countries contribute military forces to the region, in the name of stability operations, though the populist phrase "no troops for oil" and the tar baby–like trap of an inextricable commitment limit such efforts. Consuming countries must also weigh concerns about human rights violation charges against some of the oil-supplying countries even as their oil tankers offload their precious cargo in European and Asian ports. Oil and gas have helped to take once-local issues and problems in the Middle East and globalize them. Steve Yetiv focuses on the supply of oil from the Middle East, projecting the changing relationship between consumer and producer. He discusses the roller-coaster ride that both oil prices and oil supply predictions have taken over the past few years, and the impact it has had on Middle East producers in particular. While sometimes the price movements originate from supply and demand intersections, or price speculation (as occurred in 2008), they can also be a function of political decisions to disrupt petroleum supplies. The threat of such disruptions continues, as Yetiv demonstrates, particularly in the Straits of Hormuz, should Iran attempt to close that vital waterway. Other disruption threats include terrorism actions (Saudi Arabia came close to suffering major damage to oil offloading capacity in 2007 from an al-Qaeda attack) or other state efforts to curtail supplies for political purposes, such as actions that Arab oil producers took against the United States and the Netherlands in 1973. However, as Yetiv notes, the petroleum threat runs both ways, with consumers potentially posing a threat to producing countries as they switch from fossil fuels to alternative energy sources.

10

THE ISRAELI-PALESTINIAN CONFLICT

Christopher Hemmer

ONE COMMON QUIP about the Israeli-Palestinian peace process (or lack of it) is that the problem is not that there is no light at the end of the tunnel, the problem is that there is no tunnel.[1] Over the decades, countless peace proposals have been put forward for settling what has been one of the most controversial conflicts of modern times. These proposals are often remarkably similar. While details differ, in their broad outlines, most peace proposals center on a two-state solution roughly along the 1967 borders, a sharing of the city of Jerusalem, and the right of Palestinian refugees to receive compensation and to return to Palestine, but not to Israel except on an extremely limited basis. That is the light that almost everyone can see at the end of the tunnel. Given that light, why have the two parties not reached a peace agreement in their now almost century-long conflict?

"Genuine tragedies in the world," it has been observed, "are not conflicts between right and wrong. They are conflicts between two rights."[2] What has made the Israeli-Palestinian conflict so difficult to resolve is that at its core it consists of two sets of rights that are in large measure mutually exclusive. The Israelis cannot have all of what they legitimately deserve without denying the Palestinians their rights and the Palestinians cannot have all of what they legitimately deserve without denying the Israelis their rights. As the following overview of the Israeli-Palestinian conflict will make clear, peace is hard to come by in a conflict where any foreseeable resolution will require both sides to accept less than they rightfully deserve, which is what has made discovering the tunnel so difficult.

THE ORIGINS OF THE
ISRAELI-PALESTINIAN CONFLICT

While it may be tempting to view the Israeli-Palestinian clash as an age-old religious conflict between the sons of Isaac and the sons of Ishmael, the current dispute is more one of conflicting nationalisms than of competing faiths.[3] While relations between Jews and Muslims have had their historical ups and downs, the organized violence at the heart of the current Israeli-Palestinian conflict arose only in the early twentieth century when the emerging nationalism of Zionism, or Jewish nationalism, collided with a budding Arab, and ultimately a more specifically Palestinian, nationalism over the same piece of territory.

The call for creating a specifically Jewish state came in response to the increasing power of nationalism in European politics, which also led to an increase of anti-Semitism. Although Jewish families may have lived in specific states for generations, the emergence in Europe of a largely ethnically based nationalism made full political assimilation into these states problematic as Jews continued to be identified by their religion and thus not as legitimate Poles or Russians, for example. Without a state of their own in a world of nation-states, some feared, the Jewish people would be condemned to a marginal existence because they would never fully fit in anywhere. To escape such a fate required the creation of what Theodor Herzl called *Der Judenstaat* (*The Jewish State*), in the title of his influential 1896 book. While some members of the early Zionist movement were willing to consider different locations for a Jewish state, only a return to the area of Palestine, location of the biblical Jewish kingdoms, captured the imagination of the movement as a whole.[4]

The obvious problem with creating a Jewish state in Palestine, however, was that the area already had a population, a population that was also starting to develop a nationalism of its own. At first this nationalism, also coming in response to the encroachment of European ideas into the Middle East, was focused on a broader Arab identity, but it eventually gave rise to a more specific Palestinian identity.[5] This move toward a more local nationalism was given a definite boost by the influx of European Jews into the area stemming from the burgeoning Zionist movement. So just as modern Zionism, or Jewish nationalism, rose in response to the threat that European nationalism posed to Europe's Jews, Arab and Palestinian nationalism also was spurred by the threats that European and Jewish nationalism posed for them. The modern-day Israeli-Palestinian conflict stems from these competing nationalisms.

Even as late as 1880 there were only a small number of Jews living in Palestine. After 1880, however, successive waves of immigration expanded that number greatly. Some of the immigrants were religiously motivated, some were driven by the vision of creating a Jewish state, and many were simply looking to escape Europe's increasingly oppressive anti-Semitic climate. At this time, Palestine was part of the Ottoman Empire, which was struggling to hold itself together in the face of European challenges and growing nationalist movements within the empire. In World War I, the Ottoman Empire entered the war on the side of Germany and Austria-Hungary and against the Allied forces of Great Britain, France, Russia, and eventually the United States. As part of its wartime diplomacy, Britain made a series of promises related to Palestine, turning the area into the "much promised land."[6]

The first of these promises came in a series of letters exchanged between Sir Henry McMahon, the British high commissioner in Egypt, and Sherif Hussein, emir of the Hejaz region of the Arabian Peninsula, then a part of the Ottoman Empire. To encourage Hussein to lead an Arab revolt against the Ottomans, London promised to support an independent Arab state under Hussein's rule after the war was over; however, the British kept their promises regarding the specific territory this state would consist of intentionally vague.

A second ally Britain was negotiating with was France. In determining who was going to be doing what in fighting the Ottoman Empire and how the spoils of the war in the region would be divided, Britain and France concluded the Sykes-Picot Agreement (1916), which divided much of the Middle East into French and British spheres of influence. Under the agreement, Britain would control the areas we now know as Israel/Palestine, Jordan, and Iraq; while France would control Syria and Lebanon. Egypt was left out as a nominally independent state, although under British influence, as was most of the eastern portion of the Arabian Peninsula, and the western portion of the Arabian Peninsula was excluded as an area for a state under Sherif Hussein. According to Hussein's reading of the Hussein-McMahon letters, however, much of the territory blocked off there for British and French control had been promised to him.

The final pledge Britain made during the war regarding Palestine was a promise offered to the Jewish people. Calculating that Jewish support for the Allied cause could help keep Russia in the war and bring the United States into the war, trying to reward certain Jews for their efforts in the war, and in part being driven by the Christian-Zionist belief that the Jews belonged in Palestine because the area was promised to them by God, British Foreign Secretary Lord Balfour issued a letter asserting that:

> His Majesty's Government view with favour the establishment in Palestine of a national home for the Jewish people, and will use their best endeavours to facilitate the achievement of this object, it being clearly understood that nothing shall be done which may prejudice the civil and religious rights of existing non-Jewish communities in Palestine.[7]

Once the British successfully concluded the war, London needed to find some way of squaring these pledges. The eventual division of the Middle East after the defeat of the Ottoman Empire came out of the San Remo Conference. Since Britain and France were the great powers most interested in the area, not surprisingly the division they agreed upon resembled the Sykes-Picot Agreement quite closely and did much to shape the map of the Middle East today. Syria and Lebanon were put under French control, an independent Arab state under British tutelage was set up in Iraq, and Great Britain received a League of Nations mandate for Palestine and what was then called Transjordan—the territory east of the Jordan River. The mandate for Palestine also incorporated the language of the Balfour Declaration promising a national home for the Jewish people.

Ruling Palestine posed a dilemma for the British as it became difficult if not impossible to simultaneously fulfill both parts of Balfour's pledge, to allow the Jewish people to establish a national home in Palestine in a way that did not infringe upon the rights of the area's Arab and Muslim inhabitants. Refusing to allow large numbers of Jewish immigrants into the area would deny the Jews a possibility of creating a state of their own and would sentence many to death as the Nazis came to power in Germany and as European anti-Semitism reached its nadir in the Holocaust. Allowing large numbers of Jewish immigrants into the area, however, was a threat to the national aspirations of the Palestinians. These two rights were incompatible from the start. After a bout of particularly intense violence in Palestine starting in 1936, the British-appointed Peel Commission concluded that "an irrepressible conflict has arisen between two national communities within the narrow bounds of one small country" and that the best way to deal with the problem was to partition the area, thus offering the first of what would become many unrealized proposals for a two-state solution of the Israeli-Palestinian conflict.[8]

THE 1948 WAR

Being in the middle of an irrepressible conflict was a costly and uncomfortable position for London. The British found themselves under attack from the Palestinians for letting any Jewish immigrants in and for what Palestinians saw as favoritism toward the Jews. The British also found themselves under attack from the Jewish community in Palestine for not letting enough Jews in and what the Jewish community saw as favoritism toward the Palestinians. After World War II, exhausted and bankrupt as a result of the world wars, Britain needed to find a way out of Palestine. To cover this exit, Britain opted to hand the problem over to the newly created United Nations (UN), which appointed a special commission to study the issue (UNSCOP—the United Nations Special Commission on Palestine). UNSCOP's majority recommendation was embodied in UN General Assembly Resolution 181, which was passed on November 29, 1947. The resolution called for a two-state solution, partitioning the area into proposed Jewish and Palestinian states. With regard to Jerusalem and its holy sites, the resolution called for the city to be made an international city and ruled under a UN trusteeship. Making partition work on the ground, however, was complicated by the geographical interspersion of the Jewish and Palestinian population as well as a sense on both sides that the resolution gave them less than they deserved.

Immediately after the passage of Resolution 181, a new round of fighting erupted in Palestine between the Jewish and Palestinian communities. Fighting or no fighting, Britain just wanted out, so London announced that on May 15, 1948, the last British soldier would leave Palestine, regardless of what the situation was like on the ground. On May 14, the eve of the British pull-out, the Israelis declared their independence, and soon thereafter the intercommunal fighting in Palestine expanded as neighboring states entered the fray.

The two clear victors of the war were the Israelis and the Jordanians, while the Palestinians were the clear losers. The new Israeli state was not only able to hold the territory that had been allotted to it by the United Nations, but it was also able to expand upon that territory. From an allotment of 55 percent of the mandate area, Israel captured an additional approximately 2,500 square miles, giving it control of about 78 percent of mandatory Palestine. The recently independent state of Jordan also achieved its objectives in the war, taking over the West Bank, including portions of Jerusalem. With Israeli gains, Jordanian seizure of the West Bank, and Egypt's smaller gains in taking control of the Gaza Strip, the Palestinian state envisioned by Resolution 181 did not come into existence. Adding to the Palestinians' defeat, the war also made refugees of approximately 60 percent of the Palestinian community. Not surprisingly, the Israelis and the Palestinians offered different accounts of what caused these massive refugee flows, with the Israelis tending to stress the panic of war and the Palestinians tending to stress the intentional acts of the Israelis.[9] What the Israelis saw as their war of independence in 1948, the Palestinians saw as *al Nakbah*, "the catastrophe."

More than sixty years later, the Palestinian refugee issue remains central to the Israeli-Palestinian conflict. The war created about 750,000 Palestinian refugees whom Israel refused to let return to their homes in areas controlled by the new Israeli state, fearing that if hundreds of thousands of disgruntled Palestinians were allowed back within the borders of Israel, the very existence of Israel as a Jewish state would be undermined. This is another example of the conflict as a struggle between two irreconcilable rights, with the Palestinian right of return being incompatible with Israel's right to be a state for the Jewish people.

The status of Jerusalem also continues to be one of the thorniest issues in any Israeli-Palestinian peace efforts. Resolution 181 called for Jerusalem to be treated as an international city until a more permanent arrangement could be determined. Like the rest of Resolution 181, however, this was pushed aside in the fighting. Israeli forces seized most of western Jerusalem, where the large Jewish population centers were, declaring it to be the capital of the new Israeli state, and the Jordanians captured the eastern portion of the city, including the walled "Old City," where the vast majority of the city's holy sites were located. Thus, rather than an international city, Jerusalem became a divided city, but divided not between the Israelis and the Palestinians, but between the Israelis and the Jordanians.

THE "ARAB-ISRAELI" CONFLICT TAKES CENTER STAGE

The 1948 war was such a devastating defeat for the Palestinians that for the next few decades they became marginal players in the region's politics. Instead of the Israeli-Palestinian conflict, the focus shifted to a wider Arab-Israeli conflict in which the Palestinians, without a state of their own, were at best secondary actors. As a result, the wars of 1956, 1967, and 1973 were principally between Israel and its neighboring Arab states, and the Palestinians were not central actors but were largely relegated to a symbolic status or to minor roles in low-scale border skirmishes in areas with large numbers of Palestinian refugees. For example, in the 1956 war over Suez, although Palestinian attacks into Israel from the Egyptian-controlled Gaza Strip complicated the outbreak of the war, the conflict was fought not principally over Palestinian issues, but largely over issues regarding decolonization in the Middle East in the context of the expanding Cold War between the United States and the Soviet Union, as well as Israel's fears regarding Egyptian President Gamal Abdel Nasser's attempts to expand Cairo's regional influence.

Similarly, the 1967 war was largely the result of regional competition between Egypt, Syria, Jordan, and Israel. In this competition the Palestinians played a largely symbolic role as the competitors within the Arab world used their support for the Palestinians, and their associated hostility toward Israel, to justify their claims for leadership within the region. The results of the 1967 war further marginalized the Palestinians in regional politics. In the war, the Israelis seized the Gaza Strip and the Sinai Peninsula from Egypt, the Golan Heights from Syria, and East Jerusalem and the entire West Bank from Jordan. This Israeli victory made the territories taken from the Arab states the new centerpiece to the conflict, which further pushed the Palestinians into the background.

The marginalization of the Palestinians and the predominance of the Arab-Israeli conflict over the Israeli-Palestinian conflict are plainly apparent in UN Security Council Resolution 242, which became the focal point for international peace efforts in the area for the two decades after the 1967 war. Passed unanimously on November 22, 1967, Resolution 242 asserts that "the establishment of a just and lasting peace in the Middle East" requires "the application of both the following principles: (i) withdrawal of Israeli armed forces from territories occupied in the recent conflict; (ii) termination of all claims or states of belligerency and respect for the acknowledgment of the sovereignty, territorial integrity and political independence of every state in the area and their right to live in peace within secure and recognized boundaries free from threats or acts of force."[10] The central idea of this resolution is land for peace—that Israel should trade the land it has conquered for peace agreements with the surrounding states. What Resolution 242 largely omits, however, is any mention of the Palestinians and their national aspirations, referring only to solving the "refugee problem," which was now further complicated by an additional, but smaller, wave of refugees.

This smaller wave of refugees also points to a significant difference between the outcomes of the war in 1967 as opposed to 1948. In 1967, most of the Palestinian inhabitants of the areas Israel conquered stayed in their homes. After the fighting in 1948 only about 150,000 Palestinians remained in the areas that became Israel. This number was small enough to allow the Israeli leadership to offer these individuals citizenship without fear of threatening the Jewish character of the new state. In 1967, however, since most of the Palestinians stayed in their homes, Israel seized not only the land, but also over 1 million Palestinians—approximately 600,000 in the West Bank, 70,000 in East Jerusalem, and about 350,000 in the Gaza Strip. For Israelis, this meant that the post-1948 policy of offering citizenship to the Palestinians within Israel's borders was no longer feasible. To give citizenship to all the Palestinians in the areas conquered by Israeli forces in 1967 would have made close to half of Israel's population non-Jewish, which Israeli leaders calculated would pose too great a threat to the continued existence of Israel as a Jewish state. The result was that after victory in 1967, Israel became an occupying power over a large disenfranchised Palestinian population. One way Israel attempted to deal with this demographic dilemma was to encourage the creation of Jewish settlements in the occupied territories, a movement that over time would become an increasingly important issue in the Israeli-Palestinian peace process.[11]

The outcome of the fighting in 1973 did little to change the situation between the Israelis and the Palestinians as the Israelis retained control of the territories they had conquered in 1967. Indeed, perhaps the biggest impact on the Israeli-Palestinian conflict of the 1967 and 1973 wars was to help convince the Palestinians that if they were ever to achieve their national aspirations, they had to reduce their reliance on the Arab states, which had proven incapable of defeating the Israelis and far more interested in their particular interests than the objectives of the Palestinians. This led to the growth of such Palestine groups as Yasir Arafat's Fatah,[12] which eventually became the dominant voice in the Palestinian Liberation Organization (PLO), an entity that initially was created and controlled by the Arab states rather than the Palestinians themselves. At a summit in Rabat in 1974, the Arab League recognized the PLO as the "sole legitimate representative of the Palestinian people." This was both good and bad news for the Palestinians. The bad news was that it indicated that the Arab states were to some extent washing their hands of the Palestinian problem. The good news, however, was that it also meant that Palestinians now had their own organization to represent them on the world stage.

Although more autonomous, the Palestinians were still largely marginalized in the region's politics. When Egypt and Israel were negotiating the US-sponsored Camp David Accords in 1978, which would eventually result in a peace treaty between the two states, they simultaneously negotiated "A Framework for Peace in the Middle East," which was designed to offer a way forward on the Palestinian front and thus protect Egypt from charges that it was making a separate peace. The Palestinians themselves, however, were never consulted in these negotiations. Instead the United States, Israel, and Egypt negotiated for them. Not surprisingly, the Palestinians rejected the framework.[13]

While the success of the Egyptian-Israeli portion of the Camp David agreements helped to solve a key part of the Arab-Israeli conflict, its success did not advance the Israeli-Palestinian peace process. Instead, throughout the 1980s the regional focus shifted largely to the Iran-Iraq War, the Palestinians remained marginalized, and Israeli-Palestinian relations got little attention. In 1982, for example, the United States proposed the Reagan Peace Plan, putting Jordan, which had not formally relinquished its claims to the West Bank, at the center of negotiations aimed at creating a self-governing Palestinian entity in the West Bank to be federated with Jordan. While the Jordanians embraced the plan, no one else in the region did so, which caused it to quickly fade. In 1985, King Hussein of Jordan and Arafat of the PLO made a joint call for an Israeli withdrawal from the occupied territories and self-determination for the Palestinians in the context of a Palestinian-Jordanian confederation, but this proposal quickly faded as well when the United States and Israel refused to have any direct dealings with the PLO.[14]

THE RISE AND FALL OF THE OSLO ACCORDS

The political marginalization of the Palestinians in the Middle East peace process started to come to an end only with the outbreak of the Palestinian intifada in December 1987. Intifada translates as "shaking off" and is the name given to large-scale protests and acts of civil disobedience, both violent and peaceful, by the Palestinians living under Israeli occupation.[15] The death of four Palestinians at an Israeli military checkpoint in Gaza provided the initial spark for the intifada, but the underlying causes could be found in Palestinian discontent with the ongoing Israeli occupation, the continuing increase in the number of Israeli settlers in the territories, and a sense of frustration that the rest of the world, including the Arab states, were largely ignoring their plight. The intifada was also to some extent directed at the PLO leadership, headquartered in faraway Tunis and thus increasingly out of touch with the Palestinians physically living under Israeli occupation. Eventually the PLO leadership did succeed in taking greater control over the intifada from the local leadership that had emerged at its outset, but this was an early indication of what would become a greater problem for the Palestinians in the future, namely the conflict between the leadership of the PLO located outside of the occupied territories and those living in the West Bank and the Gaza Strip.

The impact of the intifada was significant primarily because it made the continued occupation of the West Bank and the Gaza Strip increasingly costly to the Israelis, in blood and treasure, and by raising uncomfortable moral questions. As the intifada continued for years, more and more of Israel's resources, especially in its military, were devoted to combating it. In addition, some Israelis began to ask how Israel, a state founded in the name of self-determination against oppression, had become an occupying power denying self-determination to another people. Israel's inability to end the intifada meant that the Palestinian issue could no longer be ignored and gave the Israelis a much greater interest in pursuing a peace deal with the Palestinians. The Jordanians were making similar calculations. After witnessing the first few months of the intifada, King Hussein decided that Palestinian nationalism meant that Jordan could never peacefully rule the West Bank, so in July 1988, he formally surrendered all of Jordan's claims to the West Bank in favor of the PLO.

It would take longer for the PLO to achieve similar recognition from the United States or Israel. To bring the PLO into the formal regional peace process the United States insisted that the PLO renounce terrorism and recognize Israel's right to exist. After a few initial limited and false starts, Arafat eventually met America's demands and direct US-PLO talks started in December 1988. Though these talks would last only a short time, an important bridge had been crossed in gaining international recognition for the PLO.

Iraq's invasion of Kuwait in August 1990 provided an unexpected external jolt to Israeli-Palestinian relations. One result of the Gulf War of 1990–1991 is that it helped isolate the PLO in the Arab world as Arafat bucked the regional consensus and opted to support Saddam Hussein's Iraq. This damaged the PLO's relationship with the Gulf states in particular that had rallied in support of the Kuwaitis. The war over Kuwait also helped bring greater international attention to the Israeli-Palestinian conflict. Seeking support for his actions and to hinder America's coalition-building efforts, Saddam Hussein attempted to link a resolution of the Kuwaiti crisis with a resolution of the Israeli-Palestinian conflict. While rejecting any explicit linkage, the United States, to keep its Gulf War coalition intact, promised that after the war it would be more active in pursuing Arab-Israeli and more particularly Israeli-Palestinian peace.

The United States fulfilled this promise after the war by convening Middle East Peace Talks in Madrid in late 1991. Sponsored jointly by the United States and the Soviet Union, the large multinational talks included delegations from Israel, Egypt, Syria, Lebanon, and a joint Palestinian-Jordanian delegation. The great achievement of Madrid was to get all these parties into the same room for direct talks, but beyond that, little was accomplished. The Madrid framework proved too unwieldy, and while the talks attracted the focus of the world, the real breakthrough came from a set of informal talks taking place in Oslo, Norway.

The Oslo Accords, also known as the Declaration of Principles, signed at an official White House ceremony on September 13, 1993, represents perhaps the high-water mark in Israeli-Palestinian relations.[16] The Declaration of Principles not only represented mutual recognition between the Israeli government and the PLO, but it also set out an ambitious agenda for a process that could lead to a final resolution of the Israeli-Palestinian conflict. Why was such an agreement possible now?

On the Palestinian side, an important part of the equation was the increasing isolation of the PLO internationally. The PLO had put itself on the losing side of the recently concluded Cold War as well as the losing side of the 1990–1991 Gulf War. The Palestinians, as well as many of the Arab states that were engaged in conflicts with Israel, had come to rely heavily on Soviet support, and with the collapse of the Soviet Union that assistance disappeared. The Palestinians were able to make up part of that loss with aid from some of the oil-rich Gulf states, but once the Palestinians sided with Iraq against Kuwait, that source of aid also dried up. Plus, many Palestinians who had been working in the Gulf states and sending money back home found themselves less welcome in the area. These defeats made the Palestinians question whether they could command the resources needed to carry on the armed struggle against the Israelis.

The Israelis had similar worries. Battling the intifada made the continuing occupation increasingly costly to Israel in terms of money, lives, and its international and moral stature. Moreover, the Iraqi missile attacks launched against Israel in 1991, which were designed to upset the anti-Iraq coalition by linking its invasion of Kuwait with the Israeli-Palestinian conflict, elevated concerns in Israel over potential future attacks that might include weapons of mass destruction. Although the missile attacks in the Gulf War did not include chemical warheads, some Israeli leaders concluded that Israel's security had to rest upon regionally accepted peace agreements rather than permanent military domination over a restive population.

Domestic factors on both sides also favored negotiation. The intifada had taken Arafat and the PLO leadership by surprise and they doubted whether they could hold on to power if the uprising continued and they were unable to produce any concrete results. Increasing pressure from more locally based groups, particularly the religious-based Hamas movement, presented a threat to Arafat and his Fatah Party's dominance over Palestinian politics, and the longer the intifada continued, the greater that threat became. Israeli Prime Minister Yitzhak Rabin likewise feared that if the intifada dragged on, it would undermine his Labor Party–led coalition government and play into the hands of his more hawkish foes in the opposition Likud Party. In addition, both sides recognized the domestic dynamics in the other and Arafat concluded that he was better off working with Labor now than Likud later, and Rabin concluded that he was better off working with Fatah now rather than Hamas later.[17]

A key first step in implementing the Oslo Accords was what was called the Gaza-Jericho First Plan. Under the plan, Israel pledged to hand over administration of most of the Gaza Strip and a small area of the West Bank around the city of Jericho (as a symbol that more of the West Bank would be coming) to a soon-to-be-created entity known as the Palestinian Interim Self Government Authority, better known simply as the Palestinian Authority (PA), which would be formed as a result of elections in the occupied territories.

Under the Oslo framework, this interim period was supposed to last a maximum of five years, during which two things were to happen. The first was that in return for the end of the intifada there would be a series of staged Israeli withdrawals so the PA would slowly take over administrative responsibility for more and more of the West Bank. The second was that during this period the two sides would engage in final status talks that would pave the way for an agreement on all outstanding differences. Despite the progress that the Declaration of Principles represented, these differences remained large, as the Oslo process pushed all of the most difficult issues to these final status talks. How was the refugee/right of return issue to be dealt with? What would be the borders between Israel and the newly created Palestinian entity and would this entity be a state or something else? What was to be done with regard to the Israeli settlers? How would critical water resources be allotted? What about the future of Jerusalem? Although a huge step forward, the Declaration of Principles pushed all of these problems down the road into the envisioned final status talks. The thinking behind this was that as the five-year interim period progressed, the two sides would grow to trust each other more, which would make it easier to tackle the most contentious issues later.

Contrary to these hopes, implementing Oslo proved difficult and divisive. Rather than building positive momentum for tackling the thorny final status issues, the implementation of interim agreements disillusioned many on both sides. Part of the problem was inherent in the process itself. If the central issues were to be decided later in final status talks, why should either side offer any generous concessions in the interim period? Why not hold back these concessions to be used as bargaining chips in the later and more consequential talks?

Moreover, if the leadership on either side did offer a significant concession during this period, they were likely to be accused by their domestic opponents of recklessly surrendering key positions before the most important negotiations even began. With both sides as a result only grudgingly offering concessions in the interim talks, rather than building confidence, the process helped convince each side that the other was not truly interested in peace.[18]

At its heart, the Oslo process was designed to be a land-for-peace deal. In return for ending Palestinian violence against Israelis, the Israelis would end their occupation of Palestinian lands. What undermined this land-for-peace deal, however, was that in the interim period "one side took unilateral liberties with the land, while the other took unilateral liberties with the peace."[19] From the Israeli standpoint, the implementation of Oslo meant that they were giving away land, but they saw themselves as getting nothing in return because assaults on their soldiers and terrorist attacks on their civilians continued. Moreover, the Israelis believed not only that Arafat was not doing enough to stop the violence, but was in many ways encouraging it. The Israelis did not believe that they were getting the peace that Oslo promised.

From the vantage point of the Palestinians, they did not believe that they were getting the land they had been promised. During the implementation phases of the Oslo Accords, Israeli settlement activity in the West Bank, East Jerusalem, and Gaza not only did not stop, but it continued at a rapid pace. For example, in the decade after the signing of the Declaration of Principles the number of Israeli settlers in the West Bank more than doubled.[20] If the Israelis were serious about a land for peace deal, the Palestinians asked, why are they continuing to add settlers to the land they were planning to cede to the Palestinians?

As the interim agreements progressed, the Israelis tended to give the PA control over most Palestinian population centers, but the Israelis kept control over most of the countryside. The result was that eventually the vast majority of Palestinians lived in areas that were at least partially under PA control, but most movement throughout the West Bank remained under the control of the Israelis. To try to decrease the possibilities of attacks on Israeli targets, the Israelis created a series of security checkpoints throughout the occupied territories, which also had the effect of subjecting Palestinians to embarrassing and time-consuming security checks if they attempted to travel throughout the West Bank. By 1999 the areas under the PA consisted of 227 separate enclaves, most smaller than 2 square kilometers, with 97 checkpoints in the West Bank, 32 in Gaza, and 250 miles of Israeli-only roads.[21] Thus, rather than a peace process, the Palestinians complained that they were getting a "piece" process, because they were getting only small parts of what they thought they had been promised and the security checkpoints meant that the everyday experience of the occupation for the Palestinians may have been increasing rather than decreasing.

The Oslo process also produced no peace dividend in the form of increased economic interaction between Israelis and Palestinians. On the contrary, in response to continued Palestinian attacks, Israel implemented a series of closure measures that made it difficult for Palestinian workers to get to jobs within Israel and limited trade between the Palestinian areas and Israel. As the more prosperous and diversified market with greater opportunities to look elsewhere for cheap labor and goods, the Israeli economy was in a far better position to weather this storm than the Palestinian economy, which was devastated by these measures. As the Oslo process stumbled forward, neither side thought it was getting what it had bargained for.

A further blow to the peace process came on November 4, 1995, when Israeli Prime Minister Yitzhak Rabin was assassinated by an Israeli who resented Rabin's efforts to make peace with the Palestinians. Rabin's death created a significant hole in the leadership of the peace camp within Israel because few could match Rabin's résumé when it came to security issues. Rabin was a brigade commander in the 1948 war, he rose quickly through the ranks and was chief of staff during Israel's dramatic victory in 1967, and he was a perennial minister of defense. Convincing the Israeli public to accept the concessions that peace with the Palestinians would require was a daunting task even for a leader with such impeccable security credentials; without him, that task was far harder.

One person who tried to take Rabin's place as leader of the peace camp was Ehud Barak, also of the Labor Party, who was elected prime minister in 1999. In dealing with the Palestinian issue, Barak altered Israel's strategy under the Oslo Accords and rather than continue with a series of interim measures, he opted instead to go directly to the final status talks. Seeing the drawbacks of the step-by-step interim approach discussed above and worrying that he would fritter away all his domestic political capital fighting for passage of a series of small agreements, Barak decided instead to pursue a single comprehensive and final agreement with the Palestinians.[22] In July 2000, in pursuit of that goal, American President Bill Clinton invited the Israelis and the Palestinians to a conference at Camp David to discuss and potentially resolve all the final status issues.

In some ways the talks at Camp David were revolutionary, as the sides started directly discussing some of the core disputes between them, such as the future of Jerusalem and the refugee/right of return issue. In pursuit of a final agreement, Barak did go to Camp David considering more far-reaching concessions than any Israeli government had previously put forward. In these discussions, the Israelis offered to withdraw from the Gaza Strip and about 90 percent of the West Bank, keeping areas where large Israeli settlements were located as well as a security presence in the Jordan Valley in the far eastern portion of the West Bank. Regarding the refugee issue, Barak offered to allow a small number of returns to Israel itself, but most of the rest would have to accept return to Palestine or an internationally funded compensation package to remain where they currently resided. With regard to Jerusalem, Barak offered the Palestinians sovereignty over certain areas of the city, but sovereignty in the Old City itself and over the holy sites remained a key point of division.[23]

The Palestinians, although they would come under criticism from some of the American mediators for not making specific enough counteroffers to the Israeli proposals, also went further than they had in the past. The Palestinians discussed allowing some Israeli settlements and settlers to stay, considered placing agreed-upon limits to what they saw as a fundamental right of return, accepted a largely demilitarized status, and discussed the division of Jerusalem.

While the Camp David talks of 2000 may, in the long run, be seen as an important breakthrough where both sides first discussed some of the fundamental issues that divided them, in the short term, the failure to reach an agreement at Camp David was a significant blow to the peace process. Both sides believed they were going about as far as their domestic situation would allow them in meeting the other side's desires. Indeed, even before Prime Minister Barak got to Camp David, his coalition government had splintered over some of the concessions he was considering and he no longer possessed a majority in the Israeli Knesset. Similarly, when President Clinton and Secretary of State Madeleine Albright tried to persuade Chairman Arafat to accept certain proposals, Arafat responded by asking if they wished to attend his funeral, implying that accepting those terms would lead to violence within the Palestinian community.[24] Thus, even with leaders on both sides going as far as they dared, there was still a significant gulf between the minimum demands of each side.

The failure at Camp David did not end the peace process, however. The Israelis and the Palestinians continued to have a number of follow-on discussions and in December 2000 the United States put out what it saw as a bridging proposal to bring the two sides together. These talks did make some additional headway. By January 2001 Israel was offering about 95 percent of the West Bank, virtually all of Gaza, and part of pre-1967 Israel to partly make up the difference to the Palestinians. The Israelis also decided to take their demand for a security zone in the Jordan Valley off the table, and the proposed borders for Palestine, although not clean, were generally contiguous. As for the settlers, with the borders as drawn, about 65 percent of them would be within Israel and the others would have to move. Palestinian refugees were to be allowed to return to Palestine, but not to Israel, except on a case-by-case basis under the control of the Israeli government. With regard to Jerusalem, based on Clinton's bridging proposal, Arab parts would go to Palestine (including sovereignty over portions of the Old City) and Jewish parts would go to Israel, but given the interspersed population of the city, making this work in practice still presented a huge challenge, especially in such key areas as what the Israelis call the Temple Mount and the Palestinians the Haram al-Sharif, where the holy sites overlap.

These talks, and with them arguably the entire Oslo process, came to an end in January and February 2001 with the change of administration in Washington and new prime ministerial elections in Israel where Ariel Sharon decisively defeated Ehud Barak. Who was being generous in these peace talks and who was being intransigent and thus responsible for their failure? Not surprisingly the two sides disagree. As the Israelis and their supporters see it, this was an incredibly generous offer. The Palestinians currently have nothing and the Israelis, despite being the stronger party, were offering them about 95 percent of the disputed territory, including a share of their capital. The Palestinians see it quite differently. Looked at from their perspective, by agreeing to accept a Palestinian state on all of the West Bank and the Gaza Strip, it is they who would be making the most concessions by ceding to Israel the approximately 80 percent of Palestine that is pre-1967 Israel.[25] For proponents of the Palestinians who would deny Israel any rights in this area, the Israeli offers are akin to someone taking over another person's house and then "generously" offering to let him keep 95 percent of one of the rooms.[26] These differing assessments are indicative of why the Oslo process failed and why this conflict has proven so difficult to resolve diplomatically; any potential peace agreement will leave both sides believing that the concessions they have made are lopsided ones that have resulted in their getting less than they deserved.

IN SEARCH OF A POST-OSLO PEACE PROCESS

The collapse of the Oslo peace process led to escalating violence between Israelis and Palestinians, often referred to as the Al-Aqsa intifada or the second intifada, which has now claimed thousands of lives. Although various efforts to restart the Israeli-Palestinian peace process have been attempted in the wake of Oslo's failure, none have made significant headway.

One attempt was put forward by the Arab League at its March 2002 summit in Beirut, where the Saudi Peace Plan called for a full Israeli withdrawal from the West Bank, Gaza, and East Jerusalem and the implementation of UN General Assembly Resolution 194 on the refugees. Although vague in how these particulars would be implemented, the novel part of the proposal was that if Israel met these Palestinian concerns (and the Syrian concerns with regard to the Golan Heights), the entire Arab world would establish full and normal relations with Israel. This proposal, however, did not have much time to serve as a basis for possible peace talks between Israelis and Palestinians, as the initiative coincided with a series of suicide attacks within Israel, including the March 27 Passover bombing in Netanya, and Israel's subsequent large-scale military action in the West Bank in response to those attacks.

Another attempt was the Quartet Plan, also known as the road map, sponsored by the United States, Russia, the European Union, and the United Nations.[27] The road map was both more specific and more modest than the Saudi Peace Plan. Instead of offering a vision of what a final agreement would look like, it outlined a series of steps that each side should take to stop the violence and eventually begin final status negotiations again. Initially put on hold in the run-up to the 2003 Iraq war, the road map was formally issued on April 30, 2003, but after both the Palestinians and the Israelis voiced objections to parts of the plan, the road map too faded from center stage.

One event that helped push the road map out of the limelight was Ariel Sharon's surprise announcement in December 2003 that Israel was going to unilaterally pull its settlers and military forces out of the Gaza Strip. Pursuing withdrawal proved to be a tough domestic battle for Sharon. First, a referendum on the plan was soundly defeated in his own party, and later he was able to secure the approval of his own cabinet for the plan by only one vote, and that margin was possible only because before holding the vote Sharon fired two members who were against the plan. The Gaza disengagement plan did have widespread support in the Knesset and with the public, and in August 2005 all Israeli settlers were removed from Gaza and by September Israel's military forces were out as well.

Although this undoubtedly represented some progress toward eventual peace, especially as it demonstrated that significant parts of even the Right in Israeli politics, as represented by Ariel Sharon, are open to ceding territory to the Palestinians, the difficulties that disengagement from Gaza presented do not bode well for tackling the far more difficult issues of the West Bank and Jerusalem. Gaza was not part of biblical Israel and thus the emotional attachment of most Israelis to it is minor. Economically, Gaza is in dire straits and will probably cost whoever controls it more than it will gain far into the future. Most important, only a small number of Israeli settlers were in Gaza, about 8,000. Compare this to the West Bank, which is at the heart of biblical Israel, is in better economic shape, and houses over 275,000 Israeli settlers (with an additional approximately 185,000 settlers in and around Jerusalem).[28]

While Israel was unilaterally withdrawing from Gaza, it was also constructing an elaborate physical barrier throughout much of the West Bank. Like much in this conflict, the two sides disagree about how to describe what is happening there. The Palestinians prefer to call what the Israelis are building a wall, or the apartheid wall. The Israelis prefer to call what they are building a fence, or the anti-terrorism or security fence. The Israelis correctly point out that well over 90 percent of the structure is fence rather than wall, so it is better to call it a fence. The Palestinians, however, also correctly point out that the wall sections are in the most populated areas, so most Palestinians experience a wall rather than a fence, so it is better to call it a wall.[29]

The purpose of the fence, the Israelis argue, is to protect Israeli citizens from terrorist attacks. The fence is not designed to be a final border, the Israelis maintain, but is more properly seen as a needed security measure. The Palestinians argue that if Israel wants to build a wall, it must do so on its side of the 1967 borders. The Palestinians maintain that building the wall represents a land grab on the part of Israelis and that it imposes additional hardships on Palestinians, who often find their families, their fields, or their place of work on the other side of the wall.

Together, disengaging from Gaza and building the barrier on the West Bank represent what can be seen as Israel's attempt to pursue a largely unilateral peace with the Palestinians. Convinced that the status quo is untenable and that a compromise solution with the Palestinians is necessary, the Israeli leadership is also largely convinced that they cannot reach an acceptable deal with any foreseeable Palestinian leadership. So how does a country get to a negotiated peace when it does not believe it has anyone to negotiate with on acceptable terms? Israel's answer in the aftermath of the failure of the Oslo peace process has been to attempt to pursue a peace with the Palestinians through unilateral initiatives rather than through negotiations.

For the optimist, the withdrawal from Gaza and the building of the barrier throughout the West Bank represents progress in the peace process, as both signify a recognition from even the hawkish end of Israeli politics that Israel cannot continue to rule over 3 million Palestinians indefinitely and that the idea of a greater Israel has to be significantly scaled down. For the pessimist, what the Israelis are offering the Palestinians is far less than what the Palestinians had already rejected in earlier negotiations, so why should anyone expect them to peacefully accept it now?

Neither are the domestic situations in both Palestine and Israel particularly ripe for bold initiatives on the peace process. In November 2004, Arafat, who had for decades led and personified the Palestinian struggle for recognition and eventual statehood, died. As some in Israel and the United States had concluded that Arafat was never going to make the concessions needed to get a final agreement, his death could be seen as opening up an opportunity for restarting the peace process.[30] Such hopes got an additional boost in January 2005 when Mahmoud Abbas, also known as Abu Mazen, was elected to succeed Arafat as the new president of the Palestinian Authority. Abbas has worked well with the Israelis in the past and has been outspoken in his beliefs that turning to violence in the intifada was a strategic mistake and the violence should stop so peace talks can begin again. His election helped to make the case that Israel did indeed have a Palestinian partner to potentially negotiate with.

Balanced against Abbas's electoral victory in 2005 was the defeat his Fatah Party suffered at the hands of Hamas in the 2006 parliamentary elections in Palestine. Hamas had never recognized Israel, rejected the Oslo Accords, and after its electoral victory gave few indications that it was eager to pursue peace talks with Israel. With Abbas and Fatah in charge of the institutions associated with the Palestinian presidency and Hamas in charge of the office of the prime minister, these two parties attempted but ultimately failed to work out a mutually acceptable power-sharing agreement. With Egypt and Saudi Arabia both attempting to broker a Palestinian unity government, the United States and Israel working to isolate Hamas and bolster Fatah, and Hamas and Fatah each fearing that the other was planning to launch a military coup against it, the protracted intra-Palestinian negotiations collapsed into a brief but bloody civil war in Palestine that resulted in Hamas's seizing control of the Gaza Strip and Fatah's seizing control of the West Bank.[31] The more intense this internal Palestinian struggle becomes, the less likely are serious peace talks with Israel. Societies in the midst of civil wars often suffer poor relations with the outside world as internal competitors for power blame outsiders for their problems and try to bolster their positions at home by showing how uncompromising they can be to their enemies abroad. Moreover, even if a significant accord is reached as a result of talks between the Israelis and Abbas, what are its prospects if it is signed without Hamas and its supporters?

The domestic situation in Israel also is not conducive to comprehensive peace talks. Part of the difficulty is inherent in the very structure of Israeli politics, with its low threshold for party representation in the Knesset, which virtually guarantees the proliferation of small parties. No political party has ever possessed an outright majority in the Knesset, which has meant that all Israeli governments have had to be coalitions, and keeping such coalitions together during contentious peace talks with the Palestinians has always proven problematic. In addition, governments in Israel are far more likely to collapse than to reach the end of their allotted terms. This creates multiple periods of stasis as Israel goes through additional electoral cycles, and even after those elections are held, the need to keep fragile coalitions together often results in sacrificing inevitably controversial talks with the Palestinians.

Consider only the most recent upheavals in Israeli domestic politics, which have included Prime Minister Sharon's departure from the Likud Party to create a new party (Kadima) to lead in the 2006 elections, his incapacitating stroke just a few months before those elections, election results that gave the victorious Kadima Party less than half the number of seats it would need for a majority in the Knesset, Prime Minister Ehud Olmert's struggles to lead Kadima in Sharon's stead and create a new governing coalition, the controversy over what was seen as the Olmert government's bungling of the 2006 war in Lebanon, multiple criminal investigations against leading Israeli politicians, including the prime minister, Olmert's eventual resignation, the inability of the anointed successor (Foreign Minister Tzipi Livni) to create a new coalition, and the subsequent need for new elections so the cycle can begin again.

The day Olmert announced his resignation as Israeli prime minister, he gave an interview to an Israeli newspaper where he argued that "we must reach an agreement with the Palestinians, meaning a withdrawal from nearly all, if not all of the [occupied] territories. . . . Without this there will be no peace." Asked if this included Jerusalem, he responded yes, including special arrangements for the holy sites. Olmert also recognized how painful this would be for Israelis to accept, calling it "difficult, awful, a decision that contradicts our natural instincts, our deepest yearnings, our collective memories, and the prayers of the nation of Israel for the past two thousand years." Hearing this, his interviewers sadly mused that "it seems that political leaders in Israel always reach this conclusion only when they themselves are no longer in a position to make this decision." Although Olmert denied that his conversion was that recent, it is clearly easier for an Israeli politician to take such stands when he no longer has to hold together a fractious coalition.[32]

One of the most recent initiatives to get Israeli-Palestinian talks back on track came in November 2007 when President George W. Bush called together forty-nine countries at Annapolis, Maryland, and secured a pledge from the Israelis and from Fatah as a representative of the Palestinians (Hamas was not included) to achieve a peace agreement by the end of 2008. However, with a lame-duck president with low approval ratings in the United States, a prime minister in Israel just trying to ward off calls for his resignation, and a civil war between the Palestinians, few took this initiative seriously or were surprised when nothing materialized.

The February 2009 elections in Israel resulted in another complicated coalition government, this one led by Benyamin Netanyahu, whose Likud Party won only 27 of the 120 seats in the Knesset. Concerns about coalition maintenance, combined with the prime minister's own ambivalence toward the peace process, have pushed Netanyahu to downplay rather than embrace talks with the Palestinians. On the Palestinian side, Hamas and Fatah remain at odds and continue to quarrel over setting dates for presidential and parliamentary elections. The most likely outcome for the future is continued weak coalition governments in Israel and a continued struggle between supporters of Hamas and Fatah for influence over Palestinian politics. Weak and divided leadership on both sides makes it increasing unlikely that both sides will be able to accept and sell the painful concessions that any peace agreement would require. As Richard Haass, after serving as a senior director for the Middle East on the National Security Council staff, cautioned over a decade ago when analyzing the then-current stalemate in the peace process, "It is often safer to espouse dreams that are whole than to accept inevitably incomplete realities."[33]

CONCLUSION: TOWARD AN UNJUST PEACE?

The pursuit of a just peace between the Israelis and the Palestinians has occupied both sides and outside mediators for over one hundred years, before Israel even existed as a state. In this case, however, the problem is that justice and peace may be mutually exclusive. Both nations advance a just claim to the area between the Mediterranean Sea and the Jordan River. Both Palestinians and

Israelis have a just claim to Jerusalem as their political capital and as religiously central to their identities. How could any international compensation program or resettlement efforts in Palestine justly compensate families of refugees that have lived for multiple generations in a stateless limbo? Given its history and the sacrifices peace with the Palestinians would entail, how can Israel ever be what the early Zionists envisioned, which was not only a Jewish state, but also a normal state?

It has been the incompatibility of justice and peace that has made the Israeli-Palestinian conflict so protracted. Both sides have preferred to fight rather than accept less than what they calculate justice demands. To end this battle between two rights, the Israelis and the Palestinians, along with the international community, are going to have to work for and lead their people to accept a settlement that offers both sides less than they deserve. If peace is ever to come between the Israelis and Palestinians, it will be an unjust one.

NOTES

1. Martin Indyk attributes this quote to Shimon Peres in "U.S. Strategy for Resolving the Israeli-Palestinian Conflict," in *Crescent of Crisis: U.S.-European Strategy for the Greater Middle East*, ed. Ivo Daalder, Nicole Gnesotto, and Philip Gordon (Washington, DC: Brookings Institution, 2006), p. 44.

2. This quote is variously attributed to Georg Friedrich Hegel or Christian Friedrich Hebbel.

3. There are numerous histories of the Israeli-Palestinian conflict. One particularly comprehensive one-volume account is Mark Tessler's *A History of the Israeli-Palestinian Conflict* (Bloomington: Indiana University Press, 1994). More current is Ian J. Bickerton and Carla L. Klausner's *A Concise History of the Arab-Israeli Conflict*, 4th ed. (Upper Saddle River, NJ: Prentice Hall, 2005). This well-balanced account also includes a number of useful primary documents. A more recent sixth edition has also been issued under the title *A History of the Arab-Israeli Conflict* (Upper Saddle River, NJ: Prentice Hall, 2009).

4. On the origins of the Jewish nationalist movement, see Howard Sachar, *A History of Israel: From the Rise of Zionism to Our Time*, 3rd ed. (New York: Alfred A. Knopf, 2007), especially pp. 3–88.

5. On the origins of the Palestinian nationalist movement, see Muhammad Muslih, *The Origins of Palestinian Nationalism* (New York: Columbia University Press, 1989), and Rashid Khalidi, *Palestinian Identity: The Construction of Modern National Consciousness* (New York: Columbia University Press, 1997).

6. The earliest use of this phrase I have found is from Ameen Rihani, "Palestine and the Proposed Arab Federation," *Annals of the American Academy of Political and Social Science* 164, no. 1 (November 1932): 66. For an overall discussion of diplomacy in the Middle East during this era, including these competing promises, see David Fromkin, *A Peace to End All Peace: The Fall of the Ottoman Empire and the Creation of the Modern Middle East* (New York: Henry Holt, 1989). For an account of the same

period that puts more emphasis on the actions and initiatives of local actors, see Efraim Karsh and Inari Karsh, *Empires of the Sand: The Struggle for Mastery in the Middle East, 1789–1923* (Cambridge, MA: Harvard University Press, 1999).

7. Bickerton and Klausner, *A Concise History of the Arab-Israeli Conflict*, p. 60.

8. For the full text of the Peel Commission Report (The Palestine Royal Commission Report, London, July 1937), see http://domino.un.org/pdfs/Cmd5479.pdf. Accessed on December 16, 2008. The quote is from p. 370.

9. See Samih K. Farsoun and Nasser H. Aruri, *Palestine and the Palestinians: A Social and Political History*, 2nd ed. (Boulder, CO: Westview Press, 2006), p. 112.

10. Bickerton and Klausner, *A Concise History of the Arab-Israeli Conflict*, p. 157.

11. On the origins of the settlement movement in Israel, see Gershom Gorenberg, *The Accidental Empire: Israel and the Birth of the Settlements, 1967–1977* (New York: Times Books, 2006).

12. Fatah means "conquest" and it is a reverse acronym in Arabic for the Movement for the Liberation of Palestine.

13. On the Egyptian-Israeli Camp David Accords, see Shibley Telhami, *Power and Leadership in International Bargaining: The Path to the Camp David Accords* (New York: Columbia University Press, 1990).

14. For an excellent treatment of US policy toward the Arab-Israeli peace process, see William B. Quandt, *Peace Process: American Diplomacy and the Arab-Israeli Conflict Since 1967*, 3rd ed. (Washington, DC: Brookings Institution, 2005).

15. Tessler, *A History of the Israeli-Palestinian Conflict*, pp. 677–696.

16. For the text of the Declaration of Principles, see www.state.gov/p/nea/rls/22602.htm. Accessed December 15, 2008.

17. For the calculations on the Palestinian side leading to an agreement at Oslo, see Ahmed Qurie, *From Oslo to Jerusalem: The Palestinian Story of the Secret Negotiations* (London: I. B. Tauris, 2006), p. 73. For the calculations on the Israeli side, see Shlomo Ben-Ami, *Scars of War, Wounds of Peace: The Israeli-Arab Tragedy* (Oxford: Oxford University Press, 2007), pp. 188–211.

18. See Hussein Agha and Robert Malley, "Camp David: The Tragedy of Errors," *New York Review of Books*, August 9, 2001.

19. David C. Unger, "Maps of War, Maps of Peace: Finding a Two-State Solution to the Israeli-Palestinian Question," *World Policy Journal* 19, no. 2 (Summer 2002): 9.

20. For information on Israeli settlement activity, see the Foundation for Middle East Peace's excellent Web site, which contains a wealth of information, www.fmep.org/settlement_info/. Accessed December 12, 2008.

21. See Sara Roy, "Palestinian Society and Economy: The Continued Denial of Possibility," *Journal of Palestine Studies* 30, no. 4 (Summer 2001): 5–21, and "Why Peace Failed: An Oslo Autopsy," *Current History* 101, no. 651 (January 2002): 8–16.

22. Ben-Ami, *Scars of War, Wounds of Peace*, pp. 255–256.

23. Since most of the exchanges at Camp David were verbal rather than written, there is some unavoidable difficulty in specifying precisely what each side proposed. In addition, during the negotiations the United States offered certain proposals to the Palestinians that went beyond what the Israelis had accepted. For example, initially Barak did not offer sovereignty over the Muslim and Christian quarters of the Old City

to the Palestinians, but he was later persuaded to tentatively accept an American proposal that included it. Later, however, he backed away from that proposal and discussions moved to debates over various types of limited sovereignty or sovereignty with arrangements. For good accounts of the talks, see Dennis Ross, *The Missing Peace: The Inside Story of the Fight for Middle East Peace* (New York: Farrar, Straus and Giroux, 2004), pp. 650–711, and Charles Enderlin, *Shattered Dreams: The Failure of the Peace Process in the Middle East, 1995–2002*, trans. Susan Fairfield (New York: Other Press, 2003), pp. 177–267. For a discussion of the contending arguments regarding what happened in these talks, see Jeremy Pressman, "Visions in Collision: What Happened at Camp David and Taba," *International Security* 28, no. 2 (Fall 2003): 5–43.

24. See Ross, *The Missing Peace*, p. 693, and Enderlin, *Shattered Dreams*, pp. 238 and 253.

25. This is a point that Saeb Erekat made to President Clinton at Camp David; see Enderlin, *Shattered Dreams*, p. 254.

26. For an example of this metaphor being used on behalf of the Palestinians, see Raymond Baker, *Islam Without Fear: Egypt and the New Islamists* (Cambridge, MA: Harvard University Press, 2003), pp. 235–236, quoting the controversial Egyptian Islamic scholar, Yusuf al Qaradawy.

27. For the full text of the road map, see www.state.gov/r/pa/prs/ps/2003/20062 .htm. Accessed December 9, 2008.

28. These numbers come from the Foundation for Middle East Peace's Website, www.fmep.org/settlement_info/. Accessed December 15, 2008.

29. For a view of the fence from the Israeli side, see the Israeli Ministry of Foreign Affairs publication "Saving Lives: Israel's Anti-Terrorism Fence," available at www.mfa .gov.il/mfa/mfaarchive/2000_2009/2003/11/saving%20lives-%20israel-s%20anti -terrorist%20fence%20-%20answ#5. Accessed December 12, 2008. For a view of the wall from the Palestinian side, see the Negotiations Affairs Department of the Palestine Liberation Organization's "Israel's Wall," July 9, 2005, www.nad-plo.org/facts/wall/ WallMagazine%207-2005.pdf, accessed October 23, 2009.

30. For example, see Ben-Ami, *Scars of War, Wounds of Peace*, pp. 215 and 259–260, and Ross, *The Missing Peace*, pp. 13 and 758–762.

31. On the struggles between Hamas and Fatah, see the International Crisis Group, "After Gaza," *Middle East Report* 68 (August 2, 2007): 1–36.

32. Ehud Olmert, "The Time Has Come to Say These Things," *New York Review of Books*, December 4, 2008, which presented a translation and excerpt of the original interview.

33. Richard N. Haass, "The Middle East: No More Treaties," *Foreign Affairs* 75, no. 5 (September/October 1996): 56.

11

CONFLICT IN
WESTERN SAHARA*

Yahia H. Zoubir

THE COLD WAR came to an end more than two decades ago; however, the conflict in Western Sahara has yet to be definitively resolved. It has become an unfortunate reality that this thirty-four-year-old dispute now belongs in the category of "forgotten" or "frozen" conflicts. The conflict itself is not the only issue to have been forgotten. Despite United Nations resolutions, the Sahrawi refugees, their struggles, the deplorable conditions under which they live, and their recognized right to self-determination through a free and fair referendum have been overlooked as well. The Western Sahara conflict attracts only sporadic attention mainly because of the national, geopolitical, and economic interests of stakeholders inside and outside the region—not because of the legitimate rights of the indigenous Sahrawis. The occupied region is often misrepresented as an empty desert, although the territory does in fact boast rich resources and a 700-kilometer Atlantic coast of strategic importance. It is also important to mention that this territory has some of the richest fishing waters in the world: waters that are currently being illegally exploited by Morocco and certain members of the European Union.[1] The Western Sahara's natural resources also extend to impressive mineral deposits. Valuable minerals such as iron ore, titanium oxide, vanadium, iron, and possibly oil may be abundant throughout the territory, which also possesses extremely rich phosphate reserves and could become one of the world's largest exporters of phosphates. Beyond the acknowledged riches of the land, the prospects of oil and natural-gas discoveries in recent years have further complicated resolution of the conflict.[2]

The objective of this work is not to provide a complete historical review of the major events related to Western Sahara;[3] still, to understand the enduring stalemate, a number of occasions deserve discussion.

DECOLONIZATION AND AFTER

What should have been a straightforward case of decolonization in the Western Sahara has become a conspicuous failure of the UN; mainly due to the disinclination of its most powerful members in the Security Council, chiefly the United States and France. This political indisposition was born from the Cold War dynamics in 1975, at which time Morocco was unequivocally anchored in the Western camp and Algeria was perceived as an ally of the former Soviet Union.[4] Having often played a proxy role for France and the United States in defeating nationalist and anticommunist forces in Africa, Morocco benefited from strong political, economic, and military support from its Western and Arab allies, which also included the wealthy Gulf monarchies. Consequentially, the United States played a key role in making it possible for Morocco to seize the Western Sahara.[5]

Power politics have overridden questions of international legality despite the unlawful occupation of the territory and the legitimacy of Sahrawi rights. The consequences of this geopolitical power play include the prevailing tension in Algerian-Moroccan relations; a freeze of the Arab Maghreb Union, instituted in 1989; the lack of feasibility of Maghrebi integration; intermittent tensions in Franco-Algerian relations; occasional friction in Moroccan-Spanish and Algerian-Spanish relations; regional insecurity and the arms race;[6] Algeria's and Morocco's arms purchases at the expense of much-needed socioeconomic development; and cyclical uprisings in the occupied territory accompanied by human rights violations against the Sahrawis. This chapter also asserts that outside powers, particularly UN Security Council members France and the United States and to a lesser degree Great Britain, have prevented the resolution of this dispute. Their interference draws from the long-standing friendship between the United States and Morocco and the services the latter renders to the former, on the one hand, and, on the other hand, France's considerable interests in Morocco. Morocco played a prominent role in the war against communism and nationalist forces in the past and now in the "Global War on Terror."

A number of points need to be reiterated before analyzing the regional and geopolitical considerations that surround the dispute. While it has become fashionable nowadays to speak about a "political solution that is mutually acceptable," many often conveniently disregard the fact that the right to self-determination of Western Sahara, a non-autonomous territory, already exists within the framework of international law and UN resolutions. The right to self-determination is inscribed in the Declaration of the Granting of Independence of

Colonial Countries and Peoples contained in General Assembly Resolution 1514 (XV) of December 14, 1960. In 1963, the United Nations recognized the Sahrawis' right to independence, and it has restated that right in every resolution since. In fact, on February 11, 2004, UN Secretary-General Kofi Annan declared at the special session of the Fourth Committee on Decolonization:

> In the twenty-first century, colonialism is an anachronism. I therefore hope that, in the year ahead, all administering Powers will work with the Special Committee, and with people in the territories under their administration [which includes Western Sahara], to find ways to further the decolonization process. After all, decolonization is a United Nations success story, but it is a story that is not yet finished.[7]

In March 2003, American and British troops invaded Iraq under the pretext that the country had not complied with UN resolutions. At the same time, the United States and France have shown no such concern for similar violations Morocco has committed since it invaded the former colony, known as Spanish Sahara, in 1975. It is also important to recognize that not a single country in the world recognizes Morocco's sovereignty over Western Sahara—not even Morocco's closest friends and allies. The territory is still de jure under Spanish administrative control. Spain's attempt to transfer administrative power to Morocco under the Madrid Accords of November 14, 1975, has no legal validity, and indeed the UN has never recognized those accords.[8] The third point is related to King Hassan II's declarations in 1981 and 1983 that stated that he was amenable to holding a referendum on self-determination in Western Sahara. It is now assumed that the king only suggested a "referendum of confirmation" and had no intention of allowing a genuine referendum to ever take place, a policy continued by his son, Mohammed VI, who succeeded him in July 1999. Furthermore, Morocco accepted the UN 1991 Settlement Plan, which included holding such a referendum. But, as shall be seen, France and the United States continue to propose solutions to the conflict that ignore these extremely valid principles. Not only do the political heavyweights choose to ignore the legal precedents and diplomatic *acquis* made over the past thirty-five years, but they also continue to demand that Sahrawis make concessions to Morocco, the occupying power, without putting any pressure on the latter to comply with UN resolutions. In fact, Morocco's refusal to comply derives from the impunity guaranteed by its two supporters.

The conflict, and negotiation efforts, has been at an impasse since the early 1990s. To fully comprehend this diplomatic deadlock, one must analyze the respective roles of the key players in this dispute, their respective positions, and the interests underlying such positions. Current analysis shows that whenever the conflict is brought to international attention, it usually means that the interests of one or several of the players have also shifted. For example, in the 1990s, the Algerian state was on the brink of collapse, so the status quo best served the interests of all (except Sahrawis). More recently, however, resolving the conflict in favor of Morocco would only serve the interests of Morocco and its traditional backers, which today also include Spain.

ALGERIA'S AND MOROCCO'S COMPETING INTERESTS

Essentially, neither Morocco nor Algeria has altered its position on Western Sahara in any fundamental way since the conflict began. Despite certain Algerian personalities having expressed differences of views, such as the former powerful Defense Minister Major General Khaled Nezzar in 2003 and President Mohamed Boudiaf (January–June 1992), or Moroccan officials such as Hassan II's right man, Driss Basri, during his self-imposed exile in France (2004–2007), the bottom line has not changed. Over the course of the years, and against its principled position, Algeria proposed dividing the territory between Sahrawis and Moroccans as a tentative to break the deadlock. On the other hand, Moroccans insist that Algerians have created an artificial conflict over Western Sahara to weaken the Kingdom of Morocco, its main rival in the region, and thwart the recovery of its "southern provinces." Moroccan scholar Abdelkhaleq Berramdane, for instance, has argued that "Algeria dug up a people [in other words, the Sahrawis]" to spoil Morocco's claims,[9] a point of view most Moroccans share today. The other debatable accusation is that Algeria's determination for an independent Western Sahara rests on an ulterior strategic motive: free access to the Atlantic.

There are historical, geopolitical, ideological, and psychological reasons that have strained Algerian-Moroccan relations since Algeria's independence in 1962.[10] Although there is a regional leadership struggle between the two countries,[11] Moroccan irredentism is a weightier factor in the Western Sahara equation. It began in the 1950s when the "greater Morocco" concept was developed by Mohammed Allal al-Fassi, leader of the nationalist Istiqlal Party. Al-Fassi's efforts to convince Moroccans to lead a struggle to liberate the region started as far back as 1956. His movement pushed for the manumission of Tangier, parts of the Sahara from Colomb-Béchar to Tindouf (both in Algeria), the Touat, Kenadza, Mauritania (only recognized in 1969—eight years after its independence), and of course Spanish Sahara. This liberation would, of course, last until the region's unification with Morocco. Thus, Morocco's new borders would extend as far south as the former French colonial capital of Saint-Louis in Senegal. Contributing greatly to rising Moroccan nationalism, the movement also inspired fear among the leaders of the Algerian nationalist movement. Morocco was becoming a potentially hostile neighbor intent on amputating parts of the territory Algerians had fought fervently to liberate through a fierce war against French colonialism. Despite the geographic proximity, a number of differences between the two countries during the colonial era were transformed into ideologies after independence. Inevitably, Moroccan irredentism, though progressively diluted, resulted in border conflicts with its eastern neighbor. In the 1970s, border issues were mostly resolved and the conflict in Western Sahara became the main bone of contention in Algerian-Moroccan relations. It is important to note that although the boundaries separating these countries were agreed upon in 1972, the Moroccan parliament did not ratify the decision, unlike Algeria, which ratified the treaty in 1973. It was King Hassan, the absolute sovereign, who confirmed the treaty in 1989. This change of heart not only put pressure on Algeria to settle the Western Sahara dispute, but also indicated that Morocco was not willing to relinquish the territory and rather would simply absorb it. The ratification of the Morocco-Algerian border treaty, however, did not mean the end of Moroccan irredentism. Thus, in January 2009, Moroccan Prime Minister Abbas al Fassi repeated the same arguments as his father by claiming that the western part of Algeria belonged to Morocco,[12] reinforcing Algeria's long-held apprehension about Morocco's irredentism. Another recent, albeit minor, manifestation of Moroccan irredentism was the call from the Front de Liberation de l'Algérie Marocain (FLAM), which in March 2006 called for the liberation of southwest Algeria and its return to Morocco.[13]

Algerian leaders used Morocco's occupation of Western Sahara as an instrument in their own struggle against Moroccan irredentist aspirations. Above and beyond the Western Sahara conflict, additional factors contribute to the rivalry between Algeria and Morocco, visible not only in the Maghreb itself, but throughout the rest of the African continent. Algeria's support of liberation movements was motivated primarily by its commitment, as a former colony, to achieving national self-determination.[14] Nevertheless, Algeria's approach to some African countries derives from its objective to thwart Morocco's ambitions and to muster support for creating an independent Sahrawi state.

The Algerian military-civilian establishment was greatly affected by the Algerian-Moroccan border dispute in 1963.[15] This partly explains why Sahrawi self-determination was so important to Algerian authorities. As in other cases of countering expansionism, in Algeria, support for Sahrawis derived from fears that Western Sahara would be absorbed into the Moroccan kingdom and would thus upset the regional balance of power in Morocco's favor, which would threaten, according to officials, Algeria's national security. As Damis rightly pointed out long ago, "Algerians fear that the absorption of the Sahara by their neighbors would only encourage Moroccan expansionist tendencies and whet the Moroccans' appetite for pursuing their unfulfilled and frequently articulated irredentist claim to territory in western Algeria."[16] The absorption of Western Sahara through military means would also create a precedent that could undermine the whole logic of the inviolability of borders—a sensitive issue not only for Algeria, but also for most members of the African Union (formerly Organization of African Unity, OAU).

Moving beyond a historical analysis of the Western Sahara conflict, certain structural discrepancies in Algerian-Moroccan relations have contributed to the policies the two countries have pursued and the animosity, and lack of trust, that has long characterized their relationship.

THE KINGDOM OF MOROCCO

Morocco has not always been against Western Sahara's independence; in fact, until 1974 it seemed favorable to Sahrawi self-determination. During the July 23–24, 1972, meeting in Agadir, Morocco concurred with Algeria and Mauritania in complying with international legality and UN resolutions and pledged its support for self-determination of Western Sahara. However, covertly, King Hassan II was convinced that the process of self-determination would eventually result in the territory's integration with Morocco. When the prospect of Sahrawi integration appeared unlikely, Hassan did not conceal his proclivity to seize the territory. At the beginning, Hassan's annexation attempts were made without seeking external support. In 1973, he first tried to obtain sanction by calling on the opinion of the International Court of Justice (ICJ). To his great disappointment, on October 16, 1975, the ICJ ruled in favor of Sahrawi self-determination. This ruling is precisely the opinion that the opponents of Sahrawi self-determination today never refer to, or seek to interpret in favor of Morocco,[17] because the judges did not agree with Moroccan and Mauritanian claims:

> The Court's conclusion is that the materials and information presented to it do not establish any tie of territorial sovereignty between the territory of Western Sahara and the Kingdom of Morocco or the Mauritanian entity. Thus the Court has not found legal ties of such a nature as might affect the application of General Assembly resolution 1514 (XV) in the decolonization of Western Sahara and, in particular, of the principle of self-determination through the free and genuine expression of the will of the peoples of the Territory.[18]

Based on this legal opinion, as well as the UN visit to the Western Sahara and UN Security Council (UNSC) Resolutions 377 (1975) of October 22, 1975, 379 (1975) of November 2, 1975, and 380 of November 6, 1975, on the situation concerning Western Sahara, UN Resolution 3458 (XXX) of December 10, 1975, declared unequivocally that the General Assembly:

> 1. *Reaffirms* the inalienable right of the people of Spanish Sahara to self-determination, in accordance with General Assembly resolution 1514(XV).

Notwithstanding international legality, Morocco and Mauritania invaded Western Sahara. On November 6, 1975, more than 350,000 Moroccans invaded the disputed territory. King Hassan II presented the march as a peaceful "repossession" by Morocco of its "southern provinces." In truth more than 25,000 troops had already crossed into Sahrawi land on October 31, 1975, and tens of thousands of soldiers could be counted within the ranks of the "peaceful" marchers. As the colonial power, Spain not only failed to meet its legal and moral obligations, but it made matters worse. Indeed, on November 14, a secret agreement, known as the Madrid Accords, was signed with Morocco and Mauritania, whereby Spain "transferred" its administrative powers over the land to these two states. Spain officially pulled out of the territory on February 27, 1976. The same day, a group claiming to represent Sahrawi interests, the Popular Front for the Liberation of Saguia el-Hamra and Río de Oro (Spanish Frente Popular para la Liberación de Saguia el-Hamra y Río de Oro, or the POLISARIO Front), proclaimed the creation of the Sahrawi Arab Democratic Republic (SADR), recognized to this day by more than seventy-five countries.

The UNSC Resolution 380 of November 6, 1975, "deplored the holding of the march" and "call[ed] upon Morocco immediately to withdraw from the Territory of Western Sahara all the participants in the march." Undiscouraged and with support from the United States and France, Morocco has strengthened the occupation of the territory through military, economic, and other repressive means. Backed by Algeria, Sahrawi combatants fought Moroccan and, until 1979, Mauritanian troops, up to the cease-fire between Morocco and Sahrawis in September 1991. This détente followed the 1988 Settlement Plan brokered by the United Nations and the Organization of African Unity. It should be pointed out that for over fifteen years the Sahrawis fought the Royal Armed Forces without ever resorting to terrorism or attacks against Moroccan territory proper.

On April 19, 1991, the UNSC finally passed Resolution 690, which outlined a detailed plan for setting up a UN mission for a referendum in Western Sahara (MINURSO) that would hold a free and fair referendum during which Sahrawis would decide their future (independence, autonomy, or integration into Morocco). Unsatisfied, Moroccans wanted nothing less than a referendum that would simply confirm their annexation of the territory. With the complicity of France, the United States, and successive UN secretaries-general, especially Boutros Boutros-Ghali, Morocco decided to use every possible stratagem to prevent the organization of a referendum with impunity. The referendum was scheduled to take place in early 1992, but due mostly to Morocco's delaying tactics, the UN was forced to postpone it repeatedly. To make matters worse, Morocco reneged on the conditions of the UN peace plan by registering thousands of Moroccans to the list of potential voters to be identified by MINURSO, thus delaying indefinitely the referendum.

From 1992 to 1997, the situation remained stalemated. Three main reasons convinced King Hassan to prevent the referendum: (1) the uncertainty of the result; (2) the unstable domestic situation in Algeria (the Sahrawis' main supporter); and (3) the decision of France and the United States to exert no pressure on Morocco, allegedly for fear of destabilizing the monarchy.

Another reason that has compelled Morocco to keep its hold on the territory is unequivocally economic.[19] Western Sahara is considerably rich in natural resources, and the huge phosphate deposits inspired heavy Spanish investment. Regardless of the territory's disputed status, Western corporations have contributed to its exploitation either through shipments of phosphates on behalf of the Moroccan government[20] or through exploration for oil by major companies such as Kerr-McGee, which, due to pressure from NGOs, eventually ceased activities there.[21] Sahrawi legal and thus economic rights were violated through illegal commercial ventures conducted in Western Sahara.[22] Furthermore, Moroccans have openly exploited Sahrawi natural resources in violation of international law, as corroborated by the UN under-secretary-general of legal affairs, Hans Corell. In 2002 Corell reaffirmed the ICJ verdict in a legal opinion to the Security Council on the matter of Western Sahara resources. He added that if exploration and exploitation of the oil resources of the territory "were to proceed in disregard of the interests and wishes of the people of Western Sahara, they would be in violation of the international-law principles applicable to mineral resource activities in Non-Self-Governing Territories."[23]

THE THIRD WAY AND "AUTONOMY"

In March 1997, Kofi Annan appointed former US Secretary of State James A. Baker as his personal representative for Western Sahara. Baker brokered the Houston Accords between the POLISARIO Front and Morocco, thus allowing MINURSO to resume the identification of voters for the referendum on self-determination. In December 1999, MINURSO finalized a provisional list of voters, and the UN made the list public in January 2000. Soon thereafter, Morocco blocked the countdown to the referendum again. Having lodged some 130,000 appeals, 95 percent of which proved to be lacking any legal or practical foundation, Morocco's goal clearly was to turn the appeals procedure into a second identification process, therefore entrenching the fait accompli of the occupation. In his report to the Security Council, Annan stated that, in addition to the fact that the referendum could not take place until at least 2002, in view of the differences between Morocco and POLISARIO, "it would be essential that the parties now offer specific and concrete solutions to the multiple problems relating to the implementation of the plan that can be agreed to or, alternatively, be prepared to consider other ways of achieving an early, durable and agreed resolution of their dispute over Western Sahara."[24]

The UN Security Council approved Annan's report and hinted that the two parties should seek the so-called third way, that is, the granting of autonomy to

Sahrawis instead of granting them the right to self-determination and the choice between independence and integration into Morocco. Once again the UNSC extended MINURSO's mandate and its resolution shifted the focus from obstacles to the 1991 peace plan to ways of circumventing it. The resolution directly resulted in the hardening of the Moroccan position. The monarchy made it plain that it would rather consider some form of autonomy for Sahrawis and abandon the holding of a referendum altogether. Morocco was not the only one to shy away from a "winner take all" outcome; both Baker and Annan started favoring an option other than the referendum. Yet Algeria and the Sahrawis categorically rejected the notion of a third way. This roadblock, as well as UN member states' attachment to UN resolutions, compelled the Security Council nevertheless to reiterate the necessity "to hold a free, fair and impartial referendum for the self-determination of the people of the Western Sahara."[25] In the end, even though the MINURSO mandate continued to be renewed, both sides remained firm in their political trenches. Nothing changed about Morocco's support for a "large autonomy" for the Sahrawis within "Moroccan sovereignty," nor in the Sahrawi and Algerian camp, which supported the 1991 UN Settlement Plan leading to the referendum on self-determination.

The situation came to a stalemate in June 2001 when Annan handed in his report.[26] The secretary-general voluntarily infringed upon international legal precedence and the fundamental principles of the UN Charter in an attempt to impose a third way. This agreement, designed without consulting the Sahrawis, was renamed the Framework Agreement. This proposal was put forth in the face of the POLISARIO's repeated and explicit rejection of any third-way strategies and despite the fact that only months earlier, the United Nations had admitted that it could rapidly solve the problems related to the identification procedure, thus eliminating the last impediment to implementing the referendum. The Framework Agreement purportedly proposed a solution other than independence, to which Sahrawis are entitled under international law, or integration, as sought by Morocco. However, if accepted, the plan submitted to POLISARIO on May 5, 2001, would simply have consecrated the integration of Western Sahara into Morocco under the cover of an illusory autonomy. This supposed solution was unsurprisingly backed by France, the United States, and Great Britain. Despite the political support of three global heavyweights, strong opposition came not only from Algeria and POLISARIO, but also from most members of the UN General Assembly. Ultimately, the Security Council did not endorse the Framework Agreement and requested that Baker produce another plan. In Washington, Senators Edward Kennedy, Patrick Leahy, and John Kerry wrote to Secretary of State Colin Powell expressing their concern over the increasingly alarming situation. They feared, perceptively, that the United Nations would "abandon the referendum and support a solution that proposes integrating the Western Sahara into Morocco against the will of the Sahrawi people."[27]

It was thus that the UNSC adopted a resolution in July 2002 that reiterated its support for implementing the 1991 UN peace plan or any other political solution acceptable to both parties. The July decision provided temporary relief to the issue, but it also created an opportunity for Baker to press for a modified version of the Framework Agreement. Disregarding the heavy opposition, Annan and Baker kept putting the third way back on the table, and by doing so, implicitly supported Morocco's claim to sovereignty over the territory.

UNSC RESOLUTION 1495
ON WESTERN SAHARA

Faced with an entrenched opposition, Baker redesigned his proposal. In January 2003 he submitted the new Peace Plan for Self-Determination of the People of Western Sahara, which described a more elaborate proposal for self-government during the five-year transition period preceding the referendum.[28] Baker believed this new proposal was a synthesis of the elements of the Settlement Plan and the proposed Framework Agreement. The plan raised a number of objections on behalf of the Moroccan government. The most unsatisfactory aspect, in Moroccan eyes, was adding an independence option to the referendum (the options being autonomy or full integration into Morocco). The UNSC adopted Resolution 1495 on July 31, 2003, endorsing the latest version of Baker's plan and establishing the enforceable character of the Settlement Plan on Moroccans and Sahrawis. The new proposal, better known as the Baker Plan II, surprisingly was accepted by both Algeria and POLISARIO after an initial period of hesitation. Algerians understood that by accepting this proposal they showed their support for a presupposed attachment to "international legality" and to the UN peace plan. The POLISARIO Front's motive for accepting Baker's new plan was to avoid a resurgence of violence or conflict with the strong-armed occupier. Morocco, with heavy French support within the UNSC, rejected Baker's new proposal, stating that it was contrary to the country's "fundamental national interests and to peace and security in the Maghreb region." Despite their numerical superiority in the occupied territory, Morocco rejected the inclusion of the holding of a referendum after the five-year transition period, only because it provided independence as an option.

One can legitimately ask why, despite the superior number of Moroccans in Western Sahara, the monarchy still opposes holding a referendum. The only logical answer is that the monarchy fears that Moroccan settlers would prefer an independent, democratic Sahrawi republic over the territory's integration into the kingdom. Another question, of course, is why Algerians and Sahrawis, who initially rejected it in March 2003, accepted the Baker Plan II four months later. Most likely the Sahrawis accepted the plan because of nudging from their friends as well as to avoid appearing to be the impediment to resolving the conflict. As for their main ally, Algeria, some analysts suggested that Algeria had now abandoned the Sahrawis. However, interviews with officials revealed that Algeria's acceptance of the plan did not mean the withdrawal of backing for the Sahrawis. Proof of this can be found in subsequent events and statements made by high officials, including President Abdelaziz Bouteflika. Algerian officials argue in private that they accepted the plan in order to corner Morocco into a position of bad faith. Algerians, based on previous interaction with Morocco, were persuaded that their neighbor would reject Baker's new plan. Their acceptance was also a way to demonstrate that Morocco, not Algeria, has been the true obstacle to a peaceful settlement of the conflict.[29] The basis of the Moroccan and French opposition to the Baker Plan II, which would not come under Chapter VII of the UN Charter, which authorizes the UNSC to undertake all actions, including military means, to execute a resolution, was linked nonetheless to UNSC efforts to impose its implementation on the parties. After the jihadist attack in Casablanca in May 2003, the French, who see themselves as the guarantors of Morocco's domestic stability, were particularly worried that implementing the Baker Plan II would destabilize the monarchy.

Faced with a new diplomatic failure and the attention-drawing war in Iraq, the situation in Western Sahara reached a stalemate. Despite the quasi veto on the Baker Plan, and with the encouragement of France, the United States, and later Spain, Morocco indicated that it would submit a proposal for a "genuine autonomy." The clear political impasse and the obvious support that Morocco obtained in Paris and Washington compelled Baker to resign in April 2004. While diplomats continued to trudge through a diplomatic gridlock, the Sahrawis continued to suffer. Near Tindouf, Algeria, refugee camps still suffer privations, including limited food supplies. Indeed, during his visit to the camps in September 2009, UNHCR High Commissioner Antonio Guterres confirmed the difficult situation in the camps and that the $12 million in food aid that the United Nations donated remains quite insufficient.[30] Within the occupied territory Sahrawis have been subjected to harsh Moroccan repression since the uprising (intifada) they launched in 2005; the repression has continued hitherto.[31] Morocco has been able to continue the occupation without suffering any retribution from the United Nations, which keeps submitting alternative options under the pretext that "Morocco has expressed unwillingness to go forward with the settlement plan."[32]

Despite their fortuitous efforts to block the Baker Plan, the Moroccan government still argued that as long as Morocco's "territorial integrity" was respected, they were willing to grant Sahrawis autonomy. If one reads between the thinly veiled lines, independence is out of the question. A former UN staff member, Anna Theofilopoulou, who worked closely with Baker, observed astutely, "The easy abandonment of the Baker Peace Plan by the secretary-general and his senior staff, following its weakened support by the Security Council, made POLISARIO and its supporters suspect that senior UN leadership was once again capitulating to Moroccan pressure."[33] Assured of French and US backing, Moroccans launched an all-out diplomatic campaign to advance their own "enhanced autonomy plan," which they eventually submitted to the United Nations in April 2007. Convinced of its allies' support, Morocco has since decided to negotiate nothing but its own "autonomy plan," which unsurprisingly France and the United States endorsed.

MOROCCO'S "OFFER"

Morocco's promise to "grant" Sahrawis some kind of autonomy is not new. King Hassan II suggested in the 1980s that, except for the "stamp and the flag," everything was negotiable. Many interpreted this as an emulation of the British Commonwealth model. Unfortunately, Algerian officials and American diplomats interviewed on this matter indicated that Hassan II's offer of Sahrawi autonomy was not genuine. On the other hand, US officials were convinced that the offer of autonomy from King Mohammed VI, who succeeded his father in July 1999, was more sincere.[34] However, it was not until the defeat of the Baker Plan II that French, American, and Spanish officials began to insist that Morocco present a "credible" offer for Sahrawi autonomy and to openly support that option. One point that needs to remain clear is that Morocco would only offer a Saharan Autonomous Region (SAR), in other words, its "southern provinces" within Morocco's "sovereignty, national unity and territorial integrity," a phrase repeated ad nauseam in all official speeches and documents.[35] Morocco has never treated the Western Sahara issue in terms of self-determination or decolonization. Moreover, the geographical limits of the proposed SAR have never been specified. Whatever Morocco's offer and whether it is genuine or not, it has no legality from an international-law point of view because Morocco has no sovereignty over the disputed territory; it is an occupying power that has seized the territory through force.

Even before the content of the autonomy proposal was unveiled, Moroccan diplomats and ministers reached around the world to garner support for their "historic initiative." Moroccans acted as if they were making a historic gesture in offering Sahrawis autonomy by holding sovereignty over the territory, sovereignty that no country in the world recognizes. The proposal, titled the Moroccan Initiative for Negotiating an Autonomy Statute for the Sahara Region, was submitted in April 2007 to UN Secretary-General Ban Ki-moon.[36] Spanish legal scholar Carlos Ruiz Miguel effectively demonstrated that the initiative is not much different from the counterproposal Morocco submitted to Baker in December 2003—yet the proposal received impressive media hype and support from Morocco's allies.[37] As Theofilopoulou points out, the new plan "follows a different strategy. Claiming to be open for negotiations, it does not go into the details of the previous autonomy project."[38] This ambiguity allegedly allows the proposal to be potentially enriched during the negotiation phase. The other novelty in the proposal is that it "shall be the subject of negotiations and shall be submitted to the populations concerned in a free referendum." Unsurprisingly, the Moroccan plan finds itself at odds with the counterproposal POLISARIO submitted to Ban Ki-moon a day earlier.[39] As long as the Moroccan initiative continues to insist that the other parties accept their territorial sovereignty, there is little chance for it to succeed. The opposing POLISARIO proposal is more consistent with international legality. The Sahrawis propose to negotiate with Morocco the holding of a referendum on self-determination (with independence as one option) and offer post-referendum guarantees:

> The Frente POLISARIO is also committed to accepting the results of the referendum whatever they are and to negotiate with the Kingdom of Morocco, under the auspices of the United Nations, the guarantees that it is prepared to grant to the Moroccan population residing in Western Sahara for 10 years as well as to the Kingdom of Morocco in the political, economic and security domains in the event that the referendum on self-determination would lead to independence.[40]

POLISARIO officials interviewed on the matter insist that autonomy is only one of the three options that are part of the Settlement Plan; therefore, POLISARIO-Morocco negotiations should focus on those options, not just on the one-sided, illegal autonomy offer. The content of the autonomy should be discussed so that should Sahrawis, during a free and fair referendum, choose autonomy, the terms would be known and agreed to by the parties.

Due to geopolitical realities, the major powers have once again granted more weight to the Moroccan proposal than to POLISARIO's. In the end, the powerful members of the UNSC have put themselves in a tenuous situation. By giving Morocco the de facto ability to veto any other solution, while maintaining their support for Sahrawi rights to self-determination, they and the UN have contributed to the continuation of the stalemate,[41] which nonetheless is favorable to Morocco since the country can continue its occupation and exploitation of the territory. On April 30, 2007, the UN passed a resolution (1754) that moved the two parties to hold direct negotiations on June 18 and 19 in Manhasset, New York. Other than agreeing to meet again in August and to maintain cordial communications, nothing of major importance occurred during that first meeting. Unfortunately, only weeks later, the king insisted that Morocco would not negotiate anything beyond autonomy,[42] once again dashing hopes for a resolution of the conflict. To no one's surprise, the second round of direct talks produced no tangible results. Contrary to UN Resolution 1754, which urged the parties not to set preconditions for their talks, Morocco held to its promise not to discuss anything but the "autonomy plan under Moroccan sovereignty." Representatives of Morocco and the POLISARIO Front met under UN auspices at the Greentree Estate on January 8 and 9, 2008. The objective was the implementation of Security Council Resolutions 1754 and 1783, both of which called on the parties to continue "negotiations without preconditions and in good faith to achieve a just, lasting and mutually acceptable political solution." Unsurprisingly, the meeting was unproductive since Morocco, in violation of the two UN resolutions cited above, set as a precondition recognition of its sovereignty over Western Sahara and discussion of autonomy only, while POLISARIO insisted that the territory's final status be decided in a referendum on self-determination that included independence as an option. The UN revealed that "the Parties discussed but did not agree on confidence-building measures. They also had preliminary discussions on thematic subjects such as administration, competencies and organs."[43] The personal envoy did not reveal that Moroccans told Sahrawis at every meeting, "We have the backing of France and the United States; so, the only thing that we will discuss is the autonomy plan which is endorsed by these two countries."[44] The fourth round took place March 16–18, 2008. Again, as anticipated, the talks were unproductive, although the two sides remained committed to pursuing negotiations in the future.

The reason why the POLISARIO Front rejects autonomy deserves some comments. First, Sahrawis remain attached to international legality and are correct in pointing out that it behooves the United Nations to conclude the process of decolonization of the territory; therefore, Morocco, which has no sovereignty, has no right to impose autonomy as a resolution to the conflict. Furthermore, the Moroccan initiative for a Saharan Autonomous Region not only is vague and dubious, but it would also require more than the promise of autonomy, no matter how large or genuine, to serve as a basis for negotiation, let alone acceptance by the Sahrawis. Assuming the latter accept autonomy under Moroccan sovereignty, they will have some prerogatives, such as levying taxes and enjoying a few legislative powers in a number of areas, such as education and health. But since the king, as Commander of the Faithful, would continue enjoying full constitutional and religious prerogatives, autonomy would be meaningless for several reasons. First, the authoritarian structure of the regime would be unaltered. Second, Sahrawis and POLISARIO, assuming the latter would be allowed to exist under such a scheme, would obviously have to proclaim allegiance to the absolute monarch, as do Moroccan society and parties, which, in essence, means the monarch can overrule any decision whenever he feels that decision has impinged upon his prerogatives. Third, Morocco has not proceeded with any real constitutional reforms that would lay the foundations of a truly democratic order. Unless such reforms have been initiated, it would be suicidal for POLISARIO as a party or for Sahrawis as a people to accept autonomy under such conditions.

UN Resolution 1813 of April 30, 2008, reiterated the need for the parties to continue the negotiations.

In early January 2009, despite Moroccan objections, Ban Ki-moon appointed former US Ambassador Christopher Ross, a fine connoisseur of the Maghreb region, as UN special envoy for Western Sahara. Given his knowledge of the region, the expectation is that Ross will carry his mission more evenhandedly than did his predecessor, the Dutch Peter van Walsum, particularly after the fourth round of negotiations. Indeed, van Walsum, arguing that since Morocco would never give up its claims and that the United States and France have not been willing to impose on Morocco a solution it does not like, Sahrawis should simply settle for autonomy and forfeit their call for self-determination, let alone independence. This statement resulted in the nonrenewal of his mandate, for he had broken the impartiality required of a UN mediator; POLISARIO insisted he no longer serve as special envoy, for he had shown his preference for Morocco.

In April 2009, Ban Ki-moon submitted his report to the UNSC, which approved it two weeks later. In Resolution 1871, the UNSC called "upon the parties to continue negotiations under the auspices of the Secretary-General without preconditions and in good faith . . . with a view to achieving a just, lasting and mutually acceptable political solution, which will provide for the self-determination of the people of Western Sahara" and, more important, support the Secretary-General's general call upon the two parties "to negotiate in good faith, without preconditions, show the political will to enter substantive discussions and ensure the success of the negotiations." Ross's idea of Morocco and the POLISARIO Front holding informal talks before the fifth round of negotiations met with approval by all interested parties. The two-day informal meeting took place in Durnstein, Austria, August 10–11, 2009; unsurprisingly, despite a fairly positive communiqué, no progress was made. The two parties committed to continuing the negotiation process, but no date was set for the fifth round.

Although the UNSC has encouraged the two parties to negotiate and find a mutually acceptable political solution, there is no doubt that any breakthrough will depend on the determination of the United States and France to ensure that such a solution is reached.

FOREIGN POWERS AS HINDRANCE TO THE RESOLUTION

The contention in this chapter is that the stalemate in Western Sahara has never been due to questions regarding international legality or technical issues concerning the eligibility of the electorate during the referendum; the absence of a solution draws from failure of powerful UNSC members, supportive of Morocco, to allow a genuine process of decolonization to move forward. Their geopolitical interests in Morocco have overridden concerns for international law and UN resolutions to which they themselves contributed. That the conflict emerged at the peak of the Cold War with the political alignments that characterized that era has also had lasting consequences on the dispute regardless of the changes that have occurred in the post–Cold War period.

When seeking explanations for the stalemate in the peace process, most analyses tend to blame technical problems, usually the alleged voter identification problems or the farfetched notion that it is difficult to organize the referendum in a desert area. Tempting as the argument might be, geopolitical considerations provide the most compelling explanation. Not only has Morocco consistently refused to allow the holding of a free and fair referendum, but it has also greatly benefited from the support of three powerful members of the UNSC—although Great Britain has been more evenhanded at times. Spain has since 2004 broken with its traditional neutrality in the conflict and the socialist government of José Luis Rodríguez Zapatero and his foreign minister, Miguel Ángel Moratinos, joined France, the United States, and Great Britain in backing Morocco.

France

Morocco has relied on France to protect its interests from the very beginning of the conflict in 1975.[45] In the event that their support was not straightforward enough, French Prime Minister Jean-Pierre Rafarin confirmed during his 2003 visit "the similarity of views and positions between Paris and Rabat concerning the question of Western Sahara."[46] Furthermore, during President Jacques Chirac's trip to Morocco in early October 2003, he stated unequivocally and candidly: "France wishes ardently for a solution to the [Western Sahara] conflict, which constitutes a barrier to the construction of a united Maghreb. We defend *a political solution . . . which takes fully into account Morocco's interests and regional stability.*"[47] Most French politicians do not mince words on the subject; Western Sahara is an integral part of the Kingdom of Morocco. Should the UN decide to impose a solution that is not acceptable to Morocco, the French made it clear that they would use their veto power at the UN Security Council.[48] Paris, which in 2003 was so vocally opposed to the United States and its war in Iraq, demonstrates in this case that power politics remains at the foundation of its foreign policy, rhetoric about human rights and international law notwithstanding. Thus, it would seem that international law applies only to countries such as Tibet or Georgia that lie outside of France's sphere of influence. It was under Chirac that France took a decidedly pro-Moroccan stance, even if Franco-Algerian relations had also witnessed remarkable improvement compared to what they had been throughout the 1990s, when civil unrest ravaged Algeria. The special relationship France has with Morocco is comparable only to the one the United States has had with Israel for the past four decades.[49]

France's opposition to an independent Western Sahara has never been a secret. In the 1970s, President Valéry Giscard d'Estaing opposed the birth of a "micro-state." Today, French officials interviewed on the question allege that another "micro-state" or a "failed state" under the influence of Algeria would not bode well for the Maghreb and would also be costly for France.[50] The French argue that the proposed referendum, which would surely favor the Sahrawis, would destabilize the kingdom, an outcome fraught with dangerous ramifications.

France has provided the Moroccan monarchy with substantial economic, political, and military support. In a juggling effort, it has managed to avoid alienating Algeria. The neighboring country has not only recovered from the instability of the 1990s, but also moved closer to the United States, thus threatening France's significant interests there.[51] French efforts to preserve good relations have not prevented the country from ignoring Algeria's national-security interests. Thus, it has sought to offset SADR's gains by coercing, through financial blackmail, African countries into withdrawing their recognition. A few weak African states (Benin, Burkina Faso, Chad, Congo-Brazzaville, and Togo) have succumbed to this pressure by withdrawing their diplomatic recognition. Despite French efforts, influential African countries such as South Africa (since September 2004) continue to recognize SADR, a blow to both France and Morocco. But South Africa is not the only country France has failed to influence on this issue. Reliable sources have indicated that during the Algerian crisis in the 1990s, France sought to exchange economic and financial aid to convince Algeria to reduce its support for an independent Western Sahara. Today the financial situation in Algeria has improved considerably, in large part due to oil revenues, and the country is no longer in the weak position that characterized it in the 1990s. The country's standing in the international arena is quite solid, especially in the African Union. Algeria's position on Western Sahara has remained relatively unchanged despite France's and Morocco's expectations. Algeria continues to support the Sahrawis' right to self-determination and respect for international legality. Such political entrenching has caused France to argue that the solution lies in Rabat and Algiers, and that these two should reach an agreement to allow for the construction of the Maghreb Union; this is precisely the argument Algeria has always opposed, considering that although Algeria is a concerned party (it shares borders with both) the conflict is one between Sahrawis and Moroccans and that the issue is one of self-determination. What is certain is that France's alignment with Morocco has added to the tension in Franco-Algerian relations in recent years.

Undoubtedly, France has heavy political and economic ties to Morocco. Not only do the French represent 25 percent of all tourists who visit the kingdom, but also thousands of French citizens and enterprises have been established in Morocco. With close to 70 percent of total foreign direct investments in

Morocco, France is Morocco's first trading partner and main investor. France's policy under Nicolas Sarkozy's presidency has remained unaltered despite his seemingly more pragmatic approach. During his brief visit to Algiers on July 9, 2007, Sarkozy declared that he would not make the question of Western Sahara a factor of dispute between France and Algeria and that the process at the United Nations was running its course.[52] Even though France wishes to keep the triangular relationship in the Maghreb intact, French authorities fully support Morocco's autonomy plan.[53] Indeed, during his visit to Morocco October 22–24, 2007, Sarkozy declared that France "sides with Morocco" at the UN Security Council and wished that Morocco's autonomy plan, described as "serious and credible," served as the basis for negotiation in the search for a "reasonable solution."[54] In April 2009, France blocked attempts to include in the UNSC resolution an additional mandate for MINURSO: the protection of human rights in Western Sahara. Instead, the resolution stressed "the importance of making progress on the human dimension of the conflict." France had even resisted the term "human," preferring "humanitarian."[55] Its permanent representative did not hide France's attachment to Morocco's autonomy plan, stating unequivocally that "Morocco's 2007 proposal deserved serious consideration by the parties."[56] Though this position has alienated Algerians, France under Sarkozy continues to provide considerable support to Morocco. But when one looks at the size of the trade agreements between the two countries—during Sarkozy's visit in October 2007, the two countries signed contracts amounting to close to 3 billion euros—it is thus not surprising that international law did not weigh much in the balance.

The current foreign minister, Bernard Kouchner, declared in the 1990s that the Western Sahara conflict was Algeria's creation and that the territory belonged to Morocco. Therefore, his position has now allowed him to act on France's convictions. Thus, since coming to power in 2007 and throughout 2008, France, especially when it took over the presidency of the European Union (EU), set as one of its objectives the granting of an "advanced status" to Morocco. By October, Morocco had obtained that status in the EU. Not only was Morocco rewarded for its role in the fight against illegal migration to Europe but the EU would also have access, illegally from an international law perspective, to fishing waters along the Western Saharan coast.[57]

The United States

Although the United States has consistently backed Morocco on the Western Sahara issue, American foreign policy indicates ambivalence. In principle, Washington supports the right to self-determination as guaranteed in the UN Charter. This notion obliges Spain to hold a referendum on self-determination. Practically speaking, though, US position rests on political, military, and economic interests. So rather than push for free and fair processes, the United States has provided steadfast support to the Moroccan monarchy, a reliable ally in the Arab world. Since the beginning of the conflict not only has the United States sided with Morocco, but it was also instrumental in Morocco's colonization of the territory.[58] This alignment and interference can be explained by Cold War politics. The United States feared Soviet expansion into sub-Saharan Africa, despite the fact that the USSR had never supported the Sahrawi nationalist movement.[59] Washington worried about the potential emergence of a pro-Soviet state. Through large-scale economic and military aid, military advisers, and logistical assistance, the United States undoubtedly tilted the balance in Morocco's favor. Morocco was important as it also served as an important surrogate for US interests in Africa and the Middle East, even dispatching its troops to troubled countries and giving the CIA and National Security Agency wide latitude to operate in the kingdom. Even though the conflict was in no way part of the East-West confrontation,[60] the United States, which then perceived Algeria—the Sahrawis' main supporter—as a close Soviet friend, sided with Morocco, despite proclaimed neutrality. In August 2004, James Baker corroborated this point by stating that US support for Morocco was justified because "in the days of the Cold War . . . the POLISARIO Front was aligned with Cuba and Libya and some other enemies of the United States, and Morocco was very close to the United States."[61] Thus, when in 1978 war in Western Sahara was raging, US military aid to Morocco was multiplied twentyfold to reach more than $99.8 million from a mere $4.1 million in 1974.[62] With the end of the Cold War, American economic and military assistance had decreased considerably due to congressional budget restrictions. However, Morocco soon managed to regain its position as an important ally. In terms of aid, one can cite a few recent figures: In 2002, Morocco received 72 percent of total US assistance to the three Maghreb countries, while in 2005 the figure amounted to 81 percent, or $58 million.[63] In 2006, military aid rose to $20 million to help Morocco not only stop clandestine immigration but also, and above all, protect its borders and continue the fight against terrorism. In fiscal year 2007, the State Department authorized the export to Morocco of defense articles and services valued at $87,475,761.[64]

American preoccupation with the survival of the pro-Western, "moderate" monarchy—as guarantor of the US and Western presence in the area—has overridden other regional concerns.[65] Morocco garners considerable support in the Congress not only because of the longtime friendship between the two countries, but perhaps primarily because Morocco is one of the few Arab countries that are friendly to Israel.

Since the attacks of September 11, 2001, the Global War on Terrorism (GWOT) has also strengthened Morocco's standing in US policy. However, there has been another important change since 2001. Neighboring Algeria is now perceived as a strategic partner in the region and has become a key actor in the GWOT. This Maghreb country has developed excellent military, security, political, and economic ties with the United States.[66] Even though US attachment to Morocco remains unwavering, this rapprochement has compelled Washington to pursue a relatively more cautious policy, at least until 2007, when Morocco submitted the autonomy proposal. Thus, when Morocco and the United States established a free trade area (FTA) in 2004 (entered into effect in January 2006), the United States made it clear that the FTA did not include Western Sahara. Until 2007, the United States called for a political solution "acceptable" to all parties. To Morocco's displeasure, the demands for the United States to impose a solution—one favorable to Morocco—have gone unmet. Washington has made it clear that it refuses to invoke Chapter VII of the UN Charter when dealing with Western Sahara. At the same time, close friendship with Morocco—which became in June 2004 a major US non-NATO ally—coupled with the need to keep the country in the antiterrorist coalition, put the United States in a delicate position. The United States tries to bridge the gaps in its foreign policy and soothe Morocco's fears by using language that does not compel the Palace to comply with UN resolutions. The country's stance could not be made more clear than in former president George W. Bush's letter to King Mohammed VI, in which he declared that the United States "understand[s] the sensibility of the Moroccan people on the question of Western Sahara and would not try to impose a solution to this conflict."[67]

Of course, this means that the United States would not undertake any action that would alienate Algerians or Sahrawis either. Following Baker's resignation in June 2004, the United States joined France's position that Morocco and Algeria should work for rapprochement "as a means to create an environment conducive to settlement of the issue."[68]

The United States began to pursue a more active policy on Western Sahara by encouraging Morocco to submit a serious proposal. Thus, Gordon Gray, deputy assistant secretary of state for Near Eastern affairs, declared that, with respect to Western Sahara,

> The United States continues to seek an acceptable political solution, within the United Nations framework, and has no desire whatsoever to impose a solution. . . . The Moroccan government has recently expressed its willingness to write up an autonomy plan for Western Sahara; the United States encouraged Morocco to present a credible proposal so that all parties can analyze it.[69]

The United States gave its full support to Morocco's 2007 autonomy proposal, describing it as "a serious and credible proposal to provide real autonomy for the Western Sahara."[70] The United States also encouraged direct negotiations between the two protagonists without preconditions. Assistant Secretary of State C. David Welch asserted during a hearing in Congress that he had "worked with them [Moroccans] on it [autonomy plan]." While he asserted that the Moroccan proposal "represents some serious efforts," he downplayed the Sahrawi proposal, stating that it "does not seem, in our judgment, to contain new ideas by comparison."[71] By "new ideas," Welch meant anything that would circumvent the principles of international law and UN resolutions that Sahrawis put forth to support their claims.

Paradoxically, while Welch rejected the Sahrawi plan because it reiterated the right to self-determination and remained attached to the Settlement Plan, he also argued that "any settlement of the Western Sahara must also take into account the concerns of the Sahrawi people and be consistent with their right of self-determination." This political contradiction is precisely the same catch-22 in which the United Nations has found itself. The ruse in Welch's statement was in recognizing Morocco's sovereignty over the disputed territory. Self-determination would be the prerogative not of the United Nations but of Morocco, which "has said its proposal would be subject to a vote by the Sahrawi people." The deputy permanent representative of the United States, Jackie Wolcott Sanders, confirmed the United States parti pris for Morocco's "initiative" following the first round of direct talks. Sanders declared: "We believe a promising and realistic way forward on the Western Sahara is meaningful autonomy. Morocco's initiative could provide a realistic framework to begin negotiations on a plan that would provide for real autonomy contingent on the approval of the local population."[72] The US position was reiterated following the second round of negotiations between Moroccans and Sahrawi nationalists. "We believe that meaningful autonomy is a promising and realistic way forward and that the Moroccan initiative could provide a realistic framework for negotiations."[73] This argument, in fact, is the same argument Morocco sought to impose upon Sahrawis. Indeed, during the talks, Moroccans declared that Sahrawis should accept their "autonomy initiative" because it enjoys the support of the United States and France. This, again, is clearly in contradiction with UN Resolution 1754, reiterated in 2009 in Resolution 1871, which urges the parties to engage in talks without preconditions.

Declarations of the United States support of the Moroccan autonomy plan, particularly after the failed fourth round of negotiations, were rather surprising. As demonstrated in this chapter, US support for Morocco in this conflict has been consistent. However, until recently official US position, at least publicly, showed a degree of commitment to international legality. The task was left to some diplomats to state that the Moroccan autonomy plan was "serious and credible," but never had the State Department openly declared its support for the Moroccan plan as the only realistic solution. Indeed, its spokesperson

stated on May 1, 2008, "An independent Sahrawi state is not a realistic option. In our view, some form of autonomy under Moroccan sovereignty is the
only realistic way forward to resolve this longstanding conflict."[74] Perhaps unwittingly, this statement placed the United States in the position of outlaw
since the stance shifted away from international legality. True, the statement
came as a result of the failure of the fourth round of negotiations, but it was
rather surprising to hold the view that because Morocco refuses any other option than autonomy, the United States should endorse that option. Obviously,
the United States could not impose the Moroccan autonomy plan by force,
but, under the Bush administration, it allowed Morocco to negotiate nothing
outside of this plan, thus contributing to the deadlock that it had been trying
to break. Undoubtedly, the weight of Deputy National Security Adviser for
Global Democracy Strategy Elliot Abrams, well-known for his pro-Moroccan
views, influenced US policy on this issue. As Clayton E. Swisher, director of
programs at the Middle East Institute in Washington, D.C., observed correctly, Abrams "is on the verge of achieving a major U.S. policy shift that
would have Washington backing Morocco's unilateral imposition of its so-
called Western Sahara Initiative, or autonomy plan upon the indigenous
Sahrawi people of Western Sahara."[75] By the end of the Bush administration,
the United States was setting an extremely dangerous precedent: Recognizing,
albeit implicitly, Morocco's sovereignty would have condoned the illegal acquisition of territory through military force. In order to lobby on behalf of
Morocco and to influence the Obama administration, some former officials,
such as Welch and Madeleine Albright, suggested that the new administration
impose a solution.[76] The support that Morocco obtained in the US Congress
for the autonomy proposal was also indicative of US willingness to breach international norms and legality to suit the interests of its ally.

There is no indication thus far that President Barack Obama will pursue Bush's
policy on Western Sahara, a policy that might not only alienate Algeria, an important partner in the GWOT, but would also put the United States in a difficult
legal position. Such a move would be in breach of the international legal position
set out in existing UN Security Council resolutions relating to Western Sahara.
Not only that, but such disregard for Sahrawis' self-determination might result in
exactly what most concerned people wish to avoid: the resumption of hostilities or
the emergence of Sahrawi desperados who may be forced to join the ranks of ji-
hadists in the region. The Moroccan government has sought, quite unsuccessfully,
to link al-Qaeda and the Sahrawi nationalist movement, POLISARIO,[77] but this
potentially self-fulfilling prophecy will not be in the interest of the region, not
even for Morocco.

Thus, it remains to be seen whether the Obama administration will provide
longtime US diplomat Christopher Ross, the UN Secretary-General's special
representative, with the necessary leverage to carry out his peace mission. The
question facing the United States is whether this "frozen conflict" and the status

quo are preferable to a lasting solution that might not be in the interest of its Moroccan ally. In June 2009, it appeared that the United States had moved away from supporting the Moroccan autonomy plan; the fact that in his letter to King Mohammed VI Obama did not mention the autonomy plan has been interpreted as a reversal in US policy on the question.[78] Citing diplomatic sources, a report suggested that "the United States no longer supports or endorses the Moroccan autonomy plan. . . . Instead, the administration has returned to the pre-Bush position that there could be an independent POLISARIO state in Western Sahara."[79] US officials refused to confirm or deny such reports, stating that the United States encourages the parties to pursue dialogue under UN auspices.[80] Undoubtedly, by referring to international legality, which in the case of Western Sahara would include the option of independence, Obama would be true to the values he promised to reinstate. However, it is too early to judge whether a shift in policy toward Western Sahara has occurred. Surely, the United States will decide whether the status quo serves its interests or whether a solution to the conflict, even one unfavorable to Morocco, would best serve its objectives in the region. Morocco has powerful friends in Washington, but Algeria has become strategic.[81] The United States has made clear that it wishes for a definitive resolution not least because the conflict has prevented greater cooperation between Algeria and Morocco in the fight against terrorism. Susan Rice stated that as a result of the conflict, "poor relations between Morocco and Algeria had prevented cooperation on issues of urgency for North Africa."[82] The United States, which is quite concerned about security in the Maghreb-Sahel region[83] and needs Algeria, a strategic partner in bringing about stability there, will definitely wish to resolve the conflict even if it is not a top priority on the administration's agenda.

Spain[84]

Spain has always maintained good rapport with the Maghreb states, adopting a bilateral policy of friendship and cooperation.[85] This approach by the former colonial power aimed at establishing a balance while seeking to strengthen political and economic ties with the neighboring southern Mediterranean states. Morocco has thus remained, except during the Spanish-Moroccan crisis (2001–2003), Spain's privileged interlocutor, even though relations with Algeria and Mauritania remained quite good. Spain's chief objective until the early 1970s had been to avoid an armed conflict with the Sahrawi militants who were openly backed by Morocco and Mauritania. Spain was more concerned over domestic politics and preoccupied with opening a new page in its history. It was the end of the Franco regime and beginning of Spain's progressive integration into the community of European democracies. Nevertheless, salient strategic interests ensured that Spain could ill afford to be antagonistic toward Morocco. The enclaves of Ceuta and Melilla, the dependency of the Spanish and Canary Islands' fishing fleets on Saharan waters, its participation in the phosphate mining company Bu-Craa in the Western Sahara, and the presence of Spaniards living and working in Morocco tightened the bonds of common interests. The Spanish government was confronted with a difficult situation: It needed to maintain good rapport with Morocco and establish stronger ties with Algeria. At the same time, it could not neglect the Western Sahara conflict. Indeed it was Spain's failure to decolonize the territory as mandated by the United Nations that led to the current situation. Madrid's position on the question of Western Sahara is ambiguous beyond doubt. Indeed, while Spain has never recognized Morocco's and Mauritania's sovereignty over the territory, it nonetheless signed fishing agreements with these two countries so Spanish vessels could operate along the coasts of the disputed territory. It also—illegally—handed the two countries the "administration of the Territory" under the terms of the November 1975 Madrid Accords.

In 2002, US Secretary of State Colin Powell mediated a resolution of Spain's contention with Morocco over Parsley Island (Perejil/Leïla Island). In that same year, Prime Minister José Maria Aznar, during talks with President Bush, declared his opposition to the annexation of Western Sahara by Morocco. If in 1975 Spain bent to US will on the Sahrawi question, in July 2002 Madrid publicly expressed opposition to Morocco's intentions. Authorities argued that "Spain's wish is that there be a peaceful solution to this problem within the framework and resolutions of the United Nations."[86] During the war in Iraq, Madrid's alignment with Washington was linked to obtaining US backing on more pressing issues, such as the security of Spain's southern borders; the defense of the Spanish enclaves of Ceuta and Melilla in northern Morocco; and access to the Atlantic zones potentially rich in hydrocarbon resources that surround the Canary Islands.

After nearly one hundred years of colonial dominance, Spain had concluded in 1974 that independence of the Western Sahara was inevitable. Although Madrid had hoped that the Sahrawis would maintain close ties with Spain after independence, they failed to keep the country's commitment to organize a referendum on self-determination. The transfer of administration (or "de-administration") to Morocco and Mauritania had been made to give Spain some flexibility as it pursued a complex policy, the aim of which was to balance its relationship with the Maghrebi protagonists. Paradoxically, though conservative governments in Spain have been closer to international legality and Spain's historic responsibilities, they also fear a Moroccan political and popular backlash. Following the March 11, 2004, bombings in Madrid that Moroccans and Spaniards of Moroccan origin committed, Zapatero's socialist government publicly feared that the result might be more bombings. The government stirred up the potential terrorist fear to reduce pressure on the government, as Spanish civil society wholeheartedly supports the Sahrawis. The Zapatero government criticized its conservative predecessor, arguing that attachment to international legality was sheer hypocrisy and that the neutrality of the Aznar government was synonymous with inertia.

Current Spanish policy vacillates between aligning with France's position and returning to a solution within the UN framework. Spanish officials rejected the Baker Plan II and promised to submit a better alternative, a promise they never fulfilled, probably because of US support for an autonomy plan. At other times, they aligned their position with France and called for a solution that was acceptable to Morocco. The Spanish government contended that since Morocco would never accept a solution that did not conform to its wishes, it was best to propose a solution that Morocco would agree to. In other words, Sahrawis can aspire to some autonomy but not an independent state. During the same period, Zapatero and his foreign minister, Moratinos, called on Morocco and Algeria to settle their differences in order to find a solution to the conflict. Moratinos even argued that Spain and France should pursue the same line in the Maghreb. These contradictions derive from a number of factors. Immediately after the fall of the Aznar government, Moratinos declared:

> Relations with Morocco are a priority for Spain. It is deplorable that the creation of a permanent crisis with Morocco has been allowed. Our priority will be to establish a privileged relation with Morocco. More than ever, complicity should exist between Spain and Morocco, between France, Spain and Morocco, and between France, Spain, Morocco and the Maghreb.[87]

While at times Spain appears to have no policy at all or is far from consistent, some observers saw in this the development of a new Paris-Madrid-Rabat axis. Shelley summarizes these contradictions and confusion in Spanish policy toward the conflict:

> Madrid does not have the strength necessary to mediate in the conflict. Fear of illegal migration, drug smuggling, terrorism, and pressure over Ceuta and Melilla have left the Spanish government frightened of offending Rabat, it seems. At the same time Madrid wants the friendship of Algiers and is unwilling to court unpopularity at home by openly repudiating Sahrawi rights. Algerian natural gas and liquefied natural gas is increasingly important to Europe, and the gradual liberalization of the upstream industry has attracted oil company interest in Europe and North America. Meanwhile, the government in Madrid is besieged by regional administrations, political parties and lobby groups that support POLISARIO.[88]

Overcoming the contradictions of its own policies may be a nearly impossible task. Spain has been trying to reassert its influence in the region but finds itself in a diplomatic hard spot. Alienating either Morocco or Algeria on the question of Western Sahara would weaken rather than increase its influence.

The dilemma explains why during Zapatero's visit to Algeria in December 2006, he and Bouteflika issued a joint communiqué that included a passage on the conflict in Western Sahara. The two parties "reaffirmed their attachment to a just and definitive solution to the conflict within international legality and pertinent United Nations resolutions, in particular resolutions 1495 and 1541 of the Security Council, which consecrate the right to self-determination of the Sahrawi people." They also committed to encouraging Sahrawis and Moroccans to establish direct dialogue within the UN framework.[89] Despite the communiqué, Algerians still blame Spain for the shift in its traditional neutrality on Western Sahara to a pro-Moroccan bias and indifference toward the plight of the Sahrawis. The result of this disaccord was Spain's failure to obtain an agreement on Algerian natural gas through which Spain would receive a preferential tariff. This gas issue has strained relations since the first half of 2007. Spain's perceived alignment with Morocco at the expense of the Sahrawis and Algeria's interests complicated the issue and the relationship as a whole. But Spanish-Algerian relations could not remain strained for too long. Even during the gas crisis, in late July 2007, Moratinos described Spain's relations with Algeria as a "model for the countries in the region."[90] For decades, Spain pursued a policy of "active neutrality" and respect for UN resolutions. But, as a Spanish analyst correctly points out, Spain also faced a dilemma:

> All democratic Spanish governments have been trapped between pressure of public opinion in support of a referendum on self-determination in Western Sahara and *Realpolitik*, out of the belief that putting too much pressure on the Moroccan regime to adhere to international legality would ultimately produce its downfall. This could initiate a period of instability and perhaps even chaos in the country, resulting in grave consequences for Spain.[91]

But the Spanish government has broken with the "active neutrality" and has decidedly supported Morocco's autonomy plan. Indeed, during his visit to Morocco in December 2008, Zapatero supported the Moroccan autonomy plan, describing it as a "positive contribution," and encouraged the parties to show flexibility.[92] Zapatero has also claimed that Spain's successful regionalization model, which grants autonomy to various provinces, would serve as a good model for Moroccans to emulate.[93] What Zapatero omitted to mention is that Spain is a constitutional monarchy, while Morocco is an absolute, authoritarian monarchy.

CONCLUSION

The stalemate in Western Sahara is a destabilizing factor throughout the Maghreb subregion. While regional integration requires normalization between

Algeria and Morocco, the Moroccan occupation of Western Sahara cannot be brushed under the carpet. Allowing Morocco to absorb Western Sahara illegally would aggravate tensions between the two countries and potentially lead to new conflict. Ceding the disputed territories would confirm Moroccan irredentism and threaten Algeria's national security interests. Furthermore, such a decision would also greatly discredit the United Nations and the charter on which it was founded. Fernando Aria Salgado, Spain's former ambassador to Morocco, explained the matter clearly. One needs to remember that the right to self-determination of the Sahrawi people is, "according to International Law, a norm of 'jus cogens' that is, one which binds not only the United Nations as an institution, but also all the member states, as established by the International Court of Justice to resolve territorial disputes derived from colonization."[94]

If genuine negotiations between Sahrawis and Moroccans regarding the post-referendum outcome actually came to pass, the impact on the region would be considerable. Unfortunately, so far such talks have not broken the stalemate. No doubt, resolving the conflict would lay the foundation for future cooperation and facilitate regional integration in North Africa. Numerous Sahrawi leaders have contended repeatedly that, should they lose a free and fair referendum, they would join with the Kingdom of Morocco. Beyond their vocal expression of goodwill, they are willing to negotiate on issues pertaining to economic, regional, political, and security affairs before the referendum is even held. Should they win the referendum, Sahrawi leaders claimed, they would allow Moroccan settlers to remain in the Western Sahara as legal residents provided they abide by the laws of the Sahrawi Republic. Unfortunately, Morocco's rejection of the Baker Plan II, which includes many elements that Moroccans themselves had proposed, proves that the monarchy wants nothing less than annexation of the territory. As many analysts have demonstrated,[95] the Moroccan autonomy plan has little chance of being accepted by Sahrawis or Algerians even as a basis for negotiation unless Morocco is willing to also discuss the independence option. In the 1950s, the example of Eritrea demonstrated how easily an occupying power, especially a kingdom where the monarch enjoys incredible prerogatives and powers, can renege on agreed arrangements. For geopolitical reasons, the United States allowed Ethiopia, a US ally, to swallow Eritrea in the 1960s. Should that same scenario occur, there is no reason to believe that the United States, France, or Spain would act differently toward Morocco today. The International Crisis Group stated the matter clearly. "The autonomy proposal . . . falls short of what is required to secure the agreement of the POLISARIO Front or Algeria to a settlement of the conflict on the basis of Moroccan sovereignty, and this proposal accordingly needs either to be amended substantially or replaced by a fresh proposal."[96] Resolution 1783, which the UN Security Council passed on October 31, 2007, reflected the United States and France's preference for Morocco's autonomy plan. This was also clear in UNSC Resolutions 1813 of April 2008 and 1871 of April 2009, which welcome "serious and credible Moroccan efforts to move the process forward towards resolution"—in other words, the autonomy plan—while only "taking note of the POLISARIO Front proposal presented 10 April 2007 to the Secretary-General," demonstrates, if need be, US (at least until recently) and French bias in favor of Morocco at the expense of Sahrawis' rights. Interestingly, though, UNSC Resolution 1813 extended MINURSO for another year, instead of the traditional six months, perhaps to give the new Obama administration time to carry on the question. UNSC 1871, too, has extended MINURSO for another year this time to perhaps give enough time for Ross to help the parties reach an agreement. In the meantime, however, the plight of the Sahrawis remains unchanged. Given the low priority that the Sahrawi question has in Washington, one can only be skeptical as to the prospects of a just solution. But the way this question is resolved will say much about the way international relations will be heading. A resolution based on international legality and a negotiated political settlement that takes into account Sahrawis' rights and Moroccan, Algerian, and Mauritanian interests will provide much more credibility to the United Nations and international law. It would undoubtedly lay the foundations for security and stability in the region. If, on the contrary, the conflict is decided without regard for international legality or the interests of the parties other than Morocco—that is, in favor of the invader and without a genuinely agreed-upon solution—then one can expect to have a powder keg in the western part of the Arab world.

NOTES

* This chapter draws from my articles "Stalemate in Western Sahara: Ending International Legality," *Middle East Policy* 14, no. 4 (Winter 2007–2008): 158–177, and "Le Conflit du Sahara Occidental: Une Décolonisation inachevée," *Les Débats* (Algiers), November 27–December 6, 2007, pp. 16–19.

1. United Nations Security Council, "Letter dated 29 January 2002 from the Under-Secretary-General for Legal Affairs, the Legal Counsel, addressed to the President of the Security Council," S/2002/161, February 12, 2002. In a conference in December 2008, Hans Corell elaborated further on the opinion. See "The Legality of Exploring and Exploiting Natural Resources in Western Sahara," www.havc.se/res/SelectedMaterial/20081205pretoriawesternsahara1.pdf, accessed October 22, 2009. See also, Marcel Brus, "The Legality of Exploring and Exploiting Mineral Resources in Western Sahara," in *International Law and the Question of Western Sahara*, ed. Karin Arts and Pedro Pinto Leite (Leiden, Netherlands: International Platform of Jurists for East Timor, 2007), pp. 201–216. Members of the European Parliament have denounced the fishing agreement between the European Union and Morocco because it allows European vessels to fish off the Western Saharan coast. Western Sahara Resource Watch (www.wsrw.org/index.php?parse_news=single&cat=105&art=683) documents the illegal exploitation of Western Sahara's resources by Morocco and foreign firms. Undoubtedly, the fishery agreements between the EU and Morocco amount to an implicit recognition of Morocco's sovereignty over Western Sahara.

2. See Jean-Paul Le Marec, "Exploitation illégale des ressources naturelles du Sahara occidental," www.arso.org/LemarecResnat0106.pdf. See also the France-Libertés Foundation's 2002 investigation in Western Sahara, which documents the exploitation of the occupied territory by the Moroccans and the exclusion of the Sahrawis from such benefits. See France-Libertés, *Report: International Mission of Investigation in Western Sahara* (Paris: France-Libertés/AFASPA, 2003).

3. Toby Shelley, *Endgame in the Western Sahara: What Future for Africa's Last Colony* (London: Zed Books, 2004); Yahia H. Zoubir and Daniel Volman, eds., *International Dimensions of the Western Sahara Conflict* (Westport, CT: Praeger, 1993); Tony Hodges, *Western Sahara: The Roots of a Desert War* (Westport, CT: Lawrence Hill, 1983); John Damis, *Conflict in Northwest Africa: The Western Sahara Dispute* (Stanford, CA: Hoover Institution Press, 1983).

4. See Yahia H. Zoubir, "The United States and Morocco: The Long-Lasting Alliance," in *Handbook on US-Middle East Relations*, ed. Robert Looney (London and New York: Routledge, 2009), and Yahia H. Zoubir, "Algeria and U.S. Interests: Containing Radical Islamism and Promoting Democracy," *Middle East Policy* 9, no. 1 (March 2002): 64–81. This observation is confirmed by former US Secretary of State James A. Baker III; see "Former U.S. Secretary of State, and former Personal Envoy of the U.N. Secretary General to Western Sahara, James A. Baker III, Discusses the Protracted Conflict in Western Sahara with Host Mishal Husain," PBS, August 19, 2004, www.pbs.org/wnet/wideangle/shows/sahara/transcript.html, accessed August 22, 2004.

5. See Jacob Mundy, "Neutrality or Complicity? The United States and the 1975 Moroccan Takeover of the Spanish Sahara," *Journal of North African Studies* 11, no. 3 (September 2006): 275–306.

6. See the special dossier, "Maghreb: les dessous d'une course à l'armement," *El Watan* (Algiers), May 21, 2009, pp. 1–4.

7. Sixteen non-self-governing territories, including Western Sahara, remain on the committee's list. Quotation is from UN Press Release SG/SM/9155-GA/COL/3091, February 11, 2004.

8. For a recent, rigorous treatment of the question of Western Sahara from a legal point of view, see Christine Chinkin, "Laws of Occupation," paper presented at the International Conference on Multilateralism and International Law, with Western Sahara as a case study, Pretoria, South Africa, December 4–5, 2008, www.arso.org/ChinkinPretoria2008.htm, accessed January 28, 2009.

9. Abdelkhaleq Berramdane, *Le Sahara occidental—Enjeu maghrébin* (Paris: Karthala, 1992).

10. For a detailed analysis, see Yahia H. Zoubir, "Algerian-Moroccan Relations and Their Impact on Maghrebi Integration," *Journal of North African Studies* 5, no. 3 (Autumn 2000): 43–74. The arguments the author discussed then have remained the same to this date.

11. Yahia H. Zoubir, "In Search of Hegemony: The Western Sahara in Algerian-Moroccan Relations," *Journal of Algerian Studies* 2 (1997): 43–61.

12. See Mohamed Sadek Loucif, "Son premier ministre revendique Tindouf: Le Maroc franchit la ligne rouge!" *L'Expression* (Algiers), January 13, 2009, p. 2, www.lexpressiondz.com/article/2/2009–01–13/59619.html, accessed January 13, 2009.

13. K. Abdelkamel, "Ses dirigeants ont saisi Kofi Annan pour 'récupérer' le sud-ouest algérien—Un parti marocain revendique Béchar," *Liberté*, March 15, 2006. Moroccan

officials condemned the organization as illegal and apparently decided to try its leader, Mohamed Alouah. See Abdellah Ben Ali, "Mohamed Alouah poursuivi par la justice marocaine—Rabat rassure Alger," *Maroc-Hebdo*, November 14–20, 2003, www.maroc -hebdo.press.ma/MHinternet/Archives_580/html_580/rabat.html. An even more recent minor incident occurred in late July 2007 when Moroccan officers entered seven meters into Algerian territory with their bulldozers to build a road, claiming they were on Moroccan territory. See C. Berriah, "Incident à la frontière algéro-marocaine," *El Watan*, July 26, 2007, online edition.

14. For an extensive study of Algeria's Africa policy, see Slimane Chikh, *L'Algérie: porte de l'Afrique* (Algiers: Casbah Editions, 1999).

15. On the conflict, see Alf Andrew Heggoy, "Colonial Origins of the Algerian-Moroccan Border Conflict of October 1963," *African Studies Review* 13, no. 1 (April 1970): 17–22.

16. John Damis, "The Western Sahara Dispute as a Source of Regional Conflict in North Africa," in *Contemporary North Africa*, ed. Halim Barakat (Washington DC: CCAS, 1985), pp. 139–140.

17. Jacques Rousselier, "Elusive Sovereignty—People, Land and Frontiers of the Desert: The Case of the Western Sahara and the International Court of Justice," *Journal of North African Studies* 12, no.1 (March 2007): 55–78.

18. www.icj cij.org/icjwww/idecisions/isummaries/isasummary751016.htm.

19. For a detailed account of Moroccan investments in occupied Western Sahara, see Yahia Zoubir, "Western Sahara Conflict Impedes Maghreb Unity," *Middle East Report* 20, no. 163 (Special Issue: North Africa Faces the 1990s, March–April 1990): 28–29.

20. Erik Hagen, "Norwegians Shipping Phosphates from Western Sahara," *Norwatch*, June 17, 2007, www.vest-sahara.no/index.php?parse_news=single&cat=49 &art=538. See also, Western Sahara Resource Watch, www.wsrw.org/index.php?parse _news=single&cat=105&art=683.

21. For a detailed analysis of the role of oil companies in Western Sahara, see Philippe Riché, "Le Maroc ouvre le territoire du Sahara Occidental à l'exploitation pétrolière," *ARSO*, July 2004, www.arso.org/ressnat3.html; see also "Campaign to Stop Oil Exploration in Western Sahara," *afrol News*, June 30, 2004, www.afrol.com/articles/13488.

22. International Mission of Investigation in Western Sahara, January 2003, fifty pages, www.france-libertes.fr.

23. UN Security Council, S/2002/161, "Letter dated 29 January 2002 from the Under-Secretary-General for Legal Affairs, the Legal Counsel, addressed to the President of the Security Council," February 12, 2002.

24. S/2000/461, May 22, 2000.

25. S/RES/ 1309, July 25, 2000.

26. S/2001/613, June 20, 2001.

27. Author's personal files.

28. A good analysis of the plan can be found in Toby Shelley, "Behind the Baker Plan for Western Sahara," *Middle East Report Online*, August 1, 2003, www.merip.org/mero/ mero080103.html.

29. Interviews with Algerian officials.

30. www.news24.com/Content/Africa/News/965/8fdc609cf4694ebd90fa1be69c 4330e9/10-09-2009-10-30/UN_W_Sahara_refugees_forgotten.

31. On the uprising in the territory, see Maria J. Stephan and Jacob Mundy, "A Battle-field Transformed: From Guerrilla Resistance to Mass Non-Violent Struggle in the Western Sahara," *Journal of Military and Strategic Studies* 8, no. 3 (Spring 2006): 1–32. Human rights abuses under Moroccan-occupied Western Sahara have been documented by governmental as well as nongovernmental organizations. See, US Department of State report 2008, www.state.gov/g/drl/rls/hrrpt/2008/nea/119123.htm; the ad hoc delegation of the European parliament, www.elpais.com/elpaismedia/ultimahora/media/200903/13/internacional/20090313elpepuint_1_Pes_PDF.pdf; and Human Rights Watch, www.hrw.org/en/reports/2008/12/19/human-rights-western-sahara-and-tindouf-refugee-camps.

32. Paragraph 48 of UN Report S/2002/178, February 19, 2002.

33. Anna Theofilopoulou, "Western Sahara—How to Create a Stalemate," US Institute of Peace briefing, May 2007, www.usip.org/resources/western-sahara-how-create-stalemate, accessed October 22, 2009.

34. Author's interview with high-level American official, US State Department, Washington, D.C., May 5, 2000.

35. See, for instance, www.moroccansahara.net/page.php?IDA=170.

36. The text of the proposal can be found on the Web site of the Moroccan Ministry of Foreign Affairs, www.maec.gov.ma/Initiative/En/Default.htm.

37. Carlos Ruiz Miguel, "The 2007 Moroccan Autonomy Plan for Western Sahara: Too Many Black Holes," *Grupo de Estudios Estratégicos GEES* (Analysis no. 196), June 15, 2007, www.gees.org/articulo/4141/.

38. Theofilopoulou, "Western Sahara—How to Create a Stalemate."

39. "Political Proposal of the Frente Polisario for a Mutually Acceptable Political Solution that Provides for the Self-Determination of the People of Western Sahara," presented to the UN Secretary-General on April 10, 2007, www.arso.org/PropositionFP 100407.htm#en.

40. Ibid.

41. For a thorough analysis of both proposals and their shortcomings, see International Crisis Group, "Western Sahara: Out of the Impasse," *Middle East/North Africa Report* no. 66, June 11, 2007.

42. "Texte du discours de SM le Roi à l'occasion de la Fête du Trône, " *Maghreb Arabe Presse*, July 30, 2007, www.map.ma/fr/sections/boite1/texte_du_discours_de/view.

43. "Communiqué of the Personal Envoy of the Secretary-General for Western Sahara," http://appablog.wordpress.com/2008/01/09/communique-of-the-personal-envoy-of-the-secretary-general-for-western-sahara-communique-de-l%e2%80%99envoye-personnel-du-secretaire-general-pour-le-sahara-occidental/, accessed January 2, 2009.

44. Interviews with Sahrawi representatives involved in the negotiations in New York.

45. Yahia H. Zoubir, "The Geopolitics of the Western Sahara Conflict," in *North Africa in Transition: State, Society, and Economic Transformation in the 1990s*, ed. Yahia H. Zoubir (Gainesville: University Press of Florida, 1999), pp. 207–208.

46. *L'Expression* (Algiers), July 27, 2003.

47. *Libération*, October 10, 2003. [emphasis added]

48. *Le Monde*, November 26, 2003.

49. The best account of the Franco-Moroccan relationship can be found in Jean-Pierre Tuquoi, *"Majesté, je dois beaucoup à votre père": France-Maroc, une affaire de famille* (Paris: Albin Michel, 2006). In a recent book, a Moroccan journalist convincingly demonstrated

the complicity between France and the monarchy. Ali Amar, *Mohammed VI—Le Grand Malentendu* (Mohammed VI, The Great Misunderstanding) (Paris: Calmann-Lévy, 2009).

50. Interview with retired French admiral, Barcelona, December 4, 2006.

51. See Yahia H. Zoubir, "American Policy in the Maghreb: The Conquest of a New Region?" *Working Paper* No. 13/2006, Real Instituto Elcano (July 2006), www.r-i -elcano.org/documentos/250.asp.

52. Amel Zemouri, "Sarkozy à Alger pour une visite de travail—Un moment fort dans les relations algéro-françaises," *El Moudjahid* (Algiers), July 10, 2007, www.elmoudjahid .com/stories.php?story=07/07/10/1456583.

53. For a good analysis of France's policy in the Maghreb, see Jean-François Daguzan, "France and the Maghreb: The End of the Special Relationship?" in *North Africa: Politics, Region, and the Limits of Transformation*, ed. Yahia H. Zoubir and Haizam Amirah-Fernandez (New York and London: Routledge, 2008).

54. Stéphanie Plasse, "Nicolas Sarkozy, Mohammed VI: une amitié économique," *Afrik.Com*, October 24, 2007, www.afrik.com/article12762.html.

55. "U.N. Council Favors Informal Talks on Western Sahara," Reuters, April 30, 2009.

56. UNSC 1871, April 30, 2009.

57. See Karima Benabdallah, "The Position of the European Union on the Western Sahara Conflict," *Journal of Contemporary European Studies* 17:3 (December 2009), pp. 417–435.

58. Mundy, "Neutrality or Complicity?"

59. Yahia H. Zoubir, "Soviet Policy toward the Western Sahara Conflict," *Africa Today* 34, no. 3 (1987): 17–32.

60. Yahia H. Zoubir, "Moscow, the Maghreb, and Conflict in the Western Sahara," in Zoubir and Volman, eds., *International Dimensions*, pp. 103–125.

61. "Former U.S. Secretary of State, and former Personal Envoy of the U.N. Secretary General to Western Sahara, James A. Baker III, Discusses the Protracted Conflict in Western Sahara with Host Mishal Husain," PBS, August 19, 2004, www.pbs.org/ wnet/wideangle/shows/sahara/transcript.html.

62. *New York Times*, July 7, 1979, cited in Stephen Zunes, "The United States in the Saharan War: A Case of Low-Intensity Intervention," in Zoubir and Volman, eds., *International Dimensions*, p. 55.

63. These figures were calculated from the statistics provided by the US State Department Congressional Budget Justification for Foreign Operations, fiscal years 2004 and 2005.

64. www.state.gov/t/pm/64727.htm.

65. For detailed analysis of US-Moroccan relations, see Yahia H. Zoubir, "Morocco and the United States: The Long-Lasting Alliance."

66. Yahia H. Zoubir, "The United States and Algeria: Hostility, Pragmatism, and Partnership," in *Handbook of US–Middle East Relations*, ed. Robert Looney (London and New York: Routledge, 2009).

67. Agence France Presse, November 19, 2003.

68. Richard Boucher, spokesman, daily press briefing, Washington, D.C., July 9, 2004, www.state.gov/r/pa/prs/dpb/2004/34290.htm.

69. Cited in, Gabriela González de Castejón, "Entretien avec Gordon Gray," *Revue Afkar/Idées* 9 (Winter 2006): 15.

70. US Department of State, Office of the Spokesman, Media Note, Western Sahara, 2006/274, April 11, 2007.

71. C. David Welch, assistant secretary for Near Eastern affairs, "U.S. Policy Challenges in North Africa," statement before the House Foreign Affairs Committee, Washington, DC, June 6, 2007, www.state.gov/p/nea/rls/rm/2007/86511.htm.

72. Patrick Worsnip, "Les discussions sur le Sahara occidental s'achèvent sans accord," Reuters, August 12, 2007.

73. See US Department of State, Office of the Spokesperson, "Question Taken at the August 13 Daily Press Briefing," Washington, D.C., August 13, 2007, www.state .gov/r/pa/prs/ps/2007/aug/90870.htm.

74. www.state.gov/r/pa/prs/dpb/2008/may/104268.htm#security.

75. Clayton E. Swisher, "Elliot Abrams' Maghreb Plot," United Press International, April 13, 2008.

76. www.potomacinstitute.org/publications/studies/NorthAfricaPolicyPaper033109 .pdf. For an excellent rebuke of the report, see Jacob Mundy, http://concernedafrica scholars.org/the-potomac-sais-report-on-north-africa.

77. In March 2007, for instance, Moroccan Minister of Justice Mohamed Bouzoubab accused POLISARIO of collaborating with al-Qaeda in the Islamic Maghreb, a baseless accusation that angered Algerians. See "Le Maroc accuse le POLISARIO de lien avec Al-Qaeda," *L'Expression* (Algiers), March 12, 2007; see also, www.meknes-net.com/ actualites/Article,5923,.html. Moroccan lobbyists sought to convince members of Congress in Washington of such links (interview with US officials in 2007 and 2008).

78. In the letter, Obama stated: "I share your commitment to the UN-led negotiations as the appropriate forum to achieve a mutually agreed solution. . . . My government will work with yours and others in the region to achieve an outcome that meets the people's need for transparent governance, confidence in the rule of law, and equal administration of justice." Cited in "Obama Reverses Bush-Backed Morocco Plan in Favor of POLISARIO State," *World Tribune*, July 9, 2009, www.worldtribune.com/ worldtribune/WTARC/2009/af_morocco0547_07_09.asp.

79. Ibid.

80. See www.elmuhajer.com/statedepartment.php.

81. The United States has expressed interest in greatly developing military cooperation with Algeria, in addition to the already strong ties in various sectors. See Sonia Lies, "Les USA veulent élargir leur coopération militaire avec l'Algérie," *Toutsurlalgerie*, July 5, 2009, www.tsa-algerie.com/Les-USA-veulent-elargir-leur-cooperation-militaire -avec-l-Al_7367.html.

82. UNSC 1871, April 30, 2009.

83. Yahia H. Zoubir, "The United States and Maghreb-Sahel Security," *International Affairs* 85, no. 5 (September 2009): 977–995.

84. This section builds upon pp. 183–184, in Yahia H. Zoubir and Karima Benabdallah-Gambier, "The United States and the North African Imbroglio: Balancing Interests in Algeria, Morocco, and the Western Sahara," *Mediterranean Politics* 10, no. 2 (July 2005): 181–202.

85. For an excellent article on Spanish policy in the Maghreb, see Miguel Hernando de Larramendi, "La politique étrangère de l'Espagne envers le Maghreb: De l'adhésion à l'Union européenne à la guerre contre l'Iraq (1986–2004)," in *L'Année du Maghreb 2004* (Paris: CNRS, 2006), pp. 27–43. See also Haizam Amirah-Fernández, "Spain's Policy towards Morocco and Algeria: Balancing Relations with the Southern Neighbors," in *North Africa: Politics, Region, and the Limits of Transformation*, ed. Zoubir and Fernández.

86. *El Watan*, July 22, 2002.

87. "Les relations avec le Maroc sont une question prioritaire pour l'Espagne. Il est lamentable que l'on ait laissé se créer une crise permanente avec le Maroc. Notre priorité va être d'établir avec le Maroc une relation privilégiée. Plus que jamais, il faut qu'il y ait une complicité entre l'Espagne et le Maroc, entre la France, l'Espagne et le Maroc et entre la France, l'Espagne, le Maroc et le Maghreb." Interview of Miguel Moratinos in *Le Figaro*, April 5, 2004.

88. Toby Shelley, "Sáhara Occidental: esperando la conflagración," *Papeles de cuestiones internacionales* 91 (Fall 2005): 69–76. I wish to thank my assistant Imogen Crowle for the translation.

89. See *El Moudjahid* (Algiers), December 15, 2006.

90. Ghada Hamrouche, "Les relations algéro-espagnoles, 'un modèle pour les pays de la région,'" *La Tribune* (Algiers), July 26, 2007.

91. Amirah-Fernández, "Spain's Policy towards Morocco and Algeria," p. 354.

92. *El País*, December 17, 2008, reported in www.algerie-dz.com/forums/international/106416-el-pais-le-net-appui-de-zapatero-au-plan-dautonomie-au-sahara-est-significatif.html, accessed February 1, 2009.

93. "Sahara: Zapatero donne en exemple le modèle espagnol d'autonomie," Maghreb Arabe Presse, December 17, 2008, www.emarrakech.info/Sahara-Zapatero-donne-en-exemple-le-modele-espagnol-d-autonomie_a17288.html?voir_commentaire=oui, accessed February 1, 2009.

94. Fernando Aria Salgado, "El Sahara, en la ONU," ABC (Spain), June 28, 2006, available in French at www.arso.org/ABC280606.htm.

95. Ruiz Miguel, "The 2007 Moroccan Autonomy Plan for Western Sahara"; Theofilopoulou, "Western Sahara—How to Create a Stalemate"; International Crisis Group, *Western Sahara: Out of the Impasse*.

96. International Crisis Group, *Western Sahara: Out of the Impasse*, p. ii.

12

THE POLITICAL ECONOMY OF MODERN IRAQ

*Eric Davis**

WHAT IS POLITICAL economy and why is it important in the study of Iraqi politics? Political economy is an appropriate conceptual approach for understanding not only Iraqi politics but also political processes generally. Having been established during the latter part of the eighteenth century, political economy is not a new approach. In this chapter, I draw upon some of the insights it offers to examine aspects of Iraqi politics that other approaches often neglect. A political economy approach not only illuminates developments in the Iraqi political system that are often ignored, but it also can help us better comprehend critical processes that have significant consequences for the larger Middle East.

Political economy may be defined as a conceptual approach that studies the impact of the interaction of political and economic variables on political processes. There are two major traditions in political economy, both of which draw upon Adam Smith's classic study *An Inquiry into the Wealth of Nations.*[1] Smith's goal was to demonstrate that the wealth of nations did not lie in Mercantilism— the idea of establishing foreign colonies and exploiting them for their natural resources. Rather than plundering colonies for their gold, silver, and other precious resources, Smith argued, productivity was the key variable in developing a country's economy and wealth. However, he felt that England's traditional political elites, namely the monarchy and large landowners, attempted to use the state to hinder increased entrepreneurial activity and the productivity that ensued, in favor of more parasitic economic behavior, especially implementing mercantilist policies abroad and collecting rents on agricultural land in the domestic economy.

Smith attempted to answer the question "What gives a product its value?" in two ways. On the one hand, Smith argued for a labor theory of value, where a product's value is determined by the amount of labor embodied in it. On the other hand, he also developed a utility theory of value, where market demand determines a product's value. These ideas structured two political economy traditions. Theorists such as David Ricardo, Karl Marx, and others built on the labor theory of value to develop a *structural* and *holistic* approach to the study of macroeconomic processes and their impact on political change. A different school of thought, developed beginning in the late nineteenth century by such economic thinkers as William Stanley Jevons, Léon Walras, and Alfred Marshall, focused on microlevel foundations of economic change. Depending on what tradition is chosen, political economy can explain much of both macrolevel and microlevel processes of change.

The first model of political economy assumes that explaining outcomes that affect the entire political system must account for the impact of large-scale structural processes of change. Examples of such processes include extensive rural-to-urban migration caused by changes in a country's agrarian system, major redistribution of income based on the state's restructuring of taxation policies or even seizure of private property, the discovery of significant new mineral resources, such as reserves of oil and natural gas, that allow a country to improve its domestic economic performance, or major changes in trading patterns that either enhance or undermine a political system's stability.

The "big picture" approach that is central to political economy requires a holistic analysis that incorporates a wide variety of structural variables derived from the type of developments mentioned above. It also requires a historical approach because large-scale structural changes invariably are conditioned by developments that occur over lengthy periods of time. The historical approach that is a corollary to political economic analysis in turn necessitates a conceptual periodization of time. In other words, we need to delineate the particular characteristics of "conceptually bounded" temporal periods in order to isolate those variables that subsequently cause significant political, social, and economic change.

The second model of political economy focuses on individual actors rather than groups and large-scale structural developments. Economic and political actors are conceptualized as "utility maximizers" whose preferences and behavior are conditioned by a cost-benefit calculus. Actors weigh the costs of their behavior against the benefits or positive outcomes they expect to receive. The focus here is on the preferences or psychology of the individual actor and what motivates her or him to behave in certain ways. This approach led to the "economic theory of politics," perhaps best articulated in Anthony Downs's *An Economic Theory of Democracy*.[2] In this chapter, I am less interested in which of these two political economy approaches is theoretically preferable than in demonstrating how, when used in tandem, they can offer an effective analytic strategy for understanding a political system such as that of Iraq. Combining insights from both macrolevel and microlevel analysis can help explain much about political processes.

Political economy has been accused in both its macroanalytic and microanalytic approaches of reducing politics to economics. This not only is a simplification of the approach, but also ignores the fact that many political economists have demonstrated that political variables are often causative, bringing about major changes in a country's economy. One need only think of Franklin Roosevelt's New Deal of the 1930s to realize that the "causal chain" is by no means unidirectional. During the Great Depression, economics affected politics but politics likewise affected economics. Other critics argue that political economists ignore human agency. While this has been true in certain instances, that is not the manner in which political economy is understood and deployed in this chapter. Whereas political economic variables may establish the "necessary conditions" for political change, human agency must always provide the "sufficient conditions."[3] Put differently, without political actors mobilizing support for political decisions and policies, change cannot occur, no matter what types of structural conditions exist.[4]

THE ARGUMENT IN BRIEF

Iraq's integration into the world market during the late nineteenth and early twentieth centuries was part of a long-term process of European economic and ultimately political encroachment on the Middle East. This process culminated with Great Britain's occupation of Iraq after invading the country in 1914 and defeating the forces of the Ottoman Empire, which collapsed in 1918. Reneging on promises made to Iraqis that it had entered their country to bring about its independence, not to control it, Britain found itself confronted by a large uprising in 1920.[5] After suppressing the uprising at great cost, the British imposed a monarchy on Iraq through a rigged referendum in August 1921. Great Britain's handpicked king, Faysal I (1921–1933), a member of the Hashemite clan of the Quraysh tribe that traced its social origins to the house of the Prophet Muhammad, controlled the two Muslim holy cities, Mecca and Medina. His father, the sharif of Mecca, Hussein bin Ali, had negotiated with the British to lead an uprising against the Ottomans in exchange for an independent Arab state once World War I ended. Faysal, who led what came to be known as the Arab Revolt (1916–1918) against the Ottomans in the Hijaz and Levant, was seen by most Iraqis as an agent of British rule in Iraq. Consequently, the Hashemite monarchy lacked legitimacy throughout its rule. British attempts to control Iraq, first through a League of Nations mandate (1920–1932) and then through indirect rule by British advisers in Iraqi ministries, and to maintain local air bases, evoked a powerful nationalist response that ultimately led to the Iraqi army overthrowing the monarchy in July 1958.

The discovery of oil in 1927 only increased Western interest in Iraq.[6] The struggle for control of this critical national resource intensified nationalist protest. However, Iraqis fought not only colonial rule but also among themselves over the definition of political community, creating additional political instability. Two competing definitions vied for dominance. One emphasized Iraqi or *watani* nationalism, namely a focus on strengthening Iraq economically and politically as a nation-state. The other, pan-Arabism or *qawmi* nationalism, sought to make Iraq part of a new pan-Arab state that would purportedly recreate the glories of the early Arab-Islamic empires.[7]

A decade of instability between 1958 and 1968 resulted in Saddam Hussein's Baathist regime, which ruled Iraq until 2003. A twentyfold increase in oil prices between 1972 and 1980 allowed the Baathist regime to develop a highly repressive security apparatus and to co-opt a large segment of Iraq's intellectual and professional classes.[8] The massive influx of oil revenues enabled the regime to develop powerful and modern armed forces, which it used to initiate two major conflicts, the Iran-Iraq War (1980–1988) and the Gulf War of 1991. The massive uprising (Intifada) that followed Iraq's defeat in the Gulf War, and the repressive sanctions the United Nations imposed on Iraq after the Gulf War until 2003 as a result of the country's weapons of mass destruction program, created great suffering for the Iraqi people, making the attempted transition to democracy after the United States' overthrow of Saddam Hussein's regime in 2003 all the more difficult.

THE POLITICAL ECONOMY OF AGRARIAN TRANSFORMATION

Drawing upon political economy, the most important concept for understanding major political, social, and economic change in Iraq is its integration into the world market and that of the larger Middle East. In Iraq, this process had a major impact on transforming Iraqi social structure, which in turn had a significant impact on the rise of the Iraqi nationalism and nationalist movements. In terms of structural change, the causal chain is thus quite clear.

Nominally, Iraq remained a province of the Ottoman Empire until it collapsed in 1918. However, as the nineteenth century progressed, Iraq's economy increasingly became tied to and dependent upon the world market dominated by the industrializing states of Western Europe, especially Great Britain. The extent to which Iraq was integrated into the world market by the end of the nineteenth century was clear from the fact that, by 1914, Western Europe accounted for 70 percent of its foreign trade.[9] Already during the 1860s, British steamers began plying the Tigris River, indicative of Britain's growing interest in

Iraq's economic affairs. While petroleum usually comes to mind as Iraq's most significant economic resource, it did not become an important component of the economy until after its discovery in 1927. The British-owned Iraq Petroleum Company (IPC) assumed a central role in the Iraqi economy and heavily influenced the Iraqi national movement and political protest and change. Iraq's oil industry further tied Iraq to the European and the world market, a relationship that still exists to this day.

Although no longer a major determinant of Iraq's gross domestic product (GDP), the agrarian system, which provided the bulk of Iraq's revenues until the 1930s, constitutes the beginning of any analysis of Iraq's modern political economy. The military and economic pressures exerted upon the declining Ottoman Empire during the late 1800s provided a strong incentive for attempting to extract greater economic resources from its remaining Arab provinces, such as Iraq. Thus the Ottomans strove to sedentize Iraq's large tribal population during the latter half of the nineteenth century so they could collect taxes on agricultural land and produce. However, the empire also offered an important incentive, especially for the tribal leader (*shaykh*). For tribes that were willing to switch to agricultural production rather than traditional pastoral and animal husbandry pursuits, tribal shaykhs were given the opportunity to obtain partial title to the lands their tribes farmed. For the Ottomans, the resulting increase in tax revenues could be used to modernize the empire's military and hence more effectively confront European colonialism. For the shaykh, the new policy offered the right to become a powerful and wealthy landowner.

An unintended consequence of the large-scale socioeconomic change that the Ottomans set in motion was to significantly transform Iraq's rural social structure, especially the manner in which tribes were organized. A key change was the transformation of the tribal shaykh, who came to think of himself as a landowner and to view his land as a source of profit. The commercialization of the land among tribes that exchanged pastoral pursuits for sedentary agriculture dramatically altered the relationship between shaykh and tribesman as the economic and social distance between them increased. The egalitarian norms that had characterized the traditional pastoral tribe now were replaced by a social hierarchy based, in effect, on social class norms rather than those of tribal solidarity. As tribesmen became peasants and were increasingly exploited by the shaykhs, resentment and conflict developed within what was now a peasant-landlord relationship.

The tensions between shaykh and peasant were further exacerbated by the tendency of wealthy shaykhs to move to urban areas and to hire agents to collect rents and administer their rural land holdings. Known as *sirkals*, these agents came to be hated by the peasantry for their lack of interest in anything beyond extracting as much tax revenue as possible from the peasantry. As exploitation increased, peasants too began to leave the land and migrate to large urban areas, such as Baghdad and Basra. This migration of peasants, especially from the south of Iraq, became a flood during the 1940s and 1950s, setting the stage for considerable political change, especially after World War II.

Another Ottoman response to increased European economic, military, and political pressures was to expand the military. One mechanism for accomplishing this end was to increase the size of the army and seek Imperial Germany's assistance in training it. This process had a significant impact on Iraq as the Ottomans recruited large numbers of junior officers from their Arab provinces for training in Istanbul. Thus another dimension of the Ottoman efforts to halt European colonial intrusion on the empire was to socially and politically mobilize elements of Iraq and other Arab provinces by incorporating them into the Ottoman military.[10]

The Young Turk Revolt of 1908, which brought the Committee of Union and Progress (CUP) to power, was based on a new generation of reformist army officers. In addition to modernizing the military, they sought to impose European notions of nationalism and political organization on the Ottoman Empire. Instead of emphasizing the traditional Ottoman policy rooted in the shared Islamic identities that had provided the "social cement" designed to unite Turks, Arabs, and Kurds within the empire, the CUP adopted a "Turkification" policy. Imitating the European model that assumed that all modern nation-states shared a single language and historical-cultural heritage, the CUP sought to emulate what it saw as the formula for Western progress and development. This break with traditional Ottoman policy required a greater emphasis on the use of Turkish within the empire's remaining provinces. In Iraq, the emphasis on Turkish culture created major social disruption as Iraqis found themselves pressured to change their nascent educational system from Arabic to Turkish language instruction. More significant, the new emphasis on Turkification forced Iraqis of Arab, Kurdish, and other ethnic origins to question their social and political identity. It is not surprising that the rise of the modern Iraqi nationalist movement can be dated to the period right after the 1908 revolt.

The induction of significant numbers of Arabs into the Ottoman officer corps promoted the rise of Arab nationalism. Not only were Arab officers, as well as bureaucrats and intellectuals who were educated and trained in Istanbul, forced to question their identity, but the spread of European ideas of nationalism by the CUP affected them as well. A large number of secret societies devoted to local provincial and pan-Arab nationalism were established in Istanbul and in Iraq and the Levant. The most famous of these was the Covenant (*al-Ahd*), which included Arab officers and established branches in Syria and Iraq. From a political economy perspective, it is clear that not only did European encroachment on the Middle East affect the regional economy, but also it had a significant effect in stimulating new forms of political organization, political culture, and nationalism and nationalist organizations.

The history of British efforts to generate an uprising against Ottoman forces among the Arab tribes of the Hijaz after the onset of World War I is well known. The Arab Revolt of 1916–1918 included large numbers of Iraqi and Levantine offers who had been trained, ironically, by the Ottomans. Although the Arab Revolt did not result in the creation of an Arab state as had been promised to the sharif of Mecca in the Hussein-McMahon correspondence, the British did create a pro-British monarchy in Iraq under the rule of the new Hashemite monarch, King Faysal I.

A second concept that can be derived from the political economy of Iraq's integration into the world market and European colonial intrusion in both the Ottoman Empire and, after its collapse in 1918, directly into the Arab world is a change in identity politics. The social structural changes set in motion by the conflict between the declining Ottoman Empire and rising European colonial influence in the Middle East forced Iraqis to confront new forms of social and political identity. When the British occupied Iraq in 1917 and refused to cede political independence to Iraq, as they had promised all Arabs once the Ottoman Empire had been defeated, a massive uprising occurred, the June–October 1920 Revolution, in which members of all Iraq's religious confessions and ethnic groups united to oppose British rule.[11] While the uprising was suppressed, at great human and financial cost to the British, it did result in the creation of a powerful nationalist movement that continued to challenge British influence in Iraq until the overthrow of the Hashemite monarchy in July 1958.

Iraq had become not only economically important to the British by the end of the nineteenth century but also strategically important as a conduit to India, the crown jewel of the British Empire. The collapse of the Ottoman Empire facilitated greater control of the Middle East by the two great colonial powers, Great Britain and France. The entire region's importance increased once oil was discovered in Persia (Iran) in the first decade of the twentieth century and after the British switched from coal to oil power for their naval fleet in 1911.

Another element of political economy that emerges from our analysis is that of resource dependency. Once oil was discovered in several areas of Iraq in 1927, and then the Arabian Peninsula in the 1930s, the British became more closely tied to and politically involved in Iraq's internal affairs and those of other Arab oil-producing countries. Plentiful, of high quality, and relatively easy to extract, especially in the south, oil extracted by the Iraq Petroleum Company became a major component of Iraq's economy. That the company was British controlled, and paid the Iraqi government relatively small royalties for each barrel it extracted, was a constant source of political tension. It is not surprising that oil was a key factor in energizing the nationalist movement, which reached the height of its strength during the 1950s.

It can be argued, then, that Iraq's and the larger Middle East's integration into the world market during the late nineteenth and early twentieth centuries caused not only major economic but political and social change as well. It led to the political and ideological restructuring of the Ottoman Empire, which in turn stimulated Iraqis to search for a new form of political identity, given their inability and/or lack of desire to become integrated into the empire's new Turkish cultural identity. The collapse of the Ottoman Empire facilitated Great Britain's further expansion of economic and political influence in Iraq, allowing it to establish a monarchy to implement its interests in the country. Increasingly British control over Iraq's political economy, especially in light of Iraqi expectations of political independence after the war's end, stimulated the creation of a powerful nationalist movement that was ethnically and religiously inclusive.

Ironically, it was Britain's development of Iraq's economic infrastructure that set in motion the conditions for major political opposition to it. Creation of a national railway system was accompanied by the rise of a strong railway workers union. Development of the port of Basra, Iraq's only outlet to the Persian Gulf, resulted in a powerful port workers union. Most significant of all was the development of a large oil workers union, both at the point of production—the oil well—and in building the pipelines that carried Iraq's oil across the western desert through Jordan and Palestine, through Turkey to the north, and to the Persian Gulf in the south. In the 1940s, these unions became more powerful, especially during World War II, when Great Britain was allied with Russia and loosened constraints on union activity as a concession to the Soviets. Workers increasingly challenged British prerogatives in Iraq by demanding not just better working conditions and higher wages, but also an end to Britain's military presence in Iraq and support for the increasingly unpopular Hashemite monarchy.[12] Weakened by two world wars, the British found it increasingly difficult to suppress nationalist dissent during the late 1940s and 1950s.

The Cold War made Iraq's oil and strategic position important not just to the British but to the United States as well. Iraq became a critical ally as the United States implemented its policy of containment during the 1950s. In 1955, Iraq joined the Central Treaty Organization (CENTO). More commonly known as the Baghdad Pact because of the place of signing, the treaty incited huge protest demonstrations that hastened the overthrow of the Hashemite monarchy on July 14, 1958. Iraq's decision to withdraw from the Baghdad Pact in 1959 and seek closer ties with the Soviet Union led CIA Director Allen Dulles to remark that Iraq represented "the most dangerous situation in the world."[13] The supposed leanings of the new Iraqi leader Gen. Abdel Karim Qasim toward the communist bloc led the United States to support a successful coup d'état by the Arab Socialist Baath Party on February 6–7, 1963. Qasim was captured and summarily executed, and the new regime rounded up and killed or tortured and imprisoned thousands of communists, reformers, and democracy activists. This first Baathist regime was so brutal and repressive that it was ousted by the military in November 1963.

Qasim was by no means a communist, but rather a mild-mannered reformist. Like President Jacobo Arbenz Guzman in Guatemala, who was overthrown by the CIA in 1954, and Mohammed Mossadegh, who was Iranian prime minister from 1951 until he was toppled by the United States and the Iranian military in 1953, Qasim sought to improve the lot of the less fortunate and poorer sectors of society. However, the British refused to support the development of political institutions in Iraq, whether during the period of occupation from 1917 to 1920, during their League of Nations mandate from 1920 to 1932, or during the period of "informal control" from 1932 to 1958. The United States made the same mistake in failing to support reforms that might have led to a democratic transition in Iraq. Instead, its support for Iraq's first Baathist regime, which jailed, tortured, and exiled a large percentage of Iraq's democracy activists as well as its professional and intellectual class, dramatically weakened those social strata who advocated the implementation of democracy and the values of political and cultural pluralism and tolerance. The reform policies that might have led to a democratic Iraq instead paved the way for the authoritarian rule of the first Baathist regime in 1963 and then the second and far more pernicious Baathist regime under Saddam Hussein in 1968.

OIL AND THE CONSOLIDATION OF THE BAATHIST REGIME

The Vietnam War created a strong demand for oil in the early 1970s. As demand outstripped supply, global oil prices increased dramatically. Between 1972 and 1980, Iraq's oil revenues increased twentyfold. These windfall profits were critical to Saddam Hussein's ability to impose a highly repressive political system on Iraq. Saddam and the Baath Party were able to not only establish a highly effective security apparatus comprising seven intelligence services, but also to use oil revenues to co-opt a large number of political figures, intellectuals, and professionals as well. Iraq's sudden abundance of oil wealth also allowed the regime to establish a number of organizations through which it sought to shape public life, such as the General Federation of Iraqi Women (*al-Ittihad al-Amm li-l-Nisat al-Iraqi*), student organizations, and cultural institutions. Many of these organizations, such as the Union of Arab Historians (*Ittihad al-Mu'arrkin al-Arab*), emphasized Iraq's pan-Arab credentials and sought to make it the leader of the Arab world.[14] None of these developments would have been possible without the dramatic increase in oil prices and the consequent resources it placed at the disposal of the Baathist regime.

The impact of Iraq's oil wealth on politics is placed in stark relief if we consider the political power of the Baath Party when it came to power in July 1968. According to British Foreign Office reports at the time, as well as the assessment of the foremost student of the era, Hanna Batatu, the Baath Party had no more than a few hundred members during the late 1960s. Having suppressed the Nasserists, who had helped them come to power, within two weeks of the initial coup, the Baathists, apart from their front man, General Ahmad Hasan al-Bakr, were little known in Iraq. Indeed, between 1968 and 1973, the party was plagued by a number of unsuccessful coups that almost brought it down.[15]

One manifestation of the Baathist regime's weakness was reflected in its attempts to terrorize the Iraqi populace, as was evident in the hanging of fourteen innocent civilians in downtown Baghdad's Liberation Square in January 1969, nine of whom were young or elderly Iraqi Jews. Cynically accused of being "Zionist spies" during a show trial, the Jews, who had not had the resources or desire to leave Iraq, were chosen due to their marginal status in Iraqi society. The real purpose of the hangings was to send a message to the Iraqi populace at large that any opposition to the new regime would be met with severe repression. The regime's weakness during its early years was also evident in the National Front coalition that it entered with its historical nemesis, the Iraqi Communist Party, in 1973. Only when the regime felt that it had consolidated its power did it dispense with the Front in 1978, executing twelve communist government ministers in the process.[16]

OIL, WAR, AND AUTHORITARIAN RULE

A political economy approach is key to helping understand how a regime that initially enjoyed little legitimacy or support among the Iraqi populace rose to become one of the most powerful in the Middle East, turning Iraq into a major military power and initiating two of the most destructive conflicts of the twentieth century. The windfall profits from oil during the 1970s do not tell the complete story. In explaining the initial success of the second Baathist regime, the Iraqi populace's "political exhaustion" after ten years of violent coups and countercoups, and the deposed Arif-Yahya regime's complete lack of legitimacy due to the Iraqi army's poor performance in the 1967 Arab-Israeli War, must also be taken into account. While it would be unwarranted to attribute all of Iraq's problems to British colonialism, had the British used their significant influence in Iraq to foster the civil society building and democratic impulses that were part and parcel of much of the Iraqi nationalist movement, especially its Iraqi or *watani* wing, much of the violence and instability of the late 1940s and afterward might have been avoided, precluding the second Baathist regime's coming to power in 1968, with all the subsequent devastating consequences to which Iraq was subjected.

Fearing the power of the nationalist movement, which was largely urban based, the British established a separate legal system for Iraq's tribal areas in 1924, the Tribal Civil and Criminal Disputes Regulations, that set powerful shaykhs against the central government, thereby promoting political instability.[17] Rather than supporting reformists such as the Ahali Group (*Jamaat al-Ahali*) and the political party that grew out of this movement, the National Democratic Party, the British threw their considerable weight behind perennial prime minister Nuri al-Said, whose authoritarian policies, corruption, and rigging of elections made him despised among Iraqis. Further, had Great Britain not insisted on maintaining air bases on Iraqi soil after 1945, and had it been more open to the Iraq Petroleum Company's sharing revenues with the Iraqi government for the purpose of social development, it is doubtful that Iraq would have experienced the level of instability that ultimately led the army to intervene and overthrow the monarchy.

WAR AND THE BAATH PARTY'S DEMISE

In September 1980, Saddam Hussein ordered the Iraqi army to attack Iran, a decision that was affected by several considerations. On the one hand, Saddam was concerned by the increase in Shia activism in Iraq, particularly that of the Islamic Call Party (*Hizb al-Dawa al-Islamiya*). Already in 1977 the police had been used to suppress a demonstration in al-Najaf by Shia who demanded to be allowed to celebrate the Ashura ritual commemorating the death of the founder of Shiism, Imam Ali ibn Abi Talib, who was martyred in 661 CE. Once Shah Muhammad Reza Pahlavi was overthrown in neighboring Iran, which fell under the forces of radical Islamists, Saddam feared that Iran's Islamic revolution might become a model that Iraq's religiously oriented as well as secular Shia might try to emulate.

From another perspective, Saddam viewed the overthrow of the shah's regime as a potential opportunity. Here we can change levels of analysis and examine Saddam's "rational calculus" at the time. Viewing the chaos that had enveloped Iran after 1979, including the execution of many of the shah's top military officers, Saddam felt that Iraq's army could quickly defeat Iran, thereby not only ridding him of Ayatollah Ruhollah Khomeini's regime, which continued to broadcast vituperative radio broadcasts castigating the Baathist regime, but he could make Iraq the dominant power in the Persian Gulf and bring the region's vast oil wealth under his control. Instead of achieving an easy victory, Iraq's army became bogged down in one of the costliest conflicts of the twentieth century. During the eight-year war, Iraq lost hundreds of thousands of soldiers and suffered severe damage to its oil industry and its larger economy. The decision to invade Iran in 1980 was the beginning of the long decline of Saddam's Baathist regime, which ended with its overthrow in April 2003.

By 1984, Iraqi forces were on the defensive. In 1986, the Iranian army threatened to cut Iraq off from the Persian Gulf by capturing the Fao Peninsula south of the port city of Basra. Clearly, Saddam underestimated the fervor with which much of the Iranian army was motivated to defeat Iraq, especially the young shock troops, or Basij, whose task was to clear minefields with Ayatollah Khomeini's promise of immediate martyrdom should they perish.[18] However, once again Iraq's oil wealth played a critical role in the country's politics. Fearing an Iranian victory, which could potentially spread Islamic radicalism throughout the Persian Gulf and Arabian Peninsula, the United States and other Western nations provided Saddam's regime with critical intelligence, financial aid, weaponry, and dual-use technology with which Saddam developed his chemical, biological, and nuclear weapons program. Saudi Arabia and Kuwait provided huge loans to offset Iraq's inability to export oil from its southern oil fields.

Saddam's development of a weapons of mass destruction (WMD) program proved critical to forcing the Iranian regime to reluctantly agree to a truce in July 1988. Following the war's end, Saudi Arabia and Kuwait, now more fearful of Saddam's million-man battle-tested army than of Iran, increased their oil output, driving down prices. They also demanded that Iraq repay the large loans they had made during the war. Saddam angrily retorted that the loans should be forgiven because Iraq had prevented Islamic revolution from spreading to the Arabian Peninsula and the Arab Gulf states. Saudi Arabia's and Kuwait's goals were to prevent Saddam from acquiring the funds that would allow his Baathist regime to rebuild the country. The drop in oil prices seriously compromised the Baathist regime's ability to return to the status quo ante and to give Iraqis the prosperity of the 1970s that Saddam had promised once the war ended. A purported coup by 178 army officers in 1988 pointed to the widespread discontent Iraqis felt at the sacrifices they had been forced to make during the war with Iran.[19] Most analysts agree that the need for funds to engage in social and economic reconstruction was a key variable in Saddam's decision to invade and seize Kuwait in August 1990.

The Gulf War of January 1991, capping months of negotiations in which the international community tried to force Saddam to withdraw from Kuwait, was a catastrophe for the Baathist regime. Estimates are that the bombing of Iraq by the UN coalition led by the United States resulted in massive destruction of its infrastructure and industrial sector, forcing Iraq back to economic levels of the early 1960s.[20] The subsequent national uprising of late February and March 1991 no doubt would have been successful had it not been for US intervention to save Saddam's regime. The most important decision the US military made was to allow Iraqi helicopter gunships to enter the air, after UN forces had forbidden Iraq at war's end to fly any of its aircraft on the threat of being shot down. The official reasons for this decision are still unclear. However, speculation was widespread that the United States feared that the collapse of Saddam's regime would lead to the breakup of Iraq, a critical oil-producing nation, and lead its neighbors to enter its domestic affairs if not parts of its territory. Further, the United States issued specific orders to its troops not to engage the Iraqi army. Perhaps most damning of all, US forces were ordered to destroy ammunition dumps in southern Iraq so they would not fall into the hands of insurgents.

UN SANCTIONS AND THE
RISE OF SECTARIAN IDENTITIES

During the 1990s, Iraq experienced one of the most severe sanction regimes ever imposed on a modern nation-state. The national economy and education system effectively collapsed. While the small political elite, whose inner circle comprised extended-family members and members of Saddam's tribe and Baathist loyalists, continued to live well through oil smuggling and funds hidden in foreign banks, the remainder of Iraq's populace experienced great suffering. Faced with salaries that were almost worthless, ration cards that failed to provide more than a small portion of a family's monthly food needs, and a lack of government services, Iraqis increasingly turned to traditional institutions, such as tribes, ethnic groups, and religion, to meet their material and psychological sustenance.

It was during this period that sectarian politics began to spread throughout Iraq. Under the guise of providing charitable services, many organizations that claimed to be religiously motivated used their activities to mobilize political and criminal groups. When Saddam implemented the so-called Faith Campaign (*al-Hamla al-Imaniya*) in 1993 that was headed by one of his trusted lieutenants, Izzat Ibrahim al-Duri, this policy provided still more opportunities for groups that claimed to be acting on religious grounds to pursue nefarious and parochial goals. Because the local community and institutions increasingly became the focus of individual Iraqis, the cross-ethnic interactions that had characterized Iraq prior to the 1990s began to break down. Iraqis no longer had the financial wherewithal to travel beyond their neighborhood, thereby reducing interactions among ethnic groups and regions. Therefore, it was no surprise that these groups emerged with a vengeance and institutionally strong in 2003 after the fall of Saddam's regime.[21]

The most powerful of these organizations was the Mahdi Army (*Jaysh al-Mahdi*, or JAM), led by the young cleric Muqtada al-Sadr. The Mahdi Army, which first became public in 2003, represented an extension of the activity carried on by Muqtada al-Sadr's father, Ayatollah Muhammad Muhammad Sadiq al-Sadr, who argued against the so-called quietist tradition of the Shia clergy. Following in the tradition of his brother Ayatollah Muhammad Baqir al-Sadr, whom the Baathist regime executed in April 1980 along with his sister Bint al-Huda, a theologian in her own right, Muhammad Sadiq al-Sadr wanted the Shia clergy to become more active in public and political life, rather than focusing on mobilizing large numbers of Shia in the poor Baghdad district of Revolution City (often called Sadr City after 2003), especially during the economically depressed years of the harsh UN sanctions. While Saddam thought initially that he might exploit Muhammad Sadiq al-Sadr's popularity after initiating the Faith Campaign, he soon realized that al-Sadr was using his ties to Saddam to attempt to undermine the regime. Realizing that al-Sadr could not be used to promote his regime's legitimacy, Saddam ordered him assassinated in 1999, along with two of his sons. Muhammad Sadiq al-Sadr's martyrdom infuriated the Shia and only increased support for the Sadrist movement, having the opposite impact from what Saddam had intended.

When the movement became known as the Mahdi Army is unclear. However, there is no question that it rose to serve the needs of poor and unemployed Shia, particularly youth, in the large, sprawling Sadr (Revolution) City area in northeastern Baghdad, as well as marginalized Shia in the cities and towns of the south of Iraq. Serving a clientele of the urban poor and migrants from rural areas, the Mahdi Army provided them with a sense of group identity and belonging, weaponry, and the idea that their actions would hasten the return of the Mahdi from occultation to make the world right according to God's will.[22] Most important of all, however, the Mahdi Army provides employment through an extensive criminal network that involves oil smuggling, extortion, kidnapping, and the seizing of property, including automobiles and houses, in neighborhoods it controls. Seen initially as protecting the collective interests of Iraq's Shia population, the Mahdi Army soon made significant enemies among the Shia middle classes due to its predatory behavior.[23] During the short period when the Sadrists were part of the Iraqi government coalition, between 2005 and 2007, it used the ministries it controlled, especially the Ministry of Health, to promote its corrupt and criminal activities as well as to promote sectarian policies, such as allowing sectarian forces to murder Sunni patients in hospitals under its control.[24]

The Mahdi Army has been largely viewed in terms of the ethnoconfessional model. This approach to understanding Iraqi politics assumes that all political actors function according to a "communal mind."[25] This implies that political attitudes and behavior are a function of one's ethnic or confessional (religious) background. Apart from this model's highly reductionist approach, it does not provide a good explanation or predictor of Iraqi political behavior. One of the main problems with this approach is that it ignores the main incentives for young Shia to join the movement. Most JAM members have a minimal formal understanding of Shiism and Islam. Indeed, many are unable to read or write. That unemployment has been as high as 60 percent to 70 percent among some segments of Iraqi youth is often ignored when analyzing JAM's appeal. If we realize that 65 percent of the Iraqi population is under the age of twenty-five and that rural-to-urban migration continues unabated, especially from the Shia south of Iraq, one does not need to draw upon sectarian identities as the main drivers of young Shia joining the movement.[26]

The ethnoconfessional model cannot explain cleavages both within JAM and between JAM and other Shia militias and political parties. A political economy approach draws our attention to the social class cleavages within the Shia community. The hostility of the Supreme Iraqi Islamic Council (formerly the Supreme Council for the Islamic Revolution in Iraq) toward JAM can be explained by the different social bases that characterize the two movements. The Supreme Council counts among its supporters many Shia merchants who distrust the urban déclassé masses, many of whom have tried to extort money from their businesses in the past or have stolen automobiles and seized houses in Shia neighborhoods.

The ethnoconfessional model cannot explain internal cleavages within JAM itself. While some are attributable to regional differences within Iraq's Shia community (especially those between the shrine cities of south central Iraq, such as al-Najaf and Karbala, and the area around the port city of Basra in the far south), there are also social class and generational fissures within JAM. The armed elements of the movement are largely uneducated and unconcerned with ideological issues. JAM units' efforts to impose social and political controls on Shia neighborhoods, whether in Baghdad or other Shia-dominated towns and cities, such as beating alcohol retailers or women who fail to wear the appropriate Islamic dress, are less about ideology than about intimidating the local populace with the goal of reducing challenges to their authority.[27]

Social class differences are noticeable within JAM itself. The clerical core of the movement is associated with the "Office of the Martyr" (*Maktab al-Shahid*) in Baghdad's Sadr City, named after the martyred of Ayatollah Muhammad Muhammad Sadiq al-Sadr. These clerics are not among Iraq's most prestigious mujahids. However, they are literate and educated in Shia religious texts. We also find parliament members associated with the Sadrist movement (*al-Tayyar al-Sadri*), such as bloc leader Nasser al-Rubai. Some of them come from professional backgrounds and look askance at the criminal activities of the armed militias. Thus social class and education have not only created cross-cutting cleavages within JAM and the larger Sadrist movement, but also have undermined its cohesiveness. While the armed wing of the movement is mainly concerned with economic gain, namely appropriating money and property, the clerics and the Sadrists' parliamentary allies' vision is to shape the movement into a powerful political party based in Baghdad and the south's large Arab Shia population.

In analyzing the Sadrist trend, we can draw upon both traditions of political economy to better comprehend JAM political behavior. In terms of macroanalysis, the structural conditions produced by the UN sanctions of the 1990s caused a major decline in the standard of living of the Iraqi populace, especially poorer elements of society, making criminal activity, such as oil and artifact smuggling, one of the few economic activities available to the poor. The collapse of the national economy and education system forced Iraqis to depend more on local institutions and notables, such as clerics and tribal leaders. These conditions were propitious for the rise of organizations led by what I call *sectarian entrepreneurs*. The continued decline of the agrarian sector, which was responsible for many youth migrating to urban areas in search of employment, provided a large recruitment base for sectarian political actors and groups. The agrarian sector's decline was further exacerbated by the unwise decision of L. Paul Bremer and the Coalition Provisional Authority (CPA) to eliminate agricultural subsidies in August 2003, which further undermined Iraq's farmers and caused a large migration to urban areas by making it more difficult for them to compete with Syrian and especially Iranian agricultural imports.

If the macroanalytical perspective helps us understand why marginalized sectors of the Iraqi populace chose to engage in criminal activity, a microanalytical perspective sheds light on how this criminal activity functioned. To sustain and expand their criminal activity, it was in the interest of sectarian entrepreneurs to promote hostility toward other ethnic and confessional groups. By promoting sectarianism, these entrepreneurs were able to impose vertical identities on the groups they controlled, thereby fostering greater social and political cohesion. In terms of a cost-benefit analysis, sectarian identities became a form of political and social currency that allowed sectarian entrepreneurs and the groups they controlled to achieve desired economic outcomes. An analysis of structural conditions and decision-making yields a convergence of the two levels of analysis when explaining sectarian identities in post-2003 Iraq. A political economy approach offers a much more instrumental understanding of sectarian-based politics in Iraq at the level of marginalized social classes than one that views such identities in "primordial" terms or some sort of static social and cultural given of Iraqi society.

This model can be applied to the post-2003 political elite, which includes more prosperous sectors of Iraqi society, namely the solid middle and upper middle classes. The arena of contestation that has preoccupied these social strata is the political disposition of Iraq's incredibly extensive and valuable hydrocarbon wealth. Specifically, there has been struggle within Iraq's political elite at multiple levels. First, and most prominently, this cleavage has pitted the Iraqi central government against the Kurdish Regional Government (KRG), which was formed after the 1991 Intifada and comprises the three Kurdish provinces in the country's northwest region. The KRG argues that it should be allowed to drill, extract, and export oil it discovers in the Kurdish region as long as it sends funds from oil sales to the central government to be distributed nationally according to population. Second, a cleavage developed after 2003 within Iraq's Arab Shia community between those who want Iraq's oil wealth controlled by the central government and those who want it controlled by a regional "Shiastan" comprising Iraq's nine southern provinces. This cleavage has set the Sadrists, al-Dawa Party, and al-Fadila Party (located in the Basra area) against the powerful Supreme Iraqi Islamic Council. Although the central government has prevailed thus far in this dispute, it may still reappear in the future. A similar dispute pits Shia politicians of the far south of Iraq, where roughly 60 percent of the country's proven oil reserves are located, against what they perceive as an attempt by Shia elites, especially the Supreme Iraqi Islamic Council, in the country's south-central shrine cities to seize control of their oil wealth. Yet another cleavage sets the rural Sunni Arab population of Ninawa, Salah al-Din, and Diyala, but especially al-Anbar province, which feels excluded by the lack of oil in the Sunni Arab regions, against the Kurds and Shia who live in provinces where oil is located. Although oil and natural gas were recently discovered along al-Anbar's border with Jordan and Syria, many Sunni Arabs still feel left out of the hydrocarbon equation—that is, they fear they will be excluded from benefiting from this critical resource.

Although the struggle over oil wealth is key to Iraqi politics and economic development given that it comprises 97 percent of the country's foreign revenues, the ethnoconfessional model tells us little about this struggle, because the political cleavages are as much within ethnic groups as they are among ethnic groups. By assuming that the political beliefs and behavior of Sunni and Shia Arabs, Kurds, Turkmen, and other ethnic groups are shaped by their ethnoconfessional background alone (the implicit notion of a communal mind), this model prevents us from understanding the important intra-ethnic divisions that shape contemporary Iraqi politics. Rather than three basic cleavages—Sunni Arab, Shia Arab, and Kurd—we find a multiplicity of divisions operating within the interstices of Iraqi politics. The existence of multiple cleavages reflecting the changing political identities given the political issue in question has important implications for a possible democratic transition in Iraq. Because issues of centralism versus regionalism divide different political elites and movements, we see that no one ethnic group or region can impose its will on the political system, thereby forcing negotiation and compromise. The important political patterns that are elucidated by the political economy model are obscured by the assumption of unitary collective behavior implicit in the ethnoconfessional model.

A political economy approach is highly effective in explaining intra-ethnic group political dynamics. In July 2009, the Change *(Goran)* List stunned the KRG by winning 41 seats in the 111-member Kurdish Regional Parliament. Once again, this development cannot be understood within the purview of a conceptual framework that emphasizes ethnic and confessional variables. Why was the Gorran List so successful?

While conducting interviews in the Kurdish region in 2005 and 2007, I found that many Kurds clearly resented the KRG for what they considered widespread corruption in the use and distribution of oil wealth. No Kurds I interviewed raised issues of hostility toward Arab Iraqis in the south (although it was likewise clear that there was still much distrust of the south). Instead, Kurds complained that, despite salary increases since 2003, inflation had outstripped these raises. A Kurdish economist informed me that data on the money supply within the KRG were unavailable, with the implication that the two main political parties, the Kurdish Democratic Party (KDP) and the Patriotic Union of

Kurdistan (PUK), did not want the populace to know how the KRG was spending its funds.

Using the ethnoconfessional model, we would assume that Kurds constitute a unitary political actor. Indeed, this is precisely the image that the KDP and PUK seek to present to the outside world. However, the PUK has always had within its ranks more reform-minded elements who seek to promote greater equity and democracy within the Kurdish community. When elements of the party broke away in 2009 to form the Change List, their main concerns were to break the political and economic stranglehold of the traditional elites within the KDP and PUK and to address the rising anger of the Kurdish population at the lack of employment opportunities in the KRG despite the availability of large amounts of oil wealth.

Another striking element of my research in Iraqi Kurdistan was the extent to which Kurdish and Arab businessmen had begun to pursue joint economic projects. Analysts who are captive to the ethnoconfessional model would not be prone to examining this type of activity. Some of this activity occurred under the auspices of the Iraqi-American Chamber of Commerce and Industry (IACCI), led by Raad Ommar, an Iraqi Arab businessman, while other activity was independent of the IACCI and resulted from Arab businessmen and engineers seeking to benefit from the stable investment environment in the north of Iraq. Once again, a political economy approach is instructive. The main incentive for Kurdish and Arab businessmen and professionals to cooperate was the ability to achieve profits from mutually beneficial economic activities. As they indicated to me, their different ethnic backgrounds were insignificant in their business transactions.

What these considerations indicate is not only the importance of oil to Iraqi politics—in contradistinction to the excessive emphasis that has been placed since 2003 on the role of ethnicity and confessionalism in the political process—but the concept of the rentier state. Many analysts feel that the main impediment to Iraq's attempted democratic transition is the ethnically and confessionally diverse character of its society. However, the March 2009 elections for provincial legislatures in the south of Iraq and the July 2009 KRG parliamentary elections in the north belie this emphasis. As the January 2010 elections approach, widespread cross-ethnic coalition-building is taking place between parties drawn from a wide variety of regions, ethnoconfessional backgrounds, and ideologies.[28]

A political economy approach suggests that the main impediment to democratization in Iraq is less its ethnoconfessional makeup than the possibility of a coalition of elites asserting monopoly control over the country's oil wealth. The rentier-state hypothesis argues that the ability of political elites to extract rents from the world market through the sale of hydrocarbons, be they petroleum or natural gas, obviates the need for the elites to respond to domestic pressures for democratic and social reforms. Put differently, the rentier state facilitates authoritarian rule by freeing the state from dependence on its citizenry for financial resources (taxes and other domestically derived revenues). Rather than focusing exclusively on ethnoconfessional politics, the political economy approach suggests the need to broaden our analytic horizons.

THE POLITICAL ECONOMY OF STATE CAPACITY

It is possible to divide Iraq's political development since 2003 into two periods. The period between the summer of 2003 and 2007 was characterized by intense ethnic-based violence.[29] The second, from 2007 to the present, could be referred to as a period of attempted democratic transition. In 2007 the Iraqi state was finally able to assert its control over areas dominated by sectarian militias such as JAM and the Islamic State of Iraq, an offshoot of al-Qaeda. The Iraqi army, which the United States had foolishly disbanded in 2003, was reconstituted and attained a sufficient level of training to allow Prime Minister Nouri al-Maliki to crack down on the Mahdi Army. Striking first in Basra in March 2008, where the Sadrists and their allies had treated the local populace in a particularly brutal manner, and then in the organization's Sadr (Revolution) City stronghold in Baghdad, the Mahdi Army proved no match for the Iraqi army, backed by US forces. Subsequently, Mahdi Army units surrendered without a fight in the critical border town of Amara, an important conduit for arms and drugs from Iran.

Maliki was assisted in asserting the central government's control by the US military's "surge" in 2007, which not only temporarily increased US force levels in Iraq, but also embedded American troops in neighborhoods to protect local inhabitants from insurgent groups and sectarian militias. Yet one of the key factors in stabilizing Iraq was confronting unemployment. The establishment of the "Awakening" (*al-Sahwa*) movement in al-Anbar province demonstrated the importance of putting young men to work. Once large numbers of rural and tribal Sunni Arab youth were given employment by the movement, with the United States providing salaries of $300 per month, not only did violence drop precipitously but the forces of al-Qaeda and the Islamic State of Iraq were quickly put on the defensive.

By late 2008, Iraq was emerging from the sectarian strife of the post-2003 era. The Awakening or "Sons of Iraq" movement had effectively defeated al-Qaeda and Islamic State of Iraq forces in al-Anbar province in northwestern Iraq, and Iraq's Shia were becoming increasingly disenchanted with the JAM and Shia militias and criminal organizations. These groups alienated and angered many of their erstwhile Shia supporters, who realized that their activities were not designed to protect the Shia community and that their ideological rhetoric was only a cover for rapacious behavior.

Once the Iraqi state was able to assert itself over most of the Arab south, Iraqis abandoned sectarian organizations. Public opinion polls since 2007 have indicated increasing support for secular political parties and revulsion at the excesses of the Mahdi Army and other sectarian militias.[30] Just when Iraq seemed to be making progress toward overcoming many of the problems it had faced since 2003, especially with improvement in the security situation, oil prices began to drop, from a high of $140 per barrel in the summer of 2008 to as low as $40 per barrel in 2009. The drop in oil prices forced the Iraqi government to scale back development projects and improvements in social services.

The drop in oil prices has made reaching an agreement with the Kurdish Regional Government over the distribution of oil revenues even more difficult. Having raised government salaries 30 percent in 2008, the Iraqi government in Baghdad found itself particularly pressed for funds. Facing pressure from nationalist deputies in the Iraqi parliament who feared a return to foreign control of Iraqi oil, the government's strict terms for oil leases led to only one contract being signed when the first auction for many of the country's oil fields that have yet to be explored was held in June 2009.[31] Thus Iraq is caught in a quandary between the need for foreign investment to modernize its aging and unproductive oil industry infrastructure and the need to assure Iraqis that the US-led invasion of 2003 was not really intended to transfer control of Iraq's oil industry to multinational corporations.

POLITICAL ECONOMY AND CONTEMPORARY IRAQI POLITICS

Due to the lack of access to the country by Western social scientists, Iraq was a relatively understudied society prior to 2003. The US-led invasion changed all that. According to the Bush administration, the fall of Saddam's regime was predicted to quickly bring about a revival of the Iraqi economy through oil revenues and an equally speedy transition toward democratization. When matters did not conform to the Bush administration's political script, and an insurgency began gaining steam during the summer and fall of 2003, many Western analysts flocked to focus on Iraq. It was at this point that many of them began blaming the disorder and violence in Iraq on the country's ethnoconfessional composition. The looting of Iraqi government ministries and offices in April 2003, when the US military was ordered not to intervene, destroyed whatever capacity to govern the state had previously enjoyed. The looting undermined Iraqi trust in American policies and confidence in the Bush administration's understanding of Iraq's political, social, and economic needs. Few Iraqis were willing to commit themselves to working with American occupation forces when they seemed to have, at worst, no plan or, at best, one that was ill defined and disorganized. The disorder that followed the collapse of Saddam's regime in

April 2003 reinforced the sinister views many Iraqis had of the US invasion. Iraqis had not forgotten the call by the administration of George H. W. Bush in 1991 to rise up and overthrow Saddam's regime, only to see the United States actively engage in preventing the uprising from succeeding.

The Interim Governing Council (IGC), was the first government since the founding of the modern state of Iraq in 1921 that was explicitly sectarian in composition. The manner in which the CPA structured the IGC in 2003 sent a message to Iraqis that sectarian identities mattered in post-Baathist politics. From a cost-benefit analysis, political actors were incentivized to behave in a sectarian manner. Because the United States relied so heavily on expatriate Iraqis to implement its policies after 2003, it became rational for many of them to organize their political programs according to sectarian criteria. However, organizing Iraqi politics along sectarian lines was not the pattern that had characterized Iraq in the past. Quite the opposite was true, as the majority wing of the Iraqi nationalist movement had emphasized cross-ethnic cooperation.

In stressing the sectarian nature of post-2003 Iraqi politics, many Western analysts largely ignored a number of critical variables that promoted ethnosectarian politics. First, they were largely unaware that the sectarian politics after 2003 was in large measure fostered by American policies, the worst of which was the disbanding of the ethnically integrated 385,000-man Iraqi conscript army in May 2003. Against the advice of Iraqi politicians and the US military, the Defense Department ordered the army disbanded. Along with firing approximately 125,000 public workers, according to the ideologically based decision that states have no right to intervene in the economy to create public sector firms, the CPA provided the growing insurgency with a large pool of potential recruits who were now unemployed but often had families for whom they were responsible. From a political economy perspective, it can be argued that the rise of the post-Baathist insurgency was as much a function of unemployment as it was ethnic or ideological variables. Many unemployed Iraqis simply joined the insurgency because they needed to provide for their families, not due to hostility toward the United States.

POLITICAL ECONOMY
AS DECISION-MAKING

As mentioned above, much current political economy eschews the large structural perspective that informs this chapter. How might the approach that emphasizes microfoundational processes, particularly decision-making on the part of significant political actors, be applied to Iraq? One way would be to examine the behavior of Saddam Hussein, whose political persona looms large in the politics of modern Iraq. Saddam was successful in building his power base within the Baath Party, and then within the Baathist regime that came to power in 1968, by focusing on controlling the intelligence services. In this sense, it could be argued that his behavior was quite rational and that he was successful in his efforts to implement his political preferences.

Yet, how do we explain the number of bad choices he made, such as invading Iran in 1980 and seizing Kuwait in 1991? These choices suggest that the environment in which Saddam made them presented a distorted view of reality. Having suppressed all opposition after removing Ahmad Hasan al-Bakr as president in 1979 and assuming the role himself, and executing all potential competitors for leadership of the Baath Party on trumped-up charges, Saddam cut himself off from one of the key prerequisites of the rational-choice underpinnings of microfoundational political economy, namely, sufficient and accurate information upon which to base decision-making. Having created narratives that distorted reality, Saddam convinced himself that these narratives about Iraqi history and society, and especially its military prowess, were true. The decisions he made after 1979 indicate much less acuity than do the decisions he made prior to that date. In other words, once Saddam had total power and had eliminated many top leaders in the Baath Party whom he viewed as potential rivals, but who could have provided him with important information and advice, he, as have many despots in the past, made choices that actually contravened his personal interests, ultimately leading to his overthrow, trial, and execution in 2006. This pattern has characterized many autocratic political leaders who have had few constraints on their behavior. Whether discussing Hitler, Mussolini, Saddam, or other would-be totalitarian dictators, there seems to be a strong correlation between autocratic rule and decision-making that works against the autocrat's interests.

Microfoundational political economy can also be applied to an understanding of many of the impediments to Iraq's attempt at a democratic transition after 2003. None of Iraq's neighbors want to see Iraq become a stable, multiethnic democracy, because such success would reflect poorly on their own authoritarian and sectarian policies. Thus the negative "neighborhood effects" that Iraq has encountered since 2003 with neighboring states interfering in its internal politics, whether Iran, Syria, Saudi Arabia, or Turkey, demonstrates that political elites in these countries have calculated that Iraq's success represents a potential loss of political influence and legitimacy. This calculation explains in large measure why these states have worked to prevent Iraq from democratizing and successfully engaging in political and social reconstruction, as evidenced by the continued bombings that afflicted Iraqi cities, even in late 2009.

WHAT POLITICAL ECONOMY CANNOT EXPLAIN

No model of politics and political change is all encompassing. This is true of political economy as well. While political economy is often very successful in delineating the "necessary" conditions for major political events, it has been less successful in explaining why political actors respond to structural change in the way that they do. As we have seen, several of the decisions Saddam made were foolhardy and actually undermined his regime. Instead of invading Iran in 1980, for example, Saddam's regime could have focused on using Iraq's vast oil wealth to transform Iraq into a modern state, a process that was already well under way before the war began.[32]

"Cultural politics" is another realm where a political economy approach is lacking. Saddam's development of a symbolic politics that drew upon Iraq's Mesopotamian civilizations, pre-Islamic Arab tribal past, Arab-Islamic heritage, and vast wealth of folklore (*al-turath al-sha'bi*) was critical in developing affective ties between the Baathist regime and the populace at large, especially those segments of society that benefitted politically and economically from regime policies. These bonds were sustained until Saddam squandered this legacy once Iraq became mired in what seemed to many Iraqis a never-ending war with Iran after 1982.

At the level of preferences, many theorists have asked why they are so frequently thwarted. Institutionalists argue that preferences always operate within a realm of constraints. These constraints present themselves in a formal manner, such as in the intricate regulations and procedures of parliaments, both Western and non-Western, and an informal manner, such as within the tribal structure of Iraq. Political economists who emphasize the microfoundational tradition need to put more effort into understanding the constraints political actors face when they make decisions that they hope will realize their preferences. For all his cunning and power, Saddam Hussein ultimately failed in his attempt to become the hegemon of the Persian Gulf and the leader of the Arab world.

SUMMARY

I have suggested that a political economy approach to the study of Iraqi politics can yield numerous conceptual and empirical insights. This is especially true once macrofoundational and microfoundational political economy are analytically integrated to bring together a focus on broad structural trends and variables with one that examines the determinants of the political behavior of important political actors and groups. Despite these benefits, political economy is not an approach that has thus far received adequate acceptance in the study of Middle East politics. Much of this resistance can be traced to the tendency of what Fareed Zakaria has termed "Islamic exceptionalism," namely the tendency to view Middle East politics through a conceptual prism based in narrow political cultural processes purportedly shaped by an ill-defined concept of Islam.[33] While the impact of Islam on politics in the Middle East cannot be denied, what we mean when we analytically deploy the concept of "Islam," and when we postulate a causal relationship between Islam, as an independent variable, and multiple dependent variables or outcomes, requires far more conceptual precision than has been exhibited to date. Resort to a political economy approach, as I have attempted to demonstrate, can not only provide an important palliative to such a political cultural approach but can potentially enrich it as well.[34]

NOTES

* The author would like to thank the Carnegie Corporation of New York for its support of research on Iraq while he was a Carnegie Scholar for 2007–2008.

1. New York: Modern Library, 1994.

2. New York: Harper, 1957.

3. In Marx's classical formulation in *The Eighteenth Brumaire of Louis Bonaparte*, "Human beings make their own history, but they do not make it as they please; they do not make it under circumstances chosen by themselves, but under circumstances directly found, given and transmitted from the past." Actors are critical, but they are constrained in what they are able to accomplish. This formulation is similar to the "New Institutionalism," which has sought to explain why individual preferences, a core concept of game theory, so often fail to be transformed into policy by political actors.

4. To continue on the New Deal analogy, had not Roosevelt and the US Congress adopted economic stimulus packages and implemented institutional change—for example, Social Security and bank regulation—it is conceivable that the American economy could have experienced an even more severe depression, if not a collapse. See Peter A. Hall, "The Role of Interests, Institutions, and Ideas in the Political Economy of the Advanced Industrialized Nations," in *Comparative Politics: Rationality, Culture and Structure*, ed. Mark Irving Lichbach and Alan S. Zuckerman (Cambridge: Cambridge University Press, 1997), pp. 174–207.

5. This uprising is known in Arabic as "the Great Iraqi Revolution," which occurred between June and October 1920. See 'Abd al-Razzaq al-Hasani, *al-Thawra al-Iraqiya al-Kubra* (*The Great Iraqi Revolution*) (Sidon: Matba'at Irfan,1952).

6. Already at the 1920 San Remo Conference, Great Britain, France, the United States, and Italy were contesting drilling rights in Iraq, even before oil had been discovered.

7. These empires included the Meccan Empire of the Rashidun, or first four "rightly guided" caliphs (632–661 CE), the Umayyad Empire (661–750 CE), which was centered in Damascus, and the Abbasid Empire (750–1258 CE), whose capital was Baghdad.

8. For a discussion of Saddam Hussein's Project for the Rewriting of History (*Mashru'a I'adat Kitabat al-Tarikh*), see Eric Davis, *Memories of State: Politics, History and Collective Identity in Modern Iraq* (Berkeley and London: University of California Press, 2005), esp. pp.148–199.

9. Mohammad Salman Hasan, "The Role of Foreign Trade in the Development of Iraq, 1864–1964," in *Studies in the Economic History of the Middle East*, M.A. Cook, ed. (London: Oxford University Press, 1970), pp. 348–353.

10. For a classic statement of the impact of social mobilization, see Karl Deutsch, "Social Mobilization and Political Development," *American Political Science Review* 54, no. 3 (September 1961): 493–514.

11. For a further discussion of the 1920 revolt, see W. J. O. Nadhmi, *The Political, Intellectual and Social Roots of the Iraqi Independence Movement, 1920*, PhD diss.,

School of Oriental Studies, Durham University, 1974; see also Davis, *Memories of State*, pp. 47–49.

12. On the Iraqi working class, see Eric Davis, "History for the Many or History for the Few? The Historiography of the Iraqi Working Class," in *Workers and Working Classes in the Middle East: Struggles, History, Historiographies*, Zachary Lockman, ed. (Albany: State University of New York Press, 1994), pp. 292–293.

13. Joe Stork, "The Soviet Union, the Great Powers and Iraq," in *The Old Social Classes Revisited*, ed. Robert Fernea and William Robert Louis (London: I. B. Tauris, 1991), p. 100.

14. Davis, *Memories of State*, pp. 145–175.

15. Ibid., pp. 153–156; Iraq's oil revenues increased from $1 billion in 1972 to $33 billion in 1980.

16. Ibid., p. 174.

17. Charles Tripp, *A History of Iraq*, Cambridge: Cambridge University Press, 3rd ed., 2007, p. 38.

18. On the Basij, see Sandra Mackey, *The Iranians: Persia, Islam and the Soul of a Nation* (New York: Penguin Books, 1998), pp. 323–324, 328–329; see also Jon Lee Anderson, "Understanding the Basij," *New Yorker*, November 8, 2009.

19. Davis, *Memories of State*, p. 229.

20. Abbas Alnasrawi, *The Economy of Iraq: Oil, Wars, Destruction of Development and Prospects, 1950–2010* (Westport, CT: Greenwood Press, 1994).

21. For an analysis of some of the activities during the 1990s, see Adil Ra'uf, *Muhammad Muhammad Sadiq al-Sadr: Marja'iyat al-Midan—Mashru'uhu al-Taghiri wa Waqa'ia' al-Ightiyal* (*Muhammad Muhammad Sadiq al-Sadr: The People's Religious Authority—His Project for Change and the Facts of His Assassination*) (Damascus: Iraqi Center for Information and Studies, 1999); and al-Sayyid Muhsin al-Nuri al-Musawi, *al-Sayyid Muqtada al-Sadr: Sadr al-'Iraq al-Thalith—Ahdafuhu, Mawqifuhu, Mashru'auhu* (*al-Sayyid Muqatada al-Sadr: Iraq's Third Sadr—His Goals, Positions and Projects*) (Baghdad: Wali Allah Center for Studies, Direction and Guidance, 2004).

22. According to Twelver Shiism, which predominates in Iraq and among Shia, the twelfth imam, Muhammad al-Mahdi, went into occultation in 869 and will return at a time designated by God to bring absolute justice to the world.

23. Sabrina Tavernese, "Shiites Grow Disillusioned with Militia in Baghdad," *New York Times*, October 12, 2007.

24. For a comparison of JAM and the crime syndicates of southern Italy, the Mafia, Camorra, and Ndrangheta, see Eric Davis, "Sectarianism, Historical Memory and the Discourse of Othering: The Mahdi Army, Mafia, Camorra and 'Ndrangheta," in *Uncovering Iraq: Trajectories of Disintegration and Transformation*, ed. Michael Hudson (forthcoming 2010).

25. Eric Davis, "10 Sins in the Analysis of Middle Eastern Politics," http://new-middle-east.blogspot.com/2009_01_01_archive.html.

26. For an elaboration of the impact of economic variables on sectarianism in post-2003 Iraq, see Eric Davis, "Rebuilding a Non-Sectarian Iraq," *Strategic Insights* 4, no. 6 (December 2007), http://fas-polisci.rutgers.edu/davis/ARTICLES/CCCdavisDec07.pdf.

27. For an excellent visual depiction of this intimidation process, see James Longley's film *Iraq in Fragments* (Typecast Films, 2006), especially the section on the JAM's attacks on alcohol sellers in a southern city of Iraq.

28. "'I'tilaf wahdat al-Iraq' - tahaluf intikhabi yadimm al-Bulani wa Abu Risha wa al-Samarra'i" ("The Iraqi Unity Alliance," an election coalition that includes al-Bulani, Abu Risha and al-Samarra'i), *al-Hayat*, October 22, 2009, where a prominent political leader and interior minister, Jawad al-Bulani formed a national political alliance with two prominent Sunni tribal leaders, Ahmad Abu Risha, head of the Awakening movement, and Ahmad Abu al-Ghaffur al-Samara'i, head of the Sunni Waqf Council.

29. Some analysts have even characterized this period as a civil war.

30. See, for example, the ABC/BBC/NHK poll, March 2009, http://news.bbc.co .uk/2/hi/middle_east/7942974.stm.

31. "Few Bidders to Develop Iraqi Oil and Gas Fields," *New York Times*, July 1, 2009; only one of Iraq's six giant oil fields was leased to a consortium of British Petroleum and the Chinese National Petroleum Company for the Rumailia field, with its estimated 17 billion barrels of oil. It should be noted that if this field were fully developed, it could more than double Iraq's current output of 2.5 million barrels per day.

32. Having spent May and June 1980 in Iraq, I can attest to the impressive level of development that had been achieved in Iraq. One indicator of this development was that by then Iraq had the most developed medical system in the Middle East.

33. See Chapter 4 of *The Future of Freedom*, "The Islamic Exception." It should be noted that, more than any other non-Western region, the Middle East suffers from being subsumed under a conceptual "cultural hermeneutic."

34. For an elaboration of this point, see Eric Davis, "Reflections on Religion and Politics in Post-Ba'athist Iraq," *Newsletter of the American Academic Research Institute in Iraq* (TAARII) 3, no. 1 (2008).

13

IRAN'S REGIONAL FOREIGN POLICY

Manochehr Dorraj

IRANIAN REGIONAL FOREIGN policy in postrevolutionary years has displayed elements of both continuity and change from the Pahlavi-era foreign policy. Broadly conceived, in both periods foreign policy was closely linked to the exigencies of domestic politics: defense of national interest and an instrument of regime survival. Under the monarchy Iran was firmly in the Western camp. It was a member of the pro-Western Baghdad Pact—known as CENTO after the 1958 Iraqi revolution that led to that country's defection from the pact. Iran's regional allies included the "Northern Tier camp" (Turkey and Pakistan), Israel, and moderate Arab states such as Egypt, Jordan, Morocco, Tunisia, North Yemen, and the Persian Gulf states of Saudi Arabia and Kuwait. After the official recognition of Israel in 1960, a strategic alliance was forged between the two countries. Iran in this period was also a pillar of support for US policy interests in the region. Under US President Richard Nixon, the Nixon Doctrine codified Iran's role as an erstwhile US ally and enforcer of a pro-Western foreign policy agenda in the region. These attributes of the monarchic foreign policy put Iran firmly in the anti-communist camp, as demonstrated by Muhammad Reza Shah's 1974 attempt to suppress the Maoist guerrilla movement in Oman that threatened the reign of that country's King Qabus. While the moderate Arab Gulf states were apprehensive about the regional ambitions of imperial Iran, their interest in containing the pro-Moscow radical Arab regimes and maintaining the viability of OPEC converged with the shah's regional political agenda. Hence Iran's chief regional rival, the Baathist Iraq that had locked horns with the shah's regime over the disputed body of water, Shatt al Arab, separating the two countries, had to come to terms with its more powerful neighbor in the Algiers Agreement of 1975. The shah's government was also one of the few regional powers to support the Camp David Peace Accords between Egypt and Israel in 1978.[1] The 1979 revolution, however, dramatically changed this regional political map and the role Iran would play in it.

POST-1979 REGIONAL FOREIGN POLICY: THE ISLAMIC REPUBLIC

Khomeini Era

The 1979 Iranian revolution was a major watershed in the Middle East. The image of an unarmed people overthrowing a powerful monarch captured the imagination of many throughout the region and the Muslim world. The demonstration effect and the appeal of revolution were far-reaching, and the revolution had its own dynamics. It changed the regional politics and the balance of power in fundamental ways. The revolution put an end to the pro-Western foreign policy orientation of the shah's regime and ushered in a new era.

Iran's regional foreign policy in the immediate aftermath of the revolution was guided by three abiding priorities: internal consolidation of power, export of Islamic revolution, and the advancement of pan-Islamism. Although after the revolution Iran decidedly defected from the camp of the moderate regimes, it nonetheless continued cooperating with its non-Arab Muslim neighbors, such as Turkey and Pakistan, that had close ties to the United States. By 1985, the former Regional Development Cooperation Organization, set up in 1964, was renamed the Economic Cooperation Organization and resumed its activities, expanding the volume of trade between the three countries.[2] In sharp contrast, Iran's relations with conservative Arab monarchies of the Persian Gulf as well as Egypt and Jordan deteriorated. While anti-Israeli rhetoric took a prominent position in the ideological repertoire of the Islamic Republic, military cooperation with the state of Israel continued during the war with Iraq (1980–1988). Iran's alliance with moderate regional powers, such as Saudi Arabia, Egypt, Jordan, and Israel, was then replaced with a new foreign policy that sought closer alliances with radical regimes and movements in the region. The slogan "neither East nor West" that characterized Iranian foreign policy in the immediate aftermath of the revolution was designed to assert the new independent Iranian ideological identity. Pan-Islamism was intended to achieve three related political objectives: to undermine conservative pro-Western Arab regimes, such as Saudi Arabia, Kuwait, Morocco, Jordan, and Egypt; to arouse the Muslim population of these countries against their respective political leaders; and to empower radical and populist Muslim opposition groups in the region, especially the Shia minorities residing in these countries.

While Iran regarded the Saudi royal family and their Wahhabi brand of Sunni Islam as illegitimate and exhorted Saudi Muslims to overthrow their regime, it supported the uprising of the marginalized Saudi Shia in the oil-rich eastern province. Tehran also supported the attempted takeover of the holy shrine in Mecca by Muslim militants in 1981. These policies alarmed the Saudi leadership and escalated tensions between the two countries.

The Islamic Republic also supported several Shia factions, including Amal and Hizbullah in Lebanon, ideologically, financially, and militarily. Regiments of Iranian Revolutionary Guards were dispatched to the Syrian-controlled Bakka Valley to train the Hizbullah and Amal fighters. The Iranian government also supported the Palestine Liberation Organization (PLO). But with the Iran-Iraq war and the PLO leadership's support of Saddam Hussein's regime, the honeymoon was over and the relationship with the PLO deteriorated. Instead, Tehran began to support smaller Palestinian factions and PLO rivals, such as Islamic Jihad and Hamas. Ideologically, the Islamic Republic felt closer to the Islamic political orientation of these two groups than to the secular vision of the PLO. The support of Palestinian militant groups set the stage for confrontation with Israel, the former erstwhile ally of the shah's regime. Although Iran and Israel have not had any direct military confrontations yet, they have fought a cold war through their surrogates—for example, Iran's support of Hizbullah, Islamic Jihad, and Hamas and Israeli military conflict with all three.[3]

The onset of the Iran-Iraq war created a wedge between pan-Islamic and pan-Arab loyalties in the region. The moderate Arab regimes, such as Egypt, Jordan, Morocco, Saudi Arabia, Kuwait, and the United Arab Emirates, supported Iraq. Syria, Libya, South Yemen, and Algeria (the latter three to a lesser extent) supported Iran. While Saudi Arabia and Kuwait provided Saddam with billions in financial support, other Arab countries (most notably, Egypt and Jordan) lent political support.

During the war, Syria proved to be Iran's closest regional ally. Linked by their common animosity toward Saddam's regime and some shared political goals, there emerged a marriage of convenience between the theocratic government in Tehran and the secular Arab Baath nationalist government in Damascus. Like Iran, Syria also supported the radical Palestinian groups opposed to the PLO, as well as Hizbullah and Amal. While the Syrian regime of Hafiz al-Asad found Palestinian radical groups and Hizbullah useful for its proxy war against Israel and the advancement of its political objectives in Lebanon, unlike the Iranian government, it did not aspire to create an Islamic republic in its former territory, which it regarded as its strategic domain. Nevertheless, Syria's financial and energy needs, Iran's willingness to export its oil to Syria at a discount price, and the Iranian regime's need for regional allies and a strategic depth in the Mediterranean that its alliance with Syria engendered made this marriage functional. However, by the late 1980s, as Syria faced its own bloody domestic confrontations with the Muslim Brotherhood and the power of Muslim groups in Lebanon increased substantially, to maintain the relationship, the Iranian government had to abandon its goal of creating an Islamic republic in

Lebanon and confine its activities to financial and military support of its ally, Hizbullah.[4]

Concerned with the threat of the Islamic Republic and Saddam's regional political ambitions, the conservative Arab monarchies of the Persian Gulf, led by Saudi Arabia, created the Gulf Cooperation Council (GCC) in 1981. The GCC was designed to create a collective security pact to protect member nations. Iran and Iraq were not included.

The new foreign policy turn of the Islamic Republic by the end of the 1980s was highlighted by such events as its defection from CENTO, severing its formal diplomatic links with Israel and South Africa, canceling the $9 billion arms contract with Western powers, and joining the nonaligned movement. In the same period Iran established relations with communist North Korea and twelve new nations in Africa while breaking diplomatic relations with Egypt, Jordan, and Morocco.[5]

The perceived Iranian threat was not merely regional. The Islamic Republic's foreign policy also posed a challenge to the existing bipolar system that marked the US-Soviet rivalry for political influence in the larger Middle East and the Muslim world. The Soviet invasion of Afghanistan in 1979 in order to prop up the pro-Moscow Najiballah government galvanized Muslim groups throughout the Middle East and North Africa in opposition to the Soviet occupation. The Islamic Republic supported the Afghan moujahidine and their struggle against Soviet troops. Similarly, the United States saw Iranian foreign policy as a threat to its regional hegemony and the security of its allies. The 1979 hostage crisis (in which US embassy personnel were taken hostage by militant Muslim students backed by the government for 444 days) was followed by breaking of diplomatic relations between the two countries, freezing billions of dollars of Iran's assets in the United States, and the imposition of sanctions on Iran that have continued to this day. Both superpowers regarded the Islamic Republic as a threat to a bipolar world in general and their regional interests in particular. Thus, they attempted to isolate Iran.[6] With the onset of the Iran-Iraq war, the US decidedly supported Iraq, providing it with intelligence on Iranian troop movements, weapons, and financial and political support. The Soviets assumed a neutral posture at first, but as the tide of war turned in Iran's favor and Iranian troops occupied the Faw Peninsula inside Iraqi territory, the Soviets began providing Iraq with military advisers and weapons that helped to turn the war in favor of Iraq.[7]

The Post-Khomeini Era

By April 1988, Iran suffered a series of setbacks on the battlefield. These demoralizing developments had a distinct impact on the decline of revolutionary zeal and strengthened the position of pragmatists led by Hojjatolislam Hashemi Rafsanjani, a key power broker in the Islamic Republic who became president in 1989. As early as June 1988, Rafsanjani expressed his undisguised critique of Iran's confrontational and isolationist foreign policy. As he put it, "One of the wrong things we did in the revolutionary atmosphere was to constantly make enemies. We pushed those who could be neutral into hostility and did not do anything to attract those who could become friends. It is part of the new plan that in foreign policy we should behave in a way not to needlessly leave ground to the enemy."[8] The second important development that served as a catalyst to change Iranian foreign policy was the death of Ayatollah Ruhollah Khomeini in 1989. In his absence the path was open for a reinterpretation of the neologism that guided the revolution, and thus more moderate regional foreign policy could emerge.

A number of other political considerations also informed the change in Iranian regional policy in the post-Khomeini era. The Iran-Iraq war drove home a bitter lesson regarding the cost of political isolation. During that war, whereas Saddam's regime received financial and military support from Western allies, many Arab countries, and the USSR, in contrast Iran found itself internationally isolated and had to buy many of its weapons on the black market at much higher financial cost. For the Rafsanjani administration it had become patently clear that the key to consolidating the revolution and the reconstruction of a war-ravaged economy lay in breaking out of international isolation. As the US economic and political sanctions continued, Rafsanjani took a two-pronged approach. First, he abandoned the policy of "neither East, nor West" in favor of normalizing and expanding relations with both East and West. In this pursuit, Rafsanjani undertook a concerted effort to normalize relations with European nations and expanded relations with Russia and China. Second, he took political initiatives to put to rest the fear of Iran's neighbors about the export of Islamic revolution, thus ending Iran's regional isolation. He reached out to all regional powers (with the exception of Israel), most notable among them the pro-Western Arab Gulf monarchies (and GCC members) Turkey and Egypt.[9]

Two important regional developments facilitated this new policy of rapprochement. First, Iraq's invasion of Kuwait in 1990 and its subsequent military emasculation by the US-led coalition in 1991 convinced the Saudis that the real threat to the security of the Persian Gulf was Saddam's regime. The Saudis also realized that the only other power in the region strong enough to contain Saddam's expansionist ambitions was Iran. Having seen their former ally (whom they had supported financially and politically during the Iran-Iraq war) turn against them, GCC countries were now seeking a more balanced policy. Saudis also hoped that rapprochement with Tehran would bestow upon them a measure of Islamic legitimacy and would dissuade Iran from exporting its revolution. While there were strong suspicions that Iranian agents were behind the terrorist bombing of the US military barracks at Dharan, Saudi Arabia, that killed nineteen Americans in 1996, since the charges were never proved, the rapprochement between the two countries continued. Thus, under Rafsanjani's tenure in office, the trade relations between the two countries expanded. The two countries also cooperated with each other in OPEC regarding production quotas and pricing.[10] However, as Rafsanjani's government was accused of bombing the Israeli embassy in Buenos Aires, Argentina, in 1992 and the Jewish center there in 1994, it became clear that the old hard-liners still wielded power in the complicated structure of the Islamic Republic.

Anwar al-Sadat's policy of providing the shah with a safe haven in Egypt in the last years of his life antagonized the Islamic Republic, and the relations between the two countries further deteriorated when Egypt supported Iraq during the Iran-Iraq war. After Sadat's assassination in 1981 and Hosni Mubarak's ascendance to power, like his predecessor, he initially continued to accuse his internal Muslim opposition of being agents of the Iranian government. Hence, the clerical establishment in Tehran accused him of being a stooge of imperialism and Zionism throughout the 1980s. Mubarak was also alarmed by Iran's support of Muslim fundamentalist government in the neighboring Sudan and by the Islamic Republic's denunciation of the Egyptian-brokered Palestinian-Israeli peace process. But with Rafsanjani's ascendance to power, some initiatives were taken to break the ice and start a new dialogue with Cairo. The lifting of pariah status that Sadat's signing of the Camp David Peace Accords brought to Egypt, and the country's return to mainstream Arab politics convinced the Islamic Republic to improve relations with one of the leaders, if not the main leader, of the Arab world.[11] One can also make the case that the Rafsanjani administration hoped that normalizing political relations with America's regional allies would send a signal to Washington about Tehran's willingness to normalize relations with the United States.

Rafsanjani also exchanged two letters with Saddam Hussein, and the two sides agreed to exchange prisoners of war and to allow Iran's Shia pilgrims to visit the Iraqi holy cities of Najaf and Karbala. But Baghdad would not meet Iran's demand for war reparations of $1 trillion. In exchange, Iran did not return to Iraq some 125 Iraqi jet fighters who during the 1991 war with the US-led coalition took refuge in Iran.[12]

Under Rafsanjani's two terms as president (1989–1997), the policy of peaceful coexistence and economic cooperation replaced export of revolution and the lofty goal of regional transformation. The priorities of reconstruction of the war-torn economy required economic reforms, inviting increased participation by the private sector and expansion of foreign investment. Hence, control of the press, suppression of civil society organizations, and restrictions on social life were relaxed. Revolution had run its course and the ideological politics of the Khomeini era were now giving way to a more moderate and pragmatic course in which the primacy of Iranian national interests replaced ideological commitment to exporting Islamic revolution. These policies paved the way for the presidency of a more reform-minded leader, Mohammad Khatami.

Khatami's surprising ascendance to political power in the 1997 presidential election in a landslide victory revealed the depth of hunger that lurked in Iranian society for reform and social change in domestic and international affairs. The majority of Iranian people longed to end their country's political isolation and be integrated into the global community. Khatami continued and expanded Rafsanjani's efforts to reach out to Iran's neighbors and the rest of the world. As a reform-minded cleric, former librarian, and minister of culture and Islamic guidance who had studied in Germany and was friends with the former head of the United Nations, Kofi Annan, Khatami was committed to reconciling Islam and democracy and democratizing the Islamic Republic. He saw reform at home linked to foreign policy. He believed that a more appealing image of the Islamic Republic would enhance its stature and influence throughout the region and the wider world. To engage the world in general and reach out to the West in particular, in response to Samuel Huntington's theory, "Clash of Civilizations" and "West against the rest," Khatami developed an initiative dubbed the "Dialogue of Civilizations."[13] While his democratic inclinations and commitments brought him into direct conflict with the conservative camp within the clerical establishment led by Ayatollah Ali Khamenei, the supreme leader, he attempted to use his popular mandate to usher in change in Iran's domestic and foreign policy, albeit with limited success.

Under Khatami's presidency, Iran inaugurated the "Good Neighbor" policy, improving relations with moderate Arab regimes and solidifying relations with Syria and Hizbullah. While Iran's relations with the United Arab Emirates (UAE) remained strained in the 1990s partially due to unresolved disputes over Iran's 1971 occupation of Abu Musa and the two Tunb Islands and UAE's financial support for the Taliban government in Afghanistan, after the overthrow of the Taliban in 2001 relations between the two countries improved. Iran also established diplomatic relations with Egypt and expanded ties with Saudi Arabia, Turkey, Jordan, and Algeria. The most significant development in Iran-GCC relations was the substantial improvement in Iran-Saudi relations. Rafsanjani's 1996 historic visit to Riyadh was reciprocated by Crown Prince Abdullah's trip to Tehran in December 1997 for the Organization of the Islamic Conference. Both sides agreed to expand cooperation and trade. This was followed by President Khatami's visit to Riyadh in 1999. Clearly, by the late 1990s it had become clear to the Saudi kingdom that the Islamic Republic was no longer interested in fomenting rebellion among Shia minorities in GCC countries. Hence, ideological conflict of the past had now given way to mutual accommodations. While the support of some of the GCC member countries, such as Saudi Arabia and the UAE, for the Taliban regime in Afghanistan, the staunch enemy of the

Islamic Republic, was not welcomed by Tehran, the bilateral relations between Tehran and Riyadh and between Tehran and Abu Dhabi were deemed significant enough to overlook this particular policy difference.[14] Although in the early 1990s the monarchy in Bahrain continuously accused the Iranian regime of fomenting dissent among its Shia population, by 1998 the two countries normalized their relationship. Hence, the tension with UAE over the three islands mentioned above has not prevented the expanding economic ties between the two countries. For example, by the year 2000, Iran emerged as the number-one trade partner of the UAE in the Muslim world.[15]

While Khatami repeatedly denounced terrorism and in 1999 hosted a conference of Islamic nations in Tehran in which the participants passed a resolution denouncing terrorism, he continued to support the Palestinian movement and its drive for a homeland, calling for an end to Israeli occupation of their land. Calling the use of violence by several Palestinian groups a "freedom seeking struggle against occupation that should be distinguished from terrorism," and regarding "confronting and fighting occupation as an inalienable right," Khatami stipulated that "supporting people who fight for the liberation of their land, is not, in my opinion, supporting terrorism. It is, in fact, supporting those who are engaged in combating state terrorism. In fact, Palestinian struggle is against Israeli state sponsored terrorism."[16] He asserted that while he considered most of the US-proposed peace initiatives to be biased against the Palestinians, his regime would support any settlement between Palestinians and Israelis that enjoyed the backing of the majority of Palestinian people. The Khatami administration's support for the Palestinian cause and Hizbullah in Lebanon, combined with his attempt to reconcile Islam and democracy at home, enhanced the popularity of his regime in the Arab world. Khatami's jubilant reception in Lebanon as a hero during his May 2003 visit was a testimony that his popularity reached beyond Iran's borders.

After the September 11, 2001, terrorist attacks against the United States, Khatami took an active role in denouncing the attacks and sent his foreign minister, Kamal Kharrazi, to the fifty-six-member Organization of the Islamic Conference in Qatar on October 10, 2001, which passed a resolution condemning the attacks in the strongest terms. However, Iran's continued support for Hamas and the Islamic Jihad in the occupied territories opened his administration to the charge that he is weak and remains beholden to the hard-line conservative camp led by the supreme leader, Ayatollah Khamenei.[17]

The major catalyst in further weakening of the Khatami administration and pursuit of his moderate regional foreign policy agenda came in 2002 when US President George W. Bush put Iran on his list of "axis of evil" countries alongside Iraq and North Korea. This was followed by the Bush administration's negative response to the Khatami government's proposal for the resolution of all outstanding issues of conflict between the two nations in 2003. Khatami's hard-line opponents alleged that for all of his moderation and concessions in foreign policy, he had nothing to show in improvement of relationship with the United States. Despite Iran's cooperation with the United States on terrorism in the immediate aftermath of September 11, 2001, and in spite of its active role in bringing stability to Afghanistan, the Bush administration remained unresponsive and seemed intent on humiliating the Islamic Republic, calling for regime change. Iran extradited a number of al-Qaeda members who fled to Iran in the face of a US military onslaught against their bases in Afghanistan back to Saudi Arabia to stand trial. Iran also contributed $560 million (the largest amount donated by any Third World nation) in Tokyo's donors' conference toward reconstructing Afghanistan. But apparently Washington was not impressed by these political initiatives and was in no mood for diplomacy or rapprochement. The political impact of American foreign policy toward Iran was to discredit Khatami and the reform movement. It also led to the strengthening of the hard-liners and the swing of the political pendulum to the right. The 2005 presidential election and the ascendancy of Mahmoud Ahmadinejad to power ushered in a right turn in Iran's foreign policy, as well as the regional policy.

As the son of a blacksmith and as a former Revolutionary Guard, Ahmadinejad came from humble origins. Cultivating the public sentiment against corruption and the inability of the Khatami administration to adequately address economic inequalities pervasive in the society, Ahmadinejad promised to distribute the oil money among the poor and to fight corruption. His background lent him a populist appeal as "ordinary folk," and his populist agenda rendered him a "man of the people."[18] His decision to reside in a modest apartment in a middle-class neighborhood in central Tehran, his simple lifestyle, his professed belief in the second coming of the Mahdi—the twelfth Shia imam, who is believed to be in occultation but who would return when the world is filled with injustice in order to restore justice on earth—and his parochial vision and political authoritarianism stood in sharp contrast to Khatami's cosmopolitan views on Islamic democracy and the dialogue of civilizations. In the foreign policy realm, Ahmadinejad attempted to revive the revolutionary foreign policy of the Khomeini era, with meager success.

Ahmadinejad purged the foreign ministry of Khatami-era reformists and filled it with his own brand of neoconservative second-generation revolutionaries who shared his vision and were loyal to him. He took initiatives to reassert the themes of pan-Islamism, Third World solidarity, nonalignment, and support for national liberation movements. To counter US pressure and a hostile political posture, he rejuvenated Iran's "Eastern strategy" (expanding ties with Russia and China) and put it on the front burner of Iran's foreign policy agenda. In this pursuit, he expanded Iran's relations with such populist left-wing governments in Latin America as Hugo Chavez of Venezuela, Daniel Ortega of Nicaragua, and Eva Morales of Bolivia. These relations lent Iran strategic alliances outside its own region that Ahmadinejad has used to push back against Washington pressures.[19] He also considerably extended trade, energy, and military ties to Russia and China. Russia became the chief provider of nuclear technology to Tehran and in 2008 Vladimir Putin became the first Russian president to visit Iran since Stalin's participation in the Tehran conference during the Second World War. China has emerged as the major consumer for Iranian oil and gas and a major investor in Iran's energy sector. Iran currently ranks second to Saudi Arabia as the major provider of energy to China in the entire Middle East, and China emerged as Iran's number-one trade partner in 2008.[20]

Regionally, in order to put to rest the anxiety of its Muslim neighbors regarding Iran's nuclear ambition, and to appeal to the "Arab Street" and play the pan-Islamic card, in 2006 Ahmadinejad convened a conference of Holocaust deniers in Tehran and opted for a more confrontational rhetoric on Israel. While these policies proved to be controversial domestically and many leading members of the reform movement, including former president Khatami, criticized Ahmadinejad for his Holocaust denial, he continued to press this idea during his first and second terms as president. In addition, in 2007, Ahmadinejad provided the Sunni fundamentalist Palestinian group, Hamas, with a $150 million package of financial aid. In reaction to these developments, Israeli rhetoric and political posture against the Islamic Republic has become harsh and antagonistic.

While the Bush administration attempted to create a coalition of pro-Western Arab states and Israel and denounced Tehran as the foremost threat to regional security, the GCC members seemed unconvinced. To prevent further erosion of legitimacy of the kingdom and establish their independence from Washington, under politically astute King Abdullah, the Saudis engaged in a balancing act. In March 2007, King Abdullah invited Ahmadinejad for a state visit in which the king described the relations between the two nations as "brotherly." On December 3, 2007, the GCC countries invited Ahmadinejad to attend the Gulf Cooperation Council meeting in Doha, Qatar, a first for any Iranian president. The warm reception Ahmadinejad received in Doha and the promise of expansion of trade and diplomatic ties portends that the GCC members have decided rather than confronting Tehran, as Washington aspired, they will accommodate "the increasing political weight of their neighbor."[21]

Ahmadinejad welcomed the overthrow of Iran's nemesis, Saddam Hussein, and considerably expanded relations with the newly elected Shia-dominated government in Baghdad. Many of these leaders had spent decades in exile in Iran, fleeing Saddam's repression and persecution of the Iraqi Shia community. In the process, a close relationship was forged between Iraqi Shia leaders in exile and their Iranian hosts. The most notable among them were the Supreme Council for Islamic Revolution in Iraq and the Al-Dawa Party. Hence, the main Shia militia that was later incorporated into Iraqi security forces, the Badr Brigade, (initially constituted from the ranks of Iraqi Shia volunteers in exile) was trained by Iran's Revolutionary Guards. Ahmadinejad provided the different factions of Iraqi Shias with financial and political support, including the radical populist leader Muqtada al-Sadr and his Mahdi Army. Trade and political ties between the two countries expanded as well. Among regional powers, Iran played a major role in reconstructing Iraq, and by 2008 the volume of trade between the two countries increased to $1.8 billion.[22]

Concerned with the implications of Iraqi disintegration on its own security, Iran supported the Nouri al-Maliki government to crush the insurgency. Keen about the possibilities of its spillover in the larger Muslim world and its negative consequences, the Ahmadinejad administration negotiated with Saudi and Iraqi leaders to contain the Sunni-Shia sectarian violence. In 2007, his administration participated in bilateral negotiation with the US government over Iraqi security. Whereas the United States was interested in using Iran's influence among the Iraqi Shia to facilitate its exit strategy, Iran hoped to use these negotiations as a stepping stone to negotiate all the outstanding issues of conflict between the two nations. Concerned with the continuous presence of the Iranian opposition group Mujahidin-i Khalq (the bitter enemy of the Islamic Republic) on Iraqi territory, Ahmadinejad's government pressured Maliki to close Camp Ashraf, the military base from which Mujahidin launched sporadic attacks against targets inside Iran. The Maliki government obliged and Iraqi troops closed the camp in August 2009. Ahmadinejad's regime also has a vested interest in the security and stability of Iraq and the defeat of Sunni insurgency. Only such an outcome would bring about the withdrawal of US troops, to which both Iranian and Iraqi leaders aspire.

Iran's relationship with Syria further solidified under the leadership of Ahmadinejad and Bashar al-Asad, as the two countries found themselves on Washington's list of states that sponsor terrorism, and more important, as their regional interests in Lebanon and Palestine converged. Iran provides Syria with financial aid and fills some of its energy needs, while Syria facilitates Iran's relations with Hizbullah and different Palestinian groups, such as Hamas and the Islamic Jihad. Syria serves as Iran's supply route to Hizbullah and Palestinian groups. In the aftermath of Lebanese Prime Minister Rafiq Hariri's assassination in 2005, in which the widely suspected involvement of Syrian agents drew global condemnation, Asad's regime found itself isolated and under pressure from the US and its allies, including the Lebanese government and people; it had to withdraw its forces from Lebanon in 2005. For all practical purposes, this development put an end to the Syrian mandate over Lebanon it enjoyed since 1976. This diminution of Syrian regional influence and its inability to use its proxies in Lebanon to gain leverage vis-à-vis Israel and other regional adversaries accentuated its isolation and need for allies. The Ahmadinejad administration rushed in to resume the mutually beneficial ties. On June 15, 2006, the two countries signed a strategic defense treaty further cementing their partnership. With Syria out of Lebanon, the days that Hafiz al-Asad could rein in Hizbullah and control it were long gone; now his son was dependent on a much more powerful Hizbullah as the major power broker in Lebanese politics. Some observers, however, regard Iran-Syria relations as a marriage of convenience between two ideologically different regimes. Given enough incentives and encouragement, Bashar al-Asad is likely to part ways with Iran.[23] The repeated shuttle diplomacy between several US congressional delegations and the mediation of Turkey between Israel and Syria in 2007–2009 is indicative of a concerted policy on the part of Washington and Tel Aviv to create a wedge between Damascus and Tehran.

Ahmadinejad also solidified his regime's relationship with Hizbullah, providing Iran with a strategic depth and enabling Tehran to be a player in the Mediterranean region. Historically, the major players in Lebanese politics have been Maronite Christians and Sunni Muslims. The Shia have been marginalized and powerless, though Iranian and Lebanese Shia communities have long maintained a relationship. The Iranian revolution of 1979 and the empowerment of Iranian Shia clergy galvanized Lebanese Shia and politicized them. By 1982, when Israel invaded Lebanon, the Iranian government was actively involved in financing and training Hizbullah fighters who were engaged in a guerrilla campaign against Israeli soldiers' occupation of the Shia stronghold in south Lebanon. The ability of Hizbullah to ultimately drive Israeli soldiers out of South Lebanon in 2000 brought the organization much prestige and popularity in the Arab and Muslim worlds. As Yitzhak Rabin once exclaimed, "The Israeli occupation of South Lebanon let the Shia genie out of the bottle."

It is widely believed that Hizbullah fighters were also responsible for the bombing of the US Marines headquarters and the US embassy in Beirut in 1983 and the taking of several US security forces and civilians as hostages throughout the 1980s. While some of these hostages were executed, others, mostly civilians, were released when Rafsanjani's government leaned on the Hizbullah leadership to free some of them in hopes of improving Iran's bilateral relations with the Bush administration.[24] In the meantime, thanks to continuous Iranian financial support, Hizbullah managed to build a network of charity organizations, hospitals, schools, endowments, and relief organizations to provide social services for the poor. These activities considerably enhanced the group's popularity in the Shia community in general and among the ranks of the underclass in particular.

Hizbullah fighters would display their military skills yet once again when they fought to a draw out the mighty army of Israel in June and July 2006. While Israeli strategy was to bombard the Lebanese infrastructure in hopes of turning the Christian and Sunni populations against the Shia community, in reality when more than 1,000 civilians lost their lives due to Israeli bombardments, Lebanese and global public opinion turned against Israel and Hizbullah emerged as the symbol of resistance against Israeli might in the region. This outcome expanded the popularity and influence of Hizbullah throughout the region. Because of this surge in popularity, however, the electoral defeat of Hizbullah in the 2009 Lebanese election took many by surprise.

The overthrow of the Sunni fundamentalist Taliban regime in Afghanistan in 2001, followed by the overthrow of Saddam's Sunni-dominated government in Iraq in 2003 and the subsequent empowerment of Iraqi Shia, coupled by the increasing power of Hizbullah in Lebanon, has made some of the leaders in the Arab world warn of an emerging "Shia Crescent" for which Tehran serves as the epicenter. While with the emergence of the first Shia-dominated government in the Arab world in Iraq and the increasing regional influence of Iran and Hizbullah, one can speak of a Shia revival,[25] it seems premature to speak of an emerging Shia political domination of the region, as some of the alarmist voices suggest. The 2009 disputed presidential election in Iran in which 3 million people in Tehran alone demonstrated against the Ahmadinejad regime revealed the eroding legitimacy of theocracy and cast doubt on its future political viability. The profound crisis of legitimacy at the heart of "the crescent," and the 2009 electoral defeat of Hizbullah in Lebanon should put to rest any worries about the specter of an emerging Shia domination of the region. Some, however, speculate that should Iran acquire a nuclear weapon, such domination would be guaranteed.

THE NUCLEAR ISSUE

Iran's nuclear program goes back to 1957, when the Eisenhower administration as a part of the US Atoms for Peace program signed a nuclear cooperation agreement with the shah's government. In 1960 a nuclear research center was established at Tehran University, and by 1967, when the United States provided Iran with a limited amount of enriched uranium, the research center became operational. Iran joined the nonproliferation treaty—a commitment not to proliferate nuclear weapons—in 1968 and ratified it in 1970. By 1974, the shah's regime had signed contracts with German and French companies to install nuclear reactors in Bushehr and Bandar-i Abbas. However, after the Islamic revolution of 1979, these contracts were canceled. Due to preoccupation with war and reconstruction, low oil income, and economic decline, Iran's nuclear ambitions were put on hold throughout the 1980s. After the Iran-Iraq war, the Islamic Republic approached the Russian government to finish the Bushehr reactor, which was damaged as a result of repeated Iraqi bombing. By 1995, under President Rafsanjani, Iran and Russia signed a contract to that end. China also agreed to provide Iran with a conversion plan. By the year 2000, Iranian officials announced the construction of two additional nuclear plants in Arak and Natanz.[26] Since then, Iran's nuclear program has become the focus of much debate and controversy among global and regional powers.

To make sense of the Islamic Republic's nuclear policy, it is helpful to see things from Tehran's perspective. During the Iran-Iraq war, Saddam received weapons from European nations and the Soviet Union and more than $50 billion from Saudi Arabia and Kuwait; in contrast, Iran found itself the target of an arms embargo and had to buy most of its weapons on the black market at exorbitant financial cost. Saddam's use of chemical and biological weapons in the battlefield against Iranian troops, to which much of the world turned a blind eye, is not forgotten by Iranian leaders; neither is the loss of more than 500,000 Iranian lives. These political realities convinced the clerical elite that they needed a deterrent. Hence, surrounded by more than 200,000 US forces that have invaded the two neighboring countries (Afghanistan and Iraq) and facing a US president who in his public pronouncements professed regime change and made repeated military threats against the Islamic Republic, the clerical establishment in Iran was imbued with an acute sense of insecurity and paranoia about its own survival as a member of the "axis of evil." Watching the fate of Iraq versus North Korea (the two other countries on the "axis of evil" list), in the eyes of the Iranian leaders the country that did not have a nuclear arsenal was invaded and its regime was overthrown, and the one that is believed to have a nuclear arsenal received a negotiated diplomatic settlement. In the absence of US security guarantees from the Bush administration, the conclusion for the guardians of theocracy in Tehran was that the only guarantor of regime survival is a credible deterrent, a clandestine nuclear arsenal that can be built under the umbrella of a civilian dual-use nuclear program.

Induced by increasing political pressure of the Bush administration on the one hand and the European Union's promise of economic, technological, and political incentives on the other, President Khatami temporarily halted uranium enrichment in 2004. But two months after Ahmadinejad's inauguration as president in June 2005, his government resumed its conversion of uranium yellowcake to uranium hexafluoride with the reopening of its Isfahan processing plant.[27] Whereas in the initial stages of the US occupation of Iraq, the Islamic Republic was preoccupied with the fear of being the next target of Bush's regime change policy, after 2006, when it became clear that the United States was bogged down in the Iraqi quagmire, the fear gave way to a sense of cockiness that the United States was stretched to its limits in Iraq and Afghanistan. The US military was in no position to invade a much larger country, such as Iran.

The reaction to Iran's nuclear drive has been mixed. Many rightly believe that should Iran acquire a nuclear arsenal, other regional powers such as Turkey, Saudi Arabia, and Egypt would follow suit, thus unleashing an arms race in one of the more volatile and militarized regions of the world. Whereas some scholars see Iran's drive for nuclear power as a drive for regional hegemony and believe that should Iran acquire a nuclear arsenal, it would be a game changer, tilting the regional balance of power decisively in favor of Tehran, others see it primarily in defensive terms, as meeting the need for a deterrent. They point out that Iran has not invaded any of its neighbors in more than two hundred years and were it to use nuclear weapons in the future, as a sector of the Israeli elite seems to suggest, it would be tantamount to committing suicide. The guardians of theocracy are interested in survival and self-preservation, not suicide.[28] Moreover, the emergence of a nuclear Iran would force the pro-Western Arab regimes to seek America's military protection, justifying US military presence in the region, an outcome that would be contrary to the professed goal of the Islamic Republic. Yet, others argue that there are ample reasons to believe that the Islamic Republic needs a nuclear program to generate electricity. Annually, the Iranian government pays between $20 billion and $30 billion in gasoline and other subsidies out of a budget of $50 billion, $5 billion of which is spent on imported gasoline. Hence, domestically subsidized gasoline is priced about 35 cents per gallon, which is very cheap compared to what Iran could receive if it sold its gasoline on the global market. Since more than 80 percent of Iran's foreign exchange comes from exporting oil and gas, if Iran's nuclear reactors can generate enough electricity to satisfy the domestic need, then the government could bring in much-needed cash by exporting a larger share of its energy production.[29]

During the Bush administration, President Ahmadinejad believed the nuclear issue was bogus, an excuse Washington used to promote its agenda of regime change, overthrow the Islamic Republic, and establish its hegemony over the region. With the election of Barack Obama, who has abandoned the idea of regime change and military threats and is engaged in direct multilateral negotiations with representatives of the Iranian government, Tehran has modified its political posture of defiance. The unexpected agreement of Iranian negotiators in Geneva, Switzerland, on October 1, 2009, to allow Iranian low-enriched uranium to be shipped to Russia for further refinement and then to France to be put into fuel rods so it can be shipped back to Iran for medical use was a major retreat from the Islamic Republic's previous position that all the enrichment should be done on Iranian soil. The uranium returned to Iran is enriched at a level suitable for generating electricity or could be used for nuclear medicine, but is not enriched enough to produce bombs. If indeed the Iranian government has revealed all of its low-enriched uranium, this new agreement may allow the international community to ensure that Iran's nuclear program is not being used for building nuclear weapons. The second major concession granted by the Iranian government was to allow the International Atomic Energy Agency (IAEA) to send inspectors to the newly declared nuclear site in the vicinity of the holy city of Qom. There was much speculation that because the Natanz facility, which is monitored by IAEA officials, cannot be used for building nuclear bombs, perhaps the previously undisclosed facility in Qom is being used for just such purposes. The agreement of Iranian nuclear negotiators that before the end of October 2009 this site would be accessible to IAEA inspectors may lay some of the anxieties of P5+1 nations (the United States, Great Britain, France, Russia, China, and Germany) and the regional powers to rest regarding Iran's nuclear program for now.[30]

This new turn in Iranian nuclear policy is also linked to internal political developments since the June 12, 2009, presidential election. The rise of the green movement and the outpouring of massive antigovernment demonstrations over the result of the disputed election that reinstated Ahmadinejad for a second term also revealed the state's erosion of legitimacy and the depth of public discontent. In such circumstances, the Islamic Republic could ill afford the possibility of a new set of paralyzing economic sanctions that may induce even more public resentment against the regime. Hence, as the regime's internal base of support has diminished substantially, it hopes to bolster its power by the legitimacy that negotiations with powerful nations such as P5+1 would bring it. Therefore, any sober analysis of the Iranian nuclear file and its possible future direction should also take into account the country's fluid internal political dynamics. While it is premature to conclude that the latest initiative from Tehran may signal that the Ahmadinejad administration may be contemplating abandoning the idea of a nuclear arsenal, it is certain that in Geneva it engaged in a tactical compromise. Whether this apparent retreat is an attempt to buy time until the regime deals effectively with its domestic opposition, and once it is firmly back in the saddle it will resume its relentless nuclear pursuit, remains to be seen. Shaken by the unexpected political uprising after the disputed presidential election, it is likely that the politics of regime survival dictates a new calculation of cost versus benefit of acquiring a nuclear arsenal.

CONCLUSION

Zbigniew Brzezinski once identified Iran as a "geopolitical pivot" that connects the Middle East, the Caucasus, and Central Asia. As the most populous and "historically entrenched" country, Iran has the potential to serve as a potent anchor of stability in a highly volatile region. Thus its integration into the global community is the key to regional security.[31]

Iranian regional policy has evolved from one preoccupied with the export of revolution and such ideological themes as pan-Islamism and fomenting Shia revolt against Sunni-dominated pro-Western Arab monarchies in the Persian Gulf throughout the 1980s under Ayatollah Khomeini's leadership, to one of peaceful coexistence and mutual accommodation since Khomeini's death. Having emerged out of revolutionary turmoil and a devastating eight-year war with Iraq, by the 1990s, Iran was poised to resume its position as the preeminent power of the Persian Gulf. While the historical tensions and mistrust between the primarily Sunni-dominated Arab world and the Persian Shia

Iran lingers, as this chapter has revealed, the pan-Islamic ideological appeal of the current regime lends it a strategic depth in the Arab and the Muslim world that the Pahlavi dynasty could not muster. But one of the inadvertent impacts of the Iran-Iraq war was that it accentuated the necessity for the infusion of Shiism with Iranian nationalism and put the primacy of Iranian national interest at the center of the Iranian foreign policy agenda. Hence, the current reality of the Islamic Republic is that increasingly the theocracy rules over a very secular and modern society. While the clerical elite utilizes Shiism as the instrument of political legitimation, what drives the foreign and regional policy is the cold calculation of national interest. It is this calculation (or miscalculation) that informs Iran's current nuclear policy.

It remains to be seen whether Iran will continue its uranium enrichment activities and mastering the fuel cycle technology. So far the country's strategy has been to expand its nuclear activity to build facts on the ground so the reality of a nuclear Iran becomes irreversible. President Ahmadinejad once described Iran's nuclear program as an unstoppable train with no brake or reverse gear. Ideally, Tehran would like to negotiate from such a position of strength. However, the current reality is that given the deep division in the ranks of the Iranian clerical elite and the eroding legitimacy of the Islamic Republic, it has to negotiate from a position of weakness.

Tehran repeatedly has complained that it is being singled out. Other regional powers have nuclear arsenals but are not the target of US sanctions and military threats, including Israel, Pakistan, and India. In light of the widely held belief that Israel has an estimated arsenal of two hundred to three hundred nuclear weapons, several regional powers including Iran and Egypt have called for declaring the entire Middle East a nuclear-free zone. But both the United States and Israel have rejected this proposal. The fear in Tel Aviv and Washington is that the emergence of a nuclear Iran would curtail if not nullify Israel's ability to engage in unilateral military action against its opponents, such as Hamas in Gaza and Hizbullah in Lebanon, as it has done in 2009 and 2006, with impunity and without fear of retaliation. Therefore, Tehran's nuclear pursuit clearly has strategic dimensions that reach far beyond Iranian borders. In this sense, it is a game changer.

It is very probable that Iran is looking for a "Japan option" in which it masters uranium enrichment, the fuel cycle, and the technological skills necessary to convert its peaceful program into a system capable of creating a nuclear arsenal in a span of a few weeks. This would allow Iran to remain within the rules set by IAEA but would still provide the option to weaponize, should political necessities dictate such a transition. The Islamic Republic sees its nuclear program as a bargaining chip in its relationships with the United Sates, the European Union, and to a lesser extent with the regional powers. What it demands instead is security guarantees, the lifting of sanctions, economic incentives, and the recognition of its role as an emerging regional power.

NOTES

1. Graham Fuller, *The Center of the Universe: The Geopolitics of Iran* (Boulder, CO, and London: Westview Press, 1991), pp. 58–135.

2. Anoushirvan Ehteshami, *After Khomeini: The Iranian Second Republic* (London and New York: Routledge, 1995), p. 130.

3. Fuller, *The Center of the Universe*, pp. 191–241.

4. Ehteshami, *After Khomeini*, p. 134. See also Augustus Richard Norton, "Lebanon: The Internal Conflict and the Iranian Connection," in *The Iranian Revolution: Its Global Impact*, ed. John L. Esposito (Miami: Florida International University, 1990), pp. 116–137.

5. Ehteshami, *After Khomeini*, p. 131.

6. James A. Bill, *The Eagle and the Lion: The Tragedy of American-Iranian Relations* (New Haven, CT: Yale University Press, 1988), pp. 261–318.

7. Mohiaddin Mesbahi, "The USSR and the Iran-Iraq War: From Brezhnev to Gorbachev," in *The Iran-Iraq War: The Politics of Aggression*, ed. Farhang Rajaee (Gainesville: University Press of Florida, 1993), pp. 69–102.

8. Scheherzade Daneshkhu, "Iran and the New World Order," in *The Gulf War and the New World Order*, ed. Tareq Y. Ismael and Jacqueline S. Ismael (Gainesville: University Press of Florida, 1994), p. 295.

9. Kaveh L. Afrasiabi, *After Khomeini: New Directions in Iran's Foreign Policy* (Boulder, CO, and London: Westview Press, 1994), pp. 57–116.

10. Gary Sick, "Iran's Foreign Policy: A Revolution in Transition," in *Iran and the Surrounding World: Interactions in Culture and Cultural Politics*, ed. Nikki R. Keddie and Ruddi Mathee (Seattle and London: University of Washington Press, 2002), pp. 363–366.

11. Assef Bayat and Bahman Bakhtiari, "Revolutionary Iran and Egypt: Exporting Inspirations and Anxieties," in *Iran and the Surrounding World*, ed. Keddie and Mathee, pp. 305–326.

12. Sick, "Iran's Foreign Policy," p. 364.

13. Mohammad Khatami, *Islam, Dialogue, and Civil Society*, http://al-islam.org/civilsociety, accessed October 5, 2009. See also Mohammad Khatami, *Islam, Freedom and Development* (Johannesburg: Global Publishers, 2001).

14. R. K. Ramazani, "Ideology and Pragmatism in Iran's Foreign Policy," *Middle East Journal* 58, no. 4 (Autumn 2004): 549–559.

15. Sick, "Iran's Foreign Policy," pp. 365–366.

16. Gary Sick, "Iran: Confronting Terrorism," *Washington Quarterly* 26, no. 4 (Autumn 2003): 89.

17. Fred Halliday, "Iran and the Middle East: Foreign Policy and Domestic Change," *Middle East Report* 204 (Autumn 2004): 42–47.

18. Kasra Naji, *Ahmadinejad: The Secret History of Iran's Radical Leader* (Berkeley: University of California Press, 2008), pp. 1–86.

19. Manochehr Dorraj and Michael Dodson, "Populism and Foreign Policy in Venezuela and Iran," *Whitehead Journal of Diplomacy and International Relations* 15, no. 1 (Winter/Spring 2008): 71–87.

20. Manochehr Dorraj and Carrie Currier, "Lubricated with Oil: Iran-China Relations in a Changing World," *Middle East Policy* 15, no. 2 (Summer 2008): 66–80.

21. Marc Lynch, "Why US Strategy on Iran Is Crumbling," *Christian Science Monitor*, January 4, 2008.

22. Mehran Kamrava, "The United States and Iran: A Dangerous but Contained Rivalry," *Middle East Institute Policy Brief* 9 (March 2008): 9–12.

23. Jonathon Gatehouse, "Syria's Next Trick: A Bargain for Power," *Maclean's*, August 14, 2006, pp. 26–28.

24. Sick, "Iran: Confronting Terrorism," pp. 83–98.

25. Vali Nasr, *The Shia Revival: How Conflict Within Islam Will Shape the Future* (New York: W. W. Norton & Company, 2007).

26. Shahram Chubin, *Iran's Nuclear Ambitions* (Washington, DC: Carnegie Endowment for International Peace, 2006).

27. Farideh Farhi, "Iran's Nuclear File: The Uncertain End Game," *Middle East Report*, October 24, 2005, www.merip.org/mero/mero102405.html.

28. See, for example, Meir Javedanfar and Yossi Melman, *The Nuclear Sphinx of Tehran: Mahmoud Ahmadinejad and the State of Iran* (New York: Carrol and Graf, 2007); Alireza Jafarzadeh, *The Iran Threat: President Ahmadinejad and the Coming Nuclear Crisis* (New York: Palgrave Macmillan, 2007); Ray Takyeh, *Hidden Iran: Power and Paradox in the Islamic Republic* (New York: Holt, 2007); and Ray Takyeh, *Guardians of the Revolution: Iran and the World in the Age of Ayatollahs* (New York and London: Oxford University Press, 2009).

29. See Alidad Mafinezam and Aria Mehrabi, *Iran and Its Place Among Nations* (Westport, CT: Praeger, 2008), pp. 91–98. See also Roger Stern, "Iranian Petroleum Crisis and the United States National Security," *Proceedings of the National Academy of Sciences* 104, no. 1 (January 2, 2007): 377–382.

30. Nicholas Kralev, "Iran Budges on Nuclear Fuel in U.S. Talks," *Washington Times*, October 2, 2009.

31. Zbigniew Brzezinski, *The Grand Chessboard: American Primacy and Its Geostrategic Imperative* (New York: Basic Books, 1997), p. 53.

14

GLOBAL ENERGY AND
THE MIDDLE EAST

Steve Yetiv

THE ARGUMENT OF this chapter is that an important race is under way in the field of energy that will help shape the contours of the twenty-first century. It is a race between alternatives to oil, and five factors that are making oil more important for the global economy and will increasingly place the Middle East even more so at the center of global oil security. It is hard to predict how the race will evolve, but one basic policy implication seems clear: Much more work needs to be done at the international level to sustain a serious search for oil alternatives, if we expect to address the factors this chapter explores. At the national level, the Obama administration has promised to put the United States on a serious path to greater reliance on alternatives. Time will tell to what extent such a move will be made and can be sustained in the coming years and decades.

The chapter begins with a brief discussion of five factors that will likely make oil and the Middle East far more important than they are today. These factors are the rising demand for global oil; peak oil and its potential effects; that the Middle East, due to its reserves, will become even more important as a supplier of global oil; that the Middle East now has and will increasingly have the lion's share of excess global oil capacity; and the likelihood that the highest potential for serious oil disruptions is in, or emanates from, the Middle East. The chapter then puts these threats into a balanced perspective, arguing that while they are very serious, a number of developments over the past thirty years can help mitigate them, to some extent at least.

The analysis then turns to alternatives to oil. Historically, their development has depended on a number of factors, with the price of oil being critical.

Price has fluctuated substantially over time, making it hard to sustain efforts to develop alternatives. This chapter's conclusion sketches some policy recommendations that follow from the basic arguments presented here.

PROJECTED DEMAND FOR GLOBAL OIL

The first trend of importance in gaining some traction on the more specific issue of Middle East oil is the rising demand for global oil. The US Department of Energy projects that the use of all energy sources, including oil, will increase through 2030.[1] This notion is fairly intuitive to most energy watchers and perhaps even to the intelligent laypeople. Indeed, we are increasingly aware that industrializing countries such as India and China will need more and more energy. Recent analysis reveals that China's demand for oil will rise rapidly through 2030.[2] China's comparative growth in oil demand is illustrated well in the figure below, from a recent study conducted by the International Energy Agency.

Even though oil demand is projected to increase, it is not expected to grow faster than that for other energy sources. In fact, the Department of Energy assumes that world oil prices will remain relatively high throughout the projection period and, based on that assumption, it projects that liquid fuels (chiefly oil) will be the world's slowest-growing source of energy, while liquids consumption increases at an average annual rate of 1.2 percent from 2005 to 2030. Renewable energy and coal are expected to be the fastest-growing energy sources, with consumption increasing by 2.1 percent and 2.0 percent, respectively. Prospects for renewable energy are expected to improve due to projected high prices for oil and natural gas, and increasing concern about the environmental impacts of fossil fuel use.

Overall, the Department of Energy projects that the liquids share of marketed world energy consumption will decline from 36 percent in 2006 to 32 percent in 2030. Even so, the projected increases in oil use are significant and will likely put serious pressure on the oil supply—a subject to which we now turn. (See www.eia.doe.gov/oiaf/ieo/world.html.)

THE PEAK OIL PROBLEMATIQUE

Although oil demand will increase over time, the opposite is likely to be true for oil production. Different estimates exist on when oil will peak. The oil peak refers to a turning point in which ever-growing production volumes will be followed by a period of shrinking volumes, until oil runs out altogether and we're left holding the global gas can. The oil peak phase follows two phases of the life cycle of oil. The first phase is called "pre-peak" and refers to continual production increases. In the second phase, production is "at peak" or stagnant.

Some analysts believe that since 1980 the world has consumed far more oil than has been discovered and that we are now at a place where one barrel of new oil is found for every four consumed; that we are well past peak oil.[3] That is a rather grim assessment.

Other thinkers believe we are facing an impending peak in oil production, if it has not already peaked recently.[4] Analysts of the Association of the Study of Peak Oil believe that oil will peak in the period 2006–2011.[5] Some of them, and other scientists,[6] use the models of M. King Hubbert, who correctly predicted the 1970 peak in US oil production, contrary to the expectations of many of his colleagues,[7] and the rapid decline of US production thereafter. Anyone who has been paying attention to the limited ability of the United States to meet its own energy needs, even if it does drill in Alaska, has a modern example of Hubbert's clairvoyance. Geologist Kenneth S. Deffeyes believes that world oil production most probably will peak before 2010. While some observers believe we can reverse this trend, Deffeyes believes that even if we did understand our predicament, it would be too late to prevent chaos in the global oil industry and economy.[8]

Pessimists believe, in part, that oil reserves are exaggerated, partly because countries in the Organization of Petroleum Exporting Countries (OPEC) want higher output quotas. These quotas are pegged to the size of the oil reserves that they claim. Thus, they exaggerate the size of their reserves. Others point to an oil production drop in the past few years in major oil-producing countries, upon which I elaborate below, and by the major oil companies as an indicator that we are depleting global oil resources faster than believed.[9] Although these companies account for only about 10 percent of global production, and while countries such as Saudi Arabia have not warned about decreasing production, the drop in production among the majors may reflect general problems in oil markets.

The pessimists also put less stock in technological fixes and in the human leadership needed to cause a major change in consumption habits. They believe that these pitfalls, combined with rising population and limited sources, spell trouble ahead.

While there are few unabashed cheerleaders of our oil future, there are reasoned optimists. The US Department of Energy has seen peak oil occurring closer to the middle of the twenty-first century than to its beginning.[10] Some oil industry leaders also assert that the world recovery rate or ability to exploit oil reserves has increased from 22 percent in 1980 to 35 percent in 2003.[11] That means that effective technology has extended the life of existing reserves.

The optimists criticize the pessimists for ignoring or not sufficiently considering changes in technology, costs, prices, or politics, all of which could significantly affect the oil peak.[12] Optimists also include many economists who have a sanguine view of market power. They believe that price incentives will drive discovery and that innovative technological fixes can yield alternatives to oil. Even as oil becomes more scarce and prices rise, other forms of energy will come on the market,[13] preempting the difficult scenarios the pessimists paint.

The pessimists were given a boost in November 2008. The authoritative International Energy Agency, the global energy watchdog for consumers, radically changed its forecast on oil. Until its November 2008 report, the agency dismissed notions that oil supplies might peak or reach a point where production no longer increased and then decreased in following years. It saw energy demand growing briskly to 2030, with abundant energy sources to meet this demand, suggesting a peak farther down the road.[14]

In its 2007 World Energy Outlook, the agency predicted a rate of decline in output from the world's existing oil fields of 3.7 percent a year. Compare that to the 2008 report, which might as well have been titled "Hey, Just Kidding About the Last Report." It projected a rate of decline of 6.7 percent—a slight problem. The findings of this unprecedented field-by-field analysis of the historical production trends of eight hundred oil fields indicates that decline rates are likely to rise significantly in the long term, from an average of 6.7 percent today to 8.6 percent in 2030.[15] As Nobuo Tanaka, executive director of the agency, points out, "Despite all the attention that is given to demand growth, decline rates are actually a far more important determinant of investment needs. Even if oil demand was to remain flat to 2030, 45 million barrels per day (MMBD) of gross capacity—roughly four times the current capacity of Saudi Arabia—would need to be built by 2030 just to offset the effect of oilfield decline."[16]

In fact, this is the first time the agency has forecast a date for an oil peak. Even more interesting, its chief economist, Fatih Birol, lead author of this study, told British journalist George Monbiot something quite startling: "In terms of non-OPEC [countries outside the big oil producers' cartel] we are expecting that in three, four years' time the production of conventional oil will come to a plateau, and start to decline. In terms of the global picture, assuming that OPEC will invest in a timely manner, global conventional oil can still continue, but we still expect that it will come around 2020 to a plateau as well, which is, of course, not good news from a global-oil-supply point of view."[17]

Why did the International Energy Agency change its forecast? The 2007 report was based on best-of-knowledge assumptions about what global oil fields could produce. The 2008 report, by contrast, is based on actual studies of the world's eight hundred largest oil fields, on the first publicly available data of their production rates. What is interesting is that Birol is no peak oil dramatist. He's a mainstream, sober economist and global leader. And he has access to very good data, compared to most other analysts. If he and the IEA are calling for peak oil around 2020, that's something to which we should give serious attention.

No one can predict an oil peak definitely or surmise its specific effects. However, there is good reason to believe that the oil peak will be important for a number of reasons. First, no matter what one thinks of peak oil prognostications, common sense tells us that oil is a finite resource. We cannot continue to discover, produce, and deliver oil forever. Even if we have twenty or thirty years from peak time to exhaustion, we are running far behind in preparing for the future. Indeed, the global economy runs on oil. It cannot switch from oil to other alternatives overnight, even if they are available at a reasonable cost.

Second, the oil crisis won't hit suddenly but oil prices will rise ahead of it. We won't wake up to the stunning headline that "We're Down to the Last Drop of Oil." Nor will future generations receive such an unwelcome shock. Oil will peak well before this news ever becomes a big surprise. Not only do opinions differ on when oil will peak, if it has not already, but also on how much time we have afterward for its production to start to decline seriously. After all, oil could peak and decline at a variety of different paces. But one thing appears to be clear: In the absence of a serious alternative energy source, the price of oil will begin to rise significantly as perceptions that it is stretching supply gain ground. The price will likely increase even more after some consensus is reached that we have peaked, especially if oil production is also viewed as likely to decline at a faster rather than slower pace, and if such realizations overlap with political and security trouble in the oil-rich Persian Gulf, as I will discuss later in this chapter. The oil peak issue is also important because it will signal changing realities to everyone who follows the oil markets.

Markets and the people that compose them make decisions often based on anticipation, well before events take place. The stock market, for instance, will go down if people anticipate that interest rates will go up. And it will go up if they believe that the economy will get better. Sometimes this happens many months before the economy actually shows serious signs of improvement. The same is likely true regarding anticipation about an oil peak arriving and oil declining thereafter.

Naturally, rising prices will decrease demand for oil and perhaps result in near-term equilibrium of supply and demand. But rising prices will also take their global toll in the form of inflation, increased input costs, reduced demands for non-oil goods and services, and lower investment in net oil-importing countries.[18] The extent of that economic dislocation is likely to depend on how well the world has prepared for it. It is fair to say that the more viable the alternatives to oil and the less dependent the world is on oil, the less serious will be the potential effects of peak oil.

Third and finally, the oil peak is important because it will signal, for a variety of reasons, an era in which the Middle East becomes even more critical for global oil. We now can turn to that issue.

INCREASING DEPENDENCE ON MIDDLE EAST OIL

Irrespective of when oil peaks, the Middle East will become increasingly important as a supplier of oil. That might sound strange since we already focus attention on much dependence on Arab oil, especially in the post–September

11 environment, during which US-Saudi relations became more strained and questions arose, often in exaggerated fashion, about how reliable the Saudis will be as oil suppliers.

As is well known, the world's oil reserves are concentrated in the Middle East. After we draw down oil reserves all over the world, Middle East oil will remain as the crucial resource base. In fact, even if we make major changes in oil consumption, the Middle East will still become more important as an oil supplier. As it stands, none of the twenty-four oil-producing nations that have already extended past peak production, except Iran, are in the Persian Gulf region.[19]

In the past two decades, the share of oil as a percentage of total energy consumption by the major industrialized countries actually declined from 55 percent in 1980 to 40 percent in 2000.[20] Arab Gulf states, in particular, have lost and not regained market share, partly as a result of the long-run impact of the 1973 oil embargo, which motivated conservation and exploration into oil alternatives and into non-OPEC oil. By 1982, oil production from areas outside the Middle East overtook oil production from the region for the first time.

Although the demand for OPEC oil has decreased since 1973, world dependence is projected to increase in the future, with the Persian Gulf serving as the principal source of supply to meet rising demand over the next two decades.[21] This will make the Gulf increasingly important to the global economy and the question of oil security even more germane.[22] Persian Gulf oil production is expected to increase from around 30 percent of world total to 39 percent by 2020.[23] According to the US Department of Energy, the region holds about two-thirds of the 1 trillion barrels of global oil reserves (or around 672 billion barrels), whereas the United States by contrast holds about 4 percent.

GLOBAL SPARE CAPACITY

It is not just that most of the world's global reserves are in the Middle East, but also that 80 percent of the world's spare oil capacity is there—a percentage that may well increase over time. Spare capacity, or idle capacity, is the amount of oil that can be brought onto the market in a short period of time, in case of a major oil disruption. Spare capacity is not just a function of how much oil a country has but to what extent it has the production capability to bring oil onto the market quickly. Saudi Arabia holds most of the world's spare capacity, and the country is carrying out plans to increase this capacity significantly, despite the serious drop in oil prices in 2008 and early 2009.[24]

Oil prices are determined by several factors, including the amount of excess ("spare") world oil production capacity relative to total world oil supply. For instance, during the mid-1990s, the world averaged around 2.5 MMBD of "spare" capacity. During that period, oil prices generally hovered below $20 per barrel. With the 1998 Asian economic crisis, oil demand growth slowed dramatically, spare production capacity rose, and prices plummeted, bottoming out around $10 per barrel in December 1998 and January 1999. World spare capacity at that point was close to 5 MMBD.

As is typical of world oil markets, this situation soon changed. Low oil prices and resurgent economic growth spurred rapid world oil demand growth in Asia and elsewhere. Combined with underinvestment in world capacity, this led to a reversal of the spare capacity situation by 2003, following a series of oil crises in Venezuela, Nigeria, and Iraq. By 2005 and 2006, spare capacity bottomed out around 11.5 MMBD, the lowest it had ever been relative to total world oil supply. Predictably, oil prices rose sharply, approaching $40 per barrel by the end of 2004, $60 per barrel by late 2005, and close to $70 per barrel during the summer of 2006.

If oil prices rise when spare capacity falls, what about the opposite? In fact, history shows that when spare capacity increases, as it did in the mid-1980s and the late 1990s, oil prices fall. When spare capacity spikes, oil prices can even collapse. (See Figure 14.1.)

Indeed, there is good reason to believe an increase in spare capacity would decrease oil prices. Imagine if the United States cut its oil consumption from currently projected levels by 3 MMBD over the next decade.[25] While spare capacity is held chiefly by Saudi Arabia and Kuwait, as a result of their ability to bring oil to market quickly in a crisis, eventually the American cut in consumption would increase world capacity. It could more than double from its 2007

FIGURE 14.1: OIL PRICES VS. SPARE CAPACITY, 1990–2006

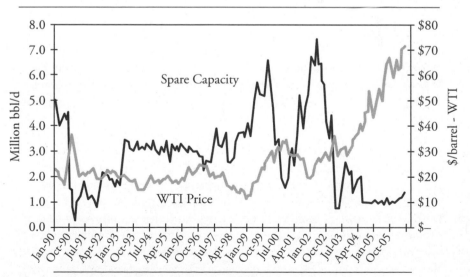

WTI="West Texas Intermediate," a standard oil price indicator.
Source: Energy Information Administration

level to over 5 MMBD, because the pressure on Saudi Arabia and other oil-rich countries to supply the market would decrease.

Yet, on our current trajectory, the United States is not projected to decrease oil consumption, and the world's oil consumption is expected to increase, making Middle East spare capacity even more important. Even more significant, such concentrated spare capacity—in addition to increasingly concentrated oil reserves—will make the region's security and political developments more important to the functioning of the world economy. These threats are discussed in the following sections.

OIL SUPPLY DISRUPTIONS

Threats to the free flow of oil certainly exist and could arise at any time. Such threats can develop anywhere in the world: Nigeria's ethnic conflicts have resulted in oil disruptions; Venezuela experiences mercurial politics under President Hugo Chavez, who at times has threatened to cut off oil to the United States; Russia has used energy for purposes of political coercion in Eastern Europe. However, historically, the most serious threats have arisen in the Middle East. While that is unlikely to change, what will change is that such threats will be weightier and produce more serious consequences for oil prices and the global economy. This is because the Middle East will become increasingly critical as a provider of oil to the world economy. Indeed, describing the results of the IEA's landmark 2008 study, Nobuo Tanaka asserted that the rising imports of oil and gas into Organisation for Economic Co-operation and Development (OECD) regions and developing Asia, "together with the growing concentration of production in a small number of countries, would increase our susceptibility to supply disruptions and sharp price hikes."[26] The sections below discuss in brief the key threats to the free flow of global oil, all of which exist in, or emerge from, the Middle East. Some of these threats may never materialize, and others may materialize very soon or many years down the road.

Military Threats to Oil Security

Various regional military threats to oil security are germane, but three are most prominent: efforts to shut down the Strait of Hormuz; to engage in interstate aggression; and to use or threaten to use weapons of mass destruction (WMD).

Much of the world's oil travels through the thirty-four-mile-wide Strait of Hormuz. At its core, it consists of two-mile-wide channels for inbound and outbound Gulf tanker traffic, as well as a two-mile-wide buffer zone. Closing the strait would require the use of alternative routes (if available), such as the Abqaiq-Yanbu natural gas liquids line across Saudi Arabia to the Red Sea. But that would impose higher transportation costs and greater lag times for delivery. Around 40 percent of the world's oil exports pass through the strait daily, a number the US Department of Energy projects will climb to 60 percent by 2030.[27]

Iran poses the key threat to the Strait of Hormuz. Iran's ability to interdict or shut down oil traffic is enhanced by anti-ship missiles, mine warfare, amphibious assets, and submarines. Such assets are not enough to challenge American military forces in a sustained, conventional engagement, but certainly offer the ability to conduct forms of unconventional warfare. Such capabilities are enhanced by Iran's long coastline dominating the strait and by its position on the Greater and Lesser Tunbs and Abu Musa, which are islands near the strait that it seized in 1992.

Prior to the US-led reflagging of Kuwaiti oil tankers in which the US Navy escorted them through the Persian Gulf in 1986–1987, Iran harassed these oil tankers. This was part of Iran's effort to prosecute the war against Iraq, which Iraq had launched in September 1980. Iran attacked Kuwaiti tankers in its war against Iraq because Kuwait was one of Iraq's financial supporters, Later, in November 1994, it began increasing troop strength and deploying anti-aircraft missiles on the Gulf islands near the strait, in ways Washington viewed as threatening oil traffic. Iran also tripled the number of missiles deployed on its Gulf coast and began fitting Chinese-built cruise missiles on its naval boats in 1995–1996, which US military officials saw as heightening the threat.[28] Since 2006, Iran has further developed various anti-ship missile capabilities[29] and anti-ship mines,[30] and plans to launch the first Iranian-built destroyer for what it calls rapid naval strikes on US ships in the Gulf.[31] It has also engaged in regular and escalating major military exercises in the Strait of Hormuz since the UN Security Council approved economic sanctions against the country on December 23, 2006.[32]

To be sure, Tehran must recognize that disrupting Gulf shipping would produce countermeasures and would diminish its own oil exports. Yet, a UN economic embargo of Iran might trigger Tehran to try to close the strait, as could the use of force against Iran's nuclear facilities. Iranian officials have suggested repeatedly that while Iran, the world's fourth largest exporter, supports the stable flow of oil, it reserves the option to shut down the strait if threatened.[33]

Iran represents the chief threat to global shipping, but it is not impossible that Iraq may become a military threat to Kuwait in the future. Democratizing states can be more violent than democracies or autocracies.[34] An autocratic or dictatorial Iraq could also threaten Kuwait, if buoyed by continuing public views that Kuwait is part of Iraq; if faced with domestic ills from which it wants to divert attention; and if in conflict with Kuwait over oil production.

If Iraq splinters into its three historic parts, Iran's influence over Iraq's Shia will likely increase, perhaps allowing it to influence Kuwait and Saudi Arabia. It is hard to determine just how much influence Iran has in Iraq and could have in future scenarios in Iraq, but it is fair to say that its influence has increased significantly since the 2003 invasion of Iraq,[35] in a variety of ways.[36] As just one sign of this, the Iraqi Shiite leader, Muqtada al-Sadr, has repeatedly asserted that his militia would defend Iran if it were attacked by the West.[37] While his star has faded in Iraq, with the increasing success of American forces in stabilizing Iraq and co-opting the Sunni insurgents, he or other Shia leaders may well cooperate with Iran in the future.

If Iran's influence increases in the future, and if it appears that its power cannot be checked at the regional or global level, Saudi Arabia and Kuwait could be more likely to accommodate Iran on various issues, including oil pricing in OPEC. This is because they would be more reluctant to challenge a powerful Iran in a region where perceptions of power count heavily. Moreover, a serious Iranian bid for regional hegemony, especially in the relative absence of influence by moderates at the domestic level, could also generate the types of broader instabilities in the region, which usually spook oil markets. As a result, it appears that even after the United States withdraws from Iraq, a strong American deterrent against increased Iranian power in Iraq will be important, even if it is over the horizon or at some distance from the actual points of potential conflict. The United States will want to pursue a well-planned role as an outside balancer in the region.[38]

In addition to threats against the Strait of Hormuz and to threats regarding Iraq, WMD represent an indirect threat to oil security. Iraq nearly developed nuclear capability prior to the 1991 Gulf War, and Iran may be able to produce nuclear weapons in the coming years. The Iranian nuclear crisis has unfolded in slow motion, but it escalated on January 10, 2006, when Iranian officials broke the International Atomic Energy Agency seals on equipment at the Natanz facility to restart prohibited uranium enrichment activities. Iran appears intent on pursuing enrichment well into the future, though it repeatedly asserts that its program is for peaceful purposes—a point accepted by a majority of Iranians.[39]

For his part, Ayatollah Ali Khamenei has referred to nuclear technology as the future of Iran. During the anniversary of the revolution in February 2007, he criticized those who say "nuclear technology is not a necessity for the country at this price," and asserted that the Iranian nation insists on the nuclear issue. Khamenei added that "the reason for the opposition to Iran's access to nuclear technology, despite [Western countries'] access to the technology, is that they wish to dominate the fate of the world's sources of energy."[40] Earlier on, Khamenei asserted that Muslim nations demand to end "nuclear monopoly headed by a greedy few" and that "many of the nations neither understand nuclear energy nor understand that it is their inalienable right. . . . Our people understand that nuclear energy is a great and palpable indicator of progress. . . . If a nation does not possess this it would be in trouble."[41]

Even a small nuclear weapon could destroy major oil facilities, and threats of radiological, chemical, and biological weapon attacks cannot be discounted. Even if Iran or other states in the region never use WMD, they could enable brinkmanship or coercion because others would be aware of their existence. This could facilitate efforts by Iran to coerce other OPEC states, such as Saudi Arabia, into lowering oil production to raise the price of oil or into launching an embargo for various political ends. Nuclear weapons could also make it harder for the United States to deploy regional forces, for the obvious reason that leaders would be less willing to take the risk of massive casualties.

Terrorism

In addition to more conventional threats, terrorists can also threaten oil security. Terrorist acts could produce significant spikes in oil prices, not only by virtue of their impact on oil supply but also because of their psychological impact on markets.[42] Traders would have to ask whether more attacks of this nature were coming.

Terrorists could do damage in various ways. They could hit sensitive points in Saudi Arabia's eight most significant oil fields, both onshore and offshore, and cause major problems in supply that could last months. Loading terminals, such as at Ras Tanura, and oil pipelines could also be hit along the broader Saudi oil system, or from Saudi oil facilities to outside markets. The Abqaiq extra light crude complex, with a capacity of 7 MMBD, is the "mother of all processing facilities" and a grand target, because a moderate to severe attack could create a loss of oil equal to that of the 1973 embargo.[43] Terrorists could also hijack ships and use them to attack ports and facilities[44] or hit large oil reservoirs, such as Kuwait's Burgan Field, which was crippled by Iraq's invasion in 1990.[45]

In fact, it is very likely that al-Qaeda has targeted such facilities. The bombing of the French-flagged supertanker *Limburg* in the Arabian Sea off Yemen's southeastern Hadramaut coast on October 6, 2002, underscored such intentions. On the same day the *Limburg* was attacked, the Al Jazeera network in Qatar broadcast an audiotape in which Osama bin Laden warned that Islamic forces were preparing to attack the crusaders' "economic lifeline,"[46] referring to the supply of oil to the American and Western world. In addition, the Saudis claimed in April 2007 that they foiled a major terrorist effort to attack their oil facilities.

Terrorism aimed at regional monarchs, if successful, could also hurt oil security, by weakening their position and slowly creating an atmosphere conducive to their overthrow. Increased domestic terrorism could dispose them to appease their anti-American domestic critics and to decrease cooperation with Washington, in the hope that they can placate at least part of the political spectrum that might sympathize with the terrorists. In fact, the Saudis moved in that direction after the September 11 terrorist attacks, while seeking to preserve their relations with the United States.[47] Meanwhile, after a lengthy national debate,[48] the United States substantially diminished its military profile in Saudi Arabia and started to build sophisticated military facilities in Qatar, where it also moved its Central Command headquarters in 2003.

The Rise of Extremists in Saudi Arabia

While terrorism could seriously affect oil security, an even bigger threat is the fall of the Saudi regime to Islamic radicals.[49] It is impossible to know exactly what such a radicalized regime would do, but based on the views of such radicals, it is likely that they would limit or cut US relations; deny the United States worst-case-scenario access to Saudi strategic facilities; oppose Mideast peace efforts; possibly align more closely with Iran; eschew antiterrorism measures at the domestic and international level; and decrease oil production to increase oil prices and oil revenues and to defy Washington. The combined effect of these actions would be to hurt oil security and raise prices, even if the new regime did not resort to oil embargoes and sought to provide a stable flow of oil to the global economy.

Saudi Regional Orientation

Short of falling to extremists, a threat also exists that the Saudi regime will genuflect more toward Iran than toward the United States. Riyadh has shown a sporadic proclivity to seek security more by accommodating than by opposing potentially threatening actors, which was true even when the Saudis faced the serious threat of Iraq's forces on their border, after the 1990 Iraqi invasion of Kuwait. They considered accommodating Saddam Hussein and exhibited much concern about letting American forces into the kingdom.[50]

To be sure, accommodating threatening actors can make sense. Even Washington blessed the Saudi-Iranian rapprochement that began in late 1997 and early 1998. But the real question is under what conditions such a rapprochement benefits oil security. Security can be threatened if a resurgent Iran slowly lures Riyadh toward its foreign policy orientation. This is because Iran, as an OPEC hawk, has sought higher oil prices than the Saudis have wanted; has at least threatened an oil embargo; seems to seek WMD capability; explicitly wants to eject US regional forces;[51] and has been far less supportive of Mideast peace efforts than Saudi Arabia. Indeed, Iran's support of Hamas and Hizbullah has hurt peace efforts, as suggested by Hizbullah's war with Israel in Lebanon and by the rejection of peace efforts by both groups. Absent Iran's strategic and political support, both actors would be less able to disrupt the peace process.

The Oil Weapon

Global attention has focused increasingly on the question of oil dependence, especially in the post–September 11 period and in light of the US-led war in Iraq. Irrespective of the fate of the Saudi regime, Arab states or Iran could be motivated independently, multilaterally, or through OPEC or the Arab League to use the oil weapon to exploit Western oil dependence. In April 2002, an official close to Crown Prince Abdullah reportedly suggested that Riyadh could use the "oil weapon," but it then dismissed that possibility.[52] Many Saudis, despite close US ties, still believe, as Gause puts it, that their "country's finest hour was when it defied the United States with the 1973 Arab oil embargo."[53] While the potential for the use of the oil weapon has probably gone down over the past three decades, it is very hard to predict the future. The Middle East can change in ways that make the oil weapon a possibility in the future. At a minimum, such a threat carried out by one or more countries cannot be discounted.

DEVELOPMENTS THAT MITIGATE THREATS TO OIL SUPPLIES

While threats to oil supplies are serious, as suggested in the previous sections of this chapter, and can arise at any time, it is important not to exaggerate threats to oil supply. The Middle East is likely to become even more important due to these threats, but several developments over the past thirty years also could help mitigate such serious disruptions.[54] It is useful to consider these developments to obtain a balanced view of the threats we are likely to face in the coming years and even decades.

In 1979, Iran's leader, Ayatollah Ruhollah Khomeini, seized power and sought to export Iran's revolution across the oil-rich Gulf. The Saudi regime appeared on the verge of falling, with massive uprisings by Iranian-inspired Shia Muslims in the eastern Hasa oil province and the seizure of the Grand Mosque at Mecca by Islamic zealots. Today's Iran, by comparison, is far less aggressive toward the oil-rich Arab states. It is true that it appears to be pursuing nuclear weapons as well as the ability to weaponize and to deliver them, and that its position as a leader of Shiites in the Middle East has probably increased. Those are serious issues, but Iran does not threaten regional oil supplies as it did in the period following the revolution.

In addition, Saddam's Iraq was a veritable powerhouse in 1979, bent on regional domination. The oil-rich Arab monarchs were scrambling to mollify Iraq, even while they feared it. Saddam is gone. His military is disbanded. Iraq is attempting to become a democracy. It could try to threaten the region again in the future. However, it is far less aggressive now than it was under Saddam. And its ability to produce oil has gone up dramatically with the end of Saddam's regime, the lifting of UN sanctions, and the increasing international investment in its oil industry.

In 1979, Washington was militarily inept at protecting Gulf oil supplies. For that, it relied on the doomed shah of Iran. Today, the United States can guard against some—though not all—of the worst-case threats to oil supplies.

Egypt and Israel made peace in 1979, but the chance of an Arab-Israeli war, which could trigger use of the Arab oil weapon, was still far higher than it is today. Back then, Egypt was ostracized for making peace; the Soviet Union was supporting Syria, Iraq, and Libya, thus emboldening them; Israel's military advantage was far less clear to Arab states than it is today; US credibility was in tatters because of its perceived inability to save the shah, and extreme pan-Arabism was much stronger. Today, no combination of Arab states can expect to defeat Israel militarily.

The world suffered two recession-causing oil shocks in the 1970s—the 1973 embargo and the 1979 Iranian revolution. Today, OPEC and Saudi Arabia often try to, albeit clumsily, increase oil supply when needed.

While OPEC's abilities have been tested recently by growing global demand, its members know that the high oil prices of the 1970s provoked alternative energy and oil exploration, which cost them market share. By enabling and motivating alternatives to OPEC oil, the rise of high technology and environmental concerns only placed added pressure on OPEC to moderate prices.

That matters less when OPEC is pumping near capacity, but more under typical circumstances. In 1973, industrialized countries lacked petroleum reserves and the know-how to use them in crises. Today, these reserves, both commercial and strategic, offer at least 90 days of import protection for most industrialized states and 141 days for the United States, and they have been used effectively in crisis and noncrisis situations.

For instance, on the eve of the military attack on Iraq on January 16, 1991, oil prices rose significantly and geopolitical fears ran amok. But the United States announced a coordinated strategic petroleum reserve sale with Europe and Japan through the International Energy Agency, and oil prices dropped precipitously, despite the fact that America sold only half of what it had announced. The drop in oil prices was also a function of reports of successful US-led military action, but there is no doubt the Strategic Petroleum Reserve (SPR) release played both a real and a psychological role in calming oil markets, underscoring the successful management of the United States and the International Energy Agency, which was created in response to the 1973–1974 Arab oil embargo.[55]

In 1979, the superpowers were locked in a dangerous global rivalry. The end of the Cold War and the events of September 11 caused a major shift in the oil sector. US-Russian business and national cooperation, despite Vladimir Putin's autocratic turn and Russia's occasional efforts to use energy for political ends, has in some ways increased in the effort to bring Russian energy to the world. During the Cold War, Soviet energy went mainly to the Soviet bloc.

Serious threats to oil supplies do exist and new ones may arise, but these broader developments are also important to understand. They put oil security into perspective. Even so, it is hard not to conclude that the tectonic plates of global oil will lie increasingly in the Middle East and be subject to its political, economic, and security earthquakes, both big and small.

ALTERNATIVES TO OIL

The foregoing analysis in this chapter makes something clear. It is important to develop alternatives to oil if we are to avoid a future in which the factors explored in this chapter make the global economy increasingly reliant on the Middle East.

The good news is that the global public increasingly has realized the importance of generating alternatives to oil.[56] Public opinion polls from 1974 through 2006 show that Americans are as concerned about the US energy situation now as they were during the nation's energy crises of the 1970s, and are more receptive to developing alternative energies and taking other steps to decrease oil dependence.[57]

However, the intensity of that realization; the actions of governments; and collective, global efforts have fluctuated over time. US energy policy has often responded to oil crises and accompanying high oil prices. The 1973 Arab oil embargo, for instance, triggered conservation, a serious search for alternatives to oil, the lower 55-mile-per-hour speed limit, the development of strategic petroleum reserves, and better US-global coordination to reduce consumption and deal with future crises. But as the oil crisis receded, so did the American appetite for serious alternatives to oil, a performance that would be repeated each time the United States suffered a major oil shock. As Figure 14.2 indicates, America has become more, not less, dependent on foreign sources of oil over time.

ANNUAL ENERGY REVIEW, 2007

Most recently, we saw yet another version of a similar story. High oil prices caused a serious change in consumer behavior and triggered serious action by the US government.

The spike in oil prices from $57 per barrel in February 2007 to $145 per barrel by summer 2008 spurred serious interest in alternatives once again in the business community, with even the famous oil man T. Boone Pickens putting forth his energy proposal based on the use of natural gas and wind power, on the way to a longer run effort to transition the United States away from oil. It seems to be a maxim or at least a strong tendency that the higher prices go, the more entrepreneurs around the world work to decrease global oil dependence. High prices triggered consideration and discussion of approaches, ranging from methanol to geothermal, to algae and bioengineering. High prices also pushed automakers to consider more seriously the potential to mass-produce more efficient, less pricey vehicles. In June 2008, for instance, General Motors changed its old business model. It closed four pickup and SUV factories, announcing a new small car that could get 45 miles per gallon. High oil prices also pushed consumers to buy more efficient vehicles. Such vehicles, such as gas-electric

FIGURE 14.2: CONSUMPTION, PRODUCTION, AND
IMPORT TRENDS, 1950–2007

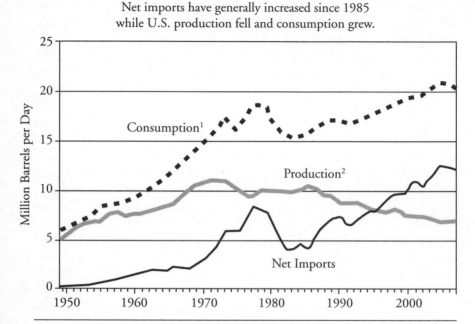

Net imports have generally increased since 1985
while U.S. production fell and consumption grew.

1. Petroleum products supplied is used as an approximation for consumption.

2. Crude oil and natural gas plant liquids production.

Source: Energy Information Administration Annual Energy Review 2007, Table 5.1. (June 2008);
June 2008 Import Highlights: August 13, 2008.

hybrids, represent a 2 percent drop in the market bucket, yet, in the summer of 2008, sales of large SUVs plummeted over 30 percent, while small car sales boomed.

By December 2008, oil prices plummeted to under $40 dollars per barrel—from $145 just months before—and the race to generate alternatives to oil was dealt somewhat of a blow, even if only temporarily.

The vast fluctuation in oil prices, and, in turn, prospects for developing alternatives to oil, is a function of the combined actions of traders on global oil markets, mainly on the New York Mercantile Exchange. When they believe oil prices will rise, they buy oil futures contracts in the hope of selling them later for a profit, and that increases oil prices.

Of course, oil prices fell in 2008 and 2009 due to the global recession, which decreased real and expected oil demand. The dollar, which had been weak, also increased in strength. Since oil is traded in dollars, a stronger dollar translates into lower oil prices. But the story was more complex than economic fundamentals alone. Oil traders pay attention to global political events, which they think may impact supply or demand or the perceptions of other traders. The big concern had been Iran. But US saber-rattling against Iran diminished in the fall, leading many to dismiss chances that a lame-duck Bush administration would attack Iran. Iraq has also largely stabilized; Venezuela's Hugo Chavez's threats to cut off oil have assumed a "boy who cried wolf" effect; and even oil-rich Nigeria's ethnic conflicts have temporarily calmed down.

The drop in oil demand also tripled the amount of idle oil capacity—a cushion of oil that can help deal with crises that disrupt oil supply. This cushion makes traders less likely to believe that oil prices will spike in the near future and, therefore, less likely to buy oil futures now.

Speculation and investment psychology were also big factors. For a while, the Oil Rush was on. Much money bought oil futures. Energy hedge funds tripled in number from 2000 to 2008. A herd mentality drove prices higher than economic fundamentals warranted.

The Wall Street meltdown of 2008 reversed the Oil Rush. Some hedge funds tied to oil futures collapsed, and big institutional investors liquidated some oil positions to raise cash and to service panicky clients.

As for OPEC, it tried to increase oil prices with production cuts. But low oil prices hurt OPEC discipline, because OPEC members are more likely to overproduce what they have promised, in order to raise enough revenue to meet their budget targets at home.

The search for alternatives to oil—the type of search that is critical for decreasing our dependence on global oil and the increasing importance of the Middle East in that equation—will depend in part on the future of oil prices. It appears that oil prices will rebound strongly at some point. Why? The US and global economies can't stay down forever. Oil demand will return and, and at some point, may well stress our finite oil supply, based on current data-driven projections.

Globally, President Barack Obama has asserted that a nuclear Iran is unacceptable. Yet, Iran has defied global pressure to abandon uranium enrichment; asserted that, if attacked, it could close down the Strait of Hormuz, through which 20 percent of the world's traded oil flows; and threatened to cut off 2.4 million barrels of its daily oil exports. This crisis, and other global hot spots, may well heat up in the future.

As for the Oil Rush, it's hard to imagine that speculators will not return, once they sense that oil prices will rise. And, for its part, OPEC's discipline to abide by production cuts should increase as well, when the price of oil rebounds.

But while oil prices may very well rebound in the future, spurring the search for alternatives and altering consumption habits, there is no telling whether such prices will remain high or will return to lower levels. The challenge for American energy policy is to try to produce a tax on carbon that does not hurt the economy.

CONCLUSION

At this time, it appears clear that the world is headed toward greater global oil demand. It also appears clear that the Middle East will become more important in the global oil picture. This is because it holds by far the largest reserves of oil in the world. As oil begins to peak in various countries, most of the world's non-peaking states will be in the Middle East, increasing the percentage of oil from the Middle East the world uses each year. In addition, even now about 80 percent of the world's spare capacity lies in the Middle East. That amount will also increase given the region's relatively massive oil reserves.

These developments and trends will make political and security developments in the region more vital. It is important not to exaggerate the number and seriousness of threats to Middle East oil, but these threats certainly exist and are unpredictable. The potential for such disruptions has been, and is likely to continue to be, far more prominent in the Middle East. As global demand rises and oil supply falls, oil disruptions in the region will produce more serious effects for global supplies and prices.

Clearly the race is on between these factors and trends, which at this time appear to be creating the potential for a highly volatile future, and the potential for developing alternatives to oil that mitigate this scenario. That makes it all the more critical to move ahead in earnest to deal with global oil dependence. A few policy points are worth making in this regard.

First, it is a myth that America has not responded to oil crises. But when oil prices dropped postcrisis, the United States lost interest in fighting its oil addiction. President Obama must convince Americans that oil dependence is a long-term problem, despite short-term oil prices. Otherwise, he'll have trouble passing his energy plans.

Second, Obama should focus on transitioning the inefficient US vehicle fleet, where most of America's oil goes, to efficient hybrid–flex fuel and hybrid-electric vehicles, so we'll be ready when the oil price bogeyman returns. Had Detroit done this years ago, it might not have run into such significant problems. Obama must also work with industrializing countries, such as China, to make a similar transition. Data show that the Chinese are buying gas guzzlers at a fast rate and repeating America's energy mistakes. As my developing research with a colleague demonstrates, even if America went 100 percent hybrid, China's fleet would consume all of the oil savings from this move by 2021, if China continued on its current path. We must get China on the right track now if we expect to deal with long-term global oil dependence.[58]

Third, to give alternatives to oil a boost in their race with global oil trends, one policy measure in particular could be very helpful. Indeed, the most direct and efficient measure from an economics point of view would be a higher gas tax, which, as I will discuss, would not be an overall tax increase. It is hard to predict the impact of taxes on consumption, but we do know that $3 per gallon of gasoline had an impact on sales of large SUVs and other gas guzzlers following Hurricane Katrina in late August–early September 2005. According to a report from the Cambridge Energy Research Associates, those gasoline prices produced the first drop in the number of miles driven by Americans in twenty-five years. Sales of SUVs and light trucks dropped from a peak of 56 percent of all vehicles sold in the United States in 2004 to just under 53 percent in 2005 and 2006.[59]

Drawing on data from the US Energy Information Administration, we can see that from 1984 to 1992, US gasoline prices rose 3.3 percent annually on average. During that same period, US gasoline demand rose 1.6 percent annually. By contrast, from 2002 to 2006, US gasoline prices rose 14.3 percent annually on average. In that same period, US gasoline demand rose just 0.9 percent annually. The fastest growth in US gasoline demand occurred in 1998, at 2.9 percent. That year, gasoline prices fell 13.7 percent.[60] Generally speaking, the rate of growth in US gasoline demand has increased when prices have fallen, and vice versa.

Dramatic and sustained changes in US gasoline consumption will likely require higher prices through the use of government tax policy. As we all know, higher US gas taxes are a hard sell politically, even though the United States has by far the lowest such taxes in the entire industrialized world. To push a gas tax hike through Congress will require the type of determined, even courageous, leadership we haven't seen in many years. It will also require serious changes in public attitudes. On the latter point, Daniel Yankelovich has suggested that the American public may be reaching a tipping point of concern on oil dependency.[61] This may be due to such rising concerns as global climate change; that oil-rich Saudi Arabia was the source of most of the 9/11 hijackers; and the costly war in Iraq, which some associate with oil dependency. Such public concerns may represent a silent, underlying level of support for gas taxes, which could be tapped by strong leaders.

The massive spike in oil prices in 2008, and any future spikes in oil prices, may further raise support for a gas tax. In addition, the Obama administration has already raised consciousness about the importance of developing a serious energy policy. And Obama's energy team, including the new energy czar, appears committed to incentivizing alternative energies, even if they are not committed to a gas tax increase.

Let's assume that gas tax increases remain politically unpalatable and require some sweetening. One approach could be to decrease taxes on other goods and services in a 1:1 ratio to any gas tax increase. A colleague of mine who worked for the Department of Energy for seventeen years and I call this the "offset plan." This "revenue neutral" approach would be easier to sell to the public than a straight tax increase. In the offset plan, the average American's overall tax burden would not go up one cent, but oil consumption—exactly what we want to reduce—would be targeted directly. Among other things, the plan would have to account for the fact that gas taxes would hit poorer Americans harder, because they are on tighter budgets. To compensate for this, one could cut other regressive taxes, such as those on food taxes or payroll. One could also increase subsidies for mass transit, giving poorer Americans more opportunities to get where they need to go without hopping in a car.

Another approach, which could be combined with the offset plan, would be to phase in any gas tax slowly and gradually. Thus, the tax increase could start at 5 cents per gallon the first year, and increase by 5 cents per gallon each subsequent year. All revenues collected could go to (a) reduce other taxes, (b) subsidize low-income people who are hit disproportionately by higher gas taxes, and (c) subsidize the purchase of highly fuel-efficient cars and trucks.

The gas tax would raise prices in a predictable manner, thus allowing for greater and more lucrative business planning and investment into alternatives. And the monies from the tax would reenter the American economy, unlike higher oil prices that embolden some of America's adversaries.

Finally, it is certainly possible to create incentives and disincentives to encourage a change in America's driving habits. For instance, one could institute a system whereby car buyers receive a rebate of $100 for every mile per gallon above mandated levels, while buyers of vehicles under that level would pay an extra $100 for every mile per gallon. Make it $200 if you want, or $500, per mile per gallon, depending on how rapidly you wanted to cut US oil consumption. Regardless, the message would be sent to consumers: Buy what you want, but be aware that the cost will now incorporate the environmental and national security impacts of your purchase.

In closing, it is worthwhile to reiterate a metaphor: The race is on. It is useful to think about alternatives to oil, and it is also useful to consider the future of oil. But the two phenomena are linked not only in that one affects the other, but also because our ability to avoid serious oil shocks in the future will depend in part on how determinedly, quickly, and sustainably we develop alternatives, without seriously hurting the US and global economies.

We should all want one of the runners to win in this race. Failure to take serious actions on oil dependence will leave the United States and the world increasingly dependent not just on oil but on oil from the Middle East. That should be viewed as a major national security concern of the first order.

NOTES

1. See www.eia.doe.gov/oiaf/ieo/world.html.

2. See www.eia.doe.gov/conf_pdfs/Monday/shealy.pdf (accessed on January 3, 2009).

3. L. F. Ivanhoe, "World Oil Supply—Production, Reserves and EOR," Hubbert Center Newsletter, January 2000.

4. C. J. Campbell and J. H. Laherrere, "The End of Cheap Oil," *Scientific American*, March 1998; Kenneth Deffeyes, *Hubbert's Peak: The Impending World Oil Shortage* (Princeton, NJ: Princeton University Press, 2001); David Goodstein, *Out of Gas: The End of the Age of Oil* (New York: W. W. Norton, 2004, 2001); Paul Roberts, *The End of Oil: On the Edge of a Perilous New World* (Boston and New York: Houghton Mifflin, 2004); and Matthew Simmons, *Twilight in the Desert: The Coming Saudi Oil Shock and the World Economy* (New York: Wiley, 2005).

5. Doris Leblond, "ASPO Sees Conventional Oil Production Peaking by 2010," *Oil & Gas Journal*, June 30, 2003, p. 28.

6. See Goodstein, *Out of Gas*, p. 17.

7. For a technical analysis of Hubbert's work, see J. H. Laherrere, "Learn Strengths, Weaknesses to Understand Hubbert Curve," *Oil & Gas Journal*, April 17, 2000, p. 63.

8. Kenneth S. Deffeyes, *Hubbert's Peak*. Also, see R. C. Duncan and W. Youngquist, "Encircling the Peak of World Oil Production," *Natural Resources Research* 8, no. 3 (1999): 219–232. Duncan sees a peak under three different scenarios as being reached between 2003 and 2016. Richard Duncan, "Three World Oil Forecasts Predict Peak Oil Production," *Oil & Gas Journal*, May 26, 2003.

9. See Alex Berenson, "An Oil Enigma: Production Falls Even as Reserves Rise," *New York Times*, June 12, 2004, pp. A1, B3.

10. *International Energy Outlook 2004* (Washington, DC: Department of Energy, Energy Information Administration, 2004), p. 15, www.eia.doe.gov/oiaf/ieo/index.html.

11. Leonardo Maugeri, "Not In Oil's Name," *Foreign Affairs* 82, no. 4 (July–August 2003): 169.

12. On possible problems with this analysis, see Deutsche Bank, "Hubbert's Pique," *Global Energy Wire*, June 2003. Also, see www.eia.doe.gov/pub/oil_petroleum/presentations/2000/long_term_supply/sld001.htm. Goodstein, *Out of Gas*, ch. 1.

13. For thinkers representative of this school, see J. L. Simon, *The Ultimate Resource 2* (Princeton, NJ: Princeton University Press, 1996); and M. Adelman, "My Education in Mineral (Especially Oil) Economics," *Annual Review of Energy and the Environment* 22 (1997): 13–46.

14. "IEA: World Energy Demand to Grow Briskly to 2030," *Oil & Gas Journal*, October 14, 2002, p. 16.

15. For the full report, including more easily accessed slide presentations and graphs, see www.energybulletin.net/node/47190.

16. See www.iea.org/textbase/press/pressdetail.asp?press_rel_id=275.

17. George Monbiot, "When Will the Oil Run Out," *The Guardian*, December 15, 2008.

18. Standing Group on Long-Term Co-operation: The Impact of Higher Oil Prices On the World Economy (World Energy Outlook.org: International Energy Agency).

19. For data, see Duncan, "Three World Oil Forecasts Predict Peak Oil Production."

20. On global dependence, see the statement by the Saudi minister of petroleum and mineral resources, Ali I. Naimi, in *OPEC Bulletin* 31 (March 2000): 6.

21. *International Energy Outlook 2006* (Washington, DC: Energy Information Administration, June 2006), pp. 34–35.

22. See *International Energy Outlook 2007* (figure 39) at www.eia.gov/oiaf/ieo/pdf/world.pdf.

23. Energy Information Agency (EIA), *International Energy Outlook 2000* (Washington, DC: US Department of Energy).

24. http://zawya.com/printstory.cfm?storyid=ZAWYA20081110045446&l=045400081110.

25. The Department of Energy uses these levels to help determine future global demand and supply.

26. See www.iea.org/textbase/press/pressdetail.asp?press_rel_id=275.

27. See www.eia.doe.gov/emeu/security/choke.html#HORMUZ.

28. Remarks by Secretary of Defense William H. Perry to the Washington State China Relations Council, October 30, 1995, *Defense Issues* (Washington, DC: Department of Defense, 1995).

29. With Chinese aid, Iran has developed the Noor radar-guided, anti-ship missile, which Hizbullah evidently used against an Israeli ship on July 14, 2006. Douglas Barrie, "Iran Acquires Additional Chinese Missile Technology," *Aviation Week & Space Technology*, April 10, 2006, p. 33.

30. See Michael Knights, "Deterrence by Punishment Could Offer Last Resort Options for Iran," *Jane's Intelligence Review*, March 20, 2006; Robert Hewson, "Iran Ready to Field Maritime Cruise Missile," *Jane's Defence Weekly*, February 24, 2004, p. 13.

31. See www.chinfo.navy.mil/clips/18apr07.doc.

32. Associated Press, "Iran Test-Fires Russian Missiles Near Strait of Hormuz," *Gulf News*, February 8, 2007, http://archive.gulfnews.com/indepth/irancrisis/General/10102714.html.

33. For instance, Parisa Hafezi, "Iran Will Never Abandon Nuclear Work," Reuters, January 8, 2007.

34. See Edward D. Mansfield and Jack Snyder, *Electing to Fight: Why Emerging Democracies Go to War* (Cambridge, MA: MIT Press, 2005).

35. See Geoffrey Kemp, "Iran and Iraq," US Institute of Peace, Special Report No. 156, November 2005, http://usip.org/pubs/specialreports/srl156.html.

36. See Kenneth Katzman, "Iran's Influence in Iraq," CRS Report to Congress, July 9, 2007, http://fpc.state.gov/documents/organization/88749.pdf.

37. See, for instance, Ellen Knickmeyer and Omar Fekeiki, "Iraqi Shiite Cleric Pledges to Defend Iran," January 24, 2006, www.washingtonpost.com/wp-dyn/content/article/2006/01/23/AR2006012301701.html.

38. On how it has not pursued such an approach over the past several decades, see Steve A. Yetiv, *The Absence of Grand Strategy: The United States in the Persian Gulf* (Baltimore: Johns Hopkins University Press, 2008).

39. "Public Opinion in Iran and America on Key International Issues, Questionnaire: (PIPA)," 2006, WorldPublicOpinion.org.

40. Vision of the Islamic Republic of Iran (Network 1), February 17, 2007.

41. Ibid., November 9, 2006.

42. "Big Oil Ready for Possible Terror Strike," *Oil Daily*, February 18, 2003.

43. Robert Baer, *Sleeping With the Devil* (New York: Crown Publishers, 2003).

44. See Eric Watkins, "Sea Terrorists Threaten Oil," *Oil & Gas Journal*, June 18, 2007, p. 30.

45. Neal Adams, *Terrorism & Oil* (Tulsa, OK: PennWell Corporation, 2003), p. 102.

46. Ed Blanche, "Tanker Terror," *Middle East* (December 2002).

47. See the view of Crown Prince Abdullah, "Abdullah Speaks Out," *Middle East Economic Digest*, February 1, 2002.

48. On this debate, see *Middle East Economic Digest*, January 25, 2002, p. 2, and *APS Diplomat News Service*, December 10, 2002.

49. For post-9/11 views of this threat, see *APS Diplomatic Operations in Oil Diplomacy*, January 28, 2002, and John E. Peterson, *Saudi Arabia and the Illusion of Security* (London: Oxford University Press for the International Institute for Strategic Studies, 2002). On Saudi stability, see Sherifa Zuhur, "Saudi Arabia: Islamic Threat, Political Reform, and the Global War on Terror," March 2005, www.carlisel.army.mil/ssi.

50. See Steve A. Yetiv, *Explaining Foreign Policy: U.S. Decision-Making and the Persian Gulf War* (Baltimore: Johns Hopkins University Press, 2004).

51. This has largely been its policy since the revolution. For a good statement of Iran's view, see "Tehran, Voice of the Islamic Republic of Iran," BBC Summary of World Broadcasts/Middle East, August 27, 1990.

52. Quoted in Patrick E. Tyler, "Saudi to Warn Bush of Rupture Over Israel Policy," *New York Times*, April 25, 2002, p. A1.

53. F. Gregory Gause III, *Oil Monarchies: Domestic and Security Challenges in the Arab Gulf States* (New York: Council on Foreign Relations Press, 1994), p. 122.

54. For this extended argument, see Steve A. Yetiv, *Crude Awakenings: Global Oil Security and American Foreign Policy* (Ithaca, NY: Cornell University Press, 2004).

55. On its efforts to deal with supply disruptions, see www.iea.org/Textbase/nppdf/free/2007/Oil_Security_flyer.pdf, accessed January 15, 2009.

56. See Daniel Yankelovich, "The Tipping Points," *Foreign Affairs* 85, no. 3 (May–June 2006): 115–125.

57. See Toby Bolsen and Fay Lomax Cook, "Public Opinion on Energy Policy," *Public Opinion Quarterly* 72, no. 2 (September 2008): 364–388.

58. For data and graphs on China's rising and projected oil consumption and vehicle usage, see www.eia.doe.gov/conf_pdfs/Monday/shealy.pdf, accessed January 15, 2009.

59. www.cera.com/aspx/cda/public1/news/pressCoverage/pressCoverageDetails.aspx?CID=8533.

60. This paragraph is based on data from www.eia.doe.gov/emeu/steo/pub/a4tab.html.

61. Daniel Yankelovich, "The Tipping Points."

GLOSSARY

Abbasid   Islamic dynasty, 750–1258 CE.

Abu Bakr   The first caliph to succeed the Prophet Muhammad.

Al-Aqsa Mosque   Islamic holy site next to the Dome of the Rock, Jerusalem.

Alawis   Religious sect found largely in Syria but also in Turkey, claims to be a branch of Shia Islam.

Ali   The Prophet Muhammad's son-in-law, who became the fourth caliph.

Allah   Arabic name for God.

Almohad   Berber dynasty that ruled parts of Spain and North Africa, twelfth and thirteenth centuries.

Almoravid   Berber dynasty that ruled parts of Spain and North Africa, eleventh and twelfth centuries.

Amal   Shia political group in Lebanon.

Arab   A person whose native language is Arabic.

Arab League   Organization of Arab states, formed in 1945.

Ashkenazi   Occidental, or "Western" Jews, largely of European origin.

Assassins   A Shia tribe living in the Zagros Mountains in Persia (modern Iran) during the Umayyad and Abbasid period.

Atatürk, Kemal   Founder of modern Turkey.

Ayatollah   Title of a high-ranking Shia leader.

Ayyubid   Islamic dynasty founded in Cairo by Salah ad-Din, 1171–1260.

BCE   Before the Common Era, used to replace BC as designating the years before the birth of Christ.

Baath   In Arabic, "renaissance," political parties organized around Arab nationalism.

Bahai   A religious group founded in nineteenth-century Persia.

Bedouins   Nomadic peoples.

Begin, Menachem   Prime minister of Israel, 1977–1982, signer of the Camp David Accords.

Berber   Family of languages identifying indigenous peoples living in North Africa.

Bey Ottoman rank for district governors, right under the rank of Pasha.

Bida Innovation, practices against Islamic tradition.

CE Common Era, the time period corresponding to AD, after the birth of Christ.

Caliph Title conferred to one who claims succession to the Prophet.

Caliphate Rule through principles of Islam, by claimant to successor to the Prophet.

Camp David Accords Israeli-Egyptian peace accord signed in 1979.

Church of the Holy Sepulcher Believed site of crucifixion of Christ, located in Jerusalem.

Civil society Nongovernmental organizations that attempt political change or influence.

Confessional A political system divided along religious lines, particularly in Lebanon.

Coptic A Christian sect, found mostly in Egypt, Sudan, Ethiopia, and Eritrea.

CSO Civil society organizations.

Dar al-harb the world outside Islam, literally "the abode of war."

Dar al-Islam the Islamic world, literally "the world of Islam."

Destour Party Tunisian nationalist party.

Dhimmi Muslim term for Christians, Jews.

Dome of the Rock Believed site of the Prophet Muhammad's ascent into heaven.

Druze Derivation of Ismaili Shia, found mostly in Lebanon, Syria, and Israel.

Emir (or Amir) Title of ruler, used mostly in the Persian Gulf Arab states.

Fatimid Shia dynasty started in North Africa around 911 CE.

Fatwa A religious advisory opinion.

Fiqh Islamic jurisprudence.

Fitna Rebellion, or disorder.

Freedom House New York–based nongovernment organization that ranks political freedom.

GCC Gulf Cooperation Council, formed in 1961, including Saudi Arabia, Qatar, Kuwait, Bahrain, the United Arab Emirates, and Oman.

GDP Gross domestic product, a measure of economic performance.

Hadith Islamic lessons based on sayings or actions of the Prophet Muhammad.

Hajj Pilgrimage to Mecca, required of all Muslims capable of performing it.

Halal Activities permissible for Muslims.

Hanafi Liberal school of Sunni Islamic law.

Hanbali Conservative school of Sunni Islamic law, prevalent in Saudi Arabia.

Haram Activities forbidden for Muslims.

Hashemites Ruling family of the Najd region of Saudi Arabia, became ruling family of Iraq (until 1958) and Jordan.

Hijab Head covering worn in public by Muslim women.

Hijrah 622 CE, the year of Muhammad's journey to Medina, and year 1 of the Islamic calendar.

Hizbullah (1) Shia political movement based largely in south Lebanon, literally "Party of God." (2) Turkish Islamist group, unaffiliated with the Lebanese Hizbullah.

Hussein ibn Ali Son of Ali, major figure in Shia religion.

Ibadi Kharijite-inspired Islamic religious sect, predominantly in Oman.

ibn Literally "son of" in Arabic.

IDF Israeli Defense Force.

Ijtihad In Islam, reasoning independent of Islamic tradition.

Imam Muslim prayer leader, spiritual leader in Shia communities.

Imamiyya Shia Muslims who follow the tradition of the Hidden, or twelfth, Imam.

IMF International Monetary Fund.

Intifada Term for two Palestinian uprisings against Israeli occupation, literally meaning "shaking off" in Arabic.

Islah "Reform" in Arabic, often the name taken by a party advocating reform.

Istiqlal Moroccan independence party.

ISI Import substitution industrialization, policies directed at economic independence through national industrial production.

Islam Religion based on the Quran and the life of Muhammad.

Ismailis ("Seveners") Shia followers of the seventh imam, Ismail.

Ithna Asharis ("Twelvers") Shia followers of the twelfth imam, born Abu-Qasim Muhammad ibn Hasan, or "Mahdi," the "Hidden Imam."

Jihad Literally, "struggle" or "striving" in Arabic.

Jizya Tax paid by non-Muslims (specifically Jews and Christians) who live in Islamic societies.

Kaaba Black building in the center of the Grand Mosque in Mecca, and the focus of Muslim prayers.

Kafir (Kefir) In Islam, an unbeliever.

Kharijite Rebellious movement against Muslim leaders, dating to seventh century.

Kurds A linguistic minority living in Turkey, Iran, Iraq, and Syria.

Levant A region of the eastern Mediterranean.

Madrasa Muslim religious school (literally "school" in Arabic).

Maghreb The part of North Africa west of Egypt.

Maliki Sunni school of law emphasizing public welfare.

Mamluk Term applied to slave soldiers who founded a dynasty of the same name in Cairo, 1260–1517.

Maronite A Monophysite Christian sect dating to the time of St. Maron. Its members live mostly in Lebanon.

Mecca (Makka)   Birthplace of the Prophet Muhammad, considered the holiest city in Islam, located in modern Saudi Arabia.

MENA   Middle East and North Africa.

Mesopotamia   Historical land now occupied largely by Iraq and parts of Syria.

Miraj   The Arab name for Muhammad's nocturnal journey to heaven.

Muhammad   The person Muslims believe received revelations from God (Allah) that became the Quran.

Muslim   A person believing in Islam.

Mutawwa   Once scholars of religion specializing in religious ritual, now the Committee to Propagate Virtue and Prohibit Vice in Saudi Arabia.

Neo-Destour Party   Tunisian political party, split from the Destour Party in 1934.

Nomenklatura   Traditionally, Russian elite, sometimes used to describe any national elite, particularly a bureaucratic state elite.

NGO   Nongovernmental organization.

OAPEC   Organization of Arab Petroleum Exporting Countries.

OECD   Organisation for Economic Co-operation and Development.

OPEC   Organization of Petroleum Exporting Countries.

Ottoman   Turkish empire, late thirteenth century to the end of World War I.

PA   Palestinian Authority.

Pasha   Ottoman title for provincial rulers, above the title of Bey, also an honorary title.

Persian   Language spoken in Iran, also called Farsi.

PLO   Palestine Liberation Organization, later to become the PA, or Palestinian Authority.

POLISARIO   Frente Popular de Liberación de Saguía el Hamra y Río de Oro (Popular Front for the Liberation of Saguia el-Hamra and Río de Oro), political group that claims the Western Sahara.

Purchasing power parity   Standardized dollar price weights applied to goods and services in a particular national economy, used to compare economic strength.

Qadi   Judge in Islamic jurisprudence.

Quran   Text Muslims believe to be collected revelations from God given to Muhammad (literally "recitation" in Arabic).

Ramadan   Ninth month of the Islamic calendar, requiring fasting and sexual abstinence for Muslims.

Rashidun   "Rightly guided," the Islamic terms for the first four caliphs after the death of the Prophet Muhammad.

Rents   Returns from ownership of natural or strategic resources.

Rentier states   States that derive a significant portion of their national income from rents from natural or strategic resources, such as petroleum.

Sahrawi Inhabitants of the Western Sahara.

Salafiyya Literally "pious" or "venerated" ancestors, a term for those who turn to the earliest Islamic community for current inspiration and guidance.

Shah Persian title for ruler.

Sharia Islamic law.

Sasanian Ancient empire stretching from Iraq and Iran into Central Asia.

Sheik Title of honor for an elderly man.

Sephardi Oriental, or "Eastern" Jews, largely of non-European origin.

Shia Islamic branch that supports the claim of Muhammad's son-in-law Ali as caliph.

Shura "Council" in Arabic, often the title of a legislature.

Sufi Form of Islamic mysticism.

Sunni Islamic branch that followed from the succession of the first three caliphs, today the majority Islamic branch.

Sultan Islamic leader title, used in the Arab world only in Oman.

Takfir In Islam, a declaration of Muslim heresy, or excommunication.

Tawhid In Islam, the unity, or "oneness" of Allah.

Ulama Muslim religious scholars.

Umar ibn Al Khattab Second of the four "rightly guided" caliphs.

Umayyad The first Sunni dynasty, 681–750 CE.

Ummah Muslim community.

UN United Nations.

Uthman ibn Affan Third of the four "rightly guided" caliphs.

Wahhabism Puritanical form of Islam inspired by Muhammad Al Wahhabi, also called al-Muwahiddun.

Waqf In Islam, a religious endowment, or those who manage such an endowment.

WMD Weapons of mass destruction, including nuclear, chemical, and biological.

Western Sahara Disputed territory southwest of Morocco, which claims it as a part of Morocco.

Western Wall Believed site of remains of Jewish Second Temple, located in Jerusalem.

Zaydi A branch of the Shia faith whose followers recognize Zayd ibn Ali, the fifth imam.

Zakat One of the five pillars of Islam, a tax fulfilling the obligation to give to the poor.

BIOGRAPHIES
OF KEY PEOPLE

Abbas, Mahmoud (1935–) Mahmoud Abbas is president of the Palestinian Authority, having succeeded Yasir Arafat in that position. Abbas (also known as Abu Mazen) extended his term in 2009 for another year, though rival Hamas does not recognize the extension. Abbas grew up in Syria and studied in Egypt and the Soviet Union. He was a founding member of the Palestine Liberation Organization in 1957, rising through the ranks to his present position.

Ahmadinejad, Mahmoud (1956–) Mahmoud Ahmadinejad is president of Iran. In 1997 he received a PhD in engineering, and served as an administrator and provincial governor before becoming mayor of Tehran. He joined the Basiji militia and claimed to have served in the Iran-Iraq war. While serving as Iranian president, Ahmadinejad became noted for calling upon God to destroy the state of Israel and for denying the Holocaust. He took a strong adversarial position against the United States and against neighboring Arab countries. In 2009, Ahmadinejad won a disputed presidential election.

Ali ibn Talib (approximately 600–661) Ali ibn-Talib was the son-in-law and cousin of the Prophet Muhammad, and the fourth caliph, from 656–661. Ali was chosen caliph only after three other companions of Muhammad served in the position, and those who supported his claim of the position were known as *Shiat Ali*, or "Partisans of Ali," shortened to Shia. Rival clans contested Ali's elevation to caliph, and after he offered to negotiate the question, a follower murdered him. His second son, Hussein ibn Ali, died at the Battle of Karbala, Iraq, in 680 at the hands of a Sunni army.

Arafat, Yasir (1929–2004) Yasir Arafat was chair of the Palestine Liberation Organization, and first president of the Palestinian Authority. Arafat was apparently born in Cairo, though he claimed to have been born in Jerusalem. He studied engineering at Cairo University and fought in the 1948 war. Later he helped to found Fatah, the Palestinian national liberation movement. Fatah launched military raids into Israel and struck at targets believed to support the Israeli cause. Arafat operated out of Jordan until 1970, when the Hashemite monarchy ousted Fatah, which moved to Lebanon until Israeli military actions forced it to Tunisia. In 1988 Arafat renounced terrorism and reduced his demands for a Palestinian state to the West Bank, Gaza, and East Jerusalem. After the Oslo-Madrid Accords of 1992, Arafat became the first president of the Palestinian Authority.

al-Asad, Bashar (1965–) Bashar Asad is the current president of Syria, taking over after the death of Hafiz al-Asad in 2001. He is an eye physician by training and was studying in London when his brother, Basil al-Asad, died in Damascus and Bashar was called back to Syria to prepare for the presidency. He suggested that he would liberalize Syria's economy and political life, but his proposed reforms ran into opposition at high levels, and Syria under Bashar is relatively unchanged from the Hafiz al-Asad years.

al-Asad, Hafiz (1928–2000) President of Syria, 1971–2000. Hafiz was a military pilot, and member of the minority Alawi religious sect, who became president after a military coup in 1970. Asad joined the Baath Party at a young age and rose through the ranks to become defense minister in 1966. He used Syria's poor performance in the 1967 war to launch a bid for power himself. Once president, he showed caution in some instances (withdrawing Syrian forces from battle against Israel in Lebanon in 1973) while showing determination in other cases, as in the 1973 war. He cracked down stridently against domestic opposition, ordering the crushing of the violent Muslim Brotherhood in 1982. He entered into peace talks later in his presidency but was unable to complete the process, dying in 2000.

al-Banna, Hassan (1906–1949) Hassan al Banna was an Egyptian nationalist and reformer who founded the Muslim Brotherhood in the 1920s. His anti-British nationalism led him to believe that Egyptians were abandoning Islam, and he began to emphasize Islamist ideas as a counter to Western influence in Egypt. The Muslim Brotherhood grew into a social network that, for al Banna, countered the lack of public provisions from a weak government. The Egyptian monarchy, fearful of the Muslim Brotherhood's widening influence, ordered it disbanded, and after unknown assailants assassinated the prime minister, another set of unknown assassins killed al Banna in February 1949.

Ben Ali, Zine el Abidine (1936–) Ben Ali is the current president of the Republic of Tunisia, having deposed President Habib Bourguiba in 1987. Ben

Ali's senior career began in internal security, serving as interior minister until October 1987, when Bourguiba appointed him prime minister, but a month later he replaced Bourguiba as president. While Ben Ali continued Tunisia's liberal economic tradition, he also continued Tunisia's restricted political system.

Ben Gurion, David (1886–1973) First prime minister of Israel. David Grün, who later changed his name to Ben Gurion, was born in Poland and migrated to Palestine in 1906. He became a journalist and helped to found the Labor Zionist movement. He later chaired the Jewish Agency and supported the original British-inspired partition plan to divide Palestine into Arab and Jewish communities. He led Jewish military forces during the 1948 war and became prime minister with the proclamation of the State of Israel in May 1948. During his first term, Ben Gurion presided over the construction of Israel, resigning in 1953, but returning as prime minister two years later. During the latter term he presided over the unsuccessful Sinai campaign in 1956 and retired in 1970.

Bourguiba, Habib (1903–2000) Habib Bourguiba served as the first president of the Republic of Tunisia from 1957 to 1987. Bourguiba was born in Tunisia, educated in the law in France, and was an advocate for Tunisian independence. French authorities initially arrested him, but a change in French leadership saw France ultimately grant Tunisia independence, with Bourguiba as founding president. Bourguiba emphasized a liberalized economic model, and a relatively pro-Western foreign policy, resisting the prevailing calls of Arab nationalism and socialism. He also advocated a liberal understanding of Islam and women's rights in society. Bourguiba was named President for Life, but in 1987 Prime Minister Zine el Abidine Ben Ali declared Bourguiba medically unfit to be president and assumed the post himself.

Erdoğan, Recep Tayyip (1954–) Recep Tayyip Erdoğan is prime minister of Turkey and chair of the Justice and Development Party (Adalet ve Kalkınma Partisi, or AKP). He served as mayor of Istanbul, and his relatively mild Islamist policies caused controversy. Turkish authorities arrested Erdoğan after he gave a speech with strong Islamist symbolism, and after his election in 2002, the authorities had to amend the constitution to permit him to serve as prime minister. He has voiced support for both secularism and the legacy of Kemal Atatürk since his electoral victory.

Fadlallah, Muhammad Hussein (1935–) Muhammad Hussein Fadlallah created the theological foundations for Hizbullah, the Lebanese political group that has both militia and social objectives. Fadlallah was born in Iraq but his family moved to Lebanon in 1952. He established many Shia social organizations, and called for resistance against Israel and the United States, which reportedly responded by attempting to assassinate Fadlallah.

Hariri, Rafiq (1944–2005) Rafiq Hariri served as Lebanon's prime minister between 1992 and 1998, and again between 2000 and 2004. He resigned in 2004 and died in February 2005 in a massive bomb blast in Beirut. His death sparked a significant political shift that forced Syria to withdraw most of its influence from Lebanon.

Hassan II (1929–1999) Hassan II was king of Morocco from 1961 until his death in 1999. He was a conservative ruler, allied with the West because of his fears of communism, but he governed without much public participation, earning criticism for Morocco's human rights record. The Moroccan military twice tried to assassinate Hassan II in the early 1970s, and, partly in response, Hassan II declared the Spanish Sahara, vacated by Spain, a sovereign part of Morocco. Hassan II died in 1999, and his son, Mohammed VI, succeeded him.

Herzl, Theodor (1860–1904) Theodor Herzl was a major founder of the Zionist movement in Europe. Born in Hungary, Herzl served as a journalist, chronicling the so-called Jewish Question regarding the status of Jews in European society, ultimately becoming president of the Zionist Congress, which advocated a Jewish state in Palestine.

Hussein ibn Ali (626–680) Hussein ibn Ali was the son of Ali ibn Talib, becoming the second Shia imam after his brother Hassan declined, or was poisoned. Hussein viewed the leaders of the Umayyad caliphate as usurpers, and journeyed to Kufa (now in modern Iraq) to support a Shia revolt there, but he and his forces were surrounded and killed by a Sunni Umayyad army in October 680, an event commemorated by Shia each year as Ashura.

Hussein ibn Talal (1935–1999) Hussein bin Talal was the third king of Jordan, following Abdullah I and Hussein's father, Talal. Hussein became king in September 1951, serving until his death in 1999. His reign emphasized modernity and studied neutrality from the great power conflicts of the Middle East, though he joined other Arab countries in the 1967 war, losing East Jerusalem and the West Bank of the Jordan River as a consequence. In 1970 Hussein ousted the Palestine Liberation Organization from Jordan after the PLO tried to instigate an uprising against the king. Hussein signed a peace accord with Israel in 1994, having relinquished Jordan's claim to the West Bank in 1988. He tried to assist peace efforts between Israel and both Syria and the Palestinians until his death in 1999.

Hussein, Saddam (1937–2006) President of Iraq between 1979 and 2003. Saddam Hussein was born in the town of Al-Auja, near the city of Tikrit, joining the pan-Arab Baath Party of Iraq in 1957. He joined an attempt to assassinate Iraqi President Qassim in 1959 and was wounded in that effort. He rose in the ranks of the Baath Party, particularly after its assumption of power in 1968. He became a general in the Iraqi armed forces and gradually eliminated political rivals in the Baath until assuming the presidency in 1979. He ordered the invasion of Kuwait in 1990, but coalition forces ousted his troops from that country a year later. After the September 11, 2001, terrorist attacks on the United States, president George W. Bush invaded Iraq, driving Saddam from power and into hiding. US forces discovered him, and the Iraqi government put him on trial for mass murder, specifically the killing of residents of the town of Dujayl in 1982. He was found guilty and hanged in December 2006.

Khamenei, Ali Hoseyni (1939–) Supreme Leader of Iran, 1989 to the present. Initially elected president of Iran, Khamenei served in that post from 1981 to 1989, when the Assembly of Experts selected him as Supreme Leader after the death of Ayatollah Khomeini. Khamenei, like Khomeini, was a Shia cleric, though he lacked the religious credentials for appointment as a grand ayatollah. Khamenei does not normally participate in daily political decision making but does sometimes intercede to correct "theologically incorrect policies," and directed that the questionable results of the 2009 presidential election be accepted.

Khomeini, Ruhollah Musavi (1902–1989) Khomeini served as Supreme Leader of Iran from 1979 to the time of his death ten years later. Khomeini was born to a family with roots to an early imam in the Shia tradition, and he built upon this position through Shia religious studies. He became an opponent of Shah Muhammad Pahlavi, who sent Khomeini into exile in 1964, first to Iraq, and then to France after Saddam Hussein exiled him from Iraq. Khomeini's followers continued to work against the shah, and in 1979, after riots forced the shah to leave Iran, Khomeini returned in triumph. He implemented his vision of Shia governance, *vilayat-e faqih*, which requires clerical rule, a concept not accepted by other Shia groups, including Hizbullah. Khomeini died of a heart attack in June 1989.

Muhammad ibn Abdullah (570–632) Muhammad ibn Abdullah is considered the last Messenger of God by Muslims. He was born in Mecca and became a merchant. While on retreat in a cave south of Mecca, he received the first of a series of revelations from God ("Allah" in Arabic), which became the Quran. Muhammad began to propagate his message and gained a small group of followers, which grew after some citizens of Medina invited him to settle a dispute in 622 (the year of hijra, now year one in the Islamic calendar). He later led an expedition that returned him to power in Mecca and later, according to tradition, performed a nocturnal journey to heaven by way of Jerusalem to receive the final revelations now contained in the Quran. He died of illness in 632 and is buried in Medina.

Nasser, Gamal Abdel (1918–1970) Nasser served as second president of the Arab Republic of Egypt. He was a career military officer who fought in the 1948 war, only to be captured by Israeli forces. In 1952 he and his fellow members of the Free Officers Movement seized power from the monarchy, and Nasser became president in 1954 after engineering the removal of Muhammad Naguib from the post. Nasser almost immediately turned against the Muslim Brotherhood, believing that it was behind assassination plots against him. He took military aid from Soviet bloc countries, leading the United States to withhold economic assistance to Egypt. Nasser did modernize the Egyptian economy, expanding electrical and industrial production while breaking up large farms and redistributing land to peasants. Nasser offered to resign after the poor performance of the Egyptian military in the 1967 war, but in the end remained in power until his death in 1970.

Netanyahu, Benyamin (1949–) Prime Minister of Israel between 1996–1999 and currently serving after the 2009 elections. Netanyahu is head of the Likud Party and has also served as foreign minister and finance minister, and as Israeli ambassador to the United Nations.

Pahlavi, Reza Khan (1878–1944) Reza Khan led a revolt that toppled the Qajar dynasty in Persia in 1925 and, taking the Pahlavi name for his dynasty, established an authoritarian state that he named Iran (from "Aryan"). He was a modernizer who built railroads, roads, and educational systems while ending restrictions on women and Iran's Jewish population. He became increasingly unpopular during his last years, and after the British and Soviets occupied his country in 1941, the British forced him into exile.

Pahlavi, Muhammad Reza (1919–1980) Shah Muhammad Reza Pahlavi was the son of Reza Khan Pahlavi, and first ruled Iran as shah after his father's exile in 1941. He continued to modernize Iran's economy while relying more on the military and a secret police network for control. His modernization efforts alienated key elements in Iranian society, and the increasingly powerful Prime Minister Mohammed Mossadegh gained political power until the CIA and British intelligence worked with Iranian supporters of the shah to topple Mossadegh and return the shah to power in 1953. In 1979 the Iranian revolution inspired by Ayatollah Ruhollah Khomeini ended the shah's reign and he fled the country, dying of cancer in Cairo in 1980.

Peres, Shimon (1923–) Current president of Israel. Initially a member of the Labor Party (initially Mapai) and long-serving Knesset member, Peres was appointed prime minister after the Yitzhak Rabin assassination, but his party lost to Likud in 1999. Peres was never elected as prime minister, and he also lost the presidential election in 2000. He served as head of several ministries and in 2005 left Labor to form the new Kadima Party with his old rival, Ariel Sharon.

Qadhafi, Muammar (1942–) Leader of Libya, though he holds no formal title. Qadhafi was a military officer who participated in the 1969 overthrow of the Sanusi monarchy. Qadhafi rejected the idea of formal government and instead created a *jamahiriya*, or "state of the people." Qadhafi also authored a series of books known collectively as the "Green Book," which was his interpretation of Islamic principles, though most Muslims do not consider it authoritative.

Qutb, Sayyid (1906–1966) Sayyid Qutb was a scholar and Islamist thinker whose work inspired the Egyptian Muslim Brotherhood, and al-Qaeda leader Ayman Zahwahiri cites Qutb. Qutb was an educator who studied in the United States, and returned disappointed in what he believed was American moral decay. Qutb authored several significant works, including *Ma'alim fi al-Tariq* (Milestones), where he argued that most Muslims had slipped into a pre-Islamic state of ignorance (*jahiliyyah*) and they could return only through a strict implementation of sharia law. Qutb criticized in particular Muslim rulers who did not implement sharia, putting him on a collision course with Gamal Abdel Nasser, Egypt's president, who had Qutb arrested numerous times. In 1966 Nasser ordered Qutb hanged, raising his status to martyr in some Islamist circles.

al-Sadr, Musa (1929–1978?) Musa al-Sadr was a Shia leader who was instrumental in founding the Lebanese political group Amal. Sadr was born in Iran but moved to Lebanon and became a Shia leader in Tyre. He traveled to Libya in 1978 and disappeared, raising suspicion that Libyan leader Muammar Qadhafi ordered his death, a charge denied in Libya.

al-Saud, Abdul Aziz (1876–1953) Founding king of Saudi Arabia, and head of the dynasty that still rules the country. Abdul Aziz al-Saud, also known as Ibn Saud, started a campaign in 1902 to take land from a rival tribe, gaining support from the Wahhabi religious family. He unified most of the Arabian Peninsula in 1932 and named it Saudi Arabia after his family. He combined tradition and modernity in his nation-building effort, justifying his tradition on the conservative Wahhabi understanding of Sunni Islam while convincing influential clerics of the need to adopt modern technology. He died in 1953 and his sons have succeeded him.

al-Saud, Abdullah (1924–) Current king of Saudi Arabia. Abdullah Bin Abdul-Aziz became regent of Saudi Arabia in 1996 after King Fahd Bin Abdul Aziz suffered a stroke and king in 2005 after Fahd's death. King Abdullah wrote a Palestinian-Israeli peace plan and sponsored several interfaith discussions.

Ibn Taymiyya, Taqi ad-Din Ahmad (1263–1368) Noted Islamic theologian whose writings and arguments have formed the basis of *salafist* Sunni Islam, emphasizing the need for the Sunni to return to the initial Islamic traditions and teachings. Ibn Taymiyya was a follower of the Hanbali school of Sunni Islam, and reified many of its teachings, particularly the duty of jihad and the identification of the Shia as apostates. His teachings are often cited as the inspiration for the later teachings of Sayyid Qutb and other contemporary Sunni Islamists.

CHRONOLOGY
OF SIGNIFICANT
MIDDLE EAST EVENTS

4000 BCE–334 BCE:	Kingdoms in Egypt, Mesopotamia
500 BCE–400 BCE:	Persian Empire
570 CE:	Birth of the Prophet Muhammad
632:	Death of the Prophet Muhammad
680:	Battle of Karbala
691–750:	Umayyad Caliphate
909–1171:	Fatimid Caliphate
750–1258:	Abbasid Caliphate
1258–1260:	Mongol invasion
1099–1290:	Crusader era
1171–1250:	Ayyubid period
1258–1260:	Mongol invasion of the Middle East
1517–1918:	Ottoman Empire
1876–1925:	Qajar dynasty
1925–1979:	Pahlavi dynasty
1914–1918:	World War I
1916:	Sykes-Picot Agreement
1916–1917:	Arab Revolt
1917:	Balfour Declaration
1920:	Treaty of Sèvres
1920:	Founding of Turkish Republic
1922:	Egyptian independence
1924:	Iraqi independence
1925:	Yemeni independence
1932:	Establishment of Saudi Arabia
1939–1945:	World War II

1941:	Syrian independence
1943:	Libyan independence
1946:	Lebanese, Jordanian independence
1948:	Emergence of the state of Israel
1951:	Omani independence
1952:	Founding of the Arab Republic of Egypt
1952:	Assassination of Jordan's King Abdullah I
1956:	Tunisian, Moroccan independence
1961:	Kuwaiti independence
1962:	Algerian independence
1967:	War between Israel and Arab states
1970:	Qatari independence
1971:	Establishment of the United Arab Emirates, Bahrain
1973:	War between Israel and Arab states
1979:	Iranian revolution
1981–1989:	Iran-Iraq war
1983–2004:	Israeli invasion and occupation of parts of Lebanon
1990–1991:	Iraqi invasion of Kuwait
1991:	Oslo-Madrid peace conference
2003:	US-led invasion of Iraq
2006:	War between Hizbullah, Israel

CONTRIBUTORS

Eric Davis is a professor of political science at Rutgers University. He received his PhD from the University of Chicago. He has written *Memories of State: Politics, History and Collective Identity in Modern Iraq* (Berkeley: University of California Press, 2004); *Challenging Colonialism: Bank Misr and Egyptian Industrialization, 1920–1941* (Princeton, NJ: Princeton University Press, 1983); *Statecraft in the Middle East: Oil, Historical Memory and Popular Culture* (with Nicolas Gavrielides) (Gainesville: University Press of Florida, 1991), along with numerous articles and chapters in edited books. He has been appointed a fellow at the Hoover Institution, Stanford University; the Institute for Advanced Study, Berlin; the Shelby Cullom Davis Center for Historical Studies, Princeton University; and the Center for the Critical Analysis of Contemporary Culture and the Rutgers Center for Historical Analysis, Rutgers University, and has received grants from the Social Science Research Council, the Ford Foundation, the National Endowment for the Humanities, and IREX, among others.

Christopher Hemmer is professor of international security studies at the US Air Force's Air War College. Before that he taught at Cornell University and Colgate University. He received his PhD in 1998 from the Department of Government at Cornell University. He is the author of *Which Lessons Matter? American Foreign Policy Decision Making in the Middle East, 1979–1987* (Albany: State University of New York Press, 2000), and articles in *Political Science Quarterly*, *Middle East Policy*, and *Orbis*, among others.

Clement M. Henry is a professor in the department of government at the University of Texas at Austin. He has authored, coauthored, or edited dozens of books, including *Globalization and the Politics of Development in the Middle East* (with Robert Springborg) (Cambridge: Cambridge University Press, 2001), *The Mediterranean Debt Crescent: Money and Power in Algeria, Egypt,*

Morocco, Tunisia, and Turkey (Gainesville: University Press of Florida, 1996), and scores of scholarly articles in *World Politics, Middle East Journal, Comparative Politics,* and many others. He previously served on the faculties of the University of California at Berkeley, the University of Michigan, American University of Cairo, and the Institut d'Etudes Politiques de Paris. His PhD is from Harvard University.

Dafna H. Rand is a senior professional staff member of the US Senate. A former Exchange Scholar in the Department of Political Science at Yale University, she has published numerous articles on North African politics. She received her PhD from the Department of Political Science at Columbia University.

Chantel Pheiffer holds a BA in government and a minor in economics from Smith College, where she graduated cum laude in 2009. A native of South Africa, she received a 2009–2010 DAAD (German Academic Exchange Service) Scholarship to Germany where she will study German-Namibian relations at the University of Freiburg and conduct an independent research project on the Herero genocide at the Arnold-Bergstraesser-Institut Freiburg.

Glenn E. Perry is a professor of political science at Indiana State University. He received his PhD in foreign (international) affairs at the University of Virginia in 1964 and later studied in the Department of Oriental Studies at Princeton. He is the author of many books, articles, and chapters on Middle Eastern politics and history, including *The Middle East: Fourteen Islamic Centuries*, 3rd ed. (Upper Saddle River, NJ: Prentice Hall, 1997), and *The History of Egypt* (Westport, CT: Greenwood Histories of the Modern Nations, 2004). Much of his recent work deals with issues related to the paucity of democracy in the area.

David S. Sorenson is a professor of international security at the US Air Force's Air War College, having previously taught at Denison University and the Mershon Center at Ohio State University. He is the author of *Introduction to the Modern Middle East* (Boulder, CO: Westview Press, 2008) and six other books, along with numerous articles and chapters in edited books. He holds a PhD from the Graduate School of International Studies, University of Denver.

Gregory White is a professor of government at Smith College. He has written *On the Outside of Europe Looking In: A Political Economy of Morocco and Tunisia* (Albany: State University of New York Press, 2001) and numerous articles and book chapters. The recipient of a Mellon Foundation grant for 2009–2010, he will be in residence at Columbia University's Department of Earth and Environmental Sciences.

Onn Winckler is an associate professor in the Department of Middle Eastern History, University of Haifa. His major fields of academic research are political demography and economy of the Arab countries; inter-Arab relations; and the modern history and politics of Arab countries. Among his recent publications are *Arab Political Demography*, 1st and 2nd eds. (East Sussex: Sussex Academic Press, 2005, 2009); *Rethinking Nasserism: Revolution and Historical Memory in Modern Egypt* (edited with Elie Podeh) (Gainesville: University Press of Florida, 2004); "The Economic Consequences of the Iraqi Crisis on the Mashreq Countries," *Mediterranean Politics* (November 2006); and "The Failure of Pronatalism of the Developed States 'with Cultural-Ethnic Hegemony': The Israeli Lesson," *Population, Place and Space* 14 (March–April 2008): 119–134. He received his PhD in 1994 from the University of Haifa.

Amy Elizabeth Young obtained her PhD in social anthropology from Harvard University in 2005 and is currently an assistant professor of anthropology at Gettysburg College. Her research is on the women's rights movement in Morocco. Among her publications is a chapter in the volume *Mirrors of Justice: Law and Power in the Post-Cold War Era*, ed. Kamari Maxine Clarke and Mark Goodale (Cambridge: Cambridge University Press, 2010).

Steve Yetiv is a professor of political science at Old Dominion University and an award-winning author and teacher. He came to ODU in 1993 after a post-doctoral position at Harvard University's Center for Middle Eastern Studies (1990–1992) and a research associate position at Harvard's Center for International Affairs (1992–1993). His recent books include *Explaining Foreign Policy: U.S. Decision-Making and the Persian Gulf War* (Baltimore: Johns Hopkins University Press, 2004); *Crude Awakenings: Global Oil Security and American Foreign Policy* (Ithaca, NY: Cornell University Press, 2004); and *The Absence of Grand Strategy: The United States and the Persian Gulf: 1972–2005* (Baltimore: Johns Hopkins University Press, 2008). His articles have appeared in *Security Studies*, the *British Journal of Political Science*, and the *Middle East Journal*.

Yahia H. Zoubir is a professor of international relations and international management at Euromed Marseille School of Management in France. Zoubir is the coauthor of *Doing Business in Emerging Europe* (Basingstoke, Hampshire, UK: Palgrave, 2003). He is also the editor and main contributor of *North Africa in Transition: State, Society & Economic Transformation in the 1990s* (Gainesville: University Press of Florida, 1999); co-editor of *L'Islamisme Politique dans les Rapports entre l'Europe et le Maghreb* (Lisbon: Friedrich Ebert Stiftung, 1996); and coeditor and main contributor of *International Dimensions of the Western Sahara Conflict* (Westport, CT: Praeger, 1993). His publications include articles in *Journal of North African Studies, MERIP, Middle East Journal, Cambridge Review of International Affairs, Third World Quarterly, Maghreb-Machrek, Géoéconomie, Middle East Policy, Cahiers du CREAD*, and chapters in edited volumes. He also contributed to various encyclopedias. He is preparing a book on US policy in North Africa and coediting a volume for Routledge Publishers, *North Africa: Region, Politics and the Limits of Transformation.*

INDEX

Abbas, Mahmoud (Abu Mazen), 297
Abdallahi, Sidi Ould Cheikh, 140
Abdel Aziz, Mohamed Ould, 140
Abdesselam, Belaid, 188–189, 202
Abduh, Muhammad, 251, 264
Abrams, Elliot, 324
Abul Magd, Kamal, 265
Achaemenids, 69, 77, 78–82, 89
al-Adad, Hariz, 94
Adalet ve Kalkinma Partisi (AKP), 95
Afghanistan, 256, 261–262, 270, 366
al-Afghany, Gamal Eddine, 264
Aflaq, Michel, 13, 21
Af-Pak theater, 256, 261–262, 270
African Command, 181
African Union, 308, 319
Agriculture, 160–161, 166, 167–168,
    172, 174–176
Ahali Group, 347
Ahmadinejad, Mahmoud, 82, 135, 143,
    278, 371–375, 376–378, 379
AKP. See Justice and Development Party
    (AKP; Turkey)
Albright, Madeleine, 294, 324
Algeria
    business-state model, 190–193,
        200–203
    conglomerates, 205
    debt service, 191–192
    de-democratization and, 118
    desalinization in, 173–174
    fertility rate, 38
    GDP, per capita, 190
    gendarmerie model, 143
    Global War on Terrorism and,
        322, 325
    military and democratization, 138
    natalist policy, 52, 53
    nongovernmental organizations in, 206
    patronage networks, 203–204
    political economy of, 185
    population growth, 36, 37
    postcolonial trajectory, 187–190
    privatization in, 161
    as rentier state, 161
    Sahrawis and, 309, 311–313
    Spain and, 325
    state-building based on gender
        difference, 228–229
    unemployment in, 44, 45
    Western Sahara and, 276–277,
        306–308
    women's roles in, 179
Algiers Agreement, 364
al-Qaeda, 32, 207, 259, 269, 280, 355,
    371, 393
Al Quds, 135
Amal movement, 365
Amin, Oasim, 236
Al-Anfal, 68
Annan, Kofi, 305, 310, 311, 369
Aoun, Michel, 141
Arab, defining, 67, 81
Arab Human Development Project, 19
Arab Human Development Reports,
    33, 100
Arabic, 1, 5, 6, 33, 64, 66, 76, 80
Arabicization, 64–67, 74–75, 89

Arab-Israeli conflict, 286–288
Arab League, 288, 295, 394
Arab Maghreb Union, 304
Arab nationalism, 16, 21–22, 87, 342
Arab Revolt, 339, 343
Arab socialism, 16–17, 158–159, 165
  gender and, 215, 230–231
Arafat, Yasir, 68–69, 207, 288, 289,
  294, 297
Aramaic, 2, 6, 66
Arms for Peace program, 375
Artesh, 135
al-Asad, Bashar, 8, 115, 138–139, 374
al-Asad, Hafiz, 8, 13, 22, 96, 131, 136,
  138, 365, 374
Ashura, 72–73, 80, 347
Association of the Study of Peak Oil, 385
Atatürk, Kemal (Mustafa Kemal), 7, 84,
  85, 131, 135, 141, 165, 267
Atlas, Ariel, 11
Authoritarian rule, 260
  inheritance of, following
    colonialism, 165
  in Iraq, 346–347
  in MENA, 97, 98–99
  natural-resource wealth and,
    102–103
Authority, gender and access to,
  221–224
Autocratic regimes
  benefits of, 94
  economic system and, 13–14
  expanding free expression and,
    107–108
  liberalized, 115
  resilience of, 106–107
Automobiles, gasoline consumption and,
  397–398, 400–402
al-Awa, Muhammad Selim, 265
Azeris, 81
Aznar, José Maria, 326

Baath Party/regime (Iraq), 13, 70, 77,
  230, 340, 344–348
Baath Party (Syria), 8, 13, 70, 94,
  131, 230
Başbug, Ilker, 142
Bacevich, Andrew, 263

Badr Brigade (Badr Organization), 68,
  372–373
Baghdad Pact, 131, 344, 363
Bahrain, 46–47, 115–116, 238, 370
Baker, James A., 310, 311, 312, 321
Baker, Raymond William, 216–217
al-Bakr, Ahmad Hasan, 346, 358
Balfour, Arthur James, 283
Balfour Declaration, 87, 283, 284
Ban Ki-moon, 314–315, 317
Banking system
  Algeria, 199, 201–202
  Morocco, 194, 199
  Tunisia, 196, 198, 199
al-Banna, Hassan, 265
Barak, Ehud, 96, 142, 293, 294, 295
Basic Law (Israel), 147
Basij militia, 136, 348
Basri, Driss, 306
Batatu, Hanna, 345
Battle of Badr, 34, 67–68
Battle of Hudaybiyyah, 68
Battle of Karamen, 134
Battle of Qadisiyyah, 69–70
Belge, Murat, 61–62
Belkheir, Larbi, 204
Belkhiria, Bechir, 191
Ben Ali, Zine al-Abidine, 102, 106,
  117–118, 180, 186, 196, 203
Ben Bella, Ahmed, 188, 228, 229
Bendjedid, Chadli, 53, 200, 204
Ben Gurion, David, 21, 22, 85, 132
Berber language, 2, 7, 66
Berbers, 75
Berramdane, Abdelkhaleq, 306
Biblical revisionism, 86
bin Laden, Osama, 86, 254, 393
Birol, Fatih, 386
al-Bishry, Tareq, 265
Bloggers, 219, 243–244
Boudiaf, Mohamed, 306
Boumediene, Houari, 52, 188, 189, 203
Bourguiba, Habib, 4, 21, 161, 165, 186,
  187, 191, 196, 203
  coup against, 117
  natalist policy, 51, 52
Bouteflika, Abdelaziz, 118, 201, 202,
  204, 328

Boutros-Ghali, Boutros, 309
Bremer, L. Paul, 352
Brown, Carl, 165
Brzezinski, Zbigniew, 378
Bu-Craa, 326
Bureaucratic de-democratization, 98, 99, 102, 117–119, 120
Bush, George H. W., 357
Bush, George W., 279, 299, 322
    Global War on Terror and, 216, 252, 253, 254, 255
    Iran and, 370–371, 372, 374
Business-state models, 190–203
    Algeria, 190–193, 200–203
    Morocco, 190–196
    Tunisia, 190–193, 196–200

Cammett, Melanie, 207
Camp David Peace Accords, 288, 364
Camp David talks of 2000, 293–294
Carter, Jimmy, 277
CEDAW. *See* UN Convention for the Elimination of All Forms of Discrimination Against Women (CEDAW)
Cell phone usage, gender relations and, 243
CENTCOM (US Central Command), 256
Central Treaty Organization (CENTO), 344, 363, 366
CGEM. *See* Confédération Générale des Entreprises du Maroc (CGEM)
Chamoun, Camille, 143, 148
Change (*Goran*) List, 353, 354
Charter of Algiers, 228–229
Chavez, Hugo, 371, 399
Chehab, Fouad, 134
Chehab, Khalid, 140–141
Cheney, Richard (Dick), 255, 280
China, 375, 384, 400
Chirac, Jacques, 318
Christianity, 2, 65, 77–78, 214
Civil law, 95
Civil liberties, 97
Civil-military relations, 125–149
    disappearance of permanent military coup, 129–130

economy and, 130, 144–146
interpreting, 130–136
military power and political power, 136–144
nation-building and, 132–135
patterns of, 126–128
political tradition, 129
security conditions, 128–129
understanding, 125–130
war, politics, and, 146–148
Civil society organizations (CSOs)
    Iraqi, 345
    in Mahgreb, 161, 206–207
    political change and, 104–106
Civil society thesis, 104–106
Climate change, 160–161, 176
Clinton, Bill, 293, 294
Coalition Provisional Authority, 352
Cold War, 23, 321, 344
Colonialism
    economic legacy of, 157–158, 164–167
    gender and aftermath of, 226–227
    legacy of in Middle East, 12
    postcolonial trajectories in Maghreb, 186–190
    Western Sahara and, 304–306
Committee of Union and Progress (CUP), 342
Committee to Protect Journalists, 109
Commodities, primary, 168–169, 170
Community-building, Islam and, 249–250
Confédération Générale des Entreprises du Maroc (CGEM), 207
Conflict
    gender and, 241–243
    religion and, 19–20
Conglomerates, 194, 205
Constraints, preferences and, 359
Corell, Hans, 310
Corruption, 160
    in Algeria, 202–203
    economic, 167
    in Maghreb, 195
    military, 130
    in Morocco, 195
    in Tunisia, 199–200, 207

Council of Chalcedon, 65, 77
Coups, military, 127, 128, 129–130, 139–144
Credit, agriculture and lack of, 168
CSOs. *See* Civil society organizations (CSOs)
Cultural politics, 359
CUP. *See* Committee of Union and Progress (CUP)

Dar al-Islam, 23
Davis, Eric, 279
Al-Dawa Party (Iraq), 68, 352, 372
Dayan, Moshe, 148
Debt service, in Mahgreb, 191–193
Declaration of the Granting of Independence of Colonial Countries and Peoples, 304–305
De-democratization, 98, 99, 102, 117–119, 120
Deffeyes, Kenneth S., 385
Democracy, 9–10, 93–94, 95, 97, 98
    economic development and, 100
    elite actors thesis and, 103
    Iraqi transition to, 355–356
    military and, 136–139
Democratic Constitutional Rally (RCD), 106, 117
Demographic gift, 41
Demographic momentum, 40
Demographic Transition Theory, 52–53
Demography, 32, 35–55, 164
    economic effects of, 176–178
    inter-Arab labor migration, 45–50
    natalist policies, 50–54
    population growth, 35–40
    socioeconomic consequences of, 40–43
    unemployment, 18, 43–45
Dependency Theory, 50
Der Judenstaat (Herzl), 282
Desalinization technology, 173–174
Development, education, gender, and, 238–241
Development theory, 259
al-Din Bitar, Salal, 13, 21
Division, memories of, 70–72
Dorraj, Manochehr, 278

Downs, Anthony, 338
Dubai, 49, 160
Dulles, Allen, 344
al-Duri, Izzat Ibrahim, 349

Eastern Mediterranean, 4, 5
East Jerusalem, 286, 287
Economic Cooperation Organization, 364
Economic development, democracy and, 100
Economic Theory of Democracy, An (Downs), 338
Economic theory of politics, 338
Economy
    economic progress, 18–19, 157
    economic themes, 13–19
    military and, 130, 144–146
    range of economic national wealth, 14–18
    See also Political economy
Education, 19
    development and, 238–241
    gender and, 237–238
    higher, 33, 238
Egypt, 5
    civil society organizations in, 105
    defense spending, 146
    family planning program, 240
    fertility rate, 38
    Iran and, 368, 369
    military, 138, 145
    Muslim Brotherhood, 143
    natalist policies, 50–52, 53
    New Islamists, 264–265
    1967 war, 146
    population growth, 36, 37
    pre-Islamic past, 75–76
    unemployment in, 43, 44–45
    women in public sphere, 227–228
ELAM. *See* Front de Liberation de l'Algérie Marocain (ELAM)
Electoral representation, 110–111
    in Kuwait, 111–114
Elite actors thesis, of political change, 103–104
Emigration, 178. *See also* Migration
Employment, in agriculture, 167

Enculturation, 237
Energy, Middle East and global. *See* Oil
Energy review (2007), 397–400
Engin, Aykut Cengiz, 142
Erbakan, Necmittin, 141
Erdoğan, Recep Tayyip, 142, 252, 268
Eritrea, 329
Erraji, Mohammed, 109
ESCWA. *See* UN Economic and Social
   Commission for Western Asia
   (ESCWA)
Ethnoconfessional model, 350–351,
   353–355, 356
European Union, 166, 205, 320
Exports, in Mahgreb, 197

al-Fadila Party, 352
Faisal II, 131
Faith Campaign, 349, 350
Family, gender and, 220–229
Family courts, 233
Family law (personal status law) reform,
   230, 231, 233–234
Family planning programs, 239–241
Fanon, Frantz, 266
FAO. *See* UN Food and Agricultural
   Organization (FAO)
Farsi, 2, 7
al-Fassi, Abbas, 307
al-Fassi, Mohammed Allal, 306
Fatah Party, 69, 287, 291, 297–298, 299
Fath, 68–69
Fatih, 69
Faulkner, William, 61
Faysal I, 339, 343
Fertility rates, 38–40, 51, 52–53, 54,
   177, 179
Finkelstein, Israel, 86
Fiqh, 251, 271
FIS (Front Islamique du Saint), 200–201
Fitnahs, 70–72
   memory of, 72–74
Flashpoints, Cold War and, 22–23
FLN, 203, 228
Food imports, population growth and, 41
Food security, 174–176
Foreign invasions and domination, 3,
   33, 99, 135

Foreign investment, 160, 180
Foreign policy, Iranian regional, 363–379
Foucault, Michel, 266
Framework Agreement, 311–312
France
   as colonial power in MENA, 3, 164
   Israeli-Palestinian conflict and,
      283, 284
   Mahgreb and, 186, 187
   Western Sahara conflict and, 304,
      305, 318–320
Freedom House rankings, 3, 6, 9, 95,
   97, 101, 102, 115, 146
Freedom of association, 107
Freedom of press, 97, 98, 107–108,
   109, 110
Freedom of speech, 97, 98, 107–108,
   109, 110
Free trade agreements, 166
Front de Liberation de l'Algérie
   Marocain (ELAM), 307
Front of National Liberation, 188
"Frozen" conflict, 24, 276, 303, 324

Gas exports, 169
Gasoline consumption, U.S., 397–398,
   400–402
Gas tax, 401–402
Gaza-Jericho First Plan, 291
Gaza Strip, 286, 287, 289, 291, 293,
   294, 296, 297
Gemayel, Amin, 141
Gemayel, Bashir, 148
Gender
   changes in women's role, 179
   conflict and, 241–243
   democracy, liberalization, and,
      100, 102
   education and development and,
      237–241
   family and, 220–226
   literacy and, 237–238
   nationalism, state-building, and
      modern family, 226–229
   overview, 219–220
   women and political movements,
      229–236
Gendered expectations, upholding, 224

Gender empowerment, 12
Gender relations, 215–216
General Federation of Iraqi
    Women, 345
Geographic boundaries of Middle East,
    4–6, 31–32
Geostrategic framework, tourism
    and, 181
al-Ghazzaly, Muhammad, 265
Gibb, Hamilton, 67
Giscard d'Estaing, Valéry, 319
Global Counterinsurgency Against
    Extremism, 252–253
Global spare oil capacity, 388–390
Global war on terror (GWOT),
    181, 216
  Islamic Awakening and, 252–262
  Morocco, Algeria, and, 321–322
Gokalp, Ziya, 85
Golan Heights, 286, 295
GONGOs. *See* Government organized
    nongovernmental organizations
    (GONGOs)
Government effectiveness, in
    Maghreb, 189
Government jobs, 203–204
Government organized nongovernmental
    organizations (GONGOs), 105
Grameen Bank, 168
Gray, Gordon, 322
Gray Wolves, 82–83
Great Britain
  as colonial power in MENA, 164
  Iraq and, 339, 340–341, 343–345,
    346, 347
  Israeli-Palestinian conflict and,
    283, 284
  Western Sahara conflict and, 304
Gross domestic product
  per capita, 14, 15, 190
  political and civil rights and, 100,
    101, 102–103
Groupe Dahli, 205
Gul, Abdullah, 142
Gulf Cooperation Council, 366, 372
Gulf War of 1991, 8, 289, 340, 348
Gur, Mordechai, 147
Guterres, Antonio, 313

Guzman, Jacobo Arbenz, 344
GWOT. *See* Global war on terror
    (GWOT)

Haass, Richard, 299
HADAS, 111, 112, 113, 114
Hadiths, 64, 249
Haj, Messali, 187
Hamas, 144, 254, 255, 261, 291,
    297–298, 299, 365, 372, 373, 379
Hamrouche, Mouloud, 200, 205
al-Haq movement, 111
Hariri, Rafiq, 373
Hasan, 71
Hassan II, 24, 52, 108, 189
  Western Sahara and, 305, 306, 307,
    308, 309–310, 314
al-Hawra (newspaper), 241
Hebraic Code, 233
Hebrew, 2, 6–7
Hegel, Georg W. F., 203
Hemmer, Christopher, 276
Henry, Clement, 161
Herzl, Theodor, 282
Higher education, 33, 238
Highly indebted poor countries, 166
Hijra, 68
Hijrah, 63
Histadrut, 159
Historical memory, 32–34, 61–62
  controlling, 88
  of early Islamic expansion, 64–67
  Iran and, 78–82
  Jewish, 85–86
  memories of division, 70–72
  memories of *fitnah,* 72–74
  memories of greatness, 64–70
  Middle East and, 62–63
  of Muhammad, 63–64
  persisting and invented, 74–78
  recent examples of use of, 67–70
  of 20th century, 86–88
  Turkey and, 82–85
Hizbullah, 3, 82, 144, 261, 275
  Iran and, 365, 366, 369, 370, 373,
    374–375, 379
Honor, 224–226
Honor crimes, 225–226

Houston Accords, 310
Hubbert, M. King, 385
al-Huda, Bint, 349
Humeini, Rudollah, 53
Husayn, 71, 72–74
Hussein, King (Jordan), 8, 289
Hussein, Saddam, 3, 8, 77, 139, 279, 372
   bad decisions made by, 357–358, 359
   Faith Campaign, 349, 350
   Iran-Iraq War, 133, 347–348
   Kuwait and, 280, 289
   oil and, 340, 345, 395
   Qadisiyyah and, 69
   Rafsanjani and, 368
   weapons of, 376
Hussein, Sherif, 283
Huwaidy, Fahmy, 265
Hydrocarbons, 168–169. *See also* Oil

IDF. *See* Israeli Defense Force (IDF)
Import substitution industrialization
   (ISI), 160, 165
Income inequality, 100, 160
Independence, military and, 127–128,
   134–135
Indo-European language family, 7
Industrialization, 158, 160, 188–189
Infitah, 166
Information Center (Israel), 88
Inquiry into the Wealth of Nations, An
   (Smith), 337
Interim Governing Council, 357
International Atomic Energy Agency,
   377–378, 379, 392
International Crisis Group, 329
International debt crisis, effect on
   Maghreb, 191–193
International Energy Agency, 384,
   386, 396
International Monetary Fund, 17, 114,
   159, 166, 192
International relations, 275–276
Internet, empowerment and, 219,
   243–244
Intifada
   Iraq, 340, 352
   Palestinian, 242, 288–289, 290
   Sahrawis, 313

Iram (Ubar), 75
Iran
   conflict with, 24–26
   democratic rule in, 94
   Egypt and, 368, 369
   family planning program, 239–240
   fertility rate, 38
   international relations and, 277–279
   IRGC and national economy, 144
   Israel and, 364, 365
   memory of Husayn and, 73–74
   mistrust of military, 135–136
   natalist policies, 51, 52, 53–54
   nuclear weapons and, 24–25,
     375–378
   oil security and, 391, 392–393, 399
   population growth, 36, 37
   pre-Islamic identity, 77
   regional allies, 363
   regional foreign policy, 363–379
   rival historical memories, 78–82, 89
   Saudi Arabia and, 364–365, 366,
     367–368, 369–370, 372, 394
   shah in, 94–95
   Shia Islamists, 265–267
   Syria and, 365, 369, 373–374
   20th-century historical memories
     of, 87
   unemployment in, 45
   United Arab Emirates and, 369–370
   United States and, 366, 370–371, 372
   women bloggers in, 219, 243–244
   youth population in, 219
Iranian New Year (*Nowruz*), 80
Iran-Iraq War, 69–70, 241, 288, 340,
   347–348, 365, 366–367
Iraq, 3
   agrarian transformation of, 340–345
   contemporary politics, 356–357
   Great Britain and, 339, 340–341,
     343–345, 346, 347
   Gulf War, 8, 289, 340, 348
   international relations and, 278–279
   invasion of Kuwait, 289
   military coup, 139
   militias, 144
   oil security and, 391–392
   political change in, 99, 355–356

Iraq *(continued)*
  political economy of, 279
  pre-Islamic identity, 77
  rise of sectarian identities, 349–355,
    356, 357
  Turkification policy, 342
  UN sanctions against, 349–355
Iraqi-American Chamber of Commerce
  and Industry, 354
Iraqi Islamic Front, 68
Iraqi nationalism, 133, 340
Iraq Petroleum Company, 341,
  343, 347
Iraq War, 269
IRGC. *See* Islamic Revolutionary Guard
  Corps (IRGC)
Irrigation, 172
ISCI. *See* Islamic Supreme Council of
  Iraq (ISCI)
ISI. *See* Import substitution
  industrialization (ISI)
Islam
  basic obligations of, 249
  divisions of, 2, 71–72
  founding, 63–64
  gender empowerment and, 12
  political, 216
  political opposition and, 21
  role in Middle East, 214–215
  state and, 19–26, 215
Islamic Action Front, 111, 252
Islamic Awakening, 216, 249–272
  community-building and, 249–250
  Global War on Terror and, 252–262
  Iranian revolution and, 265–267
  Iraq and, 355
  Islamic identity and, 262–264
  Israel and, 271–272
  New Islamists in Egypt, 264–266
  Obama and, 252–258
  Turkey and, 267–268
  United States and, 252–262,
    268–272
  Wassatteyya, 251–252, 264, 271
Islamic Call Party, 347
Islamic Constitutional Movement
  (HADAS), 111, 112, 113, 114
Islamic exceptionalism, 359–360

Islamic expansion, memories of, 64–67
Islamic Front of Salvation, 200–201
Islamic identity, 262–263
Islamic Jihad, 365, 373
Islamic-oriented parties, in Turkey,
  141–142
Islamic Revolutionary Front, 69–70
Islamic Revolutionary Guard Corps
  (IRGC), 135–136, 143, 144, 365
Islamic State of Iraq, 355
Islamic Supreme Council of Iraq
  (ISCI), 68
Islamism
  family law reform and, 233
  gender and, 229, 231–232
  women and study of religious texts,
    234–236
Islamist militants, 258–259, 260
Islamist movements, 33–34, 252,
  261, 263
Islamist Virtue Party (Turkey), 232
Islam Without Fear (Baker), 217
Isnads, 64
Israel, 5
  civil-military relations in, 146–148
  conflict over land, 23–24
  defense spending, 145
  democracy in, 95
  economic systems, 16–17
  Freedom House ranking of, 9
  historical memories, 88
  Iran and, 364, 365
  Jewish identity and, 22
  labor movement, 159
  military, 133, 142
  1948 war, 284–286
  nuclear weapons and, 25–26
  separation of Palestinians in, 11
  United States and, 257, 271–272
Israeli Defense Force (IDF), 133, 147
Israeli-Palestinian conflict, 281–300
  Arab-Israeli conflict, 286–288
  origins, 282–284
  Oslo Accords, 288–295
  search for post-Oslo peace process,
    295–299
  unjust peace, 299–300
Istikhlaf, 250

Jahiliyyah, 75, 258
JAM. *See* Mahdi Army (JAM)
Janissaries *(Yeni Ceri),* 131
Japan option, 379
Jerusalem, 20, 23, 285–286, 294, 298–299
Jeune Afrique (journal), 180
Jevons, William Stanley, 338
Jewish nationalism, 282. *See also* Israeli–Palestinian conflict
Jewish settlements, 287, 292
Jews, 214
    historical memories of, 85–86
    in Iran, 78
    in Iraq, 346
    secular, 2
Jihad, 258
Johns Hopkins University, 240
Jordan, 5, 8
    Israeli-Palestinian conflict and, 288, 289
    1948 war, 285
    military and, 134, 139, 144–145
    phosphate reserves, 169
    population growth in, 36, 37
    state socialism in, 17
    unemployment in, 43
Jordanian Arab Legion, 131
Jordan Phosphates Mines Company, 17
June-October 1920 Revolution, 343
Justice and Development Party (AKP; Turkey), 137, 142, 143, 216
Justice and Development Party (Morocco), 111, 114, 252
Justice and Development Party (Turkey), 252, 268

Kadima Party, 298
Kafala system, 48
Kallal, Abdullah, 180
Karbala, 72–74
Kata'lb militia, 148
Katsav, Moshe, 148
Kavakçi, Merve, 232
Kemal, Mustafa. *See* Atatürk, Kemal
Kennedy, Edward, 311
Kerry, John, 311

Khalifa, Abdelmoumen Rafik, 161, 201–202, 205
al-Khalifa, Hamad, 115–116
Khalifa Bank, 201, 204
Khalifa groups, 207
Khalq, Mujahidin-i, 82
Khamenei, Ali, 81, 136, 369, 370, 392
Kharrazi, Kamal, 370
Khatami, Mohammad, 143, 252, 267, 278, 369–371, 372, 376
Khawarij/Kharijites, 71–72
Khayyam, Omar, 33
Khomeini, Ruhollah, 25, 53, 73, 74, 82, 86–87, 136, 239, 266, 277, 347–348, 367, 395
al-Khoury, Bishara, 132, 134
Kibbutzim, 16, 159
Kissinger, Henry, 254
Kouchner, Bernard, 320
Kurdish, 2, 7
Kurdish Democratic Party (Iraq), 353
Kurdish Regional Government, 352, 353–354, 356
Kurds, 84, 225–226
Kuwait, 46–47, 111–114, 176, 280, 289, 348

Labor migration, inter-Arab, 43, 45–50, 159
Labor Party (Israel), 16, 159, 293
Labor theory of value, 338
Lamari, Mohamed, 138
Land, conflict over, 23–24
Land for peace, 287, 292
Languages, Middle Eastern, 1–2, 6–7
Law, 95–96
Leahy, Patrick, 311
Lebanon, 5
    civil-military relations, 148
    Iran and, 373
    military, 133–134, 140–141
    militias, 144
    population growth, 37
    pre-Islamic identity, 76
Levant, 4, 5–6
Liberalization, 97, 98
Liberalized autocracies, 115
Liberation Army (Lebanon), 133

Liberation movements, militaries formed from, 129
Libya, 15. *See also* Qadhafi, Muammar
Likud Party, 159, 291, 298
Lipkin-Shahak, Amnon, 142
Literacy rates, 237–238, 239
Livni, Tzipi, 298
Loans, nonperforming, 199

Madrid Accords, 309, 326
Mafioso, in Algeria, 188–189, 202
Maghreb
    civil society in, 206–207
    corruption in, 195
    effects of international debt crisis on, 191–193
    emigration from, 178
    exports, 197
    government effectiveness in, 189
    gross domestic product, per capita, 190
    overview of, 4–5
    political economies of, 185
    unity of, 205–208
    See also Algeria; Mauritania; Morocco; Tunisia
Mahan, Alfred Thayer, 31
al-Mahdi, Muhammad, 73
Mahdi Army (JAM), 349–352, 355–356, 373
Mahmoud II, 131
Male selving, 222–223
al-Maliki, Nouri, 68, 355, 373
Malikiyya, 134
Manufacturing, 169–171
Manufacturing value added (MVA), 170
Mao Zedong, 129
Mardam, Jamil, 139
Maronite Christians, 2, 76
Marriage, 223, 224, 238
Marshall, Alfred, 338
Marx, Karl, 203, 338
Maududi, Maulana Abul Ala, 258
Mauritania, 6, 14, 24, 104, 140
    Spain and, 325, 326
    Western Sahara and, 276, 309
    See also Maghreb
McMahon, Henry, 283
Mecca, 20, 250, 339, 365

MEDA. *See* Middle East Development Assistance (MEDA)
Medina, 63, 339
MENA (Middle East and North Africa), 5, 32
    authoritarian rule in, 97, 98–99
    drivers of political change in (*See* Political change, drivers of)
Middle class, democracy and, 100, 102
Middle East
    civil-military relations in, 130–136
    conflict in, 22–24
    economic progress in, 18–19
    economic themes, 13–14
    geographic boundaries of, 31–32
    languages of, 1–2, 6–7
    overview, 1–2
    persistent problems, 2–4
    political themes, 8–13
    regions of, 4–6
    religious theme, 19
    See also MENA; *individual countries*
Middle East Development Assistance (MEDA), 196
Middle East Institute, 324
Migration
    gender and, 239
    inter-Arab labor, 43, 45–50, 159
    rural-to-urban, 168, 338, 341–342, 350
Military
    nation-building and, 132–135
    as negative symbol, 135–136
    power of paramilitary, 143–144
    professionalization of, 126–127, 131–132
    role in politics, 96, 143
    state-building and, 13
    status quo and, 136–137
    See also Civil-military relations
Military coups, 127, 128, 129–130, 139–144
Military regimes, elite actors thesis and, 103–104
Military threats to oil security, 390–393
Militias, private, 143–144
MINURSO, 309, 311, 320, 330
Mizrahi movement, 86

Modern Iranian Persian, 7
Modernity, secularists, Islamists, and, 236
Modernization thesis, of political change, 99–106
Modesty, 235
Mohammed bin Rashid Al Maktoum Foundation, 18
Mohammed VI, 108–110, 116, 140, 234, 305, 314, 322
Monbiot, George, 386
Monophysitism, 65, 77, 78
Morales, Eva, 371
Moratinos, Miguel Ángel, 327
Moroccan Initiative for Negotiating an Autonomous Statute for the Sahara Region, 314–317
Moroccan irredentism, 306–307
Moroccan nationalism, 306–307
Morocco
    business-state model, 190–196
    civil society in, 105, 206–207
    debt service, 191, 192
    family law reform, 233–234
    free expression in, 108–110
    GDP, per capita, 190
    gendarmerie model, 143
    gender relations and cell phone use, 243
    hymen reconstruction, 224
    land disputes, 24
    literacy rates, 238
    military coup, 140
    morshidat, 235–236
    natalist policies, 52
    patronage networks, 194–195, 204
    phosphate reserves, 169
    political economy of, 185
    population growth, 36, 37
    postcolonial trajectory, 187
    privatization in, 161
    relationship with U.S., 320–325
    unemployment in, 44, 45
    Western Sahara conflict and, 276, 304, 305, 306–310
    women in, 227, 232
    See also Maghreb
Morshidat, 235–236

Mortality rates, 36, 38, 39, 177
Mosaddeq, Mohammad, 94, 345
Mubarak, Gamal, 116
Mubarak, Hosni, 53, 94, 116, 118–119, 133, 138, 368
Muhajirun, 68
Muhammad ibn Abdillah, 63–64
Mujahidin, 68
Mujahidin-i Khalq, 373
Multilateral great power politics, 165
Munafiqin, 68
Muslim Brotherhood, 17, 143, 216, 252, 265, 365
Muslim Brothers, 72
MVA. *See* Manufacturing value added (MVA)
Mythistory, 61

al-Nabulsi, Suleiman, 139
Naciri, Khalid, 109
Naguib, Muhammad, 94
al-Nahda movement, 117
al-Nahyan, Zayid bin Sultan, 95
Nakbah *(al Nakbah),* 88, 285
Nasrullah, Hasan, 82
Nasser, Gamal Abdel, 13, 22, 51, 72, 82, 96, 131, 136, 146, 165, 265, 286
Nasserists, 346
Natalist policies, 50–54
National Democratic Party (Egypt), 94, 118
National Democratic Party (Iraq), 347
National Front, 346
National identity, military and, 132–135
Nationalism
    Arab, 16, 21–22, 87, 342
    gender and, 226–229
    Israeli-Palestinian conflict and, 282
    Moroccan, 306–307
    Turkish, 84–85, 267–268
National Pact (Lebanon), 132
Nation-building, military and, 132–135
Neighborhood effects, 358
Neo-authoritarianism, 181
Neo-Destour Party (Tunisia), 186–187
Neoliberal policies, 166
Nestorianism, 2, 65, 77
Netanyahu, Benjamin, 142, 299

New Islamists, 264–265
New Persian, 80
Nezzar, Khaled, 306
1948 Arab-Israeli War, 284–286
1956 Arab-Israeli War, 286
1967 Arab-Israeli War, 146, 286, 287, 346
1973 Arab-Israeli War, 134, 286, 287
1973 oil embargo, 396
Nixon, Richard, 363
Nowruz, 80
Nuclear weapons, 24–26, 375–378, 379
Nursi, Said, 267–268
Nuwar, Ali Abu, 139

Obama, Barack, 26, 261, 262, 377, 399, 400, 401
  attitude towards Islamic world, 252–258
  Iraq War and, 279
  Western Sahara conflict and, 324–325
Obama administration, oil alternatives and, 383
Objective, 213
Offset plan, 401–402
Oil, 5
  alternatives to, 383–384, 397
  annual energy review 2007, 397–400
  developments that mitigate threats to oil supplies, 395–396
  discovery of, 340, 343
  economic expansion and decline and, 43–44
  future of supply of, 279–280
  global spare capacity, 388–390
  increasing dependence on Middle East, 387–388
  Iraq and, 345–347, 348, 352–353, 354–355
  peak oil, 384–387
  projected demand, 384
  supply disruptions, 390–395
  U.S. gasoline consumption, 400–402
Oil exports, 165–166, 168–169
Oil prices, 384, 388–390, 397–400
Olmert, Ehud, 148, 298–299
Oman, 15, 38, 46–47, 54, 145
Ommar, Raad, 354

Omnium Nord-African (ONA) bank, 187
OPEC (Organization of Petroleum Exporting Countries), 165–166, 363, 368, 385, 394, 396, 399
"Operation Anfal," 68
"Operation Badr," 67–68
Organization of Economic Co-operation and Development (OECD), 178
Organization of African Unity, 308, 309
Organization of the Islamic Conference, 369, 370
Ortega, Daniel, 371
Oslo Accords (Declaration of Principles), 288–295
Ottoman Empire, 70, 83–84, 86–87, 164, 341
El-Ouakef, Yahia Ould Ahmed, 127
Oujda clan, 188
Ouyahia, Ahmed, 207
Ozal, Turgut, 14

Pahlavi, Muhammad Reza, 3–4, 12, 24, 73, 79, 82, 94, 135, 277, 347, 363
Pahlavi, Reza Shah, 87, 96, 131, 135
Pahlavi dynasty, 78–79
Palestinian Authority, 275, 291, 297
Palestinian civil society, 105
Palestinian identity, 282
Palestinian National Authority, 105
Palestinians, 11, 285, 287, 295, 370
  conflict over land, 23–24
  gendered experiences of conflict, 242–243
  historical memories of, 87, 88
  United States and, 255
  See also Israeli-Palestinian conflict
Palestinian Uprising (1987), 85–86
Palestine Liberation Organization (PLO), 287, 288, 289, 290–291, 365
Pan-Arabism, 76, 340
Pan-Islamism, 76, 364, 371, 378
Pan-Ottomanism, 84
Pan-Turkism, 84
Paramilitary, power of, 143–144

Parti Populaire Algérien/Mouvement
    pour le Triomphe des Libertés
    Démocratiques, 187–188
Partiya Karkarên Kurdistan (PKK), 137
Patriarchal connectivity, 221
Patriotic Union of Kurdistan, 353–354
Patronage networks, 161
    Algeria, 203–204
    Morocco, 187, 194–195, 204
    Tunisia, 198, 204
Peace for Galilee, 147
Peace Plan for Self-Determination
    of the People of Western Sahara
    (Baker Plan II), 312–313, 314
Peak oil, 384–387
Peel Commission, 284
Peres, Shimon, 147
Perry, Glenn, 33
Persepolis, 79, 80
Persian, 2, 7, 78, 81
    New, 80
Personal Status Code, 102
Petrodollars, 166
Pew Charitable Trust, 10, 20–21
Pharaonism, 75–76
Pheiffer, Chantel, 160
Phosphates, 17, 161, 169, 174, 197,
    276, 303, 310, 326
Pickens, T. Boone, 397
Piety movements, 235–236
PKK. *See* Partiya Karkarên Kurdistan
    (PKK)
PLO. *See* Palestinian Liberation
    Organization (PLO)
POLISARIO Front, 276–277, 309,
    310–312, 314, 315–317, 321
Political change, drivers of, 96,
    97–120
    autocratic resilience thesis, 106–107
    bureaucratic de-democratization,
        117–119
    civil society thesis, 104–106
    electoral representation, 111–114
    elite actors thesis, 103–104
    expanding free expression, 107–110
    in MENA, 107–119
    modernization thesis, 99–103
    succession, 114–117

Political economy, 163–182
    agriculture, 167–168, 340–345
    of Algeria, 185, 187–193, 200–208
    colonial legacy and statist inheritance,
        164–167
    contemporary Iraqi politics and,
        356–357
    as decision-making, 357–358
    defined, 337
    demography, 176–178
    environmental concerns, 176
    food concerns, 174–176
    gender, 179
    immigration, 178
    of Iraq, 279, 337–360
    manufacturing, 169–171
    models, 338–339
    of Morocco, 185, 187, 190–196,
        203–208
    overview, 157–162, 163–164
    primary commodities, 168–169
    regional cooperation, 181
    security, 180–182
    of state capacity, 355–356
    tourism, 179–181
    of Tunisia, 185, 186–187, 190–193,
        196–200, 203–208
    water concerns, 171–174
    what cannot explain, 358–359
Political Islam, 216
Political movements, women and,
    229–236
Political power, military power and,
    136–144
Political rights, 97
Political socialization, 61
Politics, 9–13, 93–96
    economic theory of, 338
    of separation, 10–12
Popular Front for the Liberation of
    Saguia el-Hamra and Río de Oro.
    See POLISARIO Front
Population growth, 32, 35–40, 239
    natalist policies and, 50–54
    socioeconomic consequences of,
        40–43
Powell, Colin, 256, 269, 311, 326
Power, gender and access to, 221–224

Preferences, constraints and, 359
Pre-Islamic identities, 75–78
Primary commodities, 168–169, 170
Principal-agent theory, 127
Private militias, 143–144
Privatization, 18, 159–160, 161,
　　166, 198
Programme Complémentaire de Soutien
　　á la Croissance, 202
Putin, Vladimir, 372, 396

Qadhafi, Muammar, 15, 69, 96,
　　116–117, 131, 136
Qadisiyyah, 69–70
al-Qaradawy, Yusuf, 252, 265, 271
Qasim, Abdel-Karim, 344–345
Qatar, 5, 14, 46–47, 54, 103, 116,
　　145, 157
Quartet Plan, 295–296
Quran, 249, 251
Qutb, Sayyid, 20, 72, 217, 258
al-Quwatli, Shukri, 125

Rabin, Yitzhak, 96, 291, 293, 374
Rafarin, Jean-Pierre, 318
Rafsanjani, Ali Akbar Hashemi,
　　366–368, 375
Rahim, Mohamed Abdelouahab, 205
Ramon, Haim, 148
Rana, Dafna, 96
RCD. *See* Democratic Constitutional
　　Rally (RCD)
Reagan, Ronald, 166
Reagan Peace Plan, 288
Rebrab, Issad, 205
Regional Development Cooperation
　　Organization, 364
Religion
　　intensity of belief, 20
　　international conflict and, 19–20
　　state and, 19
　　See also individual faiths
Religious law, 21, 95–96, 233
Religious texts, participation of women
　　in studying and interpreting,
　　234–236
Remittances, 178
Renaissance Party (Tunisia), 252

Renan, Ernest, 62
Rentier states, 46, 161, 163, 165, 188,
　　354–355
Resource dependency, 343
Ricardo, David, 338
Rice, Condoleezza, 254
Rice, Susan, 325
Roosevelt, Franklin, 339
Ross, Christopher, 317, 324, 330
al-Rubai, Nasser, 351
Rule-of-law reforms, 98–99, 117
Rural-to-urban migration, 168, 338,
　　341–342, 350

Saadah, Anton, 76
al-Sabah, Ahmed al-Abdullah, 112
al-Sabah, Jaber, 112
al-Sabah, Nasser al-Mohammed al-
　　Ahmed, 112
al-Sabah family, 94, 112–114
al-Sabeeh, Nouriya, 113
al-Sadat, Anwar, 52, 67, 68, 72, 76, 82,
　　138, 265, 368
SADR, 319
al-Sadr, Muqtada, 349, 373, 392
al-Sadr, Muhammad Baqir, 349
al-Sadr, Muhammed Muhammed Sadiq,
　　349–350
al-Sadr, Sayyid Musa, 73
Sadrist movement, 351, 352
Sagr, Haj, 223–224
Saharan Autonomous Region, 314
Sahrawis, 24, 276–277, 303, 308–317.
　　See also Western Sahara,
　　conflict in
Sahwa Islamiyya. *See* Islamic awakening
al-Said, Nuri, 347
Salafi Islamist groups, 111–112
Saleh, Ali Abdullah, 22
Salgado, Fernando Aria, 329
Salifiyyist narratives, 217
Salinization, irrigation and, 172
Sanders, Jackie Wolcott, 323
San Remo Conference, 284
Saravids, 81
Sarkozy, Nicolas, 320
al-Saud, Abdul Aziz, 139
al-Saud family, 94

Saudi Arabia, 10
  coup attempts, 139–140
  defense spending, 145
  fertility rate, 38
  inter-Arab labor migration, 46–47
  Iran and, 364–365, 366, 367–368,
    369–370, 372
  Iran-Iraq War and, 348
  natalist policy, 54
  oil and, 385, 388, 390, 395
  regional reorientation of, 394
  rise of extremists in, 394
  separation of Shia areas, 11–12
Saudi Peace Plan, 295
SCIRI. *See* Supreme Council for Islamic
  Revolution in Iraq (SCIRI)
Sectarian entrepreneurs, 351–352
Sectarianism, in Iraq, 349–355, 356, 357
Secularism
  family law reform and, 233
  gender and, 229, 230, 231
  women and study of religious texts,
    234–236
Security
  civil-military relations and, 128–129
  food, 174–176
  oil, 390–395
  tourism and, 180–182
  water, 171–172, 176
Segregation by gender, 12, 234
Seljuk Turks, 83
Selving, gender and, 221–223
Semitic family of languages, 6
September 11, 2001 attacks, 115, 321,
  370, 371, 393
Shahnama (Ferdowski), 80
Sham al Nassim, 80–81
Sharia law, 21, 96, 233
Shariari, Ali, 266
Sharon, Ariel, 295, 296, 298
Shia Crescent, 375
Shia/Shiites, 2, 71, 250
  Arab *vs.* Iranian, 81–82
  in Iran, 79, 265–267
  in Iraq, 347, 349–353, 372–373
  memory of Husayn and, 72–74
Shiat Ali, 71
Shinawarra, Thaksin, 127

Shuubiyyah, 80
Silberman, Neil Asher, 86
Sinai Peninsula, 286
Sira, 64
Sirkals, 341–342
Sistani, Ali, 73, 82
Smith, Adam, 337–338
Social class
  distinctions in, 15–16
  women in public sphere and,
    227–228
Social context, 213–217
Social unrest, unemployment, poverty,
  and, 178
Society of Muslims, 72
Socioeconomic consequences, of high
  natural increase rates, 40–43
Sorenson, David, 96
Source, 213
Spain, Western Sahara conflict and,
  325–328
State
  Islam and, 19–26
  religion and, 19
State-building, 12–13
  gender and, 226–229
State capacity, political economy of,
  355–356
State feminism, 230–231
"State of the World's Children"
  (UNICEF), 239
State planning, 16–17
Statist inheritance, 164–167
Status quo, military and, 136–137
Stewart, Michael, 3–4
Strait of Hormuz, 390–391
Structural adjustment packages, 166
Structural unemployment, 44
Succession, 114–115, 120
  in Bahrain, 115–116
  in Egypt, 117
  in Libya, 116–117
  in Morocco, 116
  political reform and, 98–99
  in Qatar, 116
  in Syria, 115, 116
Sudan, 36, 37, 40
Sufism, 250, 251, 267–268

al-Sulh, Riyad, 132
Sumerians, 77, 84–85
Sunay, Cevdet, 52
Sunnis, 2, 71, 74, 250, 353
Supreme Council for Islamic Revolution
    in Iraq (SCIRI), 68, 350, 372
Supreme Iraqi Islamic Council,
    350–351, 352
Swisher, Clayton E., 324
Sykes-Picot Agreement, 87, 283, 284
Syria, 5, 8
    defense spending, 145
    democratization and military in,
        138–139
    fertility rate, 38
    Iran and, 365, 369, 373–374
    military coup, 139
    natalist policies, 50, 53
    population growth, 36, 37
    succession in, 115
Syrian National Party, 76

Talib, Ali ibn Abi, 71, 347
Taliban, 256, 369, 375
Tanaka, Nobuo, 386, 390
Tanzim, 148
Taymiyya, Taqi Al Din Ahmad ibn, 217
Terrorism
    Israeli-Palestinian conflict and, 295,
        296–297
    oil security and, 393
    September 11, 2001 attacks, 115,
        321, 370, 371, 393
al-Thani, Hamad bin Khalifa, 116
al-Thani family, 94
Thatcher, Margaret, 166
Theofilopoulou, Anna, 313–314,
    314–315
Total fertility rate, 179
Tourism, 179–182
Toynbee, Arnold, 78
Transitology thesis, 103
Transparency International, 195
Trans-Sahara Counter Terrorism
    Initiative (TSCTI), 181
Tribal Civil and Criminal Disputes
    Regualtions, 346
Tribal relations, 144, 341

TSCTI. *See* Trans-Sahara Counter
    Terrorism Initiative (TSCTI)
Tunisia
    business-state model, 190–193,
        196–200
    civil society in, 106, 206
    corruption in, 207
    debt service, 192–193
    de-democratization in, 117–119, 120
    fertility rate, 38, 179
    GDP, per capita, 190
    middle class and liberalization
        and, 102
    natalist policy, 52, 53
    patronage networks, 198, 204
    political economy of, 185
    population growth, 36, 37
    postcolonial trajectory, 186–187
    privatization in, 161
    tourism in, 180
    unemployment in, 45
    women's roles in, 179
    See also Maghreb
Tunisian Association of Democratic
    Women, 106
Tunisian Human Rights League,
    106, 118
Turkey, 5
    democracy in, 95
    fertility rate, 38
    historical memory of, 82–85
    Islamism in, 231–232, 267–268
    military, 137, 141–142, 143
    natalist policies, 50, 51, 52
    population growth, 36, 37
    pre-Islamic identity, 89
    unemployment in, 45
    women's rights groups in, 232
Turkish, 2, 7
Turkish nationalism, 84–85, 267–268
"Twelver" *(Imamiyya)* understanding of
    Shia Islam, 2, 73

UMA. *See* Union du Maghreb Arabe
    (UMA)
Ummah Party (Kuwait), 252
Unemployment, 18, 32, 43–45, 164,
    177, 178, 208, 238, 239

UNICEF, 239
Union Bank, 201
Union du Maghreb Arabe (UMA),
    205, 206
Union of Arab Historians, 345
Union of Islamic Scholars, 252
Unions, Iraqi worker, 344
United Arab Emirates, 5, 46–47, 48, 54,
    369–370
United Nations, 12
    Israeli-Palestinian conflict and,
        284–285, 286–287
    sanctions against Iraq, 340, 349–355
    Western Sahara conflict and,
        304–305, 308–318, 329–330
UN Convention for the Elimination of
    All Forms of Discrimination
    Against Women (CEDAW), 234
UN Development Programme, 105
UN Economic and Social Commission
    for Western Asia (ESCWA), 45
UN Food and Agricultural Organization
    (FAO), 175
UN Special Commission on
    Palestine, 284
United States
    alternatives to oil and, 397, 399
    Arms for Peace program, 375
    civil-military relations in, 126, 129
    energy review, 397–400
    Eritrea and, 329
    free trade agreements with MENA
        nations, 166
    Global War on Terror, Islamic
        Awakening, and, 252–262,
        268–272
    Iran and, 87–88, 277–279, 363, 366,
        370–371, 372
    Iraq and, 344, 348, 357
    Israel and, 257, 271–272
    Oslo Accords and, 290
    Palestinians and, 255
    Western Sahara conflict and, 277,
        304, 305, 320–325
U.S. Agency for International
    Development, 17, 100, 240
U.S. Department of Energy, 384,
    385, 388

Ural-Altaic language family, 7
Urbanization, 41–43, 168, 239
Utility theory of value, 338

Vall, Eali Ould Mohammed, 140
van Walsum, Peter, 317
Veiling, 226, 230, 235

Wafabank, 194
al-Walid, Khalid ibn, 131
Walras, Leon, 338
War, civil-military relations and,
    146–148
Washington Consensus, 17–18, 166
Wassetteyya, 251–252, 264, 271
Water quality, 172–173
Water scarcity, 41, 160, 163–164, 167,
    171–172
Water security, 173, 176
Weapons of mass destruction, 24–26,
    269, 348, 392–393
al-Wefaq family, 114
al-Wefaq movement, 111
Welch, C. David, 323
West Bank, 286, 287, 289, 291, 293,
    294, 296, 298
Western Sahara, conflict in, 24,
    276–277, 303–330
    Algeria and, 306–308
    decolonization and after, 304–306
    France and, 304, 318–320
    Morocco and, 306–310, 314–317,
        328–330
    natural resources and, 303, 310
    Spain and, 325–328
    third way and autonomy, 310–312
    United States and, 304, 320–325
    UNSC Resolution 1495, 312–314
White, Gregory, 160
Williamson, John, 166
Winckler, Onn, 32
Women
    access to power *vs.* authority, 221–224
    bloggers, 219, 243–244
    changes in roles of, 179
    education and, 237–239
    labor force participation rate, 40
    nationalist movements and, 227–229

Women *(continued)*
  political movements and, 229–236
  study of religious texts, 234–236
  See also Gender
Women's rights movements, 231
World Bank, 17, 100, 159, 166, 174,
    189, 194, 195, 196, 198, 202, 205
World Energy Outlook, 386
World Values Survey, 10
World War I
  Ottoman Empire and end of, 86–87
  Palestine and, 283, 284

Yad Vashem, 23, 34
Yankelovich, Daniel, 401

Yazid, 71, 72–73, 74
Yemen, 36, 37, 38, 40, 145, 157, 176,
    238, 240
Yemeni Reformist Union, 252
Yetiv, Steve, 280
Young, Amy Elizabeth, 215
Young Turk Revolt of 1908, 342

Zakaria, Fareed, 359
Zapatero, José Luis, 326, 327, 328
Zaynab, 73
Zionism, 22, 85–86, 88, 282
Ziyad, Tariq ibn, 131
Zoroastrianism, 65, 78
Zoubir, Yahia, 277